Census Substitutes & State Census Records

♦ ♦ 3rd Edition ♦ ♦

Volume 3
Northcentral States

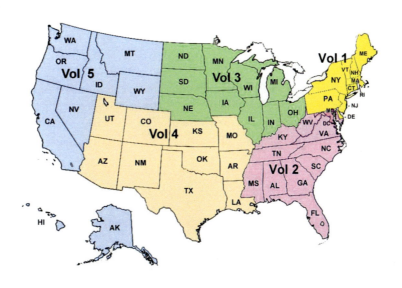

by
William Dollarhide

Copyright © 2020
William W. Dollarhide and Leland K. Meitzler
All rights reserved.

No part of this book may be reproduced in any form without permission in writing from the author or publisher except in brief quotations in articles and reviews.

Published by Family Roots Publishing Co., LLC
PO Box 1682
Orting, WA 98360-1682
www.familyrootspublishing.com

Library of Congress Control Number: 2020934867

ISBN (Paperback): 978-1-62859-288-7
ISBN (eBook): 978-1-62859-289-4

Recommended Citation:
Census Substitutes & State Census Records, 3rd Edition,
Volume Three – Northcentral States, by William Dollarhide,
publ. Family Roots Publishing Co., LLC, Orting, WA, 2020, 285 pages.

Printed in the United States of America

Contents – Vol. 3
Northcentral States

State Finder, Vols. 1 to 5 6
    Foreword 7
    Introduction 9
    Table 1: Non-State Census States 13
    Table 2: State Census States – AL -MI 14
    Table 2: State Census States – MN-WY 15
    Table 3: State Censuses in Common Years 16
    Table 4: Availability of Federal Censuses for each State 17

Vol. 3 States
    Ohio 19
    Michigan 43
    Indiana 91
    Illinois 119
    Wisconsin 159
    Iowa 179
    Minnesota 225
    Nebraska 243
    South Dakota 261
    North Dakota 273

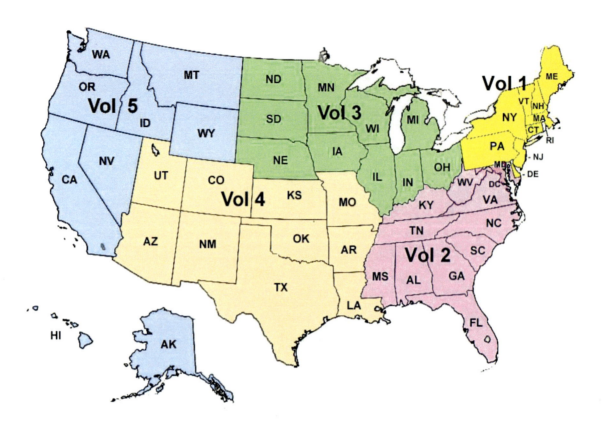

State Finder, Vols. 1-5

States	Vol.	Page
Alabama	2	233
Alaska	5	19
Arizona	4	213
Arkansas	4	75
California	5	57
Colorado	4	239
Connecticut	1	145
Delaware	1	223
District of Columbia	2	58
Florida	2	277
Georgia	2	193
Hawaii	5	37
Idaho	5	163
Illinois	3	119
Indiana	3	91
Iowa	3	179
Kansas	4	41
Kentucky	2	113
Louisiana	4	123
Maine	1	19
Maryland	2	19
Massachusetts	1	91

States	Vol.	Page
Michigan	3	43
Minnesota	3	225
Mississippi	2	259
Missouri	4	19
Montana	5	189
Nebraska	3	243
Nevada	5	107
New Hampshire	1	63
New Jersey	1	191
New Mexico	4	191
New York	1	173
North Carolina	2	145
North Dakota	3	273
Ohio	3	19
Oklahoma	4	101
Oregon	5	121
Pennsylvania	1	205
Rhode Island	1	133
South Carolina	2	177
South Dakota	3	261
Tennessee	2	161
Texas	4	169

States	Vol.	Page
Utah	4	261
Vermont	1	77
Virginia	2	79
Washington	5	141
West Virginia	2	97
Wisconsin	3	159
Wyoming	5	205

US Territories	Vol.	Page
Caribbean Region	1	245
Puerto Rico	1	246
US Virgin Islands	1	251
Panama Canal Zone	1	256
Pacific Region	1	259
Guam	1	260
No. Mariana Islands	1	262
American Samoa	1	264
The Philippines	1	268

US Nationwide	Vol.	Page
1790-1950 Maps / Descr.	5	217
US Census Substitutes	5	259

Foreword
by Leland K. Meitzler

In late 2003 Bill Dollarhide came by my office and asked if I had any ideas for *Genealogy Bulletin* articles. As it turned out, I had just finished organizing materials for a lecture on state and territorial census records and had a file folder full of data I had collected over the years on my desk. I suggested he put something together on that subject and gave him the file to review. After looking through my file, Bill decided that we needed to identify the many substitutes to censuses (statewide tax lists, voter registration lists, and such), as he quickly noted that a number of states did not take any state or territorial censuses at all. Bill began compiling a bibliography of not only extant state and territorial censuses, but substitute lists as well.

Researched and compiled by region, he added timelines of historical references to show the jurisdictions in place at the time of each census. Compiling the material by region was a logical way to go, as we quickly realized that in most cases, it would have been difficult to write about one state without writing about those surrounding it. So, if you start with Maine, for example, the adjoining state of New Hampshire would be the next chapter, then Vermont, Massachusetts, and so on.

Much of the data found in the two-volume First Edition (2008) was initially published in serial form in the old *Genealogy Bulletin (1983-2006)*. That said, the District of Columbia, for which there are many excellent sources, was never published. Also never published was The Oregon Country chapter. However, both chapters were included in the First Edition.

In the three-volume Second Edition (2016), numerous online sources were added, reflecting the ongoing efforts of both public and private companies to digitize relevant records.

In this new five-volume Third Edition (2020), the *Northeastern States* (Volume 1) adds seven (7) U.S. Territories for the first time. In addition, the *Western & Pacific States* (Volume 5) has an all-new *Maps, Descriptions, and Internet Access for the U.S. Federal Censuses, 1790-1950;* followed by an updated *U.S. Census Substitutes* chapter. Each of the 50 states & DC in this 3rd Edition has many more citations for newly added online databases and recently digitized microfilm collections – in just three years, the number went from 3,865 to 8,067 hyperlinks.

Bill also spent countless hours compiling tabulated charts that may be worth the cost of this book all by themselves. The first, found on page 13, is a chart for the non-state census states. There happens to be 13 of them (including the District of Columbia). This chart lists the states and the years covered by census substitutes. The second chart, found on pages 14-15, lists the 38 states that have extant colonial, pre-statehood, territorial, and state censuses, complete with the census year, and an indication if the census is available online as of the date of publication. The third chart, found on page 16, shows in graphic form the states that had censuses taken in common years – "on the fives." Census dates for some states are within a range. The fourth chart, on page 17, shows the availability of federal censuses for all states, 1790-1950.

Note that the title of this series of volumes is *Census Substitutes & State Census Records,* which reflects the fact that the volumes really contain a list of census substitutes, with state censuses turning out to be in the minority. Substitutes outnumber censuses by a factor of ten to one! However, the state censuses identified in this series are by far the most complete lists of Colonial, Territorial, or State Censuses published to date.

State and Territorial Censuses have long fascinated me. Many were taken in order to get congress to allow statehood. Some territories would take censuses on a nearly annual basis, in the attempt to show that they had the population base necessary to justify statehood.

Other states, like New York, had authorization of non-federal censuses written into their state constitutions. New York was one of the most prolific when it came to state censuses, as it produced numerous schedules, most falling on the ubiquitous "fives." Today we have extant New York censuses for 1825, 1835, 1845, 1855, 1865, 1875, 1892, 1905, 1915, and 1925. Some of the early years are not complete, but what is available is certainly useful. The 1925 New York census was taken as well as any other, and the population returns are largely legible and complete. However, the census was wrought with scandal, leaving New Yorkers with a taste of bitterness for such things. To make a long story short, it seems that the New York Secretary of State, a former Dean of Home Economics at Syracuse University, Florence Elizabeth Smith Knapp, took nepotism to a whole new level. As the state official in charge of the 1925 census, she put family and friends on the payroll, and while this was not illegal, most of these folks did little or nothing to earn their salaries. Even her 74-year old mother, Ella Smith, enjoyed a non-working stint as an assistant supervisor. Florence's stepdaughter, Clara Blanche Knapp, a professor at Middlebury College in Vermont, was on the payroll for over $5,000 in income, while never leaving the state of Vermont. Moreover, checks written to both Ella and Blanche seemed to have been endorsed into Florence E.S. Knapp's bank account. Numerous other family members and friends were paid substantial sums for non-work. In 1928, Mrs. Knapp finally went on trial for her misdeeds, and found guilty of first-degree grand larceny for misappropriation of state funds. She served 30 days in the Albany Jail. She could have gotten 10 years. So ended the brief political career of the first woman ever to be elected to state-wide office in New York. So also ended the state censuses of New York State.

Iowa, Kansas, Rhode Island, Florida, North Dakota, and South Dakota also took censuses up through 1925. South Dakota and Florida even took censuses in 1935 and 1945! The real value of state censuses is found in the numerous schedules enumerated in the mid-nineteenth century. Thirty-eight states took non-federal censuses that are still extant today.

And then there are the substitutes. They are of prime importance, since 12 states, as well as the District of Columbia, took no state censuses at all. And even if your ancestors lived in a state where censuses were taken "on the fives," census substitutes are helpful, especially if the family was on the move.

Although Mr. Dollarhide has used all kinds of substitutes throughout this volume, more attention has been given to tax lists, voter registration rolls, vital records, directories, statewide probate indexes, land records, and even military censuses, than most others. These records are often easily accessible and using this guide, you will be able to quickly find them for your own use. You are in for a treat, so sit back and look up the states of your ancestors. You will find information on records you never knew existed. Then... go get the records, and happy hunting!

- Leland K. Meitzler
Publisher

Introduction
Census Substitutes & State Census Records

Census Substitutes are those name lists derived from tax lists, directories, military lists, land ownership lists, voter registrations, and other compilations of names of residents for an entire state, or part of a state. A census substitute can be used to determine the names of residents in a given area when a federal or state census is missing. Moreover, a census substitute can be used as an alternative name list; confirming, contradicting, or adding to information found in a federal or state census.

This book identifies at least ten times the number of Census Substitute titles than any previous work ever published. All states are represented with significant alternative name lists – name lists that stop time for a certain year and place and name the residents of a certain place. Since all of these name lists are specific to a certain year, they are listed within each state category in chronological order. Incorporated into the lists are any State Census titles – a reference to a state census taken for a specific year.

Federal vs. State Censuses

Federal Censuses have their origins in the constitutional provision for apportionment of the U.S. House of Representatives. The first federal census was taken in 1790, and beginning about the same time, state censuses were conducted for the same reason, that is, apportionment of the various state legislatures.

Although the primary purpose of all censuses was to simply count the population, beginning with the first federal census of 1790, more information than a simple tally was added. This included the name and age of a person and progressively more details about a household for each subsequent census year. State censuses followed this same pattern.

State censuses usually add even more information than the federal censuses, and as a result, they are premier genealogical resources. Except in cases where a federal census is lost, state census records are not substitutes for the federal censuses – state censuses were almost always taken between federal census years, and usually add unique information and details about a household not found in a federal census. If a state census exists between federal census years, it may add marginally to the knowledge one gains about a family. But, more often, it will add critical information, such as more exact dates of birth, marriages, deaths; plus, additional children, different residences, other relatives living with a family; and more.

Non-State Census States

Thirteen (13) states (including DC) have never conducted a state-sponsored census. For these Non-State Census States, this review attempts to identify as many census substitutes as possible. In some cases, the census substitutes are for a single county within a state, and by listing multiple county name lists for about the same time period, regional coverage is achieved.

For an overview of the Non-State Census States, see Table 1 (page 13) showing the years for which census substitutes exist. More detail for each census substitute year indicated on the table is covered in the bibliographic sections.

State Census States

Thirty-eight (38) states have conducted censuses separate from the federal censuses. The number of censuses taken by each of the State Census States ranges from one (1) census year, e.g., the 1852 California; to twenty-four (24) census years, e.g., the 1792-1866 Mississippi territorial/state censuses. For this review, all of the state-sponsored censuses are identified, plus, to a lesser degree than the non-state census states, census substitutes available. See Table 2 (pages 14-15) for an overview of the State Census States, the year for each surviving census for a state; and an indication of which specific years are now available online as digitized databases.

Locating the Extant State Census Records

Generally, state censuses were conducted from the time of territorial status or early statehood up until about 1905, but a few continued until 1925, 1935, or 1945. The last state censuses taken by any of the states was in 1945 (Florida and South Dakota). Due to budget restraints, the Depression Era of the 1930s was a contributing factor to states ending their census-taking endeavors. Eventually, all states of the Union stopped using the population figures from state censuses and began using the federal census figures for apportionment of their state legislatures.

While the surviving federal census manuscripts are all located mostly in one repository (the National Archives), state census manuscripts are spread across the country in the various state archives or local repositories. The accessibility of state censuses may be just as good as federal censuses – but one needs to know where they are located first.

Beginning in 1941, the U.S. Bureau of the Census issued a bibliographic report attempting to identify all known state censuses, those undertaken by the various states separate from the federal censuses since 1790.[1] Prepared by Henry J. Dubester of the Library of Congress, the report was the first known attempt to research all of the state constitutions and subsequent laws related to state censuses for all of the states. The Dubester report sought, first, to identify what state censuses had ever been authorized by a state constitution or legislature; and second, to identify what census manuscripts still survive. The identification of extant state censuses was very incomplete, due to the war and under-funding of the project.

However, Dubester's review of each state's constitutional provisions for taking state censuses still stands as the best overview of what state censuses were ever authorized. The report cites the specific articles of the state constitutions or the actual state laws relating to censuses for all states.

Unfortunately, the fact that a state legislature authorized a state census does not mean one was actually taken. For example, the State Constitution of California of 1849 authorized a census in the years 1852 and 1855 and each ten years thereafter, all for the purpose of apportionment of its state legislature. Yet, only one was ever taken, that for 1852. Later, the California Constitution of 1879 provided that the decennial national census serve as the basis for legislative apportionment.[2]

This was fairly typical of all states. Even in those states for which several decades of state censuses now survive, they eventually got out of the census business, turning to the federal decennial censuses to determine apportionment. For example, New York took state censuses from 1825 and every ten years thereafter until 1925, yet, in 1938, New York decided to use the federal decennial censuses thereafter.[3]

Since the Dubester report, there have been several attempts to list all known state censuses, where they are located, and the contents of the census name lists. All of these attempts differ dramatically, because some of the lists rely on the Dubester report, which may have been accurate in identifying which state censuses were ever authorized but was not nearly complete in identifying the extant manuscripts of state census records. For example, Table 4-8 of *The Source*,[4] seems to use the census years cited in the Dubester report for "authorized state censuses" rather than those actually extant. There are lists of state censuses for each state in *The Red Book*,[5] but are only a slight improvement over those found in *The Source*. And, several Internet sites offer lists of state censuses, all of which seem to take data previously published in the *Source* or *The Red Book*, and similar publications.

Based on survey results from all states, the Family History Library prepared a two-volume publication, *U.S. State and Special Census Register: A Listing of Family History Library Microfilm Numbers,* compiled by G. Eileen Buckway and Fred Adams, a revised edition published by the FHL in 1992 (FHL book 973 X2 v. 1 & 2, and fiche #6104851 (vol. 1) and #6104852 (vol. 2). This is a particularly good guide to military censuses, school censuses, and special censuses of American Indian tribes. As a guide to state censuses, however, the list is incomplete. Since the results of the surveys from each of the states were only partially successful, there are many omissions.

Clearly, the best list of state censuses to date is Ann S. Lainhart, *State Census Records*, published by Genealogical Publishing Co., Inc., Baltimore, in 1992. The book identifies state censuses in 43 states, including 5 states without state censuses (but have major state-wide census substitutes available). For the 38 state census states, the lists generally do not include colonial or pre-territorial censuses. With a few exceptions, census substitutes such as those compiled from tax lists, voter registration lists, military lists, or other name sources, are also not included. Still, Lainhart's book stands as the most complete list ever done.

At the time when most of the previous state census lists were put together, there were some research tools unavailable to the authors. Today, the Internet as a resource for finding place-specific records is overwhelming. And, special tools such as the Periodical Source Index (PERSI)[6] which indexes articles in over 11,000 different genealogical periodicals (by subject, place, and surname) gives a big boost to the task of finding references to relevant articles using keywords such as "state census," "territorial census," or "tax list." In addition, the State Archives and/or State Libraries where obscure census originals and substitute name lists reside often have a website with an online searchable catalog.

For any genealogical research project, it helps to be close to the Family History Library (FHL) in Salt Lake City. But from any place where a researcher has access to the Internet, the FamilySearch™ online catalog as a genealogical research tool has no equal. Searching for published state censuses and census substitutes in the FHL catalog will not bring up every extant resource, but it is more complete than any other library in the world.

The Evolution of Regional Chapters to State Chapters

In the 2008 First Edition of this work, the two volumes had chapters for six (6) Eastern Regions and five (5) Western Regions of the United States.

For the 2016 Second Edition, the three volumes included an Eastern volume with five (5) regions; the Central Volume had three (3) regions; and the Western volume had four (4) regions; plus, an all-new Nationwide Chapter was added to the Western volume. A timeline for each region was prepared to put the area into a historical perspective from a genealogist's point of view.

This 2020 Third Edition was expanded to five volumes, each volume a region of the United States. Therefore, the content of each state's review now includes much of the content that was done at the regional level in the earlier editions, e.g., there is now a Timeline specific to each state.

The organization of the state bibliographic lists has changed as well. The Second Edition had several category listings for bibliographic entries, including State Resource Centers, Ancestry.com, FamilySearch.org, and others. This Third Edition has just one (1) listing where all databases from any provider are presented in chronological order.

About PERSI

PERSI (PERiodical Source Index) is a digitized database project of the Allen County Public Library (ACPL), Fort Wayne, IN. Since 1986, the PERSI extractors have indexed article titles, places, and surnames from over 11,000 genealogical & historical periodicals. The PERSI database is currently available online through the FindMyPast.com subscription website.

A number of printed articles found in periodicals were included in the state bibliography listings that follow. The Fort Wayne library has an online order form for requesting a printed copy of any article indexed in the PERSI database, see http://genealogycenter.org/docs/default-source/resources/articlerequest.pdf?sfvrsn=2.

Federal Censuses

Since the Second Edition was published in 2016, the digital images of all federal censuses 1790-1940 became accessible to the public via the Family History Library online catalog. It is now possible to view the digital images for any state's federal censuses separate from the various indexed databases at FamilySearch.org, Ancestry.com, My Heritage.com, et al. This meant adding the URL link for each state's digitized federal censuses in this Third Edition.

The Nationwide Chapter (Vol. 5) was completely reorganized into Part 1: *Maps, Descriptions, and Internet Access for the U.S. Federal Censuses, 1790-1950;* and Part 2: *U.S. Census Substitutes.* To review the federal censuses in more detail, refer to *The Census Book*[7] for each census year. The new 2019 *Census Book* has a detailed review of published federal censuses online, 1790-1950.

The maps of the changing county boundaries for all of the states shown in *Map Guide to the U.S. Federal Census, 1790-1920*[8] should also be helpful for reviewing substitute or state census years between federal census years.

- bill$hide

Notes:

1. *State Censuses: An Annotated Bibliography of Censuses of Population Taken After the Year 1790 by States and Territories of the United States*, prepared by Henry J. Dubester, Chief, Census Library Project, Library of Congress, published Washington, DC, by United States Department of Commerce, Bureau of the Census, 1941, rev. 1948.

2. Dubester, *State Censuses*, p. 3.

3. Dubester, *State Censuses*, p. 50.

4. *The Source: A Guidebook of American Genealogy*, first edition, edited by Arlene Eakle and Johni Cerny, published by Ancestry, Inc., Salt Lake City, 1984.

5. *The Red Book: American State, County & Town Sources*, edited by Alice Eichholz, rev. ed., published by Ancestry, Inc., Salt Lake City, UT, 1992.

6. Allen County Public Library, *Periodical Source Index (PERSI)*, updated semi-annually. [database online at various contracted websites] Original data: Allen County Public Library. Periodical Source Index, Fort Wayne, IN: Allen County Public Library Foundation, 1985- .

7. *The Census Book: Facts, Schedules & Worksheets for the U.S Federal Censuses,* by William Dollarhide, publ. Family Roots Publishing Co., Orting, WA, 2019, 245 pages. See www.familyrootspublishing.com/store/product_view.php?id=3643.

8. *Map Guide to the U.S. Federal Censuses, 1790-1920,* by William Thorndale and William Dollarhide, published by Genealogical Publishing Co., Inc., Baltimore, 1987-2016, 445 pages. See www.familyrootspublishing.com/store/product_view.php?id=67.

Table 1 – Non-State Census States. The following 13 states (including DC) have never conducted a state-sponsored census (or no state census survives). Census Substitutes for each state are shown for a range of years. Refer to the bibliographic listings for details about each.

State	Terr.	State	Years for which Census Substitutes are Available
Alaska	1912	1959	1870, 1873, 1878, 1885, 1887, 1890-1895, 1902-1912, 1905, 1908-1914, 1910- 1929, 1913-1916, 1917-1918, 1947, 1950, 1959-1986, and 1960-1985.
Delaware	—	1787	1609-1888, 1646-1679, 1680-1934, 1682-1759, 1684-1693, 1726, 1755, 1759, 1779, 1782, 1785, 1790, 1800, 1807, 1850-1860, and 1862-1872.
District* of Columbia	1801	1871*	1803, 1807, 1818, 1867, 1878, 1885, 1888, 1894, 1897, 1905-1909, 1912-1913, 1915, 1917, 1919, and 1925.
Idaho	1863	1890	1863, 1865-1874, 1871-1881, 1880, 1890, 1911-1937, 1911-1950, and 1930.
Kentucky	—	1792	1773-1780, 1774-1796, 1780-1909, 1781-1839, 1782-1787, 1782-1875, 1787, 1787-1811, 1787-1875, 1788-1875, 1789-1882, 1792-1830, 1792-1913, 1792-1796, 1793-1836, 1794-1805, 1794-1817, 1795, 1796-1808, 1797-1866, 1800, 1820-1900, 1851-1900, 1859-1860, 1860-1936, 1861-1865, 1862-1866, and 1895- 1896.
Montana	1864	1889	1860, 1856-1993, 1864-1872, 1868-1869, 1868-1929, 1870, 1880, 1870-1957, 1872- 1900, 1879-1880, 1881-1928, 1881-2000, 1891-1929, 1894, 1913, 1906- 1917, 1909- 1910, 1917-1918, 1921, and 1930-1975.
New Hampshire	—	1788	1648, 1709. 1723, 1736, 1740, 1763, 1767, 1775, 1776, 1779, 1789, 1795-1816, 1797, 1802, 1803, 1821, 1826, 1833, 1836, 1838, 1849, 1855 & 1865 MA, 1860, 1862-1866, 1903, and 1902-1921
Ohio	1787	1803	1787-1840, 1787-1871, 1788-1799, 1788-1820, 1790, 1800-1803, 1801-1814, 1801-1824, 1802, 1803-1827, 1804, 1807, 1810, 1812, 1816-1838, 1816-1838, 1825, 1827, 1832-1850, 1833-1994, 1835, 1846-1880, 1851-1900, 1851-1907, and 1907.
Pennsylvania	—	1787	1682-1950, 1759, 1680-1938, 1680s-1900s, 1760s-1790s, 1700s, 1780, 1798, 1740- 1900, 1887-1893, and 1870.
Texas	—	1845	1736-1838, 1700s-1800s, 1756-1830s, 1782-1836, 1809-1836, 1814-1909, 1821-1846, 1826, 1826-1835, 1820s-1846, 1820-1829, 1826-1836, 1829-1836, 1830-1839, 1835, 1835-1846, 1836, 1836-1935, 1837-1859, 1840-1849, 1840, 1846, 1837-1910, 1851-1900, 1858, 1861-1865, 1863, 1865-1866, 1867, 1874, 1882-1895, 1884, 1889-1894, 1890, 1914, 1917-1918, 1896-1948, and 1964-1968.
Vermont	—	1791	1770s-1780s, 1700s-1800s, 1654-1800, 1710-1753, 1721-1800, 1770-1832, 1771, 1782, 1788, 1793, 1796-1959, 1800s-1870, 1807, 1813, 1815, 1816, 1827-1833, 1828, 1832, 1843, 1852-1959, 1855-1860, 1861-1866, 1865, 1869, 1871-1908, 1874, 1880-1881, 1881-1882, 1882-1883, 1883-1884, 1884, 1887-1888, 1888, 1889, and 1895-1924.
Virginia	—	1788	1600s-1700s, 1600s, 1619-1930, 1623-1990, 1623-1800, 1632-1800, 1654-1800, 1704-1705, 1720, 1736-1820, 1740, 1744-1890, 1760, 1769-1800, 1779, 1779-1978, 1779-1860, 1782-1785, 1785, 1787, 1809-1848, 1810, 1815, 1828-1938, 1835, 1835-1941, 1840, 1861, 1861-1865, 1852, 1853-1896, and 1889-1890.
West Virginia	—	1863	1600s-1900s, 1777-1850, 1787, 1782-1907, 1782-1850, 1782-1860, 1782, 1783-1900, 1783-1850, 1785-1850, 1787,1850, 1789-1850, 1792-1850, 1797-1899, 1797-1851, 1799-1850, 1800, 1801-1850, 1810, 1811-1850, 1862-1866, 1863-1900, and 1899-1900.

From *Census Substitutes & State Census Records* by William Dollarhide, publ. Family Roots Publishing Co., Orting WA

Table 2 – State Census States – Alabama to Michigan

The following 38 states have state-sponsored censuses available:

State	Year a Terr.	Year a State	Years for which State Censuses are available (underlined year = an online database is available)	Notes
Alabama	1817	1819	**Colony:** 1706 1721 1764 1785 1786-1803 **AL Territory:** 1801* 1808* 1809* 1810* 1816* 1818 **State:** <u>1820</u>** 1821 1823 1832 1838 1844 <u>1850</u>** <u>1855</u> <u>1866</u>.	* as part of MS Terr. ** separate from federal.
Arizona	1863	1912	**AZ Territory:** 1831 <u>1864</u> <u>1866</u> <u>1867</u>* <u>1869</u>* <u>1874</u>* <u>1876</u>* <u>1882</u>*	*1-2 counties only
Arkansas	1819	1836	**Colony:** 1686-1791 **AR Territory:** <u>1814</u>* <u>1823</u> <u>1827</u> <u>1829</u> 1833 1835 **State:** 1838 1854 1865	* as part of MO Terr.
California	—	1850	**Colony:** <u>1790</u> <u>1790-1796</u> 1822 1834 1836 1837 **State:** <u>1852</u> only	
Colorado	1861	1876	**CO Territory:** 1861 1866* **State:** <u>1885</u>	* 2 counties only
Connecticut	--	1788	**Colony:** 1762 **State:** <u>1917</u>*	* Military census, males over 16
Florida	1822	1845	**Colony:** 1759 1763-1779 1783-1814 **FL Territory:** <u>1825</u> 1838 **State:** 1845** 1855 1864* <u>1867</u> <u>1875</u> <u>1885</u> 1895 <u>1935</u> <u>1945</u>	* Military census ** Statehood census
Georgia	—	1788	1800 federal* **State:** Partial lists only: 1827 <u>1838</u> <u>1845</u> 1852 1859 1879 1890 federal** <u>1890</u> (statewide reconstruction).	* Oglethorpe Co only ** Washington Co only
Hawaii	1900	1959	**Kingdom of Hawaii:** 1840-1866 1878 1890 1896	
Illinois	1809	1818	**IL Territory:** <u>1810</u> **State:** <u>1818</u> <u>1820</u>* <u>1825</u> <u>1830</u>* <u>1835</u> <u>1840</u>* <u>1845</u> <u>1855</u> <u>1865</u>.	* separate from federal
Indiana	1800	1816	**IN Territory:** <u>1807</u>. **State:** A few townships only: 1857 1871 1877 1883 1889 1901 1913 1919 1931	
Iowa	1838	1846	As part of **WI Territory:** <u>1836</u> **IA Territory:** <u>1838</u> **State:** <u>1844</u> <u>1845</u> <u>1847</u> <u>1849</u> <u>1851</u> <u>1852</u> <u>1853</u> <u>1854</u> <u>1856</u> <u>1859</u> <u>1873</u> <u>1875</u> <u>1885</u> <u>1888</u> <u>1893</u> <u>1895</u> <u>1896</u> <u>1897</u> <u>1905</u> <u>1915</u> <u>1925</u>	
Kansas	1854	1861	**KS Territory:** <u>1855</u> <u>1856</u> <u>1857</u> <u>1858</u> <u>1859</u> **State:** <u>1865</u> <u>1875</u> <u>1885</u> <u>1895</u> <u>1905</u> <u>1915</u> <u>1925</u>	
Louisiana	1809	1812	**Orleans District:** 1804 **State:** 1833 1837 1890 federal*	*Ascension Parish only
Maine	—	1820	<u>1837</u> only.	
Maryland	—	1788	<u>1776</u> <u>1778</u> <u>1783</u>*	* Tax list
Massachusetts	—	1788	<u>1855</u> <u>1865</u>	
Michigan	1805	1837	**MI Territory:** <u>1827</u> <u>1834</u> **State:** <u>1837</u> <u>1845</u> <u>1854</u> <u>1864</u> <u>1874</u> <u>1884</u> <u>1894</u>	

From *Census Substitutes & State Census Records* by William Dollarhide, publ. Family Roots Publishing Co., Orting WA

Table 2 – State Census States – Minnesota to Wyoming

Continuation of states with state-sponsored censuses available:

State	Year a Terr.	Year a State	Years for which State Censuses are available (underlined year = an online database is available)	Notes
Minnesota	1849	1858	**MN Territory:** 1849 1853 1855 1857* **State:** 1865 1875 1885 1895 1905	* special federal
Mississippi	1798	1817	**Colony:** 1792** **MS Territory:** 1801 1805 1809 1810 1813 1815 1816 1817 **State:** 1818 1820* 1822 1823 1824 1825 1830* 1837 1840* 1841 1845 1850* 1853 1857 1866	* separate from federal ** Natchez District only
Missouri	1805	1821	**Colony:** 1752 1791 1797 **MO Territory:** 1817 1818 1819 **State:** 1844* 1845* 1846* 1852* 1856* 1864* 1868* 1876**	* 1-2 counties only ** 28 counties
Nebraska	1854	1867	**NE Territory:** 1854 1855 1856 1865 **State:** Lancaster & Cass Co Only: 1874 1875 1876 1877 1878 1881 1882 1883 1884 1885	
Nevada	1861	1864	**NV Territory:** 1861 1862 1863 **State:** 1864 1875	
New Jersey	—	1787	1855 1865 1875* 1885 1895 1905 1915	* a few townships only
New Mexico	1850	1912	**Colony:** 1600 1750 1790 **Territory:** 1885	
New York	—	1788	1825 1835 1845 1855 1865 1875 1892 1905 1915 1925	
North Carolina	—	1789	**Pre-statehood:** 1784 -1787.	
North Dakota	1861*	1889	**Dakota Territory:** 1885 **State:** 1905 (statistics only) 1915 1925	* Dakota Territory
Oklahoma	1890	1907	**OK Territory:** 1890* **State:** 1907 federal (Seminole Co. only)	* separate from federal
Oregon	1848	1859	**OR Provisional Territory:** 1842 1843 1845 1846 **OR Territory:** 1849 1853 1854 1855 1856 1857 1858 1859 **State:** 1865* 1875* 1885* 1895* 1905	* indexes for a few counties only
Rhode Island	—	1790	1865 1875 1885 1905 1915 1925 1935	
South Carolina	—	1788	1829 1839 1869 1875	
South Dakota	1861*	1889	**Dakota Territory:** 1885 **State:** 1895 1905 1915 1925 1935 1945	* Dakota Territory
Tennessee	1790*	1796	**Southwest Territory:** 1790 (Reconstructed) **State:** 1891 (partial)	
Utah	1850	1896	**UT Territory:** 1856 only.	
Washington	1853	1889	**WA Territory:** 1851* 1856 1857 1858 1859 1861 1871 1879 1881 1883 1885 1887 **State:** 1891 1892 1894 1898	* As part of Oregon Territory.
Wisconsin	1836	1848	**WI Territory:** 1836 1838 1842 1846 1847 **State:** 1855 1865 1875 1885 1895 1905	
Wyoming	1868	1890	**WY Territory:** 1869 1885*.	*1 county only

From *Census Substitutes & State Census Records* by William Dollarhide, publ. Family Roots Publishing Co., Orting, WA

Table 3 – State Censuses Taken in Common Years. As a means of comparing state censuses taken by the 38 state census states, this table shows the common years for which many states conducted a state census. Many were done in years ending in "5." Census dates for some states are within a range, e.g., within 3 years of 1825, are indicated in the 1825 column.

	1815	1825	1835	1845	1855	1865	1875	1885	1895	1905	1915	1925	1935	1945
Alabama	•	•	•	•	•	•								
Arizona						•								
Arkansas	•	•	•		•	•								
California					•									
Colorado						•		•						
Connecticut											•			
Florida		•			•		•	•	•			•	•	•
Georgia		•	•	•	•		•							
Hawaii			•			•		•		•				
Illinois			•	•	•									
Indiana						•		•	•		•			
Iowa				•	•	•		•	•	•	•	•		
Kansas						•	•	•	•	•	•	•		
Louisiana				•										
Maine				•										
Maryland														
Massachusetts					•	•								
Michigan			•	•	•	•	•	•	•					
Minnesota					•	•	•	•	•	•	•			
Mississippi	•	•	•	•	•	•								
Missouri					•	•	•	•						
Nebraska						•	•	•	•					
Nevada							•	•						
New Jersey					•	•	•	•	•	•	•			
New Mexico									•					
New York		•	•	•	•	•	•		•	•	•	•		
No. Carolina														
No. Dakota								•		•	•	•		
Oklahoma										•	•			
Oregon				•	•	•	•	•	•	•				
Rhode Island							•	•	•	•	•	•	•	
So. Carolina		•	•			•	•							
So. Dakota								•		•	•	•	•	•
Tennessee									•					
Utah					•									
Washington						•		•	•	•				
Wisconsin			•		•	•	•	•	•	•				
Wyoming						•								
No. of States:	3	8	12	11	21	20	17	16	16	11	9	7	3	2

From *Census Substitutes & State Census Records* by William Dollarhide, published by Family Roots Publishing Co., Orting WA

Table 4 - Availability of Federal Censuses for each State

State	Year a Terr	Year a State	1790	1800	1810	1820	1830	1840	1850	1860	1870	1880	1890	1900	1910	1920	1930	1940	1950
Alabama	1817	1819				lost	●	●	●	●	●	●	lost	●	●	●	●	●	●
Alaska (to US 1867)	1912	1959	No census taken, District of Alaska, 1870, 1880, or 1890 →								--	--	--	●	●	●	●	●	●
Arizona	1863	1912									●	●	lost	●	●	●	●	●	●
Arkansas	1819	1836				lost	●	●	●	●	●	●	lost	●	●	●	●	●	●
California (to US 1848)	—	1850							●	●	●	●	lost	●	●	●	●	●	●
Colorado	1861	1876										●	lost	●	●	●	●	●	●
Connecticut	—	1788	●	●	●	●	●	●	●	●	●	●	lost	●	●	●	●	●	●
Delaware	—	1787	●	●	●	●	●	●	●	●	●	●	lost	●	●	●	●	●	●
Distr. of Columbia	1801	—		●	●	●	●	●	●	●	●	●	lost	●	●	●	●	●	●
Florida	1822	1845							●	●	●	●	lost	●	●	●	●	●	●
Georgia	—	1788	lost	lost	lost	●	●	●	●	●	●	●	lost	●	●	●	●	●	●
Hawaii (to US 1898)	1900	1959												●	●	●	●	●	●
Idaho	1863	1890									●	●	lost	●	●	●	●	●	●
Illinois	1809	1818			part	●	●	●	●	●	●	●	lost	●	●	●	●	●	●
Indiana	1800	1816		lost	lost	●	●	●	●	●	●	●	lost	●	●	●	●	●	●
Iowa (* part of WI Terr.)	1838	1846						●*	●	●	●	●	lost	●	●	●	●	●	●
Kansas	1854	1861									●	●	lost	●	●	●	●	●	●
Kentucky (*Distr. of VA)	—	1791	lost*	lost	●	●	●	●	●	●	●	●	lost	●	●	●	●	●	●
Louisiana (*OrleansTer)	1809	1812			●*	●	●	●	●	●	●	●	lost	●	●	●	●	●	●
Maine (*Distr. of MA)	—	1820	●*	●*	●*	●	●	●	●	●	●	●	lost	●	●	●	●	●	●
Maryland	—	1788	●	●	●	●	●	●	●	●	●	●	lost	●	●	●	●	●	●
Massachusetts	—	1788	●	●	●	●	●	●	●	●	●	●	lost	●	●	●	●	●	●
Michigan	1805	1837				lost	●	●	●	●	●	●	lost	●	●	●	●	●	●
Minnesota	1849	1858	MN Terr. had a special federal census in 1857 →						●	●	●	●	lost	●	●	●	●	●	●
Mississippi	1798	1817			lost	lost	●	●	●	●	●	●	lost	●	●	●	●	●	●
Missouri	1805	1821			lost	lost	●	●	●	●	●	●	lost	●	●	●	●	●	●
Montana	1864	1889									●	●	lost	●	●	●	●	●	●
Nebraska	1854	1867									●	●	lost	●	●	●	●	●	●
Nevada	1861	1864									●	●	lost	●	●	●	●	●	●
New Hampshire	—	1788	●	●	●	●	●	●	●	●	●	●	lost	●	●	●	●	●	●
New Jersey	—	1787	lost	lost	lost	lost	●	●	●	●	●	●	lost	●	●	●	●	●	●
New Mexico	1850	1912							●	●	●	●	lost	●	●	●	●	●	●
New York	—	1788	●	●	●	●	●	●	●	●	●	●	lost	●	●	●	●	●	●
North Carolina	—	1789	●	●	●	●	●	●	●	●	●	●	lost	●	●	●	●	●	●
North Dakota*	1861	1889	*1860, 1870, 1880 as part of Dakota Territory →							●	●	●	lost	●	●	●	●	●	●
Ohio (*NW Terr.)	1787	1803		*lost	lost	●	●	●	●	●	●	●	lost	●	●	●	●	●	●
Oklahoma	1890	1907	1 month prior to statehood in 1907, Oklahoma Territory had a special federal census										lost	●	●	●	●	●	●
Oregon	1848	1859							●	●	●	●	lost	●	●	●	●	●	●
Pennsylvania	—	1787	●	●	●	●	●	●	●	●	●	●	lost	●	●	●	●	●	●
Rhode Island	—	1790	●	●	●	●	●	●	●	●	●	●	lost	●	●	●	●	●	●
South Carolina	—	1788	●	●	●	●	●	●	●	●	●	●	lost	●	●	●	●	●	●
South Dakota*	1861	1889	*1860, 1870, 1880 as part of Dakota Territory →							●	●	●	lost	●	●	●	●	●	●
Tennessee (*SW Terr)	1790	1796	*tally	lost	lost	part	●	●	●	●	●	●	lost	●	●	●	●	●	●
Texas (to US 1845)	—	1845							●	●	●	●	lost	●	●	●	●	●	●
Utah	1850	1896							●	●	●	●	lost	●	●	●	●	●	●
Vermont	—	1791	●	●	●	●	●	●	●	●	●	●	lost	●	●	●	●	●	●
Virginia	—	1788	lost	lost	●	●	●	●	●	●	●	●	lost	●	●	●	●	●	●
Washington	1853	1889									●	●	lost	●	●	●	●	●	●
West Virginia	—	1863	Part of Virginia, 1790-1860								●	●	lost	●	●	●	●	●	●
Wisconsin	1836	1848							●	●	●	●	lost	●	●	●	●	●	●
Wyoming	1868	1890									●	●	lost	●	●	●	●	●	●

From *Census Substitutes & State Census Records* by William Dollarhide, publ. Family Roots Publishing Co., Orting WA

18 • *Census Substitutes & State Census Records*

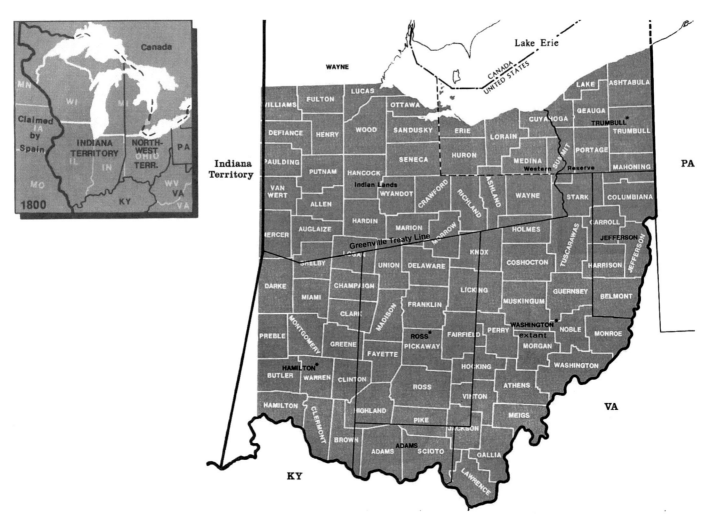

Ohio • 1800 (as part of the *Territory Northwest of the River Ohio*). The six Northwest Territory counties in the Ohio area are shown in black. The current 88 counties of Ohio are shown in white *Hamilton, Ross, and Washington are shown north to the 1795 Greenville Treaty Line. The Western Reserve was ceded by Connecticut in May 1800 and became Trumbull County, Northwest Territory in July, but only the eastern part of the county was free of Indian titles. See **http://usgwarchives.net/maps/cessions/ilcmap49.htm** for a detailed map showing all Indian Land Cessions in Ohio. The 1800 Census name lists were lost for all counties except Washington, shown as "extant" on the map. Washington County's census name lists for 1800 and 1810 were copied into the Ohio Company of Associates records. The original manuscripts are located today at Marietta College, Marrietta, Ohio. Wayne County on the map was created by Northwest Territory in 1796, its area encompassing the eastern half of the Lower Peninsula of present Michigan, plus the eastern tip of the Upper Peninsula. Most of the white population in the first Wayne County was near Fort Detroit, still occupied by the British Army; but there were also a few left-over French-Canadian fur traders near Saulte Ste. Marie. After Ohio's statehood in 1803, the name Northwest Territory was dropped, and the area of the first Wayne County was added to Indiana Territory, where the name Wayne was dropped. Ohio then created a new Wayne County in 1808; Indiana Territory created a new Wayne County in 1811; and Michigan Territory created a new Wayne County in 1815. **Map Source:** Page 268, *Map Guide to the U.S. Federal Censuses, 1790-1920*, by William Thorndale and William Dollarhide.

Ohio
Censuses & Substitute Name Lists

Historical Timeline for Ohio, 1614-1845

1614-1615. Ohio Country. Samuel de Champlain, governor of New France and the founder of Québec, was the first of the French explorers to visit the Ohio country via Lake Erie. He is believed to have entered the Maumee River in 1614 or 1615.

1668. Great Lakes region. French Jesuit missionaries Jacques Marquette and Claude Dablon established the first mission at Sault Sainte Marie.

1670. Great Lakes region. René-Robert Cavelier (Sieur La Salle) explored and claimed the Ohio country for France.

1717. French Louisiana. The *Illinois Country* was officially added to the French Louisiana jurisdiction within New France. At that time *la Louisiane Française* extended from the Wabash River, down the Ohio and Mississippi Rivers to include several ports on the Gulf of Mexico. Any trading posts or forts north of the Highlands (Terra Haute) were considered part of French Québec.

1721. Fort Philippe, later called Fort Miami, was built on the St. Mary's River, near present Fort Wayne, Indiana where the St. Mary's, St. Joseph's and Maumee Rivers meet.

1754-1763. French and Indian War. The Ohio Company of Virginia asserted the British claim to the Ohio region and began sending fur trading parties to the area. The British encroachment into "New France" and the French encroachment into "Virginia" led to a war between Britain and France. The first French Fort in the area was at the Forks of the Ohio, Fort Duquesne (now Pittsburgh) which became the focus of British forays into the western wilderness of colonial America for the first time. After the war, two wagon roads emerged (Braddock's Road and Forbes' Road) that provided overland migration routes to the Ohio River.

1763. Treaty of Paris. This was the end of the French and Indian war. (In Europe it was called the "Seven Years War.") At the 1763 Treaty, the French surrendered all their claims in North America. Spain acquired the former French areas west of the Mississippi, renamed *Spanish Louisiana*. Great Britain gained all of Québec, which they renamed the *Province of Canada*. Britain also gained control of the rest of North America east of the Mississippi River, and named their entire area *British North America*. The British continued the most important activity in the acquired areas: fur trading. The Hudson's Bay Company and the North West Fur Company, both British owned companies, were entrenched in the Great Lakes region, and the British Army was there for their protection.

1774. Québec Act. In response to increased American colonial rebellions, the British sought to solidify loyalty from their French communities in British Canada. The British Parliament passed the Québec Act, which restored the name Québec, allowed the French Canadians to retain French laws and customs, and permitted the Catholic Church to maintain all of its rights. The early French claims in present-day Ohio, Michigan, Indiana, Illinois and Wisconsin, were by the act included in the Province of Québec, under British rule.

1776-1783. Revolutionary War in the Great Lakes Area. British-held interests in the Great Lakes region suffered major defeats, losing the former French communities of Vincennes and Kaskaskia. Both victories were led by American General George Rogers Clark, who was later called the Conqueror of the Old

Northwest. But the British maintained other communities without a fight, such as Fort Detroit, Prairie du Chien, and Fort Miami (now Fort Wayne). The British left-over presence in the Great Lakes region was related to the fur trade, a lucrative source of revenue they were reluctant to leave.

1783. The Treaty of Paris recognized the United States of America as an independent nation and defined its borders from the Atlantic Ocean to the Mississippi River. Although the settlements in the Great Lakes region (formerly part of the Province of Québec) were to be included within the United States, British military forces continued to maintain control over parts of the Great Lakes area for several years after the Revolution.

1784. Ohio Country. New York, Massachusetts, Connecticut, and Virginia relinquished their claim to lands in the Ohio Country. Title transferred to the "public domain" of the United States Government. Connecticut retained ownership of the Western Reserve on Lake Erie and Virginia retained ownership of the Virginia Military District between the Scioto and Little Miami Rivers.

1787. Jul 13. Northwest Territory. The Ordinance of 1787 established the "Territory Northwest of the River Ohio," and defined the procedure for any territory to obtain statehood. The territorial capital was at Chillicothe. Present states carved out of the original area of the Northwest Territory included Ohio, Indiana, Illinois, Michigan, Wisconsin, and that part of Minnesota east of the Mississippi River.

1787-1815. Flatboat Era. The main family transportation on the Ohio River (usually beginning at Brownsville, Pittsburgh, or Wheeling) was by a flatboat designed for a one-way trip. The large, steerable rafts were constructed of lumber and nails that could be disassembled by migrating families when they arrived at their new homesites along the Ohio River and tributaries. The flatboat era continued until the classic flat-bottomed steamboats were introduced on the Ohio River in 1815.

1788. Ohio Country. Marietta was Ohio's first permanent settlement. It was founded in 1788 by General Rufus Putnam and named in honor of Marie Antoinette. Putman's Ohio Company purchased a large tract of land above the Ohio River and sold parcels to the first settlers of Ohio, most of whom arrived at Marietta by flatboat via Pittsburgh.

1790. Federal Census. The Northwest Territory was specifically left out of the 1790 enumeration. Part of the white population was around Fort Detroit and Fort Miami, two enclaves still under control of the British Army. There was a growing number of settlers arriving daily at Rufas Putnam's land office in Marrietta. But, the Northwest Territory was still mostly under control of the Indians, who had formed a Western Confederation of American Indians to defend their territory from the white invaders.

1791. Northwest Indian War. Governor Arthur St. Clair, a former Revolutionary War general, was the leader of the local militia force. In 1791, he suffered a terrible defeat against the Western Confederation of American Indians, with over 1,000 militia deaths.

1792. President George Washington had long believed that the United States did not need a large Regular Army during peacetime, and that local militia forces could handle any military needs. General St. Clair's disastrous defeat in the "Battle of a Thousand Slain" changed his mind. In 1792, Washington reactivated Major General Anthony Wayne, his favorite Revolutionary War general, to counter the Indian attacks in the Northwest Territory. General Wayne was put in charge of an all new Legion of the United States, the first post-Revolutionary War regular army force.

1794. Battle of Fallen Timbers. Led by General "Mad" Anthony Wayne, the Legion of the United States forces mounted a ferocious assault against the Indian forces concentrated on the Maumee River near present Toledo, Ohio. The American forces won a decisive victory which led to the end the Northwest Indian War.

1795. The **Treaty of Greenville** was the official end to the Northwest Indian War. A "Greenville Line" across present Ohio and Indiana defined the extent of areas opened to settlement by whites. The Greenville Line is easily seen on the 1800 map on page 18, the northwest area of "Indian Lands" is above the line.

1800. Indiana Territory was established, taken from the Northwest Territory, with William Henry Harrison as the first Governor and Vincennes the capital. The area included all of present Indiana, Illinois, Wisconsin, and the western half of Michigan. The Northwest Territory was reduced to the present-day area of Ohio and the eastern half of Michigan.

1803. Mar 1. **Ohio** was admitted to the Union as the 17th state, with boundaries nearly the same as today. Chillicothe was the first state capital. The portion of Michigan included in the Northwest Territory 1800-1803 became part of Indiana Territory. Upon Ohio's statehood, the name Northwest Territory was dropped.

1810. Ohio. The state capital was moved from Chillicothe to Zanesville.

1812-1813. Ohio in the War of 1812. Fort Meigs was constructed to protect Ohio from invasion during the War of 1812. The fort was the largest walled fortification in North America, and successfully defended the Maumee River gateway to Ohio and Indiana from two major invasions by British troops and their allied Indians in 1813.

1812-1815. Steamboats. First introduced in 1812, by 1815 steamboats had quickly become the main mode of transportation on the Ohio and Mississippi Rivers.

1814. Treaty of Ghent. The War of 1812 ended. The remaining British-held posts in the Great Lakes region were finally vacated, freeing up American settlement of the Old Northwest.

1816. Ohio. The state capital was moved from Zanesville to Columbus.

1825. Erie Canal opened. This New York route from the Hudson River to Lake Erie provided direct access to the Ohio Country. Western New York and the State of Ohio were impacted the most, with many settlements attributed to the early Erie Canal travelers.

1835. Toledo War. Michigan Territory's drive for statehood created heated arguments in Congress over the proposed Michigan-Ohio boundary. Michigan was not admitted to the Union because they would not surrender their claim to the Toledo Strip. As an adjoining state, Ohio asserted its veto power over the first attempt for statehood for Michigan Territory. Ohio had a claim to the Toledo Strip based on their original state bounds of 1803, but Ohio was really interested in the Toledo Strip as the starting point for a proposed canal to run from Lake Erie to the Ohio River.

1837. Jan 26. **Michigan** was admitted to the Union as the 26th state, soon after the Toledo Strip was finally surrendered to Ohio. The gift of the Toledo Strip was essentially Michigan's price of admission to the Union.

1845. The **Miami and Erie Canal** was opened for business by the state of Ohio. Running from Toledo to Cincinnati, it was the longest canal in America and an enterprise that probably would not have happened without the help of a major land donation by Michigan. By 1850, railroads began operating in Ohio, and the preferred method of transportation shifted from wagon roads and water canals to railroads.

Online Resources at Ohio State Websites

Ohio History Connection. The Ohio History Center in Columbus houses the largest collection of materials of interest to genealogists in the state of Ohio. The building is also the headquarters for the Ohio History Connection (formerly the Ohio Historical Society, renamed in 2014), which, among other state functions, serves as the State Archives of Ohio. To view a list of topics at the Ohio History Connection website, see **www.ohiohistory.org.**

Ohio Memory. Along with the State Library of Ohio, also located in Columbus, the Ohio History Connection hosts some online databases that have proved very useful to genealogical researchers. Ohio Memory contains over 500,000 items in a variety of materials including
- Manuscripts (letters, diaries, etc.)
- Photographs
- Maps
- Archaeological and historical objects
- Newspapers
- Video
- Government records

To view the long list of Ohio Memory collections, see **www.ohiohistoryhost.org/ohiomemory/collections.**

Ohio Network of American History Research Centers. This regional archives system was organized by the Ohio History Connection in 1970. Currently, the ONAHR is composed of four state universities and Ohio's two largest historical societies. The network preserves and makes available all forms of documentation from local governments. For more information about each of the six centers, see their separate websites:

University of Akron Libraries, Archival Services, Akron, OH. Coverage includes Ashland, Coshocton, Holmes, Portage, Richland, Stark, Summit, Tuscarawas, and Wayne counties, Ohio. See www.uakron.edu/libraries/archives/collections/local-government-records.dot.

University of Cincinnati Libraries, Archives & Rare Books Department. Coverage includes Adams, Brown, Butler, Clermont, Clinton, Hamilton, and Warren counties. See https://libraries.uc.edu/libraries/arb.html.

Ohio History Connection, Archives & Library, Columbus. Coverage includes the entire state. See http://catalog.ohiohistory.org/Presto/home/home.aspx.

Western Reserve Historical Society Library, Cleveland, OH. Coverage includes Ashtabula, Cuyahoga, Geauga, Lake, Lorain, and Medina counties. See www.wrhs.org/research/library.

Paul Laurence Dunbar Library, Special Collections and Archives, Wright State University, Dayton, OH. Coverage includes Auglaize, Champaign, Clark, Darke, Greene, Logan, Mercer, Miami, Montgomery, Preble, and Shelby Counties.
See www.libraries.wright.edu/special/localgovernment.

Youngstown Historical Center of Industry and Labor, Archives & Library, Youngstown State University, Youngstown, OH. See their webpage at the Ohio History Connection:
www.ohiohistory.org/visit/museum-and-site-locator/youngstown-historical-center-of-industry-and-labor.

Bibliography
Ohio Censuses & Substitutes

Ohio is one of 38 state census states. Although the term *census* was not used, an *enumeration* was authorized in the State Constitution of 1802, which provided for a listing of white males over the age of 21 to be taken every four years. They became known as *Quadrennial Enumerations*. In addition, there were a series of tax lists from each of the Ohio counties that became known as *Duplicate Tax Lists*. Together, these name lists provide researchers with a good starting point to find the exact place of residence for persons in Ohio.

Ohio Quadrennial Enumerations. The first of these enumerations was taken in 1803 and continued every four years until they officially ended in 1911. Tax assessors from each county were in charge of the quadrennial enumerations, and they were often taken simultaneously with lists of property owners subject to taxes. But the quadrennial enumeration lists were separate from tax assessment lists – they were compiled specifically for determining the number of males of voting age and reapportioning the state legislature every four years. Of the more than 1,800 county-wide Quadrennial Enumerations taken between 1803 and 1911, less than 100 lists have survived.

Ohio Duplicate Tax Lists. During the first half of the 19th century, numerous tax lists were taken at the county level in Ohio. The lists were gathered and maintained by county tax assessors, with a copy sent to the state auditor's office. Some of the original county tax lists have survived, but most of the surviving name lists today are the state auditor's duplicate originals. It is the Duplicate Tax Lists that now have microfilmed/digitized copies available for virtually all counties of Ohio. In just the past couple of years, online research in Ohio records now starts with the Duplicate Tax Lists – they are Ohio's best census substitutes, particularly for the period 1810-1850.

Ohio Federal Censuses. The earliest census taken in the Northwest Territory was for 1800, and the first federal census taken in the state of Ohio was for 1810. Both censuses were lost for most areas. The exception was for Washington County, where Rufus Putnam's Ohio Company of Associates kept good records beginning in 1788, and saved copies of the earliest censuses. Putnam's papers are located today at the Campus Museum of Marietta College, Marietta, Ohio.

The federal censuses, 1820 through 1940 are complete for all counties of Ohio, with the exception of the 1890, lost in a fire in Washington, DC in 1921 (like all states).

Other Censuses & Census Substitutes. An annotated list begins below:

***1787-1840 Ohio* [CD-ROM],** part of the Family Tree Maker Archives, Land and Tax Records, published by Broderbund, 1999. Contents: *Early Ohio Settlers: Purchasers of Land in Southeastern Ohio, 1800-1840*

(Marietta Land Office), compiled by Ellen T. Berry and David A. Berry; *Early Ohio Settlers: Purchasers of Land in Southeastern Ohio, 1800-1840* (Cincinnati Land Office), compiled by Ellen T. Berry and David A. Berry; *Early Ohio Settlers: Purchasers of Land in East and East Central Ohio,* compiled by Ellen Thomas Berry and David A. Berry; *First Ownership of Ohio Lands,* by Albion Morris Dyer; and Early Ohio Tax Records, by Esther Weygandt Powell. FHL CD No. 9, pt. 651.

1787-1871. *Virginia Military District Lands of Ohio; Indexes* **[Microfilm & Digital Capture].** The Northwest Territory was established by Congress in 1787 from lands ceded to the U.S. Government by Massachusetts, New York, Connecticut, and Virginia. Excluded from the cessions were any areas held in reserve by those states for land grants to veterans or others after the Revolutionary War. The *Virginia Military District* was specifically excluded from the jurisdiction of the Northwest Territory and the area was used for the express purpose of land grants to veterans of the Virginia Line of the Revolution.

The following information comes from the Ohio State Auditor's Office: "The Virginia Military District (VMD) lands lie north of the Ohio River and between the Scioto and Little Miami Rivers. It covers all the present-day counties of Adams, Brown, Clermont, Clinton, Fayette, Highland, Madison, and Union counties; and parts of Champaign, Clark, Delaware, Franklin, Greene, Hamilton, Hardin, Logan, Marion, Pickaway, Pike, Ross, Scioto, and Warren counties. The VMD lands were given by the State of Virginia as a reward to her Revolutionary War soldiers or their heirs. The rectangular survey system was not used in the VMD as used elsewhere in Ohio. To claim a warrant issued to a soldier, the soldier or his heirs sent the warrant to the Principal Surveyor of the Virginia District of Ohio. He in turn gave it to the Deputy Surveyor who gave a general description of the entry and then made a survey based on physical features such as certain trees, etc. The warrant then was sent to the U.S. Government and a U.S. Patent was made out. The first survey was made in 1787 and the first U.S. Patent was issued in 1796. In 1830 and 1852 the VMD warrants could be exchanged for land scrip and used to buy any public land open for sale. Virginia in 1852 ceded to the U.S. government any land not yet granted in the VMD. This land was given to Ohio in 1871 and they gave it to Ohio State University. The University sold these lands into the 1940s." The records were filmed by the Genealogical Society of Utah, 1995, 1958, 33 rolls, beginning with FHL film #2022655 (Index to entrymen: A – Coalier). To access the digital images, see the online FHL catalog page: www.familysearch.org/search/catalog/758280.

1787-1876. *Ohio, Biographic Sketches* **[Online Database],** digitized and OCR indexed at Ancestry.com. Original data: *The Biographical Encyclopedia of Ohio of the Nineteenth Century.* Columbus, OH, publ. Galaxy Publishing Co., 1876. This database has 1,074 records, see www.ancestry.com/search/collections/4635.

1787-1900. *The Ohio Surname Index* **[Microfilm & Digital Capture],** from a card index compiled by the Ohio Society of the Daughters of the American Revolution, under the supervision of Miss Alice Boardman, now located at the Ohio History Connection, Columbus, OH. Arranged alphabetically by surname. Some cards are out of order. Indexes individuals mentioned in various county histories and historical magazines. Film at FHL: 64 rolls, beginning with FHL film #398201 (Aarents, William - Alkire, Ruan). To access the digital images, see the online FHL catalog page:
https://familysearch.org/search/catalog/86323.
- See Also, *Ancestor Card File* **[Microfilm & Digital Capture],** from a card index at the Ohio Genealogical Society, Mansfield, OH. Year range may extend into the 1980s. The OGS card index rivals the DAR index above but is not completely digitized yet. Filmed by the Genealogical Society of Utah, 1988, 39 rolls, beginning with FHL film #1562006. To access the digital images for certain rolls, see the online FHL catalog page: www.familysearch.org/search/catalog/590587.

1787-1903. *Card Files (Bureau of Land Management, Eastern States, Alexandria, VA)* **[Microfilm & Digital Capture],** from the original index cards to public land sales in Ohio and other eastern states. The index cards are organized by Range/Township. Although the images are digitized, this particular film series does not include an index to the names of land buyers. Each card contains the following information: Certificate number, District Land Office, Kind of entry (cash, credit, warrant, etc.), Name of patentee and county of origin, Land description, Number of acres, Date of patent, and the

volume and page where document can be located. Because these index cards are arranged by township and range within each state, the researcher will need to already have an approximate legal description in order to use these cards effectively. Filmed by BLM, c1965, 160 rolls, the Ohio Townships are on the first 23 rolls, starting with FHL film #1501522 (OH Twp 1N-8N Ranges 1E-5E). To access the digital images, see the online FHL catalog page:
www.familysearch.org/search/catalog/511740.
- See also *Bureau of Land Management – General Land Office Records* [Online Database], search for the name of any land purchaser of public land in the U.S. To access the search screen, see
https://glorecords.blm.gov/search/default.aspx.

1787-1929. The *Official Roster of the Soldiers of the American Revolution Buried in the State of Ohio* [Online Database], indexed at the Ancestry.com website. Source: Ancestry cites the Adjutant General's report, 1929 (But, this 3-vol. set contains hundreds of pages regarding DAR projects in Ohio, leading one to assume that the DAR had something to do with the production of this book). This database has 1,336 pages. See
http://search.ancestry.com/search/db.aspx?dbid=20105.

1787-1973. *Ohio, Births and Christenings Index* [Online Database], indexed at the Ancestry.com website. Source: FamilySearch extractions from original and compiled records. A number of records have birthdates in the 1770s in Ohio counties that did not exist until after 1805. Each record may include name, gender, race, birthplace, birth date, date of christening, place of christening, age at christening, father's name, age, birthplace, mother's name, age, birthplace, and FHL film number. This database has 13,086,969 records. See
http://search.ancestry.com/search/db.aspx?dbid=2541.

1787-1986. *Ohio Source Records: From the Ohio Genealogical Quarterly* [Printed Book], excerpted and reprinted from The Ohio Genealogical Quarterly, publ. Genealogical Publishing Co., Baltimore, 1986. with added publisher's note, contents, index, and textual notes. Contains abstracts of probate records, marriages, cemetery inscriptions, histories, family histories, tax lists, military records, etc. FHL book 977.1 D28o.

1780s-2008. *Ohio, Church Records* [Online Database], vital records from various Ohio churches. The title date 1762 is probably incorrect. This database has 54,778 records, see
www.familysearch.org/search/collection/2787827.

1788. *The Founders of Ohio: Brief Sketches of the Forty Eight Pioneers Who, Under Command of General Rufus Putnam Landed at the Mouth of the Muskingum River on the Seventh of April, 1788, and Commenced the First White Settlement of the Northwest Territory* [Printed Book & Digital Version], by Julia P. Cutler, publ. Cincinnati: R. Clarke & Co., 1888, 28 pages, FHL book 977.1 H2. To access the digital version, see the online FHL catalog page:
www.familysearch.org/search/catalog/150281.

1788-1817. *Ohio Early Census Index* [Printed Book], edited by Ronald Vern Jackson, Accelerated Indexing Systems, Salt Lake City, 1974, 2 vols. Contents: vol. 1: Cincinnati, 1798, 1799, 1817; vol. 2: Others, 1788, 1789, 1796, 1798, 1799. FHL book 977.1 X22jr. See also *Early Ohio Census Records,* 2nd edition, 3rd printing, published by Accelerated Indexing, Bountiful, UT, 1974, which adds censuses for 1800 Northwest Territory and Ohio 1803 and 1810 (Washington County only). FHL book 977.1 X2p.

1788-1820. *Ohio Marriages Recorded in County Courts Through 1820: An Index* [Printed Book], compiled by Jean Nathan, et al, published by the Ohio Genealogical Society, Mansfield, OH, 1966, 1,167 pages. FHL book 977.1 V22o.

1788-1855. *Abstract of Probate Records, Washington County, Ohio* [Online Database], indexed at the Ancestry.com website. Source: Bernice Graham's *Abstract of Probate Records, Washington County, Ohio,* publ. 1995. When it was created in 1788, Washington County covered nearly half of the present state of Ohio. This volume contains abstracts of wills, estates, and guardian records of Washington County from 1789 to 1855 – the earliest on record. Some 4,000 early Washington residents are identified, see
http://search.ancestry.com/search/db.aspx?dbid=49011.

1788-2013. *Ohio, Marietta Cemetery Records* [Online Database], digitized and indexed at FamilySearch.org. Index and images of cemetery records from the Mound,

Harmar, and Oak Grove Cemeteries in Marietta, Washington County, Ohio. This database has 20,357 records, see
www.familysearch.org/search/collection/2492733.

1789-1898. *Ohio Marriages* **[Online Database]**, indexed at the Ancestry.com website. Source: Marjorie Smith's *Ohio Marriages. Extracted from The Old Northwest Genealogical Quarterly*. Publ. 1986. The records include name, spouse, marriage place (county, sometimes a church), and marriage date. Some records may also include details on the officiant, race, and emancipation. This database has 10,511 records. See http://search.ancestry.com/search/db.aspx?dbid=3717.

1789-1996. *Ohio Probate Records* **[Online Database]**, digitized at the FamilySearch.org website. Source: FamilySearch extractions from county courthouse records in all Ohio counties. This image only database includes Administrative dockets, Estate records, Guardianships, Journals, Wills, and Misc. files. In most cases, the files include the Name of the testator or deceased, Names of heirs, such as spouse, children, other relatives, or friends, Name of the executor, administrator, or guardian, Names of witnesses, Residence of the testator, and Document and recording dates. Browse the images, organized by Volume Title and Year. This database has 6,997,828 records. See https://familysearch.org/search/collection/1992421.
- See also, *Ohio Wills and Estates to 1850: An Index* **[Printed Book & Digital Version]**, by Carol Willsey Bell, publ. Columbus, OH, 1981, 400 pages, FHL book 977.1 P22. To access the digital version, see the online FHL catalog page:
www.familysearch.org/search/catalog/345167.

1789-1998. *Ohio, Wills and Probate Records* **[Online Database]**, digitized and indexed at the Ancestry.com website. Source: Extracts from OH county, district, and probate courts (from 85 of Ohio's 88 counties). Some dates are based on the date a will was signed, rather than the date a will was probated. It appears that the first probates begin in 1789. In most cases, probates include the names and residences of beneficiaries and their relationship to the decedent. An inventory of the estate assets can reveal personal details about the deceased's occupation and lifestyle. There may also be references to debts, deeds, and other documents related to the settling of the estate. This database has 1,372,985 records. See
http://search.ancestry.com/search/db.aspx?dbid=8801.

1789-2013. *Ohio, County Marriages* **[Online Database]**, indexed at the FamilySearch.org website. Source: FamilySearch extractions from microfilm of county records at the Family History Library. The records consist of: Licenses, Certificates, Declarations, Affidavits, Loose documents, Abstracts, and Licenses to perform marriages. The records are generally arranged by County, volume and date, License number, and Page number. This database has 5,775,847 records. See https://familysearch.org/search/collection/1614804.
- See Also *Ohio, County Marriage Records, 1774-1993* **[Online Database]**, indexed at Ancestry.com. The 1774 date is probably a mistake. This is ancestry's updated version of the FamilySearch database, with 18,873,749 records (Of course, Ancestry counts both the Groom and the Bride, while FamilySearch counts the couple as one record). See
www.ancestry.com/search/collections/61378.

1790. *Territorial Census Index Substitute, Ohio* **[Printed Book]**, edited by Sue Powell Morgan, published by Genealogical Services, West Jordan, UT, 1998, 274 pages. Includes name, town, county, record type, date and page number. FHL book 977.1 X22m 1790.

1790-1890. *Ohio, Compiled Census and Census Substitutes Index* **[Online Database]**, indexed at the Ancestry.com website. Source: Accelerated Indexing Systems, Salt Lake City, 1999. This collection contains the following indexes: 1790 Northwest Territory Federal Census (Substitute) Index; 1800 Federal Census Index (Washington County); 1810 Washington County Census Index; 1820 Federal Census Index; 1830 Federal Census Index; 1840 Federal Census Index; 1840 Pensioners List; 1850 Federal Census Index; 1860 Federal Census Index; 1870 Federal Census Index; Early Census Index; 1890 Veterans Schedule. This database has 472,914 records. See http://search.ancestry.com/search/db.aspx?dbid=3567.

1790s-1900s. *Ohio USGenWeb Archives* **[Online Database]**. The OHGenWeb Archives site offers free genealogical databases with searchable statewide name lists and for all Ohio counties. Databases may include Bibles, Biographies, Cemeteries, Censuses, Court Records, Deaths, Deeds, Directories, Histories, Marriages, Military, Newspapers, Obituaries, Photos, Schools, Tax Lists, Wills, and more. See http://usgwarchives.net/oh/ohfiles.htm.

1790s-1900s. *Linkpendium – Ohio: Family History & Genealogy, Census, Birth, Marriage, Death Vita Records & More* **[Online Databases].** Linkpendium is a genealogical portal site with links to state, county, town, and local databases. Currently listed are selected sites for Ohio statewide resources (689), Adams County (369), Allen County (828), Ashland County (546), Ashtabula County (763), Athens County (628), Auglaize County (404) and 82 more Ohio counties. See **www.linkpendium.com/oh-genealogy.**

1791-1994. *Ohio, Hamilton County Records* **[Online Database],** digitized at the FamilySearch.org website. Source: Court records from the County Recorder and the Probate Court in Cincinnati, Ohio. This image only database includes categories of Land records, Military records, Naturalization records, Probate records, and Vital records. Browse through the images, organized by category, then by Record Type, Volume, and Year Range. This database has 1,566,282 records. See **https://familysearch.org/search/collection/2141016.**

1793-1930. *Ohio, Washington County Court Records* **[Online Database],** digitized at the FamilySearch.org website. Source: Records of the Court of Common Pleas, Washington Co OH, located at the county courthouse in Marietta, OH. This image only database includes records from the Chancery court, Circuit court, Court of common pleas, District court, Justice of the Peace, and Supreme court. (The records include an *Index to Court of Common Plea, 1793-1828*; followed by one for 1795-1877; both books digitized, but the earlier dates were missed in the title of this database). Browse the images, organized by Record Type, Volume, and Year Range. This database has 91,369 records. See
https://familysearch.org/search/collection/2363038.

1795-1991. *Ohio Newspaper Archives* [Online Databases], digitized and indexed newspapers at the GenealogyBank website, for Akron, Cadiz, Canton, Chillicothe, Cincinnati, Cleveland, Clinton, Columbus, Dayton, Elyria, Lancaster, Lebanon, Marietta, New Richmond, Painesville, Ravenna, Sandusky, St. Clairsville, Steubenville, Toledo, Urbana, Warren, Williamsburg, Wooster, and Xenia, see **www.genealogybank.com/explore/newspapers/all/usa/ohio.**

1795-2010. Ohio, *Trumbull County Records* **[Online Database],** digitized at the FamilySearch.org website. Source: microfilmed records from the Trumbull Co OH courthouse. This image only database includes cemetery records, Common pleas court records, Misc. court records, Land and property records, Naturalization records, Probate records, Tax records, and Vital records. Browse through the images, organized by Record Type, Date Range, and Volume. **Note:** Perhaps the best census substitutes for Trumbull Co OH are the annual Tax Appraisement lists. They are part of this major database, beginning in 1811 and every year thereafter through 1931. This database has 800,274 records. See
https://familysearch.org/search/collection/2065327.

1796-1908. *Ohio, Homestead and Cash Entry Patents, Pre-1908* **[Online Database],** indexed at the Ancestry.com website. Source: BLM General Land Office Automated Records Project, 1996. A land patent is a document recording the passing of a land title from the government, or other proprietor, to the patentee/grantee. This is the first-title deed and the true beginning of private ownership of the land. The patent describes in legal terms the land to which the title is given. Information recorded in these records includes: Name, Land Office, Sequence, Document number, Total acres, Signature, Canceled document, Issue date, Mineral rights reserved, Metes and bounds Statutory reference, Multiple warrantee and patentee names, Act or treaty, Entry classification, and Land description. This database has 97,934 records. See
http://search.ancestry.com/search/db.aspx?dbid=2077.

1796-2004. *Diocese of Toledo, Ohio, Catholic Parish Records* **[Online Database],** indexed at the Ancestry.com website. Source: FamilySearch extractions from the microfilmed images of register books from parishes in northwestern Ohio. Entries were extracted from register books for births, confirmations, marriages, deaths, and burials, organized by county, then by community, and finally by parish within each community. Some records are available for the following Ohio counties: Allen, Crawford, Defiance, Erie, Fulton, Hancock, Henry, Huron, Lucas, Ottawa, Paulding, Putnam, Richland, Sandusky, Seneca, Van Wert, Williams, Wood, and Wyandot. This database has 102,728 records. See **http://search.ancestry.com/search/db.aspx?dbid=60099.**

1797-1947. *Ohio, Jefferson County Court Records* **[Online Database],** digitized at the FamilySearch.org website. Source: Jefferson County Courthouse, Steubenville, OH. This image only database includes the categories of Census, County Court records, Hospital records, Land and Property records, Natural-

ization records, Pensions, Probate records, and Vital records. Browse the images, organized by category, then Record Type, Volume, and Year Range. **Note. 1)** This database has a full digital index in work, a cooperative effort of FamilySearch and the Jefferson County Chapter, Ohio Genealogical Society. **2)** The only item under the category "census" is a digital capture of the 1880 federal census (Short Form) for Steubenville Township & Mingo Village. This database has 1,010,889 records. See
https://familysearch.org/search/collection/1935519.

1797-1951. *Jefferson County, Ohio, Court Records* **[Online Database],** indexed at the Ancestry.com website. Source: FamilySearch extractions from microfilm at the Family History Library, Salt Lake City, UT. Includes Probate Records, 1797-1947; Birth Records, 1797-1947; Marriage Records, 1867-1947; and Death Records, 1867-1947. This database has 1,009,365 records. See
http://search.ancestry.com/search/db.aspx?dbid=60100.

1798-1817. *Census for Cincinnati, Ohio, 1817, and Hamilton County, Ohio, Voters' Lists 1798 and 1799* **[Printed Book & Digital Version],** compiled by Marie Paula Dickoré, Publ. Historical and Philosophical Society of Ohio, 1960, 98 pages, FHL book 977.1 A1 no. 115. To access a digital version of this book, see the online FHL catalog page:
https://familysearch.org/search/catalog/70068.

1800. *Northwest Territory, Washington County, Ohio 1800 Census Index: Taken Before Ohio's Statehood* **[Printed Book],** by Fay Maxwell, publ. OH Genealogy Center, Austin, MN, 1973, 16 pages, FHL book 977.1 A1 no. 437.

1800-1803. *Second Census of the United States, 1800, Population Schedules, Washington County, Territory Northwest of the River Ohio; and Population Census, 1803, Washington County, Ohio* **[Microfilm & Digital Capture],** from the originals at the National Archives, Washington, DC. Arranged in alphabetical order by township. These two-name lists were part of the original papers of Rufus Putnam's Ohio Company of Associates, who kept a copy of the first (1800) federal census taken in Washington County, Ohio. The 1803 list was the first Quadrennial Enumeration for Washington Co OH, and lists the name of all free males over the age of 21. The area of 1800-1803 Washington County includes the modern counties of Washington, Meigs, Gallia, Lawrence, and Athens counties, Ohio. Special microfilm publication by the National Archives, 1994, series M1804, 1 roll, FHL film #2155491. To access the digital images, see the online FHL catalog page:
www.familysearch.org/search/catalog/720623.

1800-1830. See *Indexes: Census 1800, 1803, 1810; Death Notices, 1811-1830; Lives of Early Settlers - Hildreth; Account Book, 1818-1819; Supreme Court, Washington Co., 1810; Henderson-Tomlinson Journal and Papers; Nahum Ward Letters* **[Microfilm],** from a typescript at the Campus Museum, Marrietta College, Marrietta, OH. Filmed by the Genealogical Society of Utah, 1973, 1 roll, FHL film #940916. To see if this microfilm has been digitized yet, see the FHL catalog page:
www.familysearch.org/search/catalog/313722.

1800-1850. *Ohio Tax Records* **[Online Database],** digitized and indexed at the FamilySearch.org website. This project was indexed in partnership with the Ohio Genealogical Society. This database includes Images and name index of tax registers as recorded with the County Auditor of each county. Includes the following Ohio counties: Ashtabula, Belmont, Carroll, Columbiana, Guernsey, Harrison, Jackson, Jefferson, Monroe, Trumbull and Washington. The majority of the tax records in this collection are for the years 1816 through 1838. This database has 5,699,626 records. See
https://familysearch.org/search/collection/1473259.
- See also, *Ohio, Tax Records, 1800-1850* **[Online Database],** indexed at the Ancestry.com website. This database has 1,101,150 records. See
http://search.ancestry.com/search/db.aspx?dbid=60104.

1800-1942. *Ohio, Marriages* **[Online Database],** indexed at the FamilySearch.org website. Source: FamilySearch extractions from microfilm of county records at the Family History Library. This database has 3,567 records. See
https://familysearch.org/search/collection/2367319.

1800-1958. *Ohio Marriages* **[Online Database],** indexed at the FamilySearch.org website. Name index to marriage records from microfilm at the Family History Library. This database has 2,198,000 records. See https://familysearch.org/search/collection/1681001.

1800-1977. *Ohio, County Naturalization Records* **[Online Database],** indexed at the FamilySearch.org website. Source: FamilySearch extractions from microfilm of county records at the Family History Library. Information found in this collection may include: Full name of petitioner, Name of court, Date

of emigration, Place of residence, Occupation, Date and place of birth, Date of declaration, Date of marriage, Spouse's full name (usually a woman's maiden name is given), Spouse's date and place of birth, Names of children and their places of birth, Name of judge, and Names of witnesses. This database has 1,840,500 records. See
https://familysearch.org/search/collection/1987615.
- See also, *Ohio, County Naturalization Records, 1800-1977* [Online Database], indexed at the Ancestry.com website
http://search.ancestry.com/search/db.aspx?dbid=60096.

1801-1814 Tax Records of Ohio [Microfilm & Digital Capture], from the original records at the Ohio History Connection, Columbus, OH. Filmed by the Genealogical Society of Utah, 1967, 14 rolls, as follows:

- **1801. Land entries** of the lands of non-residents situated between the Scioto & Little Miami Rivers commonly known by the name of the Virginia Army Lands (Virginia Military District), vol. 1, 1801, FHL film #522837.
- **1806-1807. Tax record**, vol. 2, 1806 (Adams, Athens, Franklin, Highland, Muskingum, Ross, Scioto counties), Tax record, vol. 3, 1806 (Belmont, Fairfield, Jefferson counties); Tax record, vol. 4, 1806 (Butler, Champaign, Clermont, Greene, Montgomery counties); Tax record, vol. 5, 1806 (Hamilton and Warren counties); Tax record, vol. 6, 1806 (Trumbull, Columbiana, Gallia counties; Tax record, vol. 7, 1807 (Adams, Champaign, Clermont, Green, Highland, Ross, Scioto counties), FHL film #522838.
- **1807. Tax record,** vol. 8, 1807 (Belmont, Columbiana, Jefferson counties; Tax record, vol. 9, 1807 (non- resident sixth district resident Geauga and Trumbull counties; Tax duplicates, vol. 10, 1807 (Franklin, Fairfield, Muskingum counties); Tax duplicate, vol. 11, 1807 (Butler, Warren, Hamilton, Montgomery counties), FHL film #522839.
- **1808. Tax duplicates**, vol. 12, 1808 (Fairfield and Washington counties); Tax record, vol. 13, 1808 (non residents fifth district residents Belmont, Columbiana, Jefferson counties; Tax record, vol. 14, 1808 (Adams, Greene, Hamilton, Montgomery counties), FHL film #522840.
- **1808. Tax record**, vol. 15, 1808 (Geauga, Muskingum, Trumbull counties); Tax record, vol. 16, 1808 (Athens, Franklin, Gallia, Highland counties; Tax record, vol. 17, 1808 (non residents fourth and sixth district), FHL film #522841.
- **1809. Tax Duplicate** of land tax, vol. 18, (A - N various counties) - FHL film #522842.
- **1811. Tax Duplicate** of land tax, vol. 19, (Adams – Hamilton), FHL film #522843.
- **1811. Duplicate** of land tax, vol. 20, (Jefferson – Warren) - FHL film #522844.
- **1812. Tax Duplicate** of land tax, vol. 21, (Adams – Hamilton), FHL film #514124.
- **1812. Tax Duplicate** of land tax, vol. 22, (Jefferson – Warren), FHL film #514125.
- **1813. Tax Duplicate** of land tax, vol. 23, (Adams – Hamilton), FHL film #514126.
- **1813 Tax Duplicate** of land tax, vol. 24, (Jefferson – Warren), FHL film #514127.
- **1814. Tax Duplicate** of land tax, vol. 25, (Adams – Franklin), FHL film #514128.
- **1814. Tax Duplicate** of land tax, vol. 26-27, (Gallia – Warren), FHL film #514129.

To access the digital images, see the online FHL catalog page:
www.familysearch.org/search/catalog/451489.

1801-1824. Early Ohio Tax Records [Printed Book], abstracts compiled by Esther Weygant Powell, Ohio State Auditor, 1971, 459 pages. FHL book 977.1 R4op. See also *The Index to Early Ohio Tax Records* [Printed Book], compiled by Carol Willsey Bell, and friends of Esther Weygandt Powell in cooperation with the Ohio Genealogical Society, published Akron, OH, 1973, 173 pages. FHL book 977.1 R4op, and FHL film #1033949.

1801-1824. Ohio's Virginia Military Tract: Index of 1801 Tax List [Printed Book], compiled by Fay Maxwell, published by the Ohio Genealogy Center, 1991, 19 pages. From title page: "Index of the Virginia Militiamen who served in the revolution. The tract is located west of Ohio's Scioto River." Includes Hardin County 1821 & 1833 tax record, and Marion County 1824 tax record. FHL book 977.1 R4m.

1802 Census of Clermont County: the Northwest Territory of the United States of America [Printed Book], compiled and published by the Brown County Genealogical Society, Georgetown, OH, 1988, 9 pages. FHL book 977.1 A1 no. 323 and FHL film #6088560.

1803. Washington County, Ohio, US Territorial Census Population Schedules [Online Database], indexed at the Ancestry.com website. Source: National Archives microfilm series M1804. This database was part of the original records of the Ohio Company of Associates and was more likely a Quadrennial Enumeration than a census. Listed are males over 21 years of age. This database has 1,242 records. See
http://search.ancestry.com/search/db.aspx?dbid=2208.

1803-1827, 1831 and 1847. *Male Enumeration Lists of Adams County, Ohio* **[Printed Book & Microfilm],** by the Adams County Genealogical Society, West Union, OH, 2 vols., 1995. From FHL catalog: "These records may include some names from Brown County until Brown County was formed in 1819." Includes index. Contents: Vol. 1: 1803-1827; Vol. 2: 1831 and 1847. Library has vol. 1-2 bound together. FHL book 977.186 X2m and FHL film #2055364. To see if this microfilm has been digitized yet, see the FHL catalog page: **www.familysearch.org/search/catalog/785802.**

1803-1900. *Ohio, Marriages* **[Online Database],** indexed at the Ancestry.com website. Source: Liahona Research extractions from county records on microfilm at the Family History Library, Salt Lake City. Each record provides the names of both bride and groom, along with the marriage date. Records from the following counties may be found in this database: Allen, Ashland, Athens, Auglaize, Belmont, Columbiana, Coshocton, Clark, Crawford, Darke, Defiance, Fairfield, Franklin, Gallia, Hancock, Henry, Highland, Hocking, Holmes, Huron, Paulding, Jackson, Lawrence, Mahoning, Muskingum, Ottawa, Preble, Putnam, Richland, Ross, Sandusky, Scioto, Seneca, Shelby, and Wayne Counties. This database has 429,836 records. See **http://search.ancestry.com/search/db.aspx?dbid=5194.**

1804. *Resident Proprietors of the Connecticut Western Reserve: An Ohio Tax List of 1804* **[Printed Book, Microfilm & Digital Version],** compiled by Nellie M. Raber, published R.D. Craig, Cincinnati, 1963, 26 pages. FHL book 977.1 A1 no. 30 and FHL film #896888. Another filming, FHL film #928353. To access the digital images, see the online FHL catalog page: **www.familysearch.org/search/catalog/64010.**

1804-1958. *Ohio, Soldier Grave Registrations* **[Online Database],** digitize and indexed at Ancestry.com. Source: Ohio History Connection, Columbus, OH. his database contains grave registration cards for soldiers from Ohio who served in the armed forces, mainly from the time of the War of 1812 up through the 1950s. Information that may be found on the original records includes: Soldier's Name, Residence, Death Date, Cause of Death, Date of Burial, Name and Location of Cemetery, Date of Birth, Place of Birth, and Next of Kin. Records could also contain military service information, which may include: Branch of Service, Wars Served in, Enlistment Date, Discharge Date, Rank, and Company. This database has 330,158 records, see **www.ancestry.com/search/collections/61438.**

1805-1900. *Shaker Membership Card Index* **[Microfilm & Digital Capture],** from the original cards at the Western Reserve Historical Society in Cleveland. The index is for Shakers in several states. Shakers established several communities in the state of Ohio, the most successful were at Lebanon and North Union (now Shaker Heights, Ohio). To access the digital images, see the online FHL catalog page: **www.familysearch.org/search/catalog/54157.**

1807 Census of Butler County, Ohio **[Printed Book & Digital Version],** edited by Willard Heiss and R. Thomas Mayhill, published by Eastern Indiana Publishing Co., Knightstown, IN, 1968, 23 pages. FHL book 977.1 A1 No. 137 and FHL film #1036243. To access the digital version, see the online FHL catalog page: **www.familysearch.org/search/catalog/196754.**

1808-1820. *Tax Records of Portage, Summit and Portions of Medina Cos., Ohio, 1808-1820* **[Printed Book],** by Michael Barren Clegg, publ. Ohio Genealogical Society, Mansfield, OH, 1979, 58 pages, FHL book 977.137 R4c.

1809-1917. *Ohio, Stark County Court Records* **[Online Database],** digitized at the FamilySearch.org website. Source: Court of Common Pleas, County Recorder Center, Canton, OH. This image only database includes Appearance dockets, Common Pleas records, General Indexes, and Journals. Browse the images, organized by Record Type, Date Range, and Volume. This database has 252,043 records. See **https://familysearch.org/search/collection/1878534.**
- See also *Stark County, Ohio, Court Records, 1809-1917* **[Online Database],** indexed at the Ancestry.com website. Source: FamilySearch extractions from microfilm at the Family History Library in Salt Lake City, UT. This database has 255,616 records. See **http://search.ancestry.com/search/db.aspx?dbid=60102.**

1810. *Third census of the United States, 1810, Population Schedules, Washington County, Ohio* **[Microfilm & Digital Capture],** Includes townships of Adams, Belpre, Fearing, Grand View, Marietta, Newport, Roxburg, Salem, Warren, Waterford, Wesley, and Worcester. Lists name of head of the family and age brackets of members of the family, arranged in alphabetical order by township. Special microfilm publication by the National Archives, 1994, series M1803, 1 roll, FHL film #2155490. To access the digital images, see the online FHL catalog page: www.familysearch.org/search/catalog/720620.

***Ohio 1810 Tax Duplicate Arranged in a State-wide Alphabetical List of Names of Taxpayers: With an Index of Names of Original Entries* [Printed Book],** compiled by Gerald M. Petty, published by the author, Columbus, OH, 1976, 221 pages. Includes index. FHL book 977.1 R4p and FHL film #982373. To see if this microfilm has been digitized yet, see the FHL catalog page: **www.familysearch.org/search/catalog/75701.**

***1810 Tax Records of Various Ohio Counties* [Microfilm & Digital Capture],** from the original records at the Ohio History Connection, Columbus, Ohio. Name lists are organized alphabetically by county. Filmed by the Genealogical Society of Utah, 1967, 3 rolls, as follows:
- Counties A - Gal, FHL film #534818.
- Counties Gea – P, FHL film #534819.
- Counties R – W, FHL film #534820.

To access the digital images, see the online FHL catalog page: **www.familysearch.org/search/catalog/374800.**

1810-2016. *Ohio, Rutherford B. Hayes Presidential Center Obituary Index* [Online Database], indexed at the Ancestry.com website. This data collection is an index to newspapers obituaries and local government records, such as probate case files, funeral home records, society membership records, biographical files, brief references in history books, etc. Information extracted from these documents generally includes: Name of deceased, Death Date, Place of Death (City, State), Age at Death, Birth Date, Parents' Names, Marriage Date, Spouse Name, Newspaper Source (Title, Date, Page, Column), Newspaper Location, Newspaper Repository Location, Other Source (Title, Data, Location Description), and Notes. This database has 4,252,050 records. See **http://search.ancestry.com/search/db.aspx?dbid=1671.**

1811-2012. *Ohio, MOLO Obituary Index* [Online Database], indexed at the Ancestry.com website. Source: data gathered from several contributing libraries of the Mid Ohio Library Organization. This database is also accessible at the Northeast Ohio Regional Library website. This database has 405,566 records. See **http://search.ancestry.com/search/db.aspx?dbid=70643.**

1812. *The 1812 Census of Ohio: A Statewide Index of Taxpayers* [Printed Book], publ. T.L.C Genealogy, Miami Beach, FL, 1992, 221 pages. This is an alphabetical list of all resident land owners in Ohio, taken from county tax lists. See FHL book 977.1 R2co.

1812-1814. *Index to the Grave Records of Servicemen of the War of 1812, State of Ohio* [Printed Book & Digital Version], compiled and publ. Ohio Society, U.S. Daughters of 1812, 1969, 77 pages, FHL digitized book. To access the digital images, see the online FHL catalog page: **www.familysearch.org/search/catalog/2634756.**

1813-1932. *Ohio, Cuyahoga County Probate Files* [Online Database], digitized at the FamilySearch.org website. Source: Cuyahoga County Archives, Cleveland, OH. This image only database includes Administrative dockets, Estate records, Guardianships, Journals, Wills, and Misc. files. In most cases, the files include the Name of the testator or deceased, Names of heirs, such as spouse, children, other relatives, or friends, Name of the executor, administrator, or guardian, Names of witnesses, Residence of the testator, and Document and recording dates. Browse the images, organized by Volume Title and Year. This database has 2,622,673 records. See **https://familysearch.org/search/collection/1837736.**

1813-1815, 1836-1838. *Tax Records, Lucas County, Ohio* [Microfilm & Digital Capture], from the originals at the Ohio History Connection, Columbus, OH. Filmed by the Genealogical Society of Utah, 1967, 1 roll, FHL film #511793. To access the digital images, see the online FHL catalog page: **www.familysearch.org/search/catalog/374740.**

***1816-1838 Tax Duplicates, Adams County, Ohio* [Microfilm & Digital Capture],** from the original records now at the Ohio History Connection, Columbus, OH. Filmed by the Genealogical Society of Utah, 1967-1968, 5 rolls, as follows:
- Tax Duplicates,1816-1823, FHL film #514130.
- Tax Duplicates, 1824-1829, FHL film #514131.
- Tax Duplicates, 1830-1832, FHL film #514132.
- Tax Duplicates, 1833-1836, FHL film #514133.
- Tax Duplicates,1837-1838, FHL film #514134.

To access the digital images, see the online FHL catalog page: **www.familysearch.org/search/catalog/332827.**

1816-1838 Duplicate Tax Records of Ashtabula County, Ohio [Microfilm & Digital Capture], from the original records now at the Ohio History Connection, Columbus, Ohio. These records include resident and non-resident owners, delinquent tax properties, and personal property. From 1816-1825 arranged by first letter of surname and beginning in 1826 arranged by township then first letter of surname. Filmed by the Genealogical Society of Utah, 1967, 9 rolls, as follows:
- Tax Duplicates,1816-1822, FHL film #514136.
- Tax Duplicates,1823-1824, FHL film #514137.
- Tax Duplicates,1825-1826, FHL film #528364.
- Tax Duplicates,1827-1828, FHL film #528365.
- Tax Duplicates,1829-1830, FHL film #514138.
- Tax Duplicates,1831-1832, FHL film #514139.
- Tax Duplicates,1833-1834, FHL film #514140.
- Tax Duplicates,1835-1836, FHL film #514141.
- Tax Duplicates,1837-1838, FHL film #514142.

To access the digital images, see the online FHL catalog page:
www.familysearch.org/search/catalog/321064.
- Indexed in *Ohio Tax Records, 1800-1850* [Online Database], see
https://familysearch.org/search/collection/1473259.

1816-1838 Tax Duplicates, Athens County, Ohio [Microfilm & Digital Capture], from the original records at the Ohio History Connection, Columbus, Ohio. Filmed by the Genealogical Society of Utah, 1967-68, 4 rolls, as follows:
- Tax Duplicates, 1816-1826, FHL film #514143.
- Tax Duplicates, 1827-1830, FHL film #514144.
- Tax Duplicates, 1831-1834, FHL film #514145.
- Tax Duplicates, 1835-1838, FHL film #514146.

To access the digital images, see the online FHL catalog page:
www.familysearch.org/search/catalog/332830.

1816-1838 Tax Duplicates, Belmont County, Ohio [Microfilm & Digital Capture], from the original records at the Ohio History Connection, Columbus, Ohio. These records are duplicates that were made for the state auditors office. Filmed by the Genealogical Society of Utah, 1966, 10 rolls, as follows:
- Tax Duplicates, 1816-1823, FHL film #514147.
- Tax Duplicates, 1824-1826, FHL film #514148.
- Tax Duplicates, 1827-1828, FHL film #514149.
- Tax Duplicates, 1829-1830, FHL film #514150.
- Tax Duplicates, 1831, FHL film #830277.
- Tax Duplicates, 1832, FHL film #864973.
- Tax Duplicates, 1833, FHL film #864974.
- Tax Duplicates, 1834-1835, FHL film #864975.
- Tax Duplicates, 1836-1837, FHL film #864976.
- Tax Duplicates, 1838, FHL film #167679.

To access the digital images, see the online FHL catalog page:
www.familysearch.org/search/catalog/252683.
- Indexed in *Ohio Tax Records, 1800-1850* [Online Database], see
https://familysearch.org/search/collection/1473259.

1816-1838 Tax Duplicates of Butler County, Ohio [Microfilm & Digital Capture], from the originals at the Ohio History Connection, Columbus, Ohio. Filmed by the Genealogical Society of Utah, 1967-1968, 7 rolls, as follows:
- Tax Duplicates, 1816-1824, FHL film #514154.
- Tax Duplicates, 2516-1827, FHL film #514155.
- Tax Duplicates, 1828-1829, FHL film #514156.
- Tax Duplicates, 1830-1831, FHL film #514157.
- Tax Duplicates, 1832-1833, FHL film #514158.
- Tax Duplicates, 1834-1835, FHL film #514159.
- Tax Duplicates, 1836-1838, FHL film #514160.

To access the digital images, see the online FHL catalog page:
www.familysearch.org/search/catalog/237246.

1816-1900. See **Ohio, Clermont County Tax Records** [Online Database], from the original records at the Clermont County Treasurer's office. Includes index and images of duplicate tax records from Clermont County. This database has 116,184 records, see www.familysearch.org/search/collection/2480104.

1816-1838 Tax Duplicates of Clinton County, Ohio [Microfilm & Digital Capture], from the originals at the Ohio History Connection, Columbus, Ohio. Filmed by the Genealogical Society of Utah, 1967-1968, 4 rolls, as follows:
- Tax Duplicates, 1816-1823, FHL film #476484.
- Tax Duplicates, 1824-1828, FHL film #476485.
- Tax Duplicates, 1829-1833, FHL film #476486.
- Tax Duplicates, 1834-1838, FHL film #476487.

To access the digital images, see the online FHL catalog page:
www.familysearch.org/search/catalog/237300.

1816-1838 Tax Duplicates of Cuyahoga County, Ohio [Microfilm & Digital Capture], from the originals at the Ohio History Connection, Columbus, Ohio. Filmed by the Genealogical Society of Utah, 1967, 6 rolls, as follows:
- Tax Duplicates, 1824-1817, FHL film #476507.
- Tax Duplicates, 1825-1828, FHL film #476508.
- Tax Duplicates, 1829-1831, FHL film #476509.
- Tax Duplicates, 1832-1834, FHL film #476510.
- Tax Duplicates, 1835-1836, FHL film #476511.
- Tax Duplicates, 1838, FHL film #476512.

To access the digital images, see the online FHL catalog page:
www.familysearch.org/search/catalog/321033.

1816-1838 Tax Duplicates of Franklin County, Ohio **[Microfilm & Digital Capture],** from the originals at the Ohio History Connection, Columbus, Ohio. Filmed by the Genealogical Society of Utah, 1967, 7 rolls, as follows:
- Tax Duplicates, 1816-1825, FHL film #477110.
- Tax Duplicates, 1826-1828, FHL film #477111.
- Tax Duplicates, 1829-1830, FHL film #477112.
- Tax Duplicates, 1831-1832, FHL film #477113.
- Tax Duplicates, 1833-1834, FHL film #477114.
- Tax Duplicates, 1835-1836, FHL film #477115.
- Tax Duplicates, 1837-1838, FHL film #477116.

To access the digital images, see the online FHL catalog page:
www.familysearch.org/search/catalog/236313.

1816-1838 Tax Duplicates of Hamilton County, Ohio **[Microfilm & Digital Capture],** from the originals at the Ohio History Connection, Columbus, Ohio. Filmed by the Genealogical Society of Utah, 1967-1968, 13 rolls, as follows:
- Tax Duplicates, 1816-1817, FHL film #559350.
- Tax Duplicates, 1818-1823, FHL film #506585.
- Tax Duplicates, 1824-1826, FHL film #506586.
- Tax Duplicates, 1827, FHL film #506587.
- Tax Duplicates, 1828, FHL film #506588.
- Tax Duplicates, 1829, FHL film #506589.
- Tax Duplicates, 1830, FHL film #506590.
- Tax Duplicates, 1833, FHL film #506591.
- Tax Duplicates, 1834, FHL film #506592.
- Tax Duplicates, 1835, FHL film #506593.
- Tax Duplicates, 1836, FHL film #506594.
- Tax Duplicates, 1837, FHL film #506595.
- Tax Duplicates, 1838, FHL film #506596.

To access the digital images, see the online FHL catalog page:
www.familysearch.org/search/catalog/237430.

1816-1838 Tax Duplicates of Montgomery County, Ohio **[Microfilm & Digital Capture],** from the originals at the Ohio History Connection, Columbus, Ohio. Filmed by the Genealogical Society of Utah, 1967-1968, 7 rolls, as follows:
- Tax Duplicates, 1816-1820, FHL film #533231.
- Tax Duplicates, 1821-1825, FHL film #545129.
- Tax Duplicates, 1826-1827, FHL film #545130.
- Tax Duplicates, 1828-1830, FHL film #514165.
- Tax Duplicates, 1831-1832, FHL film #514166.
- Tax Duplicates, 1833-1835, FHL film #514167.
- Tax Duplicates, 1836-1838, FHL film #514168.

www.familysearch.org/search/catalog/237460.

1816-1838 Tax Records of Stark County, Ohio **[Microfilm & Digital Capture],** from the originals at the Ohio History Connection, Columbus, Ohio. Filmed by the Genealogical Society of Utah, 1967-1968, 7 rolls, as follows:
- Tax Records, 1816-1825, FHL film #514183.
- Tax Records, 1826-1829, FHL film #532989.
- Tax Records, 1830-1831, FHL film #514184.
- Tax Records, 1832-1833, FHL film #514185.
- Tax Records, 1834, FHL film #532990.
- Tax Records, 1835-1836, FHL film #532991.
- Tax Records, 1837-1838, FHL film #514186.

To access the digital images, see the online FHL catalog page:
www.familysearch.org/search/catalog/236327.

1817-1980. ***Ohio, Carroll County, Veteran Grave Registrations*** **[Online Database],** digitized and indexed at FamilySearch.org. This database has 2,367 records, see
www.familysearch.org/search/collection/3019664.

1818-1838 Tax Duplicates of Clark County, Ohio **[Microfilm & Digital Capture],** from the originals at the Ohio History Connection, Columbus, OH. Filmed by the Genealogical Society of Utah, 1967, 5 rolls, as follows:
- Tax Duplicates, 1818-1825, FHL film #476471.
- Tax Duplicates, 1826-1829, FHL film #476472.
- Tax Duplicates, 1830-1832, FHL film #476473.
- Tax Duplicates, 1833-1835, FHL film #476474.
- Tax Duplicates, 1836-1838, FHL film #476475.

To access the digital images, see the online FHL catalog page:
www.familysearch.org/search/catalog/321055.

1819-1936. ***Ohio, Athens County, Deceased Veteran Grave Registration Card File Index*** **[Online Database],** digitized and indexed at FAmilySearch.org. Index and images of grave registration cards. Cards include veterans name and may also include: address, date of death, place of death, cause of death, date of birth, place of birth, name of cemetery, location, lot, section, block and grave number, marker, next of kin, war served in, date enlisted, date discharged, branch of service, rank, etc. Original records at the Athens County courthouse, Athens, Ohio. This database has 323 records, see
www.familysearch.org/search/collection/3315268.

1819-1941. ***City Directories Collection at the Public Library of Cincinnati and Hamilton County*** **[Online Database],** Directories for cities and counties in Ohio and Kentucky, featuring volumes published as early as

1819. Most of the directories in this collection are located in the Genealogy and Local History and Information and Reference departments at Main Library. All directories in the collection are full-text searchable and can be downloaded for offline viewing and searching. Ohio Directories: Cincinnati, Hamilton, Cleveland, Hamilton County, Columbus, Huron County, Dayton, and Norwood. Kentucky Directories: Covington and Newport. To access a complete list of the years for each city, see http://digital.cincinnatilibrary.org/cdm/landingpage/collection/p16998coll5.

1819-1869. *Cuyahoga County, Ohio, Tax Lists* **[Online Database],** indexed at the Ancestry.com website. Source: Ancestry's World Archives Project contributors. The tax lists in this database begin in 1819, followed by a break in the records until 1823. The database includes records listing both individuals and corporate entities, such as real estate taxes levied in Cleveland and other municipalities; enumerations for assessment of both real and personal property; levies for improvements such as bridges, roads, and schools; delinquent tax lists; lists of physicians and lawyers subject to levies; fish surveys; and other items. This database has 576,973 records. See http://search.ancestry.com/search/db.aspx?dbid=2100.

1820. *Hamilton County, Ohio, 1820 Tax List* **[Microfilm & Digital Capture],** from a manuscript filmed by Wright State University, 1987, 1 roll, FHL film # 1562221. To access the digital images, see the online FHL catalog page: www.familysearch.org/search/catalog/364790.

1820-1840. *Ohio, 1820 thru 1840 Federal Census: Population Schedules* **[Microfilm & Digital Capture],** filmed by the National Archives, 1938-1960, 49 rolls, beginning with FHL film #181392 (1820: Adams, Athens, Belmont, Brown, and Champaign counties). To access the digital images, see the online FHL catalog page:
www.familysearch.org/search/catalog/745502.

1821-1962. *Ohio Births and Christenings* **[Online Database],** indexed at the FamilySearch.org website. Name index to birth, baptism and christening records from microfilm at the Family History Library. This database has 2,548,575 records. See https://familysearch.org/search/collection/1680845.

1822-2019. Ohio Search at Newspapers.com [Online Database], from the largest newspapers database on the Internet, a search for "Ohio" gives a statement of "123,530,547 matches." That is the number of times the word *Ohio* is mentioned in a newspaper obituary, article, or advertisement. You can also search for a surname, first name, etc., along with Ohio locations to narrow a search to a specific area. At the first search results screen, you can narrow your search by year/range, or you can sort the results list by a newspaper publication date, e.g., the earliest Ohio newspaper in the database appears to be one in Sandusky, published in 1822. All newspaper.com entries are accessible via Ancestry.com, or directly via the home page: **www.newspapers.com.**

1824-2001. *Ohio, Cleveland Cemetery Interment Records* **[Online Database],** indexed at the FamilySearch.org website. Cemetery interment records throughout Cleveland in Cuyahoga County. Index provided by the East Cuyahoga County Genealogical Society. This database has 346,248 records. See https://familysearch.org/search/collection/1884183.

1824-2012. *Ohio, Bloomfield Township, Brownwood Cemetery Records* **[Online Database],** images of cemetery records from the Board of Trustees in North Bloomfield, Ohio. This database has 2,550 records, see www.familysearch.org/search/collection/2109920.

1825. Index of the Ohio 1825 Tax Duplicates [Printed Book & Microfilm], compiled by Gerald M. Petty, published by the author, Columbus, OH, 1981, 189 pages. FHL book 977.1 R42p and FHL film #1597666. To see if this microfilm has been digitized yet, see the FHL catalog page:
www.familysearch.org/search/catalog/94238.

1827. *Genealogical Records in Belmont County, Ohio* **[Printed Book],** compiled and published by the Belmont County Chapter of the Ohio Genealogical Society, 10 vols., including local genealogy, cemeteries, newspapers, church records, vital records, and the 1827 enumeration of males over 21 years of age. FHL book 977.193 D29o, vol. 1-10.

1830s-1900s Ohio Original Land Owners. See the *Family Maps* series for Ohio counties, maps of original land patents, compiled by Greg Boyd, publ. Arphax Publishing Co., Norman, OK. These privately-produced computer-generated maps show the first property owners for an entire county, produced as a book of maps, each map laid out on the federal township grid, and includes indexes to help you locate a landowner, place-name, or cemetery. Additional maps added for each county show roads, waterways railroads, selected city centers, and cemeteries within a county. Visit the publisher's information and ordering website for more details and county coverage. See www.arphax.com/.

1832-1850 Duplicate Tax Records, Allen County, Ohio [Microfilm & Digital Capture], from the original records now at the Center for Archival Collections, Bowling Green State University, Bowling Green, Ohio, and the Ohio Historical Society, Columbus. Includes surname indexes. Contains records of tax assessments of real estate, with description of property. Some volumes have indexes. Volume numbers for some volumes are those assigned by the Ohio Historical Society for filing purposes. Filmed by the Genealogical Society of Utah, 1967, 1974, 9 rolls, as follows:
- Tax Duplicates, no dates, FHL film #954812.
- Tax Duplicates, 1832-1833, 1832-1838, 1836-1839, FHL film #954813.
- Tax Duplicates, 1832-1838, FHL film #514135.
- Tax Duplicates, 1840, FHL film #954814.
- Tax Duplicates, 1841-1843, FHL film #954815.
- Tax Duplicates, 1844, FHL film #954816.
- Tax Duplicates, 1845-1846, FHL film #954817.
- Tax Duplicates, 1846-1848, FHL film #954818.
- Tax Duplicates, 1850, FHL film #954819.

To access the digital images, see the online FHL catalog page: www.familysearch.org/search/catalog/249307.

1832-1900s. *Ohio's Digitized Newspapers* [Online Database], digitized and indexed at the Ohio Memory website. The Ohio History Connection has digitized over 315,000 pages of Ohio newspapers through its participation in the National Digital Newspaper Program. This content is freely-available at Chronicling America. Partnerships between the Ohio History Connection and local institutions have made additional titles freely-available on Ohio Memory. These Ohio Memory titles comprise over 265,000 pages of content. To see the list of Newspaper title, city, county, region, and time period, see the special Ohio Memory webpage. See www.ohiohistoryhost.org/ohiomemory/newspapers.
- **NOTE:** to use the Library of Congress' Chronicling America digitized newspapers index for any state, see http://chroniclingamerica.loc.gov.

1833-1994 Governor's Deeds Card Index [Microfilm & Digital Capture], from the original records at the Ohio History Connection, Columbus, Ohio, filmed by the Genealogical Society of Utah, 1995, as follows:
- A – Downing, FHL film #2022287.
- Dubois - Millirams (includes some Mills), FHL film #2022288.
- Millisor – Solomon, FHL film #2022289.
- Whalen – Z, FHL film #2022290.

To access the digital images, see the online FHL catalog page: www.familysearch.org/search/catalog/758221.

1834. *The Cincinnati directory for the year 1834* [Online Database], indexed at the Ancestry.com website. Source: 1991 reprint by E. Deming. This database has 289 pages. See http://search.ancestry.com/search/db.aspx?dbid=21299.

1834-1919. *Register of Prisoners (Ohio State Penitentiary, Columbus, OH)* [Microfilm & Digital Capture], includes indexes. Registers include name, age, birth place, occupation, description, term of sentence, crime, number, county and term of court, recording of case, discharge date and circumstance, physical description, habits, relatives and their residence, property, and education. Filmed by the Columbus Hist. Soc., 1982, 19 rolls, beginning with FHL film #928445 (Registers, 1834-1855). To access the digital images, see the online FHL catalog page: www.familysearch.org/search/catalog/40897.

1835. *Index of the Ohio 1835 Tax Duplicate* [Printed Book], compiled by Gerald M. Petty, published by Petty's Press, Columbus, OH, 1987, 320 pages. Includes information of name, county, township, town or village, type of tax record, and page. FHL book 977.1 R42pg.

1837-1838. Cleveland, Ohio Directory [Online Database], indexed at the Ancestry.com website. Source: *First Directory of Cleveland and Ohio City, 1837-38,* publ. Cleveland Directory Company, 1837. This database has 1,410 records. See http://search.ancestry.com/search/db.aspx?dbid=4228.

1840-1941. *Ohio, Summit County, Veteran Burial Cards* [Online Database], digitized and indexed at the FamilySearch.org website. Source: Burial and grave registration cards at the Summit County Library, Akron, OH. **Note:** The 1700 date is impossible. This database has 5,535 records. See https://familysearch.org/search/collection/1879059.

1840-2001. *Ohio, County Death Records* [Online Database], digitized and indexed at the FamilySearch.org website. Source: FamilySearch extractions from microfilm of county records at the Family History Library. Index and images of death records from county courthouses. Most of the records in this collection are death registers created before statewide death certificates in 1908. Each record may include the name of the person who died, date of death, and place of death. Later records have much more information. This database has 2,155,570 records. See https://familysearch.org/search/collection/2128172.

1841-2003. *Ohio, County Births* **[Online Database],** indexed at the FamilySearch.org website. Source: FamilySearch extractions from microfilm of county records at the Family History Library. Each record may include: Date birth was recorded, Full name of child, Child's birth date, Place of birth, including city, country and state, Child's gender and race, Parents' names, including mother's maiden name, Parents' place of residence, and Name of the person reporting the birth. Later records may also list the following: Parents' birth dates and places, Parents' age, Parents' occupation, and Name of attending physician or midwife. This database has 4,049,847 records. See https://familysearch.org/search/collection/1932106.

1846-1880. *Ashland County, Ohio Research Aid* **[Printed Book],** compiled and published by the Ashland County Chapter of the Ohio Genealogical Society, Ashland, Ohio, 1984, 10 vols. Includes deeds records, maps, tax and chattel lists, cemetery inscriptions, and biographical sketches. FHL book 977.129 R2a vol. 1-10.

1850. *Ohio, 1850 Federal Census: Population Schedules* **[Microfilm & Digital Capture],** filmed by the National Archives, 1964, 85 rolls, beginning with FHL film #20205 (Adams and Allen counties). To access the digital images, see the online FHL catalog page: **www.familysearch.org/search/catalog/744494**.

1850-1880. *Federal Non-Population Census Schedules, Ohio, 1850-1880, in the Custody of the State Library of Ohio: Products of Agriculture, and Products of Industry* **[Microfilm & Digital Capture],** filmed by the National Archives, 1988, 104 rolls, beginning with FHL film #1602325 (Agriculture, 1850: Adams – Auglaize counties). To access the digital images, see the online FHL catalog page: **www.familysearch.org/search/catalog/589452**.

1850-1900. *Ohio, Montgomery County, Probate Estate Files* **[Online Database],** digitized at the FamilySearch.org website. Source: Montgomery Co Records Center & Archives, Dayton, OH. This image only database includes Assignment case files, Civil case files, and Probate estate files. Browse the images, organized by Record Type, Date Range, and Volume. This database has 216,991 records. See **https://familysearch.org/search/collection/1916172**.

1850-2013. *Dayton, Ohio, Obituary Index* **[Online Database],** indexed at the Ancestry.com website. This database is also accessible at the Dayton Metro Library website. This database has 523,226 records. See **http://search.ancestry.com/search/db.aspx?dbid=70466**.

1851-1900. *Ohio Marriages, 1851-1900,* **[CD-ROM],** part of the Family Tree Maker Family Archives, Marriage Index No. 236, published by Broderbund, 1998. Lists approximately 272,000 individuals who were married in Ohio between 1851 and 1900. FHL CD-ROM no. 9 pt. 236.

1851-1907 Quadrennial Enumerations, Auglaize County, Ohio **[Microfilm & Digital Capture],** from the original records at the Archives and Special Collections, Paul L. Dunbar Library, Wright State University, Dayton, Ohio. These records are enumerations of all the male inhabitants above the age of 21 years. Filmed by Wright State Univ., 1979, 2 rolls. FHL film #1763576-1763577. To access the digital images, see the online FHL catalog page: **www.familysearch.org/search/catalog/510009**.

1852-1991. *Ohio, Southern District Naturalization Index* **[Online Database],** indexed at the FamilySearch.org website. Source: National Archives, U.S. District Court Records, card index on microfilm. The index cards include the following: Name of immigrant, Declaration number, Declaration volume number, Declaration date, Petition number, Petition volume number, and Petition date. This database has 83,982 records. See **https://familysearch.org/search/collection/2110749**.

1853-1861. *Ohio (State) Directories* **[Microfiche],** from the originals published by various publishers, filmed by Research Publications, Woodbridge, CT, 1980-1984, 41 microfiche, as follows:
- **1853-1854** W. W. Reilly & Co.'s Ohio State business directory by Morgan & Overend (11 fiche) FHL film #6044295.
- **1857** Williams' Ohio State register and business mirror, by C. S. Williams (5 fiche), FHL film #6044296.
- **1859-1860** George W. Hawes' Ohio State gazetteer and business directory by George W. Hawes (11 fiche), FHL film #6044297.
- **1860-1861** Geo. W. Hawes' Ohio State gazetteer, and business Directory, by George W. Hawes (14 fiche), FHL film #6044298.

1853-2007. *Ohio, Crawford County Church Records* **[Online Database],** digitized at FamilySearch.org. Includes baptism, marriage, and burial records from churches in North Robinson, Ohio. This collection is being published as images become available. This database has 695 images, see www.familysearch.org/search/collection/2106096.

1853-2013. *Ohio, Cleveland, Trinity Lutheran Church Records* **[Online Database],** digitized at FamilySearch.org. Includes baptisms, marriages, deaths, burials, communions, congregational registers and other miscellaneous records. This database has 1,702 images, see www.familysearch.org/search/collection/2115643.

1854-1997. *Ohio Deaths and Burials* **[Online Database],** indexed at the FamilySearch.org website. Source: FamilySearch extractions from microfilm of county records at the Family History Library. This database has 544,082 records. See https://familysearch.org/search/collection/1681000.

1855-1967. *Ohio, Northern District, Eastern Division, Naturalization Index* **[Online Database],** digitized at the FamilySearch.org website. Source: National Archives microfilm series M1893. This image only database is from microfilmed index cards for naturalizations petitions, U.S. district courts of Ohio. Browse through the images, organized by surnames in alphabetical order. This database has 196,148 records: https://familysearch.org/search/collection/2110746.

1858-1918. *State of Ohio Boys Industrial School Inmate Case Records (Fairfield School for Boys, Lancaster, OH)* **[Microfilm & Digital Capture],** Fairfield School for Boys formerly known as: State Reform Farm, 1858-1884 Boys Industrial School, 1884-1964 Fairfield School for Boys, 1964-1980. Fairfield School also served as a home for homeless and poor children. Filmed by the OH Hist. Soc., 1983, 13 rolls, beginning with FHL film #928914 (Inmate Case Records, 1858-1875). To access the digital images, see the online FHL catalog page: www.familysearch.org/search/catalog/30241.

1860. *Ohio, 1860 Federal Census: Population Schedules* **[Microfilm & Digital Capture],** filmed by the National Archives, 1967, 152 rolls, beginning with FHL film #803928 (Adams County). To access the digital images, see the online FHL catalog page: www.familysearch.org/search/catalog/705524.

1860-1970. *Ohio, Geauga County Records* **[Online Database],** digitized at the FamilySearch.org website. Source: Geauga Co Archives & Records Center, Chardon, OH. This image only database includes images of marriages, naturalizations, probates, and deeds. Browse the images, organized by Record Type, Date Range, and Volume. Included are digitized card indexes for Declarations, 1862-1959; Naturalizations, 1862-1959; and Petitions, 1880-1959. This database has 24,059 records. See https://familysearch.org/search/collection/2134457.

1860-2004. *Ohio, Crawford County Obituaries* **[Online Database],** indexed at the FamilySearch.org website. Source: Obituary file from the Crawford County Genealogical Society in Galion, Ohio. This database has 283,991 records. See https://familysearch.org/search/collection/1384728.

1861-1865. See *Official Roster of the Soldiers of the State of Ohio in the War of the Rebellion, Vols. 1-12* **[Online Database],** indexed at the Ancestry.com website. Source: *Official Roster* pub.1886-1895. This database has 2,792 pages. See http://search.ancestry.com/search/db.aspx?dbid=31412.

1861-1940. See *Cincinnati (Ohio) City Directories* **[Microfilm],** from the originals, mostly by Williams & Co., Cincinnati. Collection contains directories for a complete annual run, 1861-1940. Filmed by Research Publications, Woodbridge, CT, 1980-1984, 64 rolls, beginning with FHL film #1376706 (1861 Williams' Cincinnati Directory). For a complete list of roll numbers and contents of each roll, see the online FHL catalog page for this title. See https://familysearch.org/search/catalog/536579.

1869-1911. *State of Ohio, Girls Industrial School Inmate Case Records (Scioto Village, Delaware Co OH)* **[Microfilm & Digital Capture],** Scioto Village formerly known as: 1869-1872, State Reform and Industrial School for Girls; 1872-1878, Girl's Industrial Home 1878-1965, Girl's Industrial School 1965-Scioto Village. The village also served as a home to homeless and poor children. Filmed by the OH Hist. Soc., 1983, 2 rolls, FHL film #928912-3. To access the digital images, see the online FHL catalog page: www.familysearch.org/search/catalog/414828.

1870. *Ohio, 1870 Federal Census: Population Schedules* **[Microfilm & Digital Capture],** filmed by the National Archives, 1968, 154 rolls, beginning with

FHL film #552666 (Adams County). To access the digital images, see the online FHL catalog page: www.familysearch.org/search/catalog/698915.

1878-1980. *Ohio, Columbus, Union Cemetery, Burial Records* **[Online Database],** digitized and indexed at FamilySearch.org. This database has 54,081 records, see **www.familysearch.org/search/collection/3019070**.

1880. *Ohio, 1880 Federal Census: Soundex and Population Schedules* **[Microfilm & Digital Capture],** filmed by the National Archives, c1970, 234 rolls, beginning with FHL film #1254989 (Adams County). To access the digital images (Population Schedules), see the online FHL catalog page: **www.familysearch.org/search/catalog/676504**.

1880 Mortality Schedule. See *Schedule of Persons Who Died During the Year Ending May 31, 1880 for Ohio* **[Microfilm & Digital Capture],** filmed by the National Archives, 1972, 3 rolls, beginning with FHL film #978352 (Adams – Clinton counties). To access the digital images, see the online FHL catalog page: **www.familysearch.org/search/catalog/260524**.

1880. *U.S. Federal Census – 1880 Schedules of Defective, Dependent, and Delinquent Classes* **[Online Database],** digitized and indexed at Ancestry.com. This schedule included different forms to enumerate the following classes of individuals: Insane, Idiots, Deaf-mutes, Blind, Paupers and Indigent persons, Homeless children, and Prisoners. This database includes Ohio and 20 more states. See **www.ancestry.com/search/collections/1634**.

1880. *The Cleveland Directory, for the Year Ending June 1880* **[Online Database],** indexed at the Ancestry.com website. Source: Cleveland Directory Co, publ. 1879. This database has 717 pages. See **http://search.ancestry.com/search/db.aspx?dbid=25775**.

1880-1950. *Ohio, Cuyahoga County Records* **[Online Database],** digitized at the FamilySearch.org website. Source: Cleveland Div. of Vital Statistics. This image only database includes birth affidavits, delayed births and corrections; and voter registrations from the Cuyahoga County Courthouse in Cleveland. Browse through the images, organized by Record Type, Date Range, and Volume. This database has 36,089 records. See **https://familysearch.org/search/collection/1908531**.

- See also, *Cuyahoga County, Ohio, County Records, 1880-1950* **[Online Database],** digitized at the Ancestry.com website. See **http://search.ancestry.com/search/db.aspx?dbid=60098**.

1880-1980. *Ohio, Grace Episcopal Church Records (Galion, Crawford County, Ohio)* **[Online Database],** digitized at FamilySearch.org. Parish registers. This database has 295 images, see **www.familysearch.org/search/collection/2106724**.

1881-1962. *Ohio, Licking County, Hartford Township Records* **[Online Database].** Includes burial and cemetery deeds from Croton, Ohio. This database has 927 records, see **www.familysearch.org/search/collection/2068324**.

1882-1936. *Youngstown (Ohio) City Directories* **[Microfilm],** from the originals by various publishers. Filmed by Research Publications, Woodbridge, CT, 1995, 21 rolls, beginning with FHL #2156885 (Youngstown Directory, 1882-1883). The microfilm series is close to one directory per year (or 2 years) with a few gaps, 1882-1936.

1882-1949. *Ohio, Summit County, Coroner Inquests, Hospital and Cemetery Records* **[Online Database],** digitized and indexed at FamilySearch.org. Source: County Records Center, Akron, OH. This collection contains the following records for the listed institutions: Admittance cards, 1915-1947 and employment cards, 1915-1940 of the Edwin Shaw Hospital; burial permits, 1915-1947 of the Briar Hill Cemetery and coroner's inquest books, 1882-1922 for Summit county. This collection is being published as images become available. This database has 11,863 records, see **www.familysearch.org/search/collection/1985540**.

1884-2013. *Ohio, Washington County Newspaper Obituaries* **[Online Database].** Index and images of newspaper obituaries from the collections at the Washington County Public Library in Marietta, Ohio. This database has 57,468 records, see **www.familysearch.org/search/collection/2358414**.

1888-1919. *Ohio Soldiers Home Records* **[Online Database],** digitized at the FamilySearch.org website. Source: OH History Connection. This image only database is for the images of the admission records of

veterans, those admitted into the Ohio Soldiers Home. Browse through the images, organized by Admission Number, beginning with 1-500, 1888-1889. This database has 10,103 records. See
https://familysearch.org/search/collection/2139859.

1888-1892. *Dayton, Ohio Directories* **[Online Database]**, indexed at the Ancestry.com website. Source: Williams and Co Dayton City directories for 1888, 1890, 1891, and 1892. This database has 59,449 records. See
http://search.ancestry.com/search/db.aspx?dbid=4701.

1888-1946. *Ohio, Naturalization Petition and Record Books* **[Online Database]**, indexed at the Ancestry.com website. Source: National Archives microfilm series M1995. This database contains an index to naturalization records created in the United States District Court, Cleveland, including certificates of arrival, Declarations of Intention, Petitions for Naturalization, and other documents. This database has 395,871 records. See
http://search.ancestry.com/search/db.aspx?dbid=2363.

1889-1891. *Toledo, Ohio Directories* **[Online Database]**, indexed at the Ancestry.com website. Source: R.L. Polk Toledo Directories, 1889-1891. This database has 74,207 records. See
http://search.ancestry.com/search/db.aspx?dbid=4536.

1890 Census Substitute **[Online Database]**, indexed at the Ancestry.com website. This is nationwide collection of city directories for the time of the 1890 federal census (lost in a fire in Washington DC in 1921). A global search includes these directories from Ohio: **Canton,** 1888-1892; **Cincinnati,** 1890-1891; **Cleveland,** 1895; **Columbiana County,** 1891-1892; **Columbus,** 1887-1892; **Darke County,** 1885; **Dayton,** 1888-1892; **Fremont City,** 1889-1890; **Greenville,** 1885; **Norwalk,** 1892-1893; **Springfield,** 1890-1894; **Toledo,** 1889-1891; **Trumbull County,** 1889-1890; **Youngstown,** 1889-1890; and **Zanesville,** 1890-1891.
http://search.ancestry.com/search/group/1890census.

1890-1894. *Springfield, Ohio Directories* **[Online Database]**, indexed at the Ancestry.com website. Source: Williams and Co Springfield City directories for 1890, 1892, and 1893. This database has 51,468 records. See
http://search.ancestry.com/search/db.aspx?dbid=4856.

1890-2002. *Ohio, Stark County Coroner's Records* **[Online Database]**, digitized at the FamilySearch.org website. Source: Coroner records, now located at the Stark County Records Center, Canton, OH. This image only database includes coroner's inquest books, reports, and case files. Browse through the records, organized by Record Type, Date Range, and Volume. This database has 57,294 images. See
https://familysearch.org/search/collection/1922540.

1890-2002. *Stark County, Ohio, Coroner's Records* **[Online Database]**, digitized at the Ancestry.com website. Source: FamilySearch digital versions of microfilmed images of the Stark County Coroner's records. This database consists of images of Coroner's Inquest books, reports, and case files from the courthouse in Canton, Ohio. The following types of deaths were reported to the county coroner: Accidental deaths, Homicidal deaths, Occupational deaths, Sudden deaths (deaths of infants and young children, or deaths of individuals in any jail, confinement, or custody, Suicidal deaths, Therapeutic deaths (deaths which occurred during a medical procedure such as surgery), Any death where there is a doubt, question, or suspicion, and Deaths under any other special circumstances. Browse the images by type of record and range of years. This database has 56,154 records:
http://search.ancestry.com/search/db.aspx?dbid=60101.

1895-1916. *Ohio University Lands* **[Microfilm & Digital Capture]**, from the original records at the Ohio History Connection, Columbus, OH. Includes typescript cards referencing deeds and certificates for land sales. These records are related to the remaining public lands in Ohio never sold to individuals. In 1871, the lands were granted to the state of Ohio, who gave them to Ohio State University. The cards record the sale of lands obtained from the areas of the old Ohio Company Purchase (mostly in Athens Co OH), and the Virginia Military District (lands between the Scioto and Little Miami Rivers, see the 1787-1871 VMD description). Information on the cards includes the name of the purchaser, date of purchase, acreage and description of land; location in deed books, and certificate numbers. Filmed by the Genealogical Society of Utah, 1995, 4 rolls, as follows:
- Ohio University Land, conveyed 1895-1916 in Athens County, Township 8-9 Range 14, FHL film #2022654.
- Ohio University lands, conveyed in Athens County, Township 9 Range 14, FHL film #2022655.
- Virginia Military District, lands conveyed by Ohio State University 1890-1918, FHL film #2022655.
- Deeds, v. 1-6 1884-1916, FHL film #196146.
- Deeds, v. 7 1914-1916, FHL film #196147.

To access the digital images, see the online FHL catalog page:
www.familysearch.org/search/catalog/758279.

1896-1917. *Admission Books: Historical Conduct Record of Inmates (Ohio State Reformatory, Mansfield, OH)* **[Microfilm & Digital Capture],** filmed by the OH Hist. Soc., 1982, 21 rolls, beginning with FHL film #928464 (Index of admissions, A-Mc). To access the digital images, see the online FHL catalog page:
www.familysearch.org/search/catalog/41427.

1898-1899. *Ohio Soldiers in the War with Spain* **[Online Database],** indexed at the Ancestry.com website. Source: Adjutant General's report: *The Official Roster of Ohio Soldiers in the War with Spain, 1898-99,* publ. 1916. This database has 15,587 records.
http://search.ancestry.com/search/db.aspx?dbid=5306.

1900. *Ohio, 1900 Federal Census: Soundex and Population Schedules* **[Microfilm & Digital Capture],** filmed by the National Archives, c1970, 497 rolls, beginning with FHL film #4117686 (Adams County). To access the digital images (Population Schedules), see the online FHL catalog page:
www.familysearch.org/search/catalog/640286.

1900-1925. *Trumbull County, Ohio Marriage Record Index* **[Printed Book],** edited by Barbara Houser Layfield, publ. Trumbull Co Chapter, OH Genealogical Society, 2006, 413 pages, FHL book 977.138 V22L.

1900's-1980's. *Deaths and Graves Registration (United Spanish War Veterans, Ohio)* **[Microfilm & Digital Capture],** filmed by the Genealogical Society of Utah, 1993, 2 rolls, FHL film #1852943 (Registrations, A-L, 1900-1970) & #1853006 (Registrations, M-Z). To access the digital images, see the online FHL catalog page:
www.familysearch.org/search/catalog/656701.

1902-1960. *Ohio and Florida, City Directories* **[Online Database],** digitized and OCR indexed at Ancestry.com. This compilation has 8 Florida City Directories and 48 Ohio City Directories in a combined index. Use the Browse this Collection feature to choose a state, choose a city, and choose a year range. This database has 4,912,471 records, see
www.ancestry.com/search/collections/1988.

1907 Quadrennial Enumeration, Clinton County, Ohio **[Microfilm],** from the original records now located at the Special Collections Department, Blegen Library, University of Cincinnati, Cincinnati, Ohio. Includes townships of Adams, Chester, Clark, Green, Jefferson, Liberty, Marion, Richland, Union, Vernon, Washington, Wayne, and Wilson. Contains an enumeration of all male residents over the age of twenty-one taken during the listing of property for taxation. Filmed by the Genealogical Society of Utah, 1983, 1 roll, FHL film #973424. To see if this microfilm has been digitized yet, see the FHL catalog page: www.familysearch.org/search/catalog/140204.

1908-2007. *Ohio Death Index, 1908-1932, 1938-1944, and 1958-2007* **[Online Database],** indexed at the FamilySearch.org website. Source: OH Vital Statistic Unit (database indexed by Ancestry.com). Information found in this collection may include: Age at Death, Estimated Birth Year, Date of Death, Certificate Number or page number, Name of Deceased, Name of Father, Name of Mother, Name of Spouse, Place of Death, Sex, and Page Number. This database has 7,601,864 records. See
https://familysearch.org/search/collection/1949341.

1908-1953. *Ohio Deaths* **[Online Database],** digitized and indexed at the FamilySearch.org website. Source: FamilySearch images from microfilm of county records (death certificates or registers) at the Family History Library. Death entries include the following information: Name of deceased, Date and place of death including city, county and state, Residence of deceased; sometimes, a former residence, Gender and age of deceased in years, months, and days, Date and place of birth, Marital status, race and occupation of deceased, Spouse's name, if married, Father's name and birthplace, Mother's maiden name and birthplace, Cause of death, Name of informant, often a son, daughter or other family member, How long at current residence or length of time in United States, Occupation, and Burial information. This database has 3,544,429 records. See
https://familysearch.org/search/collection/1307272.

1908-1964. *Ohio, Birth Index* **[Online Database],** indexed at the Ancestry.com website. Source: OH Vital Statistics Unit. Extracted from a birth certificate, each record includes name, birth date, place of birth, and state file number. This database has 8,222,080 records.
http://search.ancestry.com/search/db.aspx?dbid=3146.

1908-2007. *Ohio, Deaths, 1908-1932, 1938-2007* **[Online Database],** indexed at the Ancestry.com website. Source: OH Vital Statistics Unit. Extracted from a death certificate, each record may include:

Name of the deceased, Place of residence, Death place, Death date, Age at time of death, Birth date, Race, Educational level, Father's name, and Mother's maiden name. This database has 8,266,980 records. See http://search.ancestry.com/search/db.aspx?dbid=5763.

1910. *Ohio, 1910 Federal Census: Soundex and Population Schedules* [Microfilm & Digital Capture], filmed by the National Archives, c1970, 510 rolls, beginning with FHL film #4449374 (Adams County). To access the digital images (Population Schedules), see the online FHL catalog page: www.familysearch.org/search/catalog/639620.

1914-1918. *Ohio, World War I, Enrollment Cards* [Online Database]. Source: OH Adjutant General's Office. Index and images of a card roster of Ohioans who served in World War I. Each soldier has one or two cards giving information on his/her military service, such as name, serial number, residence, place, and date of birth, military organizations he/she served in, rank, engagements participated in, wounds or injuries received, dates serving overseas, discharge date, percentage disabled, and additional remarks. See www.familysearch.org/search/collection/3029263.
- See Also, *Ohio, World War I Statement of Service Cards, 1914-1919* [Online Database], Index and images of statement of service cards for Marine Corps, Navy, and out of state enlistments. Source: OH Adjutant General's Office. See www.familysearch.org/search/collection/3010045.
- See also, *Ohio, WWI Index and Return Cards, 1916-1920* [Online Database] Index and images of index cards containing information about returning soldiers who served in the 83rd Division during World War I. See www.familysearch.org/search/collection/3039663.

1917-1918. *Ohio Soldiers in WWI* [Online Database], digitized and indexed at the Ancestry.com website. Source: *The Official Roster of Ohio Soldiers, Sailors, and Marines in the World War, 1917-18,* publ. 1926. Each record may include the soldier's name, age, birthplace, address, branch of service and enlistment date, military rank and discharge status, brief history of military career, and date and cause of death if occurred during enlistment. This database has 248,539 records. http://search.ancestry.com/search/db.aspx?dbid=7895.

1920. *Ohio, 1920 Federal Census: Soundex and Population Schedules* [Microfilm & Digital Capture], filmed by the National Archives, c1970, 583 rolls, beginning with FHL film #4966840 (Adams County). To access the digital images (Population Schedules), see the online FHL catalog page: www.familysearch.org/search/catalog/554071.

1929-1958. *Ohio, Crew List Arrivals* [Online Database], indexed at the Ancestry.com website. Source: National Archives microfilm series A3482. This database is an index to crew lists of vessels that arrived at Toledo, Ohio. Most of the crew members were U.S. and Canadian citizens. This database has 269,658 records. See http://search.ancestry.com/search/db.aspx?dbid=2139.

1930. *Ohio, 1930 Federal Census: Population Schedules* [Microfilm & Digital Capture], filmed by the National Archives, c1970, 146 rolls, beginning with FHL film #2341480 (Adams and Allen counties). To access the digital images, see the online FHL catalog page: www.familysearch.org/search/catalog/1037498.

1940. *Ohio, 1940 Federal Census: Population Schedules* [Digital Capture], digitized images from the microfilm of original records held by the Bureau of the Census in the 1940s. After microfilming, Congress allowed the Census Bureau to destroy the originals to free up space for WWII-related files. Digitizing of the 1940 census schedules was done for the National Archives and made public in 2012. To access the digital images, see the online FHL catalog: www.familysearch.org/search/catalog/2057779.

1940 Federal Census Finding Aids [Online Database]. As a guide to the release of the 1940 census to the public, the National Archives created a special website online with a detailed description of the 1940 federal census. Included at the site are descriptions of location-finding aids, such as Enumeration District (ED) Maps, Geographic Descriptions of Census EDs, and a list of 1940 City Directories available at the National Archives. This National Archives website also has a link to Search Engines using Stephen P. Morse's "One-Step" system for finding a 1940 E.D., or for a street address conversion. See www.archives.gov/research/census/1940/general-info.html#questions.

1942. *Ohio Selective Service System Registration Cards, World War II, 4th Registration* **[Microfilm & Digital Capture],** filmed by the Genealogical Society of Utah, 2004-2006, 272 rolls, beginning with FHL film #2371468 (Aab, August – Addis, Amos). To access the digital images, see the online FHL catalog page: www.familysearch.org/search/catalog/1200825.

1945-1954. *Ohio, Death Certificate Index and Death Certificates, 1951-1953* **[Microfilm & Digital Capture],** from the originals at the Ohio Connection, Columbus, OH. Filmed by the Genealogical Society of Utah, 2004, 21 rolls, beginning with FHL film #626347 (Index, Aaron, Peter – Kytos, Joseph). To access the digital images, see the online FHL catalog page: www.familysearch.org/search/catalog/1212446.

1946. *World War II Honor List of Dead and Missing – State of Ohio, June 1946* **[Microfilm & Digital Capture],** filmed by the Genealogical Society of Utah, 1960, 1 rolls, FHL film #213049. To access the digital images, see the online FHL catalog page: www.familysearch.org/search/catalog/328845.

1952-1963. *Ohio, Passenger and Crew Lists* **[Online Database],** indexed at the Ancestry.com website. Source: National Archives microfilm series A3559, A3822, A3838, and A3976. These passenger and crew lists from both ships and aircraft were recorded on a variety of forms that were then turned over to the Immigration and Naturalization Service. Details include the name of the vessel and arrival date, ports of departure and arrival (as well as future destinations on a ship's itinerary), dates of departure and arrival, shipmaster, full name, age, gender, physical description, military rank (if any), occupation, birthplace, citizen of what country, and residence. This database has 2,297 records. See http://search.ancestry.com/search/db.aspx?dbid=9126.

1952-1974. *Ohio, Passenger and Crew Lists arriving at Ashtabula and Conneaut* **[Online Database],** indexed at the FamilySearch.org website. Source: National Archives microfilm series A3405. Contains lists of immigrants, ship passengers, arrivals at seaports, passenger lists, and crew lists. This database has 79,671 records. See https://familysearch.org/search/collection/2421787.

1962-2007. *Ohio Divorce Index, 1962-1963, 1967-1971, 1973-2007* **[Online Database],** indexed at the Ancestry.com website. Source: OH Vital Statistic Unit. Extracted from filed divorce papers, each record includes name of person, year of birth, spouse's name, to whom decree was granted, county of decree, and date of divorce decree. This database has 3,850,954 records. http://search.ancestry.com/search/db.aspx?dbid=2026.

1970-2007. *Ohio Marriage Abstracts, 1970, 1972-2007* **[Online Database],** indexed at the Ancestry.com website. Source: OH Vital Statistic Unit. Extracted from a marriage return, each record includes name of bride/groom, birth year of each, county of residence, county where license was issued, and date of marriage. This database has 6,777,875 records. See http://search.ancestry.com/search/db.aspx?dbid=2025.

1985-Current. *Ohio Recent Newspaper Obituaries* **[Online Database],** digitized and indexed newspaper obituaries at the GenealogyBank website, including newspapers for Ada, Akron, Amherst, Ashtabula, Athens, Avon and 90 more Ohio cities. See www.genealogybank.com/explore/obituaries/all/usa/ohio.

Michigan Territory in 1810. The current 83 counties of Michigan are shown in white. The boundaries at the time of the 1810 federal census are shown in black. **Map Source:** Page 159, Map Guide to the U.S. Federal Censuses, by William Thorndale and William Dollarhide.

1790-1810 Census Availability: In 1790, the areas of the Northwest and Southwest territories were specifically excluded from the census enumeration. The white population in the area that became Michigan was mostly that of the British-held military post at Fort Detroit. In 1800, the Northwest Territory included an enumeration of persons living in old Wayne County – but that census was lost. In 1810, the first census taken under the name Michigan Territory included four civil jurisdictions shown on the map, but only a portion has survived for parts of Detroit and Michilimackinac.

Michigan
Censuses & Substitute Name Lists

Historical Timeline for Michigan, 1612-2019

1612-1615. French explorers Etienne Brule and Samuel de Champlain were the first Europeans to see the Great Lakes. Brule explored Lake Huron in 1612. He was followed by Champlain in 1615.

1668-1671. In 1668, French missionary Fathers Claude Dablon and Louis Marquette established the first permanent European settlement in present Michigan at Sault Sainte Marie. The same two established a mission at Mackinac Island in 1670; another at St. Ignace in 1671.

1673. French explorers Jacques Jolliet and Louis Marquette left their base in St. Ignace and made their way to the Illinois River, which they descended to become the first Frenchmen to discover the Mississippi River.

1679. Catholic priest Louis Hennepin, sailed up the Detroit River, through Lake St. Clair, which he named, and into Lake Huron and Lake Michigan. His ship, Le Griffon, was built by explorer Rene-Robert Cavelier (Sieur de La Salle). The ship disappeared during its maiden voyage.

1682. Louisiana. Following the same route as Jolliet and Marquette, René-Robert Cavelier (Sieur de LaSalle) floated down the Mississippi River and continued all the way to its mouth at the Gulf of Mexico. He then claimed the entire Mississippi Basin for Louis XIV of France, for whom Louisiana was named.

1685. The French established *La Louisiane Française* as a district of New France. The French claims in North America now included all of the present Maritime Provinces, the St. Lawrence River Valley, the Hudson's Bay area, the Great Lakes area, and the entire Mississippi Basin.

1691. Fort St. Joseph (now Niles, Michigan) was established by the French as a military and trading post.

1701. French Acadian explorer and adventurer Antoine de la Mothe Cadillac established Fort Ponchartrain du Détroit for France on the site of present Detroit, Michigan. The Wyandot Indians (named the Huron Indians by the French) allowed the fort to be built and occupied in exchange for trade goods offered by the French traders.

1713. Queen Anne's War. At the Peace of Utrecht ending the war, France ceded to Britain its claims to the present Hudsons Bay region and most of French Acadia (which the British renamed Nova Scotia). The remaining French claims in North America were now contained within *Quebéc,* including the St. Lawrence River Valley and Great Lakes region; and *La Louisiane Française,* which extended down the Ohio and Mississippi Rivers to the Gulf of Mexico.

✓ **NOTE:** For a useful historical treatise on the earliest European visitors to the area of present Michigan, and events up to the War of 1812, see *Old and New Mackinac: With Copious Extracts From Marquette, Hennepin, La Hontan, Alexander Henry, and Others,* by Rev. J.A. Van Fleet, M.A., publ. 1874, Cincinnati. A digital version is available online at the FHL catalog page. See
https://familysearch.org/search/catalog/475878.

1758-1760. During the French and Indian War, in 1758, the British captured Fort Frontenac (present Kingston, Ontario), the strategic access point to the Great Lakes.

In 1760, British Army Major Roger Rogers took possession of Fort Detroit in the name of Great Britain, ending French rule there.

1763. The **Treaty of Paris** of 1763 ended the French and Indian War (it was called the Seven Years War in Canada and Europe). France was the big loser and lost virtually all of its remaining North American claims. The areas east of the Mississippi and all of Acadia/Nova Scotia and Québec were lost to Britain; the areas west of the Mississippi went to Spain. After the Treaty of Paris, George III issued a proclamation renaming the Province of Québec as the Province of Canada. He also issued the *Proclamation Line of 1763*, in which Indian Reserves were established west of the Appalachian Mountain Range, limiting western migrations by all of the British colonies.

1763. Pontiac's Rebellion. During the French and Indian War, the Indian Tribes of the Great Lakes region supported and fought for the French. After the defeat of the French, the Ottawa Indians, led by Chief Pontiac, revolted against the British, taking possession of Fort St. Joseph, and all other trading posts and forts in present Michigan except Detroit.

1765-1773. American Rebellions. In 1765, the Stamp Act led to the formation of an anti-British group in Boston called the Sons of Liberty. In 1767, the Townshend Acts created a series of protests, led by the Sons of Liberty. In 1770, the Boston Massacre fueled the fires of rebellion, and in 1773, the Boston Tea Party in Boston Harbor protested the British tax on tea. The British Parliament responded with the Coercive Acts, taking away the right of self government in the colonies; and planting an occupation force of British Army Regulars in Boston.

1774. The Québec Act. The British reacted to the increased American rebellions by solidifying British loyalty in the Province of Canada. They enacted the Québec Act, which reversed the long-standing British policy against Catholic governments in all of their colonies. The Québec Act, just a few years after the forced deportations of Catholic Acadians, restored the name Province of Québec and granted Québec residents full British citizenship, allowed them to retain their Catholic churches and parish taxing systems, and to keep their established French Laws and Customs. The Act also expanded the physical area of Québec to include a huge area of western lands claimed by the Atlantic Colonies; including present Michigan and the rest of the Great Lakes areas. The Thirteen Colonies viewed the Québec Act as one of the *Intolerable Acts* that made the impending war justifiable.

1777-1778. During the Revolutionary War, a number of French-speaking Acadians from Spanish Louisiana joined their counterparts from the leftover French settlements of Kaskaskia, Vincennes, Sault Sainte Marie, St. Ignace, and Mackinac Island. They were added to the Virginia Militia force commanded by General George Rogers Clark. General Clark later noted that the fiercely anti-British fighters he gained from the French communities contributed greatly to his monumental victories against the British in the conquest of the Old Northwest. But General Clark was never able to lead an expedition against Fort Detroit, which remained under British control for several years after the Revolutionary War.

1780-1783. Fort St. Joseph. During the war, the British army used Fort St. Joseph to equip and train their Indian partners in the Great Lakes region. In 1780, Fort St. Joseph was raided by a combined American/French force, but the attack was repelled by the British/Indian occupants. In 1781, a Spanish/Indian force left St. Louis and marched to Fort St. Joseph, defeated the British and took possession of the fort. The Spanish flag was raised and for a brief time, Fort St. Joseph was considered Spanish territory. Although the Spanish had declared war against Britain in 1780 in support of the American rebellion, their victory at Fort St. Joseph in 1781 was their only land-based military campaign against the British during the Revolutionary War. After the war ended in 1783, the Spanish abandoned Fort St. Joseph. The British reoccupied the fort as a civilian fur trading post – and it was not officially ceded by the British to the U.S. until 1796.

1783. The **Treaty of Paris** of 1783 officially ended the Revolutionary War and recognized the United States of America as an independent nation for the first time. The area of present Michigan was included in the area defined to be part of the territory of the United States, but certain trading posts and forts in the Old Northwest region were still occupied by the British, including Prairie du Chien, Isle Royale, Fort Joseph, Fort Mackinac, and Fort Detroit.

1784. Massachusetts, Connecticut, New York, and Virginia relinquished their western claims to lands in the Great Lakes region, a large area that was to become the Northwest Territory. Titles of the state's claims were transferred to the "public domain" of the United States Federal Government.

1787. Northwest Territory. The Ordinance of 1787 established the *Territory Northwest of the River Ohio and* defined the procedure for any territory to obtain statehood. The first territory of the United States included the area of the present states of Ohio, Indiana, Illinois, Michigan, Wisconsin, and that part of Minnesota east of the Mississippi River.

1790. The Northwest Territory was specifically left out of the 1790 enumeration. Much of the white population in present Michigan was in or around Fort Detroit, still under control of the British Army. In addition, Fort St. Joseph was still held by the British as a fur trading post, and there were a few leftover French-Canadian fur trappers and traders at Sault Sainte Marie, St. Ignace, and Mackinac Island.

1796. Jay Treaty. Under terms negotiated in the Jay Treaty, Fort Detroit, Fort St. Joseph, and Fort Mackinac were officially ceded by Britain to the United States.

1796. Wayne County, Northwest Territory was created. The area including the eastern half of the Lower Peninsula of present Michigan. Except for the Fort Detroit area, old Wayne County was unceded Indian lands, and the county was never organized. In 1800, Indiana Territory was created, and old Wayne County disappeared; later it was designated as unorganized territory. The current Wayne County, Michigan was formed in 1815.

1800. Indiana Territory was established from the Northwest Territory with William Henry Harrison as the first Governor and Vincennes the capital. The area included most of present-day Indiana, Illinois, Wisconsin; part of Minnesota, and the western half of Michigan. The Northwest Territory was reduced to the present-day area of Ohio and the eastern half of Michigan. The area of 1800 Indiana Territory was nearly identical to the 1790 area of Knox County, Northwest Territory.

1803. Ohio was admitted to the Union as the 17th state, with Chillicothe as the state capital. The portion of present Michigan included in the Northwest Territory 1800-1803 became part of Indiana Territory. Upon Ohio's statehood, the name Northwest Territory was dropped.

1805. Michigan Territory was created, taken from Indiana Territory. The original area was between Lake Michigan and Lake Huron, as today, but included only the eastern tip of the Upper Peninsula, the rest was under control of Indiana Territory. The territorial capital was at Detroit.

1807. Treaty of Detroit. This was the first large Indian Land Cession in Michigan Territory, involving the Ojibwa/Ottawa, Chippewa, Wyandot, and Potawatomi Indian tribes. The cession area extended from Lake Erie, included Detroit and north to Lake Huron below Saginaw Bay. The north-south trace of the western treaty line became the *Michigan Meridian* used in surveying all Michigan lands after 1815. The 1810 map on page 42 shows the exact area of the Treaty of Detroit cession within the civil districts of Huron, Detroit, and Erie. See also Cession No. 66 on this map: **http://usgwarchives.net/maps/cessions/ilcmap29.htm.**

1809. Illinois Territory was separated from Indiana Territory, with Kaskaskia the capital. The original area included present-day Illinois, Wisconsin, a portion of the Upper Peninsula of present Michigan and that portion of Minnesota east of the Mississippi River. The area of Indiana Territory was reduced in size to the area of the present-day state, plus a portion of the Upper Peninsula of present Michigan.

1810. Federal Census. Michigan Territory was the same as when it was created in 1805, with bounds within the Lower Peninsula plus just the eastern tip of the Upper Peninsula. There were four civil districts: Michillimackinac, Huron, Detroit, and Erie. Only fragments of the census schedules from Michillimackinac and Detroit have survived. The population in Michigan Territory in 1810 was 4,762 people. See the 1810 map on page 42.

✓ **1810 NOTE:** The four civil districts of Michigan Territory in 1810 served as the means of enumerating the residents, and little else. Michillimackinac had only a population from the leftover French-Canadian settlements at St. Ignace, Mackinac Island, and Sault Sainte Marie. Of the four civil districts of 1810, Michillimackinac was the only one that became an actual county with the same name (now Mackinac). The other three civil districts of Detroit, Huron, and Erie, were within the area of the 1807 Treaty of Detroit land cession. Those three civil districts were merged together to become Wayne County in 1815, the first actual county formed in Michigan Territory.

1812-1814. At the beginning of the War of 1812, British forces occupied both Fort Mackinac and Fort Detroit. After decisive victories by American forces in the Battle of Lake Erie and the Battle of the Thames, both Mackinac Island and Fort Detroit were returned to American control. The Fort Detroit campaigns were led by General William Henry Harrison, who emerged as a national hero.

1816. Indiana was admitted to the Union as the 19th state, with the same boundaries as today. The former portion of Indiana Territory in the Upper Peninsula became Unorganized Territory.

1817. An international commission for U.S. / British boundary disputes settled on the St. Mary's River as the International Boundary between the U.S. and British North America, dividing the community of Sault Sainte Marie. The original community is now within the present Sault Sainte Marie, Michigan; and across the St. Mary's River as Sault Sainte-Marie, Ontario.

1818. Illinois was admitted to the Union as the 21st state, with the same boundaries as today. The Upper Peninsula portion of Illinois Territory was reassigned to Michigan Territory. At the same time, the unorganized lands which had been part of Indiana Territory were also added to Michigan Territory. These adjustments expanded the area of Michigan Territory into a huge, mostly uninhabited expanse, stretching all the way to the Mississippi River.

1819. Treaty of Saginaw. This was a major Indian Land Cession in Michigan Territory, involving the Chippewa, Ojibwa/Ottawa, and Potawatomi tribes. Over six million acres of land was ceded to the U.S. federal government. Cession No. 111 began at the Treaty of Detroit line to a point near present Kalamazoo, then running northeast to Thunder Bay, encompassing all of Saginaw Bay, then back to the Treaty of Detroit line. For an Indian cession map, see http://usgwarchives.net/maps/cessions/ilcmap29.htm.

1820. Federal Census. Michigan Territory now reflected the new areas obtained from Indiana and Illinois territories in 1818. The expanded territory included the Lower Peninsula and Upper Peninsula of present Michigan; plus all of present Wisconsin, and that part of present Minnesota east of the Mississippi River. The 1820 census in present Michigan was limited to areas ceded by the Indians within Monroe, Wayne, Macomb, and Oakland counties, all counties with extant census schedules. Michigan Territory created two counties in present Wisconsin in 1818: Crawford County, with an 1820 census taken for Prairie du Chien; and Brown County, with an 1820 census taken for Green Bay. Crawford and Brown became original counties of Wisconsin Territory in 1837. Michigan Territory's Upper Peninsula counties of Michillimackinac and Chippewa were almost entirely within unceded Indian lands. Exceptions were a few places like St. Ignace, Mackinac Island and Sault Sainte Marie. The population of Michigan Territory in 1820 was 8,896 people.

1820. Public Land Sales. Soon after the Treaty of Saginaw cessions, new U.S. government surveys were done in the ceded area. Public land was sold only in a local General Land Office (GLO) which the federal government sited near the land being sold. In 1820, there was just one GLO in Michigan Territory, located in Detroit. The first public land entries were in Monroe, Wayne, Macomb, and Oakland counties.

1821. Treaty of Chicago. This was a major Indian Land Cession in Michigan Territory, involving the Ottawa, Ojibwa/Chippewa, and Potawatomi Indian tribes. Cession No. 117 included all lands in Michigan Territory south of the Grand River. See Cession Map: http://usgwarchives.net/maps/cessions/ilcmap29.htm.

1825. October. **Erie Canal.** The entire route of the Erie Canal, from Albany to Buffalo, New York opened to boat traffic for the first time. It was now possible to arrive at New York harbor by sailing ship, travel up the Hudson River by steamboat, and take the same towed barge from Albany all the way to Lake Erie. Steamboat access to the Great Lakes ports in present Ohio, Michigan, and Wisconsin followed. The impact of the migrations via the Erie Canal into Michigan contributed greatly to a population that jumped from under 10,000 in 1825 to over 210,000 in 1840.

1827. Michigan Territorial Census. The territory took its first territorial census in 1827. Surviving original name lists are available for Washtenaw County only.

1830. Federal Census. The area of Michigan Territory was unchanged from 1820. The census included Crawford, Brown, and Iowa counties of the Wisconsin area; Chippewa and Michillimackinac of the Upper Peninsula; and the Lower Peninsula counties of St. Clair, Oakland, Macomb, Wayne, Washtenaw, Lenawee St. Joseph, Van Buren, Cass, and Berrien. The population of Michigan Territory in 1830 was 31,639 people. In 1830, there were GLOs in Detroit and Monroe.

1834. Michigan Territory Census. Surviving name lists are available for Crawford County (now Wisconsin) and Lenawee County only.

1835. October. The voters of Michigan Territory approved a new state constitution. Quickly submitted to Congress for admission as a state, the Michigan petition was stopped by Ohio's representatives in Congress. Any adjoining state to a proposed state had official "veto power" over the admission, if there were disputes about the legal boundaries. The other states would bow to any opposition to statehood by an adjoining state. Ohio felt justified in their opposing action because of the language of their 1802 Enabling Act – which stated that Ohio's northern boundary should extend to "the most northerly cape of the Miami Bay." But more simply put, Ohio coveted the area of the Maumee River Valley, running parallel to the Michigan Territory boundary with Ohio, where they wanted to build a canal, beginning at Toledo. The "Toledo Strip" became the issue stopping Michigan from becoming a state for another two years.

1836. March. The 13-million-acre **Treaty of Washington (1836)** was the largest Indian Land Cession in Michigan Territory, involving the Ottawa and Chippewa Indian Tribes. The cession included a large tract west of the Treaty of Saginaw, and north of the Treaty of Chicago, contained within the Lower Peninsula as well as a large part of the Upper Peninsula. To see a detailed map showing Cession No. 205, see **http://usgwarchives.net/maps/cessions/ilcmap29.htm**.

1836. July. **Wisconsin Territory** was created, reducing the size and shape of Michigan to its present boundaries, except for the "Toledo Strip," still under debate in Congress.

1837. January. **Michigan Statehood.** As a price of statehood, Michigan Territory agreed to surrender the "Toledo Strip" to Ohio, and Congress voted to admit Michigan as the 26th state in the Union. The boundary between Michigan and Ohio was adjusted by Congress as part of the enabling act. Detroit was the first state capital. NOTE: Eight years after Michigan's statehood, the Miami and Erie Canal was opened for business by the state of Ohio. Running from Toledo to Cincinnati, it was the longest canal in America and an enterprise that probably would not have happened without the help of a major land donation by Michigan.

1837. Michigan State Census. Tallies only. Individual names not included except in Kalamazoo County.

1840. Federal Census. In the first federal census for the State of Michigan, the boundaries were the same as today. Michigan's population had increased seven times over 1830, with over 212,267 people in 1840. And, in that year, Public land sales in Michigan were brisk, with GLOs located in Detroit, Genesee Township, Ionia, Kalamazoo, and Monroe.

1845. Michigan State Census. Surviving original name lists are available for St. Joseph, Lenawee, Washtenaw, and Eaton counties only.

1847. The state capital was moved from Detroit to Lansing, Michigan.

1850. Federal Census. The population of the state of Michigan was 397,654 people.

1854. Michigan State Census. Surviving original name lists are available for Eaton and Washtenaw counties only. Under a new law, Michigan began taking regularly scheduled state censuses, beginning in 1854 and every ten years thereafter.

1861-1865. Over 90,000 Michigan men were mustered into service during the Civil War.

1908. The Ford Model T was first manufactured.

1941. Auto plants were converted to the production of war vehicles, causing Michigan to become known as the "Arsenal of Democracy."

1974. Gerald R. Ford of Grand Rapids, Michigan became the 38th President of the United States.

2012. The Family Heritage Collection of the Library of Michigan was transferred to the Archives of Michigan, but all materials are still accessible at the Michigan Library and Historical Center in Lansing.

2019. August. The Census Bureau estimated the population of Michigan as 10.02 million people, making it the 10th largest state.

Resources at the Michigan Historical Center

Abrams Foundation Historical Collection. This collection was transferred from the Library of Michigan to the Archives of Michigan in 2012. The Abrams Collection emphasizes states east of the Mississippi River, including the Great Lakes region, New England, Mid-Atlantic and Southern states, and the Canadian provinces of Ontario and Quebec. Some examples include:
- County and local histories, cemetery transcriptions, vital record indexes, and more from across the U.S.
- Thousands of collective and individual family genealogies.

- Birth, death, and marriage records for a number of states across the U.S., as well as Ontario.
- A large collection of historical directories for major U.S. cities.
- Plat maps and Sanborn Fire Insurance Maps for many eastern U.S. states.
- Immigration records consisting of thousands of National Archives microfilms and a large collection of printed resources.

Primary Sources. The Archives of Michigan preserves and provides access to state and local government records, as well as private manuscripts. These primary sources include:
- Naturalization records for most Michigan counties.
- State government commission meeting minutes.
- Committee records from the Michigan State Senate and House of Representatives.
- Military records from the American Civil War to World War I.
- Records from the original land surveys that laid out Michigan's township and range system.
- Approximately fifty thousand cartographic images and over a million photographs.

Online Resources at the Archives of Michigan – Seeking Michigan

The *Seeking Michigan* collection is an online service of the Archives of Michigan. It includes digitized databases and indexes, research guides, a blog, and educator resources. New material is added frequently, and there are a number of collections ranging from pre-statehood to the late 1960s, and these include letters, diaries, photographs, postcards, and video. See http://seekingmichigan.org/about. Any of the links listed below take you to a landing page for a collection that explains what is in the collection and how to search within the collection.

List of Online Collections:
- Michigan Death Records, 1897-1920
- Michigan Death Records, 1921-1952
- State Censuses, 1827-1874
- State Censuses, 1884-1894
- Civil War Service Records
- Civil War Photographs
- Civil War Manuscripts
- Plat Maps
- Films
- Civil War Battle Flags
- Early Documents
- Early Photography
- WPA Property Inventories
- Oral Histories
- Maps
- Main Streets
- Architecture
- Lighthouses and Life-Saving Stations
- Governors of Michigan
- Civil War Volunteer Registries

Online Guides Available:
- Guide to Vital Records
- Guide to County Records
- Guide to Immigration & Naturalization Records
- Guide to Military Records

Burton Historical Collection Detroit Public Library

Genealogical materials in the BHC include federal census population schedules, family histories, cemetery inscriptions, church records of baptisms, marriages, and deaths, military records, hereditary society indexes, heraldry books, immigration records, probate indexes and records, vital records, obituaries, and land records. For a catalog/database search, see www.detroitpubliclibrary.org/featuredcollection/burton-historical-collection.

Michigan's Colonial, Territorial & State Censuses

For a thorough review of Michigan's State Censuses, see "State Censuses of Michigan: A Tragedy of Lost Treasures," by LeRoy Barnett, an article in *Family Trails* (MI State Library), Vol. 6, No. 1 (Summer-Fall 1978). The following list of censuses taken in the area of Michigan covers the French colonial period, British colonial period, Michigan Territory period; and censuses taken by the state of Michigan. (Federal censuses are noted in the bibliography). Name lists for all of the censuses were published as printed extracts/indexes, microfilm of originals, or digitized versions online. The online databases are generally indexed by groupings, e.g., 1827-1874; and 1884-1894 (*Seeking Michigan*). Refer to the bibliographic entries for more details for the following:

1710. French Colonial Census. Detroit area.
1750. French Colonial Census. Detroit area.
1762. French Colonial Census. Detroit area.
1765. British Colonial Census. Detroit area.
1768. British Colonial Census. Detroit area.
1779. British Colonial Census. Detroit area.
1780. British Colonial Census. Fort St. Joseph.
1782. British Colonial Census. Detroit, and south shore of Detroit River.

1792. British Colonial Census. Petite Côte (south shore of Detroit River).

1796. British Colonial Census. Detroit area.

1805-1806. Michigan Territorial Census. Detroit area.

1827. Michigan Territorial Census. Surviving Name lists for Wayne (Detroit), Monroe (Lawrence Twp.), Chippewa, and Washtenaw counties only.

1834. Michigan Territorial Census. Tallies only; individual names not included except in Crawford County (now Wisconsin) and Lenawee County.

1837. Michigan State Census. Tallies only; individual names not included except in Kalamazoo County.

1845. Michigan State Census. Only males over 21 years by name, and females in age categories. Includes Eaton, Lenawee, Oakland, St. Clair, St. Joseph, Van Buren, and Washtenaw counties only.

1854. Michigan State Census. Only males over 21 years by name, and females in age categories. Includes population, agricultural, and industrial schedules, for Eaton County only.

1864. Michigan State Census. Only males over 21 years by name, and females in age categories. Includes population, agricultural, and industrial schedules, with name lists for Clinton, Eaton, Houghton, and Sanilac counties only.

1874. Michigan State Census. Only males over 21 years by name, and females in age categories in population schedules for Branch, Eaton, Houghton, and Kalamazoo counties only.

1884. Michigan State Census. This detailed modern census lists the names of all members of a household, relationship to the head of house, age, sex, color, place of birth, parents place of birth, occupation, and much more. Includes population, mortality, agricultural, industrial, or social statistics schedules in Allegan, Braga, Barry, Bay, Benzie, Emmet, Hillsdale, Ingham, Iosco, Isabella, Jackson, Kalamazoo, Kent, Keweenaw, Lake, Lapeer, Leelanau, Lenawee, Menominee, Midland, Montcalm, Muskegon, Newaygo, Ottawa, Roscommon, Sanilac, St. Clair, St. Joseph, Van Buren (Paw Paw Twp.), Washtenaw, Wayne (excluding Detroit), and Wexford counties.

1894. Michigan State Census. This detailed modern census lists the names of all members of a household, relationship to the head of house, age, sex, color, place of birth, parents place of birth, occupation, and much more. Includes population, mortality, agricultural, industrial, or social statistics schedules in Allegan, Barry, Bay, Benzie, Dickinson, Emmet, Gratiot, Hillsdale, Ingham, Iosco, Isabella, Jackson, Kalamazoo, Kent, Keweenaw, Lapeer, Lenawee, Livingston, Menominee, Midland, Montcalm, Muskegon, Newaygo, Ottawa, Roscommon, Sanilac, St. Clair, St. Joseph, and Washtenaw counties.

Bibliography
Michigan Censuses & Substitutes

This bibliography identifies Michigan's censuses and substitute name lists available from the colonial period up to today. Adding the federal censuses to Michigan's state censuses totals 34 census years. Because of the great number of Michigan census name lists, the need for census substitutes between federal census years may seem less demanding – but this bibliography has many extra name lists. Michigan's federal censuses are fairly complete, but the state censuses are not. There may be many state census years, but each are incomplete, covering just a few counties in most cases. To fill out the bibliography, the added substitute name lists include Court Records, Directories, Histories, State Militia Lists, Tax Lists, Vital Records, and Voter Lists. Of Michigan's 83 counties, 25 were formed 1815-1830. Special attention was given to the early counties for any Directories, Tax Lists, and/or Deed Indexes, which are good census substitutes. All of the statewide and countywide name lists begin here in chronological order:

1700-1918. See *Deed Records, 1766-1918; Grantee-Grantor Index, 1700-1903, Wayne County, Michigan* **[Microfilm & Digital Capture],** from the original records at the Wayne County courthouse, Detroit, Michigan. Early deeds are written in French and English. Additional indexes are at front of some volumes. Filmed by the Genealogical Society of Utah, 1974, 210 rolls, beginning with FHL film #926443 (Grantee Index, A-D, 1700-1885). To access the digital images, see the online FHL catalog page: https://familysearch.org/search/catalog/244568.

1701-1710. See *Cadillac's Village, or, Detroit Under Cadillac: With a List of Property Owners and a History of the Settlement* **[Printed Book],** compiled by Clarence Monroe Burton, publ. C.M. Burton, 1896, Detroit, 43 pages, FHL book 977.434 H2bc.

1701-1710. See *First Land Owners of Wayne County, Michigan* **[Printed Book],** compiled by E. Gray Williams and Ethel W. Williams, publ. E.G. Williams, 1964, 93 pages, FHL book 973.433 R2.

1703-1869. See *Early Land Transfers, Detroit and Wayne County, Michigan, Michigan Works Progress Administration, Vital Records Project, Michigan State Library and DAR, Louisa St. Clair Chapter* **[Microfilm & Digital Capture],** from the original records (58 vols.) at the DAR Library, Washington, DC. Includes index. Filmed by the Genealogical Society of Utah, 1971, 13 rolls, beginning with FHL film #857329 (Master index to Records, vols. A, B, & C). To access the digital images, see the online FHL catalog page: **https://familysearch.org/search/catalog/241736**.

1700s-1973. See *Michigan Biography Index* **[Microfilm],** from a book by Frances Loomis, part of County and Regional Histories of the Old Northwest. Series 5, Michigan; No. 9. filmed by. Research Publications, New Haven, CT, 1973, 4 rolls, beginning with FHL film #485331 (Aagaard – Azure). To see if this microfilm has been digitized yet, see the FHL catalog page: **https://familysearch.org/search/catalog/17261**.

1700s-2000s. See *Michigan GenWeb (MIGenWeb) Archives* **[Online Databases].** MIGenWeb, of the USGenWeb Project, is hosted by Ancestry's free RootsWeb system. The MIGenWeb offers free genealogical databases on the Internet, and searchable name lists are available for all Michigan counties. Typical county records include Bibles, Biographies, Cemeteries, Censuses, Court, Death, Deeds, Directories, Histories, Marriages, Military, Newspapers, Obituaries, Photos, Schools, Tax Lists, Wills, and more. The *MIGenWeb Archives County Table of Contents* has links to each of the county web pages: See **http://usgwarchives.net/mi/mitable.htm**.

1700s-2000s. See *Linkpendium – Michigan: Family History & Genealogy, Census, Birth, Marriage, Death Vital Records & More* **[Online Databases].** Linkpendium is a genealogical portal site, with links to state, county, town, and local databases. Currently listed are selected sites for Statewide resources (528), Independent Cities, Renamed Counties, Discontinued Counties (32), and county webpages with links to databases within several categories. There are webpages for each of these Michigan counties (No. of databases): Alcona (269), Alger (146), Allegan (523), Alpena (546), Antrim (527), Arenac (156), Baraga (212), Barry (420), Bay (567), Benzie (186), Berrien (708), Branch (542), Calhoun (858), Cass (502), Charlevoix (335), Cheboygan (286), Chippewa (524), Clare (237), Clinton (426), Crawford (186), Delta (500), Dickinson (288), Eaton (516), Emmet (292), Genesee (876), Gladwin (154), Gogebic (283), Grand Traverse (387), Gratiot (269), Hillsdale (507), Houghton (959), Huron (283), Ingham (715), Ionia (660), Iosco (523), Iron (261), Isabella (219), Jackson (661), Kalamazoo (776), Kalkaska (268), Kent (1,133), Keweenaw (426), Lake (152), Lapeer (536), Leelanau (254), Lenawee (763), Livingston (497), Luce (156), Mackinac (352), Macomb (798), Manistee (404), Marquette (1,037), Mason (296), Mecosta (290), Menominee (540), Midland (217), Missaukee (230), Monroe (1,120), Montcalm (418), Montmorency (123), Muskegon (356), Newaygo (264), Oakland (1,340), Oceana (251), Ogemaw (174), Ontonagon (444), Osceola (261), Oscoda (128), Otsego (199), Ottawa (520), Presque Isle (181), Roscommon (143), Saginaw (615), Saint Clair (619), Saint Joseph (646), Sanilac (313), Schoolcraft (219), Shiawassee (402), Tuscola (852), Van Buren (453), Washtenaw (1,163), Wayne (3,169), and Wexford County (240). To access this list of Michigan counties, visit the Linkpendium Michigan welcome page: **www.linkpendium.com/genealogy/USA/MI**.

1700s–2000s. *Michigan – Collection Catalog at MyHeritage.com* **[Online Database],** 47 collections with 40,790 records for Michigan are at the MyHeritage subscription website. Free index searching is available in databases that include censuses, directories, family histories, town histories, military rosters, college/school year books, and more, see **www.myheritage.com/records/Michigan/all-records**.

1710-1810. See "State Censuses, 1710-1810" **[Printed Article],** in *Family Trails* (MI State Library), Vol. 6, No. 1 (1978).

1710. See "**Census for du Detroit de Pontchartrain, 1710**" **[Printed Article], in** *Michigan's Habitant Heritage* (French Canadian Heritage Society of Michigan), Vol. 26, No. 4 (Oct 2005).

1710-1830. See *Michigan Censuses, 1710-1830, Under the French, British and Americans* **[Printed Book],** edited by Donna Valley Russell. Name lists included:
- **1710.** French Colonial Census. Detroit area.
- **1750.** French Colonial Census. Detroit area.
- **1762.** French Colonial Census. Detroit area.
- **1765.** British Colonial Census. Detroit area.
- **1768.** British Colonial Census. Detroit area.
- **1779.** British Colonial Census. Detroit area.

- **1780.** British Colonial Census. Fort St. Joseph.
- **1782.** British Colonial Census. Detroit, and south Shore of Detroit River.
- **1792.** British Colonial Census. Petite Côte (south Shore of Detroit River).
- **1796.** British Colonial Census. Detroit area.
- **1805-1806.** Michigan Territorial Census. Detroit.
- **1810.** Michigan Territory Federal Census. Detroit & Michillimackinac areas.
- **1820.** Michigan Territory Federal Census. Includes Oakland, Wayne, Michillimackinac, Brown (now Wisconsin), Crawford (now Wisconsin), Monroe, And Macomb counties.
- **1827.** Michigan Territorial Census. Surviving fragments for Wayne (Detroit), Monroe (Lawrence Twp.), Chippewa, and Washtenaw counties only.
- **1830.** Michigan Territory Federal Census. Includes Wayne, Monroe, Oakland, Lenawee, Macomb, St. Clair, Washtenaw, St. Joseph, Berrien, Cass, Van Buren, Michillimackinac, Brown (now Wisconsin), Crawford (now Wisconsin), Chippewa, and Iowa (now Wisconsin) counties.

Published by the Detroit Society for Genealogical Research, 1982, 291 pages. FHL book 977.4 X2r.

1762. See **"Census, 1752, Detroit" [Printed Article]** in *National Genealogical Society Quarterly* (NGS, Arlington, VA), Vol. 68, No. 1 (Mar 1980).

1765. See **"Census, 1765, Detroit" [Printed Article]**, in *Detroit Society for Genealogical Research Magazine* (DSGR, Detroit), Vol. 43, No. 1 (Fall 1979).

1775-1836. *Michigan Military Records* **[Online Database]**, indexed at the Ancestry.com website. Source: Book, originally published as *Michigan Historical Commission, Bulletin No. 12,* Lansing, 1920. Although not officially a part of the United States until after the American Revolutionary War, Michigan attracted thousands of veterans who fought in both the War for Independence and the War of 1812. This database, originally compiled in 1920, is a collection of burial and pension records for residents of the state prior to 1836. It includes the names of men buried in the state and the source from which the record was taken. Also included is a list of pensioners who received land as bounty for their service. It provides the name of over 1,000 men. This database has 304 pages.
https://search.ancestry.com/search/db.aspx?dbid=4465.
For a fully digitized and OCR indexed version of the book, see
https://search.ancestry.com/search/db.aspx?dbid=48332.
- See also, *Alphabetical General Index to Public Library Sets of 85,271 Names of Michigan Soldiers and Sailors Individual Records* **[Online Database]**, digitized and OCR indexed at the Ancestry.com website. Source: An official publication by the Michigan Secretary of State, publ. 1915. See
https://search.ancestry.com/search/db.aspx?dbid=18556.

1775-1995. *Michigan Births and Christenings* **[Online Database],** indexed at the FamilySearch.org website. Includes an index to birth, baptism, and christening records extracted from microfilmed records by the Genealogical Society of Utah on site at various locations in Michigan. This database has 1,612,291 records. See
https://familysearch.org/search/collection/1675348.

1784-1980. *Michigan, Wills and Probate Records* **[Online Database],** digitized and indexed at the Ancestry.com website. Source: Ancestry extractions from Michigan County, District and Probate Courts. Probate records include Wills, Letters of Administration, Inventories, Distributions and Accounting, Bonds, and Guardianships. Each index record includes: Name, Probate date, Probate place, and Inferred death place. Case files with multiple pages have a Table of Contents with categories and numbers of images. The document image will have much more information about a parson, heirs, witnesses, etc. This database has 230,787 records. See
https://search.ancestry.com/search/db.aspx?dbid=8793.

1796. See **"Census, 1796, Detroit" [Printed Article]** in *National Genealogical Society Quarterly* (NGS, Arlington, VA), Vol. 69, No. 3 (Sep 1981).

1797-1973. *Michigan Probate Records* **[Online Database],** digitized at the FamilySearch.org website. This image-only collection includes probate records from county courthouses in Michigan. Most of the collection contains estate files. The content and time period varies by county. Some of the records date before 1837 when Michigan became a state. This database has 4,723,861 images:
https://familysearch.org/search/collection/2013878.

1799, 1806, 1827 Detroit Censuses. See *Early Michigan Census Records* **[Printed Book],** compiled by Ronald Vern Jackson, et al, published by Accelerated Indexing Systems, Bountiful, UT, 1976, 11 pages. Contains the early census records of Detroit, Wayne County, Michigan, 1799, 1806, 1827. FHL book 977.433 X2p.

1800-1850. See *Michigan Marriages to 1850* **[Online Database],** indexed at the Ancestry.com website. This database was originally compiled by Jordan R. Dodd and published by Precision Indexing, North Salt Lake, UT. Each entry includes groom, bride, marriage date, county, and state. This database has 13,000 names, see http://search.ancestry.com/search/db.aspx?dbid=2092.

1800-1995. *Michigan Deaths and Burials* **[Online Database],** indexed at the FamilySearch.org website. A name index to deaths and burials from the state of Michigan from statewide records microfilmed by the Genealogical Society of Utah. This database has 1,372,536 records. See https://familysearch.org/search/collection/1675357.

1800-2009. *Oakland County, Michigan* **[Online Databases],** indexed at the Ancestry.com website. Includes 1800-1917 Oakland County, Michigan Vital Records; 1883 Detroit and Northern Michigan Pleasure Resorts; 1891 Portrait and biographical album of Oakland County, Michigan; 1989 Directory of Birmingham; 1989 Birmingham directory: village of Birmingham and Bloomfield Township; 1912 History of Oakland County, Michigan; 1927 Birmingham directory; 1937 Telephone directory, Birmingham, Bloomfield Hills; and 1970-2009 Obituary Index. See http://search.ancestry.com/Places/US/Michigan/Oakland/Default.aspx.

1800-2010. *Indiana and Michigan, Michiana Genealogical Cemetery Index* **[Online Database],** indexed at the Ancestry.com website. Original data: MGI Cemeteries, South Bend Area Genealogical Society. Each index record includes: Name, Death date, Burial place, Age, Birth date, Notes, and a link to the SBAGS website. This database has 187,743 records: https://search.ancestry.com/search/db.aspx?dbid=70492.

1800-2012. *Kalamazoo County, Michigan* **[Online Databases],** indexed at the Ancestry.com website. Includes 1800-2012 Riverside Cemetery Index; 1880 History of Kalamazoo County; 1892 Portrait and biographical record of Kalamazoo, Allegan, and Van Buren Counties, Michigan; and 1938 Medical memoirs of 50 years in Kalamazoo. See http://search.ancestry.com/Places/US/Michigan/Kalamazoo/Default.aspx.

1805-1857. *Court Records, 1819-1857: Index to Cases, 1805-1857 (Michigan Supreme Court)* **[Microfilm & Digital Capture],** from the originals located at the Bentley Library, University of Michigan. Filmed by the Genealogical Society of Utah, 1974, 4 rolls, beginning with FHL film #955819 (Index to cases). To access the digital images, see the online FHL catalog page: www.familysearch.org/search/catalog/395479.

1806-1923. *Record of Deeds, Monroe County, Michigan, 1806-1923; Index to Deeds, 1807-1905* **[Microfilm & Digital Capture],** from the original records at the Monroe County Courthouse, Monroe, MI. Filmed by the Genealogical Society of Utah, 1983, 2003, 65 rolls, beginning with FHL film #1392545 (Index to deeds, 1807-1855). To access the digital images, see the online FHL catalog page: https://familysearch.org/search/catalog/220293.

1807-1907. *Card Files (Index to Land Entry Files of General Land Offices, Eastern States)* **[Microfilm & Digital Capture],** from the original index cards at the Bureau of Land Management, Eastern States Office, Washington, DC. The card files serve as an index to the Tract Books, Plat Books, and Case Files relating to ten million public land sales in America. **Content:** Each card contains the following information: Certificate Number, District Land Office, Kind of entry (cash, credit, warrant, etc.), Name of Patentee (Buyer, Entryman, etc.), and county of origin, Land description, Number of acres, Date of patent, Volume, and Page where document can be located. Filmed by the Bureau of Land Management, Washington, DC, c1970, 160 rolls (including 4 rolls for Michigan GLOs), beginning with FHL film #1501558 (Twp 1 North to Twp 36 North; Twp 41 North to 43 North; Ranges 3 East – 6 East). **NOTE:** The index cards in this database are arranged by township and range within each state, therefore, a researcher needs to have an approximate legal description in order to access the cards by the patentee name. See the 1807-1907 Homestead/Cash Entry statewide database at Ancestry.com. and the county databases indexed at USGenWeb sites, each with a name list of patentees, range, township, acres, and date of signature. To access the digital images, see the online FHL catalog page: https://familysearch.org/search/catalog/511740.
- See also *Bureau of Land Management – General Land Office Records* **[Online Database],** search for the name of any land purchaser of public land in the U.S. To access the search screen, see https://glorecords.blm.gov/search/default.aspx.

1807-1907. See *Michigan, Homestead and Cash Entry Patents, Pre-1908* **[Online Database],** indexed at the Ancestry.com website. This database was originally digitized by the Bureau of Land Management as part of the General Land Office Automated Records Project, 1994. The *Card Files* database listed before

this database is not indexed by the name of the person purchasing land – this database is fully indexed by the person's name, land office, and many other items. This database has 160,962 records. See
http://search.ancestry.com/search/db.aspx?dbid=2075.

1807-1907. See *Michigan, General Land Office Records, by County* **[Online Databases]**, indexed at the MIGenWeb archives, separated by each Michigan county. Each county's "Land" webpage includes an introduction to the Michigan Land Patents Database, and a name list of patentees for the township/ranges in that county. Access each county by going first to the Michigan County Table of Contents. Select a county from the list, then find "Land Records" within the county list of databases. Note other databases available for each county, such as census, military, history, cemeteries, obituaries, photos, vitals, and more. For the Michigan Counties Selection List, see
http://usgwarchives.net/mi/mitable.htm.

1809-1868. *Marriage and Death Newspaper Notices, Wayne County, Michigan, 1809-1868: Newspaper Notices from Michigan at the Michigan Historical Collections, Bentley Historical Library, University of Michigan* **[Printed Book]**, abstracted by Marguerite N. Lambert; edited and indexed by James N. Jackson. Abstracted newspapers include: *Commercial Advertiser,* 1861-1865; *Detroit Courier,* 1828-1833; *Detroit Advertiser & Tribune,* 1862-1866; *Detroit Daily Advertiser,* 1833-1862; *Detroit Daily Post,* 1861-1867; *Detroit Daily Tribune,* 1857-1865; *Detroit Gazette,* 1817-1833; *Detroit Weekly Advertiser,* 1857; *Detroit Weekly Free Press,* 1862-1868; and *Michigan Essay,* 1809. Includes separate alphabetical listings for marriages and deaths. Publ. Detroit Society for Genealogical Research, Detroit, 1998, 144 pages, FHL book 977.433 V2L.

1810. See **"Census, 1810, Detroit" [Printed Article]** In *Detroit Society for Genealogical Research Magazine* (DSGR, Detroit), Vol. 32, No. 1 (Fall 1968), and Vol. 34, No. 3 (Spring 1971).

1812-1848. *Michigan's Early Military Forces: A Roster and History of Troops Activated Prior to the American Civil War* **[Printed Book]**, compiled by LeRoy Barnett, with histories by Roger Rosentreter. Includes surname index. Contains lists of soldiers for each war, arranged in alphabetical order by surname, and gives name, rank, military unit, service dates and remarks. Also contains brief histories of Michigan and its involvement in each war: pre-territorial militia, War of 1812, Black Hawk War, 1832, Toledo War, 1835, Patriot War, 1838-1839, Mexican War, 1846-1848. Publ. Wayne State University, Detroit, MI, 2003, 518 pages, FHL book 977.4 M2ba.

1813-2012. *Monroe County, Michigan* **[Online Databases]**, digitized and indexed at the Ancestry.com website. Includes 1813 Battle and massacre at Frenchtown, Michigan; 1817-1830 Yankee meets the Frenchman: River Raisin, social, political, military; 1821-2012 Monroe County Obituary Index; 1874-1875, 1892, 1897 Monroe County Directories; 1890 History of Monroe County; and 1911 Monroe, the floral city: a city of homes and industries. See
http://search.ancestry.com/Places/US/Michigan/Monroe/Default.aspx.

1816-1836. *Records of the Territorial Court, Michigan* **[Microfilm & Digital Capture]**, from the original records at the National Archives, Washington, DC. Filmed by the National Archives, 1988, series M1111, 9 rolls, beginning with FHL film #1601888 (Unnumbered case 1816-1820). To access the digital images, see the online FHL catalog page:
www.familysearch.org/search/catalog/588854.

1817-1850. *Michigan, Compiled Marriages* **[Online Database]**, indexed at the Ancestry.com website. Source: Jordan R Dodd, compiler. 1997. Each index record includes: Name, Spouse, Marriage date, and Marriage county. This database has 13,881 records, see **https://search.ancestry.com/search/db.aspx?dbid=2092.**

1817-1999. *Michigan Newspaper Archives* **[Online Database]**, digitized and indexed newspapers at the GenealogyBank website for Adrian, Alma, Alpena, Ann Arbor, Baldwin, Bay City, Belding, Calumet, Cheboygan, Clio, Coldwater, Constantine, Copper Harbor, Crystal Falls, Dearborn, Detroit, Dowagiac, East Jordan, East Saginaw, Eastmanville, Flint, Grand Haven, Grand Rapids, Grayling, Hancock, Hillsdale, Houghton, Jackson, Kalamazoo, L'Anse, Lansing, Marquette, Monroe, Muskegon, Ontonagon, Owosso, Paw Paw, Pontiac, Saginaw, Sault Ste. Marie, St. James, Yale, and Ypsilanti See
www.genealogybank.com/explore/newspapers/all/usa/michigan.

1818-1903. *Monroe County, Michigan: Marriage Records Index* **[Printed Index]**, by Lois Vidolich, publ. Genealogical Society of Monroe Co MI, 1995, 123 pages, FHL book 977.432 V22v.

1818-1935. See *Macomb County, Michigan Deeds and Mortgages, 1818-1935; Indexes, 1818-1908* **[Microfilm & Digital Capture],** from the originals at the Macomb County Courthouse, Mt. Clemens, MI. Filmed by the Genealogical Society of Utah, 1975, 83 rolls, beginning with FHL film #979527 (Deed index, 1818-1845). To access the digital images, see the online FHL catalog page: https://familysearch.org/search/catalog/244435.

1819-1871. *Marriage Index, Macomb County, Michigan* **[Printed Book],** by Karen L. Hemme Rogers and Nancy L. Hudson Burge. 4 Vols. Contents: Vol. 1: 1819-1852; Vol. 2: 1852-1861; Vol. 3: 1861-1867; and Vol. 4: 1868-1871. Publ. K.N. Mulberry Pub., 1992, 4 vols., FHL book 977.439 V223r v.1-4.

1819-1991. *Michigan, Church Records* **[Online Database],** digitized and indexed at FamilySearch.org. This collection contains Church records from various denominations in Michigan. See the title webpage for the list of churches and range of years for each, see www.familysearch.org/search/catalog/2787825.

1820. See **"Census, 1820, Detroit and Wayne County" [Printed Article],** in *Detroit Society for Genealogical Research Magazine* (DSGR, Detroit), Vol. 12, No. 5 (May 1949) through Vol. 14, No. 2 (Dec 1950).

1820 Michigan Territory Federal Census (State Archives Copy) **[Microfilm & Digital Capture],** from Michigan Territory's manuscript copy, now located at the Archives of Michigan, Lansing, MI. The state archives and federal copies should be compared side-by-side for possible copying errors (The federal copy was made from the state's original copy). Contents: Oakland, Wayne, Michillimackinac, Brown (now Wisconsin), Crawford (now Wisconsin), Monroe, and Macomb counties. Filmed by the Genealogical Society of Utah, 1973, 1 roll, FHL film #927678. To access the digital images, see the online FHL catalog page: www.familysearch.org/search/catalog/175106. Another filming (#915334) was also digitized, see www.familysearch.org/search/catalog/339826.

1820-1840. *Michigan, 1820 Thru 1840 Federal Census: Population Schedules (Federal Copy)* **[Microfilm & Digital Capture],** from originals at the National Archives, Washington, DC. The state archives and federal copies (for 1820) should be compared side-by-side for possible copying errors (The federal copy was made from the state's original copy). Filmed by the National Archives (as part of a combined set of 1820, 1830, & 1840), 5 rolls, beginning with FHL film #506762 (Michigan 1820: Oakland, Wayne, Michillimackinac, Brown (now Wisconsin), Crawford (now Wisconsin), Monroe, and Macomb counties). To access the digital images, see the online FHL catalog page: www.familysearch.org/search/catalog/745495.

1820s-1950s. *GLO Plat Maps (Archives of Michigan)* **[Online Database],** digitized at the Seeking Michigan collection of the Archives of Michigan website. Poorly described at the website, this collection is potentially a powerful finding aid to the first land owners of Michigan. These GLO Plat Maps are from the first surveys done in Michigan, all based on the *Michigan Meridian*, first established in 1815. The first Government Land Office (GLO) was at Detroit, followed by those at Monroe, Genesee Township, Ionia, and Kalamazoo. You can browse through over 1,800 images or use the Advanced Search option to search by county, township, date, and more. The best use of these GLO Plat Maps may be after you have an exact property description (Range/Township/Section) from an original entry of land or a deed record. See http://seekingmichigan.contentdm.oclc.org/cdm/search/collection/p15147coll10.

1820-1937. *Michigan, County Marriages Index* **[Online Database],** indexed at the FamilySearch.org website. FamilySearch extractions from microfilm at the Family History Library, Salt Lake City. This database is an index to marriage registers and certificates from county records. The content and time period varies by county. This collection only includes some records from the following counties: Allegan, Alpena, Eaton, and Missaukee. This database has 22,278 records. See www.familysearch.org/search/collection/2473289.

1820-1940. *Michigan, County Marriages* **[Online Database],** digitized and indexed at the FamilySearch.org website. Includes mages of marriage registers and certificates from county records. This collection does not include the following counties: Alger, Alpena, Barry, Eaton, Gladwin, Kalkaska, Kent, Lenawee, Missaukee, Monroe, Montmorency, Oceana, Oscoda, Schoolcraft, and Shiawassee. This database has 1,030,574 records. See https://familysearch.org/search/collection/1810350.

1820-1980. *Name Index File, Monroe County, Michigan* **[Microfilm],** from the original card file index at the Monroe County Historical Commission,

Monroe, MI. From intro: "This file contains references to miscellaneous information, including funeral home records, cemetery listings, church histories, census records, Civil War records, and death, birth and marriage records. The majority of sources can be found at the Monroe County Historical Commission Archives." Filmed by the Genealogical Society of Utah, 2006, 44 rolls, beginning with FHL film #1358112 (Abbey, Alvin – Auten, Caroline). To see if this microfilm has been digitized yet, see the FHL catalog page:
https://familysearch.org/search/catalog/1324774.

1820s-1980s. *The Michigan Surname Index* **[Printed Book],** compiled by the Michigan Genealogical Council, 1984-1989, 2 vols., FHL book 977.4 D22m v.1-2.

1820-1989. *Wayne County, Michigan* **[Online Databases],** indexed at the Ancestry.com website. Includes 1820-1965 Wyandotte, Wayne County, Michigan, Death Index; 1852-1853 Shove's business advertiser, and Detroit directory; 1853-1857 Johnston's Detroit city directory; 1863-1872 Clark & Co.'s city directory of Detroit; 1869 Holland's Detroit business directory; 1872-1873 Hubbell & Weeks' city directory of Detroit; 1872-1873 Detroit city directory1873-1874 Weeks directory of Detroit; 1874-1875 Weeks directory of Detroit; 1875-1876 Weeks directory of Detroit; 1876-1877 Weeks directory of Detroit 1879 Detroit city directory; 1881-1908 Dau's Detroit blue book 1882 Detroit city directory; 1883 Detroit blue book; 1884 Detroit city directory; 1885 Detroit city directory; 1886 Detroit city and Wayne County directory; 1887 Detroit city directory; 1890 Detroit, Michigan Directory; 1893 Detroit city directory; 1894 Detroit city directory; 1895 Detroit city directory; 1897 Detroit pocket business directory. 1905-1963 Detroit Border Crossings and Passenger and Crew Lists; 1941 Polk's Dearborn (Wayne County, Mich.) city directory; 1942 The new church register of the Grosse Pointe Woods Presbyterian Church; 1943 Polk's Dearborn (Wayne County, Mich.) city directory; 1946 Dearborn (Wayne County, Mich.) city directory; 1947 Detroit? Directory; 1948 Dearborn (Wayne County, Mich.) city directory; 1952 Directory of Negro businesses, professions and churches for Detroit and environs; and 1989 Directory, Vinewood Ave Church of Christ. See http://search.ancestry.com/Places/US/Michigan/Wayne/Default.aspx.

1820-2006. *Michigan Obituaries* **[Online Database],** digitized and indexed at the FamilySearch.org website. Includes an index and images of obituary collections organized by county or newspaper and then alphabetically. Extracted information as well as newspaper clippings are represented. The originals are housed in several libraries and repositories throughout Michigan. Some collections contain obituaries from other states and nearby regions. This database has 905,098 records. See
https://familysearch.org/search/collection/2215693.

1821-1927. See *Land Records, St. Clair County, Michigan, 1821-1927; Index, 1821-1901* **[Microfilm & Digital Capture],** from the original records at the St. Clair County Courthouse, Port Huron, MI. Records include deeds 1821-1927 and mortgages 1821-1837. Filmed by the Genealogical Society of Utah, 1975, 67 rolls, beginning with FHL film #975809 (Deed index, 1821-1868). To access the digital images, see the online FHL catalog page:
https://familysearch.org/search/catalog/244706.

1821-1926. *Deed Records, Oakland County, Michigan, 1821-1926; Index, 1821-1905* **[Microfilm & Digital Capture],** from the original records at the Oakland County Courthouse, Pontiac, MI. Filmed by the Genealogical Society of Utah, 1975, 81 rolls, beginning with FHL film #975556 (Deed index, 1821-1845). To access the digital images, see the online FHL catalog page:
https://familysearch.org/search/catalog/214476.

1821-1929. See *Probate Index, Macomb County, Michigan* **[Online Database],** indexed at the Mount Clemens Public Library website. See
www.mtclib.org/search/probate.php.

1822-1940. *Michigan, County Marriage Records* **[Online Database],** indexed at the Ancestry.com website. Source: FamilySearch, various Michigan county marriages, extracted from FHL microfilm. Details vary but may include the following information for both the bride and groom: Name, Age at marriage, Marriage date, Marriage place, and Parents' names. This database has 4,451,095 records.
See https://search.ancestry.com/search/db.aspx?dbid=61374.

1822-1995. *Michigan Marriages* **[Online Database],** indexed at the FamilySearch.org website. This is a name index to marriage records from the state of Michigan taken from the microfilmed records in various locations by the Genealogical Society of Utah. This database has 1,267,961 records. See
https://familysearch.org/search/collection/1675359.

1824-1931. See *Deed Records, Saginaw County, Michigan, 1830-1931; Index, 1824-1902* **[Microfilm & Digital Capture],** from the original records at the Saginaw County Courthouse, Saginaw, MI. Filmed by the Genealogical Society of Utah, 114 rolls, beginning with FHL film #966778 (Deed index, 1824-1867). To access the digital images, see the online FHL catalog page: https://familysearch.org/search/catalog/214845.

"1827 Michigan Territorial Census, Chippewa County" [Printed Article], in *Sault Channels* (Sault St. Marie/District Branch, Ontario Genealogical Society), Vol. 12, No. 1 (Winter 1994).

1827 Detroit, Michigan Territorial Census **[Microfilm],** from a typescript (location of original not noted), filmed by the Genealogical Society of Utah, 1976, 1 roll, FHL film #928180. To see if this microfilm has been digitized yet, see the FHL catalog page: www.familysearch.org/search/catalog/322253.

1827. See *Michigan Territorial Census, Detroit, 1827* **[Microfilm & Digital Capture],** from a typescript compiled by B.F.H. Witherell, filmed by the Michigan State Library, 1960, 15 pages. Filmed by the Genealogical Society of Utah, 1973, FHL film 927477. To access the digital images, see the online FHL catalog page: www.familysearch.org/search/catalog/308956.

"1827 Michigan Territorial Census, Wayne County" [Printed Article], in *Detroit Society for Genealogical Research Magazine*, Vol. 19, No. 2 (Winter 1955).

1827 & 1834 Territorial Censuses of Washtenaw County, Michigan **[Microfilm & Digital Capture],** from the originals at the Bentley Historical Library, University of Michigan, Ann Arbor, MI. Filmed by the Genealogical Society of Utah, 1974, 1 roll, FHL film #955813. To access the digital images, see the online FHL catalog page: www.familysearch.org/search/catalog/290843.

1827-1870. *Michigan, Compiled Census and Census Substitutes Index* **[Online Database],** databases at the Ancestry.com website, originally edited and digitized by Ronald Vern Jackson, Accelerated Indexing Systems, from microfilmed territorial/state censuses, federal censuses, and/or census substitutes. This collection contains the following indexes:
- 1827 Territorial Census Index
- 1837 Kalamazoo County Index
- 1840 Federal Census Index
- 1840 Pensioners List
- 1845 State Census Index
- 1850 Federal Census Index
- 1860 Federal Census Index
- 1870 Federal Census Index
- Early Census Index.

This database has 299,144 records. The combined databases have a single search screen. See http://search.ancestry.com/search/db.aspx?dbid=3554.

1827-1874. *Michigan State Census Records* **[Online Database],** digitized and indexed at the Seeking Michigan collection at the Archives of Michigan website. This collection consists of approximately 1,000-page images of Michigan state census population schedules. The information collected varies by year and location, but only male heads of households and males over the age of 21 were listed by name. Other household members may have been counted, but not named. This collection of state census records is incomplete because many of the documents have been lost over time. It contains records from the following counties and years: Branch (1857, 1874), Clinton (1864), Eaton (1845, 1854, 1864, 1874), Houghton (1864, 1874), Lenawee (1845), Kalamazoo (1874), St. Joseph (1845), Sanilac (1864), and Washtenaw (1827, 1845, 1854). To search for a name, go to the Advanced Search option. When the menu opens, the default collection is for "Death Records, 1897-1920" which needs to be unchecked, then check "Michigan State Census Records, 1827-1874." See http://seekingmichigan.org/discover/state-census-1827-1874.

1827-1941. See *Deed Records, Lenawee County, Michigan, 1827-1920, 1940-1941* **[Microfilm & Digital Capture],** from the original records at the Lenawee County Courthouse, Adrian, MI. Filmed by the Genealogical Society of Utah, 1975, 91 rolls, beginning with FHL film #2209088 (Index, 1827-1852). To access the digital images, see the online FHL catalog page: https://familysearch.org/search/catalog/987007.

1829-1923. *Pioneer History of Ingham County* **[Microfilm & Digital Version],** from a book by Mrs. Franc L. Adams, publ. Lansing, MI, 1923, 856 pages. Filmed by W. C. Cox Co., 1974, 1 roll, FHL film #1000087. For a digital version of this book, see the online FHL catalog page for this title. See https://familysearch.org/search/catalog/22768.
- See also, *Index of Persons Mentioned in Pioneer History of Ingham County Compiled and Arranged by Mrs. Franc Adams* **[Microfilm & Digital Capture],** compiled by Theodore G. Foster, filmed by the Genealogical Society of Utah, 1941, 1 roll, FHL film #1421095. To access the digital images, see the online FHL catalog page: www.familysearch.org/search/catalog/21634.

1829-1990s. *Surname Index, Van Buren Regional Genealogical Society* **[Online Database],** includes a listing of where surnames can be found in the Local History Room at the Webster's Memorial Library in Decatur, MI. Indexed at the RootsWeb site for Van Buren Co MI. See
www.rootsweb.ancestry.com/~mivanbur/vbrgsindex.htm.

- 1840 NOTE: For the 1830 Michigan Federal Census (Microfilm/Digital Capture), see the combined listing, *Michigan, 1820 Thru 1840 Federal Census.*

1830 Federal Census: Territory of Michigan **[Printed Extract/Index & Digital Capture],** from a book transcribed and edited by Elizabeth Taft Harlan, Minnie Dubbs Milbrook, and Elizabeth Case Erwin. Includes index. Publ. Detroit Society for Genealogical Research, 1961, 1970, 150 pages, FHL book 977.4 X2h 1830. For access to a digital version of this book, see the online FHL catalog page:
https://familysearch.org/search/catalog/2512882.

1830-1860. *Tract Books Containing Abstracts of Deeds, Kent County, Michigan* **[Microfilm & Digital Capture],** from original records at the Burton Abstract Division, First American Title Insurance Co of Mid American, Grand Rapids, MI. The county's original deed books were destroyed by fire in 1860. An abstract of the deeds was made by Leonidas Scranton which eventually was lost or misplaced. The abstracts had been copied into the current tract books and held by the Burton Abstract Division. Only those volumes that have the abstracted records in them were filmed. Only those pages of each section that have abstracted records on them were filmed and only filmed up to 1860. Filmed by the Genealogical Society of Utah, 1985, 6 rolls, beginning with FHL film #1433380 (Tract Book 1-2). For a complete list of roll numbers, roll contents, and the digital images of each roll, see the online FHL catalog page:
https://familysearch.org/search/catalog/530216.

1830-1905. See *Deed Records, Cass County, Michigan, 1830-1905; Deed Index, 1871-1905* **[Microfilm & Digital Capture],** from the originals at the Cass County Courthouse, Cassopolis, MI. Filmed by the Genealogical Society of Utah, 49 rolls, beginning with FHL film #1941374 (Deed index, 1871-1898). To access the digital images, see the online FHL catalog page:
https://familysearch.org/search/catalog/216168.

1830-1924. *Deed Records, St. Joseph County, Michigan, 1830-1924; Index 1830-1902* **[Microfilm & Digital Capture],** from the original records at the St. Joseph County Courthouse, Centreville, MI. Filmed by the Genealogical Society of Utah, 1994, 46 rolls, beginning with FHL film #1941131 (Deed index, 1830-1852). To access the digital images, see the online FHL catalog page:
https://familysearch.org/search/catalog/704206.

1830-1990s. *Index to Manuscripts and Family Histories Available in the Grand Rapids Public Library* **[Printed Book],** compiled by Evelyn Sawyer for the Western Michigan Genealogical Society, Grand Rapids, MI, 1990, 28 pages, FHL book 977.4 A1 No. 727.

1831-1860. *Original Pioneer Settlers of Ottawa County, Michigan* **[Online Database],** indexed at the USGenWeb site for Ottawa Co MI. See
http://files.usgwarchives.net/mi/ottawa/settlers/s34601.txt.

1831-1884. *Gratiot County, Michigan* **[Online Databases],** indexed at the Ancestry.com website. Includes two Portrait & Biographical Albums, publ. 1884 & 1913, covering the time of the county's formation in 1831 to 1912. See
http://search.ancestry.com/Places/US/Michigan/Gratiot/Default.aspx.

1831-1895. *Tax Assessment Rolls, St. Joseph County, Michigan* **[Microfilm & Digital Capture],** from the original records at the Archives Regional History Collections, Western Michigan University, Kalamazoo, MI. Filmed by the Genealogical Society of Utah, 2001-2002, 24 rolls, beginning with FHL film #2257910 (Tax Assessments, 1831, 1836-1845). To access the digital images, see the online FHL catalog page: https://familysearch.org/search/catalog/1127419.

1831-1932. See *Deed Records, Branch County, Michigan, 1831-1932; Index, 1833-1908* **[Microfilm & Digital Capture],** from the original records at the Branch County Courthouse, Coldwater, MI. Filmed by the Genealogical Society of Utah, 1973, 59 rolls, beginning with FHL film #932686 (Deed index, 1833-1850). To access the digital images, see the online FHL catalog page:
https://familysearch.org/search/catalog/245262.

1831-2015. *Online Searchable Databases of the Western Michigan Genealogical Society* **[Online Databases],** the WMGS of Grand Rapids, MI has one of the largest collection of online databases of any genealogical group in America. Included are the following:
- 1910-2015 West Michigan Newspapers
- 1903-1925 Kent County School Census
- 1831-1877 West Michigan Church Records

- 1954-2014 *Michigana* (Quarterly) Index
- 1880-2014 Home for Veterans
- 1917-1918 World War I soldiers
- 1978-1991 WMGS manuscripts
- WMGS Members Genealogies
- 1894-1933 Monument Orders
- 1918-1926 Farm Bureau News
- 1860-1894 Michigan Censuses
- 1845-1939 Kent County Deaths
- 1903-1962 Latzek Funeral Home
- 1881 Chapman's History of Kent County
- 1905 Goss History of Grand Rapids
- Quigley files

The combined total is now over 3 million entries. For the database home page, see **http://data.wmgs.org**.

1833-1906. See *Deed Records, Calhoun County, Michigan, 1833-1906; Index, 1833-1901* **[Microfilm & Digital Capture]**, from the originals at the Calhoun County Courthouse, Marshall, MI. Filmed by the Genealogical Society of Utah, 74 rolls, beginning with FHL film #1003917 (Deed index, 1833-1848). To access the digital images, see the online FHL catalog page: **https://familysearch.org/search/catalog/213909**.

1834-1935. See *Deed Records, Barry County, Michigan, 1834-1935; Index, 1834-1903* **[Microfilm & Digital Capture]**, from the original records at the Barry County Courthouse, Hastings, MI. Filmed by the Genealogical Society of Utah, 1976, 1990, 55 rolls, beginnings with FHL film #1008282 (Deed index, 1834-1867). To access the digital images, see the online FHL catalog page: **https://familysearch.org/search/catalog/210254**.

1834-1941. See *Deed Records, Livingston County, Michigan, 1836-1941; Index, 1834-1925* **[Microfilm & Digital Capture]**, from the originals at the Livingston County Courthouse, Howell, MI. Filmed by the Genealogical Society of Utah, 43 rolls, beginning with FHL film #1005374 (Index to deeds, 1834-1867). To access the digital images, see the online FHL catalog page: **https://familysearch.org/search/catalog/213796**.

1834-1974. *Michigan, Civil Marriages* **[Online Database]**, indexed at the FamilySearch.org website. Source: various published extracts, mostly from Saginaw and Wayne counties, Michigan. Each index record includes: Name, Event type, Event date, Event place, Gender, Age, Birth year, Spouse's name, Spouse's gender, Spouse's age, Spouse's birth year, and Notes. This database has 34,763 records. See **www.familysearch.org/search/collection/2515912**.

1835-1906. See *Records of Deeds, Kent County, Michigan, 1835-1906; Index, 1835-1899* **[Microfilm & Digital Capture]**, from records at the Kent County Courthouse, Grand Rapids, MI. Filmed by the Genealogical Society of Utah, 1983, 68 rolls, beginning with FHL film #1392829 (Index to deeds, early to 1860). To access the digital images, see the online FHL catalog page: **https://familysearch.org/search/catalog/330512**.

1835-1918. See *Deed Records, Ingham County, Michigan, 1836-1918; Index, 1835-1903* **[Microfilm & Digital Capture]**, from the originals at the Ingham County Courthouse, Mason, MI. Filmed by the Genealogical Society of Utah, 1976, 51 rolls, beginning with FHL film #1010409 (Deed index, 1835-1868). To access the digital images, see the online FHL catalog page: **https://familysearch.org/search/catalog/209958**.

1835-1929. See *Deed Records, Hillsdale County, Michigan, 1835-1929; Index, 1835-1901* **[Microfilm & Digital Capture]**, from the originals at the Hillsdale County Courthouse, Hillsdale, MI. Filmed by the Genealogical Society of Utah, 1976, 71 rolls, beginning with FHL film #1009400 (Index, 1835-1861). To access the digital images, see the online FHL catalog page: **https://familysearch.org/search/catalog/210029**.

1835-1934. See **Deed Records, Bay County, Michigan, 1835-1934; Index, 1853-1907** **[Microfilm & Digital Capture]**, from the originals at the Bay County Court House, Bay City, MI. Filmed by the Genealogical Society of Utah, 1973, 43 rolls, beginning with FHL film #946292 (Deed index, 1853-1874). To access the digital images, see the online FHL catalog page: **https://familysearch.org/search/catalog/243928**.

1835-1942. See *Deed Records, Sanilac County, Michigan, 1835-1942; Index, 1835-1902* **[Microfilm & Digital Capture]**, from the originals at the Sanilac County Courthouse, Sandusky, MI. Filmed by the Genealogical Society of Utah, 1975, 29 rolls, beginning with FHL film #978659 (Deed Index, 1835-1849). To access the digital images, see the online FHL catalog page: **https://familysearch.org/search/catalog/214445**.

1836-1907. *Genesee County, Michigan* **[Online Database]**, indexed by the Ancestry.com website. Includes 1836-1934 marriages; 1867-1930 death index; 1888-1907 birth index; histories; and history indexes. **http://search.ancestry.com/Places/US/Michigan/Genesee/Default.aspx**.

1835-1916. See *Land Patents, Hillsdale County, Michigan, 1835-1850; Plat Maps, 1872-1916* **[Online Database]**, digitized and indexed at the MIGenWeb site for Hillsdale Co MI. See www.migenweb.org/hillsdale/land/index.html.

1836-1944. See *Deed Records, Shiawassee County, Michigan, 1837-1944; Index, 1836-1906* **[Microfilm & Digital Capture]**, from the originals at the Shiawassee County Courthouse in Corunna, MI. Filmed by the Genealogical Society of Utah, 1976, 66 rolls, beginning with FHL film #988468 (Index, 1836-1854). To access the digital images, see the online FHL catalog page:
https://familysearch.org/search/catalog/213984.

"1837 Michigan State Census, Ionia County" [Printed Article], in *Michigan Heritage* (Ethel W. Williams, Kalamazoo, MI), Vol. 1, No. 2 (Winter 1962) through Vol. 6, No. 2 (Winter 1964).

1837 Michigan State Census, Kalamazoo County, **(Printed Book),** compiled by Mrs. Chalmers A. (Ruth Robbins) Monteith, 46 pages. Includes index. FHL book 977.417 X2p and FHL film #925967.

1837. *Michigan 1837 Census Index* **[Printed Book]**, compiled by W. David Samuelsen, et al, published by Accelerated Indexing, Bountiful, UT, 1984, 27 pages. Kalamazoo County only. FHL book 977.417 X22j.

1837. *Directory of the City of Detroit: With its Environs, and Register of Michigan, for the Year 1837. Containing an Epitomized History of Detroit* **[Printed Book & Digital Capture]**, from a book by Julius P. Bolivar MacCabe, digitized by the Genealogical Society of Utah, 2014. To access the digital images, see the online FHL catalog page:
https://familysearch.org/search/catalog/2301954.

1837-1854. *Assessment Rolls, Washtenaw County, Michigan* **[Microfilm & Digital Capture]**, from the original records at the Washtenaw County Courthouse, Ann Arbor, MI. Filmed by the Genealogical Society of Utah, 1973, 11 rolls, beginning with FHL film #925695 (Ann Arbor Twp., 1837-1848). To access the digital images, see the online FHL catalog page:
https://familysearch.org/search/catalog/20057.

1837-1868. *Tax Records, Van Buren County, Michigan* **[Microfilm & Digital Capture]**, from the originals at Western Michigan University, Kalamazoo, MI. Includes tax assessment rolls, lands with unpaid taxes and nonresident lands returned for taxes. Filmed by the Genealogical Society of Utah, 1973, 2000, 7 rolls, beginning with FHL film #2209502 (Assessment rolls, 1838-1840). To access the digital images, see the online FHL catalog page:
https://familysearch.org/search/catalog/173228.

1837-1903. *Michigan, Index to Eastern District Naturalizations* **[Online Database]**, digitized and OCR indexed at the Ancestry.com website. This index, compiled by Loretto Dennis Szucs, pertains to the original records now in the custody of the National Archives, Chicago, IL. See
https://search.ancestry.com/search/db.aspx?dbid=6613.

1837-1928. See *Record of Deeds, Van Buren County, Michigan, 1837-1928; Index 1837-1902* **[Microfilm & Digital Capture]**, from the original records at the Van Buren County Courthouse, Paw Paw, MI. Filmed by the Genealogical Society of Utah, 1977, 54 rolls, beginning with FHL film #1019141 (Index to deeds, 1837-1862). To access the digital images, see the online FHL catalog page:
https://familysearch.org/search/catalog/209807.

1837-1935. *Detroit (Michigan) City Directories* **[Microfilm]**, from the originals published by various publishers. This series includes city directories for 1837, 1845, 1846, 1850, and every year (or two-year span) thereafter through 1935. Filmed by Research Publications, Woodbridge, CT, 1980-1984, 46 microfiche, 72 rolls of microfilm, beginning with FHL fiche #6043862. To see if this microfilm has been digitized yet, see the FHL catalog page:
https://familysearch.org/search/catalog/539682.

1838-1861. *General Roster of the Militia of the State of Michigan* **[Microfilm & Digital Capture]**, from the originals at the Michigan Adjutant General's Office. Filmed by the Genealogical Society of Utah, 1973, 2 rolls, FHL film #915335 (Roster, 1838-1848) and FHL film #915336 (Roster, 1846-1861). To access the digital images of these rolls, see the online FHL catalog page: www.familysearch.org/search/catalog/53771.

1838-1859. *Assessment Rolls, Macomb County, Michigan* **[Microfilm & Digital Capture]**, from the originals at the Archives of Michigan, Lansing, MI. Filmed by the Genealogical Society of Utah, 1973, 5 rolls, beginning with FHL film #915980 (Clinton Twp, 1838-1852). To access the digital images, see the online FHL catalog page:
https://familysearch.org/search/catalog/280414.

1838-1877. *Assessment Rolls, Kalamazoo County, Michigan* **[Microfilm & Digital Capture],** from the original records at Western Michigan University, Kalamazoo, MI. Filmed by the Genealogical Society of Utah, 1973, 40 rolls, beginning with FHL film #932044 (Assessment rolls, 1838, 1839). To access the digital images, see the online FHL catalog page: https://familysearch.org/search/catalog/176224.

1838-1880. *Tax Assessment Rolls, Ottawa County, Michigan* **[Microfilm & Digital Capture],** from the original records at the Waldo Library, Western Michigan University, Kalamazoo, MI. Includes name of owner or occupant, description, section, town, range, acres, value, total value, state tax, county tax, township tax, highway tax, school tax, total tax, and remarks. Filmed by the Genealogical Society of Utah, 1973, 2001, 19 rolls, beginning with FHL film #2257698 (Tax Assessment, 1838-1851). To access the digital images, see the online FHL catalog page: https://familysearch.org/search/catalog/176202.

1839-1987. *Prisoner Card Index* **[Microfilm & Digital Capture],** from the originals at the Michigan State Archives, Lansing, MI. This collection offers the names of prisoners serving in Michigan's correction institutions, length of sentences, dates of sentences, registration or identification numbers, and counties where the crimes occurred. There are references of any escape attempts as well as parole or discharge dates. Some of the index cards include photographs and/or physical descriptions of prisoners. Filmed by the Genealogical Society of Utah, 2002-2003, 138 rolls, beginning with FHL film #2139730 (A – Alexander, Billy, 1839-1987). To access the digital images, see the online FHL catalog page: https://familysearch.org/search/catalog/1127432.

- 1840 NOTE: For the 1840 Michigan Federal Census (Microfilm/Digital Capture), see the combined listing, *Michigan, 1820 Thru 1840 Federal Census.*

1840. *Index to 1840 Federal Population Census of Michigan* **[Printed Index],** edited by Estelle A. McGlynn, publ. Detroit Society for Genealogical Research, 1977, 165 pages, FHL book 977.4 X2p 1840.

1840-1972. *Military Veterans of Hillsdale County, Michigan* **[Online Database],** links to databases for lists of veterans, beginning with the 1840 RevWar list, War of 1812, Civil War, Spanish-American War, World War I, World War II, Korean Conflict, and Vietnam War. Indexed at the MIGenWeb site for Hillsdale Co MI. See www.migenweb.org/hillsdale/military.html.

1840-2005. *Genealogy Surname Card File Index, Lenawee County, Michigan* **[Microfilm & Digital Capture],** from the original card file at the Lenawee County Historical Society, Adrian, MI. Filmed by the Genealogical Society of Utah, 2005, 2 rolls, FHL film #1358070 (A-R) and FHL film #1358071 (S-Z). To access the digital images of these rolls, see the online FHL catalog page: www.familysearch.org/search/catalog/1318477.

1840s-2000s. *Huron Shores Genealogical Society's Names Indexes* **[CD-ROM],** prepared by Alonzo J. Sherman for the Huron Shores Genealogical Society, Oscoda, MI, 2007, 2 CDs, FHL CD No. 5627 Pt.1-2.

1841-1867. *Tax Rolls, Oakland County, Michigan* **[Microfilm & Digital Capture],** from the original records at the Michigan State Archives, Lansing, MI. Names are list alphabetically in each township. Filmed by the Genealogical Society of Utah, 1994, 28 rolls, beginning with FHL film #1928407 (Tax Rolls, 1841-1843). To access the digital images for certain rolls, see the online FHL catalog page: https://familysearch.org/search/catalog/710699.

1841-1907. *Tax Records, Berrien County, Michigan* **[Microfilm],** from the original records at the Berrien County Historical Association, Berrien Springs, MI. Includes owner's name, section, subdivision, acres, value of real estate, value of personal estate, road tax, general tax, and total tax. Filmed by the Genealogical Society of Utah, 2001, 24 rolls, beginning with FHL film #2257508 (Tax Assessment, Bainbridge Twp,1842-1883). To see if this microfilm has been digitized yet, see the FHL catalog page: https://familysearch.org/search/catalog/1131406.

1841-1999. *Iosco County, Michigan* **[Online Databases],** indexed at the Ancestry.com website. Includes 1892-1949 Tawas Herald Obituaries; 1978-1990 Obituaries; 1901-1999 Esmond-Evergreen Cemetery; 1885-1910 Naturalization Index; 1900-1910 Iosco County Gazette Index; 1869-1934 Paupers; 1903 Plat Book; 1841-1896 Early Land Owners; and 1892-1905 Glass Negatives, East Tawas: http://search.ancestry.com/Places/US/Michigan/Iosco/Default.aspx.

1842-2011. *Kent County, Michigan* **[Online Databases],** indexed at the Ancestry.com website. Includes 1842-1929 Marriage Index; 1881 History of Kent County, Michigan; 1889-1890 Grand Rapids City Directories; 1903-1925 School Census; 1905-1906 The Grand Rapids society blue book; 1910-2012 Newspapers Death Index; 1959-2011 Newspapers Marriage Index, and more. See
http://search.ancestry.com/Places/US/Michigan/Kent/Default.aspx.

1843-1895. *Assessment Rolls, Allegan County, Michigan* **[Microfilm & Digital Capture],** from the original records at the Allegan County Courthouse, Allegan, MI. Filmed by the Genealogical Society of Utah, 2000, 42 rolls, beginning with FHL film #2208022 (Assessment rolls, 1843-1847). To access the digital images, see the online FHL catalog page: https://familysearch.org/search/catalog/986472.

1844-1850. *Assessment Rolls, Saginaw County, Michigan, Vols. 1-5, 1844-1850* **[Microfilm & Digital Capture],** from the originals at the Archives of Michigan, Lansing, MI. Filmed by the Genealogical Society of Utah, 1973, 1 roll, FHL film #915993. To access the digital images, see the online FHL catalog page: www.familysearch.org/search/catalog/170034.

1844-1858. See *Assessment Rolls, Jackson County, Michigan* **[Microfilm & Digital Capture],** from the original records at the Archives of Michigan, Lansing, MI. Filmed by the Genealogical Society of Utah, 1973, 10 rolls, beginning with FHL film #915969 (1844-1848, Columbia Twp, Concord Twp, Grass Lake Twp, Hanover Twp, Liberty Twp, and Napoleon Twp). To access the digital images, see the online FHL catalog page: https://familysearch.org/search/catalog/165421.

1844-1877. *Tax Records, Genesee County, Michigan* **[Microfilm & Digital Capture],** from the original records at the Michigan State Archives, Lansing, MI. The tax assessment rolls include name of owner or occupant, legal description or lot number, number of acres comprising tract or parcel, value of each tract or parcel, value of personal estate, school district, amount of tax assessed for state, county, township highway, school, together with total tax. Delinquent tax returns are statement of lands upon which taxes were unpaid and record includes owner, description, amounts of taxes and totals. Both records arranged chronologically, then loosely alphabetically by name of township and village. Filmed by the Genealogical Society of Utah, 1973-2003, 31 rolls, beginning with FHL film #915956 (Tax rolls, 1844-1847). To access the digital images, see the online FHL catalog page: https://familysearch.org/search/catalog/311737.

1844-1895. *Tax Assessment Rolls, Eaton County, Michigan* **[Microfilm & Digital Capture],** from the original records at the Archives of Michigan, Lansing, MI. Includes name of owner or occupant, legal description of land, number of acres comprising tract or parcel, assessed value of each tract or parcel, assessed value of personal estate, amount of tax assessed for state, county, township, highway, and special purposes, together with total. Rolls are arranged chronologically, then alphabetically by name of city, township, or village. Filmed by the Genealogical Society of Utah, 2003, 28 rolls, beginning with FHL film #2365508 (Tax Assessment rolls, 1844). To access the digital images, see the online FHL catalog page: https://familysearch.org/search/catalog/262971.

1844-1904. *Tax Assessment Rolls, Calhoun County, Michigan* **[Microfilm & Digital Capture],** from the originals at Western Michigan University, Kalamazoo, MI. Includes name of owner/occupant/mortgager, description, section, town, range, acres, values, total dollars, value of personal estate, total dollars, number of school district, state tax, county tax, township tax, highway tax, school tax, total taxes, remark. Filmed by the Genealogical Society of Utah, 1973, 2001, 62 rolls, beginning with FHL film #2258799 (Tax Assessment, 1844). To access the digital images, see the online FHL catalog page: https://familysearch.org/search/catalog/262909.

1845 Michigan State Census, Eaton County **[Microfilm & Digital Capture],** from the original records at the Michigan State Archives, Lansing, MI, filmed by the Genealogical Society of Utah, 1972, 1 roll, FHL film #915300. To access the digital images of this roll, see the online FHL catalog page: www.familysearch.org/search/catalog/328232.

1845 Michigan State Census of St. Joseph, Lenawee, Washtenaw, and Eaton Counties **[Printed index],** edited by Ronald Vern Jackson, et al, published by Accelerated Indexing Systems, North Salt Lake, UT, 1988, 280 pages. FHL book 977.4 X22j.

1845 State Census, St. Joseph County, Michigan, **[Printed Book],** copied and indexed by Bette Williams, publ. B. Williams, Kalamazoo, MI, 1968, 53 pages. FHL book 977.419 X2p and FHL film #927440.

1845 Michigan State Census, Lenawee County **[Microfilm & Digital Capture],** from a typescript at the Library of Michigan, Lansing, MI. Produced by the DAR, Lucy Wolcott Barnum Chapter, Adrian, MI. Filmed by the Genealogical Society of Utah, 1973, 1 roll, FHL film #926729. To access the digital images of this roll, see the online FHL catalog page: **www.familysearch.org/search/catalog/166680**.

1845. *State Census of Oakland County, Michigan For the Year 1845* **[Printed Book],** compiled by the Oakland County Genealogical Society, Birmingham, MI, 1985, 290 pages. FHL book 977.438 X2sc 1845 and FHL film #1597984.

1845. *Index to 1845 State Census of St. Clair County, Michigan: Heads of Families and Names of White Males Over Twenty-one* **[Printed Book],** compiled by the St. Clair County Family History Group, Port Huron, MI, 1990, 78 pages. Includes name and location (usually township). Names listed alphabetically. FHL book 977.441 X22i 1845 index and FHL film #1425030.

1845 Michigan State Census, Washtenaw County **[Microfilm & Digital Capture],** from the originals at the Bentley Historical Library, University of Michigan, Ann Arbor, MI. Filmed by the Genealogical Society of Utah, 1974, 1 roll, FHL film #955813. To access the digital images of this roll, see the online FHL catalog page: **www.familysearch.org/search/catalog/290827**.

"1845 Michigan State Census, Washtenaw County" [Printed Article], in *Family History Capers*, (Gen. Soc. of Washtenaw Co, Ann Arbor, MI), beginning with Vol. 5, No. 2 (Oct 1981); and by townships in various issues through Vol. 11, No. 1 (Summer 1987).

1845-1853. *Assessment Rolls, Monroe County, Michigan* **[Microfilm & Digital Capture],** from the originals at the Archives of Michigan, Lansing, MI. Filmed by the Genealogical Society of Utah, 1973, 4 rolls, beginning with FHL film #915988 (Assessments Rolls 1845-1846). For a complete list of roll numbers, roll contents, and the digital images of each roll, see the online FHL catalog page for this title: **https://familysearch.org/search/catalog/236783**.

1845-1998. *Death Resources, Washtenaw County, Michigan* **[Online Database].** Includes Necrology Reports, 1898-1901; Genealogical Death Indexing System, 1886-1897; John Geddes Diary Extracts, 1845-1889; and Vietnam War Military Deaths, Washtenaw Soldiers. Indexed at the RootsWeb site for Washtenaw Co MI. For an archived database, see **https://web.archive.org/web/20160619172558/www.rootsweb.ancestry.com/~miwashte/washdeat.html**.

1846-1935. *Hillsdale County, Michigan* **[Online Databases],** indexed at the Ancestry.com website. Includes the following databases:
  - 1846-1849. Hillsdale Whig Standard Newspaper
  - 1865-1869. The Hillsdale Standard Newspaper
  - 1874-1875. Coldwater City Directory,
  - 1919-1924. Hillsdale Co Farm Directory
  - 1989. Hillsdale City Directory
  - 1935. Portrait and Biographical Album. See
http://search.ancestry.com/Places/US/Michigan/Hillsdale/Default.aspx.

1846-1999. *Delta County Pioneer List, Pioneer Certificate Surname Listing* **[Online Database],** indexed at the Delta County Genealogical Society website. See **http://dcmigs.org/pioneer.htm**.

1847-1848. *Michigan in the Mexican War* **[Printed Book & Digital Version],** compiled by Richard W. Welch, publ. 1967. Includes rosters of all military units, taken from the reports of the Adjutant General of Michigan located at the MI State Archives. See FHL book 977.4 M23. For access to a digital version of this book, see the online FHL catalog page: **https://familysearch.org/search/catalog/265848**.

1847-2012. *Ottawa County, Michigan* **[Online Databases],** indexed at the Ancestry.com website. Includes 1847 The immigration and early history of the people of Zeeland, Ottawa County, Michigan; 1867-1901 Ottawa County, Michigan, Death Index; 1893 Portrait and biographical record of Muskegon and Ottawa Counties, Michigan; 1910-2012 Newspapers, Death Index; 1948-1949, 1952-1976 Holland Evening Sentinel (Holland, Michigan); and 1959-2011 Newspapers, Marriage Index. See **http://search.ancestry.com/Places/US/Michigan/Ottawa/Default.aspx**.

1849-1864. *The Western Chronicle; First Newspaper Printed in Saint Joseph County, Michigan: Alphabetical Listing* **[Microfiche],** from a typescript made in 1979-1981 for the Three Rivers Public Library. Issues covered in index are for years 1849-1864. Filmed by the Michigan Genealogical Council, c1982, 1 roll, FHL fiche #6332812.

1849-1879. *Tax Assessment Rolls, Chippewa County, Michigan* **[Microfilm & Digital Capture]**, from the originals at the State Archives in Lansing, MI. Arranged alphabetically by name of township, then chronologically. Includes name of owner or occupant, legal description, number of acres comprising tract or parcel, value of each tract or parcel, value of personal estate, amount of tax assessed for state, county, township, highway and special purposes, together with total. Filmed by the Genealogical Society of Utah, 2003, 4 rolls, beginning with FHL film #2364295 (Detour Twp, 1877-1880; Sault Ste. Marie Twp, 1849-1869). To access the digital images, see the online FHL catalog page:
https://familysearch.org/search/catalog/1134606.

1845-1880. *Assessment Rolls, Cass County, Michigan, 1845-1880* **[Microfilm & Digital Capture]**, from the originals at Western Michigan University, Kalamazoo, MI. Filmed by the Genealogical Society of Utah, 15 rolls, beginning with FHL film #932054 (Assessment rolls, 1845-1848). To access the digital images, see the online FHL catalog page: **https://familysearch.org/search/catalog/176206.**

1850. See *Michigan, 1850 Federal Census: Population Schedules (Federal Copy)* **[Microfilm & Digital Capture]**, from the originals at the National Archives, Washington, DC. Filmed by the National Archives, 1964, 21 rolls, beginning with FHL film #14808 (Michigan: Allegan, Barry, and Berrien Counties). To access the digital images, see the online FHL catalog page:
www.familysearch.org/search/catalog/744485.

1850. See *Index to the Federal Population Census of Michigan* **[Printed Index]**, compiled and published by the DAR, Lansing, MI, 1976, 463 pages, FHL book 977.4 x2p 1850.

- 1850 CENSUS NOTE – State Copies vs Federal Copies. In the federal census enabling act for 1850, 1860, and 1870, every county in the U.S. was asked to make a copy of their original schedules. The county's copy was to be sent to that state's Secretary of State, who was asked to make another copy to be sent to Washington, DC. Of the three copies made in 1850, 1860, and 1870, the 1st original stayed in the county where it was created. The 2nd copy stayed in the Secretary of State's office, and the 3rd copy was sent to the Census Office in Washington, DC (as the Federal Copy). The copy that was microfilmed by the National Archives in the 1960s was the federal copy, and was used to digitize the census schedules now searchable online at FamilySearch, Ancestry, et al. The five Michigan county censuses for 1850 shown here were either state copies from the Secretary of State or original county copies. They were later transferred to the Archives of Michigan or other regional repositories They were all included in the microfilming project of the Genealogical Society of Utah in the early 1970s. Genealogists using the 1850 federal census for Michigan should be aware that there are two original sets (state copies and federal copies) for these five counties: Eaton, Barry, Kent, Montcalm, and Washtenaw. Comparing a state copy with a federal copy side-by-side will reveal copious errors, e.g., misspelled names, omitted names, duplicated entries, different dates of birth, changing a male to a female, and a myriad of mistakes caused by large, cumbersome books difficult to hand copy from one page to another.

1850 Federal Census, Eaton County, Michigan (State Copy) **[Microfilm & Digital Capture]**, from the state's original copy, now located at the Archives of Michigan. The information in this original copy may be different than the federal copy (part of the state database). Filmed by the Genealogical Society of Utah, 1972, 1 roll, FHL film #915300. To access the digital images of this roll, see the online FHL catalog page: **www.familysearch.org/search/catalog/328220.**

*1850 Federal Census, Barry County, Michigan (State Copy)***/Microfilm]**, from the state's original copy, now located at the Archives of Michigan. The information in this original copy may be different than the federal copy (part of the state database). Filmed by the Genealogical Society of Utah, 1972, 1 roll, FHL film #915278. To see if this microfilm has been digitized yet, see the FHL catalog page:
www.familysearch.org/search/catalog/328087.

1850 Federal Census, Kent County, Michigan (State Copy) **[Microfilm]**, from the state's original copy, now located at the Grand Rapids Public Library, Grand Rapid, MI. The information in this original copy may be different than the federal copy (part of the state database). Filmed by the Genealogical Society of Utah, 1972, 1 roll, FHL film #984116. To see if this microfilm has been digitized yet, see the FHL catalog page: **www.familysearch.org/search/catalog/321320.**

1850 Federal Census, Montcalm County, Michigan (State Copy) **[Microfilm]**, from the state's original copy, now located at the Archives of Michigan, Lansing, MI. The information in this original copy may be different than the federal copy (part of the state database). Filmed by the Genealogical Society of

Utah, 1972, 1 roll, FHL film #915325. To see if this microfilm has been digitized yet, see the FHL catalog page: www.familysearch.org/search/catalog/328179.

1850 Federal Census, Washtenaw County, Michigan (State Copy) **[Microfilm],** from the county's original copy, now located at the Bentley Historical Library, University of Michigan, Ann Arbor, MI. The information in this original copy may be different than the federal copy (part of the state database). Filmed by the Genealogical Society of Utah, 1974, 1 roll, FHL film #955815. To see if this microfilm has been digitized yet, see the FHL catalog page: www.familysearch.org/search/catalog/291357.

1850-1880. *Michigan Mortality Schedules* **[Online Database],** digitized and indexed at FamilySearch.org. Name index and images of mortality schedules from Michigan,1850-1880. Mortality Schedules were created in conjunction with the US Federal Census and list people who died in the year preceding the census. Mortality schedules were first included in the 1850 census. These include lists of people who died Jun 1849 - May 1850, Jun 1859 - May 1860, Jun 1869-May 1870, and Jun 1879 - May 1880. This database has 39,479 records, see www.familysearch.org/search/collection/2632078.

1850-2000. *Biography Card File, Michigan* **[Microfilm & Digital Capture],** from the original card file at the Hoyt Main Library, Saginaw, MI. Contains an alphabetized card file of brief biographical information (with source citations) extracted from newspapers, vital records, histories, and other misc. sources. Filmed by the Genealogical Society of Utah, 2006, 7 rolls, beginning with FHL film #1512857 (Abbee, Mary – Ball, Hariet). To access the digital images, see the online FHL catalog page: https://familysearch.org/search/catalog/1348295.

1850-2000. *Genealogy Vertical File Index* **[Microfilm],** from the original card file at the Hoyt Main Library, Saginaw, MI. Contains an alphabetized card index to the genealogical information within the vertical file, covering primarily Saginaw County and other areas in Michigan. Filmed by the Genealogical Society of Utah, 20065, 1 rolls, FHL film #1512884. To see if this microfilm has been digitized yet, see the FHL catalog page: www.familysearch.org/search/catalog/1348973.

1851-1875. *Michigan Marriages* **[Online Database],** indexed at the Ancestry.com website. This database was originally compiled by Jordan Dodd, Liahona Research, and contains marriage entries for Wayne, Branch, Hillsdale, Jackson, and Kent County, Michigan. Includes the names of both a bride and groom, and the date and place of the marriage. This database has 51,913 records. See http://search.ancestry.com/search/db.aspx?dbid=5299.

1852-1881. *Assessment Rolls, Barry County, Michigan* **[Microfilm],** from the original records at Western Michigan University, Kalamazoo, MI. Filmed by the Genealogical Society of Utah, 2001, 13 rolls, beginning with FHL film #2258375 (Assessment Rolls, 1852-1855). To see if this microfilm has been digitized yet, see the FHL catalog page: https://familysearch.org/search/catalog/1023761.

1852-1960 Michigan Directories, as part of ***U.S. City Directories, 1822-1995*** **[Online Database],** digitized and OCR indexed at the Ancestry.com website. See each directory title page image for the full title and publication information. This collection is one of the largest single databases on the Internet. All states are represented (except Alaska) with a total of 1.56 billion names, all indexed from scanned images of the city directory book pages. Michigan directories included in this database are listed here for a **City/County** (No. of years), and Date-Range: **Adrian** (18) 1859-1960, **Alpena** (32) 1883-1960, **Ann Arbor** (53) 1860-1960, **Battle Creek** (45) 1883-1960, **Bay City** (50) 1871-1960, **Benton Harbor** (23) 1902-1960, **Berkley** (3) 1930-1936, **Berrien County** (1) 1871, **Birmingham** (14) 1925-1960, **Cadillac** (9) 1938-1959, **Calumet** (3) 1910-1930, **Charlotte** (1) 1904, **Cheboygan** (4) 1910-1916, **Clawson** (2) 1930-1936, **Coldwater** (42) 1874-1956, **Corunna** (1) 1945, **Dearborn** (16) 1926-1959, **Detroit** (78) 1852-1958, **Durand** (1) 1945, **East Detroit** (7) 1942-1958, **East Saginaw** (2) 1868-1873, **Eaton County** (1) 1872, **Escanaba** (22) 1902-1959, **Filer City** (2) 1940-1945, **Flint** (48) 1885-1960, **Grand Haven** (10) 1936-1960, **Grand Rapids** (81) 1865-1960, **Greenville** (2) 1902-1905, **Harbor Springs** (3) 1938-1949, **Hastings** (9) 1926-1959, **Hillsdale** (9) 1870-1931, **Holland** (18) 1903-1960, **Huntington Woods** (3) 1930-1936, **Ionia** (4) 1903-1929, **Ironwood** (2) 1893-1901, **Ishpeming** (1) 1937, **Jackson** (60) 1859-1960, **Kalamazoo** (43) 1867-1960, **Kalamazoo County** (1) 1869, Kent County (1) 1870, **Lansing** (38) 1873-1960, **Lincoln Park** (11) 1929-1960, **Ludington** (13) 1883-1935, **Manistee** (19) 1902-1959, **Marquette** (25) 1894-1959, **Marshall** (4) 1926-1934, **Menominee** (25) 1887-1958, **Midland** (12) 1931-1960, **Monroe** (9) 1916-1959, **Montague** (2) 1936-1938, **Muskegon** (45) 1879-1960, **Negaunee** (1) 1937, **Niles** (9) 1940-1960, **Oak Park** (3) 1930-1936, **Owosso** (24) 1905-1960, **Perry** (1) 1945, **Petoskey** (19) 1904-1958, **Plainwell** (1) 1871, **Pleasant Ridge** (3) 1930-1936, **Plymouth** (11) 1908-1960, **Pontiac** (24) 1920-1960, **Port Huron** (9) 1904-1933, **Royal Oak** (18) 1922-1960, **Saginaw** (54) 1870-1958, **Sault Sainte Marie** (29) 1888-1960, **Shiawassee**

(1) 1917, **St. Johns** (1) 1929, **St. Joseph** (12) 1904-1956, **Three Rivers** (7) 1913-1934, **Traverse City** (14) 1901-1935, **Various Places** (4) 1863-1878, **Wenona** (1) 1875, **Whitehall** (2) 1936-1938, **Windsor** (1) 1909, **Wyandotte** (14) 1907-1958, **Ypsilanti** (16) 1873-1942, and **Zeeland** (4) 1936-1942. Use Ancestry's *Browse this Collection* feature to choose a state, choose a city, and choose a directory year available for that city. This U.S. database has 1,560,284,702 records. See
https://search.ancestry.com/search/db.aspx?dbid=2469.

1853-2000s. *Grand Traverse County, Michigan* **[Online Databases]**, indexed at the Ancestry.com website. Includes marriage and death indexes. See
http://search.ancestry.com/Places/US/Michigan/Grand-Traverse/Default.aspx.

1854 Michigan State Census, Eaton County **[Microfilm & Digital Capture]**, from the original records at the Michigan State Archives, filmed by the Genealogical Society of Utah, 1972, 1 roll, FHL film #915300. To access the digital images of this roll, see the online FHL catalog:
www.familysearch.org/search/catalog/328226.

"1854 Michigan State Census, Emmet County"[Printed Article], in *Detroit Society for Genealogical Research Magazine,* Vol. 52, No. 1 (Fall 1988) through Vol. 52, No. 2 (Winter 1989).

1854 & 1874 Michigan State Census, Branch County **[Printed Book]**, published by the Branch County Genealogical Society, Coldwater, MI, 110 pages. From preface: "The first part of the book shows Coldwater Township [and the village of Coldwater] only for 1854. The second part of the book shows all of Branch County for 1874." FHL book 977.421 X2b and FHL film #6005282.

1855-1935. See *Deed Records, Midland County, Michigan, 1855-1935; Index, 1855-1905* **[Microfilm & Digital Capture]**, from the originals at the Midland County Courthouse, Midland, MI. Filmed by the Genealogical Society, 1973, 25 rolls, beginning with FHL film #946176 (Deed index, 1855-1877). To access the digital images, see the online FHL catalog page: https://familysearch.org/search/catalog/245042.

1856-1857. *State of Michigan Gazetteer & Business Directory for 1856-1857* **[Printed Book & Digital Capture]**, digitized from the book by H.H. Lee and Co., Detroit, MI, 1856, 65 pages. To access the digital version of the book, see the online FHL catalog page for this title:
https://familysearch.org/search/catalog/2300564.

1856-1860. *Michigan (State) Directories* **[Microfilm]**, from various publishers, filmed by Research Publications, Woodbridge, CT, 1980-1984, 2 fiche, FHL fiche #6044120 (1856/1857) and FHL fiche #6044121 (1860).

1856-1935. See *Grand Rapids (Michigan) City Directories* **[Microfilm]**, from various publishers. FHL has 1856, 1859-1860, 1865-1866, 1867-1868, 1868-1869, 1870 1871, 1875-1876, 1877-1878, 1881-1882, 1882-1883, 1883-1884, 1884-1885, 1886-1887, 1888 thru 1927, 1928, 1929, 1931, 1932, 1934, and 1935. Filmed by Research Publications, Woodbridge, CT, 1980-1984, 36 film/fiche, beginning with FHL fiche #6043928 (1856 Business Directory). To see if this microfilm has been digitized yet, see the FHL catalog page: https://familysearch.org/search/catalog/543137.

1857-1911. *Emmet County, Michigan* **[Online Databases]**, indexed at the Ancestry.com website. Includes 1857-2000s marriages, 1868-2000s deaths, and 1911 history. See
http://search.ancestry.com/Places/US/Michigan/Emmet/Default.aspx.

1857-1989. *Saginaw County, Michigan* **[Online Databases]**, indexed at the Ancestry.com website. Includes 1857, 1907 Saginaw semi-centennial souvenir; 1881 History of Saginaw County; 1889-1890 Saginaw Directories; 1892 Portrait and biographical record of Saginaw and Bay Counties, Michigan; 1963 History of Saginaw County; and 1989 Views of Saginaw and Vicinity. See
http://search.ancestry.com/Places/US/Michigan/Saginaw/Default.aspx.

1858-1875. *The Grand Traverse Herald, Traverse City, Michigan* **[Online Database]**, a newspaper digitized and indexed at the Ancestry.com. Covers 1858-1861 and 1867-1875. See
http://search.ancestry.com/search/db.aspx?dbid=6573.

1859-1970s. *The Lighthouse: A Compilation of Data Taken From Actual Records, Muskegon County, Michigan* **[Online Database]**, indexed at the RootsWeb site for Muskegon Co MI. See
http://freepages.genealogy.rootsweb.ancestry.com/~muskegoncounty/Contributions/Index.htm.

1860. *Michigan, 1860 Federal Census: Population Schedules (Federal Copy)* **[Microfilm & Digital Capture]**, from the originals at the National Archives, Washington, DC. Filmed twice by the National Archives, 1960, 1967, 46 rolls total, beginning with

FHL film #803535 (Michigan, 2nd filming, Alpena, Alcona, Allegan, and Antrim Counties). To access the digital images, see the online FHL catalog page: www.familysearch.org/search/catalog/705079.

1860. *Michigan 1860 Federal Census Index* **[Printed Index],** edited by Ronald Vern Jackson, publ. Accelerated Indexing Systems, North Salt Lake, Utah, 1988, 923 pages, FHL book 977.4 X22.

- 1860 CENSUS NOTE – State Copies vs Federal Copies. Genealogists using the 1860 federal census for Michigan should be aware that there are two sets of original census records for these seven counties: Eaton, Barry, Bay, Clinton, Houghton, Kent, and Montcalm counties. Comparing a state copy with a federal copy side-by-side will reveal copious errors, e.g., misspelled names, omitted names, duplicated entries, different dates of birth, changing a male to a female, and a myriad of mistakes caused by large, cumbersome books difficult to copy from one page to another.

1860 Federal Census, Eaton County, Michigan (State Copy) **[Microfilm],** from the state's original copy, now located at the Archives of Michigan, Lansing, MI. The information in this original copy may be different than the federal copy (part of the state database). Filmed by the Genealogical Society of Utah, 1972, 1 roll, FHL film #915301. To see if this microfilm has been digitized yet, see the FHL catalog page: www.familysearch.org/search/catalog/328223.

1860 Federal Census, Barry County, Michigan (State Copy) **[Microfilm],** from the state's original copy, now located at the Archives of Michigan, Lansing, MI. The information in this original copy may be different than the federal copy (part of the state database). Filmed by the Genealogical Society of Utah, 1972, 1 roll, FHL film #915279. To see if this microfilm has been digitized yet, see the FHL catalog page: www.familysearch.org/search/catalog/328134.

1860 Federal Census, Bay County, Michigan (State Copy) **[Microfilm],** from the state's original copy, now located at the Archives of Michigan, Lansing, MI. The information in this original copy may be different than the federal copy (part of the state database). Filmed by the Genealogical Society of Utah, 1972, 1 roll, FHL film #915287. To see if this microfilm has been digitized yet, see the FHL catalog page: www.familysearch.org/search/catalog/328093.

1860 Federal Census, Clinton County, Michigan (State Copy) **[Microfilm],** from the state's original copy, now located at the Archives of Michigan, Lansing, MI. The information in this original copy may be different than the federal copy (part of the state database). Filmed by the Genealogical Society of Utah, 1972, 1 roll, FHL film #915296. To see if this microfilm has been digitized yet, see the FHL catalog page: www.familysearch.org/search/catalog/328238.

1860 Federal Census, Houghton County, Michigan (State Copy) **[Microfilm],** from the state's original copy, now located at the Archives of Michigan, Lansing, MI. The information in this original copy may be different than the federal copy (part of the state database). Filmed by the Genealogical Society of Utah, 1972, 1 roll, FHL film #915275. To see if this microfilm has been digitized yet, see the FHL catalog page: www.familysearch.org/search/catalog/328240.

1860 Federal Census, Kent County, Michigan (State Copy) **[Microfilm],** from the state's original copy, now located at the Archives of Michigan, Lansing, MI. The information in this original copy may be different than the federal copy (part of the state database). Filmed by the Genealogical Society of Utah, 1972, 2 rolls, FHL film #984116 (Schedule I) and FHL film #984117 (Schedules III-VI and another filming of schedule I). To see if this microfilm has been digitized yet, see the FHL catalog page www.familysearch.org/search/catalog/73803.

1860 Federal Census, Montcalm County, Michigan (State Copy) **[Microfilm],** from the state's original copy, now located at the Archives of Michigan, Lansing, MI. The information in this original copy may be different than the federal copy (part of the state database). Filmed by the Genealogical Society of Utah, 1972, 1 roll, FHL film #915325. To see if this microfilm has been digitized yet, see the FHL catalog page: www.familysearch.org/search/catalog/328182.

1860-1990s. *Birth, Death and Marriage Card File, Jackson County, Michigan* **[Microfilm & Digital Capture],** from the original card file at the Jackson District Library, Jackson, MI. Filmed by the Genealogical Society of Utah, 2004, 2005, 37 rolls, beginning with FHL film #2246372 (Aanstad, Thourval – Ayres, Clara). To access the digital images, see the online FHL catalog page: https://familysearch.org/search/catalog/1232617.

1861-1865. *Michigan in the Civil War* **[Printed Book & Digital Version],** compiled by John Robertson, publ. W. S. George, Lansing, MI, 1882, 1,039 pages, FHL book 974.4 M25a. For access to a digital version of this book, visit the online FHL catalog page for this title. See
https://familysearch.org/search/catalog/264728.

- For a digitized and OCR indexed version of this book, https://search.ancestry.com/search/db.aspx?dbid=7744.
- For another database, see https://search.ancestry.com/search/db.aspx?dbid=18447.
- See also, *Index to John Robertson's Michigan in the War, Revised Edition, Lansing, Michigan, 1882* **[Microfiche],** from a typescript compiled by Helen Harriet Ellis, c1960, 250 pages, filmed by University Microfilms, Ann Arbor, MI, 1989, FHL fiche #6078584.

1861-1865. *Michigan in the Civil War* **[Online Database],** digitized and indexed at the Ancestry.com website. This is a digital version of John Robertson's *Michigan in the War,* publ. 1882. See http://search.ancestry.com/search/db.aspx?dbid=7744. For another version, see http://search.ancestry.com/search/db.aspx?dbid=18447.

1861-1865. *Michigan Civil War Manuscripts* **[Online Database],** digitized and indexed at the Seeking Michigan collections of the Archives of Michigan website. See http://cdm16317.contentdm.oclc.org/cdm/search/collection/p129401coll15.

1861-1865. *Michigan Civil War Photographs* **[Online Database],** digitized and indexed at the Seeking Michigan collections of the Archives of Michigan website. See http://cdm16317.contentdm.oclc.org/cdm/search/collection/p4006coll3.

1861-1865. *Record of Service of Michigan Volunteers in the Civil War* **[Printed Book, Microfilm & Digital Capture],** from originals at the Michigan Adjutant General's Office, reprinted by Detroit Book Press, Detroit, MI, c1985, 46 vols., FHL book 977.4 M2r v.1-46, and beginning with FHL film #915948 (Alphabetical Index). For a complete list of volumes and contents of each (names of regiments and military units), a complete list of roll numbers, and access to a digital version of each volume, see the online FHL catalog page for this title. See https://familysearch.org/search/catalog/252875.
- For a digitized and OCR Indexed version of all 46 volumes of this same title, see http://search.ancestry.com/search/db.aspx?dbid=18555.

1861-1865. *Alphabetical General Index to Public Library Set of 85,271 Names of Michigan Soldiers and Sailors Individual Records* **[Printed Book & Online Database],** from the Michigan Adjutant General's Office, publ. Michael A. Hogle, Military Bookseller, Okemos, MI, 1984, 1,097 pages, FHL book 977.4 M2r Index. Also on microfilm, FHL film #915948 (Alphabetical Index). For a digital version of the index, see the online FHL catalog page: https://familysearch.org/search/catalog/37227.

1861-1865. *Michigan Civil War Service Records* **[Online Database],** digitized and indexed at the Seeking Michigan collections of the Archives of Michigan website. These documents are from the Michigan Adjutant General. See http://cdm16317.contentdm.oclc.org/cdm/search/collection/p4006coll15.

1861-1865. *Index to Compiled Service Records of Volunteer Union Soldiers Who Served in Organizations From the State of Michigan* **[Microfilm & Digital Capture],** from the originals at the US Adjutant General's Office, now at the National Archives, Washington, DC. Filmed by the National Archives, 1964, 48 rolls, beginning with FHL film #881914 (A – Aur). To access the digital images, see the online FHL catalog page: www.familysearch.org/search/catalog/98157.

1861-1930. See *Civil War Graves Registration Index Cards, ca. 1861-1930* **[Microfilm & Digital Capture],** from the original records at the Michigan State Archives, Lansing, MI. Contains graves, regiments, and counties. Filmed by the Genealogical Society of Utah, 1994, 22 rolls, beginning with FHL film #1955405 (Graves index, A-Barnes). To access the digital images, see the online FHL catalog page: https://familysearch.org/search/catalog/710418.

1862-1866. *Internal Revenue Assessment Lists for Michigan* **[Microfilm & Digital Capture],** from the originals at the National Archives, Washington, DC. From intro: "The Internal Revenue Act of July 1, 1862 (12 Stat. 432), was intended to provide Internal Revenue to support the Government and to pay interest on the public debt. Monthly specific and ad valorem duties were placed on manufactures, articles, and products ranging from ale to zinc. The lists are arranged by collection district and thereunder by division. An index that lists county names in each collection district is filmed after this introduction." Filmed by the National Archives, 1973, 15 rolls, beginning with FHL film #1534388 (District 1 annual, monthly, and special lists 1862-1863). To access the digital images, see the online FHL catalog page: https://familysearch.org/search/catalog/577914.

1863-1864. *Michigan State Gazetteer and Business Directory for 1863-1864: Embracing Historical and Descriptive Sketches of al the Cities, Towns and Villages Throughout the State* **[Microfilm],** from the book by Charles F. Clark, publ. Detroit, 1863, 611 pages. Filmed by the Genealogical Society of Utah, 1977, 1 roll, FHL film #1015815. To see if this microfilm has been digitized yet, see the FHL catalog page: www.familysearch.org/search/catalog/36348.

1864 Michigan State Census, Clinton County **[Microfilm],** from the originals at the Michigan State Archives, Lansing, MI, filmed by the Genealogical Society of Utah, 1972, 1 roll, FHL film #915297. To see if this microfilm has been digitized yet, see the FHL catalog page:
www.familysearch.org/search/catalog/328212.

1864 Michigan State Census, Eaton County, **[Microfilm],** from the original records at the Michigan State Archives, Lansing, MI. Filmed by the Genealogical Society of Utah, 1972, 1 roll, FHL film #915302. To see if this microfilm has been digitized yet, see the FHL catalog page:
www.familysearch.org/search/catalog/328128.

1864 Michigan State Census, Houghton County, **[Microfilm & Digital Capture],** from the original records at the Michigan State Archives, Lansing, MI. Filmed by the Genealogical Society of Utah, 1972, 1 roll, FHL film #915276. To access the digital images of this roll, see the online FHL catalog page:
www.familysearch.org/search/catalog/328063.

1865-1931. *Michigan Church Marriages* **[Online Database],** indexed at the FamilySearch.org website. Index to selected marriages from various churches throughout Michigan. Many of the records are from Lenawee, Manistee, Saginaw, Washtenaw, and Wayne counties. This database has 817 records. See www.familysearch.org/search/collection/2515887.

1867-1883. *Unrecorded Births of Newaygo County, Michigan, 1867-1883* **[Online Database],** indexed at the MIGenWeb site, Newaygo Co MI. See www.migenweb.org/newaygo/births.html.

1867-1907. *Deaths, Ontonagon County, Michigan, 1867-1907* **[Online Database],** indexed at the USGenWeb site for Ontonagon Co MI. See http://files.usgwarchives.net/mi/ontonagon/vitals/deaths/o53505.txt.

1867-1897. *Michigan Deaths* **[Online Database],** indexed at the FamilySearch.org website. This is a name index and images of Michigan statewide death registrations. Source: Michigan Secretary of State, Department of Vital Records, Lansing, MI. This database has 507,104 records. See https://familysearch.org/search/collection/1452402.

1867-1902. *Michigan Births* **[Online Database],** indexed at the FamilySearch.org website. This is a name index and images of Michigan statewide birth registrations. Source: Michigan Secretary of State, Department of Vital Records, Lansing, MI. This database has 1,409,989 records. See https://familysearch.org/search/collection/1459684.

1867-1911. *Michigan, Births and Christenings Index* **[Online Database],** indexed at the Ancestry.com website. Source: Index, FamilySearch, Salt Lake City, derived from digital copies of original and compiled records. This database has 916,602 records. See http://search.ancestry.com/search/db.aspx?dbid=2560.

1867-1917. *Michigan, County Births* **[Online Database],** digitized and indexed at the FamilySearch.org website. Source: FamilySearch extractions from various county records on microfilm at the Family History Library, Salt Lake City, UT. Each index record includes: Name, Event type, Event date, Event place, Gender, Father's name, Father's birthplace, Mother's name, and Mother's birthplace. The document image may have more information. This database has 136,119 records. See www.familysearch.org/search/collection/1923472.

1867-1917. *Death Records, Wayne County, Michigan* **[Microfilm & Digital Capture],** from the originals at the Wayne County Courthouse, Detroit, MI. Records are arranged by date of recording which could be quarterly. Records sent into the County Clerk are arranged within the year by village or township. Filmed by the Genealogical Society of Utah, 1983, 20 rolls, beginning with FHL film #1377692 (Deaths, 12867-1874). To access the digital images, see the online FHL catalog page:
https://familysearch.org/search/catalog/279018.

1867-1920s. *Birth Records, Otsego County, Michigan* **[Online Database],** indexed at the RootsWeb site for Otsego Co MI. For an archived database, see https://web.archive.org/web/20160818224134/www.rootsweb.ancestry.com/~miotsego/BirthsIndex.htm.

1867-1950. *Michigan, Death Records* **[Online Database],** indexed at the Ancestry.com website. Original data: Death Records. Michigan Department of Community Health, Division for Vital Records and Health Statistics, Lansing, Michigan. This collection contains death registers (1867-1897) as well as certificates (1897-1941) from the state of Michigan. While forms differ, you may find the following details among the records: Name of the decedent and place of death, Gender, Color or race, Marital status, Date of birth, Age, Occupation, Birthplace, Father's name and birthplace, Mother's name and birthplace, Name and address of informant, Date filed, Date of death, Physician's statement and cause of death, Length of residence, if in a hospital or institution, Date and place of burial, and Name and address of undertaker. Later records may include spouse's name. This database has 8,380,545 records:
https://search.ancestry.com/search/db.aspx?dbid=60872.

1867-1952. *Michigan, Marriage Records* **[Online Database],** digitized and indexed at the Ancestry.com website. This collection contains marriage registers (1868-1925) as well as licenses and certificates (1926-1952) from the state of Michigan. Usually included: a name, residence, spouse, marriage date and place, race/color, age, occupation, witnesses, father's name, and mother's name. Original data: Michigan, Marriage Records, 1867–1952. Michigan Department of Community Health, Division for Vital Records and Health Statistics. This database has 15,032,934 records:
http://search.ancestry.com/search/db.aspx?dbid=9093.
- For the FamilySearch.org version, see www.familysearch.org/search/collection/1452395.

1867-1960. *Index to Birth Records, Ottawa County, Michigan* **[Online Database],** indexed at the MIGenWeb site for Ottawa Co MI. See
http://ottawa.migenweb.net/births/index.html.

1867-1965. *Death Index, Muskegon County, Michigan* **[Online Database],** indexed at the Muskegon Co Clerk's website. See
www.co.muskegon.mi.us/clerk/websearch.cfm.

1867-1990. *Muskegon County, Michigan* **[Online Databases],** indexed at the Ancestry.com website. Includes 1867-1965 Muskegon County Death Index; 1887-1890 Muskegon Michigan Directories; 1892 The Advantages and surroundings of Muskegon, Mich.: the material interests of a progressive city; 1893 Portrait and biographical record of Muskegon and Ottawa Counties, Michigan; 1900 Lincoln, Grant, Sherman, Farragut: an account of the gift, the erection and the dedication of the bronze statues; 1910-2012 Newspapers Death Index; 1959-2011 Newspapers Marriage Index; and 1990 The Fruitport Orchard & Vineyard Company. See
http://search.ancestry.com/Places/US/Michigan/Muskegon/Default.aspx.

1867-1995. *Michigan, Deaths and Burials Index* **[Online Database],** indexed at the Ancestry.com website. Source: Index, FamilySearch, Salt Lake City, derived from digital copies of original and compiled records. This database has 1,335,443 records. See
http://search.ancestry.com/search/db.aspx?dbid=2549.

1867-1915. *Birth Index, Delta County, Michigan* **[Online Database],** indexed at the Delta County Genealogical Society website. See
http://dcmigs.org/births/birth_index.htm.

1967-1998. *Death Records, St. Joseph County, Michigan* **[Online Database],** indexed at the RootsWeb site for St. Joseph Co MI. For an archived database, see
https://web.archive.org/web/20160923111343/www.rootsweb.ancestry.com/~mistjose/death/maindeath.htm.

1867-2000s. *Branch County, Michigan* **[Online Databases],** indexed at the Ancestry.com website. Includes death records, directories, histories, and biographies. See
http://search.ancestry.com/Places/US/Michigan/Branch/Default.aspx.

1868-1887. *Births, Ontonagon County, Michigan* **[Online Database],** indexed at the USGenWeb site for Ontonagon Co MI. See
http://files.usgwarchives.net/mi/ontonagon/vitals/births/o53504.txt.

1868-1918. *Birth Records, Wayne County, Michigan* **[Microfilm & Digital Capture],** from the originals at the Wayne County Courthouse, Detroit, MI. Filmed by the Genealogical Society of Utah, 1983, 35 rolls, beginning with FHL film #1377654 (Births, 1868-1870). To access the digital images, see the online FHL catalog page:
https://familysearch.org/search/catalog/271403.

1868-1925. *Michigan Marriages* **[Online Database],** digitized and indexed at the FamilySearch.org. Source: Michigan Secretary of State, Department of Vital Records, Lansing, MI. This is a name index and images of Michigan statewide marriage records. In some cases, marriages were celebrated and recorded in a county different from the county where the marriage license was issued. This database has 1,533,863 records. See
https://familysearch.org/search/collection/1452395.

1868-2000s. *Charlevoix County, Michigan* **[Online Database],** indexed at the Ancestry.com website. Includes marriage index and death index. See http://search.ancestry.com/Places/US/Michigan/Charlevoix/Default.aspx.

1870. *Michigan, 1870 Federal Census: Population Schedules (Federal Copy)* **[Microfilm & Digital Capture],** from the originals at the National Archives, Washington, DC. Filmed twice by the National Archives, 1962, 1968, 74 rolls total, beginning with FHL film #552159 (Michigan, 2nd filming, Alcona and Allegan Counties). To access the digital images, see the online FHL catalog page:
www.familysearch.org/search/catalog/698903.

1870. *Michigan 1870 Census Index* **[Printed Index],** compiled by the library staff, Library of Michigan, Lansing, MI, 1997, 10 vols. Contents: Vol. 1: Upper Peninsula and northern half of the Lower Peninsula; Vol. 2: Western middle portion of the Lower Peninsula; Vol. 3: Mid-Michigan portion of the Lower Peninsula; Vol. 4: Genesee, Livingston, Saginaw and Shiawassee counties; Vol.. 5: Mideastern portion of the Lower Peninsula; Vol. 8: Jackson, Lenawee and Washtenaw counties; Vol. 9: Monroe, Oakland and Wayne (excluding Detroit) counties; Vol. 10: Detroit. FHL book 974.4 X22L 1870 v.1-10.

- 1870 CENSUS NOTE – State Copies vs Federal Copies. Genealogists using the 1870 federal census for Michigan should be aware that there are two sets of original census records for these thirteen counties: Barry, Bay, Benzie, Clinton, Easton, Houghton, Kent, Keweenaw, Menominee, Montcalm, St. Joseph, Van Buren, and Washtenaw. Comparing a state copy with a federal copy side-by-side will reveal copious errors, e.g., misspelled names, omitted names, duplicated entries, different dates of birth, changing a male to a female, and a myriad of mistakes caused by large, cumbersome books difficult to copy from one page to another.

1870 Federal Census, Barry County, Michigan (State Copy) **[Microfilm],** from the state's original copy, now located at the Archives of Michigan, Lansing, MI. The information in this original copy may be different than the federal copy (part of the state database). Filmed by the Genealogical Society of Utah, 1972, 2 rolls, FHL film #915280 (Towns of Woodland, Carlton, Irving, Yankee Springs, Rutland, Nashville, Castleton, Thornapple, Middleville, and Hastings); and FHL film #915283 (Towns of Assyria, Baltimore, Barry, Carlton, Nashville, Hastings, Hope, Irving, Johnstown, Maple Grove, Orangeville, Prairieville, Rutland, Thornapple, Middleville, Woodland, and Yankee Springs). To see if this microfilm has been digitized yet, see the FHL catalog page:
www.familysearch.org/search/catalog/314928.

1870 Federal Census, Bay County, Michigan (State Copy) **[Microfilm],** from the state's original copy, now located at the Archives of Michigan, Lansing, MI. The information in this original copy may be different than the federal copy (part of the state database). Filmed by the Genealogical Society of Utah, 1972, 1 roll, FHL film #915288. To see if this microfilm has been digitized yet, see the FHL catalog page:
www.familysearch.org/search/catalog/328096.

1870 Federal Census, Benzie County, Michigan (State Copy) **[Microfilm],** from the state's original copy, now located at the Archives of Michigan, Lansing, MI. The information in this original copy may be different than the federal copy (part of the state database). Filmed by the Genealogical Society of Utah, 1972, 1 roll, FHL film #915294. To see if this microfilm has been digitized yet, see the FHL catalog page: **www.familysearch.org/search/catalog/328235.**

1870 Federal Census, Clinton County, Michigan (State Copy) **[Microfilm],** from the state's original copy, now located at the Archives of Michigan, Lansing, MI. The information in this original copy may be different than the federal copy (part of the state database). Filmed by the Genealogical Society of Utah, 1972, 1 roll, FHL film #915298. To see if this microfilm has been digitized yet, see the FHL catalog page: **www.familysearch.org/search/catalog/328196.**

1870 Federal Census, Eaton County, Michigan (State Copy) **[Microfilm],** from the state's original copy, now located at the Archives of Michigan, Lansing, MI. The information in this original copy may be different than the federal copy (part of the state database). Filmed by the Genealogical Society of Utah, 1972, 1 roll, FHL film #915303. To see if this microfilm has been digitized yet, see the FHL catalog page: **www.familysearch.org/search/catalog/328131.**

1870 Federal Census, Houghton County, Michigan (State Copy) **[Microfilm & Digital Capture],** from the state's original copy, now located at the Archives of Michigan, Lansing, MI. The information in this original copy may be different than the federal copy (part of the state database). Filmed by the Genealogical Society of Utah, 1972, 1 roll, FHL film #915276. To access the digital images, see the online FHL catalog page: **www.familysearch.org/search/catalog/328066.**

1870 Federal Census, Kent County, Michigan (State Copy) **[Microfilm],** from the state's original copy, now located at the Archives of Michigan, Lansing, MI. The information in this original copy may be different than the federal copy (part of the state database). Filmed by the Genealogical Society of Utah, 1972, 1 roll, FHL film #984117. To see if this microfilm has been digitized yet, see the FHL catalog page: **www.familysearch.org/search/catalog/175151.**

1870 Federal Census, Keweenaw County, Michigan (State Copy) **[Microfilm & Digital Capture],** from the state's original copy, now located at the Archives of Michigan, Lansing, MI. The information in this original copy may be different than the federal copy (part of the state database). Filmed by the Genealogical Society of Utah, 1972, 1 roll, FHL film #915273. To access the digital images, see the online FHL catalog page: **www.familysearch.org/search/catalog/328090.**

1870 Federal Census, Menominee County, Michigan (State Copy) **[Microfilm],** from the state's original copy, now located at the Archives of Michigan, Lansing, MI. The information in this original copy may be different than the federal copy (part of the state database). Filmed by the Genealogical Society of Utah, 1972, 1 roll, FHL film #915322. To see if this microfilm has been digitized yet, see the FHL catalog page: **www.familysearch.org/search/catalog/328150.**

1870 Federal Census, Montcalm County, Michigan (State Copy) **[Microfilm],** from the state's original copy, now located at the Archives of Michigan, Lansing, MI. The information in this original copy may be different than the federal copy (part of the state database). Filmed by the Genealogical Society of Utah, 1972, 1 roll, FHL film #915325. To see if this microfilm has been digitized yet, see the FHL catalog page: **www.familysearch.org/search/catalog/328185.**

1870 Federal Census, St. Joseph County, Michigan (State Copy) **[Microfilm & Digital Capture],** from the state's original copy, now located at the Archives of Michigan, Lansing, MI. The information in this original copy may be different than the federal copy (part of the state database). Filmed by the Genealogical Society of Utah, 1972, 1 roll, FHL film #915334. To access the digital images, see the online FHL catalog page: **www.familysearch.org/search/catalog/328193.**

1870 Federal Census, Van Buren County, Michigan (State Copy) **[Microfilm & Digital Capture],** from the state's original copy, now located at the Archives of Michigan, Lansing, MI. The information in this original copy may be different than the federal copy (part of the state database). Filmed by the Genealogical Society of Utah, 1972, 1 roll, FHL film #927447. To access the digital images, see the online FHL catalog page: **www.familysearch.org/search/catalog/315380.**

1870 Federal Census, Washtenaw County, Michigan (State Copy) **[Microfilm & Digital Capture],** from the county's original copy, now located at the Bentley Historical Library, University of Michigan, Ann Arbor, MI. The information in this original copy may be different than the federal copy (part of the state database). Filmed by the Genealogical Society of Utah, 1974, 1 roll, FHL film #955813. To access the digital images, see the online FHL catalog page: **www.familysearch.org/search/catalog/290960.**

1870-1871. *Branch County Directory and Historical Record: Containing a Complete List of Residents ... Business Directory of Coldwater, Quincy, Union City and Bronson; Also a Concise History of the County* **[Online Database],** from a book compiled by Stevens & Conover, publ. Courier Steam Printing House, Ann Arbor, MI, 1871, 315 pages. Digitized by the Genealogical Society of Utah, 2014. To access the digital version of this book, visit the online FHL catalog page for this title. See
https://familysearch.org/search/catalog/2300576.

1870, 1884 & 1894 Special Schedules. See *1870 Federal Census, 1884 Michigan State Census, and 1894 Michigan State Census, Isabella County, Michigan* **[Microfilm & Digital Capture],** from the originals at the Michigan State Archives. Filmed by the Genealogical Society of Utah, 1 roll, 1972. Includes: **1870:** Schedule 2, (persons who died during the year ending 1st June, 1870), Broomfield, Chippewa, Coe, Coldwater, Lincoln, Rolland, Sherman, Union townships, (p. 685-699); **1884:** Schedule 2, persons who died during the year ending May 31, 1884); **1884:** Schedule 4, (manufactories, mines, fisheries, products of industry during the twelve months beginning with June 1, 1883 and ending with May 31, 1884); and **1894:** Schedule 4, (manufactories, mines, fisheries, products of industry) #915312. To access the digital images of this roll, see the online FHL catalog page:
www.familysearch.org/search/catalog/328164.

1870-1899. *Death Index, Schoolcraft County, Michigan* **[Online Database],** indexed at the MIGenWeb site for Schoolcraft Co MI. See
http://schoolcraft.migenweb.net/death1.htm.

1870s-1900s. *Declarations of Intent, Delta County, Michigan* **[Online Database],** indexed at the Delta County Genealogical Society website. See http://dcmigs.org/immigration/process.htm.

1870-1917. *Lenawee County, Michigan* **[Online Databases],** indexed at the Ancestry.com website. Includes 1870 Brown's city directory of Adrian, Mich.; 1879 History and biographical record of Lenawee County; 1888 Portrait and Biographical Album, Lenawee County; 1903 Polk's Adrian city directory; 1907 Polk & Co.'s Adrian city directory 1909-Polk's Adrian city directory; 1909 Lenawee County Memoirs; 1917 Polk's Adrian city directory:
http://search.ancestry.com/Places/US/Michigan/Lenawee/Default.aspx.

1871-1893. *Michigan School Censuses* **[Online Database],** indexed at the Michigan Family History Network website. Intro: During the mid to late 1800's schools were taken care of by the township government. They produced censuses to keep track of the children attending. These records show up in various archives around the state for safe keeping. For the first search screen, see
www.mifamilyhistory.org/sch-census/default.aspx.

1873. *General History of the State of Michigan: With Biographical Sketches, Portrait Engravings, and Numerous Illustrations...* **[Online Database],** digitized and OCR indexed at the Ancestry.com website. Source: Book, same title, by Charles R Tuttle, publ. Tyler & Co., Detroit, 1873. This database has 738 pages. See
https://search.ancestry.com/search/db.aspx?dbid=27702.
- A digital version of this book is also available at the FHL catalog page for this title:
www.familysearch.org/search/catalog/265806.

1873-1874. *Livingston County Directory for the Years 1873-1874: Embracing the Residents, Business Houses, Officials, Churches, Schools, Publications, Organizations, Hotels, Stage Routes, State Post Offices and Express Offices; Together With a Sketch of the County* **[Microfilm & Digital Capture],** from the book compiled and published by John W. Keating and John H. Pawling, Ann Arbor, MI, 1873, 256 pages. Filmed by W.C. Cox, Tucson, AZ, 1974, 1 roll, FHL film #1000244. To access the digital images, see the online FHL catalog page:
www.familysearch.org/search/catalog/25613.

1873-1911. *Clinton County, Michigan* **[Online Database],** indexed at the Ancestry.com website. Includes 1873, 1903, and 1911 digitized histories. See
http://search.ancestry.com/Places/US/Michigan/Clinton/Default.aspx.

1873-1911. See *Livingston County, Michigan* **[Online Databases],** indexed at the Ancestry.com website. Includes 1873-1874 Livingston County directory; 1880 History of Livingston Co Mich.; 1891 Portrait and biographical album of Ingham and Livingston Counties, Mich.; and 1911 history of the township and village of Howell, Michigan. See
http://search.ancestry.com/Places/US/Michigan/Livingston/Default.aspx.

1873-1975. *Probate Index, Delta County, Michigan* **[Online Database],** indexed at the Delta County Genealogical Society website. See
http://dcmigs.org/probate/index.htm.

1874 Michigan State Census, Eaton County, **[Microfilm],** from the original records at the Michigan State Archives, Lansing, MI. Filmed by the Genealogical Society of Utah, 1972, 1 roll, FHL film #915305. To see if this microfilm has been digitized yet, see the FHL catalog page:
www.familysearch.org/search/catalog/328107.

1874 Michigan State Census, Houghton County, **[Microfilm],** from the original records at the Michigan State Archives, Lansing, MI. Lists of names and occupations of all males over the age of 21 with some statistics on the population, agriculture and manufacturing. Arranged by townships: L'Anse, Schoolcraft, Webster, Portage, Quincy, Adams, Baraga, Catumis, Franklin, Hancock, Huron. Filmed by the Genealogical Society of Utah, 1972, 1 roll, FHL film #915277. To see if this microfilm has been digitized yet, see the FHL catalog page:
www.familysearch.org/search/catalog/328081.

1874-1989. *Mackinac County, Michigan* **[Online Databases],** indexed at the Ancestry.com website. Includes 1874, 1989 Old and new Mackinac; 1882 Mackinac Island: the wave-washed tourists' paradise of the unsalted seas; 1894 Annals of Fort Mackinac; 1897 Early Mackinac: "the fairy island;" 1898 Reminiscences of early days on Mackinac Island; 1898 Northern Michigan: handbook for travelers; 1899 The Standard guide, Mackinac Island and northern lake resorts; Mackinac Co Stories, Memories & Histories;

1899 Mackinac, formerly Michilimackinac; 1912 Early Mackinac; 1971 The Lasanen site : an historic burial locality; 1911 A brief history of Les Cheneaux Islands; 1989 Mackinaw in history; 1989 Sunlight pictures, Mackinac Island 1989 Exposition of Mackinaw City and its surroundings; 1989 The myth Wawatam, or, Alex. Henry refuted; and 1989 Old Mission Church: http://search.ancestry.com/Places/US/Michigan/Mackinac/Default.aspx?category=33.

1875-1882. *Cass County, Michigan* **[Online Database],** indexed at the Ancestry.com website. Includes three digitized histories of Cass County. See http://search.ancestry.com/Places/US/Michigan/Cass/Default.aspx.

1875-2005. *Isabella County, Michigan* **[Online Databases],** indexed at the Ancestry.com website. Includes 1875-2005 *Obituary Index*; 1884 *Portrait and biographical album of Isabella County*; and 1911 Past and present of Isabella County, Michigan. See http://search.ancestry.com/Places/US/Michigan/Isabella/Default.aspx.

1875-2012. *Southwest Michigan, Obituary Index* **[Online Database],** indexed at the Ancestry.com website. Original data: Obituary Collection. Van Buren District Library, Webster Memorial Branch, supported by the Van Buren Regional Genealogical Society. Each index record includes: Name, Publication place, page number, and a link to the VBRGS website. This database has 140,618 records,
see https://search.ancestry.com/search/db.aspx?dbid=70832.

1876. *Indexed List of Landowners From 1876, Illustrated Historical Atlas of Wayne County, MI and Maps* **[Printed Book],** compiled by Sherry Huntington, indexed by Sarah Lange, publ. Downriver Genealogical Society, Lincoln Park, MI, 1993, 87 pages, FHL book 977.433 R2h.

1877-1912. *St. Clair County, Michigan* **[Online Databases],** indexed at the Ancestry.com com website. Includes 1877 Marine history, the lake ports: historical and descriptive review of the lakes, rivers, islands, cities, towns, watering place; 1883 History of St. Clair County; 1910 Pioneer history of St. Clair County; and 1912 St. Clair County, Michigan, its history and its people. See
http://search.ancestry.com/Places/US/Michigan/St-Clair/Default.aspx.

1878-1879. *Index to Tax Assessments, Georgetown Township, Ottawa County, Michigan* **[Online Database],** indexed at the MIGenWeb site for Ottawa Co MI. See http://ottawa.migenweb.net/twprecords/Georgetw/assess/index.html.

1878-1979. *Washtenaw County, Michigan* **[Online Database],** indexed at the Ancestry.com website. Includes 1878-1879 Washtenaw County directory; 1881 History of Washtenaw County, Michigan; 1886-1887 Ann Arbor city and Washtenaw County directory; 1886, 1888-1892 Ann Arbor Directories; 1888-1889 Ann Arbor, Ypsilanti and Washtenaw County directory; 1891 Portrait and biographical album of Washtenaw; 1896 M.M. Dickson & Co.'s township and sectional; 1903 Mills Co.'s directory of the city of Ann Arbor; 1903 Mills Co.'s directory of the city of Ypsilanti; 1906 Past and present of Washtenaw County, Michigan; 1906 A history of St. Andrew's Church, Ann Arbor, Michigan; 1909 R. L. Polk & Co.'s Ann Arbor city directory; 1910 Ypsilanti City Directory; 1914 Polk's Ann Arbor, Ypsilanti and Washtenaw County directory; 1915 Polk's Ann Arbor city directory; 1916 Polk's Ann Arbor, Ypsilanti, and Washtenaw County directory; 1927 Ann Arbor, the first hundred years 1952 President as poet; 1953 The Staebler papers 1967 Notes on a tour; 1974 Old Ypsilanti town; and 1979 Toward Camelot: Admission of women to the Univ. of Michigan, see http://search.ancestry.com/Places/US/Michigan/Washtenaw/Default.aspx.

1879-1903. *Index to Biographies, Hillsdale County, Michigan* **[Online Database],** an index to biographies in the 1879, 1888, and 1903 histories of Hillsdale Co MI. Located at the MIGenWeb site. See www.migenweb.org/hillsdale/bios.html.

1880. *Michigan, 1880 Federal Census: Soundex and Population Schedules* **[Microfilm & Digital Capture],** from the originals at the National Archives, Washington, DC (ca1985). After filming, the originals (31 volumes) were transferred to the Michigan State Archives, Lansing, MI. Filmed on 119 rolls, beginning with FHL film #447332 (1880 Soundex: A000 thru A450); and FHL film #1254569 (1880 Population Schedules: Alcona Co). To access the digital images, see the online FHL catalog page:
https://familysearch.org/search/catalog/673571.

- 1880 CENSUS NOTE – 1880 Short Form. The original schedules for the 1880-1940 federal censuses were transferred from a county directly to the Census Office in Washington, DC. In 1880, a new wrinkle was added: a unique *1880 Short Form* was retained at the county courthouse in every county of the U.S. By law, the Short Form was to remain at a courthouse for one month after the 1880 census was taken, allowing for public inspection of the name list. The Short Form name list was not by family, but as an index to the full schedules with all names arranged by the first letter of their surname. The data was brief, including just a person's name, color, age, and sex. There were no relationships or full family groupings. Extant manuscripts of the 1880 county copies are rare. Of the 78 counties of Michigan in 1880, 11 county name lists have survived (Only New York has more than Michigan). All of the original Short Forms stored today in Michigan county courthouses, libraries, or archives were microfilmed by the Genealogical Society of Utah in the early 1970s. It was not always obvious where the name lists came from – few even mentioned the year 1880. But looking at the original manuscript page images reveals the same U.S. Census Office form printed in 1880.

1880 Federal Census (Short Form), Barry County, Michigan **[Microfilm],** from the county's original volumes of the 1880 name list, located at the Archives of Michigan, Lansing, MI. Filmed by the Genealogical Society of Utah, 1972, 1 roll, FHL film #915282. To see if this microfilm has been digitized yet, see the FHL catalog page:
www.familysearch.org/search/catalog/328102.

1880 Federal Census (Short Form), Eaton County, Michigan **[Microfilm],** from the county's original volumes of the 1880 name list, located at the Archives of Michigan, Lansing, MI. Filmed by the Genealogical Society of Utah, 1972, 1 roll, FHL film #915304. To see if this microfilm has been digitized yet, see the FHL catalog page:
www.familysearch.org/search/catalog/328104.

1880 Federal Census (Short Form), Ionia County, Michigan **[Microfilm],** from the county's original volumes of the 1880 name list, located at the Archives of Michigan, Lansing, MI. Filmed by the Genealogical Society of Utah, 1972, 1 roll, FHL film #915310. To see if this microfilm has been digitized yet, see the FHL catalog page:
www.familysearch.org/search/catalog/328159.

1880 Federal Census (Short Form), Kalamazoo County, Michigan **[Microfilm],** from the county's original volumes of the 1880 name list, located at the Archives of Michigan, Lansing, MI. Filmed by the Genealogical Society of Utah, 1972, 1 roll, FHL film #915313. To see if this microfilm has been digitized yet, see the FHL catalog page:
www.familysearch.org/search/catalog/328173.

1880 Federal Census (Short Form), Kent County, Michigan **[Microfilm],** from the county's original volumes of the 1880 name list, located at the Grand Rapids Public Library, Grand Rapids, MI. The FHL catalog shows the title simply as *List of Persons*. Filmed by the Genealogical Society of Utah, 1975, 1 roll, FHL film #984115. To see if this microfilm has been digitized yet, see the FHL catalog page:
www.familysearch.org/search/catalog/156549.

1880 Federal Census (Short Form), Keweenaw County, Michigan **[Microfilm],** from the county's original volumes of the 1880 name list, located at the Archives of Michigan, Lansing, MI. Filmed by the Genealogical Society of Utah, 1972, 1 roll, FHL film #915274. To see if this microfilm has been digitized yet, see the FHL catalog page:
www.familysearch.org/search/catalog/328142.

1880 Federal Census (Short Form), Lapeer County, Michigan **[Microfilm],** from the county's original volumes of the 1880 name list, located at the Lapeer County Clerk's Office, Lapeer, MI. FHL tile: *List of Persons Whose Usual Place of Abode Was Upon the 1st Day of June Within Lapeer County, Michigan.* Filmed by the Genealogical Society of Utah, 1 roll, FHL film #915317. To see if this microfilm has been digitized yet, see the FHL catalog page:
www.familysearch.org/search/catalog/328144.

1880 Federal Census (Short Form), Mecosta County, Michigan **[Microfilm & Digital Capture],** from the county's original volumes of the 1880 name list, located at the Archives of Michigan, Lansing, MI. Filmed by the Genealogical Society of Utah, 1972, 1 roll, FHL film #915321. To access the digital images of this roll, see the online FHL catalog page:
www.familysearch.org/search/catalog/53820.

1880 Federal Census (Short Form), Oceana County, Michigan **[Microfilm],** from the county's original volumes of the 1880 name list, located at the Archives of Michigan, Lansing, MI. Filmed by the Genealogical Society of Utah, 1972, 1 roll, FHL film #915328. To see if this microfilm has been digitized yet, see the FHL catalog page:
www.familysearch.org/search/catalog/328205.

1880 Federal Census (Short Form), Ottawa County, Michigan **[Microfilm],** from the county's original volumes of the 1880 name list, located at the Bentley

Historical Library, University of Michigan, Ann Arbor, MI. Filmed by the Genealogical Society of Utah, 1974, 1 roll, FHL film #915330. To see if this microfilm has been digitized yet, see the FHL catalog page: www.familysearch.org/search/catalog/328210.

1880 Federal Census (Short Form), Washtenaw County, Michigan **[Microfilm],** from the county's original volumes of the 1880 name list, located at the Bentley Historical Library, University of Michigan, Ann Arbor, MI. Filmed by the Genealogical Society of Utah, 1974, 1 roll, FHL film #955815. To see if this microfilm has been digitized yet, see the FHL catalog page: www.familysearch.org/search/catalog/291357.

1880 St. Joseph County Directory **[Microfilm & Digital Capture],** from the original published Globe Pub., Mendon, MI, 1880, 343 pages. Filmed by W.C. Cox, Tucson, AZ, 1974, 1 roll, FHL film #1000671. To access the digital images, see the online FHL catalog page: www.familysearch.org/search/catalog/784695.

1880. See *History of Shiawassee and Clinton Counties, Michigan: with Illustrations and Biographical Sketches of their Prominent Men* **[Online Database],** digitized and indexed at the Ancestry.com website. From a book by Franklin Ellis, publ. D.W. Ensign & Co., Philadelphia, 1880. See http://search.ancestry.com/search/db.aspx?dbid=17592.

1880-1890 Census Statistics. See *Population of Michigan, 1880, 1890: Showing the Population of Each County, Township, City and Village, and the Last Apportionment* **[Online Database],** a database at Ancestry.com, digitized from the book published by the Secretary of State of Michigan, 1892. See http://search.ancestry.com/search/db.aspx?dbid=20042.

1880-1892. *Van Buren County, Michigan* **[Online Databases],** indexed at the Ancestry.com website. Includes 1880 History of Berrien and Van Buren Counties, Michigan; and 1892 Portrait and biographical record of Kalamazoo, Allegan, and Van Buren Counties, Michigan. See http://search.ancestry.com/Places/US/Michigan/Van-Buren/Default.aspx.

1880-1914. See **Ingham County, Michigan [Online Databases],** indexed at the Ancestry.com website. Includes 1911 *Growth of Lansing, Michigan;* 1891 *Portrait and biographical album of Ingham and Livingston Counties, Michigan;* 1880 *History of Ingham and Eaton Counties, Michigan.* See http://search.ancestry.com/Places/US/Michigan/Ingham/Default.aspx.

1880-1915. *Eaton County, Michigan* **[Online Databases],** indexed at the Ancestry.com website. Includes 1880 history, 1904 directory, 1916 directory, and 1915 history. See http://search.ancestry.com/Places/US/Michigan/Eaton/Default.aspx.

1880-1930. See *Coldwater State School, Records of Lost & Abandoned Children: A Series of Lost Souls* **[Printed Book & CD-ROM],** compiled and published by Betty Driscoll, New Era, MI, 2004, 41 pages, FHL book 977.4 J6d and FHL CD No. 4309.

1880s-1990s. *The Detroit News Indexes* **[Online Database],** indexed at the Seeking Michigan collection at the Archives of Michigan website. This subject index of *The Detroit News* newspaper totals more than 1 million index cards. The tables are arranged alphabetically by subject and date approximately from the late 1800's to the late 1990's. An index card at Seeking Michigan indicates that there is a clipping file for those articles. Researchers may then request to look in the clippings file at the Archives of Michigan for the actual articles cited or visit a research institution that has the newspaper on microfilm. Institutions that have microfilm copies of The Detroit News include the Library of Michigan and the Detroit Public Library. See http://seekingmichigan.org/about/indexes.

1881 Voters, Delta County, Michigan **[Online Database],** indexed at the Delta County Genealogical Society website. See http://dcmigs.org/voters/1881.htm.

1881-1892. *Memorial Report from the book, Michigan Pioneer and Historical Collection, Tuscola County, Michigan* **[Online Database],** includes a list of deaths of the Tuscola County Pioneer Society for 1881-1892. Indexed at the USGenWeb site for Tuscola CO MI. See http://files.usgwarchives.net/mi/tuscola/multiple/pioneers/p56001.txt.

1881-1923. *Jackson County, Michigan* **[Online Databases],** indexed at the Ancestry.com website. Includes 1881 *History of Jackson County*; 1887-1888, 1890 *Jackson Directories*; 1903 *DeLand's History of Jackson County*; and 1918-1923 *Rural Directory*. See http://search.ancestry.com/Places/US/Michigan/Jackson/Default.aspx.

1871-1974. *Birth, Marriage and Death Records, Montmorency County, Michigan, 1881-1974* **[Microfilm & Digital Capture],** from the originals at the Montmorency County Courthouse, Atlanta, MI. Contains births, 1881-1934; deaths, 1881-1933; and marriages, 1881-1974. Filmed by the Genealogical Society of Utah, 1974, 1 roll, FHL film #965771. To access the digital images of this roll, see the online FHL catalog page:
www.familysearch.org/search/catalog/216156.
- See also, **An** *Index to Birth, Marriage and Death Records, Montmorency County, Michigan, 1881-1974* **[Printed Book],** compiled by Rhea I. LaCross and Lorrie LaCross, publ. Faded Genes, 1998, Alpena, MI, see FHL book 977.483 V223L.

1880-1890. *Population of Michigan, 1880, 1890: Showing the Population of Each County, Township, City and Village, and...* **[Online Database],** digitized and OCR indexed at the Ancestry.com website. This database has 43 pages:
https://search.ancestry.com/search/db.aspx?dbid=20042.

1882-2012. *Macomb County, Michigan* **[Online Databases],** indexed at the Ancestry.com website. Includes 1882 *History of Macomb County*; 1893, 1908, 1916 *Cutter's guide to Mt. Clemens*; 1905 *Past and present of Macomb County*; and 1945-2012 *Death Index*. See
http://search.ancestry.com/Places/US/Michigan/Macomb/Default.aspx.

1883. *List of Pensioners on the Roll, Michigan* **[Online Database],** indexed at the Michigan Family History Network website. See
www.mifamilyhistory.org/civilwar/1883Pension.

1883. *Surname Index from the History of Upper Peninsula of Michigan* **[Online Database],** indexed at the Delta County Genealogical Society website. *The History of Upper Peninsula of Michigan* was pub. by A.T. Andreas, Western Historical Co., Chicago, 1883. See http://dcmigs.org/up_history.htm.

1883. *History of Tuscola and Bay Counties, Michigan: With Illustrations and Biographical Sketches of some of their Prominent Men and Pioneers* **[Online Database],** digitized and indexed at the Ancestry.com website. From a book publ. H.R. Page & Co., Chicago, 1883. See
http://search.ancestry.com/search/db.aspx?dbid=16846.

1883-1884. *Mecosta County, Michigan* **[Online Databases],** indexed at the Ancestry.com website. Includes 1883 Portrait and Biographical Album, Mecosta County; and 1884 Directory, Michigan Western. See
http://search.ancestry.com/Places/US/Michigan/Mecosta/Default.aspx.

1883-1886. *Births From the Pioneer Tribune, Schoolcraft County, Michigan* **[Online Database],** indexed at the MIGenWeb site for Schoolcraft Co MI. See http://schoolcraft.migenweb.net/birth1.htm.

1883-1934. *Saginaw (Michigan) City Directories* **[Microfilm],** by various publishers. FHL has 1883, 1887, 1889, 1890-1896, 1898-1900, 1902-1917, 1919, 1921-1925, 1927-1934. Filmed by Research Publications, Woodbridge, CT, 1990, 23 rolls, beginning with FHL film #2156776 (1883 East Saginaw and Saginaw Directory). For a complete list of roll numbers and contents of each roll, visit the online FHL catalog page for this title. See
https://familysearch.org/search/catalog/992479.

1883-1935. *Bay City (Michigan) City Directories* **[Microfilm],** by various publishers. FHL has 1883, 1886, 1887-1888, 1889-1890, 1891-1892, 1893-1894, 1895-1897, 1899-1900, 1901-1902, 1902-1903, 1904, 1907, 1908-1913, 1914-1915, 1922, 1924, 1926, 1929, 1931, 1933, and 1935. Filmed by Research Publications, Woodbridge, CT, 1990, 13 rolls, beginning with FHL film #2156754 (1883 Bay City directory and Essexville, West Bay City). For a complete list of roll numbers and contents of each roll, visit the online FHL catalog page for this title. See
https://familysearch.org/search/catalog/992040.

1883-1935. See *Lansing (Michigan) City Directories* **[Microfilm],** from various publishers. FHL has 1883-1885, 1887-1889, 1891-1892, 1896, 1898, 1900, 1904, 1910, 1916, 1919, 1921, 1925, 1927, and 1932-1935. Filmed by Research Publications, Woodbridge, CT, 1995, 9 rolls, Beginning with FHL film #2156768 (1883-1884 Lansing City and Ingham County Directory). For a complete list of roll numbers and contents of each roll, visit the online FHL catalog page for this title. See
https://familysearch.org/search/catalog/992173.

1883-1935. *Jackson (Michigan) City/County Directories* **[Microfilm],** by various publishers. FHL has 1883, 1885-1888, 1890, 1891, 1893, 1894-1910, 1912-1918, 1920-1922, 1924, 1925, 1927-1933, and 1935. Filmed by Research Publications, Woodbridge, CT, 1990, 17 rolls, beginning with FHL film #2156763 (1883 Jackson City directory). For a complete list of roll numbers and contents of each roll, visit the online FHL catalog page for this title. See
https://familysearch.org/search/catalog/992085.

1884 Census Statistics. See *Census of the State of Michigan, 1884* **[Online Database],** digitized from the official report of the Secretary of State, state of Michigan, publ. 1886, 2 vols., with statistics on the 1884 state census, including population figures, manufacturing, and agricultural products.
http://search.ancestry.com/search/db.aspx?dbid=18557.

"1884 Michigan State Census, Wayne County" [Printed Article], in *Detroit Society for Genealogical Research Magazine,* abstracted by townships beginning with Vol. 44 (1981) and various issues through Vol. 64 (2001).

1884 Michigan State Census, Barry County, **[Microfilm],** from the original manuscripts at the Michigan State Archives, Lansing. Filmed by the Genealogical Society of Utah, 1972, 2 rolls, as follows:
- 1884 census schedules, towns of Hastings, Hope, Irving, Johnstown, Maple Grove, Orangeville, Prairieville, Assyria, Baltimore, Carlton, Castleton, Rutland, Thornapple, Woodland, Yankee Springs, Barry, and Middleville, FHL film #915281.
- 1884 census schedules, towns of Assyria, Baltimore, Barry, Carlton, Castleton, Rutland, Thornapple, Middleville, Woodland, Yankee Springs Hastings, FHL film #915284.

To see if this microfilm has been digitized yet, see the FHL catalog page:
www.familysearch.org/search/catalog/314972.

1884 Michigan State Census, Benzie County, **[Microfilm],** from the original manuscripts at the Michigan State Archives, Lansing. Filmed by the Genealogical Society of Utah, 1972, 1 roll, FHL film #915294. To see if this microfilm has been digitized yet, see the FHL catalog page:
www.familysearch.org/search/catalog/328214.

1884 Michigan State Census, Emmet County, **[Microfilm],** from the original records at the Michigan State Archives, Lansing, MI. Filmed by the Genealogical Society of Utah, 1974, 1 roll, FHL film #966509. To see if this microfilm has been digitized yet, see the FHL catalog page:
www.familysearch.org/search/catalog/92720.

1884 Michigan State Census, Ingham County, **[Microfilm & Digital Capture],** from the original records at the Michigan State Archives, Lansing, MI. Filmed by the Genealogical Society of Utah, 1972, 1 roll, FHL film #915308. To access the digital images of this roll, see the online FHL catalog page:
www.familysearch.org/search/catalog/328119.

1884 Michigan State Census, Kalamazoo County, **[Microfilm],** from the original records at the Michigan State Archives, Lansing, MI. Arranged alphabetically by name of township (Pavilion to Wakeshma Townships, only), then numerically by dwelling number. Filmed by the Genealogical Society of Utah, 1972, 1 roll, FHL film #915314.

1884 Michigan State Census, Kent County, **[Microfilm],** from the original manuscripts at the Michigan State Archives, Lansing, MI. Filmed by the Genealogical Society of Utah, 1975, 4 rolls, as follows:
- 1884 Grand Rapids wards 1-4 FHL film #984118.
- 1884 Grand Rapids, wards 5-6; Byron-Cannon Townships., FHL film #984049.
- 1884 Kent County mortality schedules, June 1883 - May 1884; Ada - Vergennes Townships, FHL film #984656.
- 1884 Walker-Wyoming Townships, Kent County manufactories, mines, fisheries; Agriculture: townships Ada - Wyoming, FHL film #984657.

To see if this microfilm has been digitized yet, see the FHL catalog page:
www.familysearch.org/search/catalog/175155.
- See Also *Index to the 1884 State Census of Kent County, Michigan* **[Printed Index],** compiled by the Western Michigan Genealogical Society, Grand Rapids, MI, 1990, 309 pages. FHL book 977.455 X22i.

1884 Michigan State Census, Keweenaw County, **[Microfilm & Digital Capture],** from the original records at the Michigan State Archives, Lansing, MI. Filmed by the Genealogical Society of Utah, 1972, 1 roll, FHL film #915273. To access the digital images of this roll, see the online FHL catalog page:
www.familysearch.org/search/catalog/328136.

1884 Michigan State Census, Lapeer County, **[Microfilm],** from the original records at the Michigan State Archives, Lansing, MI. Includes schedule 1, the listing of residents. Lists are by township followed by Lapeer City. The listing begins with Elbe Township (Missing lists: Almont, Arcadia, Attica Burlington, Burnside, Deerfield and Dryden townships). Filmed by the Genealogical Society of Utah, 1972, 1 roll, FHL film #915318. To see if this microfilm has been digitized yet, see the FHL catalog page:
www.familysearch.org/search/catalog/328147.

1884 Residents of Mecosta County, Michigan **[Printed Book],** compiled by Evelyn M. Sawyer, published 1976 by the author, 76 pages. The source is believed to be the 1884 Michigan state census. Names are listed alphabetically. Includes name, occupation, section, town/township, and postal address. FHL book 977.452 X2s.

1884 Michigan State Census, Menominee County **[Microfilm & Digital Capture]**, from, the original records at the Michigan State Archives, Lansing, MI. Filmed by the Genealogical Society of Utah, 1972, 2 rolls, as follows:
- 1884 Towns of Breen, Breitung, Cedarville, Cedar River, Ingallston, Menominee, Nadeau, and Norway, FHL film #915322.
- 1884 Towns of Spalding, Stephenson, Daggett, Menominee, Breen, Breitung, Ingallston, Nadeau, and Norway, FHL film #915323.

To access the digital images, see the online FHL catalog page: www.familysearch.org/search/catalog/53798.

1884 Michigan State Census, Montcalm County, **[Microfilm]**, from the original records at the Michigan State Archives, Lansing, MI. Filmed by the Genealogical Society of Utah, 1972, 1 roll, FHL film #915326. To see if this microfilm has been digitized yet, see the FHL catalog page:
www.familysearch.org/search/catalog/328199.

1884. See *Index to the 1884 Newaygo County, Michigan State Census* **[Printed Index]**, compiled by Evelyn M. Sawyer, published by the author, 1997, 65 pages. FHL book 977.458 X22s 1884.

1884 Michigan State Census, Ottawa County, **[Microfilm]**, from the original records at the Michigan State Archives, Lansing, MI. Filmed by the Genealogical Society of Utah, 1972, 2 rolls, as follows:
- 1884 Towns of Allendale – Polkton, FHL film #915331.
- 1884 Towns of Robinson – Zeeland, FHL film #915332.

To see if this microfilm has been digitized yet, see the FHL catalog page:
www.familysearch.org/search/catalog/328188.

1884. *The residents of the Townships of Allendale, Blendon, Georgetown, Jamestown and Zeeland of Ottawa County, Michigan From the 1884 State Census* **[Printed Book]**, compiled by Evelyn M. Sawyer, published by the author, 1996, 115 pages. Includes name, age, birthplace, years as Michigan resident, township, page and family number. Names alphabetically arranges in one listing. Data was taken from 1884 Michigan State census. FHL book 977.415 X2r 1884.

1884 Michigan State Census, Washtenaw County **[Microfilm & Digital Capture]**, from the originals at the Bentley Historical Library, University of Michigan, Ann Arbor, MI. Towns are intermixed. Filmed by the Genealogical Society of Utah, 1974, 2 rolls, FHL film #955808 (1884 inhabitants), FHL film #955809 (1884 Inhabitants, agriculture, manufactories, mines, fisheries, libraries, schools, and churches). To access the digital images, see the online FHL catalog page: www.familysearch.org/search/catalog/290923.

1884. *Portrait and Biographical Album of Midland County, Michigan: Containing Portraits and Biographical Sketches of Prominent and Representative Citizens of the County* **[Online Database]**, indexed at the Ancestry.com website. See http://search.ancestry.com/search/db.aspx?dbid=17635.

1884. *Index to Portrait & Biographical Album of Newaygo County, Michigan* **[Online Database]**, indexed at the MIGenWeb site for Newaygo Co MI.: See www.migenweb.org/newaygo/bioport.htm.

1884. *Portrait & Biographical Album of Osceola County, Michigan* **[Online Database]**, digitized at the Ancestry.com website. See
http://search.ancestry.com/search/db.aspx?dbid=17645.

1884. *Sanilac County, Michigan* **[Online Database]**, indexed at the Ancestry.com website. Includes 1884 Portrait and biographical record of Sanilac County: http://search.ancestry.com/Places/US/Michigan/Sanilac/Default.aspx.

1884. *Statistical Returns from the Census of the State of Michigan, 1884* **[Online Database]**, digitized and OCR indexed from the official report of the Secretary of State, state of Michigan, publ. 1886, 2 vols., with statistics on the 1884 state census, including population, manufacturing, and agricultural products. This database has 1,337 pages. See
https://search.ancestry.com/search/db.aspx?dbid=18557.

1884-1894. *Michigan State Census Records, 1884-1894* **[Online Database]**, digitized and indexed at the Seeking Michigan collection at the Archives of Michigan website. Both the 1884 and 1894 state censuses can be searched here, and a scanned image of the census page can be viewed and printed, as well as the indexed textual information. To search for a name, go to the Advanced Search option. When the menu opens, the default collection is for "Death Records, 1897-1920" which needs to be unchecked, then check "Michigan State Census Records, 1884-1894." This database has about 62,000-page images of Michigan state census population schedules. See http://seekingmichigan.org/discover/state-census-1884-1894.

1884-1911. *St. Joseph County, Michigan* **[Online Databases],** indexed at the Ancestry.com website. Includes 1884-1885 St Joseph Traveler Herald; 1889 Portrait and biographical album of St. Joseph County, Michigan; 1899 La Salle in the valley of the St. Joseph: an historical fragment; 1906-1909 The Weekly Press (Saint Joseph, Michigan); and 1911 History of St. Joseph County, Michigan. See http://search.ancestry.com/Places/US/Michigan/St-Joseph/Default.aspx.

1884-1922. *Huron County, Michigan* **[Online Databases],** digitized and indexed at the Ancestry.com website. Includes 1) *1884 Portrait and Biographical Album of Huron County*; and 2) *1922 Pioneer History of Huron County*. See http://search.ancestry.com/Places/US/Michigan/Huron/Default.aspx.

1884-2012. *Newaygo County, Michigan* **[Online Databases],** indexed at the Ancestry.com website. Includes 1884 Portrait and biographical album of Newaygo County, Michigan; 1910-2012 Newspapers, Death Index; and 1959-2011 Newspapers, Marriage Index. See http://search.ancestry.com/Places/US/Michigan/Newaygo/Default.aspx.

1885-1927. *Historical Register of Inhabitants (Soldiers' Home, Grand Rapids, MI)* **[Microfilm & Digital Capture],** from the originals at the MI State Archives, Lansing, MI. Includes index. Filmed by the Genealogical Society of Utah, 1972, 10 rolls, beginning with FHL film #925039 (Index). To access the digital images, see the online FHL catalog page: https://familysearch.org/search/catalog/85612.

1885-1934. See *Flint (Michigan) City Directories* **[Microfilm],** from various publishers. FHL has 1885, 1888-1889, 1892-1894, 1897-1899, 1903, 1905-1910, 1912-1932, and 1934. Filmed by Research publications, Woodbridge, CT, 1995, 17 rolls, beginning with FHL film #2156759 (1885 Flint City & Genesee Co Directory). For a complete list of roll numbers and contents of each roll, visit the online FHL catalog page for this title. See https://familysearch.org/search/catalog/992054.

1887-1916. *Alpena County, Michigan* **[Online Databases],** indexed at the Ancestry.com website. Includes directories, histories, and biographies related to Allegan county, Michigan. See http://search.ancestry.com/Places/US/Michigan/Alpena/Default.aspx.

1887-1931. *Michigan, Federal Naturalization Records* **[Online Database],** digitized and indexed at the Ancestry.com website. Source: Naturalization Records at the National Archives, Chicago, IL. Naturalizations include Petitions, Declarations, and Certificates. Each index record includes: Name, Record type, Birth date, Birth place, Arrival date, Arrival place, and Declaration, Petition, or Certificate number. The document image may have more information. This database has 430,192 records: https://search.ancestry.com/search/db.aspx?dbid=61201.

1888. *Post Office Addresses of Soldiers Residing in Michigan in 1888* **[Microfilm & Digital Capture],** from original records of the Michigan Adjutant General's Office, now located at the Michigan State Archives, Lansing, MI. Filmed by the Michigan State Archives, 1973, 1 roll, FHL film #915488. To access the digital images, see the online FHL catalog page: www.familysearch.org/search/catalog/96102.

1888 Gogebic Range Directory **[Online Database],** indexed at the MattsonWorks.com website. Includes Mining Companies of the Gogebic Range, extending from Ashland Co WI (later Iron Co WI) to Gogebic Co MI. See http://mattsonworks.com/1888/index.html.

1888-1972. See *Index to Evans-King Funeral Home, East Tawas, Iosco County, Michigan* **[Online Database],** indexed at the USGenWeb site for Iosco Co MI. See http://files.usgwarchives.net/mi/iosco/hsgs/business/fun-evans-kingfh1888-1972.txt.

1889. *Delta County City Directories* **[Online Database],** indexed at the Delta County Genealogical Society website. Includes city directories for Escanaba and Gladstone, Michigan. See http://dcmigs.org/directory/1889_esc_glada-f.htm.

1889. *Atlas of Gratiot County, Michigan* **[Online Database],** index of the patron's list at the Michigan Family History Network website. See www.mfhn.com/gratiot/atlas1889/db_paging.asp.

1889-1917. *Bay County, Michigan* **[Online Databases],** indexed at the Ancestry.com website. Includes directories, histories, and biographies related to Bay County, Michigan. See http://search.ancestry.com/Places/US/Michigan/Bay/Default.aspx.

1889-1935. *Kalamazoo (Michigan) City/County Directories* **[Microfilm],** by various publishers. FHL has 1889, 1896, 1899, 1901-1902, 1904-1917, 1919, 1921-1922, 1924, 1926-1927, 1929, 1931, and 1934-1935. Filmed by Research Publications, Woodbridge, CT, 1980-1990, 12 rolls, beginning with FHL film #2156767 (1889 Directory, Kalamazoo and Kalamazoo County). For a complete list of roll numbers and contents of each roll, visit the online FHL catalog page for this title. See
https://familysearch.org/search/catalog/620530.

1890 Michigan Census Index of Civil War Veterans or their Widows **[Printed Index],** compiled by Bryan Lee Dilts, publ. Index Publishing, Salt Lake City, UT, 1985, 236 pages, FHL book 977.4 X22d 1890.

1890 Residents oi Livingston County, Michigan **[Printed Book & Microfilm],** edited by Kennie L. King. Sources include pupil listings and censuses from local schools (1889-1891), the *1891 Portrait & Biographical Album - Ingham & Livingston Counties,* and the 1890 Union Veteran's & Widows of the Civil War. Names are listed alphabetically. From intro: "Contains transcriptions of marriage and death records from 1889 through 1891 and birth records from 1880 through 1891. Plus many other records." Publ. Livingston County Genealogical Society, Howell, MI, 2000, 990 pages, FHL book 977.436 V2r. Also on microfilm, FHL film #1145794. To see if this microfilm has been digitized yet, see the FHL catalog page: www.familysearch.org/search/catalog/990193.

1892. *Index to Tax Assessments, Georgetown Township, Ottawa County, Michigan* **[Online Database],** indexed at the MIGenWeb site for Ottawa Co MI. See
http://ottawa.migenweb.net/twprecords/Georgetw/assess/1892.html.

1892. *Portrait and Biographical Record of Genesee, Lapeer and Tuscola Counties, Michigan* **[Online Databases],** digitized and indexed at the Ancestry.com website. See
http://search.ancestry.com/search/db.aspx?dbid=23811.

1891-2012. *Ionia County, Michigan* **[Online Databases],** indexed at the Ancestry.com website. Includes 1910-2012 *Death Index*; 1959-2011 *Marriage Index*; 1891 *Ionia City Directory*; and 1891 *Portrait and Biographical Album of Ionia and Montcalm Counties, Michigan.* See
http://search.ancestry.com/Places/US/Michigan/Ionia/Default.aspx.

1891-2012. *Montcalm County, Michigan* **[Online Databases],** indexed at the Ancestry.com website. Includes 1891 *Portrait and Biographical Album of Ionia and Montcalm Counties, Michigan;* 1910-2012 *Death Index*; and 1959-2011 *Marriage Index.* See
http://search.ancestry.com/Places/US/Michigan/Montcalm/Default.aspx.

1892-1970s. *Berrien County, Michigan* **[Online Databases],** indexed at the Ancestry.com website. Includes newspapers, directories, histories, and biographies. See
http://search.ancestry.com/Places/US/Michigan/Berrien/Default.aspx.

1893. *Complete Index to the 1893 Atlas and Directory of Lapeer County, Michigan* **[Printed Index],** compiled by Dale Allison, Ila Burris and Mary Kay Townsend. Includes five indexes: landowners by township and section; directory of residents/landowners; landowners by village and city; directory of residents/landowners by village and city; places in townships and villages. Publ. Lapeer County Genealogical Society, 1997, 149 pages, FHL book 977.442 E72a.

1894. *Michigan State Census, 1894* **[Online Database],** indexed at the FamilySearch.org website. This is a name index of the Michigan State Census taken in June 1894. This collection includes Barry, Benzie, Bay, Dickinson, Emmet, Gratiot, Ingham, Iosco, Kalamazoo, Kent, Keweenaw, Lapeer, Leelanau, Menominee, Montcalm, and Washtenaw counties. Source: Michigan State Archives, Lansing, MI. This database has 381,310 records. See
https://familysearch.org/search/collection/1825187.

1894. *Michigan, State Census, 1894* **[Online Database],** indexed at the Ancestry.com website. This database contains information from the 1894 Michigan State Census for the counties of Barry, Bay, Benzie, Dickinson, Emmet, Gratiot, Iosco, Ingham, Kalamazoo, and Keweenaw. Information listed includes the name of every member of the household, and their age, race, and birthplace. The database has 173,120 records. Source: National Archives microfilm Z74. See
http://search.ancestry.com/search/db.aspx?dbid=7307.

1894 Census Statistics. See *Census of the State of Michigan, 1894* **[Online Database],** digitized from the official report of the Secretary of State, state of Michigan, publ. 1896, 3 vols., with statistics on the 1894 state census, including population figures, manufacturing, and agricultural products. Vol. 3 includes the only list of names – a list of U.S. soldiers of the Civil War residing in Michigan as of June 1, 1894. This database has 2,351 pages. See
http://search.ancestry.com/search/db.aspx?dbid=18558.

1894. *Soldiers, Sailors and Marines, Volume III, Census of the State of Michigan 1894* **[Online Database],** indexed at the Michigan Family History Network website. See
www.mifamilyhistory.org/civilwar/1894VetsCensus.

1894 Michigan State Census, Barry County **[Microfilm & Digital Capture],** from the original manuscripts at the Michigan State Archives, Lansing. Filmed by the Genealogical Society of Utah, 1972, 2 rolls, as follows:
- 1894 census schedules, towns of Johnstown, Maple Grove, Orangeville, Prairieville, Rutland, Thornapple, Middleville, Woodland, Yankee Springs, Hastings, FHL film #915285.
- 1894 census schedules, towns of Assyria, Baltimore, Delton, Barry, Carlton, Castleton, Hastings, Hope, Irving, Maple Grove, Orangeville, Prairieville, Rutland, Thornapple, Woodland, Yankee Springs, Foster, Dickinson Co., FHL film #915286.

To access the digital images, see the online FHL catalog page:
www.familysearch.org/search/catalog/53831.

1894 Michigan State Census, Benzie County **[Microfilm & Digital Capture],** from the original manuscripts at the Michigan State Archives, Lansing, MI. Filmed by the Genealogical Society of Utah, 1972, 1 rolls, FHL film #915295. To access the digital images for this roll, see the online FHL catalog page:
www.familysearch.org/search/catalog/328217.

1894 Michigan State Census, Bay County **[Microfilm & Digital Capture],** from the original manuscripts at the Michigan State Archives, Lansing, MI. Filmed by the Genealogical Society of Utah, 1972, 4 rolls, beginning with FHL film #915290.
To access the digital images for these rolls, see the online FHL catalog page:
www.familysearch.org/search/catalog/172311.

1894 Michigan State Census, Dickinson County **[Microfilm & Digital Capture],** from the originals at the Michigan State Archives, Lansing, MI, filmed by the Genealogical Society of Utah, 1972, 1 roll, FHL film #915299. To access the digital images for this roll, see the online FHL catalog page:
www.familysearch.org/search/catalog/328229.

1894 Michigan State Census, Emmet County **[Microfilm & Digital Capture],** from the original records at the Michigan State Archives, Lansing, MI. Filmed by the Genealogical Society of Utah, 1974, 1 roll, FHL film #915306. To access the digital images for this roll, see the online FHL catalog page:
www.familysearch.org/search/catalog/328113.

1894 Michigan State Census, Gratiot County **[Microfilm & Digital Capture],** from the original records at the Michigan State Archives, Lansing, MI. Arranged alphabetically by name of township (Arcadia – Newark only), then numerically by dwelling number. Filmed by the Genealogical Society of Utah, 1972, 1 roll, FHL film #915307. To access the digital images for this roll, see the online FHL catalog page:
www.familysearch.org/search/catalog/328116.

1894 Michigan State Census Index, Hillsdale County, Michigan **[Printed Book],** compiled by the Southern Michigan Genealogical Society, 1989, 208 pages. FHL book 977.429 X2hi and FHL film #6067455.

1894 Michigan State Census, Ingham County **[Microfilm & Digital Capture],** from the original records at the Michigan State Archives, Lansing, MI. Filmed by the Genealogical Society of Utah, 1972, 1 roll, FHL film #915309. To access the digital images for this roll, see the online FHL catalog page:
www.familysearch.org/search/catalog/328156.

1894. *Index to Ingham County, Michigan 1894 Census* **[Printed Index],** edited by Richard E. Lucas, Contents: Vol. 1: Townships One North; Vol. 2: Townships Two North; Vol. 3:. Townships Three North; Vol. 4:. Townships Four North; Vol. 5: Lansing City, Wards 1-3; and Vol. 6: Lansing City, Wards 4-6. Publ. Mid-Michigan Genealogical Society, 1995, 6 vols., FHL book 977.426 X22L 1894 v.1-6.

1894 Michigan State Census, Iosco County **[Microfilm & Digital Capture],** from the original records at the Michigan State Archives, Lansing, MI. Filmed by the Genealogical Society of Utah, 1972, 1 roll, FHL film #915311. To access the digital images for this roll, see the online FHL catalog page:
www.familysearch.org/search/catalog/328161.

1894 Michigan State Census, Kalamazoo County **[Microfilm & Digital Capture],** from the original records at the Michigan State Archives, Lansing, MI. Filmed by the Genealogical Society of Utah, 1972, 2 rolls, as follows:
- 1894 schedule 1, towns of Alamo-Wakeshma, FHL film #915315.
- 1894 schedule 1, city of Kalamazoo, wards 1-5, FHL film #915316.

To access the digital images of these rolls, see the online FHL catalog page:
www.familysearch.org/search/catalog/53827.

1894 Michigan State Census, Barry County **[Microfilm & Digital Capture],** from the original manuscripts at the Michigan State Archives, Lansing. Filmed by the Genealogical Society of Utah, 1972, 2 rolls, as follows:
- 1894 census schedules, towns of Johnstown, Maple Grove, Orangeville, Prairieville, Rutland, Thornapple, Middleville, Woodland, Yankee Springs, Hastings, FHL film #915285.
- 1894 census schedules, towns of Assyria, Baltimore, Delton, Barry, Carlton, Castleton, Hastings, Hope, Irving, Maple Grove, Orangeville, Prairieville, Rutland, Thornapple, Woodland, Yankee Springs, Foster, Dickinson Co., FHL film #915286.

To access the digital images of these rolls, see the online FHL catalog page:
www.familysearch.org/search/catalog/53831.

1894 Michigan State Census, Kent County **[Microfilm & Digital Capture],** from the original manuscripts at the Michigan State Archives, Lansing. Filmed by the Genealogical Society of Utah, 1975, 4 rolls, as follows:
- 1894 Nelson-Plainfield Townships; Gaines-Lowell Townships; and Grand Rapids, 12th ward, FHL film #984658.
- 1894. Grand Rapids, 11th ward, 2nd ward, and 1st ward, FHL film #984227.
- 1894 Townships of Byron – Courtland; Ada – Bowne; and Solon – Tyrone, FHL film #984228.
- 1894 Townships of Vergennes – Wyoming; and Agricultural schedules, FHL film #984229.

To access the digital images of these rolls, see the online FHL catalog page:
www.familysearch.org/search/catalog/175155.

1894. ***Index to the 1894 State Census, Kent County, Michigan*** **[Printed Book],** compiled by Evelyn Sawyer, published by the Western Michigan Genealogical Society, 1992, 266 pages. FHL book 977.455 X22i.

1894 Michigan State Census, Keweenaw County **[Microfilm & Digital Capture],** from the original records at the Michigan State Archives, Lansing, MI. Filmed by the Genealogical Society of Utah, 1972, 1 roll, FHL film #915273. To access the digital images for this roll, see the online FHL catalog page:
www.familysearch.org/search/catalog/328136.

1894 Michigan State Census, Lapeer County **[Microfilm & Digital Capture],** from the original records at the Michigan State Archives, Lansing, MI. Filmed by the Genealogical Society of Utah, 1972, 2 rolls, as follows:
- 1894 Towns of Almont, Arcadia, Attica, Burlington, Clifford, Burnside, Deerfield, Dryden, Thornville, Elba, Goodland, Hadley, Imlay, FHL film #915319.
- 1894 Towns of Lapeer Twp., Columbiaville, Marathon, Otter Lake, Mayfield, Metamora, North Branch, Oregon, Rich, Lapeer City, wards 1-4, FHL film #915320.

To access the digital images of these rolls, see the online FHL catalog page:
www.familysearch.org/search/catalog/53810.

1894 Michigan State Census, Leelanau County **[Microfilm & Digital Capture],** from the originals held by the Grand Traverse Genealogical Society, Traverse City, MI, Includes schedule 1 (enumeration of inhabitants). Filmed by the society, 1 roll. FHL copy is film #2223587. To access the digital images for this roll, see the online FHL catalog page:
www.familysearch.org/search/catalog/718941.

1894 Michigan State Census, Menominee County **[Microfilm & Digital Capture],** from the original records at the Michigan State Archives, Lansing, MI. Filmed by the Genealogical Society of Utah, 1972, 1 roll, FHL film #915324. To access the digital images for this roll, see the online FHL catalog page:
www.familysearch.org/search/catalog/328176.

1894 Michigan State Census, Montcalm County **[Microfilm & Digital Capture],** from the original records at the Michigan State Archives, Lansing, MI. Filmed by the Genealogical Society of Utah, 1972, 1 roll, FHL film #915327. To access the digital images for this roll, see the online FHL catalog page:
www.familysearch.org/search/catalog/328202.

1894 Muskegon County, Michigan Census Index; Head of Household **[Printed Book],** compiled by the Muskegon County Genealogical Society, Muskegon, MI, 1986, 101 pages. From preface: "The following index includes the names of heads of household, strays (people living in the same household with a different last name) and children over the age of 18. Parents living with children are also included." Index does not include Liber 3 (Muskegon, wards 5-8 and North Muskegon); the volume is missing. FHL book 977.457 V22m.

Michigan • 83

1894. *Index to the 1894 Newaygo County, Michigan State Census* **[Printed Book]**, compiled by Evelyn M. Sawyer, published by the author, 1997, 61 pages. FHL book 977.458 X22s 1894.

1894. *Census of Ottawa County, Michigan, 1894; Schedule 3, Statistics of Agriculture* **[Microfilm]**, from the original records at the Michigan State Archives, Lansing, MI. Filmed by the Genealogical Society of Utah, 1972. Includes name of person conducting farm, ownership, acres of land, ditches, farm value, fences, labor costs, and estimated cost of production in 1893. FHL film #915333. To see if this microfilm has been digitized yet, see the FHL catalog page: www.familysearch.org/search/catalog/328190.

1894 Michigan State Census, Washtenaw County **[Microfilm & Digital Capture]**, from the originals at the Bentley Historical Library at the University of Michigan in Ann Arbor, Michigan. Towns are intermixed. Filmed by the Genealogical Society of Utah, 1974, 3 rolls, as follows:
- 1894 Inhabitants, FHL film #955810.
- 1894 Inhabitants, FHL film #955811.
- 1894 Inhabitants, agriculture, manufactories, mines, fisheries, libraries, and churches, FHL film #955812.

To access the digital images of these rolls, see the online FHL catalog page: www.familysearch.org/search/catalog/290847.

1894. *Index of 1894 State Census for Washtenaw County, Michigan* **[Printed Book]**, prepared by Sarah Casewell Angell Chapter, National Society Daughters of the American Revolution, Ann Arbor, Michigan, published by the Genealogical Society of Washtenaw County, Michigan, 1984, 224 pages. FHL book 977.435 X22i.

1894. *An Illustrated City Directory of Hillsdale, Michigan* **[Online Database]**, digitized at the University of Michigan Digital Library site. See http://quod.lib.umich.edu/cgi/t/text/text-idx?c=micounty;idno=2745648.0001.001.

1897-1914. *Hospital Patient Records, Delta County, Michigan* **[Online Database]**, indexed at the Delta County Genealogical Society website. See http://dcmigs.org/hospital/a-b.htm.

1896-1935. *City Directory Master Index, Mount Clemens, Michigan* **[Online Database]**, and index to the collection of city directories located at the Mount Clemens Public Library. Includes 1896-1897, 1899-1900, 1901-1902, 1903-1904, 1905-1906, 1911-1912, 1913-1914, 1915-1916, 1917-1918, 1919-1920, 1921-1922, 1923-1924, 1925-1926, 1927, 1929, 1930, 1932, and 1935. The indexes for the remaining directories, 1937-1966, are still in work. Indexed at the Mount Clemens Public Library website. See www.mtclib.org/search/MCDirectory.php.

1897-1920. *Michigan Death Records* **[Online Database]**, digitized and indexed at the Seeking Michigan collections of the Archives of Michigan. A scanned image of a death certificate can be viewed and printed. See http://cdm16317.contentdm.oclc.org/cdm/search/collection/p129401coll7.
- Another version of this database is at the Ancestry.com website. See http://search.ancestry.com/search/db.aspx?dbid=1561.

1897-1920s. *Calhoun County, Michigan* **[Online Databases]**, indexed at the Ancestry.com website. Includes directories, histories, and biographies. See http://search.ancestry.com/Places/US/Michigan/Calhoun/Default.aspx.

1897-1952. *Michigan, Divorce Records* **[Online Database]**, digitized and indexed at the Ancestry.com website. Original data: Michigan. Divorce records. Michigan Department of Community Health, Division for Vital Records and Health Statistics, Lansing, Michigan. This database has 1,089,951 records. See http://search.ancestry.com/search/db.aspx?dbid=9092.

1898. *Michigan Men in the Spanish American War* **[Online Database]**, digitized and OCR indexed at the Ancestry.com website. Source: Book, same title, "by Porter." from *The Detroit Journal*, May 17-August 5, 1898. See https://search.ancestry.com/search/db.aspx?dbid=20048.

1898. *Michigan Volunteers in the Spanish American War* **[Online Database]**, indexed at the Michigan Family History Network website. Select a county at this "Veterans by County" page. See www.mifamilyhistory.org/spanam/sawcounty.aspx.

1898-1939. *Index to Michigan Soldiers Obituaries: Civil War, Spanish War, and World War I, 1898-1939* **[Printed Index]**, compiled by Kathy Tabb and Evelyn Sawyer for Western Michigan Genealogical Society, Grand Rapids, MI, 1989, 26 pages, FHL book 977.456 V42t.

1897-1935. See *Ann Arbor (Michigan) City Directories* [Microfilm], from various publishers. FHL has 1899, and 1901-1935. Filmed by Research Publications, Woodbridge, CT, 1980-1990, 16 rolls, beginning with FHL film #2156751 (1899 Directory). For a complete list of roll numbers and contents of each roll, visit the online FHL catalog page for this title. See https://familysearch.org/search/catalog/554844.

1899-1935. See *Battle Creek (Michigan) City Directories* [Microfilm], from various publishers. FHL has 1899-1916, 1918, 1921, 1922, 1924, 1926, 1927, 1929, 1931, 1933, and 1935. Filmed by Research Publications, Woodbridge, CT, 1980-1984, 10 rolls, beginning with FHL film #2156753 (1899-1900 Polk's Battle Creek City Directory), For a complete list of roll numbers and contents of each roll, visit the online FHL catalog page for this title. See https://familysearch.org/search/catalog/555523.

1900. *Michigan, 1900 Federal Census: Soundex and Population Schedules* [Microfilm & Digital Capture], from the originals held by the Bureau of the Census in the 1940s. After microfilming, Congress allowed the Census Bureau to destroy the originals to free up space for WWII-related files. Filmed on 315 rolls, beginning with FHL film #1244920 (1900 Soundex: A000 thru A223); and FHL film #1240698 (1900 Population Schedules: Alcona, Alger, and Allegan Cos). To access the digital images, see the online FHL catalog page:
https://familysearch.org/search/catalog/656796.

1900. *The Past and Present of Shiawassee County, Michigan: Historically Together with Biographical Sketches of Many of its Leading and Prominent Citizens and Illustrious Dead* [Microfilm & Online Database], originally pub. Historical Publishing Assoc., Lansing, MI, ca 1900, 557 pages. Filmed by W.C. Cox, Tucson, AZ, 1974, FHL film #1000247. To access a digital version of this book, visit the online FHL catalog page for this title. See https://familysearch.org/search/catalog/183094.
- An online index to the biographies in this book is at the MIGenWeb site for Shiawassee Co MI. See www.migenweb.org/shiawassee/bios/pastandpresent.html.

1900-1903. *Wexford County, Michigan* [Online Databases], indexed at the Ancestry.com website. Includes 1900 W. A. Norton's Cadillac city directory; and 1903 History of Wexford County, Michigan. See http://search.ancestry.com/Places/US/Michigan/Wexford/Default.aspx.

1900-1910. *Iosco County Gazette Index* [Online Database], digitized and indexed at the Ancestry.com website. See http://search.ancestry.com/search/db.aspx?dbid=5667.

1902-1912. *Declaration of Intention for U.S. Naturalization, Keweenaw County, Michigan* [Online Database], indexed at the USGenWeb site for Keweenaw Co MI. See http://files.usgwarchives.net/mi/keweenaw/naturalization/k50004.txt.

1902-1977. *Gogebic County, Michigan* [Online Databases], indexed at the Ancestry.com website. Includes newspapers from Ironwood, Bessemer, and Wakefield, MI. See http://search.ancestry.com/Places/US/Michigan/Gogebic/Default.aspx.

1903 Biographies. See *Biographical Records, Houghton, Baraga and Marquette Counties, Michigan* [Online Database], indexed at the Ancestry.com website. This database has 347 biographies. See http://search.ancestry.com/search/db.aspx?dbid=17600.

1903-1925. *Kent County, Michigan, School Census, 1903-1925* [Online Database], indexed at the Ancestry.com website. Original data: Kent County School Census. 1903-25. Western Michigan Genealogical Society. Each index record includes: Name, Residence, Residence date, and a link to the WMGS website. This database has 230,787 records. See https://search.ancestry.com/search/db.aspx?dbid=70327.

1903-1934. *Holland (Michigan) City Directories* [Microfilm], by various publishers. Filmed by Research Publications, Woodbridge, CT, 1995, 2 rolls, as follows:
- 1903-1904 Holland city directory, FHL film #2309181.
- 1906 Holland city directory, FHL film #2309181.
- 1908. The Inter-state Directory Company's directory of Holland, Mich., and Ottawa County, FHL film #2309181.
- 1921 Polk's Holland City directory, FHL film #2309181.
- 1929 Polk's Holland, Michigan city directory, including Zeeland, FHL film #2309182.
- 1931 Polk's Holland, Michigan city directory, including Zeeland, FHL film #2309182.
- 1934 Polk's Holland, Ottawa County, Mich., city directory, 1934, including Zeeland, FHL film #2309182.

1903-1965. See *Michigan Passenger and Crew Lists* **[Online Database]**, digitized and indexed at the Ancestry.com website. Original data, from National Archives publications: 1) *Manifests of Alien Arrivals at Algonac, Marine City, Roberts Landing, Saint Clair, and Sault Sainte Marie, Michigan, 1903-1955*, 2) *Crew Lists of Vessels Arriving at Alpena, Bay City, Mackinac Island, Rogers City, Saginaw, and Saint Clair, Michigan, June 1945-September 1965*, 3) *Crew Lists of Vessels Arriving at Hancock, Isle of Royale, Marquette, Menominee, and Sault Sainte Marie, Michigan, January 1946-January 1957*; and 4) *Manifests of Alien Arrivals at Port Huron, Michigan, February 1902-December 1954*. This database has 377,263 records. See
http://search.ancestry.com/search/db.aspx?dbid=1247.

1903-2000s. *Barry County, Michigan* **[Online Databases]**, indexed at the Ancestry.com website. Includes newspaper indexes, directories, histories, and biographies related to Barry County, Michigan. See
http://search.ancestry.com/Places/US/Michigan/Barry/Default.aspx.

1904 Census Statistics. See *Census of the State of Michigan, 1904* **[Online Database]**, digitized from the official report of the Secretary of State, state of Michigan, publ. 1906, 2 vols., with statistics on the 1904 state census, including population figures, manufacturing, and agricultural products. This is a book of statistics only, relating to the last state census available for Michigan. Unfortunately, the 1904 state census population schedules for all of Michigan counties were lost. See
http://search.ancestry.com/search/db.aspx?dbid=18559.

1904-1934. *St. Joseph (Michigan) City Directories* **[Microfilm]**, by various publishers. FHL has 1904-1905, 1907-1908, and 1934. Includes directory listing for St. Joseph, Benton, Harbor, Niles, and Berrien County. Filmed by Research Publications, Woodbridge, CT, 1990, 1 roll, FHL film #2309251.

1905-1932. *Owosso (Michigan) City Directories* **[Microfilm]**, by various publishers. FHL has 1905-1906, 1907-1908, 1910-1911, 1913-1914, 1915-1916, 1917-1918, 1919-1920, 1921, 1924, 1926, 1928, 1930-1931, and 1932. Most directories include Owosso, Corunna, and Shiawassee county areas. Filmed by Research Publications, Woodbridge, CT, 4 rolls, beginning with FHL film #2309224 (1905-1906 Polk's Owosso and Corunna City Directory). For a complete list of roll numbers and contents of each roll, visit the online FHL catalog page for this title. See
https://familysearch.org/search/catalog/1059486.

1905-1935. *Hillsdale (Michigan) City Directories* **[Microfilm]**, from various publishers. FHL has 1905-1906, 1908-1909, 1911-1912, 1915, 1923, 1925, 1927, 1932, 1929, 1933, and 1935. Filmed by Research Publications, Woodbridge, CT, 1 roll, FHL film #2309180 (1905-1935 Hillsdale City and County Directories, Jonesville, Reading, and all other villages in Hillsdale County).

1906 Patrons' Reference Directory of Gladwin County, Michigan **[Online Database],** indexed at the MIFamilyhistory.org website. See
www.mifamilyhistory.org/gladwin/Gladwin1906directory.htm.

1905-1963. *Detroit Border Crossings and Passenger and Crew Lists* **[Online Database]**, digitized and indexed at the Ancestry.com website. Source: National Archives, NAI 4527226. Each index record includes: Name, Gender, Age, Nationality, Birth date, Birth place, Arrival date, Arrival place, Departure contact, Arrival contact, Father, and Spouse. The document image may have more information. This database has 1,734,123 records. See
https://search.ancestry.com/search/db.aspx?dbid=1070.

1906-1954. *Michigan, Detroit Manifest of Arrivals at the Port of Detroit* **[Online Database]**, digitized and indexed at the FamilySearch.org website. Source: National Archives microfilm series M1478. This is an alphabetical card file manifest of individuals entering the United States through the Port of Detroit, 1906-1954. Includes a few records of persons entering at Port Huron, Sault St. Marie, and other Michigan ports. This database has 845,964 records. See
https://familysearch.org/search/collection/1916040.

1907-1995. See *Index Cards to the Naturalization Petitions for the United States District Court for the Eastern District of Michigan, Southern Division, Detroit, 1907-1995* **[Microfilm],** from the originals at U.S. District Court, Detroit, MI. The index cards are arranged by Soundex code. Filmed by the Genealogical Society of Utah, 1999, 280 rolls, beginning with FHL film #2116210 (A-000-A-136). For a complete list of roll numbers and contents of each roll, visit the online FHL catalog page:
https://familysearch.org/search/catalog/825447.

1907-1995. *Michigan, Eastern District, Naturalization Index* **[Online Database],** digitized at the FamilySearch.org website. Includes images of Soundex cards to naturalization petitions. The images were digitized from the microfilm series noted above. This database has 577,690 images. See https://familysearch.org/search/collection/2110745.

1910. *Michigan, 1910 Federal Census: Soundex and Population Schedules* **[Microfilm & Digital Capture],** from the originals held by the Bureau of the Census in the 1940s. After microfilming, Congress allowed the Census Bureau to destroy the originals to free up space for WWII-related files. Filmed on 307 rolls, beginning with FHL film #1370772 (1910 Soundex: A000 thru A235); and FHL film #1374647 (1910 Population Schedules: Alcona, Alger, and Allegan Cos). To access the digital images, see the online FHL catalog page:
https://familysearch.org/search/catalog/637206.

1910-1916. *Cheboygan County, Michigan* **[Online Database],** indexed at the Ancestry.com website. Includes 1910 and 1916 directories of Cheboygan city/county. See
http://search.ancestry.com/Places/US/Michigan/Cheboygan/Default.aspx.

1910-2000s. *Allegan County, Michigan* **[Online Databases],** indexed at the Ancestry.com website. Includes death indexes, marriage indexes, newspapers, histories, and biographies from Allegan county. See
http://search.ancestry.com/Places/US/Michigan/Allegan/Default.aspx.

1910-2012. Western Michigan Newspapers, Death Index [Online Database], indexed at the Ancestry.com website from a database contributed by the Western Michigan Genealogical Society. This database has 455,193 records. See
http://search.ancestry.com/search/db.aspx?dbid=9222.

1911. *A History of the Northern Peninsula of Michigan and its People, its Mining, Lumber and Agricultural Industries* **[Microfilm & Digital Capture],** from the book compiled by Alvah Littlefield Sawyer, publ. Lewis Publ. Co, Chicago, 1911, 3 vols. To access the digital images, see the online FHL page:
www.familysearch.org/search/catalog/24239.

1912 St. Clair County (Michigan) Directory **[Microfilm],** from the original book publ. Herald Printing Company, 1912. Includes the following towns and cities, Port Huron, Algonac, Capac, Emmett, Marine City, Memphis, St. Clair and Yale. FHL film #2310456. To see if this microfilm has been digitized yet, see the FHL catalog page:
www.familysearch.org/search/catalog/1940317.

1912. *Biographies, Residents in 1912, Van Buren County, Michigan* **[Online Database],** indexed at the RootsWeb site for Van Buren Co MI:
www.rootsweb.ancestry.com/~mivanbur/bioindex.htm.

1913. *Index to History of Gratiot County, Michigan* **[Online Database],** indexed at the Michigan Family History Network website.
www.mfhn.com/gratiot/tucker/index-1.html.

1914. *Index, 1914, Cass County, Michigan Land Owners* **[Printed Book & Digital Capture],** from the book compiled by Amelia B. Castle, publ. A.B. Castle, Dowagiac, MI, 1994, 30 pages. To access a digital version of this book, see the online FHL catalog page for this title:
www.familysearch.org/search/catalog/2790159.

1916. *Farm Journal Illustrated Directory of Van Buren County, Michigan, (With a Complete Road Map of the County)* **[Printed Book & digital Capture],** from the original book publ. Wilmer Atkinson, Philadelphia, 1916, 288 pages, digitized by the Genealogical Society of Utah, 2014. To access a digital version of this book, see the online FHL catalog page for this title:
https://familysearch.org/search/catalog/2301941.

1917-1918. *World War I Card Index for Michigan* **[Microfilm & Digital Capture],** from the originals at the State Archives, Lansing, MI. Card files include names of the soldiers' parents and addresses. Filmed by the Genealogical Society of Utah, 1976, 37 rolls, beginning with FHL film #1001930 (A – Ath). To access the digital images, see the online FHL catalog page: https://familysearch.org/search/catalog/434638.

1917-1918. *Deserters From Draft Index* **[Microfilm],** from the original records at the Michigan State Archives, Lansing, MI. Includes names of the organizations, soldiers, and addresses. Filmed by the Genealogical Society of Utah, 1991, 4 rolls, beginning with FHL film #1765776 (A-Colt). For a complete list of roll numbers and contents of each roll, visit the online FHL catalog page for this title. See
https://familysearch.org/search/catalog/502894.

1917-1919 Michigan Veterans Serving with Allied Forces: Census of World War I Veterans **[Microfilm & Digital Capture],** from the original records at the Michigan State Archives in Lansing. The list is alphabetical by each veteran's name. Michigan State

Archives No.: MS78-92 v. 368-373. Filmed by the Genealogical Society of Utah, 1996, 5 rolls, as follows:
- WWI Veterans (A-Cole), FHL film #2056789.
- WWI Veterans (Cole-Kee), FHL film #2056790.
- WWI veterans (Kel-Pl), FHL film #2056791.
- WWI veterans (Po-Williams, F), FHL film #2056792.
- WWI veterans (Williams, G-Z), FHL film #2056793.

To access the digital images of certain rolls, see the online FHL catalog page:
www.familysearch.org/search/catalog/727997.

1918-1923. *Farm Directory, Mecosta County, Michigan* **[Online Database],** indexed at the MIGenWeb site for Mecosta Co MI. See www.migenweb.org/mecosta/farmdirectory.html.

1920. *Michigan, 1920 Federal Census: Soundex and Population Schedules* **[Microfilm],** from the originals held by the Bureau of the Census in the 1940s. After microfilming, Congress allowed the Census Bureau to destroy the originals to free up space for WWII-related files. Filmed on 360 rolls, beginning with FHL film #1826174 (1920 Soundex: A000 thru A223); and FHL film #1820753 (1920 Population Schedules: Alcona, Alger, Areca, and Allegan Cos). To access the digital images, see the online FHL catalog page:
https://familysearch.org/search/catalog/572775.

1920-1935. *Pontiac (Michigan) City Directories* **[Microfilm],** from various publishers. FHL has 1920, 1922, 1923, 1925, 1927, 1928, 1929, 1930, 1931, and 1935. Filmed by Research Publications, Woodbridge, CT, 1984, 6 rolls, beginning with FHL film #2310333 (Polk's Pontiac Directory, 1920). For a complete list of roll numbers and contents of each roll, visit the online FHL catalog page for this title. See https://familysearch.org/search/catalog/1130597.

1920-1987. *Index to Forshee Funeral Home, Hale, Iosco County, Michigan* **[Online Database],** indexed at the USGenWeb site for Iosco Co MI. See http://files.usgwarchives.net/mi/iosco/hsgs/business/fun-forsheefh1920-87.txt.

1921-1952. *Michigan Death Records* **[Online Database],** digitized and indexed at the Seeking Michigan collections at the Archives of Michigan website. This collection consists of over 1.6 million death records created between 1921 and 1952. Records created between 1921 and 1939 include an image of the death certificate. Records from 1940-1952 are indexed only. To search for a name, go to the Advanced Search option. When the menu opens, the default collection is for "Death Records, 1897-1920" which needs to be unchecked, then check "Michigan Death Records, 1921-1952." See http://seekingmichigan.org/discover/death-records-1921-1952.

1921-1952. *Michigan Death Certificates* **[Online Database],** digitized and indexed at the FamilySearch.org website. Includes an index of death records from the Michigan Department of Community health, Division for Vital Records and Health Statistics in Lansing, MI. This database has 1,681,256 records. See https://familysearch.org/search/collection/1968532.

1924-1940. *Applications for Admission to Veteran's Facility* **[Microfilm],** from the originals at the MI State Archives, Lansing, MI. The dates are based on the date of the application for admission to the Michigan Soldiers' Home – some admissions did not occur until well into the 1960s. These records include military history, physical characteristics, and details about the immediate family. Filmed by the Genealogical Society of Utah, 2001, 53 rolls, beginning with FHL film #2217099 (Applications, 1924-1925). For a complete list of roll numbers and contents of each roll, visit the online FHL catalog page for this title. See https://familysearch.org/search/catalog/1131989.

1925. *Chippewa County, Michigan* **[Online Database],** indexed at the Ancestry.com website. Includes a 1925 history of Sault Ste. Marie. See http://search.ancestry.com/search/db.aspx?dbid=27726.

1926-1934. See *Dearborn (Michigan) City Directories* **[Microfilm],** from various publishers. FHL has 1926, 1928-1929, 1930, 1932, and 1934. Filmed by Research Publications, Woodbridge, CT, 1995, 1 roll, FHL film #2309160.

1928 History. See *Historic Michigan, Land of the Great Lakes: Its Life, Resources, Industries, People, Politics, Government, Wars, Institutions, Achievements, the Press, Schools and Churches, Legendary and Prehistoric Lore* **[Microfilm & Digital Capture],** from the book edited by George Newman Fuller, publ. National Historical Assoc., Dayton, OH, 1928, 3 vols. To access the digital versions of all 3 vols. of this book, see the online FHL catalog page:
www.familysearch.org/search/catalog/255515.

1928 Directory, Gogebic County, Michigan **[Online Database]**, indexed at the Mattsonworks.com website. See **http://mattsonworks.com/1928/index.html**.

1929-1966. *Michigan, Crew Lists for Various Ports* **[Online Database]**, digitized and indexed at the FamilySearch.org website. Source: National Archives microfilm A3432, A3413, A3418, A3421, A3430, A3443 & A3433 (Crew Lists of Vessels Arriving at Hancock, Isle Royale, Marquette, Menominee, Sault Sainte Marie, Escanaba, Algonac, Marine City, Marysville, Roberts Landing, DeTour, Alpena, Bay City, Mackinac Island, Rogers City, Saginaw, Saint Clair, Port Huron, Grand Haven, Manistee, Muskegon, and South Haven, Michigan). Each index record includes: Name, Event type, Event place, Gender, Birth Country, and Ship name. The document image may have more information. This database has 140,488 records. See **www.familysearch.org/search/collection/2426314**.

1930. *Michigan, 1930 Federal Census: Population Schedules* **[Microfilm & Digital Capture]**, from the originals held by the Bureau of the Census in the 1940s. After microfilming, Congress allowed the Census Bureau to destroy the originals to free up space for WWII-related files. Filmed on 106 rolls, beginning with FHL film #2340707 (1930 Population Schedules: Alcona, Alger, Areca, Baraga, and Allegan Cos). To access the digital images, see the online FHL catalog page: **https://familysearch.org/search/catalog/1036363**.

1933. *Census Cards, Sanilac County, Michigan, 1933* **[Microfilm]**, from the original records at the Archives of Michigan, Lansing, MI. In 1933, the legislature passed Act 237 which was designed to aid the elderly. To implement this act it was deemed wiser to have enumerators canvass the county, rather than require each adult to come to the clerk's office to register. Accordingly, a house to house survey was undertaken to record everyone 21 years of age or older as of November 15, 1933. These are the 1933 census cards for Sanilac County. (Most other counties were lost). The census cards were filmed in alphabetical order according to the first letter of the last name. Each card includes name, sex, color, date, county, city or township, precinct, street, age, date of birth, place of birth, parents' names, spouse's name, employed by, occupation, length of unemployment, source of welfare aid, U.S. citizen, naturalization data, etc. Filmed by the Genealogical Society of Utah, 2002, 6 rolls, beginning with FHL film #2139708 (A-C). To see if this microfilm has been digitized yet, see the FHL catalog page: **https://familysearch.org/search/catalog/1132766**.

1938 Directory, Gogebic County, Michigan **[Online Database]**, indexed at the Mattsonworks.com website. See **http://mattsonworks.com/1938**.

1939. *Michigan, A Centennial History of the State and its People* **[Online Database]**, digitized and OCR indexed at the Ancestry.com website. Source: Book, same title, 5 vols., publ. 1939. This database has 3,341 pages. See **https://search.ancestry.com/search/db.aspx?dbid=20041**.

1939-1944. *Michigan Casualties, World War* **[Online Database]**, digitized and OCR indexed at the Ancestry.com website. From the book by Frances Loomis, *Michigan Casualties, World War,* publ. Detroit, 1944-1948. This database has 2,901 records: **http://search.ancestry.com/search/db.aspx?dbid=23835**.

1940. See *Michigan, 1940 Federal Census: Population Schedules* **[Microfilm & Digital Capture]**, from the original records held by the Bureau of the Census in the 1940s. After microfilming, Congress allowed the Census Bureau to destroy the originals to free up space for WWII-related files. Filmed on 183 rolls, beginning with FHL film #5461556 (Alcona & Alger cos). For a complete list of roll numbers, roll contents, and the digital images of each roll, see the online FHL catalog page: **https://familysearch.org/search/catalog/2057762**.

1940 Federal Census Finding Aids **[Online Database]**. The National Archives prepared a special website online with a detailed description of the 1940 federal census. Included at the site are descriptions of location finding aids, such as Enumeration District maps, Geographic Descriptions of Census Enumeration Districts, and a list of 1940 City Directories available at the National Archives. The finding aids are all linked to other National Archives sites. The National Archives website also has a link to 1940 Search Engines using Stephen P. Morse's "One-Step" system for finding a 1940 E.D. or street address conversion. See **www.archives.gov/research/census/1940/general-info.html#questions**.

1940-1947. *Michigan, World War II Draft Registration Cards, 1940-1947* **[Microfilm & Digital Capture]**, from the originals at the National Personnel

Records Center, St. Louis, MO. From a set of 1,351 archived microfilm rolls, this collection was digitized by the Genealogical Society of Utah, 2018, beginning with FHL film #105363374 (Draft registrations cards, Hughes, Charles – Huhn, Raymond). To access the digital images, see the online FHL catalog page: www.familysearch.org/search/catalog/2999489.

1941-1945. See *World War II Honor List of Dead and Missing, State of Michigan* **[Digital Capture],** from a book by the War Department, Bureau of Public Relations, publ. 1946, 66 pages. Digitized by the Genealogical Society of Utah, 2014. For access to a digital version, see the online FHL catalog page for this title. See https://familysearch.org/search/catalog/2330656.

1941-1945. World War II Michigan Dead & MIA [CD-ROM], compiled and published by Betty Driscoll, New Era, MI, 2007, FHL CD No. 4310.

1942. *Michigan Selective Service System Registration Cards [World War II]: Fourth Registration* **[Microfilm & Digital Capture],** from the original records at the National Archives, Washington, DC. These cards represent older men, ages 45 to 65 in April 1942, that were registered for the draft. They had birth dates between 28 Apr 1877 and 16 Feb 1892. Filmed by the Genealogical Society of Utah, 243 rolls, beginning with FHL film #1669945 (Aab, Casper – Agostin, Peter). To access the digital images, see the online FHL catalog page: https://familysearch.org/search/catalog/1447661.

1938 Directory, Gogebic County, Michigan **[Online Database],** indexed at the Mattsonworks.com website. See http://mattsonworks.com/1947/index.html.

1957-1959. See *Michigan, South Haven Crew Lists* **[Online Database],** digitized at the FamilySearch.org website. This collection contains Crew Lists of Vessels Arriving at South Haven, Michigan, May 1957- October 1959. The records usually include the name of the ship, the ports and dates of arrival and departure, and the following information about each person: name, citizenship, passport number, crew position, and where the crewman was shipped or engaged. This database has 61 images. See https://familysearch.org/search/collection/2443337.

1959-2011. *Western Michigan Newspapers, Marriage Index, 1959-2011* **[Online Database],** indexed at the Ancestry.com website from a database contributed by the Western Michigan Genealogical Society. This database has 352,285 records. See http://search.ancestry.com/search/db.aspx?dbid=9221.

1965-1984. *Michigan, Naturalization Records: Index* **[Microfilm & Digital Capture],** from the manuscripts held by the National Archives, Chicago, IL. Digitized by the Genealogical Society of Utah, 2017, from 2 rolls of microfilm. To access the digital images of these rolls, see the online FHL catalog page for this title: www.familysearch.org/search/catalog/2831744.

1971-1996. *Michigan Death Index* **[Online Database],** indexed at the FamilySearch.org website. Original data: Michigan Department of Vital and Health Records. Michigan Death Index. Lansing, MI. This database has 2,052, 472 records. See https://familysearch.org/search/collection/1949333.
- Another version of this database is at the Ancestry.com website. See http://search.ancestry.com/search/db.aspx?dbid=3171.

1972. *Delta County, Michigan* **[Online Database],** indexed at the Ancestry.com website. Includes a 1972 history of Escanaba, Michigan. See http://search.ancestry.com/Places/US/Michigan/Delta/Default.aspx.

1978-1990. *Obituaries, Iosco County, Michigan* **[Online Database],** digitized and indexed at the Ancestry.com website. See http://search.ancestry.com/search/db.aspx?dbid=5480.

1989. *Centennial History of Menominee County, Michigan* **[Online Database],** digitized from a book by E. S. Ingalls, pub. Herald Power Presses, 1989, indexed at the Ancestry.com website. See http://search.ancestry.com/search/db.aspx?dbid=17633.

1995 - Current. *Michigan Recent Newspaper Obituaries* **[Online Database],** digitized and indexed newspaper obituaries at the GenealogyBank.com website, including newspapers from Adrian, Ann Arbor, Bad Axe, and 90 more Michigan cities, see www.genealogybank.com/explore/obituaries/all/usa/michigan.

90 • *Census Substitutes & State Census Records*

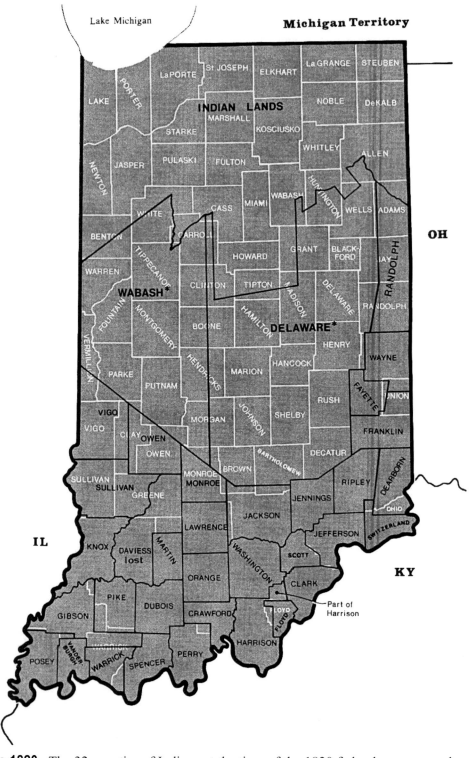

Indiana • June 1820. The 32 counties of Indiana at the time of the 1820 federal census are shown in black. The current 92 counties of Indiana are shown in white. *Note. Included are the unorganized districts of *Delaware* and *Wabash*, used as census divisions in 1820 only. The actual counties of those names were formed in 1827 and 1833, respectively. For a detailed map showing all of the Indian Cessions in Indiana, see http://usgwarchives.net/maps/cessions/ilcmap19.htm. All of the 1820 counties have extant census manuscripts except for Daviess, shown as "lost" on the map. **Map Source:** Page 108, *Map Guide to the U.S. Federal Censuses, 1790-1920*, by William Thorndale and William Dollarhide.

Indiana
Censuses & Substitute Name Lists

Historical Timeline for Indiana, 1614-1911

1614. Samuel de Champlain, Governor of New France, and the founder of Québec, was believed to be the first of the French explorers to visit the Miami du lac region between present Toledo, OH and Fort Wayne, IN. Later, the name Maumee was an anglicized spelling of the Ottawa name for the Miami Indians and became the origin of the name for the present Maumee River, the main water access to Indiana via Lake Erie.

1679-1702. In 1679, French explorer René-Robert Cavelier (Sieur de LaSalle) began negotiations with the Miami Indians to secure an area near the confluence of the St. Marys and St. Josephs rivers forming the Maumee River (at the site of present Fort Wayne, Indiana).
- For many years, the Miami Indians had enjoyed considerable influence in that area due to their control of the primary portage location between the Maumee River, flowing to Lake Erie; and the Wabash River, flowing to the Ohio River. They had maintained markings and clearings for a portage trail and charged a toll for anyone to pass.
- The first European visitors to present Indiana were French voyageurs, traversing by canoe from Lake Erie via the Maumee River into present Indiana. Those attempting to continue their canoe trips all the way to the Ohio River, however, were stopped at the site of present Fort Wayne, which sits on a continental divide separating the watershed drainage between the Great Lakes and the Ohio River.
- In 1702, a group of French voyageurs made a deal with the Miami Indians to upgrade their existing portage trail to a roadway suitable for horse-drawn wagons. The improved roadway began at the St. Mary's River (at present Fort Wayne) and covered some 10-20 miles (depending on seasonal water levels) to a point on the Little Wabash River. In exchange, the French voyageurs gained unlimited access to the only overland portage required between Lake Erie and the Ohio River.

1717 French Louisiana. The French jurisdiction, *la Louisiane Française,* extended from the Highlands along the Wabash River, down the Ohio and Mississippi Rivers, to include New Orleans and several ports on the Gulf of Mexico. The Highlands, in French, *Terra Haute*, became the division line between the Québec and Louisiana jurisdictions.

1721. The French established Fort Philippe, later called Fort Miami, on the St. Marys River, where the St. Marys and St. Josephs rivers form the Maumee River. Fort Philippe/Fort Miami was administered as part of French Québec. The fort was near the eastern portal of the Wabash-Erie Portage Road.

1732. Vincennes was established on the Wabash River, becoming Indiana's first permanent settlement. It was named after Jean Baptiste Bissot (Sieur de Vincennes), the military commander of Quebec. The town of Vincennes became the largest French settlement in Upper Louisiana.

1733-1762 French Colonies vs British Colonies. Lower Louisiana, with its ports on the Gulf of Mexico, had been the destination of colonists directly from France and other French colonies in the Caribbean. Upper Louisiana, however, was mostly inhabited by French Canadians, coming into the area from Québec. From 1733 to 1762, no new farming communities were established in French Louisiana.

The French presence in the Mississippi Basin and around the Great Lakes consisted of single French voyageurs, trappers, and traders paddling their canoes from one outpost to the next. The French established military/trading posts at strategic locations, mainly as a means of protecting the trappers during their contacts with the Indians. Unlike the French Québec settlements, French Louisiana had very few farming communities, and there was little exchanging of goods or produce, except for the trapping and trading of furs.

During this period, the French had built one road (the Wabash-Erie Portage Road), a road less than 20 miles long, and that was only to provide portage between rivers. In comparison, the British colonies by 1762 had over 2,500 miles of improved wagon roads, between Boston and Savannah. The British colonies had an economy based on town tradesmen surrounded by small farms, with the exchange of goods and produce up and down the Atlantic coast.

1763. The treaty of Paris of 1763 ended the French and Indian War. In Europe and Canada, it was called the "Seven Years War." The treaty required France to surrender all of its claims to land in North America, with the exception of fishing rights and a couple of fish-drying islands off of Newfoundland. The treaty gave Spain all of Louisiana west of the Mississippi, while Britain gained the areas east of the Mississippi River to the Appalachian Mountains. Great Britain also acquired the Province of Québec from France, which they immediately renamed the Province of Canada.

1764-1770 Transition Period. After the departure of all French military personnel by 1764, the French-colonized areas of Louisiana were still inhabited by French voyageurs, by now mostly **Métis** voyageurs (offspring of French fathers/Indian mothers). The transition from French control to Spanish or British control took several years. In former French Louisiana, French civilian settlements still operated at Prairie du Chien, now Wisconsin; Kaskaskia, now Illinois; and at Vincennes, now Indiana. In 1764, a French trading company established the trading post of St. Louis on the west side of the Mississippi River, after obtaining a trading license from the Spanish government. And, per terms of the Treaty of Paris of 1763, British forces began the evacuation of French Acadians from their homes in present Nova Scotia. The first shipload of Acadians arrived in Spanish Louisiana, just west of New Orleans, in February 1765. The Louisiana Rebellion of 1768 was an unsuccessful attempt by Acadians, Creole, and German settlers around New Orleans to stop the handover of French Louisiana to Spain. And, the French influence in Upper Louisiana continued: although part of Spanish Louisiana, St. Louis operated under French civilian control until it was actually occupied by Spanish soldiers in 1770. About the same time, the British established military jurisdiction over the French settlements at Prairie du Chien, Kaskaskia and Vincennes.

1774 Québec Act. In response to the increased rebellions by the American colonists, and after deciding not to repeat the evacuation of all French Acadians (Catholics) from Nova Scotia in the mid 1760s, the British Parliament passed the Québec Act, permitting the French Canadians to retain French laws and customs, and allowing the Catholic Church to maintain its rights. The French settlements along the Wabash River near Vincennes in present-day Indiana were included in the Province of Québec, under British rule since 1763.

1778-1779. French Acadians (the Cajuns) resettled by the British in southern Louisiana rallied in support of the American rebels during the Revolutionary War. They were joined in their support by the left-over French settlers of the Wabash Valley, who were instrumental in General George Rogers Clark's capture of Kaskaskia on the Mississippi River and Vincennes on the Wabash River.

1783. Post-Revolutionary War. The 1783 Treaty of Paris recognized the United States of America as an independent nation and defined its borders from the Atlantic Ocean to the Mississippi River. Although the old Upper Louisiana and Great Lakes regions were to be included within the United States, British forces continued to maintain control of Prairie du Chien, Fort Detroit, Fort Miami, and a few other sites for several years after the Revolution.

1784. Massachusetts, Connecticut, New York, and Virginia relinquished their western claims to lands in the Great Lakes region, a large area that was to become the Northwest Territory. Title of the state's claims were transferred to the "public domain" of the United States Federal Government.

1787 Northwest Territory. The Ordinance of 1787 established the *Territory Northwest of the River Ohio and* defined the procedure for any territory to obtain statehood.

1787-1815 Flatboat Era. After the creation of the Northwest Territory, migrating families heading to the Ohio River via horse-drawn wagons might stop at Brownsville, Pittsburgh, or Wheeling, where they would construct a flatboat to access the public lands via the Ohio River. The earliest settlements in the southern portions of Ohio, Indiana, and Illinois were mostly settled by flatboat travelers. Although steamboats were introduced to the Ohio River in 1812, they did not dominate transportation until the classic flat-bottomed steamboat design took hold in 1815. That ended the flatboat era.

1790. The Northwest Territory was specifically excluded from the 1790 census. Estimates of the population in the Knox County area that became Indiana was mostly near Vincennes, with about 1,000 persons there. Less than 100 persons were at Fort Steuben (now Jeffersonville, IN). In a 1787 enumeration of males in the Vincennes area, almost every surname was French.

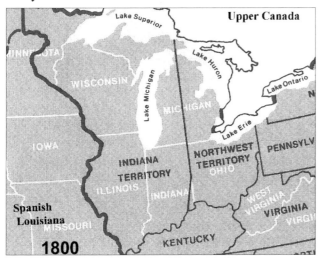

1800. Indiana Territory was established from the Northwest Territory with William Henry Harrison as the first Governor and Vincennes the capital. The area included most of present-day Indiana, Illinois, Wisconsin, and the western half of Michigan. The Northwest Territory was reduced to the present-day area of Ohio and the eastern half of Michigan. The map above shows the Northwest and Indiana territories as of the August 1800 federal census.

1803. Ohio was admitted to the Union as the 17th state, with Chillicothe as the state capital. The portion of present Michigan included in the Northwest Territory 1800-1803 became part of Indiana Territory.

1805. Michigan Territory was separated from the Indiana Territory, with Detroit the capital. The area was between Lake Michigan and Lake Huron, as today, but included just the tip of the Upper Peninsula, still mostly under control of Indiana Territory.

1809. Illinois Territory was separated from Indiana Territory, with Kaskaskia the capital. The original area included present-day Illinois, Wisconsin, a portion of the Upper Peninsula of present Michigan and that portion of Minnesota east of the Mississippi River. The area of Indiana Territory was reduced in size to the area of the present-day state, plus a portion of the Upper Peninsula of present Michigan.

1810. Indiana Territory. The 1810 population of 24,320 people was within four counties: Clark, Dearborn, Knox, and Harrison. The 1810 federal census manuscripts for all four counties were lost.

1811. Battle of Tippecanoe. Tecumseh's forces were defeated at the Battle of Tippecanoe. The American forces were led by Governor William Henry Harrison, who later used the presidential nickname "Tippecanoe." The victory over a large force of Indians opened up much of Indiana for settlement.

1813. The Indiana territorial capital was moved from Vincennes to Corydon.

1816. Dec. 11th. Indiana became the 19th state with the same boundaries as today. The first state capital was at Corydon. In 1825, the state capital was moved to Indianapolis.

About Indiana's Colonial, Territorial and Statewide Censuses

Colonial Name Lists: The only surviving colonial name lists available are from the original French settlements in and around Vincennes from the 1780s. Vincennes was first settled by the French in 1732, but only a few records have survived. Preserved name lists today are part of the early Knox County, Indiana courthouse records from the 1780s, which include land records, militia lists, and probates. A 1787 census listing the male inhabitants of the "District of Poste Vincennes" also exists, taken a few months after the creation of the Northwest Territory, but before it was organized. The 1787 published name list consists of mostly French surnames and reveals the names of the last inhabitants of the colonial era into the start of the territorial era of Indiana.

Northwest and Indiana Territory Name Lists: The Northwest Territory was created in 1787 and its first three counties of Hamilton, Knox, and Washington were created in 1790. Washington and Hamilton counties were within the land areas of present Ohio and the eastern half of present Michigan. The 1790 expansive bounds of Knox County, however, became the origin of Indiana, Illinois, Wisconsin, the western half of Michigan, and the part of Minnesota east of the Mississippi. But, only two small parts of Knox County had tracts of land ceded by the Indians in 1790. The entire 1790 non-Indian population, estimated at about 1,100 people, was centered around the Knox county seat of Vincennes, on the Wabash River; and Fort Steuben, on the Ohio River. Fort Steuben was the site of the present city of Jeffersonville, located directly across the Ohio River from Louisville, Kentucky. No federal census was taken in the 1790 Northwest Territory. Since territories did not have voting representatives in Congress, there was no need to apportion any seats. But Congress later decided that territories could benefit from census taking in other ways. From 1800 on, federal censuses were taken in all U.S. Territories – mainly as an aid to any territory in determining its population prior to becoming a state.

1800 Federal Census: Knox County, Indiana Territory's only county, was enumerated in the 1800 federal census, including small areas of present Wisconsin and Illinois. The total population was 2,632 people, but the original manuscripts containing the names of Indiana Territory's head of households were apparently lost. When the clerk of the federal district court for Indiana was asked in an 1830 law to return the original census schedules for 1800, 1810, and 1820 to Washington, DC, the Indiana clerk complied by sending the 1820 schedules only.

1807 Indiana Territory Census: This was the only census taken by Indiana Territory. A facsimile of the original manuscript was published by the Indiana Historical Society (IHS). In 1807, Indiana Territory included Dearborn, Clark, and Knox counties, plus St. Clair and Randolph counties of present Illinois. The 1807 Clark County census name list was missing, so the IHS added an 1807 voters list for Clark County, Indiana, and also for Kaskaskia (Randolph Co, IL).

1810 Federal Census: The 1810 Indiana Territory population of 24,320 people was within four counties: Clark, Dearborn, Knox, and Harrison. The 1810 federal census manuscripts for all four counties were lost. Any pre-1820 name lists from these four counties together cover a large portion of the territorial population and are identified in the bibliography that follows.

1820 Federal Census: The 1820 census was the first with surviving manuscripts for the state of Indiana. All but one county name list survives for 1820. The population of Indiana increased from 24,320 in 1810 to 147,178 people in 1820. See the IN 1820 map on page 90 and a note regarding two unorganized "counties" identified for the 1820 census only.

1830-1940 Federal Censuses. The federal censuses from 1830 through 1940 are all complete for all counties of Indiana, with the exception of the 1890 federal census, lost due to a fire in 1921 (for all states). The population of Indiana in 1830 was 343,031 people; and in 1940, 3,427,784 people.

1820-1931 Indiana State Censuses. Beginning in 1820 the state of Indiana began taking state censuses in various intervals, but few of these included name lists. Surviving original returns can be found at the Indiana State Library in Indianapolis for the following counties and years: Blackford (1857, 1871, 1877, 1883, & 1889); Henry (1919 & 1931); Ripley (1919); Starke (1919); and Washington (1901). Each of these name lists are included in the bibliography with more details, call numbers, etc.

Indiana State Digital Archives

This new service of the Indiana State Archives is a model project being developed on a multi-state basis, initiated, and sponsored by the Library of Congress. The project is administered by the lead agency of the Washington State Digital Archives. The new Indiana State Digital Archives already has several searchable databases online, with about 3 million names indexed. The databases include the following:
- **Death Records:**
  - Social Security Death Index
- **Institution Records:**
  - Women's Prison 1873-1969

- Boy's School 1867-1937
- Girl's School 1873-1935
- Prison North 1858-1897
- Prison North 1897-1966
- Prison South 1822-1897
- Indiana Life Prisoners
- Julia E. Work Training School
- School for the Deaf Admission Register
- Secretary of State Petitions
- Soldiers and Sailors Childrens Home
- Closed Nursing Schools (Database Pending)
- **Military Records:**
  - Book of Merit
  - Civil War
  - Early Military
  - Franklin County Auditor Military Service Verification – Civil War
  - Gold Star
  - Indiana Veterans Home
  - Mexican War Veterans
  - National Guard, 1898-1940
  - United Spanish War Veterans Membership Files
- **Miscellaneous Historical Records:**
  - Clark County Negro and Mulatto Register
  - Clark County Negro Register
  - Foster Children, 1892-1910
  - Franklin County Negro and Mulatto Register
  - Indiana Public Lands
  - Marion County Bar Association, 1822-1980
  - Marion County Court
  - Marion County Department of Public Safety
  - Marion County Wills
  - Orange County Department of Public Safety
  - Switzerland County Negro and Mulatto Register
  - Vigo County Negro and Mulatto Register
- **Naturalization Records.** Pending databases are in work for several Indiana counties.

Search the Records. The Indiana State Digital Archives home page starts with **Search the Digital Archives.** The search screen allows for 1) People Search, 2) Keyword Search, and 3) Detailed Search. For a People Search, choices are for Record Series (all or one), First Name, and/or Last Name. As an example, a search for just the surname Dollarhide brought up three Record Series: Military (4 results); Additional Historical Records (7 results); and Courts (15 results). The results list has the full name of the person, county name (or statewide) database, and whether an image is available. For the main Indiana State Digital Archives search screen, see **www.indianadigitalarchives.org**.

Indiana State Archives Online Collection Indexes

These databases were prepared and indexed online at the Indiana State Archives site before the State Digital Archives project was begun. For now, these special searchable databases are still available at the archives site: **www.in.gov/icpr/2355.htm**. The database titles listed below are also listed and described in more detail (by date) within the bibliography that follows.
- **Cultural Records:**
  - Indian Lands Noted on the LaPorte-Winamac Land Office (Table)
- **Military Records:**
  - Indiana Soldier's and Sailor's Children's Home
- **Court Records:**
  - State Supreme Court Cases
  - Posey County Circuit Court Records
- **Police/Criminal Records:**
  - Index to Life Prisoner's Statements: State Prison at Michigan City
- **Land Records:**
  - Land Office
  - The Indianapolis Donation
  - Hoosier Homestead Awards Database
  - Internal Improvements Projects: Contracts for Canal Structures, 1930's-1950's
- **History of Government Records**
  - Indianapolis-Marion County Employees
  - Governor Oliver P. Morton Telegraph Books

Online Databases at the Indiana State Library

These databases can be accessed at the Indiana State Library's webpage: **www.in.gov/library/databases.htm**. The following searchable databases are listed. Click on the title for more details:
- Howey Political Report 1994-2012
- Indiana Biography Index Published Before 1990
- Indiana Biography Index Published Since 1990
- Indiana Cemetery Locator Index
- Indiana Marriages 1993-2004
- Indiana Marriages Through 1850
- Indiana Memory
- Indiana World War II Servicemen
- Indianapolis Commercial Newspaper Death Listing Index
- Indianapolis Newspaper Index, 1848-1991 INSPIRE
- Logansport Newspaper Index, 1848-1855
- New Albany Newspaper Index, 1849-1889

- Online Family History Databases
- State Documents Checklist Database, 1990-2001
- USGS Topographic Quadrangle Map Database
- Vincennes Newspaper Index, 1804-1827
- VINE (Vital INformation Exchange)

Bibliography
Indiana Censuses & Substitutes

The bibliography below shows all published federal censuses for Indiana; plus unique statewide name lists, such as Territorial and State Census Records, State and County Court Records, Directories, State Military Lists (including Militia Rosters, Veteran Lists and/or Pensioner Lists), Tax Lists, Vital Records, and Voter Lists. Included as substitutes for the lost Indiana Territory censuses of 1800 and 1810 are published pre-1820 name lists for Indiana's first four counties (Clark, Dearborn, Knox, and Harrison). Other county-wide name lists are included if the database is available online.

1748-1993. Indiana, Select Marriages Index [Online Database], a FamilySearch database acquired by Ancestry.com with updates that include a few early marriages recorded at St. Francis Xavier Parish in French Vincennes. This database has 3,938,235 records, see www.ancestry.com/search/collections/60281.
- An earlier version of this database: *Indiana Marriages Index, 1780-1992 [Online Database],* indexed at FamilySearch.org website. Includes marriage records from the state of Indiana, taken from microfilm copies at the Family History Library in Salt Lake City. This database has 1,008,158 records. See www.familysearch.org/search/collection/1674830.

1773-1933. Indiana, Births and Christenings [Online Database]. indexed at FamilySearch.org. Includes name indexes to birth, baptism, and christening records from the state of Indiana, taken from microfilm copies at the Family History Library in Salt Lake City. This database has a few events taken from the parish registers of St. Francis Xavier Parish in French Vincennes. This database has 35,760 records. See www.familysearch.org/search/collection/1674814.
- For the Ancestry.com version, see www.ancestry.com/search/collections/60280.

1780-1850. Indiana State Library Genealogy Database: Marriages Through 1850 [Online Database]. To use the search screen, see www.statelib.lib.in.us/INMarriages1850/marriages_search.asp

1780-1975. Military Records, Lawrence County, Indiana [Online Database], indexed at the USGenWeb site for Lawrence Co IN. See www.ingenweb.org/inlawrence/military.htm.

1780s-2000s. Indiana Collection Catalog at MyHeritage.com [Online Database], 294 collections with 12,389,994 records specific to Indiana. Databases include censuses, directories, family histories, town histories, military rosters, college/school year books, and more. This is a subscription site, but all initial searches are free. A free search can be done for a name, place, year, or keyword. See www.myheritage.com/records/Indiana/all-records.

1780-2000s. Indiana US GenWeb Archives [Online Databases], name lists are available for all Indiana counties. Typical county records include Bibles, Biographies, Cemeteries, Censuses, Court, Death, Deeds, Directories, Histories, Marriages, Military, Newspapers, Obituaries, Photos, Schools, Tax Lists, Wills, and more. Links to all Indiana counties are located at the USGenWeb home page for Indiana. See http://usgwarchives.net/in/infiles.htm.

1783-1815 Knox County, Indiana, Early Land Records and Court Indexes [Printed Book], published by Genealogical Services and Publications, Chicago, IL, 1973, 2 vols. Contents: vol. 1: Locations entered at Vincennes, 1807-1813; Common Pleas, and county business, 1806-1810; estates; vol. 2: Lists of land donations; claims; militia donations; indexes. FHL book 977.239 R2 and R2k.

"*1787 Census, Post Vincennes, Knox County, Indiana*" [Printed Article], in *Sycamore Leaves* (Wabash Valley Genealogical Society, Terra Haute, IN), Vol. 15, No. 4 (Jun 1985).

1787 Enumeration of Males Currently Residing in the District of Poste Vincennes, 8 October 1787 [Online Database], indexed at the Genealogy Trails website. See http://genealogytrails.com/ind/knox/1787.html.

1790s-1825. Indiana Marriages, Early to 1825: A Research Tool [Printed Book], compiled, extracted & transcribed by Liahona Research, Inc.; edited by

Jordan R. Dodd and Norman L. Moyes, published by Precision Indexing, Bountiful, UT, 1991, 345 pages. Lists names of brides and grooms in alphabetical order by surname, with name of spouse, date of marriage, and county where married. See FHL book 977.2 V22i.

1780s-1991. *Soldiers and Veterans, Daviess County, Indiana* **[Online Database],** an index to county residents who served in the military, from the Revolutionary War to Desert Storm. Compiled for the USGenWeb site for Daviess Co IN. See http://www.ingenweb.org/indaviess/military.html.

1790-1829 Knox County, Indiana Deed Records **[Microfilm & Digital Capture]**, from the original records at the Knox County Courthouse, Vincennes, IN. Original deeds recorded 1790 to 1813 were destroyed in a courthouse fire, but many of the earlier deeds were brought in and recorded again soon after the fire in 1814. Filmed by the Record Registry Corp., Indianapolis, 1936, 2 rolls, FHL film #7768 (General Index to deeds) and FHL film #7769 (Deed records). To access the digital images, see the online FHL catalog page:
www.familysearch.org/search/catalog/1810523.

1798-1999. *Indiana, Wills and Probate Records* **[Online Database],** digitized and indexed by Ancestry from records in all Indiana counties. Probate records include wills, inventories, letters of administration, orphans, heirs, and details about an estate. This database has 456,004 records, see
www.ancestry.com/search/collections/9045.

1800s, *Index, Indiana Source Books* **[Printed Index]**, compiled by Dorothy Riker, published by the Indiana Historical Society, Family History Section, 1983, 406 pages. Contains an index to marriages, wills and naturalizations which appeared in the *Hoosier Genealogist* (1961-1979) and which have been compiled into three volumes, including more than 115,000 names. FHL book 977.2 D29h index.

1800s. *Surname Index to Roster of Soldiers and Patriots of the American Revolution Buried in Indiana, Vols. I & II* **[Typescript & Digital Version]**, compiled by Jane E. Darlington, typed by Linda Lauer. Published by the Fort Wayne Public Library, 1976, 140 pages, FHL book 977.2 M20 v.1-2 index. To access the digital version, see the online FHL catalog page:
https://familysearch.org/search/catalog/957313.

1800s-1900s. *Indiana Genealogy And Local History Sources Index* **[Printed Book],** by Stuart Harter. Contains a list of nearly seven thousand sources of genealogy and local history for the State of Indiana, including books, booklets, periodical articles, newspaper articles, etc. dealing with virtually every type of record useful to genealogy and local history. Published by CompuGen Systems, Ft. Wayne, IN, 1985, 195 pages, FHL book 977.2 D27h.

1800s-1900s. *Indiana Genealogical Society Ancestor File* **[Printed Book],** Vol. 1 compiled by Joan Morgan; Vol. 2 compiled by Karen Zach. Contains information compiled from 3x5 cards submitted by members of the society. Shows ancestor name and file number, birth place, spouse, Indiana county where settled, etc. Published by the society, Fort Wayne, IN, 1994-1997, 2 vols., 87 pages, FHL book 977.2 D22m v.1-2.

1800s-1900s. *Cemetery Locator File* **[Microfilm & Digital Capture],** from the originals compiled by the Indiana State Library, Indianapolis, IN. Consists of a card file alphabetically arranged by name of cemetery. Also indicates the county and township each cemetery is in. Filmed by the Genealogical Society of Utah, 1980, 4 rolls, beginning with FHL film #1292061 (Cemeteries A-Hi). To access the digital images, see the online FHL catalog page:
https://familysearch.org/search/catalog/197640.

1800s–1900s. *Cemetery Inscriptions, Indiana* **[Digital Capture],** compiled by Marc Young, a collection of handwritten cemetery transcriptions from small, abandoned cemeteries, mostly old family plots. Contents: Allen County cemeteries: Masonic, Notestine, Robinson Chapel; Carroll County cemeteries: Blizzard, Nearhoof; Cass County cemeteries: Grable Farm, Lake Cicott; De Kalb cemeteries: Dunn, Krafft, single grave (Lady Florence Link, d. Aug. 13, 1876), Stroh, Watson; Delaware County cemeteries: Ginn; Elkhart County cemeteries: Bell-Shutts, Bull, Cathcart, Cooper-Giesinger, Ivins, Middleton, Proctor/Heaton Baptist, Sailor; Hamilton County cemeteries: Paulsel; Hendricks County cemeteries: Nichols-Steetsman; Huntington County cemeteries: Arick, Furlo Beard, Lininger, Good, Rees; Jackson County cemeteries: New Hope; Koscuisko county cemeteries: Boydston, Circle, Clemmer-Fisher, Firestone, Garvin, Laing, Old Ulrey, Pendergast, Ross, Shock, single grave (William Cowan, d. Sept. 25, 1838), Stevens; La Grange County cemeteries: McCoy; La Porte County cemeteries: Coulter, Tuley;

Marion County cemeteries: Klepfer, Wright-Gentry; Miami County cemeteries: Barnhart, Brower, Butt, Clymer, Cole-Sayger-Gage, Finley, Garnard, Gettinger, Leedy, Moss, Shively, Shoemaker, Stepler, Tilden, Wilkinson, Yeich-Yich-Yike; Montgomery County cemeteries: Oliver; Noble County cemeteries: Broadway, Eagle Lake, Gragg, Hughes, Joe Ever's Farm, Kammerer, Lower-Lauer, Shobe, single stone (2 names - Secor), Stewart or Griesinger, Weston; Steuben County cemeteries: Carleton; Tippecanoe County cemeteries: First Mintonye, McCormick; Union county Cemeteries: Coe, Fosdick Farm, Ray Maddock Farm; Wabash County cemeteries: Gamble; Wells County cemeteries: Hosier, Jones, Linn, Miller; White County cemeteries: Alkire, Dilling, Flanigan, High, Rothrock II, Sheetz, Wolverton, Whitley County cemeteries: Bethel, Boggs, Jeffries, Rousseau-Pence, single grave (David Brown, d. April 17, 1895), Summit. To access the digital version, see the online FHL catalog page: **https://familysearch.org/search/catalog/1293740**.

1800s-1900s. ***Cemetery Records of Indiana*** **[Typescript & Digital Capture]**, copied and typed by members of the LDS Church in Indiana. Contains inscriptions arranged alphabetically by surname, from various cemeteries in many counties and cities of Indiana. Contents: Vol. 1: Bartholomew, Hamilton, Knox, Marion, Morgan, Owen, Saint Joseph, Vigo, and Wells counties; Vol. 2: Allen, Marion, and Montgomery counties; Vol. 3: Decatur, Elkhart, Fulton, Johnson, Marion, and Miami counties; Vol. 4: Blackford, Delaware, Fayette, Hancock, Hendricks, Marion, Monroe, Morgan, Rush, and Shelby counties; Vol. 5: Blackford, Delaware, Henry, Howard, and Wabash counties; Vol. 6: Decatur, Delaware, Hendricks, Henry, Marion, Morgan, and Shelby counties. Published 1954, 6 vols., FHL book 977.2 V39c v.1-6. Also on microfilm, FHL film #873781. To access the digital images, see the online FHL catalog page: **www.familysearch.org/search/catalog/158846**.

1800s-1900s. ***Index to Encyclopedia of American Quaker Genealogy*** **[Printed Book],** an index to the 600,000 names found in the six volumes by William Wade Hinshaw covering the records of the monthly Quaker meetings held in the states of Virginia, North Carolina, New Jersey, Pennsylvania, New York, Ohio, and Indiana. Many of Indiana's early Quaker communities were founded by people moving into the area from North Carolina meetings, and the Quaker monthly meeting records usually give details about the movement of members from one meeting to another. Quakers did not believe in civil recording of vital records, and any Quaker member of any Indiana meeting will have multiple mentions for birth, parents, marriage, death, and burial. This comprehensive index shows the name, volume, and page where to look. Published by Genealogical Publishing Co., Baltimore, 1999, 1,155 pages, FHL book 973.D2he index.

- See also, ***U.S., Encyclopedia of American Quaker Genealogy, Vol I–VI, 1607-1943*** **[Online Database],** all six volumes, digitized and indexed at Ancestry.com. See **www.ancestry.com/search/collections/3753**.

- See also, ***Indiana, Selected Quaker Meeting Directories, 1836-1921*** **[Online Database],** digitized and indexed at Ancestry.com. Contains lists of members from Indianapolis Meeting (Indianapolis, Marion Co.), Whitewater Meeting (Richmond, Wayne Co.), Walnut Ridge Meeting (Carthage, Rush Co.), and Knightstown Meeting (Knightstown, Henry Co.), as well as the yearly meeting for Indiana, 1889. See **www.ancestry.com/search/collections/8211**.

1800-1941. ***Indiana Vital Records Deaths Index*** **[CD-ROM]**, published by Heritage Quest, Bountiful, UT, 2001. Includes 867,132 entries covering the period of 1800-1941, along with a few entries outside that range of years. Each entry gives details on surname, given name, sex, ethnicity, age, death month, death day, death year, county, book, page, and fiche. FHL CD No. 1188.

1800-1941. ***Indiana, Marriage Index*** **[Online Database],** Indexed at Ancestry.com. Original data: 1) Works Progress Administration, comp. Index to Marriage Records Indiana: Indiana Works Progress Administration, 1938-1940; 2) Jordan Dodd, Liahona Research, comp. Electronic transcription of marriage records held by the individual counties in Indiana. Many of these records are on microfilm at the Family History Library in Salt Lake City, Utah. This database has 3,245,823 records, see **www.ancestry.com/search/collections/5059**.

1800-2010. ***Indiana and Michigan, Michiana Genealogical Cemetery Index*** **[Online Database],** indexed at Ancestry.com. Source: MGI Cemeteries:. South Bend Area Genealogical Society. This database has 187,743 records, see **www.ancestry.com/search/collections/70492**.

- This database is also available at the source, see **www.sbags.org/michgenidx2.htm**.

1801-1818. *Estray Book, Clark County, Indiana* **[Microfilm & Digital Capture],** from the original at the Clark County Recorder's office, Jeffersonville, IN. Filmed by the Indiana Exchange, 1968, 1 roll, FHL film #549320. To access the digital images, see the online FHL catalog page:
www.familysearch.org/search/catalog/131699.

1801-1820. *Indiana Territorial Pioneer Records* **[Printed Book],** compiled by Charles M. Franklin, published by Heritage House, 1983, 2 vols., 99 pages. Includes index. Contains miscellaneous records of election returns, military records, census returns, births, history, etc. Contents: v. 1. 1810-1815 -- v. 2. 1801-1820. FHL book 977.2 N4i vol. 1 & 2.

1801-1877. *Indiana Land Entries* **[Printed Book],** by Margaret R. Waters, originally published Indianapolis, 1948, reprinted by The Bookmark, Knightstown, IN, 1977, 2 vols. Lists names of persons who obtained (from the federal government) an original entry of land in Indiana. Contents: v. 1, Cincinnati District, 1801-1840; v. 2, Vincennes District, 1807-1877. FHL book 977.2 R2W.

1801-1899. *The Hoosier Journal of Ancestry, Clark County Special* **[Printed Book],** published by the *Hoosier Journal*, Little York, IN, 1983-1992, 2 vols., includes indexes. Contains various records of genealogical value, including township histories, marriages, probate records, census records, land records, biographies, etc., gathered from many sources in Clark County. FHL book 977.2185 B2hj vol. 1 & 2.

1801-1901 *Deed Records; Grantee/Grantor Index to Deeds, Clark County, Indiana* **[Microfilm & Digital Capture],** from records located in the Clark County Recorder's Office, Jeffersonville, IN. Filmed by the Genealogical Society of Utah, 1985, 38 rolls, beginning with FHL film #1428648 (Grantor Index, A-R, 1801-1850). To access the digital images, see the online FHL catalog page:
https://familysearch.org/search/catalog/622392.

1801-1938. *Clark County, Indiana, Index of Names of Persons and of Firms* **[Microfilm & Digital Version],** from the original book compiled by the WPA of Indiana, 1938, 319 pages. Contains an index of the names of persons and firms contained in county histories, atlases, gazetteers, and miscellaneous publications. Filmed by the Genealogical Society of Utah, 1985, 1 roll, FHL film #1428705. For a link to a digital version, see the FHL catalog page:
https://familysearch.org/search/catalog/622743.

"1802 Taxable Property, Knox County, Indiana" **[Printed Article],** in *Northwest Trail Tracer* (Northwest Territorial Genealogical Society, Vincennes, IN), Vol. 10, No. 2 (Jun 1989) through Vol. 10, No. 4 (Dec 1989).

1802, 1809 Voters, Clark County, Indiana, **[Microfilm & Digital Capture],** from a typescript located in the Jeffersonville Township Library, Jeffersonville, IN. Contains lists of voters compiled from the *National Genealogical Society Quarterly*, vol. 3, # 4, and from the *Hoosier Genealogist*, v. 2 (Mar/Apr 1961). Filmed by the Genealogical Society of Utah, 1985, 1 roll, FHL film #1428704. To access the digital images, see the online FHL catalog page:
www.familysearch.org/search/catalog/622540.

1802-1892. *Indiana, Compiled Marriages* **[Online Database],** indexed at Ancestry.com. Source: Jordan Dodd, Liahona Research. Each index record includes Name, Spouse's name, Marriage date, Location, and Source. This database has 199,807 records, see
www.ancestry.com/search/collections/7852.

1805-1830 Deed Records, Index to Deeds, 1805-1936, Dearborn County, Indiana, **[Microfilm & Digital Capture]** from the original records at the Dearborn County courthouse, Lawrenceburg, Indiana. Filmed by the Indiana State Library, 1936, 5 rolls, beginning with FHL film #209865 (Deed index, A-B, 1805-1936). To access the digital images, see the online FHL catalog page: https://familysearch.org/search/catalog/10794.

1806-1813. *Knox County, Indiana Early Land Records, Court Indexes* **[Printed Book],** by June B. Barekman and Roberta Lee Lent. Contents: Vol. 1: Locations entered at Vincennes, 1807-1813; Common Pleas, and county business, 1806-1810 estates; Vol. 2: lists of land donations; claims; militia donations; indexes. Includes index. Published by the Allen County Public Library, Ft. Wayne, IN, 1986, 2 vols., FHL book 977.239 R2b v.1-2.

1806-1833 Marriages, Dearborn County, Indiana **[Printed Book & Microfiche],** compiled by Colleen Ridlen, published Beech Grove, IN, 1989, 44 pages. Contains an index to marriages in Dearborn County, giving names of brides and grooms, name of spouse, and date of marriage. FHL book 977.211 V22r, and FHL film #6088449.

1806-1861. *Indiana, Marriage Index* **[Online Database]**, indexed at Ancestry.com. Source: Indiana State Library. Each index record includes Name, Marriage date, Marriage place, Spouse, and URL. This database has 317,373 records, see
www.ancestry.com/search/collections/9760.

1807 Indiana Territory Census **[Printed Book & Microfilm]**, facsimile of the original manuscript, published by the Indiana Historical Society, Indianapolis, 1980, 57 pages. Includes surname index. In 1807, Indiana Territory included Dearborn, Clark, and Knox counties, plus St. Clair and Randolph counties of Illinois. The 1807 Clark County census name list was missing, so the IHS added an 1807 voters list for Clark County, Indiana, and also for Kaskaskia (Randolph Co, IL). FHL book 977.2 X2c and FHL film #1033927. Another filming, FHL film #1428705. To see if this microfilm has been digitized yet, see the FHL catalog page:
www.familysearch.org/search/catalog/270021.

1807. *Indiana 1807 Census Index* **[Printed Index]**, compiled by Ronald Vern Jackson, et al, published by Accelerated Indexing Systems International, North Salt Lake, UT, 1986, 56 pages, FHL book 977.2 X22j.

1807. *Index to Clark County, Indiana Territory Census, 1807* **[Microfilm & Digital Capture]**, of a typescript located in the Jeffersonville Township Library, Jeffersonville, Indiana. Filmed by the Genealogical Society of Utah, 1985, 1 roll, FHL film #1428704. To access the digital images, see the online FHL catalog page:
www.familysearch.org/search/catalog/622583.

1807 Indiana Territory Census, Dearborn County, Indiana **[Online Database]**. Indiana Territory in 1807 had three counties in present Indiana and two counties in present Illinois. Knox, Clark, and Dearborn were the three Indiana counties. Dearborn County in 1807 included an area from Ft. Recovery, Ohio, southwest to Madison, Indiana. The area of old Dearborn today includes all or part of current Wayne, Franklin, Union, Fayette, Dearborn, Ohio, Rush, and Switzerland counties. This database was indexed at the USGenWeb site for Franklin Co IN. See
www.ingenweb.org/infranklin/pages/census/1807main.html.

"1807 Landowners Unpaid Taxes, Clark County, Indiana" [Printed Article], in *Southern Indiana Genealogical Society Quarterly* (So. Indiana Gen. Soc., New Albany, IN), Vol. 7, No. 4 (Oct 1986).

"1807 Census, Knox County, Indiana" [Printed Article], in *Sullivan County Historical Society Newsletter*, Sullivan Co Hist. Soc., Sullivan, IN), Vol. 8, No. 3 (May 1981) through Vol. 8, No. 6 (Nov 1981).

1807-1820 Land Entries, Martin County, Indiana **[Online Database]**, indexed at the USGenWeb site for Martin Co IN. See
http://files.usgwarchives.net/in/martin/1868/land/1868/land.txt.

1807-1832. *Early Marriages in Indiana, Knox County* **[Printed Book]**, by Kenneth Gene Lindsay, published by Kenma Pub., Evansville, IN, 1977, 60 pages, FHL book 977.239 V2L.

1807-1840. *Marriage Records of Knox County, Indiana* **[Printed Book & Digital Version]**, copied from the originals by Mary R. Hibel and M. Joanne Coan. Contains an alphabetical listing by surname of men, and of women showing to whom they were married and date of marriage. Published by M.R. Hibel, Vincennes, IN, 1964, 134 pages, FHL book 977.239 V2h. For a link to a digital version, see the FHL catalog page: https://familysearch.org/search/catalog/565857.

1807-1841. *Tract Book, Lands Sold, Harrison County, Indiana* **[Microfilm & Digital Capture]**, from the original at the Harrison County Recorder's Office, Corydon, IN. Filmed by the Indiana Exchange, 1968, 1 roll, FHL film #549372. To access the digital images, see the online FHL catalog page:
www.familysearch.org/search/catalog/463337.

1807-1960. *Marriage Records, Knox County, Indiana* **[Microfilm & Digital Capture]**, from the original Circuit Court marriage volumes located at the Knox County Courthouse in Vincennes, IN. Each volume indexed. Filmed by the Genealogical Society of Utah, 2009, 26 rolls, beginning with FHL film #1149418 (Marriages, 1807-1832). To access the digital images, see the online FHL catalog page:
https://familysearch.org/search/catalog/1780486.

"1808 Tax Sale, Knox County, Indiana" [Printed Article], in *Northwest Trail Tracer* (Northwest Territorial Genealogical Society of Knox County, Indiana, Vincennes, IN), Vol. 6, No. 2 (Jun 1985).

1808-1817. *Estray Book, Harrison County, Indiana* [Microfilm & Digital Capture], from the original at the Harrison County Recorder's Office, Corydon, IN Filmed by the Indiana Exchange, 1968, 1 roll, FHL film #549372. To access the digital images, see the online FHL catalog page:
www.familysearch.org/search/catalog/155742.

1809, 1812. *Indiana Election Returns* [Printed Book], compiled by John D. & Diane Stemmons. Published by Census Pub. LC, Sandy, UT, 2004, 278 pages. FHL book 977.2 N4s.

1808-1818. *Jeffersonville Land Entries* [Printed Book], compiled by Janet C. Cowen. Entries are arranged both alphabetically by surname and in numerical order. Contains an index to entries in the original land office records. Includes the counties of Bartholomew, Brown, Clark, Crawford, Decatur, Floyd, Harrison, Jackson, Jefferson, Jennings, Lawrence, Monroe, Orange, Ripley, Scott, Switzerland, and Washington counties. Published by J.C. Cowen, Indianapolis, 1984, 200 pages, FHL book 977.2 R2c.

1809-1886 *Deed Records; Grantee-Grantor Index to Deeds, 1809-1888, Harrison County, Indiana* [Microfilm & Digital Capture], from the original records located at the Harrison County Courthouse, Corydon, Indiana. Filmed by the Genealogical Society of Utah, 1984, 28 rolls, beginning with FHL film #1404902 (Grantee Index, 1809-1863). To access the digital images, see the online FHL catalog page:
https://familysearch.org/search/catalog/470691.

1809-1923. *Will Records, Harrison County, Indiana* [Microfilm & Digital Capture], from the original records at the Harrison County Courthouse, Corydon, IN. Filmed by the Genealogical Society of Utah, 1984, 4 rolls, beginning with FHL film #1404686 (Will records 1809-1832). To access the digital images, see the online FHL catalog page:
https://familysearch.org/search/catalog/90532.

1810-1813. *Early Records of Harrison County, Indiana* [Microfilm], of original manuscript compiled by Walter S. Beanblossom, published 1975. Includes index. Contains the 1810 census and the 1813 tax list of Harrison Co., Indiana. Filmed by the Genealogical Society of Utah, 1976, 1 roll, FHL film #928263. To see if this microfilm has been digitized yet, see the FHL catalog page:
www.familysearch.org/search/catalog/322520.

1810-1920. *Records of Harrison County, Indiana, from Walter Beanblossom's Collection, and Reprints From the "Ancestral News"* [Printed Book], compiled by Sherry Healy for the Ancestral Trails Historical Society, Inc., Vine Grove, KY, published by McDowell Publications, Utica, KY, 150 pages; Includes surname index. Contains abstracts from 1810 census records, tax lists of 1812-1813, voter lists of 1818, mortality schedule for 1850, naturalizations of 1841-1846, and 1855-1920, citizenships for 1852, Indiana Legion (organization of companies with lists of officers and soldiers), short histories of townships, and first marriage records of Harrison County. FHL book 977.221 H2h.

1810-1918 *Probate Records, Harrison County, Indiana* [Microfilm & Digital Capture], from the original Circuit Court records located at the Harrison County Courthouse, Corydon, IN. Includes surname indexes. Filmed by the Genealogical Society of Utah, 1984, 25 rolls, beginning with FHL film #1404691 (Index, 1810-1923). To access the digital images, see the online FHL catalog page:
https://familysearch.org/search/catalog/91332.

"1811 - Indiana's First Tax List" [Printed Article], in *American Monthly Magazine*, Vol. 87, No. 5 (May 1953); and as "Taxpayers, 1811," in *Hoosier Genealogist*, Vol. 11, No. 3 (Jul 1971); and *Genealogist*, Vol. 10 (Feb 1972).

1811-1883. *Early Land Entries, Orange County, Indiana* [Online Database], indexed at the USGenWeb site for Orange Co IN. Separate databases for each township. See
http://files.usgwarchives.net/in/orange/land/.

1811-2007. *Indiana Marriages* [Online Database], indexed at FamilySearch.org. Indexed in partnership with the Indiana Genealogical Society. Includes a groom and bride name index to marriages recorded in Indiana Territory and state of Indiana between 1811 and 2007. This collection includes searchable index data for marriage returns and licenses. This database has 1,259,299 images. See
www.familysearch.org/search/collection/1410397.
- See Also, *Indiana, Marriages, 1810-2011* [Online Database], from FamilySearch.org, indexed at Ancestry.com. This database has 11,898,007 records, see **www.ancestry.com/search/collections/60282**.

1812 Sheriff Tax Sale, Franklin County, Indiana **[Online Database]**, indexed at the USGenWeb site for Franklin Co IN. See www.ingenweb.org/infranklin/pages/census/1812sale.html.

1812. *Voters in Dearborn County, Indiana Territory (August 3, 1812)* **[Digital Version]**, from an article in *The Genealogist* (R. Bakehorn), (1971-1972). To access the digital version, see the online FHL catalog page: www.familysearch.org/search/catalog/2565849.

1812-2015. *Grant County, Indiana, Marion Public Library Death Index* **[Online Database]**, indexed at Ancestry.com. Source: Genealogy database, Marion Public Library, Marion, IN. Each index record includes: Name, Publication date, Publication place, Publication title, Notes, Record type, and URL. This database has 570,815 records, see www.ancestry.com/search/collections/9242.

1813 Tax List, Franklin County, Indiana **[Online Database]**, indexed at the USGenWeb site for Franklin Co IN. See www.ingenweb.org/infranklin/pages/census/1813taxfc.html.

1814-1824 Probate Order Book, Switzerland County, Indiana **[Online Database]**, indexed at the MyIndianaHome site. See www.ingenweb.org/inswitzer/wills/probateBook1-1814-1824.html.

1815-1855. *Posey County Circuit Court Historical Record* **[Online Database]**, digitized and indexed at the Indiana State Archives website. The Indiana State Archives holds the earliest records of the Posey County Circuit Court. The collection includes such documents as writs, summons and subpoenas, transcripts, declarations, depositions, deposition notices, certificates, cost bills, statements, affidavits, and verdicts which pertain to the litigation between early Posey County residents. The bulk of the collection dates from 1815 to 1855, with the majority of the documents created between the early 1820's and the late 1840's. There are approximately 1,200 individual court cases represented in the collection, with anywhere from one to twenty-one documents in each file. See www.in.gov/iara/2744.htm.

1815-1860. *Knox County, Indiana, Divorce Records* **[Printed Book]**, compiled by Brian Spangle. Contains an index to divorce records, arranged in alphabetical order by surname of plaintiff, giving name of spouse, year when filed, code to original record (circuit court order book, Knox County court files or common pleas order book), volume and page numbers, box and file numbers. Cases were filed between 1815 and 1860. Publisher info not given, published 1996, 14 pages, FHL book 977.239 V22s.

1815-1817. Knox County, Indiana, Index to Deed Record, A, 1815-1817 [Typescript & Digital Version], compiled by Roberta Lee Lent and June B. Barekman, 24 pages, FHL book 977.239 R2L. To access the digital version, see the online FHL catalog page: https://familysearch.org/search/catalog/167578.

1816 Indiana Territory Post Offices **[Online Database]**, index of post office, postmaster, and place of birth of postmaster, at the USGenWeb site for Indiana. See http://files.usgwarchives.net/in/post-off.txt.

"1816 Tax Levy, Harrison County, Indiana" [Printed Article], in *Hoosier Genealogist* (Indiana Historical Society, Indianapolis, IN), Vol. 1, No. 1 (Jan 1973).

1816-1884. *Mortality Records, Knox County, Indiana* **[Microfilm & Digital Capture]**, from the original manuscript prepared by the DAR, Francis Vigo Chapter, Vincennes, IN, 1946, 42 pages. Filmed by the Genealogical Society of Utah, 1970, 1 roll, FHL film #849926. To access the digital images, see the online FHL catalog page: www.familysearch.org/search/catalog/297993.

1817-1877. *Supreme Court Case Records* **[Online Database]**, digitized and indexed at the Indiana State Archives website. This database contains basic information about historic Indiana Supreme Court cases from 1817 to approximately 1877. You may use this search form to find cases of interest, and if you would like to examine the documents archived from any case, record the "box number" for the case and contact the State Archives. Some records will require conservation. An archivist will retrieve the record and determine if conservation work needs to be completed before viewing. See www.in.gov/iara/2813.htm.

1817-1900s. *Biographies and Obituaries, Daviess County, Indiana* **[Online Database]**, indexed by the USGenWeb site for Daviess Co IN. See www.ingenweb.org/indaviess/bio.html.

1817-1975. *Indiana Newspaper Archives* **[Online Database]**, digitized and indexed at the GenealogyBank.com website. This database includes historical newspapers from Brookville, East Chicago, Elkhart, Evansville, Fort Wayne, Indiana Harbour, Indianapolis, Logansport, New Albany, South Bend, Terre Haute, and Vincennes, Indiana. See www.genealogybank.com/gbnk/newspapers/explore/USA/Indiana/.

1819-1849. *Index to Probates Before 1850, Owen County, Indiana* **[Online Database]**, indexed in groups at the Sweet Owen website. See www.sweetowen.net/.

1820 Federal Census for Indiana **[Printed Extract, Index & Digital Version],** compiled by Willard Heiss. Published by the Indiana Historical Society, Indianapolis, IN, 1966, 461 pages, FHL book 977.2 X2he. For access to a digital version of this book, see the online FHL catalog page:
https://familysearch.org/search/catalog/158855.

1820. *Indiana 1820 Census Index* **[Printed Book & Digital Version]**, edited by Ronald Vern Jackson, et al, published by Accelerated Indexing Systems, 1976, 58 pages, FHL book 977.2 X2p 1820. For a link to a digital version, see the FHL catalog page for this title:
https://familysearch.org/search/catalog/167206.

1820. *The Indiana 1820 Enumeration of Males* **[Printed Book]**, compiled by Mary M. Morgan, published by the Indiana Historical Society, Family History Section, 1988, 173 pages. FHL book 977.2 X2m.

1820s-1830s. *Early Land Entries, Union County, Indiana* **[Online Database]**, indexed at the USGenWeb site for Union Co IN. See
http://files.usgwarchives.net/in/union/land/land-rec.txt.

1820-1835. *Early Landowners, Decatur County, Indiana* **[Printed Book],** by Maurice Holmes, publ. Ye Olde Genealogie Shoppe, Indianapolis, c2000, 50 pages. See
www.familysearch.org/search/catalog/2478011.

1820-1840. *Indiana, 1820 through 1840 Federal Census; Population Schedules* **[Microfilm & Digital Capture],** from the originals at the National Archives, Washington, DC. 1820, 1830, and 1840 censuses were filmed together as one microfilm series by the National Archives, 1938-1960, 21 rolls, beginning with FHL film #205607 (Indiana 1820, Dearborn, Floyd, Franklin, Gibson, Jackson, Jefferson, Pike, Posey, and Randolph counties). For a complete list of roll numbers and contents of each roll, see the online FHL catalog page for this title. See
https://familysearch.org/search/catalog/745488.

1820s–1990s. *Indiana Land Records* **[Online Database].** These titles are listed under "Land Records" at the Indiana State Archives website. See www.in.gov/iara/2355.htm. Databases included:
- **Land Office.** An index to the General Land Office entries, no dates.
- **The Indianapolis Donation.** Details regarding the donation of lands by the federal government to the new state of Indiana for the purpose of a state capital.
- **Hoosier Homestead Awards Database.** A program that recognizes farms that have been owned by the same family for one hundred years or more. This database lists the names of awarded parties from 1976 to 1994.

1820s-1850s. *Original Land Entries, Ohio County, Indiana* **[Online Database]**, indexed at the USGenWeb site for Ohio Co IN. See
http://files.usgwarchives.net/in/ohio/cemetery/land/1868/land-rec.txt.

1820s-1850s. *Original Land Entries, Morgan County, Indiana* **[Online Database]**, indexed at the USGenWeb site for Morgan Co IN. See
http://files.usgwarchives.net/in/morgan/land/.

1820s-1850s. *Original Land Entries, Scott County, Indiana* **[Online Database]**, indexed at the RootsWeb site for Scott Co IN. See
www.rootsweb.ancestry.com/~inscott/ScottLand.html.

1820s-1850s. *Original Land Entries, Rush County, Indiana* **[Online Database]**, indexed at the USGenWeb site for Rush Co IN. See
www.ingenweb.org/inrush/history1.html.

1820s-1850s. *Original Land Entries, Switzerland County, Indiana* **[Online Database]**, indexed at the USGenWeb site for Switzerland Co IN.
http://files.usgwarchives.net/in/switz/land/land-rec.txt.

1820s-1870s. *Will Books, Orange County, Indiana* **[Online Database]**, indexed at the USGenWeb site for Orange Co IN. See
http://files.usgwarchives.net/in/orange/wills/.

1820s-1930s. *Indiana Biographical Index* **[Microfiche]**, compiled by Lyman Platt and Jimmy Parker, microfiche of original typescript published by Genealogical Indexing Associates, Salt Lake City,

1983. This is an updated name index to biographical sketches in virtually all published Indiana county histories, which began as a WPA project in 1938, and was continued by the Indiana Historical Society in 1979. Earlier version: *Index to Persons and Firms*, which, along with all of the county histories referenced, can be found at the Indiana State Library in Indianapolis; the Allen County Public Library in Fort Wayne; or the Family History Library in Salt Lake City. Filmed by the Genealogical Society of Utah, 1984, 16 microfiche, FHL fiche #6331353.

"1821 Tax List, Bartholomew County, Indiana" [Printed Article], in *Hoosier Journal of Ancestry* (Naomi Keith Sexton, Little York, IN), Vol. 5, No. 1 (Jan 1978).

1821 Tax List, Bartholomew County, Indiana [Online Database], indexed at the USGenWeb site for Bartholomew Co See http://files.usgwarchives.net/in/bartholomew/land/1821tax.txt.

1821 Settlers, Shelby County, Indiana [Online Database], indexed at the Shelby County website. See www.shelbycountyindiana.org/historical_articles/history_earliest_settlers.htm.

1821-1906. *Marion County, Indiana Records Miscellanea* [Printed Book[, compiled by Jane E. Darlington. Includes surname index. Contains abstracts of: naturalizations filed 1832-1903; naturalizations filed 1904-1906; delinquent tax returns for 1842; Probate Court record A, 1822-1832; land records 1821-1824; tract book 1821-1851; hack licenses 1865-1871. Published by the Indiana Historical Society, Family History Section, Indianapolis, 1986, FHL book 977.252 P4d.

"1822 Poll Tax List, Lawrence County, Indiana" [Printed Article], in *Seedling Patch* (Lawrence County Historical & Genealogical Society, Bedford, IN), Vol. 3 (1983).

1822-1849. *Marriages and Deaths From Indianapolis Newspapers* [Printed Book & CD-ROM], compiled by Ron Darrah from information in three Indianapolis newspapers. Printed volume: 1822-1829; 2 CD volumes: 1830-1839 & 1840-1849. Also includes abstracts of divorce and probate notices. Published by the Genealogical Society of Marion County, Indiana, Indianapolis, 2001. FHL book 977.252/I1 B38d, FHL CD No. 6982 (1830-1839) and CD No. 6982 (1840-1849).

1822-1876. *History of Shelby County, Indiana* [Online Database], full text and index located at the Shelby Co History website. See www.shelbycountyindiana.org/historical_articles/history_1876.htm.

1822-1895 Coffee Creek Baptist Church Records, Jennings County, Indiana [Online Database], includes minutes, marriages, obituaries, and more. Indexed at the RootsWeb site for Jennings Co IN. See http://freepages.genealogy.rootsweb.ancestry.com/~fgww/.

1822-1940 Probate Index, Montgomery County, Indiana [Online Database], part of the Crawfordsville District Public Library Local History Database. See www.cdpl.lib.in.us/lh/probate/probate.pdf.

1823-1847. *Will Abstracts, Switzerland County, Indiana* [Online Database], indexed at the MyIndianaHome site. See http://myindianahome.net/gen/switz/records/wills/will1.html.

1823-1852 Ft. Wayne Land Office Entries [Printed Index], transcribed from the original tract books at the Indiana State Archives, Indianapolis. Tract books transcribed by Barbara S. Wolfe; data compiled by Helen S. Morrison, published by the State Archives, 199?, 138 pages. Contains an alphabetical listing by surname prepared by the Indiana State Archives of individual names of persons who purchased land in the areas now covered by the counties of Adams, Allen, Blackford, Cass, Clinton, DeKalb, Delaware, Grant, Howard, Huntington, Jay, Kosciusko, Lagrange, Madison, Miami, Noble, Randolph, Steuben, Tipton, Wabash, Wells and Whitley. This index serves a computerized database of 73,250 records that can be accessed at the Indiana State Archives in Indianapolis. See FHL book 977.2 R22f.

1824-1848. *Indiana Tax Lists* [Printed Book], compiled by Jane E. Darlington, pub. 1990, 2 vols. Includes surname indexes. Arranged by county and townships, and lists name, poll, acres, section, township, and range. Contents: v. 1: Bartholomew Co., 1843, Dearborn Co., 1842, Fayette Co., 1842, Greene Co., 1843, Harrison Co., 1844, Marshall Co., 1843 (with Starke Co.), Morgan Co., 1840, Noble Co., 1847, Perry Co., 1835, and 1824-1826, 1828, 1829, 1832,

1836-1837, 1840-1843, 1845, Scott Co., 1839; v. 2: Posey Co., 1842, Putnam Co., 1845, Spencer Co., 1846, Tippecanoe Co., 1848, Switzerland Co., 1843, Vigo Co., 1824-1828, Whitley Co., 1841. FHL book 977.2 R4d v. 1 & 2.

1825-1874 Guardian's Docket, Montgomery County, Indiana [Online Database], part of the Crawfordsville District Public Library Local History Database, see **http://history.cdpl.lib.in.us/guardian.html**.

1826-1839 Naturalization Records, Franklin County, Indiana **[Online Database]**, indexed at the USGenWeb site for Franklin Co IN. See **www.ingenweb.org/infranklin/pages/tier2/Naturalize1.html**.

1827 Complete Residential and Business Directory, Jay County, Indiana **[Online Database]**, indexed at the Distant Cousin site. See **http://distantcousin.com/Directories/IN/JayCty/1927/**.

1827 Jefferson County Tax Assessment **[Online Database]**, indexed at the Jefferson County Local History website. See **www.jeffersoncountylocalhistory.org/landtax1827jeffcotaxass**.

1828 Voter List, Republican Township, Jefferson County, Indiana **[Online Database]**, indexed at the USGenWeb site for Jefferson Co IN. See **www.ingenweb.org/injefferson/jeffvoterlist.html**.

1828-1850. *Marriages, Carroll County, Indiana* **[Online Database]**, originally indexed at the Carroll County Historical Museum website. Now archived. See **https://archive.org/details/carrollcountyind00slev**.
- See Also **Indiana, Civil Marriages, 1828-1957 [Online Database]**, index to select marriages from Carroll and Pike counties, see **www.familysearch.org/search/catalog/2469545**.

"1829 Taxpayers, Fayette County, Indiana" [Printed Article], in *Hoosier Genealogist* (Indiana Historical Society, Indianapolis, IN), Vol. 11, No. 4 (Oct 1971).

"1829 Assessment Rolls of Taxable Persons & Property, Marion County, Indiana" [Printed Article], in *Hoosier Genealogist* (Indiana Historical Society, Indianapolis, IN), Vol. 20, No. 2 (Jun 1980).

1830. *Index, 1830 Federal Population Census for Indiana* **[Microfilm]**, compiled under the supervision of Leona (Tobey) Alig, Genealogy Division, Indiana State Library. Filmed by the Indiana Historical Society, 1990, 3 microfiche, FHL fiche #6334294.

1830. Indiana 1830 Census Index [CD-ROM], compiled and published by Heritage Quest, 1999, FHL CD No. 4386.

1830. *Indiana 1830 Census Index* **[Printed Index]**, edited by Ronald Vern Jackson, et al, published by Accelerated Indexing Systems, Bountiful, UT, 1978, 137 pages, FHL book 977.2 X2p 1830.

1830s. *Tract Book, Blackford County, Indiana* **[Online Database],** indexed at the USGenWeb site for Blackford Co IN. See **http://files.usgwarchives.net/in/blackford/land/tract-bk.txte**

1830s-1840s. *Early Land Entries, Randolph County, Indiana* **[Online Database]**, indexed at the USGenWeb site for Randolph Co IN. See **http://files.usgwarchives.net/in/randolph/land/land-rec.txt**.

1830s-1930s. *Saint Joseph County Graves Registration Project* **[Online Database]**, an index to all males buried in the county who served in the military and died before 1938. Indexed at the RootsWeb site for the South Bend Area Genealogical Society, Mishawaka-Penn-Harris Public Library, Mishawaka, IN. See **www.rootsweb.ancestry.com/~insbags/grave.htm**.

1833-1855. *LaPorte-Winamac Land Office Entries* **[Online Database]**. The "land office business" in Indiana began in 1801, when public lands in the southeastern corner of the Indiana Territory were put up for sale at Cincinnati. The U.S. Congress subsequently opened land offices at Vincennes in 1804; at Jeffersonville in 1807; in 1819 at Terre Haute (later Crawfordsville) and Brookville (later Indianapolis); and at Ft. Wayne in 1822. An additional land office opened at LaPorte in 1833; six years later, the office was moved to Winamac. The LaPorte-Winamac District embraced all or part of the present counties of Benton, Carroll, Cass, Elkhart, Fulton, Howard, Jasper, Kosciusko, Lake, LaPorte, Marshall, Miami, Newton, Porter, Pulaski, St. Joseph, Starke, Wabash, and White. The first sale of land in the new district took place on 12 August 1833. After the LaPorte-Winamac Land Office closed on 31 January 1855, responsibility for unsold lands was transferred to the Indianapolis Land Office. When that closed, all records were transferred

to the State Auditor and from there to the Indiana State Archives. These land office records comprise the most detailed history available of the settlement of 19 counties, providing the names and residences of the purchaser; the date of purchase; and the legal description of the tract. All this information is now on a computerized database of 48,562 records, each structured in 12 fields documenting the details of a land sale. This searchable database is located at the Indiana State Archives website. See
www.in.gov/iara/2605.htm.

1830-1971. *Index to Saint Joseph County Wills* **[Online Database]**, indexed at the RootsWeb site for the South Bend Area Genealogical Society, Mishawaka-Penn-Harris Public Library, Mishawaka, IN. See
www.rootsweb.ancestry.com/~insbags/wills.htm.

1833-1867. *Original Land Owners, Marshall County, Indiana* **[Online Database]**, indexed at the RootsWeb site for Marshall Co IN. See
www.rootsweb.ancestry.com/~inmarsha/original.html.

1833-1860s. *Original Land Owners, Miami County, Indiana* **[Online Database]**, indexed in groups at the USGenWeb site for Miami Co IN. See
http://files.usgwarchives.net/in/miami/land/.

1834-present. *Vital Statistics From Local Newspapers, Montgomery County, Indiana* **[Online Database]**, part of the Crawfordsville District Public Library Local History Database. See
http://history.cdpl.lib.in.us/vitals.html.

1834-1910 Newspaper Index, Cass County, Indiana **[Online Database]**, indexed at the Genealogical Roots in Newspapers website. See
http://grins.freeservers.com/cass_co_,_in.htm.

1835. Lockerbie's Assessment List of Indianapolis 1835 [Printed Book], edited by Eliza G. Browning. Originally published as Volume IV, Number 7, 1909 of Indiana Historical Society. Published by the Genealogical Society of Marion County, Indiana, Indianapolis, IN, 2001, 100 pages, FHL book 977.252/11 R4b.

1835-1850s. *Original Land Owners, Kosciusko County, Indiana* **[Online Database]**, indexed at the USGenWeb site for Kosciusko Co IN. See
www.ingenweb.org/inkosciusko/OrigTract.htm.

1835-1923. *Naturalizations Index, Kosciusko County, Indiana* **[Online Database]**, indexed at the USGenWeb site for Kosciusko Co IN. See
www.ingenweb.org/inkosciusko/naturalizations.html.

"1837 Assessment List of Taxable Property, Kosciusko County, Indiana" [Printed Article], in *Our Missing Links*, (Kosciusko County Historical Society, Warsaw, IN), Vol. 6, No. 1 (Spring 1982).

1837-1970. *Indiana, United Methodist Church Records* **[Online Database]**, digitized and indexed at Ancestry.com. Source: Archives of DePauw University, Greencastle, IN. This database includes registers of baptisms, marriages, burials, memberships, and list of clergy. This database has 434,135 records, see **www.ancestry.com/search/collections/60715**.

1840. *Index, 1840 Federal Population Census, Indiana* **[Printed Index]**, compiled by the Indiana State Library, published by the Indiana Historical Society, Indianapolis, IN, 1975, 374 pages, FHL book 977.2 X2p 1840.

1844-1920 Index to Early Wills, Kosciusko County, Indiana **[Online Database]**, indexed at the USGenWeb site for Kosciusko Co IN. See
www.ingenweb.org/inkosciusko/willsndx.htm.

1845 Tax List, Carroll County, Indiana **[Online Database]**, indexed at the Carroll County Historical Museum website. To view the database online you must be a member of the Carroll Co Historical Society:
www.carrollcountymuseum.org/genealogy_databases.php.

1840. *Indiana 1840 Census Index* **[Printed Index]**, edited by Ronald Vern Jackson, published by Accelerated Indexing Systems, Bountiful, UT, 287 pages, FHL book 977.2 X22i 1840.

1840s-1930s. *Naturalization Info Gleaned from Voter Registration Records, Marshall County, Indiana* **[Online Database]**, indexed at the RootsWeb site for Marshall Co IN. See
www.rootsweb.ancestry.com/~inmarsha/naturalization.html.

1848 List of Voters, Tippecanoe County, Indiana **[Online Database]**, indexed at the RootsWeb site for Tippecanoe Co IN. See
www.rootsweb.ancestry.com/~intcags/1848Voters.html.

1848-1888. *Indianapolis Newspaper Divorce Notices* **[Microfilm & Digital Capture],** from the original index cards located at the Indiana State Library, Indianapolis. Contains a card index to divorce notices arranged alphabetically by surname, and giving date of divorce, and names of parties involved, page and column numbers, and reference to a newspaper. Filmed by the Genealogical Society of Utah, 1986, 1 roll, FHL film #1462568. To access the digital images, see the online FHL catalog page:
www.familysearch.org/search/catalog/471698.

1848-1992. *Indiana, Naturalization Records, and Indexes* **[Online Database],** digitized at FamilySearch.org. This collection contains naturalization indexes filmed at the Regional National Archives facility in Chicago, includes records from district courts in South Bend,, Hammond, Indianapolis, Fort Wayne, and Lafayette, Indiana. This database has 102,461 images. See
https://familysearch.org/search/collection/2137708.

1849 Cholera Deaths, Tippecanoe County, Indiana **[Online Database],** indexed at the USGenWeb site for Tippecanoe Co IN. See
www.ingenweb.org/intippecanoe/chlradths.htm.

1849 Delinquent Tax List, Vanderburgh County, Indiana **[Online Database],** indexed at the USGenWeb site for Vanderburgh Co IN. See
http://files.usgwarchives.net/in/vanderburgh/vitals/1849list.txt

1850. *Indiana, 1850 Federal Census: From the National Archives of the United States* **[CD-ROM],** digitized images and index by Broderbund, 1998, 5 CDs, FHL CD No. 9, Part 302, Vol. 1-5.

1850. *Indiana, 1850 Federal Census: Population Schedules* **[Microfilm & Digital Capture],** from the originals at the National Archives, Washington, DC. Filmed by the National Archives, series M432, 47 rolls, beginning with FHL film #7748 (Indiana: Adams and Allen counties). To access the digital images, see the online FHL catalog page:
https://familysearch.org/search/catalog/744478.

1850. *Indiana 1850 Census Index* **[Printed Index],** edited by Ronald Vern Jackson, published by Accelerated Indexing Systems, North Salt Lake, UT, 1976, 628 pages, FHL book 977.2 S22i 1850.

1850. *Census of Indiana Mortality, 1850: Original Returns of the Assistant Marshals, Third Series Persons Who Died During the Year Ending, 1850* **[Microfilm & Digital Capture],** from the state's original copies at the Indiana State Library. Filmed by the Frederic Luther Co., Indianapolis, 2001, 1 roll, FHL film #2259481. To access the digital images, see the online FHL catalog page:
www.familysearch.org/search/catalog/1001159.

1850 Indiana Mortality Schedules **[Printed Index],** transcribed and indexed by Lowell M. Volkel. Contents: Vol. 1: Counties Adams through Harrison; Vol. 2: Counties Hendricks through Posey; Vol. 3: Counties Pulaski through Whitley. published by the author, 1971, 3 vols., FHL book 977.2 X21p v.1-3.

1850. *Mortality Schedule, Indiana, 1850* **[Printed Index],** edited by Ronald Vern Jackson, published by Accelerated Indexing Systems, South Bountiful, UT, 1979, 159 pages, FHL book 977.2 X2j 1850.

1850-1920. *Indiana Vital Records Births Index, 1850 to 1920* **[CD-ROM],** published by Heritage Quest, Bountiful, UT, 2001. Includes 1,530,487 entries from 1850 to 1920, along with a few outside that range of years. Each entry details surname, child's name, father's given name, mother's given name, maiden name, sex, ethnicity, birth month, birthday, birth year, county, book, page, and fiche. FHL CD No. 1187.

1850-1920. *Indiana Vital Records Marriages Index, 1850 to 1920* **[CD-ROM],** by Heritage Quest, Bountiful, UT, 2 CDs, 2001. Includes 3,042,782 entries in the time period from 1850 to 1920, along with a few entries outside that range of years. Each entry details surname, given name, father's given name, spouse's given name, spouse's surname (maiden name), sex, ethnicity, age, birth month, birth day, birth year, marriage month-day-year, county, book, page, and fiche. FHL CD No. 1185.

1850-2012. *Local History Database, Evansville Newspapers, Evansville, Indiana* **[Online Database].** An index to newspaper clippings by Charles Browning from about 537,000 index cards. Digitized online at the Evansville Local History website. See
http://local.evpl.org/.

1850s-1950s Will Index, Noble County, Indiana **[Online Database],** indexed at the RootsWeb site for Noble Co IN. See
www.rootsweb.ancestry.com/~ohnoble/wills1.htm.

1852-1865. *Indiana Negro Registers* **[Printed Book],** compiled by Coy D. Robbins. Includes a surname index. The registers were compiled by the clerks of the circuit courts within the counties of Bartholomew, Floyd, Franklin, Gibson, Harrison, Hendricks, Jackson, Jefferson, Jennings, Knox, Martin, Ohio, Orange, Switzerland, and Washington counties. If free negroes could provide written evidence of their manumission, they were entitled to have their names registered. Once registered, a free negro had legal status in the county. This was a protection against slave hunters from slave states (like Kentucky) raiding Indiana areas looking for escaped slaves. Published by Heritage Books, Bowie, MD, 1994, 185 pages, FHL book 977.2 F2r.

1853 Voter List, Marshall County, Indiana **[Online Database]**, indexed at the RootsWeb site for Marshall Co IN. See
www.rootsweb.ancestry.com/~inmarsha/1853vote.html.

1854-1929 Naturalizations, Marshall County, Indiana **[Online Database]**, indexed at the RootsWeb site for Marshall Co IN. See
www.rootsweb.ancestry.com/~inmarsha/natrlz.html.

1858-1861 Indiana (State) Directories **[Microfilm]**, from originals published by various publishers, filmed by Research Publications, Woodbridge, CT, 1980-1984, 22 fiche, as follows:
- **1858-1859** G. W. Hawes' Indiana State Gazetteer and Business Directory, (10 fiche) FHL film #6043990.
- **1860-1861** George W. Hawes' Indiana State Gazetteer and Business Directory (12 fiche), FHL film #6043991.

1857-1935 Richmond (Indiana) City Directories **[Microfilm]**, from originals published by various publishers. The FHL has 1857, 1860-1861, 1883-1891, 1893-1894, 1897-1898, 1901-1908, 1910, 1912, 1914, 1916, 1918, 1921-1931, 1933 & 1935. Filmed by Research Publications, Woodbridge, CT, 1980-1984, 1995, 3 fiche, 7 rolls, beginning with FHL fiche #6044389 (1857 directory), and FHL film #2156576 (1883-1884 directory). For a complete list of fiche/roll numbers and contents of each, see the online FHL catalog page for this title:
www.familysearch.org/search/catalog/534213.

1858-1935 Fort Wayne (Indiana) City Directories **[Microfilm & Digital Version]**, from originals published by various publishers. The FHL has 1858-1862, 1864-1880, 1883-1912, and 1914-1935. Filmed by Research Publications, Woodbridge, CT, 1980-1984, 4 fiche & 31 rolls, beginning with FHL fiche #6043916 (2 fiche, 1858-1859 directory) and fiche #6043917 (2 fiche, 1860-1861 directory); and FHL roll #1376874 (1861-1862 directory. To access the digital images, see the online FHL catalog:
www.familysearch.org/search/catalog/534762.

1858-1935 Delayed Birth Records, Kosciusko County, Indiana **[Online Database]**, indexed at the USGenWeb site for Kosciusko Co IN. See
www.ingenweb.org/inkosciusko/delayedbirths.html.

1859 Old Settlers, Tippecanoe County, Indiana **[Online Database]**, "Recollections of the early settlement of the Wabash Valley," a series of articles from the *Lafayette Daily Courier*, starting in 1859. Indexed at the USGenWeb site for Tippecanoe Co IN. See **www.ingenweb.org/intippecanoe/settlers.htm.**

1859-1877. Will Book 3, Switzerland County, Indiana **[Online Database]**, indexed at the MyIndianaHome site. See
http://myindianahome.net/gen/switz/records/wills/will3.html.

1860. Indiana, 1860 Federal Census: Population Schedules **[Microfilm & Digital Capture]**, from the originals at the National Archives, Washington, DC. The 1860 federal census was filmed twice. The 2nd filming was done with a single page, while the 1st filming was done with a 2-page abreast format, thus the 2nd filming is much easier to read. However, there are some cases where the 2nd filming images are too dim to read easily, and in those cases, the 1st filming series is still available. Filmed by the National Archives, 1950, 1967, 83 rolls total, beginning with FHL film #803242 (Indiana 2nd filming, Adams County). To access the digital images, see the online FHL catalog page:
https://familysearch.org/search/catalog/704798.

1860 Indiana Census Index: Every-name Listing **[Microfiche]**, from the original book published by the Indiana Historical Society, Indianapolis, IN, 1985. Includes name, age, birthplace, county, township, and page of the 1860 census. Filmed by the Indiana Historical Society, 1990, 61 microfiche, FHL fiche #6334383.

1860. Indiana 1860 Census Index With Alternative Names, Ages and Birth Places **[Printed Index]**, compiled and published by Kratz Indexing, Salt Lake City, UT, 1986-1987, 2 vols., FHL book 977.2 X22ie 1860 v.1-2.

1860. *Indiana 1860 South Census Index* **[Printed Index],** edited by Ronald Vern Jackson, published by Accelerated Indexing Systems, North Salt Lake, UT, 1987, 991 pages, FHL book 977.2 X22in 1860.

1860. *Indiana 1860 North Census Index* **[Printed Index],** edited by Ronald Vern Jackson, published by Accelerated Indexing Systems, North Salt Lake, UT, 1987, 739 pages, FHL book 977.2 X22i 1860.

1860. *Census Records: Indiana, 1860* **[CD-ROM],** indexed by the Indiana State Historical Society, publ. Broderbund, 1997, FHL CD No. 9, part 304.

1860. *Census of Indiana Mortality, 1860: Original Returns of the Assistant Marshals, Third Series Persons Who Died During the Year Ending, 1860* **[Microfilm & Digital Capture],** from the state's original copies at the Indiana State Library. Filmed by the Frederic Luther Co., Indianapolis, 2001, 1 roll, FHL film #2259482. To access the digital images, see the online FHL catalog page:
www.familysearch.org/search/catalog/1180237.

1860 City Directory, Shelbyville, Shelby County, Indiana **[Online Database],** indexed at the Shelby County website. See
www.shelbycountyindiana.org/historical_articles/direc_1860.htm.

1860s-Present. *Veterans on File, Ripley County, Indiana* **[Online Database]**, an index to discharge papers filed at the Veterans Office, Ripley County Courthouse, dating from the Civil War era to the current DD214 (Separation from Service). Indexed at the Ripley Co Hist. Soc. Site. See
www.rchslib.org/dd214/index.html.

1860-1891 Tax Lists, DeKalb County, Indiana **[Online Database],** indexed at the USGenWeb site for DeKalb Co IN. See
http://www.ingenweb.org/indekalb/tax/.

1861-1865. *Civil War Telegrams of Governor Morton* **[Online Database],** accessible at the Indiana State Archives website. This resource, comprising over twelve thousand separate entries, represents the telegraphic communications of Governor Oliver P. Morton, his personal staff, the Adjutant General of Indiana, and scores of correspondents, both prominent and obscure, who wired their queries, comments, and responses. This resource is an important tool for the study of the Civil War, and especially Indiana's role in the conflict. Governor Morton, outspoken and indefatigable in defense of the Union cause, was in constant communication with the nation's leadership. His communications back and forth with President Abraham Lincoln, Secretaries of War Cameron and Stanton and other cabinet officials, and the leading Union generals in the field (primarily in the western theaters of operations) form an important body of documentation of the northern war effort. The records have understandably an Indiana orientation, dealing with Indiana government issues, Indiana soldiers and politicians, Indiana military units, and other matters. An index and the digital images of all of the Morton telegrams are located at the Indiana University-Purdue University Indianapolis website. See
http://ulib.iupui.edu/digitalscholarship/collections/Telegraph.

1861-1865. *Index to Compiled Service Records of Volunteer Union Soldiers Who Served in Organizations from the State of Indiana* **[Microfilm & Digital Capture],** from the original records at the National Archives, Washington, DC. Filmed by the National Archives, series M540, 1964, 86 rolls, beginning with FHL film #881722 (A-Al), To access the digital images, see the online FHL catalog page:
https://familysearch.org/search/catalog/87183.

1861-1865. *Indiana Substitutes Hired for Civil War* **[Microfilm & Digital Capture],** from the original index cards located at the Indiana State Library, Indianapolis, IN. Contains name of man hiring a substitute and the "see" reference to a service record card (with the name of the substitute). Filmed by the Genealogical Society of Utah, 1988, 1 roll, FHL film #1556875. To access the digital images, see the online FHL catalog page:
www.familysearch.org/search/catalog/545037.

1861-1865. *Civil War Soldiers, Crawford County, Indiana* **[Online Database],** indexed at the Census Diggins site. See
http://www.censusdiggins.com/crawford.html.

1861-1865. *Jasper County, Indiana GAR Records* **[Online Database]**, an index to Civil War veterans at the Jasper County Public Library website. See
www.myjcpl.org/genealogy/gar-records.

1861-1865. *Men in the Civil War, Kosciusko County, Indiana* **[Online Database],** indexed at the RootsWeb site for Kosciusko Co IN. See
www.rootsweb.ancestry.com/~inkosciu/cw.htm.

1861-1865. Civil War Rosters, Rush County, Indiana [Online Database], indexed at the ReoCities site. See www.reocities.com/Heartland/Pointe/7345/rcrosters.htm.

1861-1920s. Shelby County, Indiana in the Civil War [Online Database]. Includes excerpts from newspapers, unit rosters, historical memoirs, etc., all related to the men who served in the military during the Civil War. See www.shelbycountyindiana.org/historical_articles/history_civil_war.htm.

1861-1865. Steuben County Civil War Veterans [Online Database], indexed at the USGenWeb site for Steuben Co IN. See www.ingenweb.org/insteuben/roh/index.html.

1861-1940s. American Legion Record Book of Burials in Indiana [Microfilm], from the original record book located at the Morrison Reeves Library, Richmond, IN. Contains a list of cemeteries found in the record and an alphabetical list by surname of veterans of the Civil War, World War I, and World War II, and the cemetery in which each is buried. Filmed by the Genealogical Society of Utah, 1988, 1 roll, FHL film #1548951. To see if this microfilm has been digitized yet, see the FHL catalog page: www.familysearch.org/search/catalog/464503.

1861-2007. Indiana, Ripley, Osgood, Greendale Cemetery Records [Online Database], digitized at the Historic Record Collections of the FamilySearch website. Includes records from the Greendale Cemetery Association in Osgood, Ripley County, Indiana. The collection includes burial records, cemetery plots, and lists of veterans. This database has 3,977 images. See https://familysearch.org/search/collection/1548494.

1862 Delinquent Tax List, Lake County, Indiana [Online Database], indexed at the USGenWeb site for Lake Co IN. See http://files.usgwarchives.net/in/lake/land/non-pymt.txt.

1862-1866 Internal Revenue Assessment Lists for Indiana [Microfilm & Digital Capture], from original manuscripts located in the National Archives, Washington, DC. Lists are arranged alphabetically by surname of those being assessed for each period. Filmed by the National Archives, 1987, 42 rolls, beginning with FHL film #1491004 (District 1, division 9, special lists 1864, annual lists 1862-1864; and Divisions 9 and 11, monthly and special lists, Dec. 1862-Dec. 1866). To access the digital images, see the online FHL catalog page: https://familysearch.org/search/catalog/636046.

1862-1869 Jurors Lists, Tippecanoe County, Indiana [Online Database], indexed at the USGenWeb site for Tippecanoe Co IN. See www.ingenweb.org/intippecanoe/Jurors.html.

1862-1890 Directories, Carroll County, Indiana [Online Database], indexed at the Carroll County Historical Museum website. To view the database online you must be a member of the Carroll Co Historical Society. See www.carrollcountymuseum.org/genealogy_databases.php.

1863-1939. Carroll County, Indiana Plat Maps [Online Database], indexed at the Carroll County Historical Museum website. Data in this file includes more than 16,000 names of land owners indicated on the published plat books and maps for Carroll County in 1863, 1869, 1874, 1882, 1897, 1919, and 1939. In addition to owner name, records include township, section, and number of acres, if given. None of these are still in print but copies are in the Museum and some libraries. To view the database online you must be a member of the Carroll Co Historical Society. See www.carrollcountymuseum.org/genealogy_databases.php.

1864-1970 Burial Records, Crown Hill Cemetery, Indianapolis, Indiana [Microfilm & Digital Capture], from the original card index to burials, giving name of deceased and location of grave or crypt, and date of burial. Filmed by the Records Security Corp., Indianapolis, 1970, 23 rolls, beginning with FHL film #543343 (Burials A-Bartlein). To access the digital images, see the online FHL catalog page: https://familysearch.org/search/catalog/340557.

1866 Voter List, Clay County, Indiana [Online Database], indexed at the USGenWeb site for Clay Co IN. See http://files.usgwarchives.net/in/clay/cities/voters.txt.

1867 Voter List, Marshall County, Indiana [Online Database], indexed at the RootsWeb site for Marshall Co IN. See www.rootsweb.ancestry.com/~inmarsha/vote.html.

1867-1995. Soldiers and Sailors Childrens Home [Online Database]. This searchable database is an index to seven sets of records from the Indiana Soldiers' and Sailors' Children's Home. These are:

Applications for Admission; Admission Books; Discharge Books; Discharge Cards; School Record Cards; Indenture Papers; and the 1909 catalog of pupils published by the Home. Not all records are available for every child. Consult the index to see what is available. Names of children admitted after October 1995 are not included in this index for reasons of privacy. See
https://secure.in.gov/apps/iara/search.

1868 Business Directory, Allen County, Indiana **[Online Database],** indexed at the Allen Co IN USGenWeb site. See
http://files.usgwarchives.net/in/allen/directories/business/1868/.

1868 Business Directory, Bartholomew County, Indiana **[Online Database],** indexed at the Bartholomew Co IN USGenWeb site. See
http://files.usgwarchives.net/in/bartholomew/directories/business/1868/.

1868 Business Directory, Clinton County, Indiana **[Online Database],** indexed at the USGenWeb site for Clinton Co IN. See
http://files.usgwarchives.net/in/clinton/directories/business/1868/.

1868 Business Directory, Grant County, Indiana **[Online Database],** indexed at the USGenWeb site for Grant Co IN. See
http://files.usgwarchives.net/in/grant/directories/business/1868/.

1868 Business Directory, Howard County, Indiana **[Online Database],** indexed at the USGenWeb site for Howard Co IN. See
http://usgwarchives.net/in/howard/dir.html.

1870. *Indiana, 1870 Federal Census: Population Schedules* **[Microfilm & Digital Capture],** from the originals at the National Archives, Washington, DC. The 1870 federal census was filmed twice. The 2nd filming was done with a single page, while the 1st filming was done with a 2-page abreast format, thus the 2nd filming is much easier to read. However, there are some cases where the 2nd filming images are too dim to read easily, and in those cases, the 1st filming series is still available. Filmed by the National Archives, 1962, 1968, 104 rolls total, beginning with FHL film #545795 (Indiana 2nd filming, Adams County). To access the digital images, see the online FHL catalog page:
https://familysearch.org/search/catalog/698895.

1870. *Indiana 1870 Census Index* **[Printed Index],** compiled and published by Heritage Quest, Bountiful, UT, 1999, 3 vols., FHL book 977.2 X X22s Vol. 1: A-Goodlip; Vol. 2: Goodliss –Oralia; Vol.3: Oraluse – Z).

1870. *Census of Indiana Mortality, 1870: Original Returns of the Assistant Marshals, Third Series Persons Who Died During the Year Ending, 1870* **[Microfilm & Digital Capture],** from the state's original copies at the Indiana State Library. Filmed by the Frederic Luther Co., Indianapolis, 2001, 2 rolls, FHL film #2259483 (A-M) & film #2259484 (N-W). To access the digital images, see the online FHL catalog page:
www.familysearch.org/search/catalog/1180241.

1870. *Nationwide Index of Origin Series, Indiana: Heads of Household Listing Indiana as Birthplace in the 1870 U.S. Federal Census* **[CD-ROM],** compiled and published by Heritage Quest, Bountiful, UT 2001, FHL CD No. 1183.

1870s. *Allen County, Indiana Marriage and Death Announcements From the Monroeville (Monroe Twp., Allen Co.) Newspaper* **[Online Database].** Indexed at the USGenWeb site for Allen Co IN. See http://files.usgwarchives.net/in/allen/news/news.txt.

1874 Directory, Boone County, Indiana **[Online Database],** indexed at the USGenWeb site for Boone Co IN. See
http://files.usgwarchives.net/in/boone/enc-dir/pery-dir.txt.

1877-1896. *Will Book 4, Switzerland County, Indiana* **[Online Database],** indexed at the MyIndianaHome site (under construction). See
http://myindianahome.net.

1878 Business and Farmer Directory, Boone County, Indiana **[Online Database],** indexed at the RootsWeb site for Boone Co IN. See
www.rootsweb.ancestry.com/~inboone/directories/directories-index.htm.

1878 Business Directory, Tippecanoe County, Indiana **[Online Database],** indexed at the USGenWeb site for Tippecanoe Co IN. See
www.ingenweb.org/intippecanoe/busdir.htm.

1878 Landowners, Cass County, Indiana **[Online Database],** indexed at the USGenWeb site for Cass Co IN. See
http://incass-inmiami.org/cass/land_maps/ccland1.html.

1878-1908. *Index to Life Prisoner's Statements: State Prison at Michigan City* **[Online Database],** indexed at the Indiana State Archives website. In the early 1900's the Board of State Charities conducted interviews with inmates at the Indiana State Prison in Michigan City, Indiana. Each prisoner was given the opportunity to give his side of the story. The men often named family members and others involved in the crime for which they were sentenced and discussed whether or not attempts had been made to secure a parole or pardon. See
www.in.gov/iara/2810.htm.

1879-1905 *Death Records, Jefferson County, Indiana* **[Online Database],** indexed at the MyIndianaHome website site (under construction). See
http://myindianahome.net.

1879-1960. *Saint Joseph County Coroner Records – Index* **[Online Database],** indexed at the RootsWeb site for the South Bend Area Genealogical Society, Mishawaka-Penn-Harris Public Library, Mishawaka, IN. www.rootsweb.ancestry.com/~insbags/coroner.htm.

1880. *Indiana, 1880 Federal Census: Soundex and Population Schedules* **[Microfilm & Digital Capture],** from the originals at the National Archives, Washington, DC. Filmed by the National Archives, c1970, 160 rolls, beginning with FHL film #446821 (Soundex: A000-A354); and FHL film #1254263 (Population schedules: Adams Co – Part). To access the digital images, see the online FHL catalog page:
https://familysearch.org/search/catalog/670395.

1880. See *Census of Indiana Mortality, 1880: Original Returns of the Assistant Marshals, Third Series Persons Who Died During the Year Ending, 1880* **[Microfilm & Digital Capture],** from the state's original copies at the Indiana State Library. Filmed by the Frederic Luther Co., Indianapolis, 2001, 3 rolls, FHL film #2259485 (A-G), film #2259486, and film #2259487 (O-W). To access the digital images, see the online FHL catalog page:
www.familysearch.org/search/catalog/1180288.

1880. See *History of Hamilton County, Indiana with illustrations and biographical sketches of some of its prominent men and pioneers: to which are appended maps of its several townships* **[Digitized Book],** by Thomas B. Helm, Published 1880 by Kingman Brothers, Chicago. Available online at the Open Library site. See
https://openlibrary.org/books/OL23304573M/History_of_Hamilton_County_Indiana.

1880s. *Biographies, LaGrange County, Indiana* **[Online Database],** indexed at the Deb Murray website. See
http://debmurray.tripod.com/lagrange/lgbios.htm.

1880s. *Biographies, Morgan County, Indiana* **[Online Database],** indexed at a ReoCities site. See
www.reocities.com/Heartland/Meadows/8056/mcinbioindex.html.

1880-1920. *Indiana, WPA Birth Index* **[Online Database],** index at Ancestry.com. Birth records for the state of Indiana were recorded by the county health office beginning in 1882. The WPA began to index vital records, county-by-county for the entire state, but the agency was abolished before it was completed. This database indexes births for thirty-one of the counties indexed by the WPA. Taken from copies of the original works from the WPA, these records will prove useful for those seeking ancestors in the state of Indiana. This database has 674,773 records, see
www.ancestry.com/search/collections/4745.

1880s-1920s. *Biography Database, Cemetery Index, Naval Veterans, & WWI Veterans, Hendricks County, Indiana* **[Online Databases],** info about access to these databases can be found at the Plainfield/Guilford Township Public Library website (archived). See
http://web.archive.org/web/20130408082805/http://www.plainfieldlibrary.net/indiana/localbio.html.

1880s-1920s. *Biographies, Porter County, Indiana* **[Online Database],** indexed at the Deb Murray Tripod.com site. See
http://debmurray.tripod.com/porter/porinbio.htm.

1880s-1920s. *Biographies, Pulaski County, Indiana* **[Online Database],** indexed at the Deb Murray Tripod.com site. See
http://debmurray.tripod.com/pulaski/pulinbio.htm.

1880s-1920s. *Biographies, Rush County, Indiana* **[Online Database],** indexed at the Deb Murray Tripod.com site. See
http://debmurray.tripod.com/rush/rusbios.htm.

1880s-1920s. *Steuben County Biographies* **[Online Database],** indexed at the USGenWeb site for Steuben Co IN. See
www.ingenweb.org/insteuben/scibp/index.html.

1880s-1970s. *Death Records Index, Putnam County, Indiana* [Online Database], indexed at the USGenWeb site for Putnam Co IN. See www.ingenweb.org/inputnam/deaths/.

1882-1883 *Business Directory, Miami County, Indiana* [Online Database], indexed at the USGenWeb site for Miami Co IN. See http://files.usgwarchives.net/in/miami/business/gazete.txt.

1882-1920. *Indiana, WPA Death Index* [Online Database], indexed at FamilySearch.org, taken from the WPA index of deaths at the Indiana State Board of Health, Division of Vital Records, Indianapolis, IN. Index courtesy of Ancestry.com. This database has 793,965 records. See
www.familysearch.org/search/collection/1947977.
- For the Ancestry.com version, see
www.ancestry.com/search/collections/7834.

1883 *Military Pensioners, Clinton County, Indiana* [Online Database], indexed at the USGenWeb site for Clinton Co IN. See
http://files.usgwarchives.net/in/clinton/military/clin-1883.txt.

1883 *Military Pensioners, Vermillion County, Indiana* [Online Database], indexed at the USGenWeb site for Vermillion Co IN. See
http://files.usgwarchives.net/in/vermillion/military/pens1883.txt.

1883 *Biographies, Jasper County, Indiana* [Online Database], indexed at the Lanewood.com site. See www.lanewood.com/1883bioindex.htm.

1884 *Biographies, Orange County, Indiana* [Online Database], indexed at the USGenWeb site for Orange Co IN. See
www.ingenweb.org/inorange/prebiog.htm.

1884-1927 *Death Index, Porter County, Indiana* [Online Database], indexed at the RootsWeb site for Porter Co IN. See
www.rootsweb.ancestry.com/~innwigs/Archives/DeathIndex-PorterCounty.htm.

1886. *Index to History of Jackson County, Indiana* [Online Database], indexed by chapter at the Jackson County History website. See
www.jacksoncountyhistory.org/books/toc.asp?book=brantfuller.

1886-1894. *Enrollment of the Late Soldiers, Their Widows and Orphans of the Late Armies of the United States, Residing in the State of Indiana for the year 1886-1894* [Microfilm & Digital Capture], from original records located at the Indiana State Library, Indianapolis. Contains an enrollment of persons in the War of 1812; the War with Mexico; the Civil War' and of all wars of the United States with Indian tribes. Arranged by county and by each township within a county, alphabetically by surname. By enactment of the General Assembly of the State of Indiana, each township assessor at the time of taking lists of property for taxation, was to list all persons who served in the United States armies, as well as their widows and orphans. Assessors were to return their listings to the County Clerks who in turn sent them to the Adjutant General for the State to be put on permanent file in his office. Filmed by the Genealogical Society of Utah, 1988-1990, 89 rolls, beginning with FHL film #1605057 (Adams, Bartholomew counties, 1886- To access the digital images, see the online FHL catalog page: https://familysearch.org/search/catalog/596163.

1887 *History of Huntington County, Indiana – Biographies* [Online Database], indexed at the RootsWeb site for Huntington Co IN. See
www.rootsweb.ancestry.com/~inhuntin/1887.htm.

1892-1992. *Indiana, Federal Naturalization Records* [Online Database]. Digitized index cards at Ancestry.com. Original data: Index to Petitions for Naturalization. The National Archives at Chicago. This collection consists of several card indexes to petitions for naturalization filed in both the Southern and Northern U.S. District Courts in Indiana. The card indexes are organized by division within each district, and include the divisions of Fort Wayne, Hammond, Indianapolis, Lafayette, and South Bend. Each printed index card provides a petitioner's first and last name, the petition number, a residential street or rural route address, the town or city, the certificate of naturalization number, and either the date citizenship was granted and the certificate was issued, or the date of a court order that denied the petition. This database has 88,019 records, see
www.ancestry.com/search/collections/61197.

1898. *Steuben County Spanish American War Veterans* [Online Database], indexed at the USGenWeb site for Steuben Co IN. See
www.ingenweb.org/insteuben/SpanAm/index.html.

1889 Telephone Directory, Dearborn County, Indiana **[Online Database],** indexed by the RootsWeb site for Dearborn Co IN. See **www.rootsweb.ancestry.com/~indearbo/Pages/telebk.html**.

1889. *Early Evansville Portraits and Biographies (From History of Vanderburgh County, Indiana)* **[Online Database]**, images and text reproduced at the USGenWeb site for Vanderburgh Co IN. See **www.usgennet.org/usa/in/county/vanderburgh/portraits/index.htm**.

1889-1935. *Muncie (Indiana) City Directories* **[Microfilm],** from the original records published by various publishers. The FHL has 1889, 1897-1932, 1934-1935. Various directories include Delaware County towns of Gaston, Daleville, Albany, Cowan, Desoto, Eaton, Oakville, Royerton, Selma, Shideler, Wheeling, and Yorktown. Filmed by Research Publications, Woodbridge, CT, 1995, 10 rolls, beginning with FHL film #2156575 (Emerson's 1889 Muncie directory). For a complete list of roll numbers and contents of each roll, see the online FHL catalog page for this title. See **https://familysearch.org/search/catalog/982206**.

1890 Enrollment of Soldiers, Morgan County, Indiana **[Online Database]**, indexed at the USGenWeb site for Morgan Co IN. See **http://files.usgwarchives.net/in/morgan/war/enrl1890.txt**.

1891-1917 Dodd Funeral Home Records, Paris Crossing, Jennings County, Indiana **[Online Database],** indexed at the RootsWeb site for Jennings CO IN. See **www.rootsweb.ancestry.com/~injennin/FuneralHome/dodd.htm**.

1899-2011. *Indiana, Death Certificates* **[Online Database],** digitized and indexed at Ancestry.com. Source: IN State Board of Health, records at the IN State Archives, Indianapolis, IN. This database has 16,737,019 records, see **www.ancestry.com/search/collections/60716**.

1900. *Indiana, 1900 Federal Census: Soundex and Population Schedules* **[Microfilm & Digital Capture],** from the original records held by the Bureau of the Census in the 1940s. After microfilming, Congress allowed the Census Bureau to destroy the originals to free up space for WWII-related files. Filmed by the National Archives, c1970, 312 rolls, beginning with FHL film #1243437 (Soundex: A000-A235); and FHL film #1240361 (Population schedules: Adams & Allen counties). To access the digital images, see the online FHL catalog page: **https://familysearch.org/search/catalog/651737**.

1900s. *Indianapolis-Marion County Employees* **[Online Database].** This title listed under "History of Government Records" at the Indiana State Archives website. Index has no dates, but one sample given is for early 1900s. See **www.in.gov/iara/2807.htm**.

1900-1930 Naturalizations, Steuben County, Indiana **[Online Database],** indexed at the USGenWeb site for Steuben Co IN. See **www.ingenweb.org/insteuben/naturalizations/index.html**.

1900-2004 Wabash Valley Obituary List **[Online Database],** indexed at the Vigo County Public Library website. See **www.vigo.lib.in.us/obituaries**.

1901 Biographical Memoirs of Huntington, County, Indiana **[Online Database]**, indexed at the RootsWeb site for Huntington Co IN. See **www.rootsweb.ancestry.com/~inhuntin/1901.htm**.

1905-1967 Morocco High School Graduates, Beaver Township, Newton County, Indiana **[Online Database]**, indexed at the RootsWeb site for Newton Co IN. See **www.rootsweb.ancestry.com/~innewton/school/bv-05-67.htm**.

1907-1940. *Indiana, Birth Certificates* **[Online Database],** digitized and indexed at Ancestry.com. Source: IN State Board of Health records at the IN State Archives, Indianapolis, IN. This database includes birth records for more than 2 million children born in the State of Indiana between 1907 and 1940. Information contained in the searchable index typically includes: Child's full name, Sex, Birth date, Birth place, Registration year, Full names of both parents, and Birth certificate number. This database has 7,077,494 records, see **www.ancestry.com/search/collections/60871**.

1909 History of Shelby County, Indiana Biographical Index **[Online Database]**, indexed at the Shelby Co History site. See **www.shelbycountyindiana.org/biographies/biography_index.htm**.

1910. *Indiana, 1900 Federal Census: Population Schedules* **[Microfilm & Digital Capture],** from the original records held by the Bureau of the Census in the 1940s. After microfilming, Congress allowed the Census Bureau to destroy the originals to free up space for WWII-related files. Filmed on 52 rolls, beginning with FHL film #1374351 (Adams and Allen Cos). To access the digital images, see the online FHL catalog page: https://familysearch.org/search/catalog/653179.

1910. *Indiana 1910 Census Index* **[Printed Index],** compiled and published by Heritage Quest, North Salt Lake, UT, 2001, 6 vols. Contents: Vol. 1: A-Col; Vol. 2: Com – Grd; Vol. 3: Gre – Kum; Vol. 4: Kun – Pad; Vol. 5: Pae – Sop; Vol. 6: Sor – Z). FHL book 977.2 X22h 1910 v.1-5. Also available on CD-ROM, FHL CD No. 1176.

1914. *Index of Names, History of Huntington Count, Indiana* **[Online Database],** indexed at the RootsWeb site for Huntington Co IN. See
www.rootsweb.ancestry.com/~inhuntin/1914.htm.

1914-1919 World War I Indiana Enrollment Cards **[Microfilm & Digital Capture],** from the originals at the Indiana State Archives, Indianapolis, IN. Contains: statement-of-service cards, arranged in alphabetical order by surname, furnished primarily for historical and statistical purposes. Lists name, army serial number, race, residence, where inducted, date inducted, place of birth, age, organizations served in with dates of assignments and transfers, grades with date of appointment, engagements, wounds or other injuries received in action, service overseas, honorably discharged or demobilization date, percent disabled in view of occupation, and remarks. Filmed by the Genealogical Society of Utah, 1990, 35 rolls, beginning with Aarnink, Clifford F. – Baker, Ollie, FHL film #1674855. To access the digital images, see the online FHL catalog page:
https://familysearch.org/search/catalog/625091.
-See also *Indiana, World War I, Enrollment Cards, 1919* [Online Database], indexed at FamilySearch.org. See www.familysearch.org/search/collection/2968238.

1915 Directory, Jackson County, Indiana **[Online Database],** indexed at the Jackson County History website. See
http://history.myjclibrary.org/books/toc.asp?book=1915 directory.

1916 Biographies, Jasper County, Indiana **[Online Database],** indexed at the Lanewood.com site. See www.lanewood.com/1916bioindex.htm.

1916. *Index to Perry County, Indiana: A History* **[Online Database],** indexed at the USGenWeb site for Perry Co IN. See
http://theusgenweb.org/in/perry/hunt.htm.

1917. *Index to "The Pictorial History of Fort Wayne, Indiana; Vol. II-Biographical"* **[Online Database],** indexed at the Allen Co USGenWeb site. See http://www.acgsi.org/genweb/indexpichist.asp.

1917-1918 Draft Registrations, Ohio County, Indiana **[Online Database],** indexed at the USGenWeb site for Ohio Co IN. See
http://files.usgwarchives.net/in/ohio/cemetery/wills/draftcrd.txt.

1917-1918 World War I Selective Service System Draft Registration Cards (Indiana) **[Microfilm & Digital Capture],** from the originals at the National Archives Regional Branch in East Point, GA, part of series M1509. The draft cards are arranged alphabetically by state, then alphabetically by county or city draft board, and then alphabetically by surname of the registrants. 117 rolls cover the Indiana cards on microfilm, beginning with FHL film #1439777 (Adams County, A-Z, Allen County, A-F). To access the digital images, see the online FHL catalog page:
https://familysearch.org/search/catalog/746975.

1918 Assessments, Lake County, Indiana **[Online Database],** indexed at the USGenWeb site for Lake Co IN. See
http://files.usgwarchives.net/in/lake/land/asesmt18.txt.

1919-1970. *Cemetery Records to 1970, Washington Park Cemetery, Indianapolis, Indiana* **[Microfilm & Digital Capture],** from the original records. Includes interments in the Garden Mausoleum, Mount Vernon Mausoleum, and cemetery burials. Filmed by the Records Security Corp., Indianapolis, 1970, 6 rolls, beginning with FHL film #543440 (Garden Mausoleum, et al). To access the digital images, see the online FHL catalog page:
https://familysearch.org/search/catalog/340554.

1920. *Indiana, 1920 Federal Census: Soundex and Population Schedules* **[Microfilm & Digital Capture],** from the original records held by the Bureau of the Census in the 1940s. After microfilming, Congress allowed the Census Bureau to destroy the originals to free up space for WWII-related files. Filmed by the National Archives, c1970, 286 rolls, beginning with FHL film #1824800

(Soundex: A000-A235); and FHL film #1820420 (Population schedules: Adams & Allen counties). For a complete list of roll numbers and contents of each roll, see the online FHL catalog page for this title. See https://familysearch.org/search/catalog/534283.

1920-1940 Index to Birth Records, Orange County, Indiana [Online Database], indexed at the USGenWeb site for Orange Co IN. See www.ingenweb.org/inorange/wpa2040/index.htm.

1921 Clay County Directory [Online Database], indexed in alpha groups by the USGenWeb site for Clay Co IN. For access to all databases, see http://files.usgwarchives.net/in/clay/1921dir/.

1922 Voter's Registration Index, Kosciusko County, Indiana [Online Database], indexed at the USGenWeb site for Kosciusko Co IN. See www.ingenweb.org/inkosciusko/voterreg1922.html.

1923 Prairie Farmer's Home and County Directory of Wells County, Indiana [Online Database], indexed at the RootsWeb site for Wells Co IN. See www.rootsweb.ancestry.com/~inwells/bio/1923dir/1923index.html.

1930. *Indiana, 1930 Federal Census: Population Schedules* [Microfilm & Digital Capture], from the original records held by the Bureau of the Census in the 1940s. After microfilming, Congress allowed the Census Bureau to destroy the originals to free up space for WWII-related files. Filmed on 66 rolls, series beginning with FHL film #2340309 (Adams Co). For a complete list of roll numbers and contents of each roll, see the online FHL catalog page for this title. See https://familysearch.org/search/catalog/1035339.

1934-1949. *Obituaries (from Union City Newspapers), Randolph County, Indiana* [Online Database], indexes by year, located at the DCO Genealogical Researchers site. See www.dcoweb.org/randolph/UCobits/index.html.

1938-Present. *Obituaries printed in the Valparaiso Vidette-Messenger from 1938-1995 and the Northwest Indiana Times from 1995-present* [Online Database], search screen at the Porter County Public Library website. See http://engagedpatrons.org/database/PCPLS/obituaries/.

1940. *Indiana, 1940 Federal Census: Population Schedules* [Online Database], digitized images from the microfilm of original records held by the Bureau of the Census in the 1940s. After microfilming, Congress allowed the Census Bureau to destroy the originals to free up space for WWII-related files. Digitizing of the 1940 census schedules microfilm images was done for the National Archives and made public on April 2, 2012. No microfilm copies were distributed. To access the digital images, see the online FHL catalog page:

www.familysearch.org/search/catalog/2057753.

1940 Federal Census Finding Aids [Online Database]. The National Archives prepared a special website online with a detailed description of the 1940 federal census. Included at the site are descriptions of location finding aids, such as Enumeration District maps, Geographic Descriptions of Census Enumeration Districts, and a list of 1940 City Directories available at the National Archives. The finding aids are all linked to other National Archives sites. The National Archives website also has a link to 1940 Search Engines using Stephen P. Morse's "One-Step" system for finding a 1940 E.D. or street address conversion. See www.archives.gov/research/census/1940/general-info.html#questions

1941-1945 World War II Enlistments, Knox County, Indiana [Online Database], extracted from local newspapers, indexed at the USGenWeb site for Knox Co IN. See www.ingenweb.org/inknox/wwii.htm.

1941-1945. *Men and Women of Perry County, Indiana Who Served in the Military during World War II* [Online Database], indexed at the USGenWeb site for Perry Co IN. See http://theusgenweb.org/in/perry/wwiimem.htm.

1940-1947. *Indiana, World War II Draft Registration Cards* [Digital Capture], from the original records at the National Personnel Records Center, St. Louis, MO. digitized by FamilySearch International, 2017. To access the digital images, see the online FHL catalog page:

www.familysearch.org/search/catalog/2852766.

- See also, *Indiana Selective Service System Registration Cards (World War II): Fourth Registration (1942).* [Microfilm & Digital Capture] of original records at the National Archives and Records Administration, Great Lakes Region, Chicago,

Illinois. These cards represent older men, ages 45 to 65 on April 27, 1942, that were registered for the draft. They had birth dates between 28 April 1877 and 16 Feb 1897. The cards are arranged in alphabetical order by surname. Includes name, place of residence, age, place of birth, date of birth, race, weight, height, employer's name and address, name and address of person who would always know their address, color of eyes and hair. Filmed by the Genealogical Society of Utah, 2001, 203 16mm rolls, beginning with FHL film #2240128 (Aabel, Hans - Alexander, Harley J.). To access the digital images, see the online FHL catalog page: https://familysearch.org/search/catalog/1106813.

1960-2005. *Indiana, Marriage Certificates* **[Online Database]**, digitized and indexed at Ancestry.com. Source: IN State Board of Health records at the IN State Archives, Indianapolis, IN. This database has 8,081,464 records, see www.ancestry.com/search/collections/61009.

1963-1973. See *Hoosier Ancestors Index* **[Microfilm & Digital Capture]**, compiled by Eloise R. Means and Pearl Brenton. Contains all newspaper columns and an index to all queries and responses published in the *Hoosier Ancestors*, a column written by Pearl Benton, and appearing in the Indianapolis Sunday Star between June 1963 and June 1973. The original copy is located at the Martinsville Public Library. Filmed by the Genealogical Society of Utah, 1987, 2 rolls, FHL #1502906 (Index, June 1963-Dec 1970 ; column, July 1967-Sep 1969), and FHL film #1502907, (Column, Sept 1969 – June 1973). To access the digital images, see the online FHL catalog page: www.familysearch.org/search/catalog/452912.

1984-1998. *Index to County Deaths, Marshall County, Indiana* **[Online Database]**, indexed at the RootsWeb site for Marshall Co IN. See www.rootsweb.ancestry.com/~inmarsha/1984-98deathindex.html.

1984-2012. *Indiana, Daviess County, Washington Times Herald Obituaries* **[Online Database]**, digitized and indexed at FamilySearch.org. Includes obituary clippings from the Washington Times Herald bound in book form. Contains deaths from Daviess, Martin, Pike and Knox Counties and other areas. This database has 31,930 records, see www.familysearch.org/search/collection/2300886.

1988 – Current. *Indiana Newspaper Obituaries* **[Online Database]**. Digitized and indexed at the GenealogyBank.com website. One search screen for obituaries published in over 60 city newspapers. See www.genealogybank.com/gbnk/obituaries/explore/USA/Indiana/.

1993-2015. *Indiana, County Marriages Index* **[Online Database]**, indexed at Ancestry.com. Source: Marriage License Public Lookup. State of Indiana Supreme Court. This database has 1,886,818 records, see www.ancestry.com/search/collections/70802.
- This database is also available at the source, see https://publicaccess.courts.in.gov/mlpl/Search.

Illinois • 1820. The 19 counties of Illinois at the time of the August 1820 federal census are shown in black. The current 102 Illinois counties are shown in white. Madison, Bond, and Clark counties are shown within the areas ceded by the Indians; statutorily, their lines extended all the way to the border with Michigan Territory. For detailed maps showing the Indian Cessions in Illinois, see **http://usgwarchives.net/maps/cessions/ilcmap17.htm.** (Royce Map Illinois 1-Map 17) and **http://usgwarchives.net/maps/cessions/ilcmap18.htm.** (Royce Map Illinois 2-Map 18). Many of the first Illinois communities were established by people who had floated down the Ohio River on flatboats from points such as Brownsville, Pittsburgh, or Wheeling. The sparse formation of counties by 1820 confirms that the settlement of Illinois began in the south and moved north. For example, Chicago was not founded until 1837; and Springfield, the present capital of Illinois since 1839, had exactly one cabin in 1820.

Illinois
Censuses & Substitute Name Lists

Historical Timeline for Illinois, 1673 – 2016

1673. French explorers Jacques Marquette and Louis Jolliet discovered the upper portions of the Mississippi River. They descended the Mississippi to the mouth of the Arkansas River then returned to the Great Lakes via the Illinois River.

1675. Jacques Marquette founded a mission at the Great Village of the Illinois River, near present-day Utica, Illinois.

1680. French explorer René-Robert Cavelier (Sieur de LaSalle) and trader Henri deTonti built Fort Crève Coeur on the Illinois River, near present-day Peoria.

1682. René-Robert Cavelier (Sieur de LaSalle) erected a cross near the confluence of the Mississippi River and the Gulf of Mexico, after floating down river from the Illinois Country. He claimed the entire Mississippi Basin for Louis XIV of France, for whom Louisiana was named. All of the rivers and streams flowing into the Mississippi were part of the Mississippi Basin and included in the Louisiana claim.

1696. Jesuit priest Pierre François Pinet established a mission near the site of present-day Chicago. The Mission l'Ange Gardie (Mission of the Guardian Angel) was abandoned in 1700.

1699. Cahokia. Québec priests founded the Holy Family Mission at Cahokia, named for the Indians there, near present-day East St. Louis on the Mississippi River. Cahokia was the first permanent settlement in the Illinois Country.

1703. Kaskaskia. The French established a mission and settlement at Kaskaskia, named for the river and Indians there, near the Mississippi River. Kaskaskia became the capital of Upper Louisiana after Fort de Charles was built there in 1718.

1717-1762. French Louisiana. In 1717, the Illinois Country was officially added to the French Louisiana jurisdiction within New France. At that time, *la Louisiane Française* extended from the Wabash River, down the Ohio and Mississippi Rivers to include several ports on the Gulf of Mexico. Any trading posts or forts north of the Highlands (Terra Haute) were considered part of French Québec.

By 1721, several hundred French colonists had abandoned Arkansas Post, the capital of Lower Louisiana, and the largest settlement of all of French Louisiana since 1686. A few French trading forts between the Great Lakes and New Orleans remained and continued to be the focal point for trade with the Indians in the region. As a failed farming community, Arkansas Post was typical of the French efforts to colonize North America south of the Great Lakes. They were much more interested in trading for furs with the Indians.

From 1721 to 1762, no new farming communities were ever established. Arkansas Post continued as a trading fort, and the French presence in the Mississippi Basin consisted mainly of single French voyageurs, trappers, and traders paddling their canoes from one trading post to the next. The French established military forts at strategic locations, partly as a means of protecting the voyageurs during their contacts with the Indians.

In comparison, the British colonies by 1762 had over 2,500 miles of improved wagon roads, between Boston and Charles Town. The British colonies had an economy based on town tradesmen surrounded by small farms, with the exchange of goods and produce up and down the Atlantic coast. During this same period, the French had built one 20-mile long road, and that was only to provide portage between rivers. Unlike the French Québec settlements, French Louisiana had very few farming communities, and there was little exchanging of goods or produce, except for the trapping and trading of furs.

1763. The Seven Years War (in Europe), which was called the French and Indian War in colonial America, ended with the 1763 Treaty of Paris. France lost virtually all of its North American claims – the western side of the Mississippi was lost to Spain, and the eastern side of the Mississippi was lost to Britain. The British also gained Québec from the French. They immediately renamed it the *Province of Canada*. Also in the 1763 treaty, the British acquired Florida from the Spanish in exchange for Cuba.

1774. Québec Act. As a means of gaining loyalty from French Canadians, the British Parliament passed into law the Québec Act, which permitted the French Canadians to recover the name Québec, keep their French laws and customs, and the Catholic Church to maintain its position there. The former French settlements in the Old Northwest (including Illinois) were by the act now part of the British Province of Québec.

1778-1779. During the Revolutionary War, General George Rogers Clark of the Virginia Militia led the American forces to celebrated victories over the British, with the capture of Kaskaskia in 1778 and Vincennes in 1779. Because the British ceded the entire Great Lakes region to the U.S. in the 1783 treaty of Paris, Clark was often hailed as the "Conqueror of the Old Northwest."

1781. Prairie du Chien. The first American settlement on the Mississippi River was at Prairie du Chien near the present border of Wisconsin and Illinois. A former French fur trading post, the American interest there was to exploit the lead deposits discovered nearby.

1783. Post-Revolutionary War. The 1783 Treaty of Paris recognized the United States of America as an independent nation and defined its borders from the Atlantic Ocean to the Mississippi River. However, British military forces continued to maintain control of much of the Great Lakes area for several years after the Revolution.

1787. Northwest Territory. The Ordinance of 1787 established the *Territory Northwest of the River Ohio* and defined the procedure for any territory to obtain statehood. States carved out of the original area of the Northwest Territory included Ohio, Indiana, Illinois, Michigan, Wisconsin, and that part of Minnesota east of the Mississippi River.

1787-1815. Flatboat Era. The main family transportation on the Ohio River (usually beginning at Brownsville, Pittsburgh, or Wheeling) was by a flatboat designed for a one-way trip. The large, steerable rafts were constructed of lumber and nails that could be disassembled by migrating families when they arrived at their new homesites along the Ohio River and tributaries. The flatboat era continued until the classic flat-bottomed steamboats were introduced on the Ohio River in 1815.

1795. Jay Treaty. Great Britain finally relinquished control of a series of military forts from Lake Champlain to the Mississippi River, including Fort Detroit, Fort Mackinac, and Fort Miami (now Ft. Wayne) in the Northwest Territory. In exchange, the British-owned fur-trading companies were allowed to continue their operations in the Great Lakes region, and their employees residing in the U.S. were given the option of becoming U.S. citizens.

1800. Indiana Territory was established from the Northwest Territory with William Henry Harrison as the first Governor and Vincennes the capital. The area included all of present-day Indiana, Illinois, Wisconsin, and the western half of Michigan. The Northwest Territory was reduced to the present-day area of Ohio and the eastern half of Michigan.

1800. Louisiana. Napoleon acquired title of Louisiana from Spain. At the Third Treaty of San Ildefonso, the Spanish acknowledged that it was too costly to explore the country and could not see the rewards being worth the investment. Spain retroceded Louisiana to France in exchange for the Grand Duchy of Tuscany (now part of Italy).

1803. Louisiana Purchase. The United States purchased Louisiana from France. Sent by President Jefferson to attempt the purchase of New Orleans, the American negotiators (James Madison and Robert

Livingston) were surprised when Napoleon offered the entire tract to them. The Louisiana Purchase was officially described as the "drainage of the Mississippi and Missouri River basins." Adding the area doubled the size of the United States.

1804-1805. Louisiana District and Orleans Territory. In 1804, Congress divided the Louisiana Purchase into two jurisdictions: Louisiana District and Orleans Territory. The latter had north and south bounds the same as the present state of Louisiana but did not include land east of the Mississippi River, and its northwestern corner extended on an indefinite line west into Spanish Texas. For a year, Louisiana District was attached to Indiana Territory for judicial administration but became Louisiana Territory with its own Governor in 1805.

1809. Illinois Territory was created from Indiana Territory, with Ninian Edwards the first governor, and Kaskaskia the territorial capital. The original area included present-day Illinois and Wisconsin; as well as a portion of the Upper Peninsula of Michigan, and Minnesota east of the Mississippi.

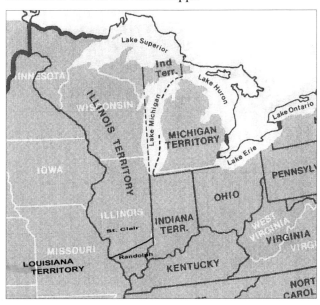

1810. The above map shows Illinois Territory at the time of the 1810 Federal Census. There were two counties: Randolph County (census extant), and St. Clair County (census lost). The territory's population was at 12,282 people.

1812-1815. Steamboats. First introduced in 1812, steamboats would soon become the main mode of transportation on the Ohio and Mississippi Rivers. The classic flat-bottomed steamboat design began in 1815. Before that, the boats had too much draft for the Ohio River low water seasons.

1818. December. **Illinois** became the 21st state in the Union, with the same boundaries as today. The territorial capital of Kaskaskia continued as the first state capital. The capital was moved to Vandalia in 1820.

1837. Chicago was incorporated as a city.

1839. The state capital of Illinois was moved from Vandalia to Springfield.

1846. The Mormons left Nauvoo, Illinois for the Great Salt Lake Basin in Utah.

1846. The Donner party left Springfield, Illinois by wagon train for California; forty-two persons perished in the Sierra Mountains due to heavy snowstorms.

2016. The Chicago Cubs won the World Series, defeating the Cleveland Indians 4 games to 3.

Online Databases at the Illinois State Archives and IRAD

The Illinois State Archives is the official depository for records of governments within the state of Illinois, including state, county, and local records. Statewide government records are housed at the State Archives (Norton) Building in Springfield; while county and local records are held at regional facilities. **IRAD** (Illinois Regional Archives Depositories), is a system administered by the State Archives, with regional depositories located at various state universities in Illinois. The main State Archives website has searchable databases for the statewide records as well as from each of the regional depositories. Each database title is listed below by category, and listed again in more detail within the bibliography, by year of origin.

State Archives Online Databases. See www.cyberdriveillinois.com/departments/archives/databases/. At this site, click on the links for the following indexed databases:
Land, Slavery, & Military Databases:
- Public Domain Land Tract Sales
- Illinois Servitude and Emancipation Records
- Illinois Veterans' History Project

- Illinois War of 1812 Veterans
- Illinois Winnebago War Veterans
- Illinois Black Hawk War Veterans
- Illinois Mexican War Veterans
- Illinois Civil War Muster and Descriptive Rolls
- Illinois Civil War Veterans in the U.S. Navy
- Illinois Civil War Veterans of Missouri Units
- Illinois Spanish-American War Veterans
- 1929 Illinois Roll of Honor
- Illinois Soldiers' and Sailors' Home Residents

Statewide Vital Records Databases:
- Illinois Statewide Marriage Index, 1763-1900
- Illinois Statewide Death Index, Pre-1916
- Illinois Statewide Death Index, 1916-1950

IRAD Online Databases. See www.cyberdriveillinois.com/departments/archives/databases/. Click on the links for the following indexed databases:

Guides to IRAD Records:
- Name Index to Illinois Local Governments. See www.ilsos.gov/isa/localgovnameindexsrch.jsp.

Records at Eastern Illinois University:
- Arthur Local Registrar's Birth Certificates Index (1868–1925)
- Mattoon Death Certificate Registers Index (1899–1918)
- Mattoon Court of Common Pleas Case Files Index (1869–1873)
- Shelby County Circuit Court Case Files Index (1828–1871)
- Wayne County Coroner's Inquest Record Index (1888–1960)

Records at Illinois State University:
- DeWitt County Coroner's Inquest Files Index (1924–1977)
- Livingston County Probate Case Files Index (1837–1958)
- Logan County Circuit Court Criminal Case Files Index (1857–1945)
- McLean County Probate Record Index (1834–1934)
- McLean County Will Record Index (1838–1940)
- Vermilion County Coroner's Inquest Files Index (1908–1956)
- Woodford County Almshouse Registers Index (1868–1957)

Records at Northeastern Illinois University:
- Chicago City Council Proceedings Files, 1833–1871
- Cook County Coroner's Inquest Record Index, 1872–1911
- Chicago Police Department Homicide Record, 1870–1930

Records at Northern Illinois University:
- Carroll County Birth Certificates Index (1877–1913)
- JoDaviess County Almshouse Registers Index (1846–1938)
- Kane County Circuit Court Case Files Index (1836–1870)
- Lake County Circuit Court Case Files Index (1840–1898)
- Ogle County Almshouse Register Index (1878–1933)
- Ogle County Naturalization Papers (County Court) Index (1872–1906)

Records at Southern Illinois University:
- East St. Louis City Court Naturalization Papers Index (1874–1906)
- Madison County Probate Case Files Index (1813–1903)
- St. Clair County Circuit Court Chancery Case Files Index (1815–1870)
- St. Clair County Farm Board Record Index (1874–1879)

Records at the University of Illinois at Springfield:
- Macon County Circuit Court Case Files Index (1829–1861)
- Macoupin County Coroner's Inquest Files Index (1835–1928)
- Morgan County Poor Farm Records Index (1850–1932)
- Sangamon County Guardian's Case Files Index (1825–1901)
- Sangamon County Probate Case Files Index (1821–1906)

Records at Western Illinois University:
- Adams County Almshouse Register Index (1873–1898)
- Brown County Almshouse Registers Index (1882–1963)
- Fulton County Circuit Court Case Files Index (1825–1876)
- McDonough County Probate Case Files Index (1833–1925)
- McDonough County Guardian's Case Files Index (1838–1933)
- Mercer County Almshouse Register Index (1859–1948)
- Peoria County Probate Case Files Index (1825–1887)
- Rock Island Probate Case Files Index (1834–1899)
- Stark County Almshouse Register Index (1868–1941)

Global Database Search. This powerful search engine will examine all databases on the Illinois State Archives website for the personal name you enter. The Global Database Search includes all online records of the State Archives databases, as well as the IRAD Records. A list of all databases containing the name you enter will be returned. Simply click on a database from the list to search for the record in that database.

✓ **NOTE:** The **Public Domain Land Tract Sales** webpage of the Illinois State Archives has Quick Links to the following:
- **Bureau of Land Management Federal Land Patents Database.** A search can be done here by surname for original land patents issued in Illinois.
- **Federal Township Plats of Illinois.** Includes federal Township/Range/Section maps for all of Illinois.
- **Illinois Public Domain Land Tract Sales Map.** An excellent map of Illinois showing Counties, Townships, and Ranges, with Principal Meridians and Base Lines.

Genealogy in the Illinois State Archives. See www.cyberdriveillinois.com/departments/archives/services.html. This webpage serves as a home page for genealogists, with online guides to research, as follows:

1. Getting Started in Genealogy: An online essay organized into 1) Where to Begin, 2) Download a *Record of Ancestry* chart, 3) Links to researching at the Illinois State Archives, 4) Illinois State Genealogical Society, and 5) Other Genealogy Links.

2. Genealogical Research: State and Related Federal Government Records in the Illinois State Archives. Includes 1) Guidelines for Research at the Illinois State Archives, 2) Censuses, 3) Military Service Records, 4) World War I Draft Registration Records, 5) Veterans' Homes, Pensions, and Burials, 6) Vital Records, and 7) Land Sale Records.

3. Genealogical Research: Local Governmental Record in IRAD. Q & A about IRAD records.

4. Genealogical Research Series Pamphlets:
- Genealogical Research Series Pamphlet 1: Land Sales Records
- Genealogical Research Series Pamphlet 2: Probate Records
- Genealogical Research Series Pamphlet 3: Military Records
- Genealogical Research Series Pamphlet 4: Federal Census Records
- Genealogical Research Series Pamphlet 5: State Census Records
- Genealogical Research Series Pamphlet 6: African–American Records
- Genealogical Research Series Pamphlet 7: Death Records
- Genealogical Research Series Pamphlet 8: Illinois State Genealogical Society Microfilm Collection
- Genealogical Research Series Pamphlet 9: Illinois State Genealogical Society Prairie Pioneer Certificates

Bibliography
Illinois Censuses & Substitutes

Censuses and other name lists were created in French Louisiana before the British took over the region in 1763. Original manuscripts from both the French and British eras exist today. Some of the colonial records reside in the county courthouses for the first two counties of Illinois: both St. Clair and Randolph County have surviving French and British land records created prior to the Revolutionary War. More colonial records from the French and British eras are located today at the State Archives in Springfield.

The first American census taken in what was to become Illinois was the 1807 Indiana territorial census. Illinois' two original counties, St. Clair, and Randolph, were inherited from Indiana Territory when Illinois Territory was created in 1809. In the 1810 Illinois territorial census, which was separate from the federal census of 1810, the two original counties were also included. An Illinois territorial census was taken again in 1818, mainly to determine if Illinois Territory had the minimum residents required for statehood. In just a few weeks after the 1818 territorial census, Illinois became a state.

After statehood, the Illinois legislature authorized state censuses for 1820, 1825, 1830, 1835, 1840, 1845 1855, and 1865, all separate from the federal censuses. Unfortunately only the 1820, 1855, and 1865 state censuses have survived reasonably intact. Most of the county returns for 1825, 1830, 1835, and 1845 are missing and nearly half of the 1840 state census was lost.

Since Illinois chose to conduct several of its state censuses in the same years as the federal censuses, it may not be obvious that there are potentially two statewide name lists available for 1810, 1820, 1830, and 1840 (although the state versions are mostly incomplete for those years).

The bibliography shows published and online territorial, state, and federal census records plus other statewide name lists unique to Illinois. Included are county-wide name lists for the earliest counties, plus a selection of name lists from any county.

♦ ♦ ♦ ♦ ♦

1678-1814. *Raymond H. Hammes Collection (Land Transfers)* **[Microfilm & Digital Capture],** from the original manuscripts at the Illinois State Archives. The sale of Illinois land began in the late 17th century, nearly 100 years before the establishment of the United States. While under the control of three separate and distinct governmental authorities: France (1678–1763), England (1763–1778), and the state of Virginia (1778–1784), individuals residing in what was to become the state of Illinois received and conveyed title to lands there. Throughout these periods respective government agents registered land transactions. After the United States established its control over Illinois in 1784, the federal government eventually began a review process to determine the legitimacy of preexisting land claims. When examinations were completed in 1814, federal authorities had confirmed title to less than half of the claims presented to them.

Record Contents: The Raymond H. Hammes Collection at the State Archives chronicles Illinois land transfers during 1678–1814. The collection consists of 157 microfilm reels and includes selected governmental records and private papers. In 12 years of independent research Raymond Hammes abstracted these records and recorded more than 10,000 ancient land grants, transfers, and other contract transactions. These abstracts usually detail the names and relationships of sellers and purchasers, a description and location of the real estate and/or personal property in question, the selling price, and sale and filing dates. Often provided are the names and relationships of prior owners, ancestors, and neighbors. See *Genealogical Research Series Pamphlet No. 1,* a downloadable PDF file at the Illinois State Archives for more information on the Hammes Collection and how to access the records:
www.cyberdriveillinois.com/publications/pdf_publications/ard124.pdf.

- The microfilm from the Hammes Collection is also located at the FHL in Salt Lake City, and several digitized databases have been created from the Hammes Collection. See the titles listed below by their inclusive dates:

1678-1814. *Consolidated Index for the Raymond H. Hammes Collection at the Illinois State Archives* **[Microfilm & Digital Capture],** from the original manuscripts at the Illinois State Archives, Springfield, IL. This is a comprehensive alphabetical surname index of the principal individuals involved in land transfers as well as cited individuals who were neighbors or witnesses to transactions. Filmed by the Genealogical Society of Utah, 1988, 1 roll, FHL film #1543598. See *Genealogical Research Series Pamphlet No. 1,* a downloadable PDF file at the Illinois State Archives for more information on the Hammes Collection and how to use this index to access the records. See www.cyberdriveillinois.com/publications/pdf_publications/ard124.pdf.

- See also *Consolidated Index for the Raymond H. Hammes Collection* **[Microfilm & Digital Capture].** To access the digital images, see the online FHL catalog page:
www.familysearch.org/search/catalog/533302.

1722-1784 *Land Records* **[Microfilm & Digital Capture],** from the original records at the Illinois State Archives, Springfield, IL, part of the Raymond H. Hammes Collection. This volume contains abstracts of Illinois land transactions, 1722-1784, translated from the original French. Includes a general index by transaction number. Some personal names are found under "Occupations" in the index. Lists of military & religious personnel are also found in the index. Filmed by the Genealogical Society of Utah, 1988, 1 roll, FHL film 1543598, Item 1 (Land Records). To access the digital images, see the online FHL catalog page:
www.familysearch.org/search/catalog/534081.

- See also, *Miscellaneous Land Records: Insinuations, Grants, Confirmations, Lists of Inhabitants, Lists of Militia Men Entitled to Land, Etc., 1722-1812* **[Microfilm & Digital Capture],** from the original manuscript at the Illinois State Archives, Springfield, IL, part of the Raymond H. Hammes Collection. Indexed in the Consolidated Index, Hammes Collection. Filmed by the Genealogical Society of Utah, 1988, 1 roll, FHL film #1543598. To access the digital images, see the online FHL catalog page: **www.familysearch.org/search/catalog/534081.**

1722-1863. *Illinois Servitude and Emancipation Records* **[Online Database],** an index to approximately 3,400 names found in government records involving the servitude and emancipation of Africans and, occasionally, Indians in the French and English eras of colonial Illinois (1722-1790) and African Americans in the American period of Illinois (1790-1863). The Illinois State Archives extracted the names of servants, slaves, or free persons and masters, witnesses, or related parties from selected governmental records to produce this database. After searching the database, researchers can see an abstract of the record by clicking the record number of the appropriate entry. See www.cyberdriveillinois.com/departments/archives/databases/servant.html.

- See also *Illinois Servitude and Emancipation Records, 1720-1865* [Online Database], indexed at the Ancestry.com website. This database has 2,055 records. See
https://search.ancestry.com/search/db.aspx?dbid=3749.

1729-1956. *Illinois, Diocese of Belleville, Catholic Parish Records* [Online Database], digitized at the FamilySearch.org website. This database has 34,135 images of parish registers recording the events of baptism, first communion, confirmation (to 1907), marriage (to 1930) or death (to 1956) in the Diocese of Belleville (Illinois), Roman Catholic Church. In addition to traditional parish registers, this collection includes a small number of census, church history, family, and financial records. Taken from the microfilm at the FHL in Salt Lake City, UT, "Catholic Church of Southern Illinois, Belleville." See
www.familysearch.org/search/collection/1388122.

1763-1916. *Illinois Marriage Records Index* [Microfiche], compiled by the Illinois State Genealogical Society, from records located at the Illinois State Archives, Springfield, IL. This index is an ongoing project of the Illinois State Archives and the Illinois State Genealogical Society to produce an index of Illinois marriages prior to 1901. Filmed by the Archives and the Society, 1994, 94 microfiche, beginning with FHL fiche #6334564 (Unknown, incomplete names - Adams, David). To see if this microfiche has been digitized yet, see the FHL catalog page: **www.familysearch.org/search/catalog/705931**.

1763-1900 Illinois Statewide Marriage Index [Online Database], indexed at the Illinois State Archives website. Since 1985 the Illinois State Genealogical Society (ISGS) has cooperated with the Illinois State Archives to create an index to Illinois marriages occurring prior to 1901. Today more than one million marriages, or two million names, are included in the Illinois Statewide Marriage Index. The sources for this index include original county clerks' marriage records, such as marriage registers and licenses, as well as publications of county genealogical societies and private individuals. For each marriage, the index includes the names of the groom and bride, the date of the marriage or issuance of the license, the name of the county in which the marriage was performed, and a citation to the original record. See
www.cyberdriveillinois.com/departments/archives/databases/marriage.html.

1673-1818. *Names of Early Illinois Settlers (as listed in the Pioneer History of Illinois)*, [Online Database], indexed at the GenealogyTrails.com website: **www.genealogytrails.com/ill/ILSettlers.html**.

1772-1999. *Illinois, Wills and Probate Records* [Online Database], indexed at the Ancestry.com website. Original data: Illinois County, District and Probate Courts. Each record includes: Name, Probate Date, Probate Place, Inferred Death year, Inferred Death Place, and Item Description (Type, Book, Page, Year, Etc.). The contents of a probate file can vary from case to case, but certain details are found in most probates, most importantly, the names and residences of beneficiaries and their relationship to the decedent. An inventory of the estate assets can reveal personal details about the deceased's occupation and lifestyle. There may also be references to debts, deeds, and other documents related to the settling of the estate. This database has 898,073 records. See
https://search.ancestry.com/search/db.aspx?dbid=9048.

1774-1974. *Illinois Soldier Burial Places* [Online Database], indexed at the FamilySearch.org website. Source: IL State Archives. From an index card file of soldiers buried in Illinois. Most of these soldiers served from 1774-1898. This database has 144,735 records. See **www.familysearch.org/search/collection/2171435**.

1775-1850. *Illinois, Revolutionary War Veteran Burials* [Online Database], indexed at the. Ancestry.com website. This database has 185 pages:
https://search.ancestry.com/search/db.aspx?dbid=48613.

1775-1995. *Illinois, Databases of Illinois Veterans Index* [Online Database], indexed at the Ancestry.com website. Source: IL State Archives. Each record includes: Name, Cemetery, Burial Place, Volume, Page, Record Source, and a link to the URL of the IL State Archives website. This database has 414,835 records. See
https://search.ancestry.com/search/db.aspx?dbid=9759.

1775-1850. *Illinois, Revolutionary War Veteran Burials Index* [Online Database], indexed at the Ancestry.com website. Original data: Harriet J. Walker, *Revolutionary Soldiers Buried in Illinois,* publ. Los Angeles, CA, 1917. Each record includes: Name,

Birthplace, and Comments (which are often quite extensive). This database has 666 pages. See
https://search.ancestry.com/search/db.aspx?dbid=4508.

1775-1860. *Illinois Pensioners List of the Revolution; 1812 & Indian Wars* **[Printed Book & Digital Version],** by Homer A. Walker, digitized 2018 by FamilySearch International. To access the digital images, see the online FHL catalog page:
www.familysearch.org/search/catalog/2842999.

1778-1790 Cahokia Records **[Online Database],** a digitized book (with OCR index) at the Ancestry.com website. Original data: Cahokia records, 1778-1790. Springfield, Ill.: Trustees of the Illinois State Historical Library, 1907. Cahokia was the first county seat of St. Clair County, an original county of Illinois. This database has 822 pages:
https://search.ancestry.com/search/db.aspx?dbid=19761.

1785-1898. *U.S. Indexed Early Land Ownership and Township Plats* **[Online Database],** indexed at the Ancestry.com website. This database has 165,796 records, with extracted names from the township plat maps from the Public Lands Survey in the United States initiated by the Land Ordinance Act of 1785. This collection includes maps of townships in all or parts of Alabama, Illinois, Indiana, Iowa, Kansas, Mississippi, Missouri, Ohio, Oklahoma, Oregon, Washington, and Wisconsin. The Public Lands Survey divided public lands west of the original colonies into a grid of townships and sections. A township was a square six miles to a side and contained 36 one-square-mile (or 640 acre) sections. These maps became the basis for property claims as public domain lands were transferred to private ownership. Search the entire collection by name, location, years; or browse the database by state, principal meridian, and range of Ranges/Townships. See
http://search.ancestry.com/search/db.aspx?dbid=2179.

1787 Census of Kaskaskia **[Online Database],** indexed at the GenealogyTrails.com website. Kaskaskia was the first county seat of Randolph County, an original Illinois county, see
www.genealogytrails.com/ill/1787kaskcensus.html.

1790-1857 Indexes to Court Records (St. Clair County, IL), by Plaintiff and Defendant **[Microfilm & Digital Capture],** from originals at the Illinois State Archives, Springfield, IL. Filmed by the archives, 1986, 1 roll, FHL film #1689038. To access the digital images, see the online FHL catalog page:
www.familysearch.org/search/catalog/558957.

1790-1860. *Illinois, Compiled Marriages* **[Online Database],** indexed at the Ancestry.com website. This database has 163,917 records compiled by Liahona Research, Provo, UT, from FHL microfilm. Information for each individual includes a name, spouse's name, date and location of marriage, and source. The search/browse screen at Ancestry.com has a table showing the Illinois counties covered, the inclusive dates of marriages, and the FHL film source:
http://search.ancestry.com/search/db.aspx?dbid=7851. - Another version of this database was published by Jordan Dodd (aka Liahona Research) with the dates 1791-1850, see
https://search.ancestry.com/search/db.aspx?dbid=2086.

1791-1810. *St. Clair County, Illinois, Book A, Marriage Certificates and Licenses, Feb. 1807-July 1810: Some Additional Records from Deed Book A & Loose Papers* **[Printed Book],** by Peggy Lathrop Sapp. Includes surname index. Published by Folk Works Research, Springfield, IL, 1993, 23 pages, FHL book 977.389 V2sp.

1796-1814. See *St. Clair County, Illinois Court Records, Marks, and Brands, 1807-1831 and 1796-1797, Tavern Licenses Granted 1808-1814* **[Printed Book],** by Peggy Lathrop Sapp. Includes surname index. Published by Folk Works Research, Springfield, IL, 1993, 45 pages, FHL book 977.389 R2s.

1799-1813 Land and Property Records, St. Clair County, Illinois **[Microfilm & Digital Capture],** from the original manuscripts at the Illinois State Archives, Springfield, IL. St. Clair (with Randolph) was one of the two original counties of Illinois and covered the northern 3/4^{ths} of the present state of Illinois. These records are mostly for the first settled areas along the Mississippi River north of Fort Kaskaskia. Some marriage information may be found among the deeds. Filmed by the state archives, 1985, 1 roll, FHL film #1689031. To access the digital images, see the online FHL catalog page:
www.familysearch.org/search/catalog/558920.

1800-1820. *Cahokia Books B & C, Land Records* **[Microfilm & Digital Capture],** vols. 4-5 of the Raymond H. Hammes Collection. Text mostly in English, some in French. All entries pertain to St. Clair

County as it existed in the late 1700s and early 1800s, and to the inhabitants of the villages then within its borders: Cahokia (the county seat), Prairie du Pont, Harrison, Peoria, Michilimackinac, and Bellefontaine. Filmed by the Genealogical Society of Utah, 1988, 1 roll, FHL film #1543598. To access the digital images, see the online FHL catalog page:
www.familysearch.org/search/catalog/533302.

1800-1940. *Illinois, County Marriage Records* **[Online Database],** indexed at the Ancestry.com website. Source: Ancestry extractions from various Illinois county collections. Each record may include: Name, Gender, Age, Birth Date, Marriage Date, Marriage Place, Father, Mother, Spouse, and Film Number. This database has 5,268,844 records. See https://search.ancestry.com/search/db.aspx?dbid=61370.

1800-1840. *McLean County, White County, Will County Genealogical Records* **[Online Database],** digitized and indexed at the Ancestry.com website. Original data: *McLean County, White County, Will County Genealogical Records,* Evanston, IL: Illinois Society, D.A.R., 1945. Browse this collection for Title page, Front matter, Table of contents, McLean County, White County, Will County, Index. This database has 137 pages. See
https://search.ancestry.com/search/db.aspx?dbid=27154.

1800-1850. *Randolph County, Where Illinois Began* **[Printed Book],** compiled by the Randolph County Genealogical Society. Includes 1807, 1825 & 1840 censuses; marriages; deeds; participants in court cases; deaths from administrators' lists, 1844-1848; cemetery records (those born before 1851); probate index, and surname index. Published by the society, Chester, IL, 369 pages, FHL book 977.392 V3r.

1800-1998. *Illinois, County Naturalization Records* **[Online Database],** digitized and indexed at the FamilySearch.org website. Includes naturalization records from county courthouses in Illinois. This database has 1,059,509 records. See
www.familysearch.org/search/collection/1989159.

1800-1999. *DeKalb County, Illinois Naturalizations* **[Online Database],** indexed at the Ancestry.com website. Original data: DeKalb County Clerk and Recorder, Sycamore, Illinois, 2012. Each record includes (at least): Name, and Naturalization Date. This database has 22,521 records. See
https://search.ancestry.com/search/db.aspx?dbid=5392.

1804. *Early Court Records of Randolph County, Illinois: Beginning in 1804 – Census, Court Cases, Marriages, Probates & Wills, Relocation of County Seat, Roads and Bridges* **[Printed Book],** compiled and published by the Randolph County Genealogical Society, 2009, 292 pages, FHL book 977.392 P2rce.

1804-1814 Kaskaskia French and English Deed Records **[Microfilm & Digital Capture],** from the original records at the Randolph County Courthouse, Chester, IL. Kaskaskia was the capital of Upper Louisiana during the French era; the first county seat of Randolph County, an original Illinois county of 1809; and the first capital of Illinois Territory. These records provide names of land owners during the transition from the early French to the English eras; and later American settlements in Illinois. Filmed by the Genealogical Society of Utah, 1977, 3 rolls, as follows:
- Deeds vol. A45-B46 1804-1806, FHL film #1012401.
- Deeds vol. C47-D48 1804-1814, FHL film #1012402.
- Translation of French deeds in vol. A-D, vol. 49 1804-1814, FHL film #1012403.

To access the digital images, see the online FHL catalog page:
www.familysearch.org/search/catalog/231287.

1805-1985. *Illinois, Church Marriages* **[Online Database],** indexed at the FamilySearch.org website. Source: FamilySearch extractions from various churches in Illinois. This database has 4,715 records:
www.familysearch.org/search/collection/2534491.

1807. Colonial and Territorial Research Collection of Illinois: Land Sales, Squatters [Microfilm & Digital Capture], vol. 18 of the Raymond H. Hammes Collection. Includes list of land applicants. This material is concerned with what is now Southern Illinois. Filmed by the Genealogical Society of Utah, 1988, 1 roll, FHL film 1543598. To access the digital images, see the online FHL catalog page:
www.familysearch.org/search/catalog/533302.

1807 Census of Indiana Territory [Printed Facsimile], from the original manuscript, published by the Indiana Historical Society, 1980, 57 pages. In 1807, Indiana Territory included St. Clair and Randolph counties, now in Illinois. (Illinois Territory was formed in 1809). Includes name index. FHL book 977.2 X2c and FHL film #1033927. To see if this microfilm has been digitized yet, see the FHL catalog page:
www.familysearch.org/search/catalog/270021.

1807. *Election Held at Kaskaskia in the County of Randolph to Elect a Representative to the Assembly of the Indiana Territory on 02 Feb 1807* **[Online Database]**, indexed at the Genealogy Trails.com website. See
www.genealogytrails.com/ill/randolph/election1807.htm.

1807-1977. *Surname Index of the Genealogy Society of Southern Illinois* **[Printed Book & Digital Version]**, compiled by Louise Morehouse, publ. Carterville, IL, Gen. Soc. of So. Illinois, 1977, 61 pages, FHL book 977.3 D22. To access the digital version, see the online FHL catalog page:
www.familysearch.org/search/catalog/586239.

1810 Federal Census of Illinois Territory **[Printed Index]**, an alphabetized name list, compiled by Accelerated Indexing Systems, North Salt Lake, UT, 1987, 27 pages. Includes only Randolph County, Illinois Territory, which then included the area of several modern counties of southern Illinois. (The only other Illinois county in 1810 was St. Clair, whose 1810 census schedules were lost). See FHL book 977.3 X28i.

1810-1818 Illinois Census Returns **[Printed Book & Online Database]**, edited by Margaret Cross Norton, originally published by the Trustees of the Illinois State Historical Library, Springfield, IL, 1935, as *Collections of the Illinois State Historical Society*, vol. 24, (reprint, Genealogical Publishing Co., Inc., Baltimore, 1969), 329 pages. The volume is devoted to the schedules available from the 1810 state census, to returns from the 1818 state census, and to an index of names. FHL book 977.3 B4i v. 24. Also on FHL film #897331.
- See also, *Illinois Census Returns, 1810 and 1818* **[Online Database]**, *digitized and indexed* at Ancestry.com, see
http://search.ancestry.com/search/db.aspx?dbid=48327.

1810-1848. See *Illinois, Soldiers of the Frontier, 1810-1813; the Black Hawk War, 1831-1832; and the Mexican War, 1846-1848* **[Online Database]**, digitized and OCR indexed at the Ancestry.com website. Source: IL Adjutant General, 1882. This database has 372 pages. See
https://search.ancestry.com/search/db.aspx?dbid=28914.

1810-1820. **[Illinois People in]** *Midwest Pioneers* **[CD-ROM]**, a publication of Broderbund's Family Tree Maker Archives in collaboration with Genealogical Publishing Co., Inc., Baltimore, 1999. Illinois Contents: *Pioneer families of the Midwest*, by Blanche L. Walden (vols. I-III); *Illinois Census Returns, 1810 and 1818*, edited with introduction and notes by Margaret Cross Norton; *Illinois Census Returns, 1820*, edited by Margaret Cross Norton; *Revolutionary Soldiers Buried in Illinois*, by Harriet J. Walker, FHL CD-ROM no. 9, pt. 508.

1810-1861. *Name Index to Early Illinois Records* **[Microfilm & Digital Capture]**, from 3x5 card indexes located at the Illinois State Archives, Springfield, IL, this major work includes indexes to the IL state and federal censuses of 1810, 1818, 1820, 1825, 1830, 1835, 1840, 1845, 1850, and 1855; plus executive records to 1861; election returns of 1818-1847; House and Senate journals through 1830's; and early laws to 1849. Part of the Perrin Collection at the IL State Archives. Filmed by the archives, 1975, 248 rolls. FHL film begins with film #1001592 (Aacer – Adams). To access the digital images, see the online FHL catalog page:
www.familysearch.org/search/catalog/40879.

✓ **NOTE:** *Name Index to Early Illinois Records*, has nearly one million original index cards. Until statewide census indexes for all states were created for the Internet by various providers, this card index from Illinois was unique, the largest census index for any state in the U.S., dating back to the 1930s. Like many other publications of the Illinois State Archives, this 1810-1861 card index is a legacy of the person responsible, Margaret Cross Norton, the first state archivist of Illinois (who happened to be an amateur genealogist). See the IL State Archives information website with a link to *Genealogical Research Series Pamphlet 4: Federal Census Records*; and *Pamphlet 5: State Census Records*. To access all pamphlets, see
www.cyberdriveillinois.com/departments/archives/services.html.

1810-1890. *Illinois Compiled Census and Census Substitute Index* **[Online Database]**, indexes originally edited by Ronald V. Jackson, Accelerated Indexing, Salt Lake City, UT. Electronic files were acquired in 1999 by Ancestry, Inc. which has these Illinois lists indexed at their website. A combined index contains the following:
- 1810 Randolph Co Census
- 1818 Territorial Census Index
- 1820 State Census Index
- 1825 State Census Index
- 1830 Federal Census Index

- 1830 State Census - Morgan Co only
- 1835 State Census Index
- 1840 Federal Census Index
- 1840 State Census Index
- 1840 Pensioners List
- 1850 Federal Census Index
- 1855 State Census Index
- 1860 Federal Census Index
- 1870 Federal Census Index
- 1880 Cook County Census Index
- 1890 Veterans Schedule

See http://search.ancestry.com/search/db.aspx?dbid=3545.

1810-1940. *Illinois, County Marriages* **[Online Database],** digitized and indexed at the FamilySearch.org website. Source: FamilySearch extractions from various county offices in Illinois. Each record may include: Name, Event Type, Event Date, Event Place, Gender, Age, Birth Year (estimated), Father's Name, Mother's Name, Spouse's Name, Spouse's Gender, Spouse's Age, Spouse's Birth Year (estimated), Spouse's Father's Name, Spouse's Mother's Name, and Page Number. This database has 2,632,093 records. See www.familysearch.org/search/collection/1803970.

1810-1990s. *Illinois Collection Catalog at MyHeritage.com* **[Online Database],** 96 collections with 6,896,401 records specific to Illinois. Databases include censuses, directories, family histories, town histories, military rosters, college year books, and more. This is a subscription site, but a free search can be done for a name, place, year, or keyword. See www.myheritage.com/research/catalog?location=illinois.

1811-1990. *Illinois, Compiled Records from Lockport Area Genealogical and Historical Society* **[Online Database],** a name index at the Ancestry.com website. Original data: Genealogical Records. Lockport Area Genealogical and Historical Society, Lockport, Illinois. This database has 99,167 records. See https://search.ancestry.com/search/db.aspx?dbid=61104.

1811-1995. *Lockport Area, Illinois, Church, Cemetery, and Other Records* **[Online Database],** indexed at the Ancestry.com website. Original data: Genealogical Records. Lockport Area Genealogical and Historical Society, Lockport, Illinois. Each record includes: Name, Event Type, Residence Place, and Record Place. This database has 141,422 records. See https://search.ancestry.com/search/db.aspx?dbid=61412.

1812-1814. *Illinois War of 1812 Veterans* **[Online Database],** indexed at the Illinois State Archives website. This database indexes the names of Illinois militiamen listed on the War of 1812 muster rolls included in the ninth volume of the *Report of the Adjutant General of the State of Illinois* (1902). The original muster rolls, first published in the Adjutant General's 1882 report, recorded approximately 1,500 names appearing in 24 rosters of officers, companies or units. See www.cyberdriveillinois.com/departments/archives/databases/war1812.html.

1813-1903. *Madison County Probate Case Files Index* **[Online Database],** indexed at the Illinois State Archives website. See www.cyberdriveillinois.com/departments/archives/databases/madison.html.

1813-1909. *Illinois, Public Land Purchase Records* **[Online Database],** indexed at the Ancestry.com website. Source: State of Illinois. Land sales from the Illinois public domain were recorded by a variety of persons employed by the federal, state, or local governments. The records in this database were transferred to the Illinois State Archives and detail the sale of over 54,000 square miles of public land. Each entry includes the purchaser's name, purchase date, number of acres, price per acre, and in some cases the purchaser's sex and residence. This database has 546,064 records. See https://search.ancestry.com/search/db.aspx?dbid=3780.

1814 Jurors List, Madison County, Illinois **[Online Database],** indexed at the Genealogy Trails website: http://genealogytrails.com/ill/madison/grandjury1814.htm.

1814-1816. *Colonial and Territorial Research Collection of Illinois: Land Sales, Preemptions* **[Microfilm & Digital Capture],** vol. 19 of the Raymond H. Hammes Collection. These records identify squatters who wanted to claim land in southern Illinois. They are listed in alphabetical order. Filmed by the Genealogical Society of Utah, 1988, 1 roll, FHL film #1543598. To access the digital images, see the online FHL catalog page: www.familysearch.org/search/catalog/534379.

1814-1872 Original Land Patents, Randolph County, Illinois **[Printed Book],** abstracted by Lola Frazer Crowder, 1991, 174 pages. As one of two original counties of Illinois, the federal land sales during the early period represent a large part of the early population. These name lists are county records relating to the original public land buyers in Randolph County. FHL book 977.392 R28c.

1814-1872. *Kaskaskia Land Warrants, Military Certificates, Randolph County, Illinois* **[Printed Book]**, by Peggy Lathrop Sapp of Springfield, Illinois, from film at the Illinois State Archives. Includes four alphabetical indexes. See FHL book 977.392 R2s.

1814-1925. *Public Domain Sales Land Tract Record Listing (Index)* **[Microfiche]**, from a computer printout made in 1984 at the Illinois State Archives, Springfield, IL, with reference to public land sales from the U.S. Government to individuals in Illinois. This alphabetically arranged index includes the name of a land purchaser, type of sale, description of the land purchased (including section, township, range, and principal meridian), number of acres purchased, total purchase price, date of purchase, and volume and page of the original land record on which the transaction was entered. This project was originally called the Public Domain Computer Conversion Project. It indexes over 550,000 individual entries obtained from sales records of the U.S. General Land Office, Illinois officials, and the Illinois Central Railroad. Filmed by the IL Archives, 1984, 144 microfiche, all under FHL fiche #6016848.

1814-1925. *Index to Public Domain Sales – Land Tract Record Listing for Illinois* **[Online Database]**, a searchable online index by Legal Description or by Name of Purchaser at the IL State Archives website. Each record includes the name of purchaser, type of sale, description of the land purchased (including section, township, range, and principal meridian), number of acres purchased, total purchase price, date of purchase, and volume and page of the original land record on which the transaction was entered. It indexes over 550,000 individual entries obtained from sales records of the U.S. General Land Office, Illinois officials, and the Illinois Central Railroad. See www.cyberdriveillinois.com/departments/archives/databases/data_lan.html.

1814-1925. Illinois Original Land Owners. See the *Family Maps* series for Illinois counties, maps of all original land patents, compiled by Greg Boyd, publ. Arphax Publishing Co., Norman, OK. These privately-produced computer-generated maps show the first property owners for an entire county, produced as a book of maps, each map laid out on the federal township grid, and includes indexes to help you locate a person, place-name, or cemetery. Additional maps are added for each county to show roads, waterways, railroads, selected city centers, and cemeteries within a county. Visit the publisher's information and ordering website for more details and updated county coverage. See **www.arphax.com/**.

1814-1900s. The Illinois Archives, a Digital Library of the USGenWeb Archives Project. A city/town list and a county-by-county files list leads to hundreds of genealogical databases. A typical county has an array of databases from Bibles, Biographies, Cemeteries, Census, Churches, Court, Deaths, Deeds/Land, History, Marriages, Military, News, Obituaries, Post Cards, Wills, and more. See http://usgwarchives.net/il/ilfiles.htm.

1815-1870. *St. Clair County Circuit Court Chancery Case Files Index* **[Online Database]**, indexed at the Illinois State Archives website. See www.cyberdriveillinois.com/departments/archives/databases/stcchan.html.

1815-1935. *Illinois, Marriages* **[Online Database]**, indexed at the FamilySearch.org website. Includes a name index to marriage records from the state of Illinois, taken from the microfilm copies available at the Family History Library in Salt Lake City. This database has 636,536 records. See www.familysearch.org/search/collection/1680829.

1816 List of Taxpayers, Monroe County, Illinois [Online Database], indexed at the USGenWeb site for Monroe Co IL. See http://monroe.illinoisgenweb.org/1816_taxpayers.htm.

1818 Illinois State Census Index **[Printed Index]**, edited by Ronald Vern Jackson, et al, Accelerated Indexing, North Salt Lake, UT,1997, 93 pages. The name list was generated from the originals. Records on 14 of the 15 counties in existence at the time of the census have been preserved. (Edwards County missing). See FHL book 977.3 X28i. **NOTE:** Illinois became a state in 1818, but the census noted above was taken a few weeks before that and was actually the "1818 Territorial Census."

1818-1848 Illinois Election Returns **[Printed Book, Microfilm & Digital Version]**, from the publication edited by Theodore Calvin Pease, published by the

Trustees of Illinois State Historical Library, vol. 18, *Collections of the Illinois State Historical Library: Statistical Series*, 1923. Filmed by the Genealogical Society of Utah, 1984, 1 roll, FHL book 977.3 B4i v.18 and FHL film #1035628. To access the digital version, see the online FHL catalog page:
www.familysearch.org/search/catalog/197977.

1818-1968. *Illinois Cemetery Records* [Online Database], digitized and OCR indexed at the Ancestry.com website. Source: Book, same title, prepared by the DAR, Illinois Society. This database has 110 pages. See
https://search.ancestry.com/search/db.aspx?dbid=29748.

1818-2016. *Illinois Newspaper Archives* [Online Database], digitized and indexed at the GenealogyBank.com website. Includes newspapers from the following Illinois cities: Alton, Belleville, Bloomington, Canton, Centralia, Charleston, Chester, Chicago, Dixon, East Moline, East Saint Louis, Edwardsville, Elgin, Elizabethtown, Evanston, Farmer City, Freeport, Galena, Galesburg, Greenville, Havana, Highland, Jacksonville, Joliet, Kaskaskia, Knoxville, Mattoon, Nashville, Nauvoo, Oquawka, Oregon, Ottawa, Paris, Peoria, Pittsfield, Quincy, Rock Island, Rockford, Rushville, Shawneetown, Shiloh, Springfield, Sterling, Tuscola, Vandalia, Wheaton, and Woodstock. See
www.genealogybank.com/gbnk/newspapers/explore/USA/Illinois/.

1819-1970. *Illinois Probate Records* [Online Database], digitized at the FamilySearch.org website. This database has 1,137,607 images of a collection of probate records, which includes wills, indexes, and other documents created to track the distribution of estates of deceased individuals who lived in Illinois. Probates were generally recorded in the county of residence. This collection covers probate records created by Illinois courts. See
www.familysearch.org/search/collection/1834344.

1820 Federal Census of Illinois [Printed Index], compiled by Lowell M. Volkel and James V. Gill, published by Heritage House, Danville, IL, 1966, 79 pages, FHL book 977.3 X2v 1820.

1820. *Fourth Census of the United States, 1820, Illinois Population Schedule* [Printed Index], transcribed by Larry C. Bohannan, published by Century Enterprises, Huntsville, AR, 1968, FHL book 977.3 X2p 1820.

1820. *Illinois 1820 Census Index* [Printed Index], edited by Ronald Vern Jackson, et al, published by Accelerated Indexing Systems, Bountiful, UT, 1977, 155 pages, FHL book 977.3 X2j 1820.

1820-1825 Residents of early Randolph County, Illinois [Printed Book], compiled by Lucille Wittnenborn Wiechens, published 1989, 26 pages. Names are in alphabetical order. Includes names from the 1825 state census and names from 1820 land records. Includes short history of Illinois and Randolph County. FHL book 977.392 X2w.

1820-1840. *Illinois, 1820 thru 1840 Federal Census: Population Schedules* [Microfilm & Digital Capture], from the originals at the National Archives, Washington, DC. Filmed as a series, 1820-1840, 11 rolls total, beginning with FHL film #506763 (1820); FHL film #7647 (1830); FHL film #7641 (1830); and FHL film #7643 (1840). To access the digital images, see the online FHL catalog page:
www.familysearch.org/search/catalog/745487.

1820 Illinois State Census [Originals], at the Illinois State Archives, Record Series 103.002, 2 vols., no microfilm. Each county return includes name of county and for each household name or head of household and numbers of free white males twenty-one years of age and older, other white inhabitants, slaves and servants, and free Negroes and mulattoes. Returns are included for 18 of 19 counties exiting at that time: Alexander, Bond, Clark, Crawford, Franklin, Gallatin, Jackson, Jefferson, Johnson, Madison, Monroe, Pope, Randolph, St. Clair, Union, Washington, Wayne, and White counties. Only Edwards county is missing. (Indexed in *Name Index to Early Illinois Records, 1810-1855* by the Illinois State Archives). See the Illinois State Archives *Genealogical Research Series Pamphlet No. 5 – State Census Records*, an online PDF file downloadable at
www.cyberdriveillinois.com/publications/pdf_publications/ard128.pdf.

1820. *Illinois Census Returns, 1820* [Printed Book & Online Database], from the 1820 Illinois State Census, separate from the 1820 federal census, edited by Margaret Cross Norton, published Springfield, IL: Trustees of the Illinois State Historical Library, 1934, 466 pages, as part of *Collections of the Illinois State Historical Library, Statistical Series*, Vol. 3. The 1820 IL State Census originals were never microfilmed, mainly because this book was so complete and beautifully indexed. From preface: "This book contains

not only the 1820 state census schedules but also notes comparing all discrepancies between the names as written in the 1818 territorial, the 1820 state, and the 1820 federal censuses." Includes an index of names FHL book 977.3 B4i v. 26 and FHL film #6051147. **Online versions:** This 1820 state census book was digitized and indexed at the Ancestry.com site as *Illinois Census, 1820.* See
http://search.ancestry.com/search/db.aspx?dbid=48328.

1821-1848 Probate Index, Greene County, Illinois [Online Database], indexed at the RootsWeb site for Greene Co IL. See
www.rootsweb.ancestry.com/~ilmaga/greene/misc/probate_index.htm.

1821-1885 Probate Case Files Index, Sangamon County, Illinois [Online Database], indexed at the GenealogyTrails.com website. See
http://genealogytrails.com/ill/sangamon/probate_1821-85.html.

1821-1906 Probate Case Files Index, Sangamon County, Illinois [Online Database], indexed at the Illinois State Archives website. See
www.cyberdriveillinois.com/departments/archives/databases/sangprob.html.

1824-1940. *Illinois, Births and Christening* **[Online Database],** indexed at the FamilySearch.org website. This is a name index to birth, baptism, and christening records from the state of Illinois. Microfilm copies of these records are available at the Family History Library and Family History Centers. This database has 507,005 records. See
www.familysearch.org/search/collection/1676968.

1824-2009. *Illinois, Select United Methodist Church Records* **[Online Database],** digitized and indexed at the Ancestry.com website. Each record may include: Name, Event Type, Event Date, Baptism Type, Baptism Date, and Baptism Place. This database has 112,750 records. See
https://search.ancestry.com/search/db.aspx?dbid=9062.

1825 Illinois State Census [Originals], at the Illinois State Archives, Springfield, IL. Entries for each household include name of head of household; number of free white males twenty-one years of age and older, including heads of families; number of free white males under twenty-one years of age, including heads of families; number of free white females, including heads of families; numbers of male and female servants and slaves, and free persons of color; and type (e.g., mill, distillery) and number of manufacturing establishments. Returns are included for 3 of 43 counties existing at that time: Edwards, Fulton, and Randolph. (Indexed in *Name Index to Early Illinois Records, 1810-1855* by the Illinois State Archives). See the Illinois State Archives *Genealogical Research Series Pamphlet No. 5 – State Census Records,* an online PDF file downloadable at
www.cyberdriveillinois.com/publications/pdf_publications/ard128.pdf.

1825 Illinois State Census Index **[Printed Index],** compiled by W. David Samuelsen, published by Accelerated Indexing Systems, North Salt Lake, 1985, 26 pages. FHL book 977.3 X2j.

1825 Census of Randolph County, Illinois **[Printed Extract & Index],** transcribed by Mrs. Harlin B. Taylor, published by Vio-Lin Enterprises, Decatur, IL, 1972, 29 pages. Includes index.

1825 Tax List, Peoria County, Illinois [Online Database], indexed at the GenealogyTrails.com website. See
http://genealogytrails.com/ill/peoria/tax/index.htm#1825.

1825-1837 Will Book Index, Morgan County, Illinois [Online Database], indexed at the RootsWeb site for Morgan Co IL. See
www.rootsweb.ancestry.com/~ilmaga/morgan2/wills-probates/early-wills.html.

1825-1865. *Illinois, State Census Collection, 1825-1865* **[Online Database],** digitized and indexed at Ancestry.com, acquired in 2008 from the Illinois State Archives microfilm for the following: 1825 IL State Census (3 counties, 1 roll); 1830 IL State Census (1 county, 1 roll); 1835 IL State Census (4 counties, 1 roll); 1845 IL State Census (3 counties, 1 roll); 1855 IL State Census (31 counties, 13 rolls); and 1865 IL State Census (99 counties, 18 rolls). The collection also contains the federal Non-population Census Schedules for Illinois, 1850-1880, 2 rolls. This database has 690,833 records. See
http://search.ancestry.com/search/db.aspx?dbid=1079.

1825-1876. *Fulton County Circuit Court Case Files Index* **[Online Database],** indexed at the Illinois State Archives website. See
www.cyberdriveillinois.com/departments/archives/databases/fulton.html.

1825-1887. *Peoria County Probate Case Files Index* **[Online Database],** indexed at the Illinois State Archives website. See www.cyberdriveillinois.com/departments/archives/databases/peoria.html.

1825-1901. *Sangamon County Guardian's Case Files Index (1825-1901)* **[Online Database],** indexed at the Illinois State Archives website. See www.cyberdriveillinois.com/departments/archives/databases/sang.html.

1827. *Illinois Winnebago War Veterans* **[Online Database],** indexed at the Illinois State Archives website. This database indexes the names of 412 militiamen found on the 1827 company rosters of the 20th Regiment of mounted volunteer riflemen included in the record series, Militia Files. This unit, raised in Sangamon and Morgan counties under the command of Colonel Thomas M. Neale, proceeded to Peoria to complete its organization. The militiamen then traveled to the Galena vicinity, where the regiment disbanded. This military action also became known as the Fever River Expedition. See www.cyberdriveillinois.com/departments/archives/databases/winebago.html.

1828-1871. *Shelby County Circuit Court Case Files Index* **[Online Database],** indexed at the Illinois State Archives website. See www.cyberdriveillinois.com/departments/archives/databases/shelby.html.

1829-1861. *Macon County Circuit Court Case Files Index* **[Online Database],** indexed at the Illinois State Archives website. See www.cyberdriveillinois.com/departments/archives/databases/macon.html.

1830 Illinois State Census **[Originals & Microfilm],** at the Illinois State Archives, Springfield, IL. Each county return includes: name of head of household; numbers of white males and females in each decennial age group (e.g., ages 0–9, 10–19, 20–29); numbers of male and female Negroes and mulattoes, indentured or registered servants, and French Negroes and mulattoes held in bondage; total number of inhabitants in household; number of males subject to duty in state militia; and type (e.g., gristmill) and number of manufacturing establishments. Of the 51 counties existing at that time, the only return included is for Morgan County. (Indexed in *Name Index to Early Illinois Records, 1810-1855* by the Illinois State Archives). See the Illinois State Archives *Genealogical Research Series Pamphlet No. 5 – State Census Records,* an online PDF file downloadable at www.cyberdriveillinois.com/publications/pdf_publications/ard128.pdf.

1830 Illinois State Census Index **[Printed Index],** by W. David Samuelsen, et al, published by Accelerated Indexing Systems, Bountiful, UT, 1984, 34 pages. FHL book 977.3 X2j.

1830. *Census, 1830, Gallatin County, Illinois* **[Online Database],** IL State Census indexed at the Ancestry.com website. This database appears to be a county copy, as no 1830 Gallatin Co IL name list is at the IL State Archives collection. See http://search.ancestry.com/search/db.aspx?dbid=24481.

1830. *Index to the 1830 Federal Census* **[Printed Index],** compiled by James V. Gill and Maryan R. Gill, published by Illiana Genealogical Pub. Co., Danville, IL, 1968, 4 vols., FHL book 977.3 X22g 1830.

1830 Federal. *Illinois 1830 Census Index* **[Printed Index],** edited by Ronald Vern Jackson, et al, published by Accelerated Indexing Systems, Bountiful, UT, 1976, 63 pages. FHL book 977.3 X2ja 1830.

1830-1848 Membership of The Church of Jesus Christ of Latter-day Saints **[Printed Book & Online Database],** compiled by Susan Black from more than 300 primary and secondary sources, identifying LDS members who lived in the U.S., Canada, and Great Britain. The largest number of Mormons during this period were in Illinois. The Mormon population in Nauvoo, Illinois began in 1839 and by 1844, Nauvoo rivaled Chicago as the largest city in Illinois, with over 12,000 inhabitants. Nearly the entire population of Nauvoo migrated to Utah, beginning in 1846. This database has 112,820 records, See www.ancestry.com/search/collections/5333.

1830-1884. *Illinois State Canal Commission's Land Sales Record* **[Microfilm],** from the original transcripts at the Illinois State Archives, Springfield, IL. Includes names of purchasers for Chicago, Lockport, Ottawa, and LaSalle. Other land sales described by section – no towns listed. Filmed by the archives, 19??, 1 roll, FHL film #1689049.

1830-1954. *Illinois, Lee County Records* **[Online Database],** digitized at the FamilySearch.org website. Includes Naturalization and Probate records from the Lee County Courthouse at Dixon, IL. This database has 108,387 images. See
www.familysearch.org/search/collection/2068938.

1830s-2001. *Master Index to the South Suburban Genealogical and Historical Society Cemetery Census Series* **[Printed Book],** compiled and published by the society. Cemeteries are primarily in Cook and Will Counties, IL, with 2 cemeteries in Lake County, IN. Published South Holland, IL, 2001, 742 pages, FHL book 977.3 V32m.

1831-1832. *Illinois Black Hawk War Veterans* **[Online Database],** indexed at the Illinois State Archives website. This database of Black Hawk War Veterans indexes the first volume of Ellen M. Whitney's *The Black Hawk War 1831-1832.* That volume contains a comprehensive listing of Illinois' Black Hawk War soldiers. It includes the muster rolls for all of the 1831 and 1832 companies including 2 Indian companies. Approximately 1,800 men served in the 1831 campaign and 9,000 in the 1832 campaign. The Illinois State Historical Library possesses in either original or on microfilm the records from which this database was extracted. See
www.cyberdriveillinois.com/departments/archives/databases/blkhawk.html.

1831-1937. *DeKalb County, Illinois Births* **[Online Database],** indexed at the Ancestry.com website. Source: DeKalb County Clerk and Recorder, Sycamore, Illinois, 2012. Each record includes: Name, and Birth Date. This database has 13,178 records. See
https://search.ancestry.com/search/db.aspx?dbid=5339.

1831-1841 *Delinquent Tax List, Clinton County, Illinois* **[Online Database],** indexed at the Clinton Co IL GenWeb site. See
http://clintonilgenweb.net/misc/taxes/delinq1831.htm.

1832-1900 *Will and Estate Index, Knox County, Illinois* **[Online Database],** indexed at the USGenWeb site for Knox Co IL. See
www.usgennet.org/usa/il/county/knox/will_estate_index.htm.

1833 *Tax List, Champaign County, Illinois* **[Online Database],** indexed at the Champaign Co IL GenWeb site (archived). See
http://web.archive.org/web/20080720010355/http://champaign.ilgenweb.net/other/taxassess.html.

1833 *Delinquent Tax List, Madison County, Illinois* **[Online Database],** indexed at the Genealogy-Trails.com website. See
http://genealogytrails.com/ill/madison/mc_1833_tax_list.htm.

1833-1871. *Chicago City Council Proceedings Files* **[Online Database],** indexed at the Illinois State Archives website. See
www.cyberdriveillinois.com/departments/archives/databases/chicago_proceedings/home.html.

1833-1889. *Cook County, Illinois, Marriage and Death Indexes* **[Online Database],** indexed at the Ancestry.com website. This database has 182,100 records, compiled by Sam Fink from marriage and death notices in Chicago newspapers, plus Cook County death records. Marriages cover the years 1833–1871. Death records are extracted from newspapers for the years 1856–1889 and from Cook County death records for 1878–1884. Marriage entries include names, marriage date, and source. Death entries extracted from newspapers include name, death date, and source. This database appears to be the same as FHL microfilm #1321939. The Ancestry website has the online database. See
http://search.ancestry.com/search/db.aspx?dbid=2433.

1833-1889. *Illinois, Civil Marriages* **[Online Database],** indexed at FamilySearch.org. Source: DAR and Hancock County Clerk of Courts. This is an index to selected civil marriages from published transcripts for the counties of Boone, Champaign, Christian, Cook, DeKalb, DuPage, and Hancock. This database has 8,971 records. See
www.familysearch.org/search/collection/2515894.

1834-1899. *Rock Island Probate Case Files Index* **[Online Database],** indexed at the Illinois State Archives website. See
www.cyberdriveillinois.com/departments/archives/databases/riprob.html.

1833-1925. *Illinois, Chicago, Catholic Church Records* **[Online Database],** digitized and indexed at FamilySearch.org. Source: extractions from microfilmed records of the Catholic Bishop of Chicago at the FHL in Salt Lake City. Each record may include: Name, Event Type, Event Date, Event Place, Father's Name, and Mother's Name. This database has 302,566 records, See
www.familysearch.org/search/collection/1452409.

1833-1925. *McDonough County Probate Case Files Index* **[Online Database],** indexed at the Illinois State Archives website. See www.cyberdriveillinois.com/departments/archives/databases/mcdonoughpro.html.

1834-1934. *McLean County Probate Record Index* **[Online Database],** indexed at the Illinois State Archives website. See www.cyberdriveillinois.com/departments/archives/databases/mclean.html.

1835 Illinois State Census **[Originals & Microfilm],** at the Illinois State Archives, Record Series 103.005, 1 roll. Each county return includes name of county and for each household name of head of household; numbers of free white males and females in each decennial age group (e.g., ages 0–9, 10–19, 20–29); numbers of male and female Negroes and mulattoes, indentured or registered servants and their children, and French Negroes and mulattoes held in bondage; total number of inhabitants in household; number of males subject to duty in state militia; and type (e.g., gristmill) and number of manufacturing establishments. Returns at the state archives are included for 4 of 60 counties existing at that time: Fayette, Fulton, Jasper, and Morgan. (Indexed in *Name Index to Early Illinois Records, 1810-1855* by the Illinois State Archives). See the Illinois State Archives *Genealogical Research Series Pamphlet No. 5–State Census Records*, an online PDF file downloadable at **ns/ard128.pdf**.

1835 Illinois State Census Index **[Printed Index],** edited by W. David Samuelsen, et al, published by Accelerated Indexing Systems, Bountiful, UT, 1984, 58 pages. FHL book 977.3 X2j 1835.

1835 Illinois State Census **[Printed Articles],** certain countywide name lists were published in various genealogical journals and do not all seem to be available at the Illinois State Archives – thus, these name lists may be from county resources only:
- *1835 Illinois State Census, Cass, Morgan, Scott Counties* **[Printed Article],** in *Jacksonville, Illinois Genealogical Society Journal*, Vol. 26, No. 1 (Mar 1998).
- *1835 Illinois State Census, Edwards County* **[Printed Article],** in *Edwards County Historical Society Newsletter*, Vol. 4, No. 2-3 (Summer 1983).
- *1835 Illinois State Census, Iroquois County* **[Printed Article],** in *Iroquois Stalker*, Vol. 31, No. 2 (2001).
- *1835 Illinois State Census, Union County* **[Printed Article],** in *Saga of Southern Illinois*, Vol. 5, No. 1 (Spring 1978), and Vol. 23, No. 3 (Fall 1996).

1835 Tax List, Sangamon County, Illinois **[Online Database],** indexed at the RootsWeb site for Sangamon Co IL. See www.rootsweb.ancestry.com/~ilmaga/sangamon/1835_taxlist.html.

1835-1928. *Macoupin County Coroner's Inquest Files Index* **[Online Database],** indexed at the Illinois State Archives website. See www.cyberdriveillinois.com/departments/archives/databases/macoupin.html.

1836-1870. *Kane County Circuit Court Case Files Index* **[Online Database],** indexed at the Illinois State Archives website. See www.cyberdriveillinois.com/departments/archives/databases/kane.html.

1836-1962. *Winnebago County, Illinois, Marriages* **[Online Database],** indexed at the Ancestry.com website. Original data: Winnebago County Clerk Genealogy Records. Winnebago, IL, 2008. Each record includes: Name, Marriage Date, and Spouse. This database has 75,634 records. See https://search.ancestry.com/search/db.aspx?dbid=5393.

1837-1958 Probate Case Files Index, Livingston County, Illinois **[Online Database],** indexed at the Illinois State Archives website. See www.cyberdriveillinois.com/departments/archives/databases/pontiac.html.

1838 Tax Rolls, Schuyler County, Illinois **[Online Database],** indexed at the GenealogyTrails.com website. See www.genealogytrails.com/ill/schuyler/1838taxroll.html.

1838-1927. *Illinois, DeKalb County Land Records* **[Online Database],** digitized at the FamilySearch.org website. Includes deed books, grantor, and grantee indexes from the courthouse in Sycamore, IL. This database has 57,179 images. See www.familysearch.org/search/collection/2043772.

1838-1933. *McDonough County Guardian's Case Files Index* **[Online Database],** indexed at the Illinois State Archives website. See www.cyberdriveillinois.com/departments/archives/databases/mcdonuogh.html.

1838-1940. *McLean County Will Record Index* **[Online Database],** indexed at the Illinois State Archives website. See
www.cyberdriveillinois.com/departments/archives/databases/mcleanwills.html.

1839 Personal Property Assessment, Jo Daviess County, Illinois **[Online Database],** indexed at the GenWeb site for Jo Daviess Co IL (archived). See
http://web.archive.org/web/20120703050231/http://jodaviess.ilgenweb.net/tax/1839PP.htm.

1839 Tax List, Morgan County, Illinois **[Online Database],** indexed at the RootsWeb site for Morgan Co IL. See
www.rootsweb.ancestry.com/~ilmaga/morgan2/mc-1839tx.html.

1839-1929. *Chicago (Illinois) City Directories* **[Microfilm],** from the originals published by various publishers. Filmed by Research Publications, Woodbridge, CT, 1980-1984, 96 microfiche and 64 microfilm rolls. The FHL has 1839, 1843-1905, 1907-1917, 1923, 1928-1929. The fiche starts with FHL fiche #6043786 (1839 Fergus' Directory of the City of Chicago) through fiche #6043808 (1860-61 D.B. Cook's Chicago City Directory); and the microfilm starts with FHL film #1376659 (1861-62 Halpin & Bailey's Chicago City Directory) through film #1759649 (1928/29 Polk's Chicago City Directory). For a complete list of fiche/roll numbers, see the online FHL catalog page for this title:
www.familysearch.org/search/catalog/533804.

1839-1845 Voters Lists, Menard County, Illinois **[Online Database],** indexed at the Genealogy Trails website. See
www.genealogytrails.com/ill/menard/voters/ev_a.html.

1839-1846. *Illinois, Hancock County, Nauvoo Community Project* **[Online Database],** indexed at the FamilySearch.org website. Family history students at Brigham Young University's Center for Family History and Genealogy are working to identify the residents of Nauvoo, Illinois, from 1839 to 1846. Wherever possible, each resident will be documented from birth to death in original records kept during their lifetime. Each record may include: Name, Event Type, Event Date, Event Place, Birth Date, Birthplace, Death Date, Death Place, Father's Name, Mother's Name, Note, and Image ID. This database has 4,403 records. See
www.familysearch.org/search/collection/2769728.

1839-1845. *Marriages in the Nauvoo Region* **[Online Database],** indexed at the Ancestry.com website. Source: Black, Susan Easton, *Marriages in the Nauvoo Region, 1839–1845,* Provo, Utah, 1981. Each record includes: Name, Gender, Birth Date, Birth Place, Marriage Date, Marriage Place, Spouse's Name, Father's Name, and Mother's Name. This database has 792 records. See
https://search.ancestry.com/search/db.aspx?dbid=5286.

1839-1963 Probate File Index, Menard County, Illinois **[Online Database],** indexed at the RootsWeb site for Menard Co IL. See
www.rootsweb.ancestry.com/~ilmaga/menard/menprobate.htm?cj=1&netid=cj&o_xid=0001231185&o_lid=0001231185.

1840. *Illinois 1840 Federal Census Index* **[Printed Index],** edited by Ronald Vern Jackson, et al, published by Accelerated Indexing Systems, Bountiful, UT, 1977, 192 pages, FHL book 977.3 X2i 1840.

1840 Illinois State Census **[Microfilm & Digital Capture],** from originals at the Illinois State Archives, Springfield, IL. Each county return includes name of county and occasionally the names or legal descriptions of legal subdivisions contained in counties (e.g., townships, cities, villages). Under each of these categories entries for each household include name of head of household; numbers of free white males and females in each decennial age group (e.g., ages 0–9, 10–19, 20–29); numbers of male and female Negroes and mulattoes, indentured and registered servants and their children, and French Negroes and mulattoes held in bondage; number of males subject to duty in the state militia; total number of inhabitants in household; and type (e.g., sawmill, gristmill) and number of manufacturing establishments. Returns are included for 35 of 87 counties existing at that time: Adams, Bond, Brown, Calhoun, Champaign, Clark, Clay, Clinton, Coles, Cook, Crawford, Edgar, Effingham, Franklin, Fulton, Hamilton, Hardin, Jackson, Jasper, Jo Daviess, Johnson, Knox, LaSalle, Lawrence, Livingston, Monroe, Randolph, Rock Island, Schuyler, Stark, Tazewell, Union, Vermillion, White, and Whiteside. (Indexed in *Name Index to Early Illinois Records, 1810-1855* by the Illinois State Archives). Filmed by the Genealogical Society of Utah, 1976, 2 rolls. FHL film #1004694 and #1004695. To access the digital images, see the online FHL catalog page:
www.familysearch.org/search/catalog/270278.

- See the Illinois State Archives *Genealogical Research Series Pamphlet No. 5 – State Census Records*, an online PDF file downloadable at www.cyberdriveillinois.com/publications/pdf_publications/ard128.pdf.

1840. *Illinois 1840 State Census Index* **[Printed Index]**, compiled by W. David Samuelsen, et al, published by Accelerated Indexing Systems, Bountiful, UT, 1984, 294 pages. FHL book 977.3 X2j 1840.

1840s-1970s. *Index to Journal History* **[Microfilm]**, from the originals compiled by the Historical Department, Church of Jesus Christ of Latter-day Saints. This huge index to names of people and places is related to early church history and includes the early days of the LDS church in Illinois. *The Journal History of the Church* is on FHL film #1259729 to 1259975. This index is on 58 rolls, filmed by the Genealogical Society of Utah, 1973, beginning with FHL film #1233503 (A – Anderson, Oliver Martel). To see if this microfilm has been digitized yet, see the FHL catalog page: www.familysearch.org/search/catalog/52690.

1840 Voters List, Kane County, Illinois **[Online Database]**, voters in the 1840 Presidential Election, from the *History of Kane Co Illinois*, 1908. Indexed at the GenealogyTrails.com website. See http://genealogytrails.com/ill/kane/voterlists.html#1840voters.

1840-1858 Death Notices, Will County, Illinois **[Online Database]**, indexed at the USGenWeb site for Will Co IL. See http://files.usgwarchives.net/il/will/vitals/death/1840-58.txt.

1840-1898. *Lake County Circuit Court Case Files Index* **[Online Database]**, indexed at the Illinois State Archives website. See www.cyberdriveillinois.com/departments/archives/databases/lake.html.

1840-1950. *Illinois, Northern District Naturalization Index* **[Online Database]**, digitized and indexed at the FamilySearch.org website. This database has 1,491,586 records taken from National Archives publication M1285. This card file is an index to petitions for residents of northern Illinois, northwestern Indiana, southern and eastern Wisconsin, and eastern Iowa. Filed by Soundex codes, the entries prior to 1906 differ from those after 1906. After 1906 the entries generally include the name of petitioner; address; name of the court in which naturalization occurred; certificate, petition, or other identifying document number; country and date of birth; date and place of arrival in the United States; date of naturalization; and name and address of witnesses. Although space was provided for this information, it is not always present on every card. Index cards for naturalizations taking place prior to 1906 typically contain only the name of the petitioner, the name of the court in which naturalization occurred, document number, country of origin, and the date of naturalization. See www.familysearch.org/search/collection/1838804.

- See also *Soundex Index to Naturalization Petitions for U.S. District & Circuit Courts, Northern District of Illinois and Immigration and Naturalization Service District 9, 1840-1950* **[Microfilm & Digital Capture]**, filmed by the Genealogical Society of Utah, 1988, 183 rolls, beginning with FHL film #1432001 (A-000 to A-234). To access the digital images, see the online FHL catalog page: www.familysearch.org/search/catalog/232846.

1840s-2000s. *Births in Whiteside County, Illinois* **[Online Database]**, indexed at the Genealogy-Trails.com website. See www.genealogytrails.com/ill/whiteside/birthsb.html.

1842 Tax List Index, Nauvoo, Hancock County, Illinois **[Online Database]**, names indexed at the Ancestry.com websute. See http://search.ancestry.com/search/db.aspx?dbid=4221.

1842 Tax Assessment, Kendall County, Illinois **[Online Database]**, indexed at the USGenWeb site for Kendall Co IL. See http://kendallkin.org/records/property-tax/assessment-1842.html.

1842 Roll of Property Owners, Will County, Illinois **[Online Database]**, indexed at the USGenWeb site for Will Co IL. See http://genealogytrails.com/ill/will/earlyhistory.html#1842tax.

1843. *Directory of the City of Chicago, Illinois for 1843* **[Online Database]**, a digitized book with OCR index at the Ancestry.com website. This database has 126 pages. See https://search.ancestry.com/search/db.aspx?dbid=18550.

1843-1847 Probate Index, White County, Illinois **[Online Database]**, indexed at the USGenWeb site for White Co IL (archived). http://web.archive.org/web/20120814143105/http://white.ilgenweb.net/probates4347.html.

1843-1871 Delinquent Tax Lists, Coles County, Illinois [Online Database], indexed at the GenealogyTrails.com website. See www.genealogytrails.com/ill/coles/.

1843-1992. *DeKalb County, Illinois Deaths* [Online Database], indexed at the Ancestry.com website. Source: DeKalb County, Illinois Death Index, 1843–1992. DeKalb County Clerk and Recorder, Sycamore, Illinois, 2012. Each record includes: Name, and Death Date. This database has 40,907 records. See https://search.ancestry.com/search/db.aspx?dbid=5388.

1844 City Directory, Chicago, Illinois [Online Database], indexed at the GenealogyTrails.com website. See http://genealogytrails.com/ill/cook/1844directory.html.

1844-1846 Delinquent Tax List, Edgar County, Illinois [Online Database], indexed at the GenealogyTrails.com website. See http://genealogytrails.com/ill/edgar/edgar_1845_taxlist.htm.

1844-1870 Delinquent Tax Lists, Cumberland County, Illinois [Online Database], indexed at the GenealogyTrails.com website. See www.genealogytrails.com/ill/cumberland/taxindex.html.

1844-1872 Delinquent Tax Lists, Jersey County, Illinois [Online Database], indexed at the GenWeb site for Jersey Co IL (archived). See http://web.archive.org/web/20120325020219/http://www.ilgenweb.org/jersey-county/census-records/tax-lists/.

1844-1901. Chicago City Directories [Microfilm], from originals published by various publishers. Includes directories for the years 1844, 1854-1855, 1859-1860, 1865, and 1869-1901. Filmed by W.C. Cox, Tucson, AZ, 1974, 16 rolls, beginning with FHL film #1000739 (Chicago Directories, 1844-1869). For a complete list of roll numbers and the contents of each roll, see the online FHL catalog page for this title: www.familysearch.org/search/catalog/308691.

1844-1992. *Winnebago County, Illinois, Deaths* [Online Database], indexed at the Ancestry.com website. Source: Original data: Winnebago County Clerk Genealogy Records. Winnebago, IL: Winnebago County Clerk, 2008. Each record includes: Name and Death Date. This database has 106,761 records. See https://search.ancestry.com/search/db.aspx?dbid=5397.

1845 Illinois State Census [Originals & Microfilm], at the Illinois State Archives, 1 roll. Each county return includes name of county and for each household name of head of household; numbers of free white males and females in each decennial age group (e.g., ages 0–9, 10–19, 20–29); numbers of male and female Negroes and mulattoes, indentured or registered servants, and French Negroes and mulattoes held in bondage; total number of inhabitants in household; number of males subject to duty in state militia; and type (e.g., gristmill) and number of manufacturing establishments. Returns are included for 3 of 98 counties existing at that time: Cass, Putnam, and Tazewell. See the Illinois State Archives *Genealogical Research Series Pamphlet No. 5 – State Census Records*, an online PDF file downloadable at www.cyberdriveillinois.com/publications/pdf_publications/ard128.pdf.

1846-1848. *Illinois Mexican War Veterans* [Online Database], indexed at the Illinois State Archives website. This database indexes the names of Illinois Mexican War veterans appearing in the ninth volume of the publication, *Report of the Adjutant General of the State of Illinois* (1902). In 1881 U. S. War Department clerks transcribed the Illinois rosters from their records and sent copies to the Adjutant General for publication. The 1882 Report of the Adjutant General of the State of Illinois first included Mexican War veterans. The names of approximately 6,500 men, organized into the First through the Fourth Regiments and four independent companies, are found in the 1882 report and the 1902 republication. See www.cyberdriveillinois.com/departments/archives/databases/mexwar.html.

1846-1898. *Report of the Adjutant General of the State of Illinois* [Microfilm & Digital Capture], from the original published by Phillips Bros., Springfield, IL, 1900-1902, 9 volumes. Includes index. This is an alphabetical index of men and 9 vols. of rosters of officers and men in the Mexican War, Indian Wars, Civil War, and the Spanish-American War. Filmed by the Genealogical Society of Utah, 1974, 64 rolls, beginning with FHL film #1001124 (Index, Mexican War: A- Smith, J.). To access the digital images, see the online FHL catalog page: www.familysearch.org/search/catalog/277178.

1846-1938. *JoDaviess County Almshouse Registers Index (1846-1938)* **[Online Database],** indexed at the Illinois State Archives website. See www.cyberdriveillinois.com/departments/archives/databases/jodavalms.html.

1847-1860 *Illinois (State) Directories* **[Microfilm],** from originals published by various publishers. Filmed by Research Publications, Woodbridge, CT, 1980-1984, 41 microfiche, as follows:
- **1847** Illinois annual register, and Western business directory (3 fiche), FHL film #6043985.
- **1854-1855** Montague's Illinois and Missouri state directory (9 fiche), FHL film #6043986.
- **1855-1856** The Northern counties gazetteer and directory. The Chicago city directory, and business advertiser (8 fiche), FHL film #6043987. film #6043988
- **1858-1859** Illinois state gazetteer and business directory... by George W. Hawes (7 fiche), FHL
- **1860** Illinois state business directory ... by J. C. W. Bailey & Co., FHL film #6043989.

1849-1861 *Deaths Abstracted from Administrators Bonds, Morgan County, Illinois* **[Online Database],** indexed at the USGenWeb site for Morgan Co IL (archived). See
http://web.archive.org/web/20120325232802/http://morgan.ilgenweb.net/deaths/1849-61.htm.

1849-1903 *Deaths, Schuyler County, Illinois* **[Online Database],** indexed at the USGenWeb site for Schuyler Co IL (archived). See
http://web.archive.org/web/20110509172529/http://schuyler.ilgenweb.net/schuylernewhome/indexdeaths.html.

1850. *Illinois, 1850 Federal Census: Population Schedules* **[Microfilm & Digital Capture],** from the originals at the National Archives, Washington, DC. Filmed by the National Archives, 1964, 38 rolls, beginning with FHL film #7670 (Adams Co). To access the digital images, see the online FHL catalog page: www.familysearch.org/search/catalog/744477.

1850. *Illinois 1850 Census Index* **[Printed Index],** edited by Ronald Vern Jackson, published by Accelerated Indexing Systems, Bountiful, UT, 580 pages, FHL book 977.3 X2p 1850.

1850-1877 *Birth Index, Peoria County, Illinois* **[Online Database],** indexed at the Genealogy Trails website. See
www.genealogytrails.com/ill/peoria/birth/1850_1877.htm.

1850-1880. *Illinois, Non-Population Census Schedules* **[Online Database],** digitized at FamilySearch.org. This is an image-only database of the 1850-1880 Agriculture, Manufactures/Industry, and Social Statistics schedules. Browse through 33,726 images, see
www.familysearch.org/search/collection/2287447.

1850-1880. *Illinois, Mortality Schedules, 1850-1880* **[Online Database],** digitized and indexed at the FamilySearch.org website. Mortality Schedules were created in conjunction with the US Federal Census and list people who died in the year preceding the census. Mortality schedules were first included in the 1850 census. These include lists of people who died Jun 1849 - May 1850, Jun 1859 - May 1860, Jun 1869-May 1870, and Jun 1879 - May 1880. This database has 97,928 records. See
www.familysearch.org/search/collection/2334599.

1850-1881 *Probate Index, Macoupin County, Illinois* **[Online Database],** indexed at the Macoupin City Genealogy website. See
http://macoupinctygenealogy.org/probate-a/index.html.

1850-1932. See *Morgan County Poor Farm Records Index (1850-1932)* **[Online Database],** indexed at the Illinois State Archives website. See
www.cyberdriveillinois.com/departments/archives/databases/morganalms.html.

1850-2007. *Illinois, Stephenson County, Cedarville Cemetery Records* **[Online Database],** digitized and indexed at FamilySearch.org. This database has 8,511 records, see
www.familysearch.org/search/collection/1430678.

1851-1900. *Illinois, Compiled Marriages* **[Online Database],** indexed at the Ancestry.com website. This database indexes approximately 660,000 individuals in selected areas of Illinois, compiled by Liahona Research, Orem, UT, from FHL microfilm. Each entry includes: Name, Spouse's name, Date and location of marriage, and Source information. This database has 659,028 records. See.
http://search.ancestry.com/search/db.aspx?dbid=7857.

1852-1951. *Will County, Illinois, Saint Dennis Catholic Church Vital Records* **[Online Database],** indexed at the Ancestry.com website. Original data: Will County, Illinois, Saint Dennis Catholic Church Vital Records, 1852-1951. Vol. 1–9. Lockport, Will County, Illinois: Saint Dennis Catholic Church. Each record includes: Name, Record Type, Marriage Date, Marriage Place, and Spouse's Name. This database has 8,284 records. See
https://search.ancestry.com/search/db.aspx?dbid=1945.

1853 Delinquent Tax List, Clinton County, Illinois **[Online Database],** indexed at the Clinton Co IL GenWeb site. See
http://clintonilgenweb.net/misc/taxes/delinq001.htm.

1853-1898. *Children of Orphan Trains: From New York to Illinois and Beyond* **[Printed Book],** compiled by Janet Coble and members of the Elgin Genealogical Society. Includes index. Includes name of child, place and date of birth, age, date of trip, family taking child, address, informant, and a reference to file if more information is available. By January 1853, the New York Juvenile Asylum opened a House of Reception to accommodate children who were orphaned or had parents unable or unfit to care for them, or who were otherwise without homes. The Department of Charities determined that children would benefit from being sent to Illinois where they were apprenticed to farm families. Children between ages 7-14 were sent to Illinois from 1853 until the fall of 1898. The names and facts are extracted from records of the Asylum and their reports from the families or the children who were apprenticed. Published by the Illinois State Genealogical Society, 1994, 122 pages, FHL book 973 J3c.

1853-2009. *Illinois Cemetery Transcriptions* **[Online Database],** digitized at the FamilySearch.org website. Includes images of cemetery transcriptions and records in Illinois. Although the database contains records from Elmwood cemetery in Centralia, IL, more cemeteries will be added. This database has 5,040 images. See
www.familysearch.org/search/collection/2043817.

1854 City Directory, Galena, Illinois **[Online Database],** indexed at the GenWeb site for Jo Daviess Co IL (archived). See
http://web.archive.org/web/20120415060607/http://jodaviess.ilgenweb.net/Directories/1854Galena.htm.

1854-1855 County Directory, DeKalb County, Illinois **[Online Database],** indexed at the DeKalb Co IL GenWeb site (Archived). See
http://web.archive.org/web/20110818052002/http://dekalb.ilgenweb.net/HTMLs/Dir1854.htm

1854-1983. *Illinois, Stephenson County, Lena Park Cemetery Transcriptions* **[Online Database],** digitized and indexed at FamilySearch.org. Includes transcriptions of grave markers from originals at the Freeport Public Library, Freeport, IL. This database has 4,815 records, see
www.familysearch.org/search/collection/1430683.

1855. *Springfield, Illinois City Directory* **[Online Database],** indexed at the Ancestry.com website. Each record includes: Name of Resident/Business, Trade, and Home (address). This database has 1,579 records:
https://search.ancestry.com/search/db.aspx?dbid=3846.

1855 State Census of Illinois [Microfilm & Digital Capture& Digital Capture], from originals at the Illinois State Archives, Springfield, IL. Several counties missing, including Carroll, Champaign, Franklin, Gallatin, Henry, Jefferson, Jo Davies, Lake, Stark, Will and Woodford. (Indexed in *Name Index to Early Illinois Records, 1810-1855* by the Illinois State Archives). Census schedules filmed by the Genealogical Society of Utah, 1975, 15 rolls, as follows:
- Adams Co. - FHL film #976178.
- Alexander - Clay counties, FHL film #976179.
- Clinton - Cook counties, FHL film #976180.
- Crawford - Effingham counties, FHL film #976181.
- Fayette - Hamilton counties, FHL film #976182.
- Hancock - Kane counties, FHL film #976183.
- Kankakee - LaSalle counties, FHL film #976184.
- Lawrence and Lee counties, FHL film #976185.
- Livingston - McHenry counties, FHL film, #976186.
- McLean - Massac counties, FHL film #976670.
- Menard - Ogle counties, FHL film #976671.
- Peoria - Putnam counties, FHL film #976672.
- Randolph - Sangamon counties, FHL film #976673.
- Schuyler - Wabash counties, FHL film #977062.
- Warren - Winnebago counties, FHL film #977063.

To access the digital images, see the online FHL catalog page:
www.familysearch.org/search/catalog/271754.
- See the Illinois State Archives *Genealogical Research Series Pamphlet No. 5 – State Census Records*, an online PDF file downloadable at
www.cyberdriveillinois.com/publications/pdf_publications/ard128.pdf.

1855. *Illinois State Census, 1855* **[Online Database],** digitized and indexed at the FamilySearch.org website. This database has 256,004 records, taken from the FHL microfilm. See
www.familysearch.org/search/collection/1803969.

1855 Tax List, Jo Daviess County, Illinois **[Online Database],** indexed at the GenWeb site for Jo Daviess Co IL. See
http://jodaviess.illinoisgenweb.org/tax/1855PPGK.htm.

1856 Delinquent Tax List, Marshall County, Illinois **[Online Database],** indexed at the Genealogy-Trails.com website. See
www.genealogytrails.com/ill/marshall/history/1856TaxList.html.

1856-1991. *Illinois, Federal Naturalization Records* **[Online Database],** indexed at the Ancestry.com website. Source: National Archives, Chicago. Each record includes: Name, Gender, Record Type, Birth Date, Birth Place, Arrival Date, Arrival Place, Spouse, and Petition Number. This database has 4,252,176 records. See
https://search.ancestry.com/search/db.aspx?dbid=61196.

1857-1929 Church Records, Chicago, Illinois **[Online Database],** indexed at the Genealogy Trails website. See http://genealogytrails.com/ill/cook/churchdata.html.

1857-1900s Birth Records Index, Jersey County, Illinois **[Online Database],** indexed at the GenWeb site for Jersey Co IL. (Archived). See
https://web.archive.org/web/20130910184043/http://jersey.illinoisgenweb.org/birthindex.html.

1857-1937. *Winnebago County, Illinois, Births* **[Online Database],** indexed at the Ancestry.com website. Original data: Winnebago County Clerk Genealogy Records. Winnebago, IL, 2008. Each record includes: Name, and Birth Date. This database has 64,821 records. See
https://search.ancestry.com/search/db.aspx?dbid=5335.

1857-1945. *Logan County Circuit Court Criminal Case Files Index* **[Online Database],** indexed at the Illinois State Archives website. See
www.cyberdriveillinois.com/departments/archives/databases/logan.html.

1858-1878 Delayed Birth Records, Morgan County, Illinois **[Online Database],** indexed at the USGenWeb site for Morgan Co IL (Archived). See:
http://web.archive.org/web/20111210142133/http://morgan.ilgenweb.net/births/d-1858-78.htm

1859-1860 City Directory, Quincy, Illinois **[Online Database],** indexed at the Genealogy Trails website. http://genealogytrails.com/ill/adams/dir/1859qcydir1.htm.

1859-1860 City Directory, Kane County, Illinois **[Online Database],** indexed at the Genealogy Trails website. See
www.genealogytrails.com/ill/kane/1859directory.html.

1859-1948. *Mercer County Almshouse Register Index* **[Online Database],** indexed at the Illinois State Archives website. See
www.cyberdriveillinois.com/departments/archives/databases/mercer.html.

1860. *Illinois, 1860 Federal Census: Population Schedules* **[Microfilm & Digital Capture],** from originals at the National Archives, Washington, DC. Filmed twice by the National Archives, 1950, 1967, 107 rolls total, beginning with FHL film #803154 (2nd filming, Adams Co, City of Quincy). To access the digital images, see the online FHL catalog page:
www.familysearch.org/search/catalog/704761.

1860. *Illinois 1860 North* **[Printed Index],** edited by Ronald Vern Jackson, et al. Contains the counties of Adams, Boone, Brown, Bureau, Calhoun, Carroll, Champaign, De Kalb, Du Page, Ford, Fulton, Grundy, Hancock, Henderson, Henry, Iroquois, Jo Daviess, Kane, Kankakee, Kendall, Knox, Lake, LaSalle, Lee, Livingston, Marshall, McDonough, Mc Henry, Mc Lean, Mercer, Ogle, Peoria, Pike, Putnam, Rock Island, Schuyler, Stark, Stephenson, Tazewell, Vermillion, Warren, Whiteside, Will, Winnebago, and Woodford, Published by Accelerated Indexing Systems, North Salt Lake, UT, 1987, FHL book 977.3 X22jr 1860 (North).

1860. *Illinois 1860 South* **[Printed Index],** edited by Ronald Vern Jackson, et al. Contains the counties of Alexander, Bond, Cass, Christian, Clark, Clay, Clinton, Coles, Crawford, Cumberland, De Witt, Douglass, Edgar, Edwards, Effingham, Fayette, Ford, Franklin, Gallatin, Greene, Hamilton, Hardin, Jackson, Jasper, Jefferson, Jersey, Johnson, Lawrence, Logan, Macon, Macoupin, Madison, Marion, Mason, Massac, Menard, Monroe, Montgomery, Morgan, Moultrie, Perry, Piatt, Pope, Pulaski, Randolph, Richland, St. Clair, Saline, Sangamon, Scott, Shelby, Union, Wabash, Washington, Wayne, White, and Williamson. Published by Accelerated Indexing Systems, North Salt Lake, UT, 1987, FHL book 977.3 X22j 1860 (South).

1860. *Illinois 1860 [Census] Chicago-Cook County* **[Printed Index],** edited by Ronald Vern Jackson, et al. Published by Accelerated Indexing Systems, North Salt Lake, UT, 1986, 643 pages, FHL book 977.31 X2j 1860.

1860 Federal Census Index of Cook County, Illinois **[Printed Index],** compiled by Bernice G. Richard, from a card index prepared for the Illinois State Archives, FHL book977.31 X22f. Also on microfilm, 1 roll, FHL film #1421582.

1860. *Illinois Mortality Schedule, 1860* **[Printed Index],** transcribed and indexed by Lowell M. Volkel, published by Heritage House, Indianapolis, IN, 1979, FHL book 977.3 X2j.

1860. *Illinois 1860 Mortality Schedule* **[Printed Index],** edited by Ronald Vern Jackson, published by Accelerated Indexing Systems, North Salt Lake, UT, 1988, FHL book 977.3 X22i 1860.

1860-1862 Death and Administration Notices, Joliet, Will County, Illinois **[Online Database],** indexed at the USGenWeb site for Will Co IL. See http://files.usgwarchives.net/il/will/vitals/death/1860dea.txt.

1860-1920. *Illinois, Marriage Index* **[Online Database],** digitized and indexed at the Ancestry.com website. Source: Original data: Illinois State Marriage Records. Online index. Illinois State Public Record Offices. Each record includes: Name, Gender, Marriage Date, Marriage Place, Spouse Name, and Spouse Gender. This database has 2,294,483 records: https://search.ancestry.com/search/db.aspx?dbid=60984.

1861 Delinquent Tax List, Menard County, Illinois **[Online Database],** indexed at the Genealogy-Trails.com website. See www.genealogytrails.com/ill/menard/tax/tax1861.html.

1861-1862 Illinois Military Census **[Microfilm],** from the original records at the office of Secretary of State, Springfield, IL. A list, by county, of able-bodied male citizens between the ages of eighteen and forty-five in pursuance of General Orders No. 99 of the War Department and instructions of the Adjutant General of the State of Illinois. Includes Adams, Cook, Jo Daviess & Lake counties. Filmed by the IL Office of the Secretary of State, 1979, 1 roll, FHL film #2209347. To see if this microfilm has been digitized yet, see the FHL catalog page: www.familysearch.org/search/catalog/967547.

1861-1865 Rosters of Illinois Regiments of the Civil War **[Microfilm],** from the original *Report of the Adjutant General of the State of Illinois*, published Springfield, IL, 1867, 8 vols. Contents: Vol. 1: 7th to 46th regiment; vol. 2: 47th to 157th regiment; vol. 3: 1st to 17th cavalry regiment, 29th United States colored infantry; 1st & 2nd regiments and independent batteries of artillery; also rosters of enlisted men numbered from the 7th to the 20th regiment; vol. 4: 21st to 47th regiments; vol. 5: 48th to 76th regiment; v. 6: 1861-1866; 77th to 117th regiment; vol. 7. 1861-1865; 118th to 156 infantry regiment; 1st to 3rd cavalry regiment; v. 8. 1861-1866; 4th to 17th cavalry regiment; 1st & 2nd regiments & independent batteries of artillery; colored troops; 1st army corps; recruits for regular army. The 1st to the 3rd vols. contain rosters of Civil War officers. The 3rd vol. also contains rosters of enlisted men which continues to the end of the 8th vol. Filmed for the FHL by the Library of Congress, 1989, 3 rolls, beginning with FHL film #1674241. To see if this microfilm has been digitized yet, see the FHL catalog page: www.familysearch.org/search/catalog/379629.

1861-1865. *Illinois Civil War Muster and Descriptive Rolls* **[Online Database],** indexed at the Illinois State Archives website. This database is a transcription of each soldier's entry in the record series, Muster and Descriptive Rolls, and contains information about over 285,000 soldiers from Illinois who served in the Union Army during the War of the Rebellion. Each entry includes all of the information that was recorded by the Illinois Adjutant General in the original Muster and Descriptive Rolls. Entries for each roll include soldier's name; rank; age; height; colors of eyes, hair, and complexion; occupation; marital status; birthplace; residence; date, place, and term of enrollment; name; name of mustering officer; date and place of muster out; name of mustering-out officer; and remarks concerning transfers, promotions, injuries, or special duty. Fred Delap of Kansas, Illinois, a volunteer with the Edgar County Genealogical Society, entered the information found in this database from microfilm of the 89 volumes of original Muster and Descriptive Rolls provided by the Illinois State Archives. Delap discovered that the published Adjutant General's Reports included soldiers that were not included in the original Muster and Descriptive Rolls. To make the database as comprehensive as possible, he also extracted the information from the first eight volumes of the nine-volume publication, Report of the Adjutant General of the State of Illinois. (The ninth volume lists veterans of Black Hawk, Mexican, and Spanish-American Wars. See www.cyberdriveillinois.com/departments/archives/databases/datcivil.html.

1861-1865. *Illinois Civil War Veterans Serving in the U.S. Navy* **[Online Database]**, This database indexes the Illinois State Archives record series, Roster of Illinois Men in the U.S. Navy During the Civil War. This record of approximately 3,000 men came from the Illinois Adjutant General. The database includes the name and birthplace of each sailor. See www.cyberdriveillinois.com/departments/archives/databases/ilnavy.html.

1861-1865. *Illinois Civil War Veterans of Missouri Units* **[Online Database]**, This database indexes the names of 5,610 Illinois citizens appearing on the rosters of Missouri's Federal Civil War units. Illinoisans occasionally joined military units raised in other states. In December 1863, the Missouri Adjutant General compiled rosters of Illinois men, extracting the names from his unit rolls. He then sent them to the Illinois Adjutant General. The rosters are a part of the Archives' record series, Company Muster Rolls. See www.cyberdriveillinois.com/departments/archives/databases/missouri.html.

1861-1865. *Index to Compiled Service Records of Volunteer Union Soldiers Who Served in Organizations from the State of Illinois* **[Microfilm & Digital Capture]**, from the originals at the National Archives, Washington, DC. Filmed by the National Archives, series M539, 101 rolls, beginning with FHL film #881621 (A – Alle). To access the digital images, see the online FHL catalog page: www.familysearch.org/search/catalog/92181.

1861-1916 *Will Record Index, Pope County, Illinois* **[Online Database]**, indexed at the USGenWeb site for Pope Co IL. See http://pope.illinoisgenweb.org/willA.htm.

1862-1864 *Naturalization Records, Sangamon County, Illinois* **[Online Database]**, indexed at the USGenWeb site for Sangamon Co IL (Archived). See http://web.archive.org/web/20090513052341/http://sangamon.ilgenweb.net/nat-1862.htm

1862-1866 *Internal Revenue Assessment Lists for Illinois* **[Microfilm & Digital Capture]**, from originals at the National Archives, Washington, DC. Includes a locality index (filmed at the beginning of each roll of film) that references counties to districts and film roll numbers. The lists are arranged by collection district and then by division. They are filmed in the order in which they are bound in the volumes. Counties included in each district are as follows: **District 1:** Cook. **District 2:** Boone, De Kalb, Kane, Lake, McHenry, and Winnebago. **District 3:** Carroll, Jo Daviess, Lee, Ogle, Stephenson, and Whiteside. **District 4:** Adams, Hancock, Henderson, Mercer, Rock Island, and Warren. **District 5:** Bureau, Henry, Knox, Marshall, Peoria, Putnam, and Stark. **District 6:** Du Page, Grundy, Kankakee, Kendall, La Salle, and Will. **District 7:** Champaign, Coles, Cumberland, Douglas, Edgar, Ford, Iroquois, Macon, Moultrie, Piatt, and Vermilion. **District 8:** De Witt, Livingston, Logan, McLean, Sangamon, Tazewell, and Woodford. **District 9:** Brown, Cass, Fulton, McDonough, Mason, Menard, Pike, and Schuyler. **District 10:** Bond, Calhoun, Christian, Greene, Jersey, Macoupin, Montgomery, Morgan, Scott, and Shelby. **District 11:** Clark, Clay, Crawford, Effingham, Fayette, Franklin, Hamilton, Jasper, Jefferson, Lawrence, Marion, Richland, and Wayne. **District 12:** Clinton, Madison, Monroe, Randolph, St. Clair, and Washington. **District 13:** Alexander, Edwards, Gallatin, Hardin, Johnson, Massac, Perry, Pope, Pulaski, Saline, Union, Wabash, White, and Williamson. Filmed by the National Archives, series M764, 63 rolls, beginning with FHL film #1534562 (District 1, 1862-1863). To access the digital images, see the online FHL catalog page: www.familysearch.org/search/catalog/577851.

1862 Military Census, Logan County, Illinois **[Online Database]**, indexed at the USGenWeb site for Logan Co IL (archived). See http://web.archive.org/web/20111106075246/http://logan.ilgenweb.net/1862military.htm

1862-1928. *Records of the Russian Consular Offices in the United States* **[Microfilm & Digital Capture]**, includes records from the Russian Consulate Office located in Chicago, IL. These records contain data on subjects of the Russian Empire (Jews, Poles, Ukrainians, Lithuanians, Finns, and others) who came to the U.S. between 1862 and 1928. Included are passports and applications, visas, nationality certificates, certificates of origin,, inheritance information, contracts, and correspondence. The records are primarily in Russian, although a variety of other languages are used, including some English. Filmed by the Genealogical Society of Utah, 1986, 169 rolls, beginning with FHL film #1463389 (Chicago Consulate). To access the digital images, see the online FHL catalog page: www.familysearch.org/search/catalog/534673.
- See also, *The Russian Consular Records Index and Catalog (in English)* **[Microfilm]**, by Sallyann

Amdur Sack and Suzan Fishi Wynne, publ. Garland Pub. Co., New York, 1987, 897 pages. To see if this microfilm has been digitized yet, see the FHL catalog page: www.familysearch.org/search/catalog/548652.

1863-1900s. *Illinois, Quaker Records* [Online Database], indexed at the FamilySearch.org website. Original data: Quaker Records: Illinois Monthly Meetings. USA, 19??. Each record includes: Name, Birth Date, and possible other items, such as "Relatives." This database has 7,029 records. See https://search.ancestry.com/search/db.aspx?dbid=4752.

1863-1941 Plat Books, Lee County, Illinois [Online Database], indexed at the RootsWeb site for Lee Co IL. See www.rootsweb.ancestry.com/~illee/platbooks.htm.

1864-1962. DeKalb County, Illinois Marriages [Online Database], indexed at the Ancestry.com website. DeKalb County Clerk and Recorder, Sycamore, Illinois, 2012. Each record includes: Name, Spouse's Name, and Marriage Date. This database has 28,790 records. See https://search.ancestry.com/search/db.aspx?dbid=5377.

1864-1989. *Illinois, Archdiocese of Chicago, Cemetery Records* [Online Database], indexed at the FamilySearch.org website. The majority of the collection is comprised of burial index cards. A small percentage of the collection includes burial registers, daily burial logs and registers of cemetery lot owners. Cemeteries within the Archdiocese of Chicago are located in both Cook and Lake counties, Illinois. This database has 1,921,208 records. See www.familysearch.org/search/collection/1503083.

1865 Illinois State Census [Microfilm & Digital Capture], from original records at the Illinois State Library, Springfield, IL. At the time of filming, the state library was missing the 1865 census schedules for Gallatin, Mason & Monroe counties. Only Elm Grove Township is included for Tazewell County. Filmed by the Genealogical Society of Utah, 1964, 1977, 25 rolls, as follows:
- Adams, Bureau, Edwards, Ford, and Effingham counties, FHL film #972746.
- Fayette, Franklin, Grundy, Henderson, and Fulton counties, FHL film #972747.
- Jo Daviess, Pulaski, Alexander, Bond, and Boone counties, - FHL film # 972748.
- Clinton, Champaign, Clark, Cumberland, and Christian counties, FHL film #972749.
- Crawford, Carroll, DeWitt, DeKalb, Douglas, DuPage, and Brown counties, FHL film #972750.
- Coles, Calhoun, Cass, Clay, and Greene counties, FHL film #972751.
- Edgar, Jasper, Pike, Hardin, and Jefferson counties, FHL film #972752.
- Jackson, Johnson, Henry, and Hancock counties, FHL film #972753.
- Hamilton, Iroquois, Kankakee, and Knox counties, FHL film #972754.
- Jersey County, FHL film #972755.
- Kane, Kendall, and Logan counties, FHL film #972756.
- Lake, Lawrence, Lee, and Livingston counties, FHL film #972757.
- McHenry, Montgomery, Macoupin, and Ogle counties, FHL film #1012404.
- Madison and Macon counties, FHL film #972758.
- Menard, Morgan, Pope, and Richland counties, FHL film #972759.
- Cook Co. (Chicago wards 1-12), FHL film #972760.
- Cook Co. (Chicago wards 12-16; other towns), FHL film #972761.
- Randolph, Saline, Mercer, McDonough, and McLean counties, FHL film #972762.
- Marshall, Peoria, Piatt, Perry, and Putnam counties, FHL film #972763.
- Rock Island Co., FHL film #972764.
- Sangamon, St. Clair, and Tazewell (Elm Grove Township only) counties, FHL film #972765.
- Vermilion, Will, and La Salle counties, FHL film #972766.
- Marion, Massac, Moultrie, Shelby, Stephenson, Schuyler, and Stark counties, FHL film #972767.
- Scott, Union, Wayne, White, Woodford, and Washington counties, FHL film #972768.
- Williamson, Winnebago, Wabash, and Warren counties, FHL film #972769.

To access the digital images, see the online FHL catalog page:
www.familysearch.org/search/catalog/259412.
- See the Illinois State Archives *Genealogical Research Series Pamphlet No. 5 – State Census Records*, an online PDF file downloadable at
www.cyberdriveillinois.com/publications/pdf_publications/ard128.pdf.

1865. *Illinois State Census, 1865* [Online Database], digitized and indexed at the FamilySearch.org website. This database has 380,262 records, including Chicago, taken from the FHL microfilm. See www.familysearch.org/search/collection/1803971.

1866 Directory, Madison County, Illinois [Online Database], indexed at the GenealogyTrails.com website. See
http://genealogytrails.com/ill/madison/mcdirectory.htm.

1866-1939. *Birth Records, 1866-1916; Index, 1866-1939, Saline County, Illinois* [Online Database], indexed at the USGenWeb site for Saline Co IL. See http://files.usgwarchives.net/il/saline/vitals/birth/1866_1916.txt.

1868 Delinquent Tax, Shelby County, Illinois [Online Database]. indexed at the Ecolitgy.com site (archived): http://web.archive.org/web/20061101082020/http://www.ecolitgy.com/it/1868TaxList.pdf

1868-1925. *Arthur Local Registrar's Birth Certificates Index* [Online Database], indexed at the Illinois State Archives websites. See www.cyberdriveillinois.com/departments/archives/databases/arthurbirths.html.

1868-1941. *Stark County Almshouse Register Index* [Online Database], indexed at the Illinois State Archives website. See www.cyberdriveillinois.com/departments/archives/databases/stark.html.

1868-1957. *Woodford Almshouse Registers Index* [Online Database], indexed at the Illinois State Archives website. See www.cyberdriveillinois.com/departments/archives/databases/wood.html.

1869 Illinois Central Directory [Microfilm & Digital Capture], from the original published 1869, filmed by the Genealogical Society of Utah, 1975, 1 roll, FHL film #969494. To access the digital images, see the online FHL catalog page: www.familysearch.org/search/catalog/47591.

1869 Businesses & Property Owners, Stark County, Illinois [Online Database], indexed at the GenealogyTrails.com website. See http://genealogytrails.com/ill/stark/BradfordHistory.html.

1869-1873. *Mattoon Court of Common Pleas Case Files Index* [Online Database], indexed at the Illinois State Archives website. See www.cyberdriveillinois.com/departments/archives/databases/mattoon.html.

1870. *Illinois, 1870 Federal Census: Population Schedules* [Microfilm & Digital Capture], from the original records at the National Archives, Washington, DC. Filmed twice by the National Archives, 1962, 1968, 156 rolls total, beginning with FHL film #545685 (2nd filming, Adams Co, part). To access the digital images, see the online FHL catalog page: www.familysearch.org/search/catalog/698894.

1870. *Illinois 1870 Census Index* [Printed Index], edited by Raeone Christensen Steuart, published by Heritage Quest, Bountiful, UT 1999, 5 vols., FHL book 977.3 X22j 1870 v.1-5.

1870-1871. *J.S. Lothrop's Champaign County Directory* [Online Database], digitized and OCR indexed at the Ancestry.com website. This database has 459 records. See https://search.ancestry.com/search/db.aspx?dbid=24609.

1870-1880 Proof of Death Index, St. Clair County, Illinois [Online Database], indexed at the St Clair IL GS site. See www.stclair-ilgs.org/prd1.htm.

1870-1898 Probate Index, Iroquois County, Illinois [Online Database], indexed at the RootsWeb site for Iroquois Co IL. See www.rootsweb.ancestry.com/~ilicgs/moredata/proba_k.htm.

1871-1902 Cook County. See *Minors and Old Soldiers Naturalization Index and Final Naturalization Index* [Microfilm], from original records at the Cook County Courthouse, Chicago, IL. Filmed by the Genealogical Society of Utah, 1978, 1 roll, FHL film #1023961. To see if this microfilm has been digitized yet, see the FHL catalog page: www.familysearch.org/search/catalog/407643.

1871-1906 *Indexes to Naturalization Records, Cook County, Illinois* [Microfilm], from originals at the Cook County Courthouse, Chicago, IL. Filmed by the Genealogical Society of Utah, 1980, 2 rolls, FHL film #1023967 (1871-1906 Naturalizations, A-L) & #1023968 (1871-1906 Naturalizations, M-Z). To see if this microfilm has been digitized yet, see the FHL catalog page: www.familysearch.org/search/catalog/114790.

1870s-1915. *Illinois Statewide Death Index Pre-1916* [Online Database], indexed at the Illinois State Archives website. The Pre–1916 Illinois Statewide Death Index is an ongoing project and data entry is far from complete. The list of counties and years at this webpage should be consulted to determine the status of data entry for a particular county. At this writing, data entry was complete through December 1915 for 22 of the 102 counties in Illinois. This database includes death data from 45 counties in Illinois and currently contains over 1,162,017 records. Counties that have been completed are capitalized on the list: www.cyberdriveillinois.com/departments/archives/databases/deathlst.html.

1870-1930 Police Department Homicide Record, Chicago, Illinois [Online Database], indexed at the Illinois State Archives website. See www.cyberdriveillinois.com/departments/archives/databases/homicide.html.

1870-1992. *Kankakee County, Illinois Death Index* **[Online Database],** indexed at the Ancestry.com website. Original data: Kankakee County Clerk Genealogy Records. Kankakee, IL, 2008. Each record includes: Name, and Death Date. This database has 51,108 records. See
https://search.ancestry.com/search/db.aspx?dbid=4214.

1871-1915. *Illinois, Cook County, Birth Registers* **[Online Database],** digitized and indexed at the FamilySearch.org website. This database has 962,515 records, including Chicago, taken from the FHL microfilm of the originals from the Illinois Department of Public Health, Division of Vital Records, Springfield, IL. See
www.familysearch.org/search/collection/1463129.

1871-1920. Illinois, Cook County Marriages **[Online Database],** digitized and indexed at the FamilySearch.org website. Name index of marriage licenses and returns. This database has 865,669 records, taken from the FHL microfilm of the originals from the Illinois Department of Health, Springfield, IL:
www.familysearch.org/search/collection/1463145.
- This database is also at the Ancestry.com website (with 1,730,670 records). See
https://search.ancestry.com/search/db.aspx?dbid=2556.

1871-1916. *Cook County Death Record Index* **[Microfiche],** from the originals at the Cook County Courthouse, Chicago, IL. Filmed by the Genealogical Society of Utah, 1982, 70 microfiche, beginning with FHL fiche #6016533 (Aaberg, Emma M. – Anderson, Jane E). For a complete list of fiche numbers and contents of each, see the online FHL page for this title:
www.familysearch.org/search/catalog/78612.

1871-1933. *Indexes to Deaths in the City of Chicago During the Years 1871-1933: Showing Name, Address, and Date of Death* **[Microfilm & Digital Capture],** from original records at the Cook County Courthouse, Chicago, IL. These indexes are believed to be for burial permits, the actual deaths having occurred both in and outside the city of Chicago, often times out of state. Filmed by the Genealogical Society of Utah, 1980, 13 rolls, beginning with FHL film #1295943 (Deaths, A-Bou 1871-1933). To access the digital images, see the online FHL catalog page:
www.familysearch.org/search/catalog/293534.

1871-1922. *Cook County, Illinois, Birth Certificates Index* **[Online Database],** indexed at the Ancestry.com website. Source: IL Dept of Public Health, Springfield, IL. Each record includes: Name, Birth Date, Father, Mother, FHL film number, and Page number. This database has 6,946,882 records:
https://search.ancestry.com/search/db.aspx?dbid=2545.

1871-1940. *Illinois, Cook County, Birth Certificates* **[Online Database],** digitized and indexed at the FamilySearch.org website. Source: FamilySearch extractions from the Cook County Courthouse, Chicago, IL. This database is an index to birth records and includes the city of Chicago. Each record may include: Name, Event Type, Event Date, Event Place, Registration Place, Gender, Father's Name, Mother's Name, and Certificate Number. This database has 3,231,003 records. See
www.familysearch.org/search/collection/1462519.

1871-1948. *Chicago Delayed Birth Indexes, 1871-1948* **[Microfilm],** from the originals at the Cook County Courthouse, Chicago, IL. Not in strict alpha order. Filmed by the Genealogical Society of Utah, 1981, 7 rolls, beginning with FHL film #378352 (Aabel – Crabb). To see if this microfilm has been digitized yet, see the FHL catalog page:
www.familysearch.org/search/catalog/263696.

1872-1911. *Cook County Coroner's Inquest Record Index* **[Online Database],** indexed at the Illinois State Archives website. See
www.cyberdriveillinois.com/departments/archives/databases/cookinqt.html.

1872-1906. *Ogle County Naturalization Papers (County Court) Index* **[Online Database],** indexed at the Illinois State Archives website. See
www.cyberdriveillinois.com/departments/archives/databases/ogle.html.

1873-1898. *Adams County Almshouse Register Index* **[Online Database],** indexed at the Illinois State Archives website. See
www.cyberdriveillinois.com/departments/archives/databases/adamsalms.html.

1874-1879. *St. Clair County Farm Board Record Index* **[Online Database],** indexed at the Illinois State Archives website. See
www.cyberdriveillinois.com/departments/archives/databases/stcboard.html.

1874-1906. *East St. Louis City Court Naturalization Papers Index* **[Online Database],** indexed at the Illinois State Archives website. See
www.cyberdriveillinois.com/departments/archives/databases/eslnat.html.

1875 Tax List, Adams County, Illinois **[Online Database]**, indexed at the GenealogyTrails.com website. See
http://genealogytrails.com/ill/adams/1875tax.html.

1875-1876. *Wilson's History and Directory for Southeast Missouri and Southern Illinois, Giving Descriptions of Counties, Towns, and Villages, With Valuable Historical and Statistical Information* **[Printed Book & Digital Version]**, by Lewis A. Wilson, publ. Cape Girardeau, MO, 1875-76, 343 pages. To access the digital images, see the online FHL catalog page:
www.familysearch.org/search/catalog/2086388.

1876. *The Voters and Tax-Payers of DeKalb County, Illinois* **[Online Database]**, a digitized book with OCR index at the Ancestry.com website.
This database has 342 pages. See
https://search.ancestry.com/search/db.aspx?dbid=24740.

1876. *The Voters and Tax-Payers of Kendall County, Illinois* **[Online Database]**, a digitized book with OCR index at the Ancestry.com website. This database has 113 pages. See
https://search.ancestry.com/search/db.aspx?dbid=7892.

1877 Tax List, Adams County, Illinois **[Online Database]**, indexed at the GenealogyTrails.com website. See
http://genealogytrails.com/ill/adams/1877tax.html.

1877. *Bureau County, Illinois Voters and Tax-Payers Directory, 1877* **[Online Database]**, indexed at the Ancestry.com website. See
http://search.ancestry.com/search/db.aspx?dbid=7932.

1877 Voters and Taxpayers Lists, Henry County, Illinois **[Online Database]**, indexed at the IllinoisAncestors.org website. See
www.illinoisancestors.org/henry/VotandTaxList.htm.

1877 Directory, McHenry County, Illinois **[Online Database]**, indexed at the Genealogy Trails website:
www.genealogytrails.com/ill/mchenry/1877index.html.

1877-1886 Birth Records, Schuyler County, Illinois **[Online Database]**, indexed at the USGenWeb site for Schuyler Co IL (archived). See
http://web.archive.org/web/20110509173121/http://schuyler.ilgenweb.net/BirthRecords/Birthrecordsindexpage.html.

1877-1913. *Carroll County Birth Certificates Index* **[Online Database]**, indexed at the Illinois State Archives website. See
www.cyberdriveillinois.com/departments/archives/databases/carroll.html.

1877-1916. *Illinois, Select Deaths Index* **[Online Database]**, digitized and indexed at the Ancestry.com website. Original data: Illinois Statewide Death Index, Pre-1916. Illinois State Archive. Each record includes: Name, Birth Year, Gender, Age, Death Date, Death Place, Volume, Page, URL, This database has 1,162,513 records. See
https://search.ancestry.com/search/db.aspx?dbid=9758.

1877-1916 Death Index, Kankakee County, Illinois **[Online Database]**, indexed at the Kankakee Valley Genealogical Society website. See
www.kvgs.org/deathindex/.

1877-1888 Directories, Grundy County, Illinois **[Microfilm & Digital Capture]**, from the originals published by Lawrence & Thompson, filmed by W.C. Cox Co., Tucson, AZ, 1974, 1 roll, FHL film #934985. To access the digital images, see the online FHL catalog page:
www.familysearch.org/search/catalog/35962.

1877-1910 Death Records, Menard County, Illinois **[Online Database]**, indexed at the RootsWeb website for Menard Co IL. See
www.rootsweb.ancestry.com/~ilmaga/menard/deaths/1_index.html.

1877-1950 Death Records, Peoria County, Illinois **[Online Database]**, indexed at the Genealogy Trails website. See
http://genealogytrails.com/ill/peoria/deathrec/index.htm.

1877-1990. *Illinois, Adams County, Card Index to Deaths* **[Online Database]**, digitized and indexed at the FamilySearch.org website. Source: FamilySearch extractions from the courthouse in Quincy, IL. This database has 95,523 records. See
www.familysearch.org/search/collection/2174942.

1878 Residents, Champaign County, Illinois **[Online Database]**, indexed at the Champaign Co IL GenWeb site (archived). See
http://web.archive.org/web/20100826064745/http://champaign.ilgenweb.net/patrons/patintro.html.

1878-1887 Birth Records, Menard County, Illinois **[Online Database]**, indexed at the RootsWeb site for Menard Co IL. See
www.rootsweb.ancestry.com/~ilmaga/menard/births/1_index.html.

1878-1915 Death Records, Cass County, Illinois **[Online Database]**, indexed at the RootsWeb site for Cass Co IL. See
www.rootsweb.ancestry.com/~ilmaga/cass/deaths/1_index.html.

1878-1917 Index to Death Records, DeWitt County, Illinois [Online Database], indexed at the DeWitt Co IL GenWeb site (archived). See http://web.archive.org/web/20120513191742/http://dewitt.il genweb.net/death-recordsindx-1878-1917.htm

1878-1900s Death Records Index, Jersey County, Illinois [Online Database], indexed at the GenWeb site for Jersey Co IL. (Archived) See https://web.archive.org/web/20130910190251/http://jersey.illinoisgenweb.org/deathindex.html.

1878-1916 Birth Index, Kankakee County, Illinois [Online Database], indexed at the Kankakee Valley Genealogical Society website. See www.kvgs.org/birthindex/index.htm.

1878-1922. Illinois, Cook County, Birth Certificates [Online Database], digitized and indexed at the Ancestry.com website. This database has 1,431,946 records, taken from the FHL microfilm of the originals from the Illinois Department of Health, Division of Vital Records, Springfield, IL. See https://search.ancestry.com/search/db.aspx?dbid=2552. - This database is also at the FamilySearxch.org website. See www.familysearch.org/search/collection/1462519.

1878-1994. Illinois, Cook County Death Records [Online Database], digitized and indexed at the FamilySearch.org website. This database has 7,025,208 records (including the city of Chicago), taken from the FHL microfilm of the originals from the Illinois Department of Health, Division of Vital Records, Springfield, IL. See www.familysearch.org/search/collection/1463134.

1878-1933. Ogle County Almshouse Register Index [Online Database], indexed at the Illinois State Archives website. See www.cyberdriveillinois.com/departments/archives/databases/oglealms.html.

1879 Taxpayers List, Coles County, Illinois [Online Database], indexed at the Genealogy Trails website: www.genealogytrails.com/ill/coles/1879taxpayers.html.

1879 Tax Records, Edgar County, Illinois [Online Database], indexed at the USGenWeb site for Edgar Co IL. See http://usgwarchives.net/il/edgar/tax.htm.

1879. Index to Biographies, 1879 History of Greene County, Illinois [Online Database], indexed at the RootsWeb site for Greene Co IL. See www.rootsweb.ancestry.com/~ilmaga/greene/1879bios/gc-1879dex.html.

1879-2007. Illinois, Macon County, Decatur Public Library Collections [Online Database], digitized at the FamilySearch.org website. This database has 64,268 images of card indexes from the Decatur Public Library. Obituary indexes are by year range. The World War I Soldiers Cards give soldiers, deaths, and enlistees. See www.familysearch.org/search/collection/1447337.

1880. *Illinois, 1880 Federal Census: Soundex and Population Schedules* [Microfilm & Digital Capture], from the originals at the National Archives, Washington, DC. Filmed by the National Archives, c1970, 232 rolls, beginning with FHL film #446678 (Soundex: A000-A234); and FHL film #1254174 (Population schedules: Adams Co – Part). To access the digital images, see the online FHL catalog page: www.familysearch.org/search/catalog/670393.

1880-1905 Index, Declarations of Intent, Jefferson County, Illinois [Online Database], indexed at the GenWeb site (archived). See http://web.archive.org/web/20080703214353/http://jefferson.ilgenweb.net/DeclarationsofIntent.htm.

1881-1899 Delayed Birth Records, Pulaski County, Illinois [Online Database], indexed at the GenealogyTrails.com website. See http://genealogytrails.com/ill/pulaski/delayedbirths81-99.html.

1881-2010. *DuPage County, Illinois, Bronswood Cemetery Burial Index* [Online Database], indexed at the Ancestry.com website. From a database at the website of the Oak Brook Historical Society. Each record includes: Name Birth Date, Death Date, Burial Place, Cemetery, Notes, and a link to the source website. This database has 10,521 records. See https://search.ancestry.com/search/db.aspx?dbid=9255.

1882-1892. *Rock Island and Moline, Illinois Directories* [Online Database], indexed at the Ancestry.com website. Each record includes: Name, Location, and Occupation. This database has 40,140 records. See https://search.ancestry.com/search/db.aspx?dbid=4684.

1882-1963. *Brown County Almshouse Registers Index* [Online Database], indexed at the Illinois State Archives website. See www.cyberdriveillinois.com/departments/archives/databases/brown.html.

1883 Delinquent Tax List, Coles County, Illinois [Online Database], indexed at the Genealogy Trails website. See www.genealogytrails.com/ill/coles/1884deltaxes.html.

1883-1899 Birth Records, Pulaski County, Illinois **[Online Database]**, indexed at the Genealogy Trails website. See http://genealogytrails.com/ill/pulaski/births83-99.html.

1883-1899 Death Records, Pulaski County, Illinois **[Online Database]**, indexed at the Genealogy Trails website. See http://genealogytrails.com/ill/pulaski/deathrecords1883-1899.html.

1884-1889 Birth Register Index, Peoria County, Illinois **[Online Database]**, indexed at the Genealogy Trails website. See www.genealogytrails.com/ill/peoria/birth/bookc.htm.

1884-1892. See *Joliet, Illinois Directories* **[Online Database]**, indexed at the Ancestry.com website. Each record includes: Name, Location, and Occupation. This database has 84,075 records. See https://search.ancestry.com/search/db.aspx?dbid=4422.

1884-1917 Index to Births, Hardin County, Illinois **[Online Database]**, indexed at the US GenWeb site: http://files.usgwarchives.net/il/hardin/vitals/birth/index_vol1.txt.

1885. *Index to Biographies, 1885 History of Greene County, Illinois* **[Online Database]**, indexed at the RootsWeb site for Greene Co IL. See www.rootsweb.ancestry.com/~ilmaga/greene/1885bios/1885index.html.

1885-2002. *Illinois, Cook County, Maywood, Maywood Herald Obituary Card Index* **[Online Database]**, digitized at the FamilySearch.org website. This database has 61,564 images, taken from the microfilmed card index from *Maywood Herald*, 1920-2001 at the FHL in Salt Lake City, UT. See www.familysearch.org/search/collection/1929848.

1886 Directory, Hancock County, Illinois **[Printed Book]**, reprinted 1988, from the original published 1886. See FHL book 977.343 E4. Also on microfilm, FHL film #1320883. To see if this microfilm has been digitized yet, see the FHL catalog page: www.familysearch.org/search/catalog/580490.

1886-1898 Wills & Probate Books Index, Jefferson County, Illinois **[Online Database]**, indexed at the GenWeb site for Jefferson Co IL (archived). See http://web.archive.org/web/20120415042018/http://jefferson.ilgenweb.net/wills/wills.htm.

1887-1890. *Quincy, Illinois Directories* **[Online Database]**, indexed at the Ancestry.com website. Each record includes (at least): Name, and Location. This database has 32,140 records. See https://search.ancestry.com/search/db.aspx?dbid=5134.

1887-1903 Birth Records, Kendall County, Illinois **[Online Database]**, indexed at the USGenWeb site for Kendall Co IL. See http://files.usgwarchives.net/il/kendall/vitals/kbircomb.txt.

1887-1903 Death Records, Kendall County, Illinois **[Online Database]**, indexed at the USGenWeb site for Kendall Co IL. See http://files.usgwarchives.net/il/kendall/vitals/kcdearev.txt.

1887-1916. *Illinois Soldiers' and Sailors' Home Residents* **[Online Database]**, indexed at the Illinois State Archives website. This database indexes the names of male residents of the Illinois Soldiers' and Sailors' Home admitted from its opening in 1887 through September 1916. Female residents are also included from their first admissions in 1908 through September 1916. The database contains more than 14,000 entries. The 1st – 16th Biennial Reports of the Illinois Soldiers' and Sailors' Home are the sources of the names included in the database. In 1885 the General Assembly created the Illinois Soldiers' and Sailors' Home at Quincy to provide subsistence and a home for honorably discharged and disabled veterans of the Mexican and Civil Wars. In succeeding years Illinois veterans of all wars and veterans' wives, mothers, and daughters became eligible for admission. In 1973 the General Assembly changed the home's name to the Illinois Veterans' Home. Since 1976 the Department of Veterans' Affairs has administered the home. See www.cyberdriveillinois.com/departments/archives/databases/quincyhome.html.

1887-2000. *Woodford County, Illinois, Prairie District Library, Obituaries* **[Online Database]**, indexed at the Ancestry.com website. Original data: The Woodford Sentinel Newspaper and The Metamora Herald Newspaper. Woodford County, IL. Each record includes: Surname, Number, Death, Age, Newspaper, Newspaper Date, Page No., and Column No. This database has 31,936 records. See https://search.ancestry.com/search/db.aspx?dbid=6109.

1888 Chicago Voter Registration **[Online Database]**, indexed at the Ancestry.com website. The handwritten 1888-1892 ledgers were microfilmed by the Illinois State Archives. Ancestry.com used the 25 microfilm rolls to create an electronic index of this collection. Fields in the original index include names of individuals, nativity (country of birth), date and place of naturalization; term of residence in precinct, county, and state; current address. This electronic index has 169,236 records and lists just a name and the person's nativity. See http://search.ancestry.com/search/db.aspx?dbid=5991.

1888 Voter Lists, Pope County, Illinois [Online Database], indexed at the USGenWeb site for Pope Co IL. See http://usgwarchives.net/il/pope/popehist.html.

1888-1960. Wayne County Coroner's Inquest Record Index [Online Database], indexed at the Illinois State Archives website. See www.cyberdriveillinois.com/departments/archives/databases/wayne.html.

1889. Danville, Illinois Directory [Online Database], indexed at the Ancestry.com website. Each record includes: Name, City, State, Occupation, and Year. This database has 6,324 records. See https://search.ancestry.com/search/db.aspx?dbid=5265.

1889. Directory and Gazetteer of Sangamon County, Illinois [Printed Book & Online Database], original published by Illinois State Register Book and Job Printing, Springfield, IL, 1989, 1 vol., FHL book 977.3 A1 No. 260. A digital version of this directory is available at the Ancestry.com website. See https://search.ancestry.com/search/db.aspx?dbid=5391.

1889 Delinquent Tax List, Menard County, Illinois [Online Database], indexed at the Genealogy Trails.com website. See www.genealogytrails.com/ill/menard/tax/tax1889.html.

1889-1890. East St. Louis, Illinois Directory, 1889-1890 [Online Database], indexed at the Ancestry.com website. Each record includes: Name, City, State, Occupation, Year, Location 2 (street address, etc.). This database has 6,648 records. See https://search.ancestry.com/search/db.aspx?dbid=5365.

1889-1962. Kankakee County, Illinois Marriage Index [Online Database], indexed at the Ancestry.com website. Original data: Kankakee County Clerk Genealogy Records. Kankakee, IL, 2008. Each record includes: Name, Marriage Date, and Spouse. This database has 67,442 records. See https://search.ancestry.com/search/db.aspx?dbid=4172.

1890 United States Federal Census Fragment (includes Illinois locations) [Printed Index & Online Database]. Illinois was one of eight states that had fragments survive from the 1921 fire and water damaged census schedules. The surviving 1890 census population schedules for Illinois were just some fragments from McDonough County, Mound Township. A national index to the 6,160 names from all surviving fragments was published by the Family History Library and others. See FHL book 973 X2. Online version: See *1890 United States Federal Census Fragment* [Online Database], indexed at Ancestry.com, see www.ancestry.com/search/collections/5445.

1890. Alton, Illinois Directory [Online Database], indexed at the Ancestry.com website. Each record includes: Name, City, State, and Occupation. This database has 4,285 records. See https://search.ancestry.com/search/db.aspx?dbid=5107.

1890 Tax List, Iroquois County, Illinois [Online Database], indexed at the RootsWeb site for Iroquois Co IL. See www.rootsweb.ancestry.com/~ilicgs/hospital/hsptlind.htm.

1890 Chicago Voter Registration [Online Database], indexed at the Ancestry.com website. The handwritten 1888-1892 ledgers were microfilmed by the Illinois State Archives. Ancestry.com used the 25 microfilm rolls to create an electronic index of this collection. Fields in the original index include names of individuals, nativity (country of birth), date and place of naturalization; term of residence in precinct, county, and state; current address. This electronic index has 168,461 records and lists just a name and the person's nativity. See http://search.ancestry.com/search/db.aspx?dbid=5997.

1890. Metamora, Illinois Directory [Online Database], indexed at the Ancestry.com website. Each record includes: Name, Occupation, City, and State. This database has 749 records. See https://search.ancestry.com/search/db.aspx?dbid=5316.

1890. Peoria, Illinois Directory [Online Database], indexed at the Ancestry.com website. Each record includes: Name, Location, and Occupation. This database has 42,774 records. See https://search.ancestry.com/search/db.aspx?dbid=4595.

1890-1893. Evanston, Illinois Directories, 1890-1893 [Online Database], indexed at the Ancestry.com website. Each record includes: Name, Occupation, Business Address, Home Address, City, State, and Year. This database has 30,982 records: https://search.ancestry.com/search/db.aspx?dbid=4445.

1891. *Index to Portrait and Biographical Album of DeWitt and Piatt Counties, Illinois* **[Online Database],** indexed at the DeWitt Co IL GenWeb site (archived). See http://web.archive.org/web/20120718003127/http://dewitt.ilgenweb.net/portrait-biographical-album.htm.

1891-1995. *The Denni Hlasatel Obituary Index* **[Printed Book],** compiled by Joe Novak, et al. Contents: Vol. 1: 1891-1970, Vol. 2: 1971-1995, Vol. 3: 1891-1899, Vol. 4: 1930-1939, Vol. 5: 1940-1949. From intro: "The *Denni Hlasatel* is a Czech (Bohemian) newspaper that has been published in the Chicago area since 1891." Published by the Polish Genealogical Society of Illinois, 5 vols., FHL book 977.3 11 V32d v.1-5.

1891, 1900, 1920 Directories, Jackson County, Illinois **[Online Database],** indexed at the GenealogyTrails.com website. See http://genealogytrails.com/ill/jackson/index_directory.htm.

1892. *Adams County, Illinois Directory* **[Online Database],** indexed at the Ancestry.com website. Each record includes: Name, Location, and Occupation. This database has 13,001 records. See https://search.ancestry.com/search/db.aspx?dbid=5281.

1892 Chicago Voter Registration **[Online Database],** indexed at the Ancestry.com website. The handwritten 1888-1892 ledgers were microfilmed by the Illinois State Archives. Ancestry.com used the 25 microfilm rolls to create an electronic index of this collection. Fields in the original index include names of individuals, nativity (country of birth), date and place of naturalization; term of residence in precinct, county, and state; current address. This electronic index has 236,684 records and lists just a name and the person's nativity. See http://search.ancestry.com/search/db.aspx?dbid=6001.

1892. *Champaign, Illinois Newspaper Index* **[Online Database],** indexed at the Ancestry.com website. Original data: Fuller, Mary, ed.. *Vital Statistics Entries in the Champaign Daily Gazette, 1892.* Each record includes: Surname, Residence, License, Spouse, Published, and Note. This database has 314 records. https://search.ancestry.com/search/db.aspx?dbid=4070.

1892-1902. *Encyclopaedia of Biography of Illinois* **[Printed Book & Digital Version],** by Hyland MacGrath, publ. Century Pub. Co., Chicago, 1892-1902, 3 vols., 1250 pages. This is the best "mug book" for Illinois, with hundreds of biographies of the "prominent men of Illinois." Note that women are often mentioned in passing). To access the digital version, see the online FHL catalog page: www.familysearch.org/search/catalog/2087549.

1892-1913. *Illinois, Stark County, Circuit Court Naturalization Records* **[Online Database],** digitized and indexed at FamilySearch.org. Digital images of originals held by the Circuit Court Clerk in Toulon, IL. This database has 56 records, see www.familysearch.org/search/collection/3158025.

1894 Historical Directory, Edgar County, Illinois **[Online Database],** indexed at the USGenWeb site for Edgar Co IL. See http://files.usgwarchives.net/il/edgar/directories/1894.txt.

1895-1956 Funeral Card Images, Monroe County, Illinois **[Online Database],** indexed at the USGenWeb site for Monroe Co IL (archived). See http://web.archive.org/web/20090416112207/http://monroe.ilgenweb.net/funeralcard_index.html.

1897 Jury List, McDonough County, Illinois **[Online Database],** indexed at the USGenWeb site for McDonough Co IL (archived). See http://web.archive.org/web/20120727131136/http://mcdonough.ilgenweb.org/grjurors997.html

1898 Biographies, from Biographical Record of Kane County, Illinois **[Online Database],** indexed at the GenealogyTrails.com website. See http://genealogytrails.com/ill/kane/bioindex.html.

1898-1902. *Illinois Spanish-American War Veterans* **[Online Database],** indexed at the Illinois State Archives website. This database of Illinois Spanish–American War Veterans indexes the portion of the ninth volume of the nine-volume publication, *Report of the Adjutant General of the State of Illinois,* which lists veterans of that war. (The remainder of the ninth and the other eight volumes list veterans of the Black Hawk, Mexican, and Civil Wars.) This 1902 publication, originating from the rosters maintained by the Illinois Adjutant General, is the result of an 1899 Illinois statute mandating that the rosters of Illinois volunteers be printed. The names of approximately 1,000 men, organized into 10 regiments, are found in its pages. The volume includes a roster and history for each regiment. See www.cyberdriveillinois.com/departments/archives/databases/spanam.html.

1898-2000s. *Illinois Veterans' History Project* **[Online Database],** index to participants at the Illinois State Archives website. The Illinois Veterans' History Project began in 2004 and seeks to honor those men and women from Illinois who have served their country by recording their stories. Veterans or their family members complete and submit to the Illinois State Archives Illinois Patriot Information Forms, which contain information about their service to their country. In addition to filling out the form, veterans and their family members also are encouraged to write down their remembrances and recollections of their service. The purpose of this database is to provide an index to the names of Illinois veterans whose stories have been preserved on Illinois Patriot Information Forms and submitted to the Illinois State Archives for permanent retention. This database will allow you to search for persons who have Illinois Patriot Information Forms on file. You may search by name, branch of service or war fought. www.cyberdriveillinois.com/departments/archives/databases/ilvetproject.html.

1899-1918. Mattoon Death Certificate Registers Index [Online Database], indexed at the Illinois State Archives website. See www.cyberdriveillinois.com/departments/archives/databases/matdth.html.

1900. *Illinois, 1900 Federal Census: Soundex and Population Schedules* **[Microfilm & Digital Capture],** from the original records held by the Bureau of the Census in the 1940s. After microfilming, Congress allowed the Census Bureau to destroy the originals to free up space for WWII-related files. Filmed on 597 rolls, beginning with FHL film #1242962 (Soundex, A000-A165), and FHL film #1240237 (Population schedules, Adams Co-part). To access the digital images, see the online FHL catalog page: **www.familysearch.org/search/catalog/650144.**

1900-2004 Wabash Valley Obituary Index **[Online Database],** indexed at the Vigo County Public Library website. See **www.vigo.lib.in.us/obituaries.**

1903-1912 Death Records Index, Saline County, Illinois **[Online Database],** indexed at the US Gen Web site for Saline Co IL. See http://files.usgwarchives.net/il/saline/vitals/death/deathind.txt.

1905. *Index to Biographies, 1905 History of Greene County, Illinois* **[Online Database],** indexed at the RootsWeb site for Greene Co IL. See www.rootsweb.ancestry.com/~ilmaga/greene/1905bios/index1905.html.

1906-1918 Index to Births, Hardin County, Illinois **[Online Database],** indexed at the USGenWeb site for Hardin Co IL. See http://files.usgwarchives.net/il/hardin/vitals/birth/index_vol2.txt.

1906-1994. *Illinois, Northern District Petitions for Naturalization* **[Online Database],** digitized at the FamilySearch.org website. This is an image-only database, taken from National Archives records of District Courts of the United States. Browse through the images, organized by county, court district, year(s), and Vol./No. This database has 2,046,215 images. See **www.familysearch.org/search/collection/2212212.**

1907 Biographies Index, McDonough County, Illinois **[Online Database],** indexed at the USGenWeb site for McDonough Co IL (archived): http://web.archive.org/web/20120728235115/http://mcdonough.ilgenweb.org/Biographies/morgan_biosIndex.html.

1908. *Early Families in Kane County* **[Online Database],** names extracted from History of Kane County, Illinois, 1908. Indexed at the RootsWeb site for Kane Co IL. See www.rootsweb.ancestry.com/~ilkane/family/family.htm.

1908-1956. *Vermilion Coroner's Inquest Files Index* **[Online Database],** indexed at the Illinois State Archives website. See www.cyberdriveillinois.com/departments/archives/databases/vermcor.html.

1908-1988. *Cook County, Illinois Death Index* **[Online Database],** indexed at the Ancestry.com website. Original data: Cook County Clerk. Cook County Clerk Genealogy Records. Cook County Clerk's Office, Chicago, IL: Cook County Clerk, 2008. Each record includes: Name, Death Date, Death Location, File Number, Archive Collection Number, Archives Repository Location, and Archive Repository Name. This database has 2,746,806 records. See https://search.ancestry.com/search/db.aspx?dbid=1501.

1910. *Illinois, 1910 Federal Census: Soundex and Population Schedules* **[Microfilm & Digital Capture],** from the original records held by the Bureau of the Census in the 1940s. After microfilming, Congress allowed the Census Bureau to destroy the originals to free up space for WWII-related files. Filmed on 599 rolls, begins with FHL film #1369810

(Soundex, A000-A165), and FHL film #1374243 (Population schedules, Adams, Bond, and Alexander Co). To access the digital images, see the online FHL catalog page:
www.familysearch.org/search/catalog/648376.

1910. *Chicago and Cook County, Illinois 1910 Federal Census Index* **[CD-ROM],** compiled by Heritage Quest, Bountiful, UT, 2003, FHL CD-ROM No. 1280.

1912-1942. *Cook County, Illinois Marriage Indexes* **[Online Database],** indexed at the Ancestry.com website. Source: Ancestry extractions from an unnamed private donor's database. Each record includes: Name, Gender, Spouse Name, and Spouse Gender. This database has 674,692 records. See
https://search.ancestry.com/search/db.aspx?dbid=2273.

1912-1985. *Wunders Cemetery, Chicago, Illinois* **[Online Database],** indexed at the Ancestry.com website. Original data: *A Transcription of Wunders Cemetery,* Chicago, Illinois, Chicago Genealogical Society, 1985. Each record includes: Name, On the same stone with, Birth, and Death. This database has 5,568 records. See
https://search.ancestry.com/search/db.aspx?dbid=5738.

1914-2007. *Tazewell County, Illinois, Obituary Card Index from the Pekin Times* **[Online Database],** digitized at the FamilySearch.org website. This database has 91,822 images taken from the Obituary Card Index at the Pekin Public Library, Pekin, Illinois. www.familysearch.org/search/collection/1447328.
- This same database is located at Ancestry.com, see https://search.ancestry.com/search/db.aspx?dbid=60279.

1916-1919. *Illinois, World War I Soldiers Card File* **[Digital Capture],** from a card file located at Decatur Public Library, Decatur, IL. Records are of Christian, Coles, Douglas, Effingham, Fayette, DeWitt, Logan, Marion, Moultrie, and Montgomery counties, Illinois. Digitized 2007, Genealogical Society of Utah. To access the digital images, see the online FHL catalog page: www.familysearch.org/search/catalog/1448989.

1915-1936. *Kankakee County, Illinois Birth Index* **[Online Database],** indexed at the Ancestry.com website. Original data: Kankakee County Clerk Genealogy Records, 2008. Each record includes: Name, and Birth Date. This database has 4,832 records.
https://search.ancestry.com/search/db.aspx?dbid=4097.

1916-1947. *Illinois Deaths and Stillbirths* **[Online Database],** digitized and indexed at the FamilySearch.org website. This database has 2,879,598 records, taken from the FHL microfilm of the originals from the Illinois Department of Health, "Certificates of Death." See
www.familysearch.org/search/collection/1438856.

1916-1935. *Cook County, Illinois Birth Index* **[Online Database],** indexed at the Ancestry.com website. Original data: Cook County, Clerk, comp. Cook County Clerk Genealogy Records. 2008. Each record includes: Name, Birth Date, Birth Location, File Number, Archive Collection Name, and Archive Repository Location. This database has 1,275,307 records. See
https://search.ancestry.com/search/db.aspx?dbid=1499.

1916-1947. *Illinois Deaths and Stillbirths Index* **[Online Database],** indexed at the Ancestry.com website. This database has 2,881,376 records, taken from the FHL microfilm of the originals from the Illinois Department of Health, "Certificates of Death."
http://search.ancestry.com/search/db.aspx?dbid=2542. This database is also available at the FamilySearch.org website. See
www.familysearch.org/search/collection/1438856.

1916-1950 *Illinois Death Certificates* **[Online Database],** indexed at the Illinois State Archives website. This database provides listings of death certificates filed with the Illinois Department of Public Health between 1916 and 1950. As a result of 1989 legislation, that agency makes available for public inspection at the Illinois State Archives only copies of death certificates produced 50 years ago or longer. Certificates show county and city in which death took place; certificate number; address where death took place; sometimes the voting ward of that address; the deceased's full name, sex, marital status, birth date, age at death, occupation, employer, and city and state of birthplace; father's name and birthplace; mother's maiden name and birthplace; name of the informant providing the above information; the filing date; and the name of the registrar. Also included are the date of death; indication if an inquest was held; sometimes the duration of the causal condition and the type of secondary contributory cause; the coroner's signature, address, and telephone number; the date of the coroner's signature; See
www.cyberdriveillinois.com/departments/archives/databases/idphdeathindex.html.

1917 Farmer's Directory, Cass, Mason, Menard and Sangamon Counties, Illinois **[Online Database],** indexed at the RootsWeb site for Cass Co IL. See www.rootsweb.ancestry.com/~ilmaga/cass/farm-dir_ak.html.

1917 Farmers Directory, Fulton County, Illinois **[Online Database],** indexed at the Ancestry.com website. Each record includes: Name, Spouse (Maiden Name if female), Name of farm, Post Office, Rural Route, Township, Section, Ownership, Acres, and Year became resident. This database has 4,319 records. https://search.ancestry.com/search/db.aspx?dbid=4773.

1917 Farmers Directory, Lawrence County, Illinois **[Online Database],** indexed at the RootsWeb site for Lawrence Co IL. See www.rootsweb.ancestry.com/~illasall/farmdir/.

1917 Farmers Directory, Livingston County, Illinois **[Online Database],** indexed at the Ancestry.com website. Each record includes: Name, Spouse (Maiden Name if female), Name of farm, Post Office, Rural Route, Township, Section, Ownership, Acres, and Year became resident. This database has 4,093 records. See https://search.ancestry.com/search/db.aspx?dbid=4845.

1917 Prairie Farmers' Directory of McHenry and Boone Counties, Illinois **[Online Database],** indexed at the GenealogyTrails.com website. See http://genealogytrails.com/ill/mchenry/1917index.html.

1917 Prairie Farmer's Reliable Directory of Morgan and Scott Counties, Illinois **[Online Database],** indexed at the RootsWeb site for Morgan Co IL. See www.rootsweb.ancestry.com/~ilmaga/morgan2/farmdir/1917index.html.

1917 Farmer's Directory, Scott County, Illinois **[Online Database],** indexed at the RootsWeb site for Scott Co IL. See www.rootsweb.ancestry.com/~ilmaga/scott/farm.html.

1917 Farmer's Directory, Stephenson County, Illinois **[Online Database],** indexed at the Ancestry.com website. Each record includes: Name, Spouse (Maiden Name if female), Name of farm, Post Office, Rural Route, Township, and Section. This database has 8,105 records. See https://search.ancestry.com/search/db.aspx?dbid=4371.

1917 Prairie Farmer's Directory, Woodford County, Illinois [Online Database], indexed at the GenealogyTrails.com website. See http://genealogytrails.com/ill/woodford/Washburn.html#1917.

1917-1918 World War I Draft Registrations, Edgar County, Illinois **[Online Database],** indexed at the USGenWeb site for Edgar Co IL. See www.usgwarchives.net/il/edgar/worldwari.htm.

1917-1918. *Illinois, World War I Selective Service System Draft Registration Cards* **[Microfilm & Digital Capture],** filmed by the National Archives, 1987-1988, 290 rolls, beginning with FHL film #1452428 (IL Adams Co, A-Z). To access the digital images, see the online FHL catalog page: www.familysearch.org/search/catalog/746976.

1917-1919. *Illinois, World War I American Expeditionary Forces, Deaths* **[Digital Capture],** digitized from archived microfilm, 2018, FamilySearch International. To access the digital images, see the online FHL catalog page: www.familysearch.org/search/catalog/3023923.

1918 Farmer's Directory, Coles County, Illinois **[Online Database],** indexed at the Genealogy Trails website. See www.genealogytrails.com/ill/coles/farmerindex.html.

1918 Farmer's Directory, Kane County, Illinois **[Online Database],** indexed at the Genealogy Trails website. See http://genealogytrails.com/ill/kane/index.html.

1918 Prairie Farmer's Directory, Schuyler County, Illinois **[Online Database],** indexed at the USGenWeb site for Schuyler Co IL. See http://schuyler.illinoisgenweb.org/PrairieDirectory/PrairieFD.html.

1918 Prairie Farmer's Reliable Directory, St. Clair and Monroe Counties, Illinois **[Online Database],** indexed at the USGenWeb site for Monroe Co IL (archived). See http://web.archive.org/web/20080820234425/http://monroe.ilgenweb.net/Prarie_farmers/prairie_farmer.html.

1920. *Illinois, 1820 Federal Census: Soundex and Population Schedules* **[Microfilm & Digital Capture],** from the original records held by the Bureau of the Census in the 1940s. After microfilming, Congress allowed the Census Bureau to destroy the originals to free up space for WWII-related files. Filmed on 634 rolls, beginning with FHL film #1824290 (Soundex, A000-A165), and FHL film #1820296 (Population schedules, Adams-part). To access the digital images, see the online FHL catalog page: **www.familysearch.org/search/catalog/534280.**

1920 Prairie Farmer's Reliable Directory of Farmers and Breeders, Clinton County, Illinois **[Online Database],** indexed at the Clinton Co IL GenWeb site. **http://clintonilgenweb.net/history/farm/index.htm.**

1920 Prairie Farmer's Directory, Saline County, Illinois [Online Database], indexed at the Angelfire.com website. See **www.angelfire.com/ok4/moore/pfrbd.html.**

1922-2017. *Illinois, Kane County, Elgin, Gail Borden Public Library District, Local Newspaper Obituary Digital Index* **[Online Database].** This index will be updated as more records become available. This database has 66,820 records, see **www.familysearch.org/search/collection/3319741.**

1924-1977. *DeWitt County Coroner's Inquest Files Index* **[Online Database],** indexed at the Illinois State Archives website. See **www.cyberdriveillinois.com/departments/archives/databases/dewtcor.html.**

1925-1977. *Illinois, Order Sons of Italy in America, Lodge Records* **[Online Database],** indexed at the Ancestry.com website. Most of the records relate to death benefit claims. Each record includes: Name, Birth Date, Age at Death, Death Date, Death Location, Claim Number, Document Type, Archive, Archive Location, Collection Title, and Folder Title. This database has 1,805 records. See **https://search.ancestry.com/search/db.aspx?dbid=1915.**

1926-1979. *Illinois, Northern District (Eastern Division), Naturalization Index* **[Online Database],** digitized and indexed at the FamilySearch.org website. Includes a card index to naturalization records for the U.S. District Court for the Eastern Division of the Northern District of Illinois in Chicago. This database has 550,931 images. See **www.familysearch.org/search/collection/2040533.**

- This database is also available at Ancestry.com: **https://search.ancestry.com/search/db.aspx?dbid=60724.**

1927. *History of Illinois and her People* **[Online Database],** digitized and indexed at the Ancestry.com website. This definitive six-volume history of Illinois by George Washington Smith was published by the American Historical Society, Chicago, 1927. See **http://search.ancestry.com/search/db.aspx?dbid=28006.**

1929 Illinois Roll of Honor **[Online Database],** an index to the 1929 publication, *Roll of Honor*, which contains the locations of the burial places of soldiers, sailors, marines, and army nurses who served in any of the wars of the United States and are buried in Illinois. The database contains more than 72,000 names. The General Assembly mandated in 1927 and 1929 that Illinois publish the Roll of Honor as an aid to patriotic and veteran organizations honoring deceased veterans on Memorial Day. The Grand Army of the Republic, United Spanish-American War Veterans, Veterans of Foreign Wars, were among the organizations that gathered the information. See **www.cyberdriveillinois.com/departments/archives/databases/honorroll.html.**

1929-1953. *Lombard, Illinois Newspaper Obituaries* **[Online Database],** indexed at the Ancestry.com website. Original data: Database by David Jackson, *1929-1953 Lombard Illinois Spectator Newspaper Obituaries,* publ. 1999. Each record includes: Name, Date, and page from the *Spectator*; and Date and page from the *Lombardian*. This database has 2,065 records. **https://search.ancestry.com/search/db.aspx?dbid=3683.**

1930. *Illinois, 1930 Federal Census: Population Schedules* **[Microfilm & Digital Capture],** from the original records held by the Bureau of the Census in the 1940s. After microfilming, Congress allowed the Census Bureau to destroy the originals to free up space for WWII- related files. Filmed on 169 rolls, beginning with FHL film #2340140. To access the digital images, see the online FHL catalog page: **www.familysearch.org/search/catalog/1035337.**

1930-1960. *Cook County, Illinois Marriage Index* **[Online Database],** indexed at the Ancestry.com website. Original data: Cook County Clerk, comp. Cook County Clerk Genealogy Records. Cook County Clerk's Office, Chicago, IL: Cook County Clerk, 2008. Each record includes: Name, Marriage Date,

Spouse, Marriage Location, Marriage License (Number), File Number, Archive Repository Location, and Archive Repository Name. This database has 2,035,378 records. See https://search.ancestry.com/search/db.aspx?dbid=1500.

1935-1970. *Chicago and North Western Railroad Employment Records* **[Online Database],** indexed at the Ancestry.com website. Original data: Chicago and North Western Railroad Employee Records. Chicago & North Western Historical Society, Berwyn, Illinois. This collection includes Chicago & North Western Work Cards and Social Security applications for the years 1937–1970 and retiree records from the Chicago, St. Paul, Minneapolis & Omaha Railway, a smaller semi-independent railway the CNW owned a controlling interest in. Each record may include: Employee Names, Occupations within the company, with dates and locations of service, Residences, Social Security numbers (redacted for those born after 1912), Birth dates, Death dates, Start dates with the company, Employee signatures, Absences from service of the company, and Parents' names (on Social Security apps). This database has 1,095,643 records. See https://search.ancestry.com/search/db.aspx?dbid=6944.

1937. *Lurie Index of People in Chicago in 1937 as well as all of the Voters' Registration for Chicago* **[Microfilm & Digital Capture],** author's full name not noted, filmed by Reproduction, Inc., Tucson, AZ, 1975, 38 rolls, beginning with FHL film #933501 (Aabel, Harry H. – Balek, Rudolph F.). To access the digital images, see the online FHL catalog page: www.familysearch.org/search/catalog/360204.

1940. *Illinois, 1940 Federal Census: Population Schedules* **[Online Database],** digitized images from the microfilm of original records held by the Bureau of the Census in the 1940s. After microfilming, Congress allowed the Census Bureau to destroy the originals to free up space for WWII-related files. Digitizing of the 1940 census schedules microfilm images was done for the National Archives and made public on April 2, 2012. This was the first census released only as digitized images on the Internet. To access the digital images, see the online FHL catalog page: www.familysearch.org/search/catalog/2057801.

1940. *Federal Census Finding Aids* **[Online Database].** The National Archives prepared a special website online with a detailed description of the 1940 federal census. Included at the site are descriptions of location finding aids, such as Enumeration District maps, Geographic Descriptions of Census Enumeration Districts, and a list of 1940 City Directories available at the National Archives. The finding aids are all linked to other National Archives sites. See www.archives.gov/research/census/1940/general-info.html#questions.

1940-1947. *Illinois, World War II Draft Registration Cards* **[Digital Capture],** digitized 2016, FamilySearch International, from records located at the National Personnel Records Center, St. Louis, MO. To access the digital images, see the online FHL catalog page: www.familysearch.org/search/catalog/2832983.

1941-1945. *WWII Army Enlistments, by Illinois County,* part of the USGenWeb Archives Project. All Illinois county links available at the USGenWeb home page for the state of Illinois. See http://usgwarchives.net/il/ilfiles.htm.

1942. *Illinois Selective Service System Registration Cards (World War II), Fourth Registration (1942)* **[Microfilm & Digital Capture],** filmed by the Genealogical Society of Utah, 2001-2004, 326 rolls, beginning with FHL film #2240540 (Gustave Renus Aaby – Ivan James Adams). To access the digital images, see the online FHL catalog page: www.familysearch.org/search/catalog/1049164.

1943-1963. *Illinois, Passenger and Crew Lists, 1943-1963* **[Online Database],** indexed at the Ancestry.com website. Source: National Archives microfilm A3716. Each record includes: Name, Nationality, Birth Date, Birth Place, Arrival Date, Arrival Place, Age, and Airline Flight. This database has 273,301 records. See https://search.ancestry.com/search/db.aspx?dbid=9122.

1956. *Veterans of all Wars Buried in Clinton County, Illinois, and Surrounding Areas* **[Online Database],** indexed at the Clinton Co IL GenWeb site. See http://clintonilgenweb.net/military/1956honor/index.htm.

1959-1981. *Illinois, Mildred Hooper Obituary Collection* **[Online Database],** indexed at the FamilySearch.org website. Index and images of obituaries for West Central Illinois and North Eastern Missouri. This database has 34,695 records. See www.familysearch.org/search/collection/2258572.

1968-1969. *Bible Records Compiled by Illinois Society, D.A.R.* **[Online Database],** indexed at the Ancestry.com website. This database has 83 pages: https://search.ancestry.com/search/db.aspx?dbid=29760.

1970-1990. *Illinois, Cook County, Obituaries* **[Online Database],** digitized and indexed at the FamilySearch.org website. Index and images of obituaries from various newspapers in southern Cook County, Illinois, compiled by the South Suburban Genealogical and Historical Society in South Holland, Illinois. The collection also contains obituaries from Hammond, Indiana. Each record includes: Name, Event Type, Event Date, Event Place, Gender, Relationship to Deceased, Death Date, and Newspaper. This database has 38,777 records. See www.familysearch.org/search/collection/2258580.

1979-1993. *Index to the Newsletters, Journals, and Bulletins of the Polish Genealogical Society of America* **[Printed Book],** compiled by Rosemary A. Chorzempa. Published by the Polish Genealogical Society of America, Chicago, IL, 1994, 95 pages, FHL book 943.8 D25p index.

1985-Current. *Illinois Newspaper Obituaries* **[Online Database].** Digitized and indexed at the GenealogyBank.com website. One search screen for obituaries in over 195 city newspapers: www.genealogybank.com/gbnk/obituaries/explore/USA/Illinois/.

1988-1907. *Chicago Tribune, Obituary Index, 1988-1997* **[Online Database],** indexed at the FamilySearch.org website. Source: John Stoddard, comp. Original data: Chicago Tribune. Chicago, IL, USA: Chicago Tribune, 1988-1997. Each record includes a Name (plus Maiden Name of a woman), and the Date of Death. This database has 238,764 records. https://search.ancestry.com/search/db.aspx?dbid=7304.

1988-1995. *Chicago Sun-Times Obituaries, 1988-1995* **[Online Database],** indexed at the Ancestry.com website. Original data: Chicago Sun-Times. Chicago, IL. Each record includes: Name (and Maiden name of a woman), and Date (of obituary). This database has 3,790 records. See https://search.ancestry.com/search/db.aspx?dbid=5607.

1988-1998. *Elmhurst Press (Elmhurst, Illinois) Obituaries* **[Online Database],** indexed at the Ancestry.com website. Original data: John Stoddard, comp.. Elmhurst, Illinois Press Publications. Each record includes: Name (and Maiden name of a woman), and Death Date. This database has 12,005 records. See https://search.ancestry.com/search/db.aspx?dbid=5341.

1994. *Index to Prairie Pioneers of Illinois: As of September 1, 1994 with a Cross-Index to Spouses* **[Printed Book],** compiled and published by the Illinois State Genealogical Society, Springfield, IL. This is an index to all applications for Illinois Prairie Pioneer Certificates, issued by the IL State Genealogical Society. The names of persons applying for the certificate, their spouses, and the names of their Illinois ancestors are included in the index. See FHL book 977.3H22i.

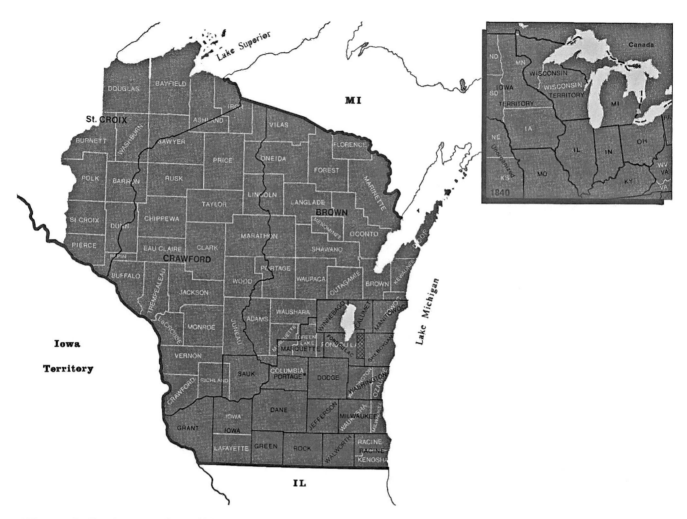

Wisconsin Territory • June 1840. The 22 counties of Wisconsin Territory at the time of the 1840 Federal Census are shown in black. The current 72 counties of Wisconsin are shown in white. Wisconsin became a territory in 1836. The area of Wisconsin Territory in 1840 included the part of present Minnesota east of the Mississippi; the territory's population was at 30,945 people. *** Notes:** Portage County was expanded northward in 1841, and in 1856, Portage assumed its present, modern bounds, having thus "migrated" completely north of its position shown on this 1840 map. The cross-hatched area was mistakenly overlooked by the Wisconsin laws in 1840 but is assumed to be part of Fond du Lac County. **Map Source:** Page 367, *Map Guide to the U.S. Federal Censuses, 1790-1920*, by William Thorndale and William Dollarhide.

Wisconsin
Censuses & Substitute Name Lists

Historical Timeline for Wisconsin, 1671-1848

1671. The French established a Jesuit mission at La Baie des Puants (now Green Bay).

1673. French explorers Jacques Marquette and Louis Jolliet descended the Illinois River to discover the Mississippi River. They spent a few days exploring the area between the Illinois and Wisconsin Rivers, then floated down the Mississippi as far as the mouth of the Arkansas before returning to the Great Lakes.

1682. René-Robert Cavelier (Sieur de LaSalle) erected a cross near the confluence of the Mississippi River and the Gulf of Mexico, after floating down river from the Illinois Country. He claimed the entire Mississippi Basin for Louis XIV of France, for whom Louisiana was named. All of the rivers and streams flowing into the Mississippi were part of the Mississippi Basin and included in the Louisiana claim.

1685. French fur traders established a trading post at Prairie du Chien, the point where the Wisconsin river enters the Mississippi. During the entire French Era, any French in other Wisconsin areas were single voyageurs engaged in fur trading with the Indians.

1717. French Louisiana. The *Illinois Country* was officially added to the French Louisiana jurisdiction within New France. At that time *la Louisiane Française* extended from the Wabash River, down the Ohio and Mississippi Rivers to include several ports on the Gulf of Mexico. Any trading posts or forts north of the Highlands (Terra Haute) were considered part of *French Québec*.

1754-1763. French and Indian War. The Ohio Company of Virginia asserted the British claim to the Ohio region and began sending fur trading parties to the area. The British encroachment into "New France" and the French encroachment into "Virginia" led to a war between Britain and France. The first French Fort in the area was at the Forks of the Ohio, Fort Duquesne (now Pittsburgh) which became the focus of British forays into the western wilderness of colonial America for the first time. The war escalated into a world-wide conflict called the Seven Years War. It involved most of the European great powers of the time, and affected Europe, the Americas, West Africa, India, and the Philippines.

1763-1764. At the 1763 Treaty of Paris ending the Seven Years War, the British acquired all of the French claims east of the Mississippi. The French were asked to leave North America. While the French military left immediately, the Voyageurs / Métis had lost their ties to France and remained. The few French settlements in the Great Lakes region accepted British rule without protest. In 1764, the first British fur trading settlement was established at Green Bay, planted with families from Quebéc by the Hudson's Bay Company.
- The British saw the strategic importance of the former French settlement at Prairie du Chien and established a military garrison there in 1764. The British then consolidated all of their fur trading enterprises at Prairie du Chien, with voyageurs, trappers, traders, and Indians coming together with furs collected in the Upper Mississippi region.

1774. Québec Act. In response to increased American colonial rebellions, the British sought to solidify loyalty from their French communities in British Canada. The British Parliament passed the Québec Act, which restored the name Québec, allowed the French Canadians to retain French laws and customs, and permitted the Catholic Church to maintain all of its rights. The early French settlements in present-day Michigan, Indiana, Illinois and Wisconsin, were by the act included in the Province of Québec, under British rule.

1778-1779. During the Revolutionary War, General George Rogers Clark of the Virginia Militia led the American forces to celebrated victories over the British, with the capture of Kaskaskia in 1778 and Vincennes in 1779.
- Unlike other British-held French settlements, Prairie du Chien was never lost by the British during the war. The British Army used Prairie du Chien as their mustering point with their Indian allies during the Revolutionary War. The town became an attractive refuge to French-Canadian traders, as well as American Loyalists fleeing the war zones. After the war, the British refused to cede their post at Prairie du Chien, continuing their fur trading operations there for another 15 years.

1783. The Treaty of Paris recognized the United States of America as an independent nation and defined its borders from the Atlantic Ocean to the Mississippi River.
- The Wisconsin area was part of the Old Northwest ceded by Britain to the U.S. in the 1783 Treaty of Paris. Between 1783 and 1814, nearly the entire white residential population lived in the villages of Green Bay and Prairie du Chien, still under control of the British military.
- Although the settlements in the Great Lakes region (formerly part of the Province of Québec) were to be included within the United States, British military forces continued to maintain control over parts of the Great Lakes area for several years after the Revolution, e.g., Fort Detroit remained in British control until 1796, and the Isle Royale in Lake Superior was a mustering point for the British and their allied Indians, and also remained in British control until after the War of 1812.

1787. Jul 13. Northwest Territory. The Ordinance of 1787 established the "Territory Northwest of the River Ohio," and defined the procedure for any territory to obtain statehood. Present states carved out of the original area of the Northwest Territory include Ohio, Indiana, Illinois, Michigan, Wisconsin, and that part of Minnesota east of the Mississippi River.

1790. Wisconsin was part of the Northwest Territory, which had no census taken. Prairie du Chien was under British occupation during and after the Revolutionary War, and not vacated by the British Army until after the War of 1812. Green Bay was still under control of British fur trading companies.

1796. Jay Treaty. The British officially ceded Fort Detroit, Fort Miami, and several more British-held military posts from the Great Lakes to Lake Champlain. In exchange, the British retained rights to fur trading operations in the U.S. by private companies, with their employees given the option to become U.S. Citizens. However, two British-held posts in Wisconsin were left out of the Jay Treaty. The British did not cede Green Bay or Prairie du Chien until the Treaty of Ghent ending the War of 1812.

1800. Indiana Territory was established from the Northwest Territory with William Henry Harrison as the first Governor and Vincennes the capital. The area included all of present Indiana, Illinois, Wisconsin, and the western half of Michigan. The Northwest Territory was reduced to the present-day area of Ohio and the eastern half of Michigan. The 1800 federal census for Indiana Territory was lost.

1800-1803. Louisiana. In 1800, Napoleon defeated the Spanish in battle and gained title to Louisiana again after trading them a duchy in Italy. However, Napoleon's troops in the Caribbean were under siege and unable to provide any help in establishing a French government in Louisiana. A couple of years later, when American emissaries showed up trying to buy New Orleans, Napoleon offered the entire tract to them. In 1803, President Thomas Jefferson urged Congress to vote in favor, and the U.S. purchased the huge tract from France, doubling the size of the United States.

1810. The Wisconsin area was part of St. Clair County, Illinois Territory, whose 1810 schedule was lost. There was no attempt to enumerate the two British-held villages of Green Bay and Prairie du Chien.

1814. The treaty of Ghent officially ended the War of 1812. The British Army agreed to vacate Prairie du Chien and Green Bay, but the civilian employees of the Hudson's Bay Company remained at their posts. Per the treaty, they were given the option to become naturalized citizens of the U.S.

1812-1815. Steamboats. First introduced in 1812, the early steamboats were built like ocean vessels, with more draft than the rivers allowed. Introduced in

1815, the classic flat-bottomed steamboat quickly become the main mode of transportation on the Ohio and Mississippi Rivers; as well as their tributaries.

1816. Wisconsin Area. The U.S. Army established Fort Howard at Green Bay and Fort Shelby was built at Prairie du Chien (then renamed Fort Crawford). The two forts asserted an American presence in the Wisconsin area for the first time.

1820 Federal Census – Wisconsin Area (as part of Michigan Territory). Nearly all whites lived near Fort Howard/Green Bay, Brown County, Michigan Territory; or near Fort Crawford/Prairie du Chien, Crawford County, Michigan Territory. The two counties had a combined population of 1,444 people. The 1820 census name lists have survived.

1825. Erie Canal. The entire route of the Erie Canal, from Albany to Buffalo, New York opened to boat traffic in 1825. It was now possible to arrive at New York harbor by sailing ship, travel up the Hudson River by steamboat, and take the same towed barge from Albany all the way to Lake Erie. Steamboat access to the Great Lakes ports in present Ohio, Michigan, and Wisconsin followed. The impact of the migrations via the Erie Canal into Wisconsin contributed greatly to a population that jumped from under 3,700 in 1830 to over 305,000 in 1850.

1830-1835. In the 1830 federal census, the Wisconsin Area population was contained in Brown, Crawford, and Iowa counties, Michigan Territory – the three counties had a combined population of 3,635 people. The census name lists survive for 1830 as well.
- The migrations into Wisconsin really accelerated in the early 1830s, with the main entry points at the Lake Michigan ports of Green Bay, Milwaukee, Racine, and Kenosha.
- Between 1832 and 1834, the first public land surveys were completed, and land sales commenced at the first three federal GLOs at Green Bay, Milwaukie, and Mineral Point.
- 1835-1837. The US Army constructed the *Military Ridge Road*, connecting Fort Howard with Fort Crawford via Fond du Lac, Fort Winnebago, Madison, and Dodgeville. The new wagon road opened an East-West access for many new settlements.

1836. Wisconsin Territory was created in 1836, including lands west of the Mississippi River to the Missouri River. The first territorial capital was at Belmont, where the first session of the legislature met for 42 days and selected Madison as the new capital. The same session dictated that Burlington (now Iowa) serve as a temporary site for legislative sessions until a capitol building could be erected in Madison.

1838. WI Territory Reduction. After the creation of Iowa Territory, Wisconsin's western line ended at the Mississippi River.

1840. WI Territory Federal Census. The territory's population was at 30,945 people. Refer to the 1840 WI map on page 158.

1848. May 29. **Wisconsin** was admitted to the Union as the 30th state, with boundaries the same as today. Madison continued as the state capital.

Online Resources at the Wisconsin Historical Society

The Library-Archives Division of the WHS is the home of the Genealogy and History Collection, one of the largest and most comprehensive family history library collections in the world. Online databases include vital records, biographies, cemeteries, censuses, histories, immigration records, land records, maps, military records, naturalizations, newspapers, obituaries, and probate records. The WHS databases for Civil War records, Vital Records, and the Wisconsin Name Index are outstanding genealogical tools. View the WHS resources available online, see www.wisconsinhistory.org/Content.aspx?dsNav=N:1133.

Bibliography
Wisconsin Censuses & Substitutes

Wisconsin Territory Censuses: Territorial censuses were taken in the years 1836, 1838, 1842, 1846 and 1847. A few counties are missing from the 1846 territorial census, but the others are fairly complete. The WI territorial censuses are all head of household censuses. All surviving originals, 1836-1847, are located today at the WI Historical Society in Madison. Censuses Online: Ancestry's Compiled Census & Census Substitutes database includes indexes to the 1836 through 1846 WI Territorial Censuses.

Wisconsin State Censuses: The state constitution of 1848 mandated state censuses every ten years for the purpose of apportionment of the state legislature. Accordingly, Wisconsin conducted state sponsored censuses for the years 1855, 1865, 1875, 1885, 1895, and 1905. Of these, the 1865 state census has only a handful of counties extant, while the others are mostly complete. All of the censuses 1855-1895 are head of household censuses, and they vary in content with added information, e.g., no. of males and females, no. of persons of foreign birth, deaf, dumb, blind, insane, etc. In the 1885 and 1895 state censuses, a special added list was prepared, giving the names of living war veterans. The only Wisconsin census to list the names of all family members was the 1905 state census. As the culmination of all Wisconsin territory and state censuses, it is in every way a detailed and useful genealogical tool, showing relationships, parent's birthplace, etc. An every-name index to the 1905 state census was prepared by the State Historical Society, a card index organized by county. Censuses Online: all of the surviving state censuses taken in Wisconsin have been digitized and indexed online: 1855-1905 combined in one database at Ancestry.com; individual years at FamilySearch.org. In addition, all of the FHL microfilms for WI 1855 thru WI 1905 were digitized, so another set of the images is accessible at the online FHL catalog.

Wisconsin Federal Censuses (Federal Copies), 1840-1940: The only federal census taken under the name Wisconsin Territory was in 1840, with all 22 counties extant and 30,945 people. After statehood in 1848, the 1850 through 1940 federal censuses for Wisconsin are complete for all counties (with the exception of the 1890, lost for all states).

Wisconsin Federal Censuses (State Copies), 1850-1870: Adding to the superb array of territorial and state censuses available, Wisconsin also has the original state copies of its 1850, 1860, and 1870 federal censuses. These original schedules have not been microfilmed, but the WI Historical Society has prepared every-name indexes to each of their state copies.

Census Substitutes. Although the array of federal and state censuses for Wisconsin is impressive, there are many more substitute databases available. They are identified in an annotated list beginning below in chronological order:

♦ ♦ ♦ ♦ ♦

1685-1850. *Prairie du Chien: French, British, American* **[Online Database],** digitized and indexed at the Ancestry.com website. Source: book, same title, by Peter Lawrence Scanlan, publ. 1937. The names of the French explorers, traders, and settlers in and around Prairie du Chien are given for the 80 years of French rule, plus the main players of the British era, 1763-1814; and the American possessors thereafter. This database has 267 pages. See
http://search.ancestry.com/search/db.aspx?dbid=27459.

1800-1987. *Wisconsin, Wills and Probate Records* **[Online Database],** digitized and indexed at the Ancestry.com website. Source: Ancestry extracts from original records at district, county, and probate courts of Wisconsin. Searchable database fields include the Probate Place, Place of Death, and Item Description (estate, will, petition, etc.). View a digitized original document, which may add substantial details about the deceased personal and real property, names of witnesses, heirs, and more. This database has 210,019 records. See
http://search.ancestry.com/search/db.aspx?dbid=9088.

1800s-1900s. *Wisconsin USGenWeb Archives* **[Online Database].** The WIGenWeb Archives site offers free genealogical databases with searchable statewide name lists and for all Wisconsin counties. Databases may include Bibles, Biographies, Cemeteries, Censuses, Court Records, Deaths, Deeds, Directories, Histories, Marriages, Military, Newspapers, Obituaries, Photos, Schools, Tax Lists, Wills, and more. See
http://usgwarchives.net/wi/wifiles.htm.

1800s-1900s. *Linkpendium – Wisconsin: Family History & Genealogy, Census, Birth, Marriage, Death Vita Records & More* **[Online Databases].** Linkpendium is a genealogical portal site with links to state, county, town, and local databases. Currently listed are selected sites for Wisconsin statewide resources (451), Renamed/Discontinued Counties (4), Adams County (188), Ashland County (188), Barron County (211), Bayfield County (176), Brown County (450) and 67 more Wisconsin counties. See
www.linkpendium.com/wi-genealogy.

1800s-1900s Wisconsin Original Land Owners. See the *Family Maps* series for Wisconsin counties, maps of original land patents, compiled by Greg Boyd and published by Arphax Publishing Co., Norman, OK. These privately-produced computer-generated maps show the first property owners for an entire county, produced as a book of maps, each map laid out on the federal township grid, and includes indexes to help you locate a person, place-name, or cemetery. Additional maps are added for each county to show roads, waterways, railroads, selected city centers, and cemeteries within a county. *Family Maps* books have been published for the following Wisconsin counties:. Barron, Bayfield, Buffalo, Chippewa, Clark, Crawford, Dane, Dodge, Dunn, Eau Claire, Fond du Lac, Green, Iowa, Jackson, Langlade, Lincoln, Monroe, Oneida, Pepin, Pierce, Portage, Price, Racine, Rock, Rusk, Sawyer, Sheboygan, St. Croix, Taylor, Vernon, Vilas, Washburn, Washington, and Waushara counties, Wisconsin. Visit the publisher's information and ordering website for more details and updated county coverage. See **www.arphax.com/**.

1801-1928. *Wisconsin, Births and Christenings Index* **[Online Database],** indexed at the Ancestry.com website. Source: FamilySearch extractions from original and compiled records on microfilm at the Family History Library, Salt Lake City, UT. Each record may include name, gender, race, birthplace, birth date, christening place, christening date, father's name, age, birthplace; mother's name, age, birthplace; paternal grandparents, maternal grandparents, and FHL film number. This database has 4,138,236 records. See **http://search.ancestry.com/search/db.aspx?dbid=2544**.

1807-1907. *Card Files (Index to Land Entry Files of General Land Offices, Eastern States)* **[Microfilm & Digital Capture],** from the original index cards at the Bureau of Land Management (BLM), Eastern States Office, Washington, DC. The card files serve as an index to the Tract Books, Plat Books, and Case Files relating to ten million public land sales in America. **Content:** Each card contains the Certificate Number, District Land Office, Kind of entry (cash, credit, warrant, etc.), Name of Patentee (Buyer, Entryman, etc.), and county of origin, Land description, Number of acres, Date of patent, Volume, and Page where document can be located. Filmed by the Bureau of Land Management, Washington, DC, c1970, 160 rolls (including 4 rolls for Wisconsin GLOs), beginning with FHL film #1501664. To access the digital images, see the online FHL catalog page: **www.familysearch.org/search/catalog/511740**.
- **NOTE:** The index cards in this database are arranged by township and range within each state, not by name of purchaser. An online index at the BLM website can be used to find the name of a purchaser with the land description for that person.
- See also *Bureau of Land Management – General Land Office Records* **[Online Database],** search for the name of any land purchaser of public land in the U.S. To access the search screen, see **https://glorecords.blm.gov/search/default.aspx**.

1807-1907. *Land Patents, Brown County, Wisconsin* **[Online Database],** index to the patents issued to private purchasers of land at the first General Land Office in Wisconsin at Green Bay, Brown County. The first land patent took place in 1807, when Green Bay was still part of Michillimackinac County, Michigan Territory. (Brown County was created by MI Terr. in 1818 and was an original county of Wisconsin Territory in 1836). The index gives the name of the land purchaser, no. of acres, and land description (Section, Township, Range). Indexed at the USGenWeb archives website for Brown Co WI, see **www.usgwarchives.net/wi/brown/old/brland.htm**.

1816-1866. *Index to Crawford County Marriages* **[Printed Book],** compiled by Carol Higgins, publ. Lower Wisconsin River Genealogical & Historical Research Center, Wauzeka, WI, 1994, 96 pages, FHL book 975.574 V22h.

1818-1907. *Land Patents, Crawford County, Wisconsin* **[Online Database],** index to the patents issued to private purchasers of land in Crawford County, Wisconsin. Crawford County was created by Michigan Territory in 1818 and was an original county of Wisconsin Territory in 1836. The index gives the name of the land purchaser, no. of acres, and land description (Section, Township, Range). Indexed in alpha groups at the USGenWeb archives website for Crawford Co WI. See **http://files.usgwarchives.net/wi/crawford/land**.

1820 Michigan Territory Federal Census (MI State Archives Copy) **[Microfilm & Digital Capture],** from Michigan Territory's original manuscript copy, now located at the Archives of Michigan, Lansing, MI. This state archives copy, and the national archives copy should be compared side-by-side to see if there are differences. This MI Territory set was used to make a copy to be sent to Washington, DC (the federal copy). Contents: Oakland, Wayne, Michillimackinac, Brown (now Wisconsin), Crawford (now Wisconsin), Monroe, and Macomb counties. Filmed by the Genealogical Society of Utah, 1973, 1 roll, FHL film #927678. To access the digital images, see the online FHL catalog page: **www.familysearch.org/search/catalog/175106**.

1820 & 1830. See *Michigan, 1820 thru 1840 Federal Census: Population Schedules (Federal Copy)* **[Microfilm & Digital Capture],** from originals at the National Archives, Washington, DC. In 1820, Crawford and Brown counties (now Wisconsin) were part of Michigan Territory. In 1830, Crawford, Brown

and Iowa counties were part of Michigan Territory. These federal copies were filmed by the National Archives (as part of a combined set of 1820, 1830, & 1840), as follows:
- **1820 MI Territory:** Oakland, Wayne, Michillimackinac, Brown (now Wisconsin), Crawford (now Wisconsin), Monroe, and Macomb counties, FHL film #506762.
- **1830 MI Territory:** Wayne, Monroe, Oakland, Lenawee, Macomb, St. Clair, Washtenaw, St. Joseph, Berrien, Cass, Van Buren, Michillimackinac, Brown (now Wisconsin), Crawford (now Wisconsin), Chippewa, and Iowa (1836 Wisconsin Terr.; 1838 Iowa Terr.) counties, FHL film #363348.

To access the digital images, see the online FHL catalog page:
www.familysearch.org/search/catalog/745495.

1820-1839. *Deeds, Brown County, Wisconsin* **[Microfilm & Digital Capture],** from the original records at the WI Historical Society, Madison, WI. Includes general deeds, tax deeds, quit claim deeds, warranty deeds, and any grantor/grantee indexes within certain volumes. Filmed by the Genealogical Society of Utah, 2003, 45 rolls, beginning with FHL film #2367060 (Deed Records, Vol. A, Nov 1820-Jan 1826). To access the digital images, see the online FHL catalog page:
https://familysearch.org/search/catalog/1137284.

1820-1890. *Wisconsin, Compiled Census and Census Substitutes Index* **[Online Database],** indexed at the Ancestry.com website. Originally compiled by Accelerated Indexing Systems, Salt Lake City, acquired by Ancestry in 1999. This collection contains the following Wisconsin indexes:
- 1820 Federal Census Index (MI Territory)
- 1821-1829 Early Census Index
- 1830 Federal Census Index (MI Territory)
- 1836 WI Territorial Census Index
- 1837 WI Territorial Census Index
- 1838 WI Territorial Census Index
- 1840 Federal Census Index
- 1840 Pensioners List
- 1842 WI State Census Index
- 1846 WI State Census Index
- 1850 WI Federal Census Index
- 1855 WI State Census Index
- 1860 WI Federal Census Index
- 1890 WI Veterans Schedule

This database has 182,605 records. See
http://search.ancestry.com/search/db.aspx?dbid=3581

1820-1907. *Wisconsin Birth Index* **[Online Database],** indexed at the FamilySearch.org website. Source: WI Dept of Health. Each record includes a name, date of birth, place of birth, and film numbers and record numbers. This database has 985,659 records. See
https://familysearch.org/search/collection/1946789.
- See also, *Wisconsin, Birth Index, 1820-1907* **[Online Database],** indexed at the Ancestry.com website. Source: Pre-1907 Vital Records Collection, WI Historical Society. The records have a link to the Wisconsin Historical Society website, where a copy of the original record can be ordered. This database has 1,368,708 records. See
http://search.ancestry.com/search/db.aspx?dbid=4997.

1820-1907. *Wisconsin Death Index* **[Online Database],** indexed at the FamilySearch.org website. Source: WI Dept of Health. Each record includes a name, date of death, place of death, and page number. This database has 435,208 records. See
https://familysearch.org/search/collection/1940759.
- See also, *Wisconsin, Deaths, 1820-1907* **[Online Database],** indexed at the Ancestry.com website. Source: Pre-1907 Vital Records Collection, WI Historical Society. The records have a link to the Wisconsin Historical Society website, where a copy of the original death record can be ordered. This database has 439,245 records. See
http://search.ancestry.com/search/db.aspx?dbid=4984.

c1820-1992. *Wisconsin, County Naturalization Records* **[Online Database],** digitized at the FamilySearch.org website. Images only database, from FamilySearch imaging of naturalization records at Wisconsin county courthouses. The starting date of 1807 (in the title) is probably in error and was changed to the time of the earliest counties of Wisconsin before territorial status (about 1820). The records usually include the following information: Full name, Current residence, Birth date and place of birth, Date Naturalized, Name of court, Age when naturalized, Spouse's name, married, Names of children, Arrival date and port of entry, and Certificate number. Browse through the records, organized by county, then by Record Type, Year Range, and Volume No. This database has 1,135,393 records. See
https://familysearch.org/search/collection/2046887.

1824-1910. *Probate Index, Brown County, Wisconsin* **[Microfilm & Digital Capture],** from the original records at the WI Historical Society, Madison, WI. Although the index covers probate and guardianship matters, it is mostly an index to court records. Adoptions have been blanked out before filming. Filmed by the Genealogical Society of Utah, 1991, 1 roll, FHL film # 1753115. To access the digital images, see the online FHL catalog page:
www.familysearch.org/search/catalog/462336.

1825-1980. *Wisconsin, Outagamie County Records* **[Online Database],** indexed at the FamilySearch.org website. Source: Outagamie County Register of Deeds, Appleton, WI. This is an image only database of land and probate records. Browse through the records, organized by Land and Property records or Probate records, then Record Type, Volume, and Year Range. This database has 70,159 records. See
https://familysearch.org/search/collection/1463639.

1826-1926. *Wisconsin Births and Christenings* **[Online Database],** indexed at the FamilySearch.org website. Source: FamilySearch extractions from county records on microfilm at the Family History Library, Salt Lake City, UT. Each record includes a name, gender, date of birth, place of birth, race, father's name and birthplace, Mother's name and birthplace and FHL film number. This database has 1,440,965 records. See
https://familysearch.org/search/collection/1708703.

1830 Census Index, Michigan Territory, Iowa County **[Online Database],** indexed at the USGenWeb Archives website. See
http://files.usgwarchives.net/wi/territory/census/1830/cens1830.txt.

1830-1850. *Iowa County (Wisconsin) Heritage* **[Printed Book & Microfilm],** abstracts of censuses from the 1830 Michigan Territory census; the 1836, 1838, 1840, 1842, and 1847 Wisconsin Territory censuses; and the Wisconsin federal census of 1850. Published in 4 vols., 1967. FHL book 977.5 B4f vol. 1-4. (Vols. 1 & 2 relate to Iowa County, WI; Vol. 3 relates to Grant Co., WI; & Vol. 4 relates to Jo Daviess County, IL). From introduction: "When organized as a county, under the territorial government of Michigan, in 1829, Iowa county contained within its jurisdiction the present counties of Dane, Green, Grant, LaFayette, and a part of Rock, thus embracing almost one-half of Wisconsin which lies south of the Wisconsin River." Filmed by the Genealogical Society of Utah, 1987, FHL film #1320510.

1832-1907. *Wisconsin, Homestead and Cash Entry Patents, Pre-1908* **[Online Database],** indexed at the Ancestry.com website. Source: BLM General Land Office Automated Records Project. This database is the Wisconsin portion of the GLO patents issued by the federal government within the public domain of the United States. The patent was the first-title deed and the true beginning of private ownership of the land. The deeds recorded in these records includes: Name, Land Office, Sequence, Document number, Total acres, Signature, Canceled document, Issue date, Mineral rights reserved, Metes and bounds, Statutory reference, Multiple warrantee and patentee names, Act or treaty, Entry classification, and Land description (usually Section, Range, Township). This database has 187,635 records. See
http://search.ancestry.com/search/db.aspx?dbid=2079.

1833-1992. *Wisconsin Newspaper Archives* **[Online Databases],** digitized and indexed newspapers at the GenealogyBank website, for Appleton, Beloit, Chilton, Fond du Lac, Fort Atkinson, Fox Lake, Galesville, Grafton, Gratiot, Green Bay, Janesville, La Crosse, Lancaster, Madison, Mauston, Milwaukee, Monroe, New Lisbon, Oshkosh, Racine, Sheboygan, and Waukesha, WI. See
www.genealogybank.com/explore/newspapers/all/usa/wisconsin.

1835-1900. *Wisconsin Marriages* **[Online Database],** indexed at the Ancestry.com website. Source: Jordan Dodd, compiler, Liahona Research, from Grant County, Jackson County, and Monroe County, WI records on microfilm at the Family History Library, Salt Lake City, UT. This database has 27,383 records:
http://search.ancestry.com/search/db.aspx?dbid=5230.

1835-1968. *Wisconsin Deaths and Burials* **[Online Database],** indexed at the FamilySearch.org website. Source: FamilySearch extractions. This database is a name index to death and burial records from microfilm at the Family History Library, Salt Lake City, UT. This database has 34,943 records. See
https://familysearch.org/search/collection/1708699.

1836. *The First Census of the Original Counties of Dubuque and Demoine (Iowa) Taken in July 1836* **[Online Database],** indexed at Ancestry.com. Source:

book, same title, edited by Benjamin F. Shambaugh, originally published by the Historical Department of Iowa, Des Moines, IA, 1897-1898, 93 pages. Contents: pt. 1. Dubuque County, pt. 2. Demoine County. From the original manuscript returns preserved in the office of the Secretary of State of Wisconsin. Census taken in accordance with the act of Congress erecting the territory of Wisconsin (of which these two counties at the time formed a part) comprising the present states of Wisconsin, Iowa, Minnesota and part of North and South Dakota. This database has 90 pages. See http://search.ancestry.com/search/db.aspx?dbid=23732.

1836 Wisconsin Territory Census [Online Database], extracted and indexed at the WIGenWeb Archives website. See
http://files.usgwarchives.net/wi/territory/census/1836/1836cens.txt.

1836 Wisconsin Territorial Census [Microfilm & Digital Capture], from the original records at the WI Historical Society, Madison, WI. This is a head of household census similar in format to the 1830 federal census. Originals filmed by the Genealogical Society of Utah, 1980, 1 roll, FHL film #1293919. To access the digital images, see the online FHL catalog page: **www.familysearch.org/search/catalog/218173**.
- The 1830 WI State Census name list was published in *Collections of the Wisconsin State Historical Society*, vol. 13, (1895), p. 247-270; reprinted as **"The Territorial Census For 1836,"** Reuben Gold Thwaites, editor. The article was also filmed (and digitized) by the Genealogical Society of Utah, 1980, 1 roll, FHL film #1293922. To access the digital images, see the online FHL catalog page: **www.familysearch.org/search/catalog/235270**.
- See also, *Wisconsin 1836 Census Index* [Printed Index], edited by Ronald Vern Jackson and Gary Ronald Teeples, published by Accelerated Indexing, Bountiful, UT, 1976, 24 pages. FHL book 977.5 X2 1836.

1836-1911. *Wisconsin, County Marriages* [Online Database], indexed at the FamilySearch.org website. Source: WI Historical Society. Each record may include: Name of the groom, Name of the bride, Names of the officiator and witnesses, Names of the parents or guardians of the bride and groom, Date of the marriage, Race and Birthplaces of the bride and groom, Residences of the bride and groom, and Occupation of the groom. This database has 755,345 records. See https://familysearch.org/search/collection/1803973.

1836-1930. *Wisconsin Marriages* [Online Database], indexed at the FamilySearch.org website. Source: FamilySearch extractions. This database is a name index to marriage records from microfilm at the Family History Library, Salt Lake City, UT. This database has 197,702 records. See
https://familysearch.org/search/collection/1708704.

1838 Wisconsin Territorial Census [Microfilm & Digital Capture], from the original records at the WI Historical Society, Madison, WI. Head of household census similar in format to the 1836 territorial census. Originals filmed by the Genealogical Society of Utah, 1980, 1 roll, FHL film #1293919. To access the digital images, see the online FHL catalog page: **www.familysearch.org/search/catalog/234130**.
- See also, *Wisconsin 1838 Census Index* [Printed Index], edited by Ronald Vern Jackson, et al, Accelerated Indexing Systems, Bountiful, UT, 1984, 27 pages. FHL book 977.5 X22j 1838.

1840-1970. *Oshkosh Area, Wisconsin, Naturalizations Index* [Online Database], indexed at the Ancestry.com website. This database is also accessible at the University of Wisconsin Oshkosh Archives and Area Research Center website. Each record may include a name, case type, date, place, archives, title, court, role (immigrant, returning citizen, etc.), call no. and location data. This database has 54,394 records. See
http://search.ancestry.com/search/db.aspx?dbid=70824.

1842 Wisconsin Territorial Census [Microfilm & Digital Capture], from the original records at the WI Historical Society, Madison, WI. This is a head of household census similar in content to the 1838 territorial census. Filmed by the Genealogical Society of Utah, 1980, 1 roll, FHL film #1293919. To access the digital images, see the online FHL catalog page: **www.familysearch.org/search/catalog/235220**.
- See also, *Wisconsin 1842 Census Index* [Printed Index], edited by Ronald Vern Jackson, et al, published by Accelerated Indexing Systems, Bountiful, UT, 1984, 110 pages. FHL book 977.5 X22j 1842.

1846 Wisconsin Territorial Census [Microfilm], from the original records at the WI Historical Society, Madison, WI. Includes name of head of family; number of males and females by color, those of foreign birth, deaf, dumb, blind, or insane. Incomplete schedules for

The counties of Crawford and Fond du lac; and Grand Rapids in Portage County. No schedules at all for Chippewa, LaPointe, or Richland counties. Filmed by the Genealogical Society of Utah, 1980, 1 roll, FHL film #1293920.

1847 Wisconsin Territorial Census [Microfilm & Digital Capture], from the original records at the WI Historical Society, Madison, WI. This was a heads of household census with a format similar to the 1846 territorial census, complete for all counties except Sheboygan county is missing. Filmed by the Genealogical Society of Utah,
1980, 2 rolls, as follows:
- **1847 WI territorial census**, Brown to Sheboygan Co. (Sheboygan missing), FHL film #1293921.
- **1847 WI territorial census**, Walworth to Winnebago Co., FHL film #1293922.

To access the digital images, see the online FHL catalog page:
www.familysearch.org/search/catalog/235228.

1848-1948. *Wisconsin Probate Estate Files* [Online Database], digitized at the FamilySearch.org website. Source: WI Historical Society. This image only database includes probate estate case file from Barron County (1910-1930), Bayfield County (1874-1919), Door County (1862-1938), Dunn County (1858-1940), Fond du Lac County (1848-1948), Green County (1848-1885), Jackson County (1897-1935), La Crosse County (1877-1935), Pepin County (1900-1935), Shawano County (1861-1933), and Trempealeau County (1900-1920). Browse through the records, organized by County, then Case File Number and Year Range. This database has 1,399,485 records. See
https://familysearch.org/search/collection/1874190.

1848-1977. *Oshkosh Area, Wisconsin, Court Records Index* [Online Database], indexed at the Ancestry.com website. This database is also accessible at the University of Wisconsin Oshkosh Archives and Area Research Center website. Each record may include a name, case type, date, place, archives, title, court, role (immigrant, returning citizen, etc.), call no and location data. This database has 43,624 records:
http://search.ancestry.com/search/db.aspx?dbid=70823.

1848-1980. *Wisconsin, Fond du Lac Public Library Records* [Online Database], digitized at the FamilySearch.org website. This image-only database includes images of three separate card index files: 1) Calvary Cemetery, 1900-1980; 2) Marriage Applications, 1899-1930; and 3) Divorces, 1848-1950. Browse through the images, organized by category, then alphabetically by surname. This database has 22,198 images. See
https://familysearch.org/search/collection/1391196.

1848-1990. *Wisconsin, Milwaukee Naturalization Index* [Online Database], digitized and indexed at the FamilySearch.org website. Source: National Archives publication ID #6948573. This database reproduces the card index to naturalizations produced by the District Court of the Eastern District of Wisconsin (Milwaukee). The index cards include the following information: Certificate number, Full name of citizen, Residence, Birth date, Admission date, Certificate date, Name and place of court, Petition and Alien registration number. This database has 76,412 records. See
https://familysearch.org/search/collection/2138589.

1848-1991. *Wisconsin, Milwaukee Petitions for Naturalization* [Online Database], digitized at the FamilySearch.org website. Source: National Archives publication ID #7267811. This image-only database includes the petitions for naturalizations produced by the District Court of the Eastern District of Wisconsin (Milwaukee). Browse through the records, organized by volume and date range. This database has 176,312 images/records. See
https://familysearch.org/search/collection/2174939.

1848-1992. *Wisconsin, Federal Naturalization Records* [Online Database], indexed at the Ancestry.com website. Source: Microfilm of Naturalization Records from U.S. District Courts, originals at the National Archives, Chicago, IL. These records are searchable by Name, Birth Date, Birth Place, and Immigration Year. Additional information in the original records may include: Place of Residence, Occupation, Date of Departure, Place of Departure, Place of Arrival, Spouse's Name, Birth Date, and Residence, Number of Children, Each child's Name, Birth Date, Birth Place, and Residence. This database has 331,780 records. See
http://search.ancestry.com/search/db.aspx?dbid=61213.

1850. *Wisconsin, 1850 Federal Census: Population Schedules (Federal Copy)* [Microfilm & Digital Capture], from the original records at the National Archives, Washington, DC. The census schedules show the names of all members of a family, age, sex, and place of birth. Since Wisconsin has the state copies of the same federal census schedules, a comparison can made between the federal and state copies. This federal set was filmed by the National Archives, 1964, 16 rolls, beginning with FHL film #34508 (Adams, Brown, Calumet, Chippewa, and Columbia Counties). To access the digital images, see the online FHL catalog page: **https://familysearch.org/search/catalog/745188.**

- See also, *Index to 1850 Federal Census of Wisconsin (State Copy)* **[Microfilm]**, from the original card index at the WI Historical Society, Madison, WI. The index is to the state copy, and volumes and page numbers given in the census index do not always match the federal copy of the census. The alphabetized list of names is for the entire state, regardless of county of residence. Filmed by the University of Wisconsin Film Laboratory, 1971, 36 rolls, beginning with FHL film #933599 (Aaby – Autthouse). To see if this microfilm has been digitized yet, see the FHL catalog page: **https://familysearch.org/search/catalog/283885.**

1850-2007. *Wisconsin, Shawano and Oconto Counties, Indexes and Records* **[Online Database],** digitized at the FamilySearch.org website. Source: This image-only database has images of original records now located at the Shawano Wisconsin Family History Center. The collection includes a partial obituary index, original obituaries, 1928-2005; land plat books, 1905-1911; and an index to the 1910 US Census for Shawano County. A few records originated in Oconto County, the parent county of Shawano. Browse through the records, organized by Record Type, Volume, and Year Range. This database has 27,614 records. See **https://familysearch.org/search/collection/1930024.**

1853-2012. *Outagamie County, Wisconsin, Appleton Public Library Obituary Index* **[Online Database],** indexed at the Ancestry.com website. This database is also accessible at the Appleton Public Library website. Each record may include: Name, Birth Date, Birth Place, Death Date, Burial Place, Cemetery, Date of Obituary, Place of Obituary, Title of Newspaper, Spouse's name, Notes, and the URL link to the database at the Appleton Public Library. This database has 128,147 records. See **http://search.ancestry.com/search/db.aspx?dbid=9254.**

1855 Wisconsin State Census **[Microfilm & Digital Capture],** from the original records at the WI Historical Society, Madison, WI. This is a head of household census similar in format to the 1847 census layout. Complete for all counties except Kewaunee County, which is missing. Filmed by the Genealogical Society of Utah, 1979, 4 rolls, as follows:
- **1855 WI state census**, Adams - Dane, Douglas, Dunn counties, vols. 1-3, FHL film #1032686.
- **1855 WI state census**, Dodge, Fond du Lac - LaPointe counties, vols. 4-9, FHL film #1032687.
- **1855 WI state census**, Manitowoc - Rock counties, vols. 10-14, FHL film #1032688.
- **1855 WI state census**, St. Croix – Winnebago counties, vols. 15-18, FHL film #1032689.

To access the digital images, see the online FHL catalog page: **www.familysearch.org/search/catalog/176546.**

-See also, *Wisconsin 1855 Census Index* **[Printed Index],** edited by Ronald Vern Jackson, et al, published by Accelerated Indexing, Bountiful, UT, 1984, 417 pages. FHL book 977.5 X22w 1855.

- See also, *Wisconsin State Census, 1855* **[Online Database],** digitized and indexed at the FamilySearch.org website. Source: WI Historical Society. Includes name index and images of the population schedules for 1855, a head of household census listing, including: Name of head of family, Number of white males and white females in each household, Number of colored males and colored females in each household, Number of individuals who are deaf and dumb, blind, or insane, and the Number of individuals who are foreign born. The database is searchable by a first name, last name, or residence. This database has 133,164 records. See **https://familysearch.org/search/collection/1443825.**

1855-1905. See *Wisconsin, State Censuses, 1855-1905* **[Online Database],** digitized and indexed at Ancestry.com. Source: microfilm of originals held by the Wisconsin Historical Society, Madison, WI. This database contains a combined index to the 1855, 1865, 1875, 1885, 1895, and 1905 WI State Censuses. The index records are all linked to an actual image of the census page. The 1865 WI State Census has 6 surviving counties; all other census years are complete for all counties organized at the time of the census. This database has 3,427,739 records, see **www.ancestry.com/search/collections/1055.**

1857-1859 Wisconsin (State) Directories **[Microfiche]**, from the originals published by various publishers. Filmed by Research Publications, Woodbridge, CT, 1980-1984, 17 microfiche, as follows:
- **1857-1858**, The Wisconsin State directory, by Smith, Du Moulin & Co. (7 fiche), FHL fiche #6044651.
- **1858**, Strickland's North-Western almanac and business directory by Strickland & Co. (2 fiche), FHL fiche #6044652.
- **1858-1859**, The Wisconsin State directory by Strickland & Co. (8 fiche), FHL fiche #6044653.

1857-2013. *Milwaukee, Wisconsin, Catholic Archdiocese Burial Index* **[Online Database]**, indexed at the Ancestry.com website. This database is also accessible at the Catholic Archdiocese of Milwaukee website. Each record may include: Name, Birth Date, Age at death, Burial date, Name of Cemetery, and Location of Cemetery. This database has 15,900 records. See
http://search.ancestry.com/search/db.aspx?dbid=70645.

1860. *Wisconsin, 1860 Federal Census: Population Schedules (Federal Copy)* **[Microfilm & Digital Capture]**, from the original records at the National Archives, Washington, DC. The 1860 census was filmed twice. The second filming is listed first and is usually easier to read. Filmed by the National Archives, 1962, 1968, 49 rolls, beginning with FHL film #805399 (2nd filming, Adams and Bad Ax Counties). To access the digital images, see the online FHL catalog page:
https://familysearch.org/search/catalog/708785.

1860. *Index to the 1860 Federal Census of Wisconsin (State Copy)* **[Microfilm]**, from the original index cards at the WI Historical Society, Madison, WI. The index is to the state copy, and volumes and page numbers given in the index do not always match the federal copy of the census. The alphabetized list of names is for the entire state, regardless of county of residence. Filmed by the University of Wisconsin Film Laboratory, 1971, 95 rolls, beginning with FHL film #933635 (Aaby – Ambrosch). To see if this microfilm has been digitized yet, see the FHL catalog page https://familysearch.org/search/catalog/283919.

1861-1865. *Roster of Wisconsin Volunteers, War of the Rebellion* **[Online Database]**, digitized and indexed at the Ancestry.com website. Source: Book, same title, publ. Madison, WI, 1886. This database has 1,834 records. See
http://search.ancestry.com/search/db.aspx?dbid=29993.

1861-1865. *Index to Compiled Service Records of Volunteer Union Soldiers Who Served in Organizations From the State of Wisconsin* **[Microfilm & Digital Capture]**, from the original records at the National Archives, Washington, DC. Filmed by the National Archives, 1964, series M0559, 33 rolls, beginning with FHL film #882486 (Index, A-Bak, 1861-1865). To access the digital images, see the online FHL catalog page:
https://familysearch.org/search/catalog/317099.

1865 Wisconsin State Census **[Printed Index & Microfilm & Digital Capture]**. The state's original set was destroyed, but there are duplicate copies that exist for six counties, Dunn, Green, Jackson, Kewaunee, Ozaukee, Sheboygan. A transcription and index was compiled by Barry Christopher Noonan, published by the author, Madison, WI, 1993, 353 pages. Copy at the State Historical Society library, call no. F580 N66 1993. The original manuscripts of the six surviving counties are available on microfilm, as follows:
- *1865 WI State Census, Dunn County,* microfilm of original records now located at the Stout Area Research Center at Menomonie, WI. Head of household census. Filmed by the Genealogical Society of Utah, 1981, 1 roll, FHL film #1298908. To access the digital images, see the online FHL catalog page:
www.familysearch.org/search/catalog/317931.
- *1865 WI State Census, Green County, WI,* microfilm of original records at the WI Historical Society, Madison, WI. Head of household census. Filmed by the Genealogical Society of Utah, 1981, 1 roll, FHL film #1306084. To access the digital images, see the online FHL catalog page:
www.familysearch.org/search/catalog/106852.
- *1865 WI State Census, Jackson County, WI,* microfilm of original records at the WI Historical Society, Madison, WI. Head of household census. Filmed by the Genealogical Society of Utah, 1981, 1 roll, FHL film #1306084. To access the digital images, see the online FHL catalog page:
www.familysearch.org/search/catalog/106852.
- *1865 WI State Census, Kewaunee County, WI,* microfilm of originals at the WI Historical Society, Madison, WI. Head of household census. Filmed by the WI Historical Society, 2003, 1 roll, FHL film #2311106. To access the digital images, see the online FHL catalog page:
www.familysearch.org/search/catalog/744954.

- *1865 WI State Census, Ozaukee County, WI,* microfilm of originals at the WI Historical Society, Madison, WI. Head of household census. Filmed by the WI Historical Society, 2003, 1 roll, FHL film #2311107. To access the digital images, see the online FHL catalog page:
  www.familysearch.org/search/catalog/1122739.
- *1865 WI State Census, Sheboygan County, WI,* microfilm of original records at the Sheboygan County courthouse, Sheboygan, WI. Heads of household census. Filmed by the Genealogical Society of Utah, 1983, 1 roll, FHL film #1392915. To access the digital images, see the online FHL catalog page:
  www.familysearch.org/search/catalog/4960307.
   - See also *Copy of the Sheboygan County Census, 1865, State of Wisconsin: Enumeration of the Inhabitants in Sheboygan County*, copied by the Sheboygan County Genealogical Society, Sheboygan Falls, WI, 1985, 123 pages. FHL book 977.569 X2c.

- See also, *1865 Wisconsin State Census* **[Online Database]**, digitized and indexed at the FamilySearch.org website. Source: WI Historical Society. The original state copies of the 1865 state census were purposely destroyed. This database is for six counties only – county copies transferred to the WI Historical Society (Dunn, Green, Jackson, Kewaunee, Ozaukee, and Sheboygan County, WI). Includes name index and images of the population schedules for 1865, a head of household listing, including: Name of head of family, Number of white males and white females in each household, Number of black males and black females in each household, and the Number of individuals who are foreign born. This database has 21,162 records. Source: See
https://familysearch.org/search/collection/2058670/.

1867-1907. *Wisconsin, Death Records* **[Online Database]**, indexed at the FamilySearch.org website. Source: WI Historical Society. A database extracted from death registers, including: Full name of deceased, Maiden name (if deceased is a married woman), Color, Sex, Race, Occupation, Age, Name of father, Birthplace of father, Name of mother, Birthplace of mother, Birthplace of deceased, Name of spouse, Birth date of deceased, Marital status of deceased, Death date, Residence of deceased, Cause of death, Place of death, duration of disease, Was deceased a soldier or in the service of the United States, Burial place, Name of undertaker, Date of certificate, Number of burial permit, Place of burial permit, and Other remarks. This database has 432,959 records. See
https://familysearch.org/search/collection/1803975.

1874. *Green Bay and Fort Howard Directory. Containing Historical Information of Their Early Settlement and Growth; Their Present Standing; Schools, Churches, Societies, etc. Also Business Directory of Principle Dealers. Street Directory, Ward Boundaries, etc., publ. Reid and Miller, 1874* **[Online Database]**, digitized and indexed at the Univ. of Wisconsin Digital Collection website. See
http://digicoll.library.wisc.edu/cgi-bin/WI/WI-idx?id=WI.NLHGBayDir1874.

1870. *Wisconsin, 1870 Federal Census (Federal Copy)* **[Microfilm & Digital Capture],** from the original records at the National Archives, Washington, DC. The 1870 census was filmed twice. Filmed by the National Archives, 1962, 1968, 60 rolls, beginning with FHL film #553202 (Adams, Ashland, Barron, Bayfield, and Brown Counties). To access the digital images, see the online FHL catalog page:
https://familysearch.org/search/catalog/698928.

- See also, *Index to the 1870 Federal Census of Wisconsin (State Copy)* **[Microfilm],** from the original card index at the WI Historical Society, Madison, WI. The index is to the state copy, and volumes and page numbers given do not always match the federal copy of the census. The alphabetized list of names is for the entire state, regardless of county of residence. Filmed by the University of Wisconsin Film Laboratory, 1971, 135 rolls, beginning with FHL film #933730 (Aaby – Allen, Myron). To see if this microfilm has been digitized yet, see the FHL catalog
page: https://familysearch.org/search/catalog/284025.

1875 Wisconsin State Census **[Microfilm & Digital Capture],** from the original records at the WI Historical Society, Madison, WI. Head of household census similar to the 1855 state census format. Filmed by the Genealogical Society of Utah, 1979, 6 rolls, as follows:
- *1875 WI State Census,* Adams - Calumet (part) counties, vol. 1, FHL film #1032689.
- *1875 WI State Census,* Calumet (cont.) – Eau Claire counties, vol. 1-3, FHL film #1032690.
- *1875 WI State Census,* Fond du Lac- Juneau counties, vol. 4-5, FHL film #1032691.
- *1875 WI State Census,* Kenosha- Milwaukee counties, vol. 6-, FHL film #1032692.
- *1875 WI State Census,* Monroe- Sheboygan counties, vol. 8-10, FHL film #1032693.
- *1875 WI State Census,* Sheboygan – Wood counties, vol. 10-12, FHL film #1032694.

To access the digital images, see the online FHL catalog page:
www.familysearch.org/search/catalog/176663.

- See Also, *Wisconsin State Census, 1875* **[Online Database]**, indexed at the FamilySearch.org website. Source: WI Historical Society. Includes name index and images of the population schedules for 1875, a head of household listing, including: Name of head of family, Number of white males and white females in each household, Number of black males and black females in each household, and the Number of individuals who are foreign born. This database has 296,899 records. See
https://familysearch.org/search/collection/1443778.

1876-1907. *Vital Records Index, Crawford County, Wisconsin* **[Online Database]**, an index to births, marriages, and deaths. Indexed at the USGenWeb Archives website for Crawford Co WI. For the parent directory, see
http://files.usgwarchives.net/wi/crawford/vitals.

1880. *Wisconsin, 1880 Federal Census: Soundex and Population Schedules* **[Microfilm & Digital Capture]**, filmed by the National Archives, c1970, 88 rolls, beginning with FHL film #1255417 (Population: Adams, Ashland, Barron, Bayfield, Buffalo, and Burnett counties). To access the digital images (Population Schedules), see the online FHL catalog page: www.familysearch.org/search/catalog/676542.

1880 Mortality Schedules. see *Schedule of Persons Who Died During the Year Ending May 31, 1880, Wisconsin* **[Microfilm & Digital Capture]**, filmed by the Genealogical Society of Utah, 1979, 3 rolls, beginning with FHL film #1032684 (Adams – Fond du Lac counties). To access the digital images, see the online FHL catalog page:
www.familysearch.org/search/catalog/176498.

1880. *Wisconsin Soldiers and Sailors Reunion: Containing the Post Office Address, Occupation and Name of Every Wisconsin Soldier and Sailor Now Living ... Also the Name of Every Wisconsin Soldier Who Perished in the War ... Also, a Complete Roster of Wisconsin's Armed Military Organizations* **[Microfiche]**, contributed by J. A. Kellogg, et al, original published Fond du Lac, WI by Star Steam Job and Book Printing House, 1880, 309 pages. Reprinted by University Publications of America, Bethesda, MD, 1993, filmed by the Genealogical Society of Utah, 4 microfiche, FHL film #6118307.

1880-1979. *Wisconsin, Milwaukee, Pilgrim's Rest Cemetery, Interment Records* **[Online Database]**, digitized and indexed at FamilySearch.org, see www.familysearch.org/search/collection/3246496.

1885 Wisconsin State Census **[Microfilm & Digital Capture]**, from the original records at the WI Historical Society, Madison, WI. Head of household census, schedules complete for all Wisconsin counties. Also includes county by county "Enumeration of Soldiers and Sailors of the Late War" (Civil War). Filmed by the Genealogical Society of Utah, 1979, 10 rolls, as follows:
- **1885 WI State Census**, Adams – Clark counties, FHL film #1032695.
- **1885 WI State Census**, Columbia – Dunn counties, FHL film #1032696.
- **1885 WI State Census**, Dunn – Green Lake counties, FHL film #1032697.
- **1885 WI State Census**, Iowa – Lincoln counties, FHL film #1032698.
- **1885 WI State Census**, Manitowoc, Marathon, Marinette, Marquette, Monroe, Milwaukee County, & Milwaukee City, wards . FHL film #1032699.
- **1885 WI State Census**, Milwaukee City, wards 4-13; Oconto – Portage counties, FHL film #1032700.
- **1885 WI State Census**, Portage, Price, Pepin, Pierce, Racine, Richland, Rock, St. Croix, and Sauk counties, FHL film #1032701.
- **1885 WI State Census**, Sauk – Walworth counties, FHL film #1032702.
- **1885 WI State Census**, Waukesha - Wood counties; and Enumeration of Soldiers & Sailors, Adams - Dunn counties, FHL film #1032703.
- **1885 WI State Census**, Enumeration of Soldiers & Sailors, Eau Claire - Wood counties, FHL film #1032704.

To access the digital images, see the online FHL catalog page:
www.familysearch.org/search/catalog/176742.
- See Also, *Wisconsin State Census, 1885* **[Online Database]**, indexed at the FamilySearch.org website. Source: WI Historical Society. Includes name index and images of the population schedules for 1885, a head of household listing, including: Name of head of family, Number of white males and white females in each household, Number of colored males and colored females in each household, and the Number of individuals in the family whose Nativity was U.S., Great Britain, Ireland, France, British America, Scandinavian, Holland, or All Other Countries. A

separate schedule includes the name of a Civil War veteran, with military rank, military regiment, and place of military service. This database has 407,138 records. See
https://familysearch.org/search/collection/1443713.

1885. *Tabular Statements of the Census Enumeration, and the Agricultural, Mineral and Manufacturing Interests of the State: Also Alphabetical List of the Soldiers and Sailors of the Late War Residing in the State, June 20, 1885* **[Printed Book & Microfilm],** an official report published for the Wisconsin Secretary of State by Democrat Printing Company, State Printers, Madison, WI, 1886, 791 pages. FHL book 977.5 X2w and FHL film #962237.

1887-1945. *Wisconsin, Dane County Naturalization Records* **[Online Database],** digitized at the FamilySearch.org website. Image only database of naturalization records from Dane County, Wisconsin. The records include declarations (1887-1915), petitions (1906-1945), photographs (1841-1955), depositions (1910-1929) and certificate stubs (1907-1926). Browse through the records, organized by Record Type, Year Range, and Volume No. This database has 34,494 records. See
https://familysearch.org/search/collection/1384564.

1889-1890. *Milwaukee, Wisconsin Directory* **[Online Database],** indexed at the Ancestry.com website. Source: Wright's 1889 and 1890 *Milwaukee Directory*. This database has 147,772 records. See
http://search.ancestry.com/search/db.aspx?dbid=4749.

1890 Census Substitute **[Online Database],** indexed at the Ancestry.com website. This is nationwide collection of city directories for the time of the 1890 federal census (lost in a fire in Washington DC in 1921). A global search includes directories from several Wisconsin cities. Too see an alpha list of all U.S. cities included, go to the *View all collections included in this search* tab. See
http://search.ancestry.com/search/group/1890census.

1890-1892. *Racine, Wisconsin Directories* **[Online Database],** indexed at the Ancestry.com website. Source: Curtis & Co directories for 1890 and 1892. This database has 21,231 records. See
http://search.ancestry.com/search/db.aspx?dbid=5201.

1895 Wisconsin Soldiers in Soldier Homes **[Printed Book],** compiled by Bev Hetzel, published by the author, West Bend, WI, 19[--], 24 pages. Names, with annotations, are in alphabetical order. The list was taken from an 1895 census report & from a two-volume set on the Civil War. FHL book 977.5 M2he.

1895 Wisconsin State Census – Veterans Home **[Online Database],** index to the residents of the King Veterans Home, Town of Farmington, Waupaca County, Wisconsin, as part of the 1895 state census. Indexed at the WIClarkCountyHistory.org website: **www.wiclarkcountyhistory.org/clark/facts/1895_KingVets.htm**.

1900-2001. *Wisconsin, Calumet County, New Holstein Public Library Records* **[Online Database],** digitized at the FamilySearch.org website. The collection consists of an obituary card file from the New Holstein Public Library. The obituaries came from the *New Holstein Report*.. Browse through the images, organized in alphabetical order. Each index card may contain: Name of deceased, including maiden name of married women, Date and Place of Birth, Date and Place of Death, Date and Place of Burial, Marriage Date, Name of spouse, Death date of spouse, Nickname of the deceased, and Names of survivors, This database has 10,139 records. See
https://familysearch.org/search/collection/1391206.

1895 Wisconsin State Census **[Microfilm & Digital Capture],** from the original records at the WI Historical Society, Madison, WI. Head of household census, complete for all Wisconsin counties. Also includes, "Enumeration of Soldiers and Sailors," a separate name list of living veterans for each county. Filmed by the Genealogical Society of Utah, 1979, 12 rolls, as follows:
- **1895 WI State Census**, Adams – Columbia counties, FHL film #1032705.
- **1895 WI State Census**, Columbia – Dunn counties, FHL film #1032706.
- **1895 WI State Census**, Dunn – Green Lake counties, FHL film #1032707.
- **1895 WI State Census**, Iowa – La Crosse counties, FHL film #1032708.
- **1895 WI State Census**, Lafayette – Monroe counties, FHL film #1032709.
- **1895 WI State Census**, Milwaukee County, Milwaukee City, wards 1-9, FHL film #1032710.
- **1895 WI State Census**, Milwaukee City, wards 10-18, Milwaukee County, FHL film #1032711.

- **1895 WI State Census**, Milwaukee County & Oconto - Racine counties, FHL Film #1032712.
- **1895 WI State Census**, Racine – Taylor counties, FHL film #1032713.
- **1895 WI State Census**, Taylor – Waupaca counties, FHL film #1032714.
- **1895 WI State Census**, Waushara – Wood counties; and Enumeration of Soldiers & sailors, Adams – Jefferson counties, FHL film #1032715.
- **1895 WI State Census**, Enumeration of Soldiers & sailors, Jefferson – Wood counties, FHL film #1032716.

To access the digital images, see the online FHL catalog page:
www.familysearch.org/search/catalog/176967.

- See also, *Wisconsin State Census, 1895* **[Online Database]**, indexed at the FamilySearch.org website. Source: WI Historical Society. Includes name index and images of the population schedules for 1895, a head of household listing, including: Name of head of family, Number of white males and white females in each household, Number of colored males and colored females in each household, and the Number of individuals in the family whose Nativity was U.S., Great Britain, Ireland, France, British America, Scandinavian, Holland, or All Other Countries. A separate schedule includes the name of a Civil War veteran, with military rank, military regiment, and place of military service. This database has 494,911 records. See
https://familysearch.org/search/collection/1443712.

1895-1905. See *Wisconsin, State Censuses, 1895 and 1905* **[Online Database]**, indexed at the Ancestry.com website. Source: WHS, Madison. This database contains an index to the 1895 and 1905 Wisconsin state censuses. Both censuses cover all counties that existed at the time. This is basically all modern counties with the exceptions of Rusk (not included in the 1895 census because it was not created until 1905) and Menominee (not included in either year since it wasn't created until 1961). Information listed includes: Name of individual, and Place of enumeration. For the 1905 census the following information is also listed: Date of enumeration, Relationship to head of household, Race, Gender, Age, Marital status, Birthplace, Additional information about an individual, such as their occupation, may be available on the actual census record. This database has 2,690,489 records. See
http://search.ancestry.com/search/db.aspx?dbid=1055.

1900. *Wisconsin, 1900 Federal Census: Soundex and Population Schedules* **[Microfilm & Digital Capture]**, filmed by the National Archives, c1970, 237 rolls, beginning with FHL film #1241777 (Population: Adams, Ashland, and Barron counties). To access the digital images (Population Schedules), see the online FHL catalog page:
www.familysearch.org/search/catalog/655060.

1900-2001. *New Holstein, Calumet, Wisconsin, Obituary Records* **[Online Database]**, indexed at the Ancestry.com website. Source: FamilySearch image only database. The collection consists of an obituary card file from the New Holstein Public Library. The obituaries came from the *New Holstein Report*. Browse through the images, organized in alphabetical order. Each index card may contain: Name of deceased, including maiden name of married women, Date and Place of Birth, Date and Place of Death, Date and Place of Burial, Marriage Date, Name of spouse, Death date of spouse, Nickname of the deceased, and Names of survivors, This database has 10,139 records. See
http://search.ancestry.com/search/db.aspx?dbid=60373.

1903-1988. *Wisconsin, Employment Records* **[Online Database]**, digitized and indexed at Ancestry.com. This collection contains records several WI State licensing boards with details about a person applying for a license, including Education, Watchmaking, Boxing, and Barbering. Details may include a Name, Street Address and Residence City, Birth Date and Birthplace, Race, Occupation and Industry, License or Application Date, Previous Training or Education, and Photographs. his database has 47,717 records, see
See www.ancestry.com/search/collections/61705.

1905 Wisconsin State Census **[Microfilm & Digital Capture]**, from the original records at the WI Historical Society, Madison, WI. Contents: Name of each individual; relationship to head of household; color/race; sex; age at last birthday; marital status; place of birth, by state or country; place of birth of parents; occupation, if 14 years or older; number of months unemployed; and whether a home or farm was owned outright, mortgaged, or rented. The 1905 WI state census schedules are complete for 71 of Wisconsin's 72 modern counties. (Menominee Indian Reservation became co-extensive with a newly formed

Menominee County in 1959). Filmed by the WI Historical Society, 1952, 36 rolls, as follows:
- **1905 WI State Census**, Adams, Ashland, Barron counties, FHL film #1020439.
- **1905 WI State Census**, Bayfield and Brown counties, FHL film #1020440.
- **1905 WI State Census**, Buffalo, Burnett, Calumet counties, FHL film #1020441.
- **1905 WI State Census**, Chippewa and Clark counties, FHL film #1020442.
- **1905 WI State Census**, Columbia and Crawford counties, FHL film #1020443.
- **1905 WI State Census**, Dane County, FHL film #1020444.
- **1905 WI State Census**, Dodge and Door counties, FHL film #1020445.
- **1905 WI State Census**, Douglas and Dunn counties, FHL film #1020446.
- **1905 WI State Census**, Eau Claire and Florence counties, FHL film #1020447.
- **1905 WI State Census**, Fond du Lac and Forest counties, FHL film #1020448.
- **1905 WI State Census**, Grant and Green counties, FHL film #1020449.
- **1905 WI State Census**, Green Lake, Iowa Iron, & Jackson counties, FHL film #1020450.
- **1905 WI State Census**, Jefferson and Juneau counties, FHL film #1020451.
- **1905 WI State Census**, Kenosha, Kewaunee, La Crosse counties, FHL film #1020452.
- **1905 WI State Census**, Lafayette, Langlade, Lincoln counties, FHL film #1020453.
- **1905 WI State Census**, Manitowoc County, FHL film #1020454 .
- **1905 WI State Census**, Marathon County, FHL film #1020455.
- **1905 WI State Census**, Marinette, Marquette, Monroe counties, FHL film #1020978.
- **1905 WI State Census**, Milwaukee County; and city of Milwaukee, Ward 1, FHL film #1020991.
- **1905 WI State Census**, city of Milwaukee, wards 2-8, FHL film #1020992.
- **1905 WI State Census**, city of Milwaukee, wards 8-11, FHL film #1020993.
- **1905 WI State Census**, city of Milwaukee, wards 11-14, FHL film #1020994.
- **1905 WI State Census**, city of Milwaukee, wards 15-19, FHL film#1020995.
- **1905 WI State Census**, city of Milwaukee wards, 19-23, FHL film #1020996.
- **1905 WI State Census**, Oconto, Oneida, Outagamie counties, FHL film #1020979.
- **1905 WI State Census**, Ozaukee, Pepin, Pierce, Polk counties, FHL film #1020980.
- **1905 WI State Census**, Portage and Price counties, FHL film #1020981.
- **1905 WI State Census**, Racine and Richland counties, FHL film #1020982.
- **1905 WI State Census**, Rock and Rusk counties, FHL film #1020983.
- **1905 WI State Census**, St. Croix, Sauk, Sawyer counties, FHL film #1020984.
- **1905 WI State Census**, Shawano and Sheboygan counties, FHL film #1020985.
- **1905 WI State Census**, Taylor, Trempealeau, Vernon, Vilas counties, FHL film #1020986.
- **1905 WI State Census**, Walworth, Washburn, Washington counties, FHL film #1020987.
- **1905 WI State Census**, Waukesha and Waupaca counties, FHL film #1020988.
- **1905 WI State Census**, Waushara and Winnebago counties, FHL film #1020989.
- **1905 WI State Census**, Wood County, FHL film #1020990.

To access the digital images, see the online FHL catalog page: www.familysearch.org/search/catalog/44737.

- See also, *Wisconsin State Census, 1905* **[Online Database]**, indexed at the FamilySearch.org website. Source: WI Historical Society. Facts found in Wisconsin State Censuses for the year 1905 are: Town and county in which census was taken, Name of each person in family, Relationship to head of household, Age, gender and birth place, Parents' names and their birthplace, Race, and marital status of each person, Occupation, Home owner or renter, Whether living on a farm or in a house. This database has 2,228,391 records. See

https://familysearch.org/search/collection/1443899.

- See also, *1905 Wisconsin State Census Index* **[Microfilm]**, from the original card indexes (by county) at the WI Historical Society, Madison, WI. Surname, first name indexes in alphabetical order for each county. All 77 county-wide indexes filmed by the Genealogical Society of Utah, 1978-1985, 444 rolls, beginning with FHL film #1266809 (Adams Co). To see if this microfilm has been digitized yet, see the FHL catalog page:

www.familysearch.org/search/catalog/11508.

1910. *Wisconsin, 1910 Federal Census: Population Schedules* **[Microfilm & Digital Capture]**, filmed by the National Archives, c1970, 237 rolls, beginning with FHL film #1375713 (Adams, Bayfield, Ashland, and Barron counties). To access the digital images, see the online FHL catalog page:

www.familysearch.org/search/catalog/646891.

1913. *Biographical Index: History of Brown County, Wisconsin: Past and Present, Vol. II* **[Online Database],** indexed at the USGenWeb Archives website for Brown Co WI. See
http://files.usgwarchives.net/wi/brown/bios/1913ndex.txt

1917-1918. *Wisconsin's Gold Star List: Soldiers, Sailors, Marines, and Nurses from the Badger State Who Died in the Federal Service During the World War* **[Online Database],** indexed at the Ancestry.com website. Source: book, same title, compiled by John Goadby Gregory, publ. WHS, 1925.
This database has 221 pages. See
http://search.ancestry.com/search/db.aspx?dbid=27947.

1917-1918. *Wisconsin, World War I Selective Service System Draft Registration Cards* **[Microfilm & Digital Capture],** filmed by the National Archives, 1987, 103 rolls, beginning with FHL film #1685061 (Adams Co, A-Z; and Ashland Co, A-M). To access the digital images, see the online FHL catalog page:
www.familysearch.org/search/catalog/747003.

1917-1919. *Wisconsin, World War I American Expeditionary Forces, Deaths* **[Digital Capture],** from originals at the National Archives, digitized 2018 FamilySearch International. To access the digital images, see the online FHL catalog page:
www.familysearch.org/search/catalog/3023959.

1920. *Wisconsin, 1920 Federal Census: Soundex and Population Schedules* **[Microfilm & Digital Capture],** filmed by the National Archives, c1970, 240 rolls, beginning with FHL film #1821975 (Population: Adams, Buffalo, and Ashland counties). To access the digital images (Population Schedules), see the online FHL catalog page:
www.familysearch.org/search/catalog/558337.

1922-1958. *Minnesota, Duluth and Wisconsin, Superior Crew Lists* **[Online Database],** digitized and indexed at the FamilySearch.org website. Source: National Archives microfilm series A3452. Each record is indexed with a name, event type, event date, event place, gender, and name of ship. The digitized original document may have more details. This database has 186,334 records. See
https://familysearch.org/search/collection/2140606.

1922-1963. *Wisconsin, Milwaukee Passenger and Crew Lists* **[Online Database],** indexed at the FamilySearch.org website. Source: National Archives microfilm series A3399. Each record may contain: Port and date of departure, Port and date of entry, Name of ship, Country of citizenship, Name of passenger, including maiden name of women, Names of persons accompanying passenger, Age, gender, marital status and occupation of passenger, Date and place of birth of passenger, Address of last permanent residence, Name and address of friend or relative at last address, Final destination, Name and address of friend or relative in U.S., Physical description and distinguishing marks, Who paid for the passage, and the Purpose of visit. This database has 62,820 records. See
https://familysearch.org/search/collection/2421844.

1922-1963. *Wisconsin, Passenger and Crew Lists* **[Online Database],** indexed at the Ancestry.com website. Source: National Archives microfilm series A3399. The index includes given name, surname, age, gender, ethnicity, nationality, destination, arrival date, port of arrival, port of departure, ship or airline name, microfilm roll and page number. This database has 324,017 records. See
http://search.ancestry.com/search/db.aspx?dbid=2138.

1925-1969. *Wisconsin Crew Lists* **[Online Database],** indexed at the Ancestry.com website. Source: National Archives microfilm series A3397, M2044, and M2045. This database is an index to crew lists (and a few passenger lists) of vessels (as well as a few aircraft) that arrived at various Wisconsin ports, departed from a Canadian or other foreign port. The index includes the following ports and years: **Green Bay** (1925-1969) (missing 1960, 1961, 1967); **Manitowoc** (1925-1956); **Ashland** (1955-1956); **Kenosha** (1937-1940); **Marinette** (1929-1940); **Sheboygan** (1929-1956); **Sturgeon Bay** (1946-1952); and **Washburn** (1925-1928). Each record may include: Given name and surname of crew member, Age, Gender, Ethnicity or nationality, Last Residence, Birth date, Birthplace, Port of departure, Port of arrival, Date of arrival, and Name of vessel. This database has 37,770 records. See
http://search.ancestry.com/search/db.aspx?dbid=1005.

1925-1956. *Wisconsin, Crew Lists of Ship Arrivals* **[Online Database],** indexed at the FamilySearch.org website. Source: National Archives microfilm series

M2044. Images of crew lists for ship arrivals at **Ashland**, 1955-1956; **Kenosha**, 1937-1940; **Marinette**, 1929-1940; **Sheboygan**, 1929-1956; **Sturgeon Bay**, 1946-1952; and **Washburn**, 1925-1928. Crew lists may contain any of the following: Port and date of departure, Port and date of entry, Name of ship, Country of citizenship, Name of passenger, including maiden name of women, Names of persons accompanying passenger, Age, gender, marital status and occupation of passenger, Date and place of birth of passenger, Address of last permanent residence, Name and address of friend or relative at last address, Final destination, Name and address of friend or relative in U.S., Physical description and distinguishing marks, Who paid for passage, and Purpose of visit. This database has 3,993 records. See
https://familysearch.org/search/collection/2299361.

1925-1956. *Wisconsin, Crew Lists of Vessels Arriving at Manitowoc* [Online Database], digitized and indexed at the FamilySearch.org website. Source: National Archives microfilm series M2045. This database has 3,937 records. See
https://familysearch.org/search/collection/2299401.

1930. *Wisconsin, 1930 Federal Census: Population Schedules* [Microfilm & Digital Capture], filmed by the National Archives, c1970, 61 rolls, beginning with FHL film #2342294 (Adams, Bayfield, Ashland, and Barron counties). To access the digital images, see the online FHL catalog page:
www.familysearch.org/search/catalog/1037544.

1940. *Wisconsin, 1940 Federal Census: Population Schedules* [Online Database], digitized images from the microfilm of original records held by the Bureau of the Census in the 1940s. After microfilming, Congress allowed the Census Bureau to destroy the originals to free up space for WWII-related files. Digitizing of the 1940 census schedules microfilm images was done for the National Archives and made public on April 2, 2012. No microfilm copies were distributed. To access the digital images, see the online FHL catalog page: www.familysearch.org/search/catalog/2057799.

1940 Federal Census Finding Aids [Online Database]. The National Archives prepared a special website online with a detailed description of the 1940 federal census. Included at the site are descriptions of location finding aids, such as Enumeration District maps, Geographic Descriptions of Census Enumeration Districts, and a list of 1940 City Directories available at the National Archives. The finding aids are all linked to other National Archives sites. The National Archives website also has a link to 1940 Search Engines using Stephen P. Morse's "One-Step" system for finding a 1940 E.D. or street address conversion. See
www.archives.gov/research/census/1940/general-info.html#questions.

1942. *Wisconsin Selective Service System Registration Cards, World War II: Fourth Registration* [Microfilm & Digital Capture], filmed by the Genealogical Society of Utah, 2006, 118 rolls, beginning with FHL film #1572506 (Aabert, Alfred – Allen, Wyeth). To access the digital images, see the online FHL catalog page:
www.familysearch.org/search/catalog/1373136.

1959-1997. *Wisconsin Death Index* [Online Database], indexed at the FamilySearch.org website. Source: WI Dept of Health. The index includes: Name of Deceased, Sex, Age at death, Date and place of death, Name of Father, Name of Mother, Name of Spouse, Certificate number/Page number, and FHL film number. This database has 1,629,093 records. See
https://familysearch.org/search/collection/1947978.
- This database is also located at Ancestry.com, see http://search.ancestry.com/search/db.aspx?dbid=8790.

1965-1984. *Wisconsin Divorce Index* [Online Database], digitized and indexed at the FamilySearch.org website. Source: WI Dept of Health. The index includes: Name of husband, Name of wife, Docket number, Divorce date, Divorce place, and Reference number (page, volume, entry number). This database has 231,499 records. See
https://familysearch.org/search/collection/1967741.
- This database is also located at Ancestry.com, see http://search.ancestry.com/search/db.aspx?dbid=1244.

1973-1997. *Wisconsin Marriage Index* [Online Database], indexed at the FamilySearch.org website. Source: WI Dept of Health. The index may include the following information: Name of bride and groom, Marriage date and place, Name of spouse (May only list surname) Reference ID-Page, Volume, Entry, and Certificate Number. This database has 948,961 records. See https://familysearch.org/search/collection/1946794.
- This database is also located at Ancestry.com, see http://search.ancestry.com/search/db.aspx?dbid=8744.

1989-Current. *Wisconsin Recent Newspaper Obituaries* [Online Database], digitized and indexed newspaper obituaries at the GenealogyBank website, including newspapers for Ashland, Baraboo, Bay View, Bayside, Beaver Dam, Beloit, Black River Falls, Brookfield, Cambridge, Deerfield, Cedarburg, Chippewa Falls, Columbus, Cottage Grove, DeForest,

Dousman, Edgerton, Fort Atkinson, Franklin, Germantown, Greenfield, Hartford, Hartland, Hayward, Kenosha, La Crosse, Lake Mills, Lodi, Madison, Mauston, McFarland, Menomonie, Milton, Milwaukee, Minocqua, Mukwonago, Muskego, New Berlin, Oconomowoc, Oneida, Park Falls, Phillips, Portage, Poynette, Racine, Reedsburg, Rhinelander, Rice Lake, Ripon, Sauk City, Spooner, State-Wide County, Sun Prairie, Superior, Tomah, Viroqua, Washburn, Waterloo, Waukesha, Waunakee, Wauwatosa, West Bend, West Salem-Onalaska-Holmen, and Westby. See www.genealogybank.com/explore/obituaries/all/usa/wisconsin.

Declaration of Intention to Become A Citizen of the United States, filed in the District Court of Portage Co, Wisconsin, part of *Wisconsin County Naturalizations, 1820-1892*, a database with 1,135,393 records, See https://familysearch.org/search/collection/2046887.

Census Substitutes & State Census Records

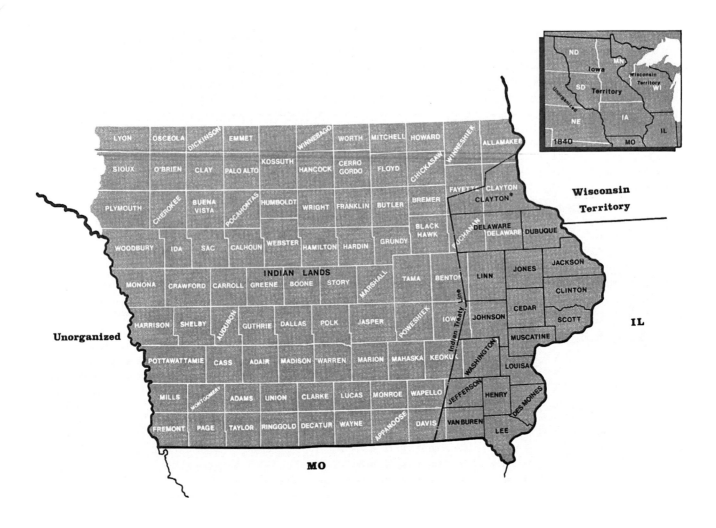

Iowa Territory in 1840. The 18 counties of Iowa Territory at the time of the June 1840 Federal Census are shown in black. The current 99 counties of Iowa are shown in white. After the 1832 Black Hawk War, in 1833 a new treaty with the Sauk and Fox Indians was signed, creating the "Indian Treaty Line" shown on the map. The line defined the western limit of the area first opened for white settlement in the Ioway Country. At that time, Iowa was part of the "Unorganized Territory." (See **http://usgwarchives.net/maps/cessions/ilcmap24.htm** for a detailed map of the Indian Land Cessions in Iowa). In 1836, the Iowa area was part of Wisconsin Territory until Iowa Territory was established in 1838. Iowa statehood came in 1846. **Map Source:** Page 114, *Map Guide to the U.S. Federal Censuses, 1790-1920*, by William Thorndale and William Dollarhide.

Iowa
Censuses & Substitute Name Lists

Historical Timeline for Iowa, 1673-1857

1673. Mississippi River. French explorers Jacques Jolliet and Louis Marquette left their mission base at Sault Ste Marie, and made their way to the Illinois River, which they descended to become the first Europeans to discover the Mississippi River. After canoeing up river to discover the mouth of the Wisconsin River, they floated down the Mississippi, passing by the present states of Illinois, Iowa, Missouri, Kentucky, Tennessee, Arkansas, and Mississippi, as far south as the mouth of the Arkansas River. Returning to the Great Lakes area, their journals reported the location of several streams flowing into the west side of the Mississippi from the interior of present Iowa. The three largest of the rivers were later identified as the Demoine, Ioway, and Cedar rivers.

1682. Louisiana. Following the same route as Jolliet and Marquette, René-Robert Cavelier (Sieur de LaSalle) floated down the Mississippi River, but continued all the way to its mouth at the Gulf of Mexico. He claimed the entire Mississippi Basin for Louis XIV of France, for whom Louisiana was named.

1685-1720. During this period, *La Louisiane Française* extended from the Highlands (Terra Haute) on the Wabash River, down the Ohio and Mississippi Rivers to include New Orleans. The French also considered the early ports of Biloxi, Mobile, and Pensacola as part of La Louisiane. Forts and settlements established by the French in the Mississippi Basin during this period were Prairie du Chien (now Wisconsin) in 1685; Arkansas Post in 1686; Kaskaskia (now Illinois) in 1703; Natchez (now Mississippi) in 1716; New Orleans in 1718; Baton Rouge in 1719; And Fort de Charles (at Kaskaskia) in 1720. Of these settlements, just two of them included farming activities (Prairie du Chien and Arkansas Post), the others were mostly trading posts established to support the French Fur Trade.

1721. In this year, French colonists abandoned Arkansas Post, the largest settlement of all of French Louisiana. As a failed farming community, Arkansas Post was typical of the French efforts to colonize North America south of the Great Lakes. Arkansas Post continued as a small trading post, but the French presence in the Mississippi Basin became one of single French voyageurs paddling their canoes from one trading post to the next.

1722-1762. During this period of *La Louisiane Française,* a few more trading posts were established as river ports in present Illinois, Missouri, Kansas, and Tennessee. By 1762, the French had built one road (the Wabash-Erie Portage Road). That road was less than 20 miles long and was only built to provide portage between rivers for the French Voyageurs and their canoes. Unlike the French Québec settlements, French Louisiana had very few farming communities, and there was little exchanging of goods or produce, except for the trapping and trading of furs. In comparison, the British colonies by 1762 had over 2,500 miles of improved wagon roads, between Boston and Charles Town. The British colonies had an economy based on town tradesmen surrounded by small farms, with the exchange of goods and produce up and down the Atlantic coast.

1763. Treaty of Paris. The Seven Years War (in Europe and Canada), was called the French and Indian War in colonial America and ended with the 1763 Treaty of Paris. France lost virtually all of its North American claims – the western side of the Mississippi was lost to Spain, the eastern side of the Mississippi and all of Québec was lost to Britain. In another provision of the 1763 treaty, the British acquired Florida from the Spanish in exchange for Cuba.

1763-1770. Transition Period. St. Louis was founded in 1764 by French Trader Pierre Laclede Liguest, after obtaining a trading license from the Spanish governor in New Orleans. There was little government or military interference by anyone in former French La Louisiane (Spanish Luisiana and British Louisiana). The entire region was still inhabited mostly by French voyageurs. French settlements and trading posts still operated in Lower Louisiana (including Arkansas Post, Baton Rouge, and Natchez); and in Upper Louisiana (including Prairie du Chien, Kaskaskia, and Vincennes).

St. Louis operated under French civilian control until it was occupied by Spanish soldiers in 1770. About the same time, the British established their military jurisdiction over the main Upper Louisiana French settlements at Prairie du Chien, Kaskaskia and Vincennes.

1783. United States of America. The treaty of Paris of 1783 officially ended the Revolutionary War, and first recognized the United States as an independent nation. The U.S. borders were from the Atlantic Ocean to the Mississippi River, and from present Maine to Georgia. The treaty also reaffirmed the claims of Britain to present Canada; and Spain's claim to East Florida, West Florida, Mexico (including Texas), and Louisiana west of the Mississippi River.

1788-1798. Iowa. French Canadian Julien Dubuque became the first white settler in present Iowa, near the present city that bears his name. He was given permission by the Meskwaki Indians to mine for lead there in 1788 and given a land grant from the Spanish Government in 1798.

1800. Louisiana. Napoleon acquired title of Louisiana from Spain. At the Third Treaty of San Ildefonso, the Spanish acknowledged that it was too costly to explore the country and could not see the rewards being worth the investment. Spain retroceded Louisiana to France in exchange for the Grand Duchy of Tuscany (now part of Italy).

1803. Louisiana Purchase. The United States purchased Louisiana from France. Sent by President Jefferson to attempt the purchase of New Orleans, the American negotiators (James Madison and Robert Livingston) were surprised when Napoleon offered the entire tract to them. The Louisiana Purchase was officially described as the "drainage of the Mississippi and Missouri River basins." Adding the area doubled the size of the United States. The area of Iowa became part of the United States for the first time.

1804. Lewis and Clark's Corps of Discovery left St. Louis, then headed up the Missouri River in search of a passage to the Pacific Ocean. Soon after, Spanish troops were dispatched from Santa Fe into present Colorado and Kansas to intercept and arrest them, but Lewis and Clark had already passed by present Iowa and Nebraska and were well into present South Dakota by the time the Spanish troops finally gave up looking for them.

1804-1805. Louisiana District and Orleans Territory. In 1804, Congress divided the Louisiana Purchase into two jurisdictions: Louisiana District and Orleans Territory. The latter had north and south bounds the same as the present state of Louisiana but did not include land east of the Mississippi River, and its northwestern corner extended on an indefinite line west into Spanish Tejas. For a year, Louisiana District was attached to Indiana Territory for judicial administration but became Louisiana Territory with its own Governor on July 4, 1805.

1805. 1st Pike Expedition. U.S. Army Lieutenant Zebulon Pike led a small party of soldiers to investigate the Mississippi River above St. Louis. He was given specific orders to find the source of the Mississippi, and while doing so, to note "…any rivers, prairies, islands, mines, quarries, timber, and any Indian villages and settlements encountered." As instructed, Pike drew some maps and recorded the location of the Demoine, Ioway, and Cedar rivers in present Iowa.

1805. Michigan Territory was created, taken from the early Indiana Territory. After the statehoods of Ohio, Indiana, and Illinois, Michigan Territory was increased in size. By 1818, the entire region north of those three states became part of a Michigan Territory that extended west to the Mississippi River.

1805-1806. Louisiana Territory in 1805 had five original subdivisions: St. Louis District, St. Charles District, Ste. Genevieve District, Cape Girardeau District and New Madrid District. In 1806, the territorial legislature created the District of Arkansas from lands ceded by the Osage Indians. The unpopulated area north of these original districts was known as "Upper Louisiana Territory," and included the area of present Iowa.

1806-1807. 2nd Pike Expedition. Zebulon Pike, now a Captain, was again sent out, this time to explore and locate the source of the Red River in Lower Louisiana. Pike followed the Arkansas River through present southwest Kansas into Colorado and on to the Rocky Mountains, where Pike's Peak was named for him. On his return, he skirted south in search of the headwaters of the Red River, putting him in an area claimed by the Spanish. Pike and his men were arrested by Spanish soldiers, taken to Santa Fe, but treated well and returned to the Arkansas River a short time later. Pike wrote a book about his travels in 1810 that was a best seller in both America and Europe. In addition to the first English language observations of the Spanish culture in North America, Pike's descriptions of the Rocky Mountains became the inspiration for a whole generation of "mountain men."

1812. June 4th. Louisiana Territory was renamed **Missouri Territory**. This was to avoid any confusion after Orleans Territory became the State of Louisiana on April 30, 1812. The General Assembly of the Territory of Missouri met in October and converted the first five original districts into counties: Cape Girardeau, New Madrid, St. Charles, St. Louis, and Ste. Genevieve. The area of present Iowa was without any enumerated population, lying north of St. Charles District in the "Unattached" region of the territory.

1819. Arkansas Territory was created, taken from the southern area of Missouri Territory. The area included all of present-day Arkansas and most of Oklahoma.

1819. Adams-Onis Treaty. The treaty included the purchase of Florida, but also set the boundary between the U.S. and New Spain (now Mexico), from Louisiana to the Oregon Country. The treaty established the Sabine and Red River border with Spanish Tejas; the Arkansas River border with Nuevo Mexico; and the 42nd Parallel border with Spanish California. The treaty was named after John Quincy Adams, U.S. Secretary of State, and Luis de Onis, the Spanish Foreign Minister, the parties who signed the treaty at Washington on February 22, 1819. John Quincy Adams was given credit for a brilliant piece of diplomacy by adding the western boundary settlements with Spain to the Florida Purchase.

1820. The "Missouri Compromise" in Congress allowed Missouri to enter the Union as a slave state and Maine as a free state, thus keeping the balance of slave and free states equal in Congress. Although Missouri was allowed to enter as a slave state, the remainder of Missouri Territory areas north of Latitude 36° 30,' including present Iowa, were supposed to be forever free of slavery. After Missouri became a state, the remaining part of old Missouri Territory was described as "Unorganized Territory."

1830. At the time of the 1830 federal Census, present Iowa was part of the "Unorganized Territory" and had no enumerated population.

1832. Black Hawk War. Indian leader Black Hawk of the Sauk and Fox tribe led a sizable force of warriors across the Mississippi River into Illinois, seeking to reclaim lands they had lost to the whites earlier. The U.S. met the threat with a voluntary force of militia raised mostly in Illinois. (Abraham Lincoln's only military service was in this war, where he was elected a militia Captain by his New Salem neighbors). As a result of the defeat of Black Hawk's forces at the battle of Bad Axe, the Sauk and Fox, natives of lands near the Ioway River, were forced to cede land on the west side of the Mississippi River to the United States.

1833. 1 June. The Ioway country was open for legal white settlement for the first time. It is estimated that before that date, there were fewer than 40 non-Indians living in the present Iowa region. Most were left-over French-Canadian fur traders. The area was still part of "Unorganized Territory."

1836. Wisconsin Territory was split off from Michigan Territory. At that time, Wisconsin Territory included all of present Wisconsin, Minnesota, and Iowa; and North and South Dakota east of the Missouri River – same as the combined areas of Wisconsin and Iowa Territory shown on the 1840 map below.

1838. Iowa Territory was created, taken from Wisconsin Territory, including lands between the Mississippi and Missouri Rivers. Iowa City was named the territorial capital, but Burlington served as the interim capital until Iowa City could provide facilities for a governor and legislature, which it did in 1841.

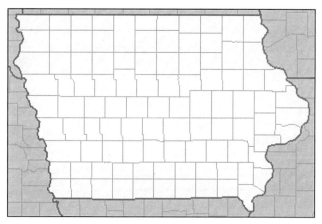
Iowa's 99 counties since 1857

Iowa and Wisconsin Territory in 1840

1838-1857. Iowa County Formation. The first appointed governor of Iowa Territory was Robert Lucas, who served from 1838 to 1841. Lucas was an army general during the War of 1812 and an elected governor of Ohio, 1832-1836. Early in his term as Governor of Iowa Territory, Lucas proposed to the legislature a method of county formation in Iowa that was based on the Range/Township lines, with a dedicated section (1 square mile) of land set aside for a courthouse/county seat for each county near its geographic center. However, Lucas had poor relations with the legislature, and they rejected his proposal. Although Lucas' county plan was never officially adopted, a very similar method was followed for the formation of virtually all of Iowa's counties. By 1857, all of Iowa's current 99 counties had been formed, and there have been very few changes to the boundaries since. Iowa has more "box counties" and the fewest number of counties formed along the lay of the land than any other state.

1840. Iowa Territory. In the 1840 Federal Census, Iowa Territory's population of 43,112 persons was limited to the 18 counties formed within the Indian Cession lands of 1832-1837. Although destined to become a free state, a total of 6 male and 10 female slaves were counted, all in Dubuque County. See the 1840 Iowa County Map on page 178.

1846. Leaving their home in Nauvoo, Illinois, about 20,000 Mormons crossed the Mississippi River and proceeded across the entire length of Iowa. They were headed to their winter quarters on the Missouri River, near present Council Bluffs, Iowa.

1846. Dec. 28th. Iowa became the 29th state. Iowa City continued as the state capital.

1857. The capital of Iowa was moved from Iowa City to Des Moines.

State Historical Society of Iowa

The State Historical Society acts as the State Archives, with two major facilities in Iowa, both with public reading rooms friendly to amateur genealogists:

State of Iowa Historical Building, Des Moines, Iowa. This facility houses a State Historical Museum, State Historical Society Library and Archives.

Centennial Building, Iowa City, Iowa. This facility houses a State Historical Society Library and Archives, with a unique archival collection of historical materials, photographs, and manuscripts not repeated at the Des Moines facility. In addition, the Iowa City facility holds the same microfilm collection as the Des Moines facility.

Libraries and Special Collections:
- Books and Periodicals
- Photo Collections
- Newspapers
- County Government Records
- Birth, Marriage, and Death Records
- Manuscripts, Audio-Visual, and Map Collections
- Census Materials.

For more information about their holding, see https://iowaculture.gov/history/research/collections.

Guide to Iowa County Records. At an online map of the 99 counties of Iowa, click on a county to display a list of the related county records available on microfilm at the State Historical Society of Iowa, Des Moines Library. Then scroll down below the map to see a listing along with date ranges of that county's microfilmed records holdings. See https://iowaculture.gov/history/research/collections/county-records.

Bibliography
Iowa Censuses & Substitutes

Jurisdictions: After the 1832 Black Hawk War, the area first called Ioway was opened for white settlement in 1833. In 1836, the area was added to Wisconsin Territory; then part of Iowa Territory in 1838; and became the state of Iowa in 1846.

Censuses: Territorial Censuses include Iowa areas taken by Wisconsin Territory in 1836, and Iowa Territory in 1838, 1844 and 1846. The state of Iowa has surviving statewide censuses for 1847, 1849, 1851, 1852, 1853, 1854, 1856, 1859, 1881, 1885, 1888, 1889, 1891, 1892, 1893, 1895, 1896, 1897, 1905, 1915, and 1925. Federal censuses are complete for 1840 through 1940 (with the exception of the 1890, lost for all states).

Census Substitutes: Adding the federal censuses to Iowa's territorial and state censuses totals 35 census years, more than any other state in the Union. Because of the great number of Iowa census name lists, the need for census substitutes between federal census years may seem less demanding – but this bibliography has many extra name lists. Together, they include Territorial, State, and Federal Censuses, Court Records, Directories, County Indexes, State Military Lists, Tax Lists, Vital Records, and Voter Lists. The censuses and substitute name lists begin below in chronological order:

◆ ◆ ◆ ◆ ◆

1833–1850. *Iowa Marriages, Early to 1850: A Research Tool* **[Printed Book]**, compiled and published by Liahona Research, Orem, UT, 1990, 373 pages, FHL book 977.7 V22i.

1833–1900s. *Biography Files* **[Microfilm],** from originals at the Iowa State Historical Society, Des Moines, IA. Filmed by the Genealogical Society of Utah, 1978, 4 rolls, beginning with FHL film #1023616 (Albrock – Blanchard). To see if this microfilm has been digitized yet, see the FHL catalog page: www.familysearch.org/search/catalog/409055.

1833-1900s. *Biographical Data Collection* **[Microfilm],** from originals at the Iowa State Historical Society, Des Moines, IA. Filmed by the Genealogical Society of Utah, 1978, 6 rolls, beginning with FHL film #1023885 (Adams – Curtiss). To see if this microfilm has been digitized yet, see the FHL catalog page: www.familysearch.org/search/catalog/409051.

1833-1900s. *Iowa Biography Index* **[Printed Book]**, an index to county histories, biographical records, town, county, church, fraternal, governmental, vital, state, etc. covering all 99 counties in the State of Iowa available from the State of Iowa Lending and Research Library, Menlo, IA, 1986, 167 pages, FHL book 977.7 D22.

1833-1900s. Iowa Original Land Owners. See the *Family Maps* series for Iowa counties, maps of all original land patents, compiled by Greg Boyd and published by Arphax Publishing Co., Norman, OK. These privately-produced computer-generated maps show the first property owners for an entire county, produced as a book of maps, each map laid out on the federal township grid, and includes indexes to help you locate a person, place-name, or cemetery. Additional maps are added for each county to show roads, waterways, railroads, selected city centers, and cemeteries within a county. *Family Maps* books have been published for the following Iowa counties: Benton, Black Hawk, Cedar, Clayton, Decatur, Dubuque, Fayette, Henry, Iowa, Jasper, Jefferson, Johnson, Jones, Keokuk, Linn, Madison, Mahaska, Page, Poweshiek, Ringgold, Story, Union, Warren, Washington, Wayne, and Winneshiek counties. Visit the publisher's information and ordering website for more details and updated county coverage. See **www.arphax.com/**. Arphax's entire *Family Maps* series is also available as a subscription service online. See **www.historygeo.com**.

1833-1940s. *A Reference Guide to the DAR Volumes* **[Printed Book],** an alphabetical listing by county of Iowa cemetery, marriage, death and probate records produced by the DAR and the WPA which are housed at the State Historical Society of Iowa, Iowa City, Iowa. This guidebook leads a researcher to the wealth of indexed materials for all Iowa counties. FHL book 977.7 V22in.

1833-1950. *Iowa, Births and Christenings* **[Online Database],** an index to births, baptisms, and Christenings, taken from FHL microfilm records. The beginning date is impossible. This database has 608,253 records. See **https://familysearch.org/search/collection/1674820**.
- A later version of this database is at the Ancestry.com website with the title, *Iowa, Births and Christenings Index, 1800-1999*, a database acquired from FamilySearch with 4.6 million records. The 1800 date is impossible in Iowa. See **https://search.ancestry.com/search/db.aspx?dbid=2547**.

1833-1992. *Iowa Marriages* **[Online Database],** indexed at the FamilySearch.org website. Source: FamilySearch extractions from microfilm at the Family History Library. The date of 1809 is impossible for Iowa. Each index record includes: Name, Spouse's name, Event date, Event place, and Spouse's Father's name. This database has 1,261,966 records. See **www.familysearch.org/search/collection/1674842**.
- A later version of this database is at the Ancestry.com website with the title, *Iowa, Select Marriages Index, 1758-1996*, a database with over 5 million records, acquired from FamilySearch. The FamilySearch information page reveals that the original source of most of these marriages came from the International Genealogy Index (IGI), a huge database of genealogical data originally submitted by LDS Church members on Family Groups Sheets, before the age of personal computers. The data was submitted and recorded without anyone checking to see if the data was correct. That explains the myriad of births, marriages, and deaths supposedly taking place in Iowa in the 1700s. Unless your ancestors belonged to the Sauk and Fox, Sioux, or Ioway tribes of Iowa, the dates are probably wrong – but visit the ancestry.com version anyway, see **https://search.ancestry.com/search/db.aspx?dbid=60284**.

1833-1999. *Iowa, Cemetery Records* **[Online Database],** indexed at the Ancestry.com website. Original data: Works Project Administration. Graves Registration Project. Washington, D.C. These cemetery records represent seventy-six counties in Iowa which were transcribed by the Works Project Administration, Graves Registration Project. Records in this database include: WPA index page number, Name of the deceased, Birth date, Death date, Age, Cemetery name, and Town name. There were twenty counties that were not indexed by the WPA and therefore are not included in this database. The counties not included are Appanoose, Benton, Cherokee, Clinton, Dallas, Des Moines, Hamilton, Henry, Howard, Humboldt, Ida, Iowa, Jasper, Lucas, Lyon, Monona, Osceola, Pottawattamie, Warren, and Winnebago. This database has records. See **https://search.ancestry.com/search/db.aspx?dbid=4711**.
- See also *WPA-Work Projects Administration 1930's Graves Registration Survey* **[Online Database],** indexed at the IowaWPAGraves website. This database has 656,621 records. See **https://iowawpagraves.org/**.

1833–2000s. *Iowa Collection Catalog at MyHeritage.cm* **[Online Database],** 47 collections can be searched at the MyHeritage website. Databases include censuses, directories, family histories, town histories, military rosters, college/school year books, and more. This is a subscription site, but all initial searches are free. A free search can be done for a name, place, year, or keyword. See **www.myheritage.com/research/catalog?q=iowa**.

1833-2000s. *Iowa US GenWeb Archives* **[Online Databases],** name lists are available for all Iowa counties. Typical county records include Bibles, Biographies, Cemeteries, Censuses, Court, Death,

Deeds, Directories, Histories, Marriages, Military, Newspapers, Obituaries, Photos, Schools, Tax Lists, Wills, and more. The Special Projects include:
- Iowa Family Group Sheet Project
- Iowa Genealogy Boards
- Iowa Gravestone Photo Project
- Iowa History Project
- Iowa in the Civil War (See 1861-1865 entry)
- Iowa in the Great War
- Iowa in World War II
- Iowa Old Press
- Iowa State Census Project (See 1836-1895 entry)
- Orphan Train Riders to Iowa
- Iowa WPA Graves Registration Survey

Links to all Iowa counties and projects are located at the USGenWeb home page for Iowa. See http://iagenweb.org/.

1833-2000s. *Iowa Gravestone Photo Project* **[Online Database],** a project of Iowa GenWeb. To access this database directly from the IA Gravestone website, see https://iowagravestones.org/. This project has partnered with Ancestry.com. See *Web: Iowa Gravestones Index* **[Online Database],** indexed at the Ancestry.com website. Original data: Iowa Gravestone Photo Project. IAGenWeb. The Ancestry.com index includes: Name, Cemetery, Burial place, and a link to the Iowa Gravestones website, where a photo of the gravestone can be viewed. This database has 698,890 records. See https://search.ancestry.com/search/db.aspx?dbid=70558.

1835-1850. *Iowa, Compiled Marriages* **[Online Database],** indexed at the Ancestry.com website. Source: Jordan Dodd, *Early American Marriages: Iowa to 1850,* 1997. Each entry includes groom, bride, marriage date, county, and state. This database has 21,236 records. See https://search.ancestry.com/search/db.aspx?dbid=2088.

1835-1998. *Armed Forces Grave Registrations* **[Online Database],** indexed at the FamilySearch.org website. Index to grave registrations from the Soldiers Relief Commission (Polk County, Iowa). The grave registrations contain information on United States military veterans buried in Iowa, ranging from Revolutionary War veterans (ca. 1835) to 1998. These records were acquired from the Iowa State Historical Society in Des Moines. The collection is arranged alphabetically. This database has 289,493 records. See www.familysearch.org/search/collection/2515886.

1836. *The First Census of the Original Counties of Dubuque and Demoine (Iowa) Taken in July 1836* **[Microfilm & Digital Capture],** edited by Benjamin F. Shambaugh, microfilm of original published by the Historical Department of Iowa, Des Moines, 1897-1898. 2 parts in 1 vol., 93 pages. Contents: part 1: Dubuque County; part 2: Demoine County. From the original manuscript returns preserved in the office of the Secretary of State of Wisconsin. The census was taken in accordance with the act of Congress erecting the territory of Wisconsin (of which these two counties at the time formed a part) comprising the present states of Wisconsin, Iowa, Minnesota and part of North and South Dakota. Includes names of heads of households with number of males and females by age brackets. Filmed by the Genealogical Society of Utah, 1978, 1 roll, FHL film #989450. To access the digital images, see the online FHL catalog page: http://search.ancestry.com/search/db.aspx?dbid=23732.

1836. *Iowa 1836 Territorial Census Index* **[Printed Book],** edited by Ronald Vern Jackson, et al, published by Accelerated Indexing Systems, Bountiful, UT, 1976, 35 pages. FHL book 977.7 X22j.
NOTE: Mr. Jackson probably knew that the names were from Wisconsin Territory, not Iowa, but that's OK, he was trying to sell books in Iowa, not Wisconsin.

1836 Wisconsin Territorial Census, Des Moines County (now Iowa) **[Online Database],** indexed at the USGenWeb site for Des Moines Co IA. See http://iagenweb.org/muscatine/1836census/desmoines1836.htm.

1836-1895. *Iowa State Census Project* **[Online Database],** an index to census transcriptions from across multiple Iowa counties. Included are newly discovered state census records (outside of the State Historical Society of Iowa) and indexed online for the first time at USGenWeb Iowa sites. See http://iagenweb.org/census/.

1836-1925. *Iowa, State Census Collection* **[Online Database],** digitized and indexed at the Ancestry.com website in 2007, from microfilm of the mostly complete, every-name state censuses for 1856, 1885, 1895, 1905, 1915, 1925; as well as various special state censuses from 1836-1897, (and a few added federal censuses), all obtained from the State Historical Society of Iowa. This combined database has 9,549,935 records. See http://search.ancestry.com/search/db.aspx?dbid=1084
- Below is a list of all the years and counties included in this database:
1836: Des Moines & Dubuque
1838: Van Buren
1844: Keokuk
1846: Louisa, Polk & Wapello

1847: Clinton, Louisa, Scott, Wapello, Davis, Marion & Van Buren
1849: Benton, Boone, Clinton, Jackson, Louisa, Madison, Poweshiek, Scott, Van Buren & Washington
1850: Van Buren (✓)
1851: Cedar, Clinton, Decatur, Guthrie, Iowa, Jackson, Johnson, Madison, Mahaska, Page, Pottawattamie, Scott & Washington
1852: Appanoose, Black Hawk, Boone, Bremer, Buchanan, Butler, Cass, Cedar, Clarke, Clayton, Clinton, Davis, Des Moines, Fayette, Fremont, Guthrie, Henry, Iowa, Jackson, Jasper, Jefferson, Johnson, Jones, Keokuk, Lee, Linn, Louisa, Mahaska, Marshall, Mills, Monroe, Muscatine, Polk, Pottawattamie, Poweshiek, Scott, Tama, Taylor, Van Buren, Wapello, Warren & Washington
1853: Warren (Allen, Greenfield, Lynn, and Richland townships)
1854: Adair, Allamakee, Benton, Black Hawk, Boone, Bremer, Chickasaw, Clarke, Clayton, Clinton, Crawford, Dallas, Decatur, Des Moines, Dubuque, Fayette, Fremont, Hardin, Harrison, Henry, Jackson, Jasper, Jefferson, Johnson, Jones, Keokuk, Lee, Linn, Louisa, Madison, Mahaska, Marion, Marshall, Monona, Montgomery, Muscatine, Page, Polk, Pottawattamie, Poweshiek, Ringgold, Scott, Shelby, Story, Tama, Taylor, Union, Wapello, Washington, Wayne & Webster
1856: All counties that were organized at the time except Warren (80 total)
1859: Black Hawk, Buchanan, Carroll, Montgomery, Palo Alto, Plymouth, Pocahontas, Sac, Scott, Union, & Washington
1860: Calhoun, Carroll, Cerro, Gordo, Clay, Crawford, Dickinson, Emmet, Fayette, Greene, Hancock, Humboldt, Iowa, Kossuth, Mitchell, Monona, Palo Alto, Plymouth, Sac, Shelby, Van Buren (✓), Webster, Winnebago, Woodbury, Worth & Wright
1870: Van Buren (✓)
1881: Cerro Gordo (Mason City)
1885: All 99 counties.
1888: Kossuth (Algona), Polk (North Des Moines) & Montgomery (Villisca)
1889: Cherokee (Cherokee) & Emmet (Emmetsburg)
1891: Clay (Spencer)
1892: Carroll (Carroll), Emmet (Estherville), Greene (Jefferson), Tama (Tama) & Wright (Eagle Grove)
1893: Davis (Bloomfield), Franklin (Hampton) & Story (Ames and Nevada)
1895: Adair, Adams, Allamakee, Appanoose, Audubon, Benton, Buchanan, Hardin, Henry, Jones, Lee, Mills, Page, Polk, Pottawattamie, Washington, Wayne, Webster, Winnebago, Winneshiek, Woodbury, Worth & Wright
1896: Fayette (Oelwein)
1897: Chickasaw (New Hampton)
1905: All 99 counties.
1915: All 99 counties.
1925: All 99 counties.

✓ **1836-1925 Notes:** Van Buren County was the only Iowa county listed for 1850 and 1870, and the 1850, 1860 and 1870 Van Buren County censuses are each limited to a one-page typescript, with a few families listed for Link Township, Van Buren County. They have the look of a typewritten extract done in the 1920s.

The 1860 censuses listed for the remaining 24 counties are all very brief extracts, all on the 1860 federal census forms, usually one page per township; but poorly microfilmed. After state-of-the-art digitizing, they still have dark, unreadable top headings. By comparison, the federal set of the 1860 federal censuses has enhanced images, with clear, readable text. Placing two versions of the same page side-by-side and comparing the 1860 SHSI census pages with Ancestry's federal set, seems to indicate that the SHSI pages are state copies of the federal census. There are significant differences in the two sets, including different handwriting, omitted names and data, and different spellings of names. See the 1850 NOTE for a discussion on census copies.

1836-1979. *Early Settlers and County Histories, Mills County, Iowa* **[Online Database],** indexed at the USGenWeb site for
http://iagenweb.org/mills/history/index.htm.

1836-1992. *Iowa, Marriages* **[Online Database],** indexed at the FamilySearch.org website. The beginning dates indicated for this database are impossible if the marriage took place in Iowa. Taken from FHL marriage records on microfilm, this database has 1,320,389 records. See
https://familysearch.org/search/collection/1674842.

1836-1997. *Iowa, Wills and Probate Records* **[Online Database],** digitized and indexed at the Ancestry.com website. One packet of papers in this database included a 1758 deed from New York as part of the deceased's property. The rest of the papers were dated 1836 in Iowa, where the probate court was located. Records may include Wills, Letters of Administration, Inventories, Distributions and Accounting, Bonds, and Guardianships. Each index record includes: Name, Probate date, Inferred death place, Case number, and Item description. A Table of Contents showing the number of images for each type of document allows a direct jump to a certain page/image. This database has 594,492 records. See
https://search.ancestry.com/search/db.aspx?dbid=9064.

1837-1915. *The Old Settlers Association of Linn County, Iowa* **[Online Database],** indexed at the USGenWeb site for Linn Co Ia. See
http://files.usgwarchives.net/ia/linn/history/old-set.txt.

1837-1976. *Iowa Newspaper Archives* [Online Database], digitized and indexed newspapers at the GenealogyBank website for the following cities: Anamosa, Atlantic, Boone, Burlington, Corning, Council Bluffs, Creston, Davenport, De Witt, Denison, Des Moines, Dubuque, Eddyville, Eldora, Fairfield, Independence, Iowa City, Jefferson, Keokuk, La Porte City, Lenox, Marion, Mount Ayr, Mount Pleasant, Ogden, Sibley, and Sioux City. See www.genealogybank.com/gbnk/newspapers/explore/USA/Iowa/.

1837-1989. *Iowa, Church and Civil Marriages* [Online Database], indexed at the FamilySearch.org website. FamilySearch extractions from multiple archives. Each index record includes: Name, Event type, Event date, Event place, Gender, Age, Birth year, Spouse's name, Spouse's gender, Spouse's age, and Spouse's birth year. This database has 12,474 records. See www.familysearch.org/search/collection/2366605.

1838. *Iowa 1838 Territorial Census Index* [Printed Book], edited by Ronald Vern Jackson, et al, published by Accelerated Indexing Systems, Bountiful, UT, 1984. FHL book 977.7 X22ji 1838.

1838. See "The Census of 1838" [Printed Article], by Marie Haefner, in *The Palimpsest* (State Historical Society of Iowa, Iowa City, IA), Vol. 19 (May 1938), pp 185-192.

1838 Census, Henry County, Iowa [Online Database], indexed at USGenWeb site for Henry Co IA. See
http://iagenweb.org/henry/census/1838henry.htm.

1838 Grand Jurors, Slaughter County, Wisconsin Territory [Online Database], indexed at the USGenWeb for Washington Co IA. See
http://files.usgwarchives.net/ia/washington/history/1838gj.txt.

✓ **1838 NOTE:** Slaughter County was formed by Wisconsin Territory in January 1838, and the area was included in the new Iowa Territory, created in July 1838. Slaughter was renamed Washington a year later.

1838-1845 Original Land Entries, Clinton County, Iowa [Online Database], indexed at the USGenWeb site for Clinton Co IA. See
http://iagenweb.org/clinton/places/land/original_land_entries.htm.

1838-1865. See *1838 Census, Clayton County, Wisconsin Territory and 1865 Gazetteer, Clayton County, Iowa* [Online Database], originally indexed at the Sharyl's Cabin site. For an archived database:
https://web.archive.org/web/20160807083554/http://sharylscabin.com/Clayton/directory/gazetteer_p126.htm.

1838-1870. *Iowa Census, 1830-1870* [Online Database], indexed at the Ancestry.com website, from indexes compiled by Jordan Dodd and Liahona Research, and from digitized indexes edited by Ronald Vern Jackson, Accelerated Indexing Systems. This collection contains the following indexes:
- 1838 Territorial Census
- 1840 Federal Census Index
- 1840 Pensioners List
- 1841-1849 Tax Lists
- 1850 Federal Census Index;
- 1851 State Census Index
- 1852 State Census Index
- 1860 Federal Census Index
- 1870 Federal Census Index

This database has 48,152 records. See
http://search.ancestry.com/search/db.aspx?dbid=3547.

1838-1934. *Iowa, County Marriages* [Online Database], indexed at the FamilySearch.org website. Currently, portions of the following counties are represented in this collection: Adair, Appanoose, Audubon, Boone, Buchanan, Calhoun, Clarke, Clinton, Crawford, Davis, Decatur, Des Moines, Dickinson, Dubuque, Franklin, Hamilton, Hancock, Hardin, Harrison, Henry, Jackson, Jefferson, Johnson, Jones, Keokuk, Lee, Louisa, Lucas, Madison, Mahaska, Marshall, Mitchell, Monroe, Muscatine, Plymouth, Shelby, Tama, Van Buren, Webster, Winneshiek, and Wright. (in 2015) Check for recently added counties – this database is nearing completion for all 99 counties of Iowa. This database base currently (2018) has 2,271,641 records. See
https://familysearch.org/search/collection/1805551.

1839-1841 Jurors, Johnson County, Iowa [Online Database], originally indexed at the USGenWeb site for Johnson Co IA. For an archived database, see
https://web.archive.org/web/20150619082408/http://iagenweb.org/johnson/JCdistrictCourtJurors.htm.

1839-1841 Jurors, Washington County, Iowa [Online Database], indexed at the USGenWeb site for Washington Co IA. See
http://files.usgwarchives.net/ia/washington/history/jurors.txt.

1839-2004. *Iowa, Church Records* **[Online Database],** digitized and indexed at FamilySearch.org. Church records from different denominations in several counties of Iowa. See
www.familysearch.org/search/collection/2790247.

1840. *Iowa, 1840 Federal Census: Population Schedules* **[Microfilm & Digital Capture]**, from the original records at the National Archives, Washington, DC. Filmed by the National Archives, 1938, 1950, 1 roll, FHL film #7790. To access the digital images, see the online FHL catalog page:
www.familysearch.org/search/catalog/745489.

1840. *The 1840 Iowa Census* **[Printed Book]**, compiled by Rowene Obert, Helen Blumhagen, and Wilma Adkins, published Salt Lake City, UT 1968. Includes index. Includes the 18 original counties and several precincts which comprised the entire area of Iowa Territory. FHL book 977.7 X2p 1840 and FHL film #844885.

1840s-1850s. *Settlement of Ringgold County, Iowa* **[Online Database]**, text at the USGenWeb site for Ringgold Co IA. See
http://iagenweb.org/ringgold/history/misc/hist-beforestatehood-settlement.html.

1840s-1860s. *Stories of Early Fayette County History* **[Online Database]**, published at the USGenWeb site for Fayette Co IA. See
http://files.usgwarchives.net/ia/fayette/history/stories.txt

1840s-1860s. *Original Land Owners, Warren County, Iowa* **[Online Database]**, published at the USGenWeb site for Warren Co IA. See
http://iagenweb.org/warren/land/land_dg.html.

1840s-1970s. *Military Information & Links, Madison County, Iowa* **[Online Database]**, includes info for veterans who lived in Madison Co IA. See
http://iagenweb.org/madison/military/military_index.html.

1841-1849. *Iowa Census Records* **[Printed Index]**, edited by Ronald Vern Jackson, et al. The actual years are not noted, but it is probable that the Iowa territorial and state censuses of 1844, 1846, 1847, and 1849 are included in this combined index. Published by Accelerated Indexing Systems, Salt Lake City, UT, 1979, 1981, FHL book 977.7 X22i.

1842. *First Tax Assessment Roll of 1842, Delaware County, Iowa* **[Online Database]**, indexed at the USGenWeb site for Delaware Co IA. See
http://iagenweb.org/delaware/taxes/1842-1stax.htm.

1844-1886 *Indentured Children, Des Moines County, Iowa* **[Online Database]**, indexed at the USGenWeb site for Des Moines Co IA. See
http://files.usgwarchives.net/ia/desmoines/court/indent.txt.

1845-1851 *County Probate Book A, Marion County, Iowa* **[Online Database]**. Originally indexed at the USGenWeb site for Marion Co IA. For an archived database, see
http://iagenweb.org/marion/otherRecords/probateRecords/probateBookA.php.

1845-1900s. *Index to Monroe County, Iowa Will Books A, B, and C* **[Online Database]**, indexed a the USGenWeb site for Monroe Co IA. See
http://iagenweb.org/monroe/Wills/wills.html.

1845-1995. *Index, Pioneer History, Calhoun County, Iowa* **[Online Database],** indexed at the USGenWeb site for Calhoun Co IA. See
http://iagenweb.org/calhoun/records/histories/pioneer/index.php.

1846 Iowa Territorial Census **[Microfilm]**, from the originals at the State Historical Society of Iowa, Des Moines, Iowa. FHL title: *1846 Census of Louisa, Polk, and Wapello Counties, Iowa*. This filming includes a 4-page typescript of the Polk County census that was done by the Iowa Writers Project of the Works Progress Administration in 1940. Filmed by the Genealogical Society of Utah, 1978, 1 roll, FHL film #1022202. To see if this microfilm has been digitized yet, see the FHL catalog page:
www.familysearch.org/search/catalog/409026.

✓ **1846 NOTE:** The last of three territorial censuses for Iowa Territory was dated Sept 16, 1846 and was for all of the 18 counties of Iowa Territory at that time. But apparently only the three counties of Louisa, Polk, and Wapello are extant. The results of this census gave Iowa the evidence that it had met the minimum population requirement for statehood, which was granted on Dec 29, 1846. The peopling of Iowa began on June 1, 1833, and at statehood, 13 years later, Iowa's population was over 96,000.

1846 Iowa Territorial Census Index, Polk County, Iowa Territory **[Online Database]**. This name index came from a typescript created in 1940 as a WPA project, originally available online at the USGenWeb site for Polk Co IA. For an archived database, see
http://iagenweb.org/polk/census/1849census.html.

1846 Iowa Territorial Census, Wapello County, Iowa **[Online Database]**, indexed at the USGenWeb site for Wapello Co IA. See
http://files.usgwarchives.net/ia/wapello/census/1846.txt.

1846 Directory. See *A glimpse of Iowa in 1846* **[Microfiche]**, from the original 1846 directory by John B. Newhall; published by Thurston and Tizzard, 2 fiche, FHL fiche #6043998.

1846 Directory, Davenport, Iowa **[Online Database]**, indexed at the Celtic Cousins website. See
www.celticcousins.net/scott/1846dir.htm.

1846-1850s. Wills and Probates, Polk County, Iowa **[Online Database]**. Includes Will Book 1 and Probate Book A. This webpage gives the address for the Clerk of the Court of Polk County, the availability of indexes to the probate records, 1847- present, and the fee for copies. Originally indexed at the USGenWeb site for Polk Co IA. For an archived version, see
http://iagenweb.org/polk/vitals/wills.html.

1846-1860. See *Early Pioneers of Warren County, Iowa* **[Online Database]**, indexed at the USGenWeb site for Warren Co IA. See
http://files.usgwarchives.net/ia/warren/history/pioneers.txt.

1846-1865 Probate Index, Jasper County, Iowa **[Online Database]**, indexed at the USGenWeb site for Jasper Co IA. See
http://iagenweb.org/jasper/probate/.

1847 Iowa State Census **[Microfilm]**, from the originals at the State Historical Society of Iowa, Des Moines, IA. FHL title: **Census of Clinton, Davis, Louisa, Marion, Scott, Van Buren, and Wapello counties, Iowa, 1847.** Includes a 9-page typescript of the Davis County census transcribed by Joe and Madeline Huff in 1975 and an 8-page photocopy of a typescript of the Louisa County census transcribed by Madeline Huff in 1974. Names heads of households and total numbers in the family. Filmed by the Genealogical Society of Utah, 1978, 1 roll, FHL film #1022202.

✓ **1847 NOTE:** The Iowa Constitution of 1846 provided that within one year after its ratification and within every subsequent term of two years, an enumeration of all the white inhabitants of the state should be made. In accordance with this provision an act was passed by the First General Assembly, and approved January 20, 1847, requiring the assessors to take an enumeration of white inhabitants on or before the first day of August 1847. In the census of 1847, thirty-two counties in all were included. The total population was 116,454. See
http://iavanburen.org/1847index.htm.

"**1847 Iowa State Census, Clinton County, Iowa**" **[Printed Article & Online Database]**, name list in *The American Genealogist* (American Society of Genealogists, et al), Vol. 43, No. 1 (Jan 1967); and in *Hawkeye Heritage* (Iowa Genealogical Society, Des Moines, IA), Vol. 10, No. 3 (Jul 1975). This name list was digitized and indexed at the USGenWeb site for Clinton Co IA. See
http://files.usgwarchives.net/ia/clinton/census/1847cen.txt.

"**1847 Iowa State Census, Davis County, Iowa**" **[Printed Article & Online Database]**, in *The American Genealogist*, Vol. 42, No. 4 (Oct 1966); and in *Hawkeye Heritage*, Vol. 11, No. 1 (Jan 1976). This name list was indexed online at the USGenWeb site for Davis Co IA. See
http://iagenweb.org/davis/census_1847.htm.

"**1847 Iowa State Census, Marion County**" **[Printed Article & Online Database]**, in *Hawkeye Heritage*, Vol. 3, No. 2 (Apr 1968). This name list was indexed online at the USGenWeb site for Marion Co IA. See
http://iagenweb.org/marion/mci1847.html.

"**1847 Iowa State Census, Van Buren County**" **[Printed Article & Online Database]**, in *Hawkeye Heritage*, Vol. 1, No. 1 (Winter 1966); and in *Van Buren Iowa Quill*, beginning with Vol. 2, No. 1 (Winter 1967). This name list of the 1847 Iowa State Census for Van Buren County, Iowa was indexed at the USGenWeb site for Van Buren Co IA. See
http://iavanburen.org/1847index.htm.

1847 Iowa State Census, Wapello County, Iowa **[Online Database]**, indexed at the USGenWeb site for Wapello Co IA. See
http://files.usgwarchives.net/ia/wapello/census/1847.txt.

1847 Non-Resident Tax List, Louisa County, Iowa **[Online Database]**, indexed at the RootsWeb site for Louisa Co IA. See
www.rootsweb.ancestry.com/~ialcgs/nrltx47.htm.

1847-1851. Military Land Warrants, Jefferson County, Iowa [Online Database], indexed at the USGenWeb site for Jefferson Co IA. See
http://iagenweb.org/jefferson/Land_Records/Military_Land_grants.html.

1848 Delinquent Taxes, Louisa County, Iowa [Online Database], indexed at the RootsWeb site for Louisa Co IA. See
www.rootsweb.ancestry.com/~ialcgs/ldtx48.htm.

1848-1849 Personal Tax Lists, Louisa County, Iowa [Online Database], indexed at the RootsWeb site for Louisa Co IA. See
www.rootsweb.ancestry.com/~ialcgs/perstx48-49.htm.

1848-1900. See *Shelby County, Iowa Early Pioneers* [Online Database], originally indexed at the USGenWeb site for Shelby Co IA. For an archived database, see
https://web.archive.org/web/20131022062751/http://iagenweb.org/shelby/pioneer_early.htm.

1849 Iowa State Census [Microfilm], from the typescript copies of the extant population schedules at the State Historical Society of Iowa,, Des Moines, Iowa. FHL title: **Census of Benton, Boone, Clinton, Jackson, Louisa, Madison, Poweshiek, Scott, Van Buren and Washington counties, Iowa. 1849.** Heads of households. Includes photocopies of typescript material transcribed by Madeline and Joe Huff, Lida Lisle Greene, Mary A. Fullbright, and Robert Fisher. The typescript of Washington County was filmed with the Madison County record. See FHL film #1022202. To see if this microfilm has been digitized yet, see the FHL catalog page:
www.familysearch.org/search/catalog/4323.

"**1849 Iowa State Census, Boone County**" [Printed Article], name list in *Hawkeye Heritage*, Vol. 1, No. 2 (Spring 1966).

1849 Iowa State Census, Clinton County, Iowa [Online Database], indexed at the USGenWeb site for Clinton Co IA. See
http://files.usgwarchives.net/ia/clinton/census/1849cen.txt.

1849 Iowa State Census, Van Buren County, Iowa [Online Database], index in alpha groups at the USGenWeb site for Van Buren Co IA. See
http://iavanburen.org/1849vbc_census.html.

1849 Tax List, Warren County, Iowa [Online Database], an index to the "First Tax List of Warren County, Iowa, August 20, 1849," indexed at the USGenWeb site for Warren Co IA. See
http://iagenweb.org/warren/tax_lists/1849ataxlist.html.

1849-1850 Poll Tax List, Jasper County, Iowa [Online Database], indexed at the USGenWeb for Jasper Co IA. See
http://iagenweb.org/jasper/resources/polltax1849.htm.

1849-1853 First Land Entries, Fremont County, Iowa [Online Database], originally listed at the USGenWeb site for Fremont Co IA. For an archived database, see
http://iagenweb.org/fremont/court/early_land_deeds.htm.

1849-1853 Earliest Land Entries, Tama County, Iowa [Online Database], listed at the USGenWeb site for Tama Co IA. See
http://files.usgwarchives.net/ia/tama/deeds/tama-lnd.txt.

1849-1925. See *Iowa State Censuses, Madison County, Iowa* [Online Database], includes 1849, 1851, 1852, 1854, 1856, 1859, 1873, 1885, 1895, 1905, 1915, and 1925 state censuses, indexed at the USGenWeb site for Madison Co IA. See
http://iagenweb.org/census/madison/.

1850 Personal Tax List, Louisa County, Iowa [Online Database], indexed at the RootsWeb site for Louisa Co IA. See
www.rootsweb.ancestry.com/~ialcgs/tax50.htm.

1850. *Iowa, 1850 Federal Census: Population Schedules (Federal Copy)* [Microfilm & Digital Capture], from the originals at the National Archives, Washington, DC. Filmed by the National Archives, 1964, 8 rolls, beginning with FHL film #7791 (Allamakee, Appanoose, Benton, Black Hawk, Boone, Buchanan, Cedar, Clarke, Clayton, Clinton, Dallas, and Davis Counties). To access the digital images, see the online FHL catalog page:
www.familysearch.org/search/catalog/744479.

1850. *Federal Census of Iowa for 1850 (State Copy)* [Microfilm], from the Iowa Secretary of State's originals at the State Historical Society of Iowa, Des Moines, IA. Filmed by the Genealogical Society of Utah, 1977, 7 rolls, beginning with FHL film #1021283 (Allamakee, Appanoose, Benton, Buchanan, Black Hawk, Clayton, Cedar, Clinton, Clarke, Des Moines, & Lucas counties). To see if this microfilm has been digitized yet, see the FHL catalog
page: www.familysearch.org/search/catalog/280372.

✓ **1850 NOTE:** The above item for the 1850 Federal Census of Iowa (State Copy) needs clarification. Three (3) copies of the 1850 census were made for every county of the United States: 1) the original documents prepared by the door-to-door census takers stayed at the county courthouse on public display for a specified period of time – but locating any of the 1,623 (1850) county copies today is very rare. It is estimated that less than 50 counties in the U.S. still have a copy of their original 1850 census schedules. 2) In every county of the U.S., the county census supervisor (an assistant marshal of the federal district court) made a copy of the original set. That copy was sent to the state's Secretary of State. In this case, the Iowa Secretary of State's office was at the state capital at Iowa City, Iowa. Of the 31 U.S. states and 4 territories enumerated in the 1850 federal census, only the full sets of state copies from Wisconsin, Minnesota, and Iowa are known to still exist. 3) The Secretary of State made a copy for his entire state that was sent to the Census Office in Washington, DC. This third copy was the one that was eventually microfilmed for public use, as well as the version digitized and indexed online at various websites. In any case where copies can be compared, there will be unexplained differences, i.e., copying errors, such as different spellings, names omitted, different first names, different ages, different place of births, etc.

1850. *Federal Census for Iowa, 1850, Dubuque County* **[Printed Book]**, a transcription of the original manuscript (state copy) at the Iowa State Historical Society, Des Moines, IA. Published by the Iowa Genealogical Society, Des Moines, IA, 1975, 244 pages, FHL book 977.739 X2f.
- NOTE: Compare this 1850 printed transcription (state copy) for Dubuque County with the 1850 federal census originals (federal copy) for Dubuque County.

1850. *Iowa, Pottawattamie County, Annotated Record of US Census, 1850* **[Online Database]**, digitized and indexed at the Ancestry.com website. Pottawattamie County lies on Iowa's western edge, bordered by the Missouri River, and was organized in 1848. This annotated census for 1850 Pottawattamie County was created by Susan Easton Black, Harvey Bischoff Black, Sarah Allen, and Rebecca Allen. The authors used a number of different sources to flesh out biographical details, including later censuses and LDS church membership records. These additional sources provide details for the individuals listed in the census well beyond 1850. This database has 7,814 records: http://search.ancestry.com/search/db.aspx?dbid=3208.

1850-1880. See *Iowa Non-Population Census Schedules, 1850-1880* **[Online Database]**, indexed at the FamilySearch.org website. Source: National Archives microfilm T1156. This is an image-only database. Browse the images, organized by Year, Type of Schedule, and County. Included are Industry Schedules; Social Statistics Schedules, and Agriculture Schedules. This database has 23,397 images. See www.familysearch.org/search/collection/2274801.

1850-1880. See *Iowa Mortality Schedules, 1850-1880* **[Online Database]**, indexed at the FamilySearch.org website. Source: National Archives microfilm T1156. Mortality Schedules were created in conjunction with the US Federal Census and list people who died in the year preceding the census. Mortality schedules were first included in the 1850 census. These include lists of people who died Jun 1849 - May 1850, Jun 1859 - May 1860, Jun 1869-May 1870, and Jun 1879 - May 1880. This database has 39,148 records. See www.familysearch.org/search/collection/2659389.

1850-1880 *Agricultural Schedules, Jones County, Iowa* **[Online Database]**, includes 1850, 1860, 1870, and 1880 federal Ag schedules; and the 1856 IA state Ag schedules. Indexed at the USGenWeb site for Jones Co IA. See http://iowajones.org/agri/agri.htm.

1850-1895 *Federal and State Census Records, Allamakee County, Iowa* **[Online Database]**, originally indexed at the USGenWeb site for Allamakee Co IA. See http://iagenweb.org/allamakee/census.html.

1850-1900. *Census of Taylor County, Iowa* **[Online Database]**. This census compilation has the federal census of 1850, 1860, 1870, 1880, 1900 and the state census of 1856, 1885, 1895 for Taylor County, Iowa. They are recorded by townships for each year as enumerated by the census taker and also in one composite alphabetical listing. An index by alpha groups was prepared at the USGenWeb site for Taylor Co IA. See http://iagenweb.org/taylor/census/tci49.htm.

1850-1990. *Iowa Deaths and Burials* **[Online Database]**, indexed at FamilySearch.org website. FamilySearch extractions, taken from FHL microfilm. Each index record may include: Name, Gender, Burial date, Burial place, Death date, Death place, Age, Birth date, Birthplace, Race, Father's name, Father's birthplace, Mother's name, and Mother's birthplace This database has 398,901 records. See https://familysearch.org/search/collection/1674841.

1850-1925 *Federal & State Census Records, Iowa County, Iowa* **[Online Databases]**, transcribed censuses for 1850 federal; 1851, 1852, 1854, and 1859

state; 1860, 1870, and 1880 federal; 1885 state; 1900 federal; 1905 state; 1910 federal; 1915 state; 1920 federal; and 1925 state. Indexed at the USGenWeb site for Iowa Co IA. See
http://iagenweb.org/iowa/census/.

1850-1925 Federal & State Census Records, Jones County, Iowa [Online Databases], transcribed censuses for 1850 federal; 1852, 1854, and 1856 state; 1870 federal; 1885, 1895 state; 1910 federal; and 1925 state. Indexed at the USGenWeb site for Jones Co IA. See http://iowajones.org/census/census.htm.

1850-1925 Federal & State Census Records, Mitchell County, Iowa [Online Databases], transcribed censuses for 1850 federal; 1856, 1859 state; 1860, 1870, 1880 federal; 1885, 1895 state; 1900 federal; 1905 state (full), 1905 state (register), and 1915 state; 1910 and 1920 federal; 1925 state; and 1930 federal. Indexed at the USGenWeb site for Mitchell Co IA. http://iagenweb.org/census/mitchell/index.htm.

1850s-1900s. *Birth Records, Madison County, Iowa* [Online Database], indexed at the USGenWeb site for Madison Co IA. See
http://iagenweb.org/madison/birth_records/birth_rec_idx.html.

1850s-1900s. *Biographies, Poweshiek County, Iowa* [Online Database], indexed at the USGenWeb site for Poweshiek Co IA. See
http://iagenweb.org/boards/poweshiek/biographies/index.cgi.

1850s-1900s. *Probates, Wapello County, Iowa* [Online Database], an index to probate records, with the subject's name, date, and file number. Indexed at the USGenWeb site for Wapello Co IA. See http://iagenweb.org/wapello/PROBATE-A.htm.

1850s-1900s. *Pioneers of Wayne County, Iowa* [Online Database], text originally at the USGenWeb site for Wayne Co IA. For an archived version, see http://iagenweb.org/wayne/.

1850s-1980s. *Ringgold County History* [Online Database], includes Pictorial History Book, Settlement Before Statehood, Honey War, Formation of Ringgold County, Major Samuel Ringgold, Jr., Iowa's Defense, Agricultural History, Centennial Decade at Ringgold Co., 1980s, Bohemian Settlers, and much more. Indexed at the USGenWeb site for Ringgold Co IA. See http://iagenweb.org/ringgold/history/history.html.

1850-1939. *Iowa, Delayed Birth Records* [Online Database], indexed at the FamilySearch.org website. Index and images of delayed birth records from the State Historical Society of Iowa. Each index record includes: Name, Event type, Event date, Event place, Gender, Father's name, and Mother's name. The document image may include more information, such as types of documents submitted, names of persons swearing affidavits, and etc. This database has 540,796 records. See
www.familysearch.org/search/collection/2527591.

1850-1954. *Poweshiek County Probate, School, and Court Records* [Online Database], indexed at the FamilySearch.org website. Source: Poweshiek County Clerk's Office, Montezuma, IA. This is an image-only database with probate case files, school records, circuit and district court records from Poweshiek County, Iowa. The records include estate files, wills, administrations, minutes, guardianships and other records. Browse through the images, organized by Volume Title, and Year(s). This database has 169,128 images. See
www.familysearch.org/search/collection/2211980.

1850-1990. *Iowa, Deaths and Burials* [Online Database], indexed at the Ancestry.com website. Source: FamilySearch extractions from FHL microfilm. Each index record includes: Name, Gender, Marital Status, Race, Age, Birth date, Birth place, Death date, Death place, Burial date, Burial place, Father, Mother, FHL film number, and Reference ID. This database has 703,870 records. See
https://search.ancestry.com/search/db.aspx?dbid=60283.

1851 Iowa State Census [Microfilm], from the extant population schedules at the State Historical Society of Iowa, Des Moines, Iowa. FHL title: *Census of Cedar, Clinton, Decatur, Guthrie, Iowa, Jackson, Jasper, Jefferson, Johnson, Madison, Mahaska, Page, Pottawattamie, Poweshiek, Scott, and Washington Counties, Iowa, 1851.* Heads of households. Filmed by the Genealogical Society of Utah, 1978, FHL film #1022203. To see if this microfilm has been digitized yet, see the FHL catalog page:
www.familysearch.org/search/catalog/3824.

1851 Iowa State Census Index, Page County, Iowa [Online Database], indexed at the USGenWeb site for Nodaway Co MO. See
www.mogenweb.org/nodaway/census/pageindx.htm.

1851-1859. *Iowa Census Records, 1851-1859* **[Printed Index]**, edited by Ronald Vern Jackson, et al. Actual years not noted, but the index probably includes the Iowa state censuses of 1851, 1852, 1853, 1854, 1856, and 1859. Published by Accelerated Indexing Systems, North Salt Lake, UT, 1981, FHL book 977.7 X2i 1851-1859.

1851 & 1854 Iowa State Census, Page County, Iowa **[Online Database]**, images at the RootsWeb site for the jrbakerjr Iowa Genealogy site. See http://freepages.genealogy.rootsweb.ancestry.com/~jrbakerjr/iowa/iowa.html.

1851-1900. See *Iowa (Marriages), 1851-1900* **[CD-ROM]**, Family Tree Maker's Family Archives, Marriage Index. From back of case: "Contains information on approximately 157,000 individuals who were married between 1851 and 1900 in select Iowa counties, including Adair (1854-1900), Appanoose (1851-1900), Carroll (1854-1900), Chickasaw (1853-1900), Dallas (1851-1886), Delaware (1851-1860), Des Moines (1862-1879), Guthrie (1852-1899), Hamilton (1857-1900), Louisa (1851-1899), Lucas (1851-1899), Marion (1851-1877), Monona (1856-1880), Monroe (1887-1900), Muscatine (1851-1900), Plymouth (1860-1891), Polk (1851-1861), Scott (1855-1860), Taylor (1851-1865), Warren (1851-1879), Webster (1853-1890), Woodbury (1881-1899), Worth (1858-1900), and Wright (1855-1869)." You can generally obtain an individual's name, spouse's name, marriage date, and the county where the marriage was recorded. See FHL CD #222. This CD database is also available online at the Ancestry.com website.
- See also, *Iowa, Compiled Marriages, 1851-1900* **[Online Database]**, indexed at the Ancestry.com website. This database 197,647 has records. See https://search.ancestry.com/search/db.aspx?dbid=4460.

1851-1905 Vital Records, Mills County, Iowa **[Online Database]**. Includes Birth Records, 1880-1887, and Delayed Births to 1924; Marriage Records 1851-1905; and Death Records, 1880-1897. Originally indexed at the USGenWeb site for Mills Co IA. For an archived version, see http://iagenweb.org/mills.

1851-1928. *Iowa, Fayette County Probate Records* **[Online Database]**, digitized at the FamilySearch.org website. Includes probate case files located at the Fayette County courthouse in West Union, Iowa. The case files are organized by year, and within each set of files, the documents are in loose alphabetical order by the 1st letter of the surname of the subject (deceased, guardian, heir, etc.). This database has 230,855 images. See https://familysearch.org/search/collection/1978346.

1852 Iowa State Census **[Microfilm]**, from the extant population schedules at the State Historical Society of Iowa, Des Moines, Iowa. FHL title: *1852 Census of Various Counties in Iowa*. Heads of households. Filmed by the Genealogical Society of Utah, 1978, 2 rolls, as follows:
- Appanoose - Lucas Counties, FHL film #1022204.
- Madison - Wayne counties, FHL film #1022205.

To see if this microfilm has been digitized yet, see the FHL catalog page: www.familysearch.org/search/catalog/409030.

✓ **1852 NOTE:** For the 1852 microfilm set, the FHL catalogers did not give us the full list of 42 counties, yet it was the second largest head of household state census taken in Iowa. See the entry, *1836-1925 Iowa State Censuses Available at Ancestry.com*, which identifies the names of all 42 counties available for 1852.

1852. *Iowa 1852* **[Printed Index]**, edited by Ronald Vern Jackson, published by Accelerated Indexing Systems, 1988, 610 pages. FHL book 977.7 X22io.

1852 Iowa State Census, Appanoose County **[Online Database]**, indexed at the USGenWeb site for Appanoose Co IA. See http://files.usgwarchives.net/ia/appanoose/census/1852.txt.

1852 Iowa State Census, Bremer County, Iowa **[Online Database]**, indexed at the USGenWeb site for Bremer Co IA. See http://iagenweb.org/census/textdisplay.php?file=/census/bremer/1852-IA-bremer.txt.

1852 Iowa State Census, Buchanan County, Iowa **[Online Database]**, indexed at the USGenWeb site for Buchanan Co IA. See http://iagenweb.org/census/textdisplay.php?file=/census/buchanan/1852-IA-buchanan.txt.

1852 Iowa State Census, Butler County, Iowa **[Online Database]**, indexed at the USGenWeb site for Butler Co IA. See http://iagenweb.org/census/textdisplay.php?file=/census/butler/1852-IA-butler.txt.

1852 Iowa State Census, Cedar County, Iowa [Online Database], indexed at the USGenWeb site for Cedar Co IA. See
http://iagenweb.org/census/textdisplay.php?file=/census/cedar/1852-IA-cedar.txt.

1852 Iowa State Census, Clayton County, Iowa [Online Database], indexed by township at the USGenWeb site for Clayton Co IA. See
http://files.usgwarchives.net/ia/clayton/census/1852/.

1852 Iowa State Census, Fremont County, Iowa [Online Database], indexed by township at the USGenWeb site for Fremont Co IA. See
http://iagenweb.org/fremont/census/census1852/index1852.htm.

1852 Iowa State Census Index, Henry County, Iowa [Online Database], indexed at the USGenWeb site for Henry Co IA. See
http://iagenweb.org/henry/census/1852henry.htm.

1852 Iowa State Census, Monroe County, Iowa [Online Database], indexed at the USGenWeb site for Monroe Co IA. See
http://files.usgwarchives.net/ia/monroe/census/1852.txt.

1852 Iowa State Census, Pottawattamie County, Iowa [Online Database], indexed at the USGenWeb site for Pottawattamie Co IA. See
http://files.usgwarchives.net/ia/pottawattamie/census/1852pot.txt.

1852 Iowa State Census, Tama County, Iowa [Online Database], indexed at the USGenWeb site for Tama Co IA. See
http://iagenweb.org/census/textdisplay.php?file=/census/tama/1852-ia-tama-all.txt.

1852 Iowa State Census, Taylor County, Iowa [Online Database], indexed at the USGenWeb site for Taylor Co IA. See
http://files.usgwarchives.net/ia/taylor/census/taylcocen1852.txt.

1852 Iowa State Census, Washington County, Iowa [Online Database], indexed at the USGenWeb site for Washington Co IA. See
http://iagenweb.org/washington/washington52.htm.

1852-1930 State & Federal Censuses, Mills County, Iowa [Online Database]. Includes 1852, 1856, 1885, and 1895 state censuses; and 1860, 1870, 1880, and 1930 federal censuses. Indexed at the USGenWeb site for Mills Co IA. See
http://iagenweb.org/mills/census/index.htm.

1853 Iowa State Census, Warren County, Iowa [Online Database], indexed at the USGenWeb site for Warren Co IA. See
http://files.usgwarchives.net/ia/warren/census/1853.txt.

1853 Landowners, Mills County, Iowa [Online Database], originally indexed at the USGenWeb site for Mills Co IA. For an archived version, see
http://web.archive.org/web/20131022050251/http://iagenweb.org/mills/land/lndown53.htm.

1853-1980 Probate Index, Harrison County, Iowa [Online Database], indexed at the USGenWeb site for Harrison Co IA. See
http://iagenweb.org/harrison/probate/probate.htm.

1854 Census of Various Counties in Iowa [Microfilm & Digital Capture], from the originals of extant population schedules at the State Historical Society of Iowa, Des Moines, Iowa. Heads of households. Filmed by the Genealogical Society of Utah, 1978, 3 rolls, as follows:
- Adams - Lee Counties, FHL film #1022206.
- Linn - Winneshiek Counties, FHL film #1022207.
- Duplicate film of Page, Polk, Pottawattamie, and Poweshiek Counties, FHL film #1022210.

To access the digital images, see the online FHL catalog page:
www.familysearch.org/search/catalog/409034.

✓ **1854 NOTE:** For the 1854 microfilm set, the FHL catalogers did not give us the full list of 51 counties, yet it was the largest head of household state census taken in Iowa. See Ancestry's 1836-1925 list of Iowa state censuses online, which identifies the names of all counties available for 1854.

1854 Iowa State Census, Allamakee County, Iowa [Online Database], indexed at the Sharyl's Cabin (USGenWeb) site. See
www.sharylscabin.com/Allamakee/1854/1854_index.htm.

"1854 Iowa State Census, Clarke County, Iowa" [Printed Article], full name list in *Hawkeye Heritage*, Vol. 3, No. 4 (Oct 1968), and index of surnames in *Clarke County Roots & Branches*, Vol. 6, No. 3 (Sep 1997).

1854 Iowa State Census, Crawford County, Iowa [Online Database], indexed at the USGenWeb site for Crawford Co IA. See
http://iagenweb.org/crawford/census/1854census.html.

1854 Iowa State Census, Dubuque County, Iowa **[Online Database]**, indexed by township at the USGenWeb site for Dubuque Co IA. See http://iagenweb.org/dubuque/census/1854/.

1854 Iowa State Census, Hardin County, Iowa **[Online Database]**, indexed at the USGenWeb site for Hardin Co IA. See http://iagenweb.org/census/textdisplay.php?file=/census/hardin/1854-IA-Hardin-Hardin.txt.

1854 Iowa State Census, Harrison County, Iowa **[Online Database]**, indexed at the USGenWeb site for Harrison Co IA. See http://iagenweb.org/harrison/census/1854_Census.htm.

1854 Iowa State Census Index, Henry County, Iowa **[Online Database]**, indexed at the RootsWeb site for Henry Co IA. See http://iagenweb.org/henry/census/1854henry.htm.

1854 Iowa State Census Index, Madison County, Iowa **[Online Database]**, indexed at the USGenWeb site for Madison Co IA. See http://us-census.org/pub/usgenweb/census/ia/madison/1854/1854-state-index.txt.

1854 Iowa State Census, Mahaska County, Iowa **[Online Database]**, indexed a the USGenWeb site for Mahaska Co IA. See http://iagenweb.org/state/textdisplay.php?file=/mahaska/Census/1854census.txt.

1854 Poll Book of First Election, Iowa County, Iowa **[Online Database]**, indexed at the USGenWeb site for Iowa Co IA. See http://iagenweb.org/iowa/dir/1845-poll.htm.

1854 Tax List, Montgomery County, Iowa **[Online Database]**, indexed at the USGenWeb site for Montgomery Co IA. See http://iagenweb.org/montgomery/taxes/FirstRecorded_Taxes.htm.

1854 Iowa State Census, Tama County, Iowa **[Online Database]**, indexed at the USGenWeb site for Tama Co IA. See http://iagenweb.org/census/textdisplay.php?file=/census/tama/1854-ia-tama-all_twps.txt.

1854, 1856, 1860 Census Indexes, Wayne County, Iowa **[Microfilm & Digital Capture]**, from the original records at the Wayne County Courthouse, Corydon, Iowa. Filmed by the Genealogical Society of Utah, 1990, 1 roll, FHL film #1673539. To access the digital images, see the online FHL catalog page: www.familysearch.org/search/catalog/524396.

1855 Tax List, Warren County, Iowa **[Online Database]**, indexed at the USGenWeb site for Warren Co IA. See http://iagenweb.org/warren/tax_lists/1855TaxList.htm.

1855-1934. *Iowa, Poweshiek County Land Records* **[Online Database]**, indexed at the FamilySearch.org website. Source: State Historical Society of Iowa, Des Moines. This is an image-only database of land records including deeds and town lot records, originating from the county recorder of deeds and the county auditor. Browse the images, organized by Record Type, Volume, and Year Range. This database has 16,268 images. See www.familysearch.org/search/collection/2235530.

1855-1935 City Directories, Davenport, Iowa [Microfiche & Microfilm], from originals published by various publishers. Filmed by Research Publications, Woodbridge, CT, 1980-1984, 16 microfiche and 21 microfilm rolls, beginning with FHL fiche #6043849 (1855-1856 Davenport city directory, 3 fiche). For a complete list of fiche and roll numbers, and the contents of each, see the online FHL catalog page for this title: www.familysearch.org/search/catalog/536168.

1856 State Census of Iowa [Microfilm & Digital Capture], from the extant population schedules at the State Historical Society of Iowa, Des Moines. The first modern state census for Iowa, the 1856 identifies all members of family listed by name, age, nativity, occupation, length of time in Iowa, etc., plus agriculture, domestic and general manufactures. Filmed by the Genealogical Society of Utah, 1977, 26 rolls, beginning with FHL film #1021290 (Adair-Audubon counties). To access the digital images of certain rolls, see the online FHL catalog page: www.familysearch.org/search/catalog/409022.

✓ **1856 NOTE:** Ancestry's 1836-1925 state census collection indicates that all counties in Iowa in 1856 have extant census schedules except Warren County, and that a total of 80 counties were digitized and indexed at the Ancestry.com. A good list of Iowa counties is at a Wikipedia site, where the counties can all be sorted by date established. See https://en.wikipedia.org/wiki/List_of_counties_in_Iowa.

1856 Iowa State Census **[Online Database]**, digitized and indexed at the Ancestry.com website, included in the series, *Iowa, State Census Collection, 1836-1925*: http://search.ancestry.com/search/db.aspx?dbid=1084.

"1856 Iowa State Census, Adair County, Iowa" [Printed Article], name list published serially in the *Adair County Anquestors*, beginning with Vol. 9, No. 1 (Dec 1996). This name list was indexed at the USGenWeb site for Adair Co IA. See www.iagenweb.org/adair/census/1856census.htm.

1856 Iowa State Census, Allamakee County, Iowa [Online Database], indexed by township at the USGenWeb site, Allamakee Co IA. See http://uscensus.org/pub/usgenweb/census/ia/allamakee/1856/.

1856 Iowa State Census, Appanoose County, Iowa [Online Database], indexed at the USGenWeb site for Appanoose Co IA. See http://files.usgwarchives.net/ia/appanoose/census/1856/.

1856 Iowa State Census, Audubon County, Iowa [Online Database], indexed at the USGenWeb site for Audubon Co IA. See http://iagenweb.org/census/audubon/.

1856 Iowa State Census, Benton County, Iowa [Online Database], indexed at the USGenWeb site for Benton Co IA. See http://iagenweb.org/benton/1856_census/1856idxa.htm.

1856 Iowa State Census, Butler County, Iowa [Online Database], indexed at the USGenWeb site for Butler Co IA. Se http://files.usgwarchives.net/ia/butler/census/1856/.

"1856 Iowa State Census, Calhoun County, Iowa" [Printed Article], name list published in *Hawkeye Heritage*, Vol. 5, No. 4 (Oct 1970).

1856 Iowa State Census, Cass County, Iowa [Online Database], indexed at the USGenWeb site for Cass Co IA. See http://iagenweb.org/cass/census/1856census.htm.

"1856 Iowa State Census, Clarke County, Iowa" [Printed Article], name list in *Clarke County Roots & Branches*, beginning with Vol. 5, No. 4 (Dec 1996).

1856 Iowa State Census, Crawford County, Iowa [Online Database], indexed at the USGenWeb site for Crawford Co IA. See http://iagenweb.org/crawford/census/1856censusx.html.

"1856 Iowa State Census, Davis County, Iowa" [Printed Article], name list in *Davis County Genealogical Society Newsletter*, beginning with Vol. 5, No. 3 (Fall 1987).

1856 Iowa State Census, Decatur County, Iowa [Online Database], indexed at the USGenWeb site for Decatur Co IA. See www.usgwarchives.net/ia/decatur/census.html.

1856 Iowa State Census, Des Moines County, Iowa [Online Database], indexed by township at the USGenWeb site for Des Moines Co IA. See http://iagenweb.org/desmoines/Census/Census.htm.

"1856 Iowa State Census, Franklin County, Iowa" [Printed Article], name list in the *Franklin Record*, beginning with the April 1988 issue; and in *Hawkeye Heritage*, Vol. 22, No. 3 (1987).

1856 Iowa State Census, Fremont County, Iowa [Online Database], indexed by township at the USGenWeb site for Fremont Co IA. See http://iagenweb.org/census/fremont/.

"1856 Iowa State Census, Greene County, Iowa" [Printed Article], name list in *Greene Gleanings*, beginning with the February 1993 issue. This name list was indexed online at the USGenWeb site for Greene Co IA. See http://iagenweb.org/census/textdisplay.php?file=/census/greene/1856-IA-greene-jefferson.txt.

"1856 Iowa State Census, Hardin County, Iowa" [Printed Article], name list in *Hawkeye Heritage*, Vol. 3, No. 3 (Jul 1968). This name list was indexed online at the USGenWeb site for Hardin Co IA. See http://iagenweb.org/hardin/56census/56census.html.

1856 Iowa State Census, Harrison County, Iowa [Online Database], indexed at the USGenWeb site for Harrison Co IA. See http://iagenweb.org/harrison/census/1856_Census.htm.

1856 Iowa State Census, Tippecanoe Twp., Henry County, Iowa [Online Database], indexed at the USGenWeb site for Henry Co IA. See http://iagenweb.org/census/textdisplay.php?file=/census/henry/IA-1856-Henry-Tippecanoe.txt.

1856 Iowa State Census, Center Twp., Henry County, Iowa [Online Database], indexed at the USGenWeb site for Henry Co IA. See http://iagenweb.org/census/textdisplay.php?file=/census/henry/1856-IA-henry-center.txt.

1856 Iowa State Census, Jasper County, Iowa [Online Database], indexed at the USGenWeb site for Jasper Co IA. See http://iagenweb.org/census/textdisplay.php?file=/census/jasper/1856-IA-jasper_index.txt.

"1856 Iowa State Census, Jones County, Iowa" [Printed Article], in *News 'N' Notes*, beginning with Vol. 3, No. 1 (Jan 1992).

"1856 Iowa State Census, Kossuth County" [Printed Article], name list in *Hawkeye Heritage*, Vol. 3, No. 1 (Jan 1968).

1856 Iowa State Census, Louisa County, Iowa [Online Database], indexed at the USGenWeb site for Louisa Co IA. See www.usgwarchives.net/ia/louisa/census.html.

1856 Iowa State Census, Monroe County, Iowa [Online Database], indexed by township at the USGenWeb site for Monroe Co IA. See http://iagenweb.org/monroe/Census/1856/.

"1856 Iowa State Census, Allen Township, Polk County" [Printed Article], name list in *Pioneer Trails*, Vol. 7, No. 4 (Dec 1987).

1856 Iowa State Census, Poweshiek County, Iowa [Online Database], indexed at the USGenWeb site for Poweshiek Co IA. See http://iagenweb.org/census/textdisplay.php?file=/census/poweshiek/1856/pow56inx.txt.

"1856 Iowa State Census, Sac County, Iowa" [Printed Article], in *Sacoge News*, beginning with Vol. 7, No. 1 (Jan 1986).

"1856 Iowa State Census, Story County, Iowa" [Printed Article], in *Hawkeye Heritage*, Vol. 13, No. 4 (Fall 1978). This name list was indexed at the IA Story site. See http://iastory.com/1856/.

1856 Iowa State Census, Van Buren County, Iowa [Online Database], indexed at the USGenWeb site for Van Buren Co IA. See http://iavanburen.org/1856-VanBurenCoIACensus-A-F.htm.

1856 Iowa State Census, Wayne County, Iowa [Printed Book], compiled by Wayne County Genealogical Society, Corydon, Iowa. Published by the Iowa Genealogical Society, 1985, FHL book 977.788 X2c 1856.

1856 State Census, Webster County, Iowa [Microfilm], from a typescript transcribed by Hamilton Heritage, 97 pages. Filmed by the Genealogical Society of Utah, 1990, 1 roll, FHL film #1672462. To see if this microfilm has been digitized yet, see the FHL catalog page: www.familysearch.org/search/catalog/569245.

1856 Iowa State Census of Woodbury County [Printed Book], compiled in 1994 by Peggy Powell and MaryAnn Haafke for the Woodbury County Genealogical Society, Sioux City, Iowa. FHL book 977.741 X29p.

1856 Iowa State Census, Wright County, Iowa [Online Database], indexed at the USGenWeb site for Wright Co IA. See http://iagenweb.org/wright/1856WrightCounty.htm.

1856 Old Settlers Register, Book One, Muscatine County, Iowa [Online Database], indexed at the USGenWeb site for Muscatine Co IA. See http://iagenweb.org/muscatine/settlersone/settlersregindex.htm.

1856 City Directory, Muscatine, Iowa [Online Database], indexed at the USGenWeb site for Muscatine Co IA. See http://iagenweb.org/muscatine/citydirectory1856/dir1856index.htm.

1856-1897 City Directories, Dubuque, Iowa [Microfilm & Digital Capture], from originals published by Hardie & Scharle, Dubuque, IA. Filmed by the Genealogical Society of Utah, 1976, 1978, 5 rolls, as follows:
- **1861, 1856-1859, 1867, 1874-1876, 1884-1887** Dubuque directories, FHL film #985427.
- **1888-1889** Dubuque directories, FHL film #985428.
- **1863, 1870-1871, 1873-1874, 1883-1885** Dubuque directories, FHL film #1024142.
- **1880-1881, 1894-1897** Dubuque directories, FHL film #1024143.
- **1858, 1884-1885** Dubuque directories, FHL film #1024843.

To access the digital images, see the online FHL catalog page. www.familysearch.org/search/catalog/299446.

1856-1899 City Directories, Davenport, Scott County, Iowa [Microfilm & Digital Capture], from the originals published by H.N. Stone, Davenport, IA. Filmed by the Genealogical Society of Utah, 1976, 1978, 8 rolls, as follows:
- **1856-1863**, 1866-1870 directories, FHL film #989491.

- **1873-1878**, 1880-1881 directories, FHL film #989492.
- **1876** directory, FHL film #1024842.
- **1882-1888**, directories, FHL film #989493.
- **1890-1891**, 1894-1895 directories, FHL film #989494.
- **1896-1899** directories, FHL film #989495.
- **1874-1875**, **1885-1886**, **1894-1897** directories, FHL film #1024141.
- **1892-1893** directories, FHL film #1024843.

To access the digital images, see the online FHL catalog page:
www.familysearch.org/search/catalog/299483.

1856-1910 Directories, Mills County, Iowa **[Online Database]**. Includes the 1856-1890 Masonic Directories; 1865 Iowa State Gazetteer & Directory; 1880-1887 Medical Attendants; 1882-1883 Business Directory; and 1910 Farmer Directory. Indexed at the USGenWeb site for Mills Co IA. See http://iagenweb.org/mills/direct-gaz/index.htm.

1856-1937. *Iowa, Federal Naturalization Records* **[Online Database],** digitized and indexed at the Ancestry.com website. Source: Records of District Courts of the U.S. at the National Archives. The records include Petitions, Declarations, and Certificates. Each index record includes: Name, Gender, Record type, Birth place, Arrival date, Arrival place, and Declaration number. The document image may have more information. This database has 26,820 records. See
https://search.ancestry.com/search/db.aspx?dbid=61198.

1856-1940. *Iowa, Delayed Birth Records* **[Online Database],** digitized and indexed at the Ancestry.com website. Source: State Historical Society of Iowa, Des Moines. Delayed birth records were necessary for someone about to qualify for a Social Security pension but had no official birth certificate as proof of age. Every county in the U.S. was encouraged to provide the service of recording a delayed birth record. This began in most states at about the time of the 1935 onset of Social Security. The dates from the birth records may relate to the birth years found on them, so these records, created between about 1935 and 1940 have births as early as 1856. Each index record includes: Name, Gender, Race, Birth date, Birth place, Father, Mother, and Certificate number. The document image has more information. This database has 1,616,005 records. See
https://search.ancestry.com/search/db.aspx?dbid=61441.

1857-1900 City Directories, Iowa City, Johnson County, Iowa **[Microfilm & Digital Capture],** from originals published by A.G. Tucker, Iowa City, IA. Filmed by the Genealogical Society of Utah, 1976, 1978, 2 rolls, as follows:
- **1857, 1868, 1875, 1878, 1891-1894 & 1897-1900**, FHL film #989476.
- **1857**, FHL film #1024845.

To access the digital images, see the online FHL catalog page:
www.familysearch.org/search/catalog/299426.

1858-1886 Will Book A, Taylor County, Iowa **[Online Database]**, listed by date at the USGenWeb site for Taylor Co IA. See
http://iagenweb.org/taylor/courthouse/tci16.htm.

1858-1924 Delayed Birth Records, Mills County, Iowa **[Online Database],** originally indexed at the USGenWeb site for Mills Co IA. For an archived version, see
http://web.archive.org/web/20110902033121/http://iagenweb.org/mills/vr/DelayedBirths/delbirthindex.htm.

1858-1979 Abstracted Newspaper Index of Page and Taylor Counties, Iowa **[Online Database]**, indexed at the USGenWeb site for Taylor Co IA. See
www.mogenweb.org/nodaway/obits/index.htm.

1859 Iowa State Census, Carroll and Sac Counties **[Microfilm]**, from the extant population schedules at the State Historical Society of Iowa, Des Moines, Iowa. Includes name lists for Carroll and Sac counties only. Filmed by the Genealogical Society of Utah, 1978, 1 roll, FHL film #1022208. To access the digital images, see the online FHL catalog page:
www.familysearch.org/search/catalog/3720.

1859 Iowa Land Map, Index to Names, Linn County, Iowa **[Online Database]**, indexed at the RootsWeb site for Linn Co IA. See
www.rootsweb.ancestry.com/~ialinn/1859land/index.htm.

1859-1860 Directory, Henry County, Iowa **[Microfilm]**, from the original published by Watson Bowron, Burlington, Iowa. See the online FHL catalog page for this title
www.familysearch.org/search/catalog/50554.

1859 City Directory, Muscatine, Iowa **[Online Database]**, indexed at the USGenWeb site for Muscatine Co IA. See
http://iagenweb.org/muscatine/atlas/city-countyresidentsindex.htm.

1859-1912. See *Iowa City Assessor's Book* **[Microfilm & Digital Capture],** from originals at the Iowa State Historical Society, Des Moines, IA. Filmed by the Genealogical Society of Utah, 1990, 6 rolls, beginning with FHL film #1728635 (Iowa City Assessor's book, 18589-1860). To access the digital images, see the online FHL catalog page: www.familysearch.org/search/catalog/551040.

1860. *Iowa, 1860 Federal Census: Population Schedules (Federal Copy)* **[Microfilm To access the digital images, see the online FHL catalog page:],** from the originals at the National Archives. Filmed twice by the National Archives, 1950, 1957, 43 rolls, beginning with FHL film #803310 (2nd filming: Adair, Adams, and Allamakee Counties). To access the digital images, see the online FHL catalog page: www.familysearch.org/search/catalog/704803.

1860. *Iowa 1860* **[Printed Index]**, edited by Ronald Vern Jackson, published by Accelerated Indexing Systems, North Salt Lake, UT, 1987, 741 pages, FHL book 977.7 X22ij.

1860. *Greene County, Iowa Census, 1860 Federal, Annotated* **[Printed Book],** compiled by the Greene County Genealogical Society. Includes surname index. Contains names of head of household and other members of household, ages, place of birth, occupation, value of real estate owned, as well as (annotated) information of marriage date and place and maiden name of wife, birth dates and birth places of children, burial places of former spouses and deceased children, etc. Published by the Iowa Genealogical Society, Des Moines, IA, 1998, 66 pages, FHL book 977.7466 X2g.

1861-1949. *Grand Army of the Republic Records, Iowa Posts: Indexes to Veterans; Post Membership Records* **[Microfilm & Digital Capture],** from the originals at the State Historical Society of Iowa, Des Moines, IA. Contains indexes made by members of the Daughters of the American Revolution chapters in Iowa, giving names of soldiers, birth dates and places, death dates (if available) and cemeteries where buried, and the G.A.R. posts which veterans belonged to, as well as their membership records. The membership records are arranged by county and then by posts within each county. They include veteran's name, residence, occupation, date and place of birth, date and place of death, cemetery where buried, war record, dates of enlistment and discharge, names of parents, spouse, children (if given), and sources of information. Filmed by the Genealogical Society of Utah, 1978, 1987, 69 rolls, beginning with FHL film #1487370 (Surname Index to Veterans and their GAR Posts – Aaker, Drengman Oleson – Boyce, William H.). To access the digital images, see the online FHL catalog page: www.familysearch.org/search/catalog/155392.

1861-1949. *Iowa, Grand Army of the Republic Membership Records* **[Online Database],** indexed at the FamilySearch.org website. Index and images of the Department of Iowa Grand Army of the Republic membership records. The records are arranged by county and then by posts within each county. They include veteran's name, residence, occupation, date and place of birth, date and place of death, cemetery where buried, war record, dates of enlistment and discharge, names of parents, spouse, children (if given), and sources of information. This database has 87,376 records. See www.familysearch.org/search/collection/2351982.

1861-1865. *Iowa Colonels and Regiments: Being a History of Iowa Regiments in the War of the Rebellion and Containing a Description of the Battles in Which They Have Fought* **[Printed Book],** by Addison A. Stuart, published by Mills, Des Moines, IA, 1865, 656 pages, FHL book 977.7 M2s.

1861-1865. *Index to Compiled Service Records of Volunteer Union Soldiers Who Served in Organizations from the State of Iowa* **[Microfilm],** from the originals at the National Archives, Washington, DC. Filmed by the National Archives, 1964, 29 rolls, FHL film #881808 (Index, A-Bam 1861-1865). For a complete list of roll numbers and contents of each roll, see the online FHL catalog page for this title: www.familysearch.org/search/catalog/315985.

1861-1865. *Iowa in the Civil War* **[Online Database],** a project of the USGenWeb Iowa website. For a name search box for all of Iowa, see http://iagenweb.org/civilwar/.

1861-1865. *United States Civil War Soldiers Index* **[Online Database],** an index to soldiers who served in the Civil War, culled from 6.3 million soldier records in the General Index Cards to the Compiled Military Service Records in the National Archives. This index was a joint project of the U.S. National Park Service, the Federation of Genealogical Societies (FGS), and the Genealogical Society of Utah (GSU). Each record provides the full name of the soldier, state, regiment, whether Union or Confederate, the company, the soldier's rank, sometimes alternate names, the NARA publication and roll numbers. See https://familysearch.org/search/collection/1910717.
- See also *Soldiers and Sailors Database* **[Online Database],** indexed at the National Park Service website. This is the original database containing information about the men who served in the Union

and Confederate armies during the Civil War. Other information on the site includes histories of Union and Confederate regiments, links to descriptions of significant battles, and selected lists of prisoner-of-war records and cemetery records, which will be amended over time. This database has 6.3 million records. See www.nps.gov/civilwar/soldiers-and-sailors-database.htm.

1861-1865. *Scott County Men Who Served in the Civil War* **[Online Database],** indexed at the RootsWeb site for Scott Co IA. See www.rootsweb.ancestry.com/~iascott/civilwar.htm.

1861-1866. *Iowa Civil War Soldier Burial Records* **[Online Database],** digitized and indexed at the Ancestry.com website. At least 75,000 soldiers enlisted from the state of Iowa during the Civil War and thousands more who served from other states settled in Iowa following the Rebellion. This database currently contains a listing of over 18,800 of these service men (and a few women) who died and were buried in the state, or who enlisted from the state of Iowa and are buried elsewhere. In addition to those who served in the Union army, burials include those serving in the Confederate Army, the US Regular army, US Colored Troops and the Navy and Marines between 1861 and 1866. See http://search.ancestry.com/search/db.aspx?dbid=3854.

1861-1865. See *Civil War Soldiers from Black Hawk County, Iowa* **[Online Database],** indexed at the Census Diggins site. See www.censusdiggins.com/blkhwkiacw.html.

1861-1865. *Residents of Poweshiek County, Iowa, who served in the Civil War* **[Online Database],** includes List of Pensioners on the Roll January 1, 1883. Originally indexed at the USGenWeb
site for Poweshiek Co IA. For an archived version, see http://iagenweb.org/poweshiek/mil/military.htm.

1861-1865. See *Civil War Soldiers, Ringgold County* **[Online Database],** indexed at the Census Diggins website. See www.censusdiggins.com/ringgoldcw.html.

1861-1865. *Civil War Soldiers, Wayne County* **[Online Database],** indexed at the USGenWeb site for Wayne Co IA. See http://iagenweb.org/wayne/warofreb.htm#cw.

1861-1866. See *Roster and Records of Iowa Soldiers in the War of the Rebellion: Together with Historical Sketches of Volunteer Organizations, 1861-1865* **[Printed Book],** prepared by the Iowa Adjutant General's office, published by authority of the General Assembly, Des Moines, IA: E. H. English, 1908-1911, 6 vols., FHL book 977.7 M2i. To view a digital version, (Vols. 1, 2, 3, 4, & 6), see the online FHL online catalog page for this title: www.familysearch.org/search/catalog/27.
- See also *Index to Iowa Soldiers* **[Typescript],** an index to *Roster and Records of Iowa Soldiers in the War of Rebellion*, by the Iowa Adjutant General. Contents: vol. 1: A-C, vol. 2: D-G, vol. 3: H-K, vol. 4: L-Mc, vol. 5: N-R, vol. 6: S-T, vol. 7: U-Z., compiled by the Idaho State Historical Society, Boise, ID, 1979, FHL book 977.7 M21 Index, v.1-7.

1861-1865. *Iowa Soldiers Residing in Kansas* **[Printed Book],** compiled by Keo-Mah Genealogical Society. From intro: "This publication was copied from a small booklet housed at the Nelson Pioneer Farm in Oskaloosa, Iowa. It evidently was a publication of a magazine called *The Western Veteran,* printed after the Civil War, in Topeka, Kansas. Its purpose was to keep veterans updated as to the whereabouts of their friends and comrades. Therefore, the original booklet was organized by regiments, and contains an alphabetical listing by surname of veterans of the Civil War, giving name and rank, company, regiment and Kansas town of residence." Published by the Iowa Genealogical Society, Des Moines, IA, 1996, 80 pages, FHL book 977.7 M2io.

1861-1898 Military Records, Iowa County, Iowa **[Online Database],** an index to records of the Civil War, 188 3 Pensioners, and Spanish-American War rosters at the USGenWeb site for Iowa Co IA. See http://iagenweb.org/iowa/mil/.

1861-1914 Military Records, Page County, Iowa **[Online Database],** an index to records of the Civil War, Ex-Soldiers, & World War I, indexed at the USGenWeb site for Page Co IA. See http://iagenweb.org/page/military/index.htm.

1861-1918 Pottawattamie County Military Service **[Online Database].** Includes the following histories/name lists:
- The Battle of Pea Ridge (Civil War)
- Deceased Service Personnel
- Draft Board Bulletin (circa 1940)

- The Mormon Battalion
- The Roster of Enlisted Men from Council Bluffs or Pottawattamie County, Iowa Who Served in the Civil War
- The War of 1898
- World War I Military Registration List for Pottawattamie County, Iowa

Indexed at the RootsWeb site for Pottawattamie Co IA. See **www.rootsweb.ancestry.com/~iapcgs/military.htm**.

1861-1945 Military Records, Linn County, Iowa **[Online Database]**, an index to records of the Civil War, World War I, and World War II at the RootsWeb site for Linn Co IA. See **www.rootsweb.ancestry.com/~ialinn/military/index.htm**.

1861-1945 Military Records, Montgomery County, Iowa **[Online Database]**, an index to records of the Civil War, Spanish-American War, World War I, and World War II, originally at the USGenWeb site for Montgomery Co IA. For an archived version, see **http://web.archive.org/web/20120703142606/http://iagenweb.org/montgomery/militarycenter.htm**.

1861-1952 Military Information, Civil War to Korean War, Mills County, Iowa **[Online Database]**, indexed at the USGenWeb site for Mills Co IA. See **http://iagenweb.org/jones/military/index.html**.

1861-1972 Military Information, Civil War to Vietnam War, Clay County, Iowa **[Online Database]**, indexed at the USGenWeb site for Clay Co IA. See **http://iagenweb.org/clay/military.htm**.

1861-1972 Military Information, Civil War to Vietnam War, Osceola County, Iowa **[Online Database]**, indexed at the USGenWeb site for Osceola Co IA. See **http://iagenweb.org/osceola/military/index.htm**.

1861-1972 Military Information, Civil War to Vietnam War, Lyon County, Iowa **[Online Database]**, indexed at the USGenWeb site for Lyon Co IA. See **http://iagenweb.org/lyon/military/mili_dex.htm**.

1861-1972 Military Records, Plymouth County, Iowa **[Online Database]**, includes info for the Civil War, Spanish-American War, World War I, World War II, Korean War, and Vietnam War. Indexed at the USGenWeb site for Plymouth Co IA. See **http://iagenweb.org/plymouth/MilitarilySpeaking.html**.

1861-1990. *Iowa, Grand Army of the Republic Membership Records* **[Online Database]**, indexed at the FamilySearch.org website. Index and images of the Department of Iowa Grand Army of the Republic membership records. The records are arranged by county and then by posts within each county. They include veteran's name, residence, occupation, date and place of birth, date and place of death, cemetery where buried, war record, dates of enlistment and discharge, names of parents, spouse, children (if given), and sources of information. This database has 87,376 records. See **www.familysearch.org/search/collection/2351982**.

1861-1995. See *(Iowa Cities) in U.S. City Directories, 1822-1995* **[Online Database]**, digitized and indexed at the Ancestry.com website. This collection is one of the largest single databases on the Internet, with a total of 1.56 billion names, all indexed from full scanned images of the city directory book pages. All states are represented except Alaska, and there are 32 cities of Iowa beginning with 1861 (Davenport), 1866 (Council Bluffs, Des Moines), and 1868 (Iowa City). The complete list of Iowa cities with directories: Ames, Boone, Burlington, Cedar Falls, Cedar Rapids, Charles City, Clarinda, Clear Lake, Clinton, Council Bluffs, Creston, Davenport, Des Moines, Dougherty, Dubuque, Fort Dodge, Fort Madison, Grinnell, Iowa City, Keokuk, Marshalltown, Mason City, Muscatine, Nevada, Newton, Oelwein, Osceola, Ottumwa, Shenandoah, Sioux City, Spirit Lake, and Waterloo. Use Ancestry's *Browse this Collection* feature to choose a state, choose a city, and choose a directory year available for that city. See **https://search.ancestry.com/search/db.aspx?dbid=2469**.

1861-2004. Military Records, Fremont County, Iowa **[Online Database]**, indexed at the USGenWeb site for Fremont Co IA. See **http://iagenweb.org/fremont/military/index.htm**.

1862 Iowa State Census (Statistics) [Microfilm & Digital Capture], FHL title: *Census Returns of the Different Counties of the State of Iowa for the Year 1862: Showing in Detail the Population, Agricultural Statistics, Domestic and General Manufactures, &c.*, Iowa Census Board, 1863. Filmed by W. C. Cox Co., Tucson, AZ, 1974, 1 roll, FHL film #1000025. To access the digital images, see the online FHL catalog page: **www.familysearch.org/search/catalog/328360**.

1862, 1863, 1864 County Tax Assessments, Delaware County, Iowa **[Online Database]**, indexed at the USGenWeb site for Delaware Co IA. See http://iagenweb.org/delaware/taxes/index.htm.

1862-1866 Internal Revenue Assessment Lists for Iowa **[Microfilm & Digital Capture]**, from the originals at the National Archives, Washington, D C. See beginning of film for list of the counties and what districts they are in. Filmed by the National Archives, Washington, D.C., Series M0766, 16 rolls, beginning with FHL film #1534648 (Assessment Lists, District 1, division 1-11, annual 1862). To access the digital images, see the online FHL catalog page: www.familysearch.org/search/catalog/577929.

1862-1866 Internal Revenue Assessment Lists for Clayton County, Iowa **[Online Database]**, indexed at the USGenWeb site for Clayton Co IA. See http://iagenweb.org/clayton/tax/tax_index.htm.

1862-1866 Internal Revenue Assessment Lists for Jones County, Iowa **[Online Database]**, indexed at the USGenWeb site for Jones Co IA. See http://iowajones.org/taxes/taxes.htm.

1862-1866 Internal Revenue Assessment Lists for Mills County, Iowa **[Online Database]**, indexed at the USGenWeb site for Mills Co IA. See http://iagenweb.org/mills/taxes/1862.htm.

1862-1879 Naturalization Records, Wright County, Iowa **[Online Database]**, indexed at the USGenWeb site for Wright Co IA. See http://iagenweb.org/wright/naturalizations.htm.

1862-1910. *Persons Subject to Military Duty, ca. 1862-1910* **[Microfilm & Digital Capture]**, from original records of the Iowa Adjutant General's Office, located at the Iowa State Historical Society, Des Moines, IA. Names are organized by county. Filmed by the Genealogical Society of Utah, 1978, 94 rolls, beginning with FHL film #1024847 (Adair co). To access the digital images, see the online FHL catalog page: www.familysearch.org/search/catalog/388617.
- See also, *Iowa, Records of Persons Subject to Military Duty* **[Online Database]**, digitized and indexed at FamilySearch.org, see www.familysearch.org/search/collection/2821291.

1862-1930 Tax Records, Allamakee County, Iowa **[Online Database]**, indexed at the USGenWeb site for Allamakee Co IA. See http://iagenweb.org/allamakee/taxes_index.htm.

1863 Militia Roll, Monroe County, Iowa, Part 1, Surnames A-I **[Online Database]**, indexed at the USGenWeb site for Monroe Co IA. See http://iagenweb.org/monroe/Military/1863_a-i.html.

1863 Militia Roll, Monroe County, Iowa, Part 2, Surnames J-Y **[Online Database]**, indexed at the USGenWeb site for Monroe Co IA. See http://iagenweb.org/monroe/Military/1863_j-y.htm.

1863-1871 Men Eligible for Military Duty, Pocahontas County, Iowa **[Online Database]**, indexed at the USGenWeb site for Pocahontas Co IA: http://iagenweb.org/pocahontas/military/1871milit.htm.

1863-1900 Pioneers, Pocahontas County, Iowa **[Online Database]**, indexed at the USGenWeb site for Pocahontas Co IA. See http://iagenweb.org/pocahontas/pocapion.html.

1865. *Iowa State Gazetteer* **[Printed Book, Microfilm & Digital Capture]**, by James T. Hair, a very thorough listing and description of Iowa places at the time of the end of the Civil War. Published by Bailey & Hair, Chicago, 1865, 722 pages, FHL book 977.7 E4. Also on microfilm, FHL film #1024846. To access the digital images, see the online FHL catalog page: www.familysearch.org/search/catalog/146783.
- See also, *1865 Iowa State Gazetteer* **[Online Database]**, digitized and OCR indexed at the Ancestry.com website. See https://search.ancestry.com/search/db.aspx?dbid=26474.

1865 First Families of Jefferson County, Iowa **[Online Database]**, indexed at the USGenWeb site for Jefferson Co IA. See http://iagenweb.org/jefferson/First_Families.html.

1865-1867 Amnesty Papers: Name Index to Pardon Application Files. Group 2, Pardon Applications Submitted by Persons from Iowa **[Microfilm & Digital Capture]**, from original records of the U.S. Adjutant General's Office, at the National Archives, Washington, DC. Filmed by the National Archives, series M1003, 73 rolls, beginning with FHL film #1578739 (Name Index). See FHL film #1578811 (Roll 73) containing the pardon applications from persons from the north and west, including Iowa residents. To access the digital images, see the online FHL catalog page: www.familysearch.org/search/catalog/573048.

1866 City Directory, Muscatine, Iowa [Online Database], indexed at the USGenWeb site for Muscatine Co IA. See http://iagenweb.org/muscatine/citydirectory1866/dir1866index.htm.

1866 City Directory, Des Moines, Iowa [Online Database], indexed at the USGenWeb site for Polk Co IA. See http://iagenweb.org/polk/directories/DirectoriesIndex.html.

1866-1935 City Directories, Des Moines, Polk County, Iowa [Microfilm], from originals published by various publishers. Filmed by Research Publications, Woodbridge, CT, 1980-1984. FHL has 41 rolls, beginning with FHL film #1376808 (1866, 1869, 1871, 1873, & 1874 Des Moines city directory).

1866, 1886, 1902 & 1914 Plat Maps and Land Owners, Clayton County, Iowa [Online Database], indexed at the Sharyl's Cabin site. See http://sharylscabin.com/Clayton/land/land_index.htm.

1867 Iowa State Census (Statistics) [Microfilm & Digital Capture], FHL title: *The Census of Iowa, as Returned in the Year 1867,* Iowa Census Board, 1867. Filmed by W. C. Cox Co., Tucson, AZ, 1974, 1 roll, FHL film #1000025. To access the digital images, see the online FHL catalog page: www.familysearch.org/search/catalog/57551.

"1867 Iowa State Census (Statistics), Newton, Jasper County, Iowa" [Printed Article], in *Jasper County Gleaner*, Vol. 8, No. 1 (Jan 1986).

1867-1970. Iowa, Consecutive Registers of Convicts [Online Database], indexed at the Ancestry.com website. Source: State Historical Society of Iowa, Des Moines. Every new inmate in an Iowa prison was assigned an ID number upon arrival. The name, offence, dates, location of crime, and other facts were recorded in a Register book, entered in consecutive order by the ID number of the inmate. This database is a copy of the images of the register books, from 1867-1970, and a complete index to the inmates listed therein. This database has 93,470 records. See https://search.ancestry.com/search/db.aspx?dbid=60384.

1869 Iowa State Census (Statistics) [Microfilm & Digital Capture], FHL title: *The Census of Iowa as Returned in the Year 1869.* Filmed by W. C. Cox Co., Tucson, AZ, 1974, 1 roll, FHL film #1000025. To access the digital images, see the online FHL catalog page: www.familysearch.org/search/catalog/57555.

1869 City Directory, Muscatine, Iowa [Online Database], indexed at the USGenWeb site for Muscatine Co IA. See http://iagenweb.org/muscatine/citydirectory1869/dir1869index.htm.

1870. Iowa, 1870 Federal Census: Population Schedules [Microfilm & Digital Capture], from the originals at the National Archives, Washington, DC. Filmed twice by the National Archives, 1962, 1968, 70 rolls, beginning with FHL film #545873 (2nd filming: Adair, Adams, and Allamakee Counties). To access the digital images, see the online FHL catalog page: www.familysearch.org/search/catalog/698896.

1870. Iowa 1870 [Printed Index], edited by Ronald Vern Jackson, published by Accelerated Indexing Systems, North Salt Lake, UT, 2 vols., FHL book 977.7 X22i.

1870. Iowa 1870 Census Index [Printed Index], edited by Raeone Christensen Steuart, published by Heritage Quest, Bountiful, UT, 2000, 3 vols., FHL book 977.7 X22s.

1870s-1920s. Declarations of Intent (Naturalization Records), Montgomery County, Iowa [Online Database], indexed at the USGenWeb site for Montgomery Co IA. See http://iagenweb.org/montgomery/naturalization/intentindex.htm.

1870s-1920s. Inventors and Inventions of Union County, Iowa [Online Database], indexed by town at the USGenWeb site for Union Co IA. See http://files.usgwarchives.net/ia/union/history/inventors.txt.

1871 Enrollees, Pioneer Association, Van Buren Co IA [Online Database], indexed at the USGenWeb site for Van Buren Co IA. See http://files.usgwarchives.net/ia/vanburen/history/1871.txt.

1871-1879 Birth Records, Plymouth County, Iowa [Online Database], indexed at the USGenWeb site for Plymouth Co IA. See http://iagenweb.org/plymouth/HistoryCenter/earlybirths.html.

1873-1901 Naturalization Records, Lyon County, Iowa [Online Database], indexed at the USGenWeb site for Lyon Co IA. See http://iagenweb.org/lyon/naturalz/natu_dex.htm.

1873-1976 Jury Duty, Miscellaneous Jurors, Allamakee County, Iowa **[Online Database]**, indexed at the USGenWeb site for Allamakee Co IA. See http://iagenweb.org/allamakee/history4/jury.htm.

1873-1976 Biographies from Allamakee County, Iowa **[Online Database]**, indexed at the USGenWeb site for Allamakee Co IA. See http://iagenweb.org/allamakee/.

1874 Landowners, Lee County, Iowa **[Online Database]**, indexed at the USGenWeb site for Lee Co IA. See http://iagenweb.org/lee/land/index.htm.

1875 Iowa State Census (Statistics) **[Printed Book & Digital Version]**], full title: *The Census of Iowa as Returned in the year 1875: Thirteenth State Census, Showing in Detail the Population, Agricultural Statistics, Domestic and General Manufactures and Other Items of Interest,* published under the direction of the executive council, printed Des Moines, IA, R.B. Clarkson, State Printer, 1875. Book is in off-site Storage. To view a digital version of this book, see the online FHL catalog page: www.familysearch.org/search/catalog/1781303.

1875 Biographies. As part of *A. T. Andreas' Illustrated Historical Atlas of the State of Iowa, 1875* **[Microfilmed Book & Digital Capture]**, by A. T. Andreas, published by Lakeside Press, Chicago, 1875. This is the standard history of Iowa and includes biographical sketches of Iowa's earliest settlers and statistics from the 1875 state census of Iowa, fully indexed. Filmed by the Genealogical Society of Utah, 1975, 1 roll, FHL film #980875. To access the digital images, see the online FHL catalog page: www.familysearch.org/search/catalog/291264.

1875 Andreas Atlas: Businesses: Butler County, Iowa **[Online Database]**, indexed at the USGenWeb site for Butler Co IA. See http://files.usgwarchives.net/ia/butler/history/butlerb.txt.

1875 Andreas Atlas: Patron's Directory, Butler County, Iowa **[Online database]**, indexed at the USGenWeb site for Butler Co IA. See http://files.usgwarchives.net/ia/butler/history/butlerp.txt.

1875 Andreas Atlas: Patron's Directory, Scott County, Iowa **[Online database]**, indexed at the Celtic Cousins website. See www.celticcousins.net/scott/1875dirindex.htm.

1875 Andreas Atlas: Patron's Directory, Wapello County, Iowa **[Online database]**, indexed at the USGenWeb site for Wapello Co IA. See http://iagenweb.org/wapello/1875Patrons.htm.

1875 Andreas Atlas: Township Maps and Index of Farmers, Jasper County, Iowa **[Online database]**, indexed at the USGenWeb site for Jasper Co IA. See http://iagenweb.org/jasper/history/1875/.

1875 Crawford County Residents Who Were Patrons of Illustrated Historical Atlas of the State Of Iowa **[Online Database]**, indexed at the USGenWeb site for Crawford Co IA, see http://iagenweb.org/crawford/res/1875atlaspeople.html.

1875 Business Directory, Davis County, Iowa **[Online Database]**, indexed at the USGenWeb site for Davis Co IA. See http://iagenweb.org/davis/PatronBus1875.htm.

1875 Andreas Atlas: Township Maps, Polk County, Iowa **[Online database]**, indexed at the USGenWeb site for Polk Co IA. See http://iagenweb.org/polk/maps/maps.html.

"**1875 Iowa State Census, Webster County**" **[Printed Article]**, name list in *Webster County Genie Gleaners*, Vol. 12, No. 3 (Jul 2000).

1875 Andreas Atlas: Patron's Directory, Henry County, Iowa **[Online database]**, indexed at the USGenWeb site for Henry Co IA. See http://iagenweb.org/henry/Maps/MapsIndex.htm.

1875 Andreas Atlas: Patron's Directory, Page County, Iowa **[Online database]**, indexed at the USGenWeb site for Page Co IA. See http://iagenweb.org/page/atlas/andreas/patrons.htm.

1875 Andreas Atlas: Patron's Directory, Warren County, Iowa **[Online database]**, indexed at the USGenWeb site for Warren Co IA. See http://iagenweb.org/warren/directories/patrons1875.html.

1875 Andreas Atlas: Business Directory, Warren County, Iowa **[Online Database]**, indexed at the USGenWeb site for Warren Co IA. See http://iagenweb.org/warren/directories/busdir1875.html.

1875 History & 1882 Business Directory, Marshall County, Iowa **[Online Database]**, indexed at the USGenWeb site for Marshall Co IA. See http://files.usgwarchives.net/ia/marshall/history/.

1875-1938 County Business Directories, Palo Alto County, Iowa **[Online Database]**, includes 1875, 1907-1908, 1922, and 1938-1939 Business Directories. Indexed at the RootsWeb Site for Palo Alto Co IA. See www.rootsweb.ancestry.com/~iapaloal/dirs.htm.

1875-1897 Birth Index, Grundy County, Iowa **[Online Database]**, indexed at the USGenWeb site for Grundy Co IA. See http://iagenweb.org/grundy/vitals/vitalbirth1875-1897partial.html.

1876 Business Directory, Des Moines, Iowa **[Online Database]**, indexed at the USGenWeb site for Polk Co IA. See http://iagenweb.org/polk/directories/DirectoriesIndex.html.

1876-1877 History and Directory, Muscatine County, Iowa **[Online Database]**, indexed at the USGenWeb site for Muscatine Co IA. See http://iagenweb.org/muscatine/CountyDir1876/Contents.htm.

1878. *Iowa Biographical Dictionary, 1878* **[Online Database]**, digitized and OCR indexed at the Ancestry.com website. See http://search.ancestry.com/search/db.aspx?dbid=7722.

1878 Biographies, Benton County, Iowa **[Online Database]**, indexed at the USGenWeb site for Benton Co IA. See http://iagenweb.org/benton/1878_bios/1878_bios.htm.

1878 History, Fayette County, Iowa **[Online Database]**, indexed at the USGenWeb site for Fayette Co IA. See http://iagenweb.org/fayette/hist/1878/ndx.htm.

1878, 1886, 1903 Biographies, Appanoose County, Iowa **[Online Database]**, indexed at the USGenWeb site for Appanoose Co IA. See http://iagenweb.org/appanoose/biographies.html.

1879 Biographies, Dallas County, Iowa **[Online Database]**, indexed by township at the RootsWeb site for Dallas Co IA. See www.rootsweb.ancestry.com/~iadallas/twp.

1879 Pioneer Settlers of Jefferson County, Iowa **[Online Database]**, indexed at the USGenWeb site for Jefferson o IA. See http://iagenweb.org/jefferson/Pioneers/Pioneers.html.

1879 Biographical Index, History of Muscatine County, Iowa **[Online Database]**, indexed at the USGenWeb site for Muscatine Co IA. See http://iagenweb.org/muscatine/biographies1879/contents1879.htm.

1879 County Directory, Warren County, Iowa **[Online Database]**, indexed at the USGenWeb site for Warren Co IA. See http://iagenweb.org/warren/directories/1879-history/1879directory.html.

1879-1915 Biographies, Madison County, Iowa **[Online Database]**, indexed at the USGenWeb site for Madison Co IA. See www.usgwarchives.net/ia/madison/bios.html.

1879-1979 Biographies, Montgomery County, Iowa **[Online Database]**, indexed at the USGenWeb site for Montgomery Co IA. See http://iagenweb.org/montgomery/bios/ndx.htm.

1880. See *Census of Iowa for 1880, and the Same Compared With the Findings of Each of the Other States: And Also With all Former Enumerations of the Territory Now Embraced Within the Limits of the State of Iowa, With Other Historical and Statistical Data* **[Microfilm & Digital Capture]**, by John A. T. Hull, Secretary of State, printed by order of the General Assembly. Original published by F.M. Mills, Des Moines, 1883, 744 pages. This is an invaluable listing of Iowa territorial, state, and federal censuses, 1836-1880. It contains historical and statistical data about the state of Iowa and its counties but does not enumerate the population by name or household. Population totals from various enumerations of each county, as well as totals for towns and villages are given. Filmed by W.C. Cox Co., Tucson, AZ, 1974, FHL film #1000024. To access the digital images, see the online FHL catalog page: www.familysearch.org/search/catalog/322685.

1880. See *Iowa, 1880 Federal Census: Soundex and Population Schedules* **[Microfilm & Digital Capture]**, from the originals at the National Archives. Filmed by the National Archives, ca1970, 125 rolls, beginning with FHL film #446919 (Soundex: A000 thru A435), and FHL film #1254325 (Population schedules: Adair, Adams, and Allamakee Co-part). To access the digital images, see the online FHL catalog page: www.familysearch.org/search/catalog/673551.

1880 Federal Census (Short Form), Floyd County, Iowa [Microfilm & Digital Capture], from the county's original volumes of the 1880 name list, located at the Floyd County Courthouse in Charles City, Iowa. Includes name, color, age, and sex. Filmed by the Genealogical Society of Utah, 1987, 1 roll, FHL film #1481693. To access the digital images, see the online FHL catalog page:
www.familysearch.org/search/catalog/429005.

1880 Federal Census (Short Form), Hardin County, Iowa [Microfilm & Digital Capture], from the county's original volumes of the 1880 name list, located at the Hardin County Courthouse in Eldora, Iowa. Includes name, color, age, and sex. Filmed by the Genealogical Society of Utah, 1988, 2 rolls, FHL film #1547838 (Ackley, Etna, Iowa Falls, Hardin, Alden, Ellis Buckeye, Jackson, Clay, and Eldora (A-T); and FHL film #1547839 (Eldora (T-Z), Pleasant, Sherman, Tipton, Concord, Grant, Providence, and Union). To access the digital images, see the online FHL catalog page:
www.familysearch.org/search/catalog/619407.

✓ **1880 NOTE:** The 1880 Short Form was copied from the original schedules. The full schedules were organized by house and family; but the Short Form was designed to be an index, with the names in general alpha order – 1st letter of surname only. Each person was listed by name, color, sex, and age only. The Short Form was the copy that stayed at the county courthouse for public review, while the main 1880 schedules were transmitted to the Census Office in Washington, DC. The Short Form sets cited above for Floyd and Hardin counties are the only known surviving 1880 county originals for all of Iowa.

1880 Biographies, Davis County, Iowa [Online Database], indexed at the RootsWeb site for Davis Co IA. See
www.rootsweb.ancestry.com/~iabiog/davis/d1882/d1882.htm.

1880 Birth Register, Hardin County, Iowa [Online Database], indexed at the USGenWeb site for Hardin Co IA. See
http://iagenweb.org/hardin/hc1880birthregister.htm.

1880 Death Register, Hardin County, Iowa [Online Database], indexed at the USGenWeb site for Hardin Co IA. See
http://iagenweb.org/hardin/hc1880deathregister.htm.

1880 History, Washington County, Iowa [Online Database], full text at the USGenWeb site for Washington Co IA. For an archived version, see http://web.archive.org/web/20120722014047/http://www.usgennet.org/usa/topic/historical/LightOn/1880wash_1.htm.

1880-1881 Iowa State Gazetteer & Business Directory, Calhoun County Extraction [Online Database], indexed at the USGenWeb site for Calhoun Co IA. See
http://iagenweb.org/calhoun/records/directories/gazetteer/1881.php.

1880-1885 Birth Records, Lee County, Iowa [Online Database], indexed at the USGenWeb site for Lee Co IA. See
http://iagenweb.org/lee/vr/births/index.htm.

1880-1888 Birth Records, Pocahontas County, Iowa [Online Database], indexed at the USGenWeb site for Pocahontas Co IA. See
http://iagenweb.org/pocahontas/pocbirth.html.

1880-1889 Deaths, Wright County, Iowa [Online Database], indexed at the USGenWeb site for Wright Co IA. See
http://files.usgwarchives.net/ia/wright/vitals/wrideath1_old.txt.

1880-1895 & 1907-1912. Death Records, Buena Vista County, Iowa [Online Database], indexed at the USGenWeb site for Buena Vista Co IA:
http://iagenweb.org/buenavista/DeathRecords/BuenaVistaDeathRecords(1880-1895&1907-1912)/deathrecords.html.

1880-1896 Birth Records, Hamilton County, Iowa [Online Database], indexed at the USGenWeb site for Hamilton Co IA. See
http://iagenweb.org/hamilton/vr/vr_index.html.

1880-1897 Death Records, Page 1, Pocahontas County, Iowa [Online Database], indexed at the USGenWeb site for Pocahontas Co IA. See
http://iagenweb.org/pocahontas/deaths.html.

1880-1897 Death Records, Page 2, Pocahontas County, Iowa [Online Database], indexed at the USGenWeb site for Pocahontas Co IA. See
http://iagenweb.org/pocahontas/deaths2.html.

1880-1897 Death Records Sioux County, Iowa **[Online Database]**, indexed at the USGenWeb site for Sioux Co IA. See http://iagenweb.org/sioux/deaths/courthouse_deaths_1.htm.

1880-1900 Death Records, Davis County, Iowa **[Online Database]**, indexed at the USGenWeb site for Davis Co IA. See http://iagenweb.org/davis/death1.htm.

1880-1907 Death Records, Clinton County, Iowa **[Online Database]**, indexed at the USGenWeb site for Clinton Co IA. See http://iagenweb.org/clinton/records/deaths.htm.

1880-1909 Birth Records, Clinton County, Iowa **[Online Database]**, indexed at the USGenWeb site for Clinton Co IA. See http://iagenweb.org/clinton/records/births.htm.

1880-1910 Death Records, Harrison County, Iowa **[Online Database]**, indexed at the USGenWeb site for Harrison Co IA. http://iagenweb.org/harrison/obit/death_index.htm.

1880-1913 Vital Records, Fremont County, Iowa **[Online Database]**, indexed at the USGenWeb site for Fremont Co IA. See http://iagenweb.org/fremont/vr/vitalrecords.htm.

1880-1919 Death Records, Pottawattamie County, Iowa **[Online Database]**, indexed at the RootsWeb site for Pottawattamie Co IA. See www.rootsweb.ancestry.com/~iapcgs/Deaths.html.

1880-1925 Germans from Russia Census Records, Montgomery County, Iowa **[Online Database]**, an extraction of apparent Germans from Russia taken from the 1880 federal; 1885, 1895 state; 1900, 1910 federal; and 1915, 1925 state census for Montgomery County. Indexed at the USGenWeb site for Montgomery Co IA: http://iagenweb.org/montgomery/census/grcensus.htm.

1880-1935. *Iowa, County Births* **[Online Database]**, indexed at the FamilySearch.org website. Taken from county birth records on microfilm at the FHL in Salt Lake City, taken from all 99 Iowa counties. Each index record includes: Name, Event type, Event date, Event place, Gender, Father's name, and Mother's name. This database has over 2,282,689 records. See https://familysearch.org/search/collection/1821206.

1880-1992. *Iowa, County Death Records* **[Online Database]**, indexed at the FamilySearch.org website. Taken from county death records on microfilm at the FHL in Salt Lake City, taken from 98 of 99 Iowa counties. Each index record includes: Name, Event type, Event date, Event place, Age, Birth year, Father's name, Mother's name, Certificate number, and page number. This database has 543,429 records. See **www.familysearch.org/search/collection/2110820**.

1880-1940. *Iowa, Marriage Records* **[Online Database]**, indexed at the FamilySearch.org website. Source: IA Dept of Public Health Records at the State Historical Society of Iowa, Des Moines. This collection includes indexed images of marriage records held at the State Archives of Iowa for the years 1880 through 1940 for all counties. Some of the marriage returns will be on certificate forms, while others were entered into registers. Each index record may include: groom's name, bride's name, bride and groom's current ages, or age at next birthday; marriage application date, marriage date, marriage county, places of residence for both parties, occupations, how many marriages for each party, places of birth for the bride and groom, color and nationality, parents' names for the bride and groom (including mother's maiden name), location of the marriage, name of the officiant, and names of witnesses. This database has 7,272,471 records. See https://search.ancestry.com/search/db.aspx?dbid=8823.

1881 Biographies, Fremont County, Iowa **[Online Database]**, indexed at the USGenWeb site for Fremont Co IA. See http://iagenweb.org/fremont/bios/bios1881.htm.

1881 Biographies, Lucas County, Iowa **[Online Database]**, indexed at the RootsWeb site for Lucas Co IA. See www.rootsweb.ancestry.com/~iabiog/lucas/hl1881/hl1881.htm.

1881-1940 Biographies, Iowa County, Iowa **[Online Database]**, includes biographical sketches from county histories published in 1881, 1893, and 1915; and the 1940 *Who's Who in Iowa* for the county. Indexed at the USGenWeb site for Iowa Co IA. See http://iagenweb.org/iowa/bios/.

1882 Iowa State Gazetteer & Business Directory **[Online Database]**, indexed for all of Iowa at the USGenWeb Archives website. Table of contents, see www.usgwarchives.net/ia/1882gaz.htm.

1882 Iowa State Gazetteer & Business Directory, Adair County, Iowa **[Online Database]**, text at the USGenWeb site for Adair Co IA. See http://iagenweb.org/adair/directories/1882polk.htm.

1882 Iowa State Gazetteer & Business Directory, Scott County, Iowa **[Online Database]**, indexed at the Celtic Cousins website. See **www.celticcousins.net/scott/1882gazeteerindex.htm**.

1882 Iowa State Gazetteer & Business Directory, Webster County, Iowa **[Online Database]**, indexed at the USGenWeb site for Webster Co IA. See http://files.usgwarchives.net/ia/webster/history/web1882.txt.

1882 Biographies, Allamakee County, Iowa **[Online Database]**, indexed at the USGenWeb site for Allamakee Co IA. See http://iagenweb.org/allamakee/bio_index.htm.

1882 Biographies, Clayton County, Iowa **[Online Database]**, indexed at the USGenWeb site for Clayton Co IA. See http://iagenweb.org/clayton/biographies/bio_index.htm.

1882 Index to History of Winneshiek County **[Online Database]**, indexed at the USGenWeb site for Winneshiek Co IA. See http://files.usgwarchives.net/ia/winneshiek/history/.

1882 Index to History of Woodbury County **[Online Database]**, indexed at the USGenWeb site for Woodbury Co IA. See http://files.usgwarchives.net/ia/woodbury/history/.

1882-1883 Iowa State Gazetteer & Business Directory, Calhoun County Extraction **[Online Database]**, indexed at the USGenWeb site for Calhoun Co IA. See http://iagenweb.org/calhoun/records/directories/gazetteer/1883.php.

1882-1883 Iowa State Gazetteer & Business Directory, Carroll County Extraction **[Online Database]**, indexed at the USGenWeb site for Carroll Co IA. See http://files.usgwarchives.net/ia/carroll/history/1882mtc.txt.

1882-1883 Iowa State Gazetteer & Business Directory, Davis County Extraction **[Online Database]**, indexed by township at the USGenWeb site for Davis Co IA. See http://files.usgwarchives.net/ia/davis/history/.

1882-1883 Iowa State Gazetteer & Business Directory, Decatur County Extraction **[Online Database]**, indexed by township at the USGenWeb site for Decatur Co IA. See http://files.usgwarchives.net/ia/decatur/history/.

1882-1883 Iowa State Gazetteer & Business Directory, Des Moines County, Iowa **[Online Database]**, indexed for Danville and Dodgeville at the USGenWeb site for Des Moines Co IA. See http://files.usgwarchives.net/ia/desmoines/history/.

1882-1883 Iowa State Gazetteer & Business Directory, Dubuque County Extraction **[Online Database]**, indexed by townships at the USGenWeb site for Dubuque Co IA. See http://files.usgwarchives.net/ia/dubuque/history/.

1882-1883 Iowa State Gazetteer & Business Directory, Fayette County Extraction **[Online Database]**, indexed by townships at the USGenWeb site for Fayette Co IA. See http://files.usgwarchives.net/ia/fayette/history/.

1882-1883 Iowa State Gazetteer & Business Directory, Jackson County Extraction **[Online Database]**, indexed for La Motte at the USGenWeb site for Jackson Co IA. See http://files.usgwarchives.net/ia/jackson/history/la-motte.txt.

1882-1883 Iowa State Gazetteer & Business Directory, Mills County Extraction **[Online Database]**, indexed by township at the USGenWeb site for Mills Co IA. See http://iagenweb.org/mills/direct-gaz/index.htm.

1882-1883 Iowa State Gazetteer & Business Directory, Washington County Extraction **[Online Database]**, indexed at the USGenWeb site for Washington Co IA. See http://files.usgwarchives.net/ia/washington/history/1882wash.txt.

1882-1883 Iowa State Gazetteer & Business Directory, Wayne County Extraction **[Online Database]**, indexed by townships at the USGenWeb site for Wayne Co IA. See http://files.usgwarchives.net/ia/wayne/history/.

1883 Biographies, Butler County, Iowa **[Online Database]**, indexed at the USGenWeb site for Butler Co IA. See http://iagenweb.org/butler/bios/bio_index-1883.htm.

1883 Biographies, Franklin County, Iowa [Online Database], indexed at the USGenWeb site for Franklin Co IA. See http://iagenweb.org/franklin/1883Biographies/1883Biography_index.htm.

1883 Pensioners, Butler County, Iowa [Online Database], indexed at the USGenWeb site for Butler Co IA. See http://iagenweb.org/butler/list_of_pensioners1883.htm.

1883 Pensioners on the Roll, Davis County, Iowa [Online Database], indexed at the USGenWeb site for Davis Co IA. See http://iagenweb.org/davis/pension.htm.

1883 Pensioners on the Roll, Monroe County, Iowa [Online Database], indexed at the USGenWeb site for Monroe Co IA. See http://iagenweb.org/monroe/Military/1883_militia.htm.

1883 Pensioners on the Roll, Tama County, Iowa [Online Database], indexed at the USGenWeb site for Tama Co IA. See http://iagenweb.org/tama/resource/pensioners1883.html.

1883 Pensioners on the Roll, Washington County, Iowa [Online Database], indexed at the USGenWeb site for Washington Co IA. See http://files.usgwarchives.net/ia/washington/military/civilwar/1883pen.txt.

1883 History, Chickasaw and Howard Counties, Iowa [Online Database], indexed at the USGenWeb site for Howard Co IA. See http://iagenweb.org/howard/history/1883%20Howard%20Co%20Biographical%20Sketches.htm.

1883 History, Tama County, Iowa [Online Database], indexed at the USGenWeb site for Tama Co IA. See http://iagenweb.org/tama/history/toc2.html.

1883-1948. *Iowa, Kansas and Nebraska Civil War Veterans: Compilation of the Death Rolls of the Departments of Iowa, Kansas and Nebraska, Grand Army of the Republic, 1883-1948* [Printed Book], by Dennis Northcott. Names of veterans are listed in alphabetical order for each state. Published by D. Northcott, St. Louis, MO, 2007, 688 pages, FHL book 973 M2nde.

1884 Landowners, Grundy County, Iowa [Online Database], indexed at the USGenWeb site for Grundy Co IA. See http://iagenweb.org/grundy/land/landowners1884.html.

1884 Landowners, Muscatine County, Iowa [Online Database, indexed at the USGenWeb site for Muscatine Co IA. See http://iagenweb.org/muscatine/atlas/atlas1884intro.htm.

1884 Biographies, Guthrie County, Iowa [Online Database], indexed at the USGenWeb site for Guthrie Co IA. See http://iagenweb.org/guthrie/bios/guthsttc.htm.

1884 History Index, Harrison County, Iowa [Online Database], indexed at the USGenWeb site for Harrison Co IA. See http://iagenweb.org/harrison/1884/1884.htm.

1884 County Directory, Ida County, Iowa [Online Database], indexed at the USGenWeb site for Ida Co IA. See http://iagenweb.org/ida/directories/1884/1884directory.html.

1884-1885. See *Iowa Gazetteer and Business Directory* [Online Database], digitized and OCR indexed at the Ancestry.com website. Source: R.L. Polk & Co, Chicago, 1884. This gazetteer covers each city, town, village, and settlement in Iowa and includes a description of each place and a directory of the people engaged in business or the professions located there. The business directory portion of this work is comprised of lists of all trades and professions, with the names and post office addresses of the businesses arranged under headings according to line of business. This database has 1,381 pages. See https://search.ancestry.com/search/db.aspx?dbid=7669.

1884-1919 Record of Burial Permits, Iowa City, Johnson County, Iowa [Online Database], indexed at the USGenWeb site for Johnson Co IA. See http://iagenweb.org/johnson/cem/BurialRecords1/BurialsIndex.htm.

1884-1935 City Directories, Sioux City, Woodbury County, Iowa [Microfilm], from the originals published by various publishers, filmed by Research Publications, 1980-1995. FHL has 20 rolls, beginning with FHL film #2156595 (**1884, 1887, 1888 & 1889** Sioux City directory). To see if this microfilm has been digitized yet, see the FHL catalog page: www.familysearch.org/search/catalog/698946.

1885 Iowa State Census **[Microfilm & Digital Capture]**, from the originals at the State Historical Society of Iowa, Des Moines, IA. Some townships are missing, but every county is represented with census schedules of the population. The census schedules provide detailed information for all members of a family, relationship to head of house, an exact property location, whether a street address in a town or an indication of a Range-Township-Section of a farm; age, birthplace by county for a person born in Iowa, or the state/country of birth; nativity of parents, whether first papers filed for aliens; and more, such as occupation and military information. Filmed by the Genealogical Society of Utah, 1977, 95 rolls, beginning with FHL film #1021316 (Adair County). To access the digital images, see the online FHL catalog page:
www.familysearch.org/search/catalog/388625.

1885 Iowa State Census **[Online Database]**, indexed at the Ancestry.com website. Source: database compiled for Ancestry.com by Gary Quigg, 2003. This database contains information from the 1885 Iowa State Census for 39 (of 99) counties of Iowa. Information listed includes the names of every member of the household, their sex, ages, birthplaces, location (town, county, state), marital status, and much more. A reference to the location of each entry in the original record is provided. This database has 411,324 records. See
http://search.ancestry.com/search/db.aspx?dbid=6812.
- See also *1885 Iowa State Census* **[Online Database]**, digitized and indexed at the FamilySearch.org website. Source: State Historical Society, Des Moines. Includes a name index for all 99 counties of the Iowa state census taken in 1885. The population schedule names every person in a household. This database has 1,737,228 records. See
https://familysearch.org/search/collection/1803643.

1885. *Iowa Soldiers, Sailors, and Marines, 1885* **[Online Database],** digitized and OCR indexed at the Ancestry.com website. Source: Alexander, William L., *List of Ex-Soldiers, Sailors and Marines, Living in Iowa,* Publ. Des Moines, 1886. Presumably, this list was extracted from the 1885 IA State Census, which had a question re military service. This database has 781 pages. See
https://search.ancestry.com/search/db.aspx?dbid=7715.
- See also, *List of Ex-Soldiers, Sailors and Marines Living in Iowa* **[Online Database],** digitized and OCR indexed at the Ancestry.com website. This database has 781 pages/records. See
https://search.ancestry.com/search/db.aspx?dbid=28266.

1885 Iowa State Census, Buena Vista County, Iowa **[Online Database],** indexed at the USGenWeb site for Buena Vista Co IA. See
http://iagenweb.org/census/buenavista/.

1885 Iowa State Census, Crawford County, Iowa **[Online Database],** indexed at the USGenWeb site for Crawford Co IA. See
http://iagenweb.org/crawford/census/1885censusx.html.

1885 Iowa State Census, Davis County, Iowa **[Online Database],** indexed at the USGenWeb site for Davis Co IA. See
http://iagenweb.org/davis/1885census.htm.

1885 Iowa State Census, Decatur County, Iowa **[Online Database],** indexed at the USGenWeb site for Decatur Co IA. See
http://iagenweb.org/decatur/CensusDocs/1885StateCensus.html.

1885 Iowa State Census, Harrison County, Iowa **[Online Database],** indexed at the USGenWeb site for Harrison Co IA. See
http://iagenweb.org/harrison/census/1885_Census.htm.

1885 Iowa State Census Index, Jasper County, Iowa **[Online Database],** indexed at the USGenWeb site for Jasper Co IA. See
www.usgwarchives.net/ia/jasper/census.html.

1885 Iowa State Census, Madison County, Iowa **[Online Database],** indexed at the USGenWeb site for Madison Co IA. See
www.usgwarchives.net/ia/madison/statecen.html.

1885 Iowa State Census, Palo Alto County, Iowa **[Online Database],** indexed by township at the USGenWeb site for Palo Alto Co IA. See
http://iagenweb.org/census/counties/paloalto/1885/.

1885 Iowa State Census, Story County, Iowa **[Online Database],** indexed at the IA Story site. See
http://iastory.org/1885/.

"1885 Iowa State Census, Wapello County, Iowa" **[Printed Article],** in *Southern Genealogists Exchange Quarterly,* Vol. 22, No. 100 (Winter 1981).

1885 Iowa State Census, Warren County, Iowa **[Online Database],** indexed at the USGenWeb site for Warren Co IA. See
http://iagenweb.org/warren/census/1885index.html.

1885 Iowa State Census, Wayne County, Iowa; Index to 1885 Wayne County, Iowa State Census **[Printed Index]**, compiled by Wayne County Genealogical Society, Corydon, Iowa, published by the Iowa Genealogical Society, Des Moines, Iowa, 1998, 90 pages. FHL book 977.788 X22w 1885, and FHL film #795989.

1885 Iowa State Census, Webster County, Iowa **[Printed Book]**, compiled by Webster County Genealogical Society, Fort Dodge, IA, published by the Iowa Genealogical Society, 1990. FHL book 977.751 X2w and FHL film #6104038.

1885 Delinquent Tax Lists, Polk County, Iowa **[Online Database]**, indexed by township at the USGenWeb site for Polk Co IA. See http://iagenweb.org/polk/taxes/del-tax.html.

1885. See *List of Ex-Soldiers, Sailors and Marines Living in Iowa* **[Online Database]**, from the book published by the state of Iowa, a special listing of veterans taken from the 1885 Iowa state census schedules. Several Iowa counties have reproduced their lists with the title, *1885 Census of Veterans.* The full statewide list was Digitized and indexed at Ancestry.com. See http://search.ancestry.com/search/db.aspx?dbid=28266.

1885 Old Settlers Association, Humboldt County, Iowa **[Online Database]**, indexed at the USGenWeb site for Humboldt Co IA. See http://iagenweb.org/humboldt/history/logcabin.htm.

1885 Plat Book (Landowners), Ida County, IA **[Online Database]**, *indexed at the USGenWeb site* for Ida Co IA. See http://iagenweb.org/ida/maps/Platbook1885.htm.

1885 Veterans Living in Monroe County, Iowa **[Online Database]**, indexed at the USGenWeb site for Monroe Co IA. See http://iagenweb.org/monroe/Census/spec1885_1.htm.

1885 & 1895 Iowa State Census, Plymouth County, Iowa **[Online Database]**, indexed by township at the USGenWeb site for Plymouth Co IA. See http://iagenweb.org/plymouth/Census/.

1885 Business Directory, Pottawattamie County, Iowa **[Online Database]**, indexed at the USGenWeb site for Pottawattamie Co IA. See http://iagenweb.org/pottawattamie/dir/atlas-1885.htm.

1885-1926. Polk County, Iowa, Newspapers, Des Moines Capital, Index **[Printed Book]**, compiled by Ankeny Genealogical Society. 3 volumes contain alphabetical listings by surname of persons, events (births, deaths, marriages, marriage licenses, miscellaneous data, divorces, and killed in action in war), date of the event and publication date of the newspaper. Published by the Iowa Genealogical Society, Des Moines, IA, 1996-1997, 3 vols., FHL book 977.758/D1 B32po v.1-3.

1886 Veterans Living in Page County, Iowa **[Online Database]**, indexed at the USGenWeb site for Page Co IA. See http://iagenweb.org/page/military/1886a-j.htm.

1886 Biographical Sketches, Clarke County, Iowa **[Online Database]**, indexed at the USGenWeb site for Clarke Co IA. See http://iagenweb.org/clarke/bio.html.

1886-1960s. See Funeral Home Records, Jasper County, Iowa **[Online Database]**, indexed at the USGenWeb site for Jasper Co IA. See http://iagenweb.org/jasper/funeral_homes/.

1887 Business Directory, Carroll County **[Online Database]**, indexed at the RootsWeb site for Carroll Co IA. See www.rootsweb.ancestry.com/~iacarrol/data/busdir.htm.

1887 Biographies, Washington County, Iowa **[Online Database]**, indexed at the USGenWeb site for Washington Co IA. See http://freepages.books.rootsweb.ancestry.com/~cooverfamily/album_1b.html.

1887-1888 Iowa State Gazetteer & Business Directory, Calhoun County Extraction **[Online Database]**, indexed at the USGenWeb site for Calhoun Co IA. See http://iagenweb.org/calhoun/records/directories/gazetteer/1888.php.

1888 Newspaper Article, "Log Cabin Reunion," Published Indianola, Warren County, Iowa **[Online Database]**. The article includes a list of "Veterans of 1840," those living in Warren County who had voted for William Henry Harrison in the Presidential election of 1840. The list gives the voter's name, 1840 residence; and for some, their town of residence in Warren County in 1888. The Log Cabin Reunion was a rally held in Indianola to line up support for Benjamin

Harrison in the Presidential Election of 1888. Indexed at the USGenWeb site for Warren Co IA. See http://files.usgwarchives.net/ia/warren/history/1840voters.txt

1889 Biographies, Audubon County, Iowa [Online Database], indexed at the RootsWeb site for Audubon Co IA. See www.rootsweb.ancestry.com/~iabiog/audubon/bh1889/bh1889.htm.

1889 Biographies, Clay County, Iowa [Online Database], indexed at the USGenWeb site for Clay Co IA. See http://iagenweb.org/clay/hist/bibliography.htm.

1889 Biographies, Muscatine County, Iowa [Online Database], indexed at the USGenWeb site for Muscatine Co IA. See http://iagenweb.org/muscatine/biographies1889/contents1889.htm.

1889 Biographies, Shelby County, Iowa [Online Database], indexed at the RootsWeb site for Shelby Co IA. See www.rootsweb.ancestry.com/~iabiog/shelby/bh1889/bh1889.htm.

1889 Petitioners, Clarke County, Iowa [Online Database], indexed at the USGenWeb site for Clarke Co IA. See http://iagenweb.org/clarke/rrpet.html.

1889-1890 Iowa State Gazetteer & Business Directory, Calhoun County Extraction [Online Database], indexed at the USGenWeb site for Calhoun Co IA. See http://iagenweb.org/calhoun/records/directories/gazetteer/1890.php.

1889-1935 City Directories, Council Bluffs, Pottawattamie County, Iowa [Microfilm], from originals by various publishers. Filmed by Research Publications, Woodbridge, CT, c1990. FHL has 11 rolls, beginning with FHL film #2156587 (**1889**, **1892**, **1893** & **1894** Council Bluffs city directory) To see if this microfilm has been digitized yet, see the FHL catalog page: **www.familysearch.org/search/catalog/982742**.

1891 Historical Directory, Davis County, Iowa [Online Database], indexed at the USGenWeb site for Davis Co IA. See http://iagenweb.org/davis/1891historicaldirectory.htm.

1891 Biographies, A-K, Fayette County, Iowa [Online Database], indexed at the USGenWeb site for Fayette Co IA. See http://iagenweb.org/fayette/bios/1891/ndx_A-K.htm.

1891 Biographies, L-O, Fayette County, Iowa [Online Database], indexed at the USGenWeb site for Fayette Co IA. See http://iagenweb.org/fayette/bios/1891/ndx_L-O.htm.

1891 Biographies, P-Z, Fayette County, Iowa [Online Database], indexed at the USGenWeb site for Fayette Co IA. See http://iagenweb.org/fayette/bios/1891/ndx_P-Z.htm.

1891 Newspaper Article, "Pioneer Days in Plymouth County," [Online Database], indexed at the USGenWeb site for Plymouth Co IA. See www.iagenweb.org/plymouth/HistoryCenter/WLClark.html.

1891 Biographies, Pottawattamie County, Iowa [Online Database], indexed at the USGenWeb site for Pottawattamie Co IA. See http://iagenweb.org/pottawattamie/biographiesandfamilyhistories/Bios1891/Bios1891.htm.

1892 Farm Directory. See *Farmers of Iowa: A List of Farmers of Each County With Post Office* [Microfilm & Digital Capture], from the original book published 1892 (publisher not noted). Filmed by the Genealogical Society of Utah, 1978, FHL film #1024846. To access the digital images, see the online FHL catalog page: **www.familysearch.org/search/catalog/198058**.
- See also, *1892 Farm Directories* [Online Databases] for several individual counties, part of a statewide project by the Iowa GenWeb. See **http://iagenweb.org/**.

1892 Plat Book (Landowners), Winnebago County, Iowa [Online Database], indexed at the RootsWeb site for Winnebago Co IA. See www.rootsweb.ancestry.com/~iawinneb/land/surnames_1892.htm.

1892. *History of Osceola County, Iowa* [Online Database], full text at the USGenWeb site for Osceola Co IA. See http://iagenweb.org/osceola/history92/toc.htm.

1892 Tama City Census, Tama County, Iowa [Online Database], indexed at the USGenWeb site for Tama Co IA. See http://iagenweb.org/tama/census/1892tamacensus.html.

1893 Biographies, Crawford County, Iowa [Online Database], indexed at the USGenWeb site for Crawford Co IA. See http://iagenweb.org/crawford/biography/1893bioindex.html.

1893 Biographies, Ida County, Iowa [Online Database], indexed at the USGenWeb site for Ida Co IA. See http://iagenweb.org/ida/bios/bios.htm.

1893 Iowa State Census, Ames, Story County, Iowa [Microfilm & Digital Capture], from originals at the Iowa State Historical Society, Des Moines, IA. Filmed by the Genealogical Society of Utah, c1980, 1 roll, FHL film #1022210. To access the digital images, see the online FHL catalog page: www.familysearch.org/search/catalog/3927.

1893-1899 Death Records, Ida County, Iowa [Online Database], indexed at the USGenWeb site for Ida Co IA. See http://iagenweb.org/ida/births_deaths/births_deaths.html.

1894 Biographies, Clayton County, Iowa [Online Database], indexed at the USGenWeb site for Clayton Co IA. See http://iagenweb.org/clayton/bio94/bio_index94.htm.

1895 Iowa State Census [Microfilm & Digital Capture], from originals at the State Historical Society of Iowa, Des Moines, Iowa. Complete for all counties. The census schedules provide detailed information about persons, similar to the 1885 but adding special questions for military service in the Civil War and the Spanish American War, including the exact company and regiment of service. Also, the 1895 asks for a person's "Religious Belief." Filmed by the Genealogical Society of Utah, 1977. 121 rolls, beginning with FHL film #1021706 (Adair County). To access the digital images, see the online FHL catalog page: www.familysearch.org/search/catalog/388621.
- See also *1895 Iowa State Census* [Online Database], digitized and indexed at the Ancestry.com website. This database contains information from the 1895 Iowa State Census for all counties. Information listed includes the name of every member of the household, their sex, age, birthplace, and location (town and county). This database has 1,934,349 records. See http://search.ancestry.com/search/db.aspx?dbid=7321.
- See also *1895 Iowa State Census* [Online Database], digitized and indexed at the FamilySearch.org website. Includes a name index of the Iowa state census taken in 1895. The population schedule names every person in a household. This database has 2,110,508 records. See https://familysearch.org/search/collection/1803957.

1895-1897. Polk County, Iowa Newspapers, The Record Indexes [Printed Book], compiled by Ankeny Genealogical Society, published by the Iowa Genealogical Society, 1995, 22 pages, FHL book 977.7 A1 No. 262.

1896 County Directory, Warren County, Iowa [Online Database], indexed at the USGenWeb site for Warren Co IA. See http://iagenweb.org/warren/directories/1896Res.htm.

1896 Business Directory, Warren County, Iowa [Online Database], indexed at the USGenWeb site for Warren Co IA. See http://iagenweb.org/warren/directories/directory1896ad.html.

1896-1907 Death Records, Lee County, Iowa [Online Database], indexed at the USGenWeb site for Lee Co IA. See http://iagenweb.org/lee/vr/deaths/index.htm.

1897 History of O'Brien County, Iowa, On-Line Index [Online Database], indexed at the USGenWeb site for O'Brien Co IA. See http://iagenweb.org/obrien/history/1897.htm.

1897 City Directory, Des Moines, Iowa [Online Database], digitized at the Archive.org website. See https://archive.org/details/1897DesMoinesAndPolkCountyIowaCityDirectory.

1897-1904. See *Iowa City Register of Voters, 1897-1904* [Microfilm], from originals at the State Historical Society of Iowa, Des Moines, IA. Filmed by the Genealogical Society of Utah, 1990, 4 rolls, beginning with FHL film #1728631 (Register of voters, ward 1, 1897-1903). For a complete list of roll numbers and contents of each, see the online FHL catalog page for this title: www.familysearch.org/search/catalog/551006.

1897-1898 County Directory, Story County, Iowa [Online Database], indexed at the IA Story site. See http://iastory.com/1898/.

1899 History. See *Biographies and Portraits of the Progressive Men of Iowa: Leaders in Business, Politics and the Professions; Together With an Original and Authentic History of the State* [Printed Book], by B.F. Gue & Benjamin Franklin Shambaugh,

published by Conaway and Shaw, Des Moines, IA, 1899, 2 vols., FHL book 977.7 D3b. For access to a digital version of this book, see the online FHL catalog page for this title:
www.familysearch.org/search/catalog/166616.

1899 Biographies Index, Carroll County, Iowa [Online Database], indexed at the RootsWeb site for Carroll Co IA. See
www.rootsweb.ancestry.com/~iacarroll/reineke/1899idx.htm.

1899 Landowners, Muscatine County, Iowa [Online Database], indexed at the USGenWeb site for Muscatine Co IA. See
http://iagenweb.org/muscatine/atlas/atlas1899intro.htm.

1900. Iowa, 1900 Federal Census: Soundex and Population Schedules [Microfilm & Digital Capture], from the original records held by the Bureau of the Census in the 1940s. After microfilming, Congress allowed the Census Bureau to destroy the originals to free up space for WWII-related files. Filmed on 269 rolls, beginning with FHL film #1243691 (Soundex: A000 August C. thru A252 Fredrick) and FHL film #1240415 (Population schedules: Adair, Adams, and Allamakee Co.-part). To access the digital images (Population Schedules), see the online FHL catalog page:
www.familysearch.org/search/catalog/651832.

1900-1911 Death Roll of Pioneers of Crawford County, Iowa [Online Database], indexed at the USGenWeb site for Crawford Co IA.
http://iagenweb.org/crawford/deaths/xcrdec.html.

1901 Biographies, Fremont County, Iowa [Online Database], indexed at the RootsWeb site for Fremont Co IA. See
www.rootsweb.ancestry.com/~iabiog/fremont/hfmc1901/hfmc1901.htm.

1901 Biography Index, Linn County, Iowa [Online Database], indexed at the RootsWeb site for Linn Co IA. See
www.rootsweb.ancestry.com/~ialinn/bios/1901index.htm.

1901 Historical Atlas, Jasper County, Iowa [Online Database], indexed at the USGenWeb site for Jasper Co IA. See
http://iagenweb.org/jasper/history/1901/.

1901-1919 Iowa State Directories [Microfilm], from originals published by various publishers. Filmed by Research Publications, Inc., Woodbridge, CT, 1980-1984, 9 rolls at FHL, as follows:
- **1901-1902** Polk's Iowa state gazetteer and business directory, FHL film #1759801.
- **1903-1904** Polk's Iowa state gazetteer and business directory, FHL film #1759802.
- **1905-1906** Polk's Iowa state gazetteer and business directory, FHL film #1759803.
- **1908-1909** Polk's Iowa state gazetteer and business directory, FHL film #1759804.
- **1910-1911** Polk's Iowa state gazetteer and business directory, FHL film #1759805.
- **1912-1913** Polk's Iowa state gazetteer and business directory, FHL film #1759806.
- **1914-1915** Polk's Iowa state gazetteer and business directory, FHL film #1759807.
- **1916-1917** Polk's Iowa state gazetteer and business directory, FHL film #1759807.
- **1918-1919** Polk's Iowa state gazetteer and business directory, FHL film #1759808.

To see if this microfilm has been digitized yet, see the FHL catalog page:
www.familysearch.org/search/catalog/527427.

1901-1935 City Directories, Waterloo, Black Hawk County, Iowa [Microfilm], from originals in various libraries and societies. Filmed by Research Publications, Woodbridge, CT, c1980, 5 rolls at FHL, beginning with FHL film #2308832 (**1901**, **1904**, **1906** & **1908** Waterloo city directories). To see if this microfilm has been digitized yet, see the FHL catalog page:
www.familysearch.org/search/catalog/1060629.

1902 Landowners, Harrison County, Iowa [Online Database], indexed at the USGenWeb site for Harrison Co IA. See
http://iagenweb.org/harrison/1902/1902.htm.

1902 Landowners (Township Atlas), Page County, Iowa [Online Database], indexed at the USGenWeb site for Page Co IA. See
http://iagenweb.org/page/atlas/1902/index1.htm.

1902 Landowners (Township Atlas), Pottawattamie County, Iowa [Online Database], indexed at the RootsWeb site for Pottawattamie Co IA. See
www.rootsweb.ancestry.com/~iapcgs/1902index_index.htm.

1902 Landowners (Township Atlas), Story County, Iowa [Online Database], indexed at the IA Story site. See http://genloc.com/1902/.

1903 History. *History of Iowa From the Earliest Time to the Beginning of the Twentieth Century* **[Printed Book & Digital Version],** by Benjamin F. Gue, Contents: Vol. 1: Pioneer period; Vol. 2: Civil War; Vol. 3: from 1866 to 1903; Vol. 4: Iowa biography. Published by Century History Co., New York, NY, 4 vols., includes index. FHL book 977.7H2g. To access a digital version of this book (in 4 vols), see the online FHL catalog page:
www.familysearch.org/search/catalog/166700.

1903. *Excerpts from the History of Iowa for Webster, County, Iowa* **[Online Database],** text at the USGenWeb site for Webster Co IA. See
http://files.usgwarchives.net/ia/webster/history/1903webs.txt.

1903 *Biographies, Monroe County, Iowa* **[Online Database],** indexed at the USGenWeb site for Monroe Co IA. See
http://iagenweb.org/monroe/Bios/bio.html.

1903-1935 *City Directories, Cedar Rapids, Linn County, Iowa* **[Microfilm],** from the originals by various publishers. Filmed by Research Publications, Woodbridge, CT. ca1980. FHL has 8 rolls, beginning with FHL film #2308784 (**1903, 1904, 1906 & 1907** Cedar Rapids city directory). To see if this microfilm has been digitized yet, see the FHL catalog page:
www.familysearch.org/search/catalog/1049272.

1904 *Business Directory, Hamilton County, Iowa* **[Online Database],** indexed at the USGenWeb site for Hamilton Co IA. See
http://files.usgwarchives.net/ia/hamilton/history/misc/hambd1904.txt.

1904-1951. *Iowa Death Records* **[Online Database],** digitized and indexed at FamilySearch.org. From records held by the State Historical Society of Iowa. This database has 475,273 images, see
www.familysearch.org/search/collection/2531337.

1905 *Iowa State Census Schedules* **[Microfilm & Digital Capture],** from the original records located at the State Historical Society of Iowa, Des Moines, Iowa. Includes name of each member of a family, age, nativity, time in US, time in Iowa, nativity of parents, and extensive military information, including branch of service, company, regiment, and war. Filmed by the Genealogical Society of Utah, 1985, 453 rolls, beginning with FHL film #1430251 (Adair County). To access the digital images, see the online FHL catalog page: www.familysearch.org/search/catalog/486033.

- See also, *Iowa, State Census, 1905* **[Online Database],** digitized and indexed at the FamilySearch.org website. Index and images of the Iowa state census taken in 1905. Each individual was recorded on a single card which includes name, age, and place of birth. The cards are filed alphabetically by county, then by surname of the individual. The population schedule names every person in the household. See
https://familysearch.org/search/collection/2126961.

- See also, *Iowa, State Census, 1905* **[Online Database],** digitized and indexed at the Ancestry.com website. This 1905 database was acquired by Ancestry.com from FamilySearch and is separate from Ancestry's combined series, *Iowa State Census, 1836-1925*. This database has 2,171,126 records. See
https://search.ancestry.com/search/db.aspx?dbid=60725.

1905 *Iowa State Census, Buena Vista County, Iowa* **[Online Database],** indexed at the USGenWeb site for Buena Vista Co IA. See
http://iagenweb.org/census/buenavista/.

1905 *Iowa State Census, Crawford County, Iowa* **[Online Database],** indexed at the USGenWeb site for Crawford Co IA. See
http://iagenweb.org/crawford/census/1905censusx.html.

1905 *Iowa State Census Index, Fremont County, Iowa* **[Online Database],** indexed at the USGenWeb site for Fremont Co IA. See
http://iagenweb.org/fremont/census/index.html.

1905 *Iowa State Census Index, O'Brien County, Iowa* **[Online Database],** originally indexed at the USGenWeb site for O'Brien Co IA. For an archived version, see
http://iagenweb.org/obrien/census/1905/Census_TOC.htm.

1905 *Iowa State Census Register* **[Microfilm],** from the originals at the State Historical Society of Iowa, Des Moines. Taken from the full census schedules, the *Census Register* is a series of cards, organized by township within each county, showing a page number, surname, first name, post office, township, and town or city. The Register provides a quicker look-up of names in the full census schedules. Filmed by the Genealogical Society of Utah, 1978, 45 rolls, beginning with FHL film #1026366 (Adair and Adams counties). To see if this microfilm has been digitized yet, see the FHL catalog page:
www.familysearch.org/search/catalog/411798

1905 Iowa State Census Register, Buena Vista County, Iowa [Online Database], indexed at the USGenWeb site for Buena Vista Co IA. See http://iagenweb.org/census/buenavista/.

1905 Iowa State Census Register, Story County, Iowa [Online Database], indexed at the IA Story site. See http://genloc.com/1905/index.htm.

1906 Farmers Directory, Ida County, Iowa [Online Database], indexed at the USGenWeb site for Ida Co IA. See http://iagenweb.org/ida/directories/1906/1906twp.htm.

1906 Biographies, Mahaska County, Iowa [Online Database], indexed at the USGenWeb site for Mahaska Co IA. See http://iagenweb.org/mahaska/past/index.html.

1906-1907 Farmers & Business Directory, Plymouth County, Iowa [Online Database], indexed at the USGenWeb site for Plymouth Co IA. See http://files.usgwarchives.net/ia/plymouth/history/.

1907 Biographies, Dallas County, Iowa [Online Database], indexed at the RootsWeb site for Dallas Co IA. See www.rootsweb.ancestry.com/~iabiog/dallas/pp1907/pp1907in-a.htm.

1908 Historical Atlas of Sioux County, Iowa [Online Database], surname index to each section at the USGenWeb site for Sioux Co IA. See http://iagenweb.org/sioux/Atlas1908/at1908_index.htm.

1909 Old Settlers Association, Buena Vista County, Iowa [Online Database], indexed at the USGenWeb site for Buena Vista Co IA. See http://iagenweb.org/buenavista/History/OldSettlersAssociation/OldSettlers1.html.

1910. *Iowa, 1910 Federal Census: Population Schedules* [Microfilm & Digital Capture], from the original records held by the Bureau of the Census in the 1940s. After microfilming, Congress allowed the Census Bureau to destroy the originals to free up space for WWII-related files. Filmed on 41 rolls, beginning with FHL film #1374403 (Population schedules: Adair, Adams, Allamakee, and Appanoose Co-part). To access the digital images (Population Schedules), see the online FHL catalog page: www.familysearch.org/search/catalog/653183.

1910. See *Iowa 1910 U.S. Federal Census Index* [CD-ROM], compiled and published by Heritage Quest, Bountiful, UT, 2002, FHL CD#973.

1911 Farmers Directory, Calhoun County, Iowa [Online Database], indexed at the USGenWeb site for Calhoun Co IA. See http://iagenweb.org/calhoun/records/directories/farmers/1911.php.

1911 Biographies, Crawford County, Iowa [Online Database], indexed at the USGenWeb site for Crawford Co IA. See http://iagenweb.org/crawford/biography/1911bioindex.html.

1911 Farmers Directory, Grundy County, Iowa [Online Database], indexed at the USGenWeb site for Grundy Co IA. See http://iagenweb.org/grundy/land/landowners1911.html.

1911 Farm Directory, Mitchell County, Iowa [Online Database], indexed in alpha groups at the USGenWeb site for Mitchell Co IA. See http://files.usgwarchives.net/ia/mitchell/history/.

1911 Biographies, Muscatine County, Iowa [Online Database], indexed at the USGenWeb site for Muscatine Co IA. See http://iagenweb.org/muscatine/biographies1911/1911contents.htm.

1911-1912 Directory, Henry County, Iowa [Online Database], indexed at the Celtic Cousins site for Henry Co IA. See www.celticcousins.net/henry/1911to1912dir.htm.

1912 Biographies, Carroll County, Iowa [Online Database], indexed at the RootsWeb site for Carroll Co IA. See www.rootsweb.ancestry.com/~iacarrol/bios/1912indx.htm.

1914 Biographies, Butler County, Iowa [Online Database], indexed at the USGenWeb site for Butler Co IA. See http://iagenweb.org/butler/bios/bio_index-1914.htm.

1914 Biographies, Franklin County, Iowa [Online Database], indexed at the USGenWeb site for Franklin Co IA. See http://iagenweb.org/franklin/1914Biographies/1914Biography_index.htm.

1914 Atlas and Directory of Rural Taxpayers, Linn County, Iowa **[Online Database]**, indexed at the USGenWeb site for Linn Co IA. See www.usgennet.org/usa/ia/county/linn/census/1914/index.htm.

1914 County Directories, Osceola County, Iowa [Online Database], indexed at the USGenWeb Site for Osceola Co IA. See www.iagenweb.org/osceola/dir/dir.htm

1914-1924. *Iowa, Polk County Probate Records* **[Online Database]**, indexed at the FamilySearch.org website. Source: State Historical Society of Iowa, Des Moines. This is an image-only database of probate case files in loose paper format. Browse through the images, organized by Record Type, Volume, and Year Range. This database has 157,848 images. See www.familysearch.org/search/collection/2138591.

1915 Iowa State Census **[Microfilm & Digital Capture]**, from the extant census records located at the State Historical Society of Iowa, Des Moines, Iowa. The 1915 census name lists were prepared on cards and organized alphabetically within each county. Cards that were illegible or that contained only a first name appear at the beginning of each county under the heading "miscellaneous." There are a number of duplicate filming of various counties included in the set. The 1915 census gives a name for each member of a family, relationship to head, age, occupation, total earnings, birthplace, if foreign born, if naturalized, years in Iowa and U.S., marital status, etc. Filmed by the Genealogical Society of Utah, 1985-1986, 1989, 583 rolls, beginning with FHL film #1379445 (Adair County, Abbott, A. – Fredricks, J.). To access the digital images, see the online FHL catalog page: www.familysearch.org/search/catalog/539259.

- See also, *Iowa, State Census, 1915* **[Online Database]**, digitized and indexed at the Ancestry.com website. Included with Ancestry's combined series, *Iowa State Census, 1836-1925*. See http://search.ancestry.com/search/db.aspx?dbid=1084.

- See also *Iowa State Census, 1915* **[Online Database]**, digitized and indexed at the FamilySearch.org website. Source: State Historical Society of Iowa, Des Moines. Each index record includes: Name, Event type, Event date, Event place, Gender, Age, Marital Status, Race, Birth year, Birthplace, Father's birthplace, and Mother's birthplace. The card image may have more information. This database has 2,574,691 records. See www.familysearch.org/search/collection/2240483.

1915. *Index of "History of Adair County and its People,"* [Online Database], indexed at the USGenWeb site for Adair Co IA. See http://iagenweb.org/adair/history/1915index.htm.

1916 Biographies, Clayton County, Iowa [Online Database], indexed at the USGenWeb site for Clayton Co IA. See http://iagenweb.org/clayton/bio16/bio_index16.htm.

1916 Farmers Directory, Tama County, Iowa [Online Database], indexed at the USGenWeb site for Tama Co IA. See http://iagenweb.org/tama/family/farmdir.html.

1916-1917 Iowa State Gazetteer & Business Directory, Calhoun County Extraction [Online Database], indexed at the USGenWeb site for Calhoun Co IA. See http://iagenweb.org/calhoun/records/directories/gazetteer/1917.php.

1916-1951 Naturalization Records, Wapello County, Iowa [Online Database], indexed at the USGenWeb Site for Wapello Co IA. See http://iagenweb.org/wapello/Natural.htm.

1917 Farmers Directory, Benton County, Iowa [Online Database], indexed at the USGenWeb site for Benton Co IA. See http://iagenweb.org/benton/1917_atlas/1917_index.htm.

1917-1918. See *Soldiers who Served in World War I from Wright County, Iowa* [Online Database], indexed at the USGenWeb site for Wright Co IA. See http://iagenweb.org/wright/WorldWarISOLDIERS.htm.

1917-1918. See *The Scott County Honor Roll: List of Soldiers, Sailors, and Nurses Who Died in the Service* [Online Database], indexed at the RootsWeb site for Scott Co IA. See www.rootsweb.ancestry.com/~iascott/ww1dead.htm.

1918 Landowners, Hamilton County, Iowa [Online Database], indexed at the USGenWeb site for Hamilton Co IA. See http://iagenweb.org/hamilton/dir/1918landowners_index.html.

1918 Township Maps (Landowners), Pocahontas County, Iowa [Online Database], indexed at the USGenWeb site for Pocahontas Co IA. See http://iagenweb.org/pocahontas/townshipandmaps/1918index.htm.

1918 Draft Registrations, Ida County, Iowa [Online Database], indexed at the USGenWeb site for Ida Co IA. See http://iagenweb.org/ida/military/draft.htm.

1918. *"Soldiers Going to Camp Dodge," from a Mitchell County, Iowa Newspaper* [Online Database], indexed at the USGenWeb site for Mitchell Co IA. See. http://iagenweb.org/mitchell/military/wwi_troo.htm.

1918 Biographies, Mitchell County, Iowa [Online Database], indexed at the RootsWeb site for Mitchell Co IA. See www.rootsweb.ancestry.com/~iaworth/data/worvol2.htm.

1918-1919 Iowa State Gazetteer & Business Directory, Calhoun County Extraction [Online Database], indexed at the USGenWeb site for Calhoun Co IA. See http://iagenweb.org/calhoun/records/directories/gazetteer/1919.php.

1919 Biographies, Chickasaw and Howard Counties, Iowa [Online Database], indexed at the USGenWeb site for Howard Co IA. See http://iagenweb.org/howard/history/volume_two.html.

1919 Farmers Directory, Clay County, Iowa [Online Database], indexed at the USGenWeb site for Clay Co IA. See http://iagenweb.org/clay/farmers/1919ndx.html.

1919 Rural Residents, Muscatine County, Iowa [Online Database], indexed at the USGenWeb site for Muscatine Co IA. See http://iagenweb.org/muscatine/residents1919.htm.

1920. *Iowa, 1920 Federal Census: Soundex and Population Schedules* [Microfilm & Digital Capture], from the original records held by the Bureau of the Census in the 1940s. After microfilming, Congress allowed the Census Bureau to destroy the originals to free up space for WWII-related files. Filmed on 227 rolls, beginning with FHL film #1825030 (Soundex: A000 A.H. thru A261) and FHL film #1820476 (Population schedules: Adair, Audubon, Adams, and Allamakee counties.) To access the digital images, see the online FHL catalog page: www.familysearch.org/search/catalog/568294.

1920 Farmers Directory, Crawford County, Iowa [Online Database], indexed at the USGenWeb site for Crawford Co IA. See http://iagenweb.org/crawford/landowner/indx1920.html.

1920 Merchants, Tradesmen & Manufacturers, Davis County, Iowa **[Online Database]**, indexed at the USGenWeb site for Davis Co IA. See http://iagenweb.org/davis/merchants.htm.

1920 Merchants, Tradesmen & Manufacturers, Wapello County, Iowa **[Online Database]**, indexed at the USGenWeb site for Wapello Co IA. See http://iagenweb.org/wapello/1920Merchants.htm.

1920-1921 & 1923-1933. *Death Certificate Index, Wapello County, Iowa* **[Online Database]**, this downloadable PDF listing has over 6,200 deaths; and for each, includes a Name, Birth Date, Death Date, County (Wapello), Mother's Maiden Name, File No. & Box No., available at the USGenWeb site for Wapello Co IA. See http://iagenweb.org/wapello/Deaths_1923to1933.pdf.

1920-1940. *Iowa, Death Records* **[Online Database]**, indexed at the Ancestry.com website. Source: State Historical Society of Iowa, Des Moines. Each index record includes: Name, Gender, Age, Birth year, Death date, Death place, Father, Mother, and Spouse. This database has 1,708,424 records. See https://search.ancestry.com/search/db.aspx?dbid=61442.

1921-1935. *Cedar Rapids Record of Deaths* **[Microfilm & Digital Capture]**, from originals at the Linn County Courthouse, Cedar Rapids, IA. Filmed by the Genealogical Society of Utah, 1990, 1 roll, FHL film #1728034. To access the digital images, see the online FHL catalog page: www.familysearch.org/search/catalog/608905.

1921-1940. *Iowa, Death Records* **[Online Database]**, digitized and indexed at the FamilySearch.org website. Source: State Historical Society of Iowa, Des Moines. Each index record includes: Name, Event type, Event date, Event place, Gender, Age, Birth year, Father's name, Mother's name, Spouse's name, and Certificate number. The full death certificate image may have more information. This database has 516,904 records. See www.familysearch.org/search/collection/2531337.

1921-1942. *Iowa, Birth Records* **[Online Database]**, digitized and indexed at FamilySearch.org. From records at the State Historical Society of Iowa, includes birth records from all Iowa counties. See www.familysearch.org/search/collection/2849548.

1922 Patrons, Atlas of Wapello County, Iowa **[Online Database]**, indexed at the USGenWeb site for Wapello Co IA. See http://iagenweb.org/wapello/1922_wapello_county_iowa_patrons.htm.

1922 Farmers of Harrison County, Iowa **[Online Database]**, indexed at the USGenWeb site for Harrison Co IA. See http://iagenweb.org/harrison/1922/1922.htm.

1923 Farmers Directory, Ida County, Iowa **[Online Database]**, indexed at the USGenWeb site for Ida Co IA. See http://iagenweb.org/ida/directories/1923/1923directory.htm.

1923 City Directory, Mason City, Cerro Gordo County, Iowa **[Online Database]**. originally indexed at the Distant Cousin website. For an archived database, see https://web.archive.org/web/20160428003227/http://distantcousin.com/Directories/IA/MasonCity/1923/.

1924 Telephone Directory, Lee County, Iowa **[Online Database]**, indexed at the USGenWeb site for Lee Co IA. See http://iagenweb.org/lee/directories/index.htm.

1925 Iowa State Census **[Microfilm & Digital Capture]**, from original records at the State Historical Society of Iowa, Des Moines, IA. In addition to a person's name, age, marital status, and nativity, this census recorded the full names of each person's parents – the only census ever taken by any state to give a *Father's Name* and *Mother's Maiden Name* for every person listed. Then, incredibly, the 1925 Iowa state census adds the age of both parents, their place of marriage, and where each were born. (Iowa researchers have discovered that when a parent's age is missing, it usually means that parent was deceased). The 1925 also gives religion, details about military service, and more. This was the most comprehensive and final state census taken by the state of Iowa. Filmed by the State Historical Society of Iowa, 1976, 434 rolls, beginning with FHL film #1429191 (Adair County). To access the digital images, see the online FHL catalog page: www.familysearch.org/search/catalog/501121.
- See also, *Iowa, State Census, 1925* **[Online Database]**, digitized and indexed at the Ancestry.com website. Included with Ancestry's combined series,

Iowa State Census, 1836-1925. See the microfilm description for details. See http://search.ancestry.com/search/db.aspx?dbid=1084.

- See also, *Iowa State Census, 1925* [Online Database], digitized and indexed at the FamilySearch.org website. Source: State Historical Society of Iowa, Des Moines. Each index record includes: Name, Event type, Event date, Event place, Gender, Age, Marital Status, Relationship to Head of Household, and Birth year. The full schedule (7 pages) image will add extensive information. See the microfilm description for more details. This database has 2,487,170 records. See www.familysearch.org/search/collection/2224537.

- See also, *1925 Iowa State Census Index (for Selected Cities)* [Microfilm], for residents of selected cities, from the original records at the State Historical Society of Iowa, Des Moines, Iowa. Arranged by city, then alphabetically by surname. Index lists name, address, book/line (from schedules), county of residence, for the following cities:
- **Boone** (Boone Co.).
- **Cedar Falls** (Black Hawk Co.).
- **Centerville** (Appanoose Co.),
- **Cedar Rapids** (Linn Co.).
- **Clinton** (Clinton Co.).
- **Council Bluffs** (Pottawattamie Co.).
- **Dubuque** (Dubuque Co.).
- **Ottumwa** (Wapello Co.).
- **Sioux City** (Woodbury Co.).
- **Waterloo** (Black Hawk Co.).
- **Davenport** (Scott Co.).
- **Des Moines** (Polk Co.).

Filmed by the State Historical Society of Iowa, Des Moines, IA, 1980, 29 rolls, beginning with FHL film #1430705 (Boone, Cedar Falls, Centerville, & Cedar Rapids, pt. 1). To see if this microfilm has been digitized yet, see the FHL catalog page: www.familysearch.org/search/catalog/494967.

1925 Iowa State Census, Butler County, Iowa [Online Database], indexed at the USGenWeb site for Butler Co IA. See http://iagenweb.org/census/butler/1925/.

1925 Iowa State Census, Crawford County, Iowa [Online Database], indexed at the USGenWeb site for Crawford Co IA. See http://iagenweb.org/crawford/census/1925censuscontents.html.

1925 Iowa State Census Index, Iowa City, Johnson County, Iowa [Online Database], indexed at the US GenWeb site for Johnson Co IA. See http://iagenweb.org/johnson/census/1925ICcensus/1925ICcensusA.htm.

1925 Iowa State Census Index, Johnson County (Except Iowa City), Iowa [Online Database], indexed at the US GenWeb site for Johnson Co IA: http://iagenweb.org/johnson/census/1925JCCensus/1925JC-A.HTM.

1925 Iowa State Census, Muscatine County, Iowa [Online Database], indexed at the USGenWeb site for Muscatine Co IA. http://iagenweb.org/muscatine/1925census/index-census1925.htm.

1925 Iowa State Census Index, O'Brien County, Iowa [Online Database], originally indexed at the USGenWeb site for O'Brien Co IA. For an archived version, see http://web.archive.org/web/20080724153738/http://iagenweb.org/obrien/1925/Census_TOC.htm.

1925 Iowa State Census, Story County, Iowa [Online Database], indexed at the IA Story site. See http://iastory.org/1925/.

1925 Iowa State census, Taylor County, Iowa [Online Database], indexed by township at the USGenWeb site for Taylor Co IA. See http://iagenweb.org/taylor/census/1925/index.htm.

1925 Iowa State Census, Webster County, Iowa [Printed Book], compiled by Webster County Genealogical Society, researched and typed by Marion Martin Pliner, published by the Iowa Genealogical Society, Des Moines, Iowa, 1994. Contains an index arranged in alphabetical order by surname of persons in each household, and book number of original census. FHL book 977.751 X22w 1925, and FHL film #2055296.

1930. *Iowa, 1920 Federal Census: Population Schedules* [Microfilm & Digital Capture], from the original records held by the Bureau of the Census in the 1940s. After microfilming, Congress allowed the Census Bureau to destroy the originals to free up space for WWII-related files. Filmed on 52 rolls, beginning with FHL film #2340375 (Population schedules: Adair, Audubon, Adams, and Allamakee counties). To access the digital images (Population Schedules), see the online FHL catalog page: www.familysearch.org/search/catalog/1035340.

1930-1949 Naturalizations, Union County, Iowa [Online Database], indexed at the USGenWeb site for Union Co IA. See http://files.usgwarchives.net/ia/union/court/unionnat.txt.

1930-1981 Obituaries, Ames, Story County, Iowa **[Microfilm]**, from original manuscripts at the City Clerk's Office, Ames, IA. Obituaries are listed alphabetically by name of deceased. Filmed by the Genealogical Society of Utah, 1986, 8 rolls, beginning with FHL film #1462778 (Aasheim, Raymond – Carlsen, Lillian). To see if this microfilm has been digitized yet, see the FHL catalog page: www.familysearch.org/search/catalog/478748.

1934-1937 Old Age Assistance Tax List **[Online Database]**, indexed at the USGenWeb site for Davis Co IA. See
http://iagenweb.org/davis/tax_list.htm.

1934-1946. *Iowa, Old Age Assistance Records* **[Online Database]**, indexed at the FamilySearch.org website. Source: FamilySearch extractions from various county auditor's records. This database is an Index to old-age tax records captured in fifty-five counties. These records include principal name, date, and place of birth; parents' names; and contemporary addresses. The birth information is especially significant as it applies to Iowa settlers who may not appear in regular birth records. This database has 546,417 records. See
www.familysearch.org/search/collection/2573700.

1937 Farm Directory, Decatur County, Iowa **[Online Database]**, indexed at the USGenWeb site for Decatur Co IA. See
http://iagenweb.org/decatur/directories/FarmDirectory1937index.html.

1938-1940s. See *Biographical Sketches of Iowans* **[Microfilm]**, from a typescript by the Citizens Historical Association (Indianapolis), filmed by the Genealogical Society of Utah, 1976, 3 rolls, as follows:
- Biographies, A – Choate, FHL film # 985407.
- Biographies, Choate – Stampfer, FHL film #985408.
- Biographies, Stampfer – Z, FHL film #985409.

To see if this microfilm has been digitized yet, see the FHL catalog page:
www.familysearch.org/search/catalog/49887.

1939 Farmers Directory, Clinton County, Iowa **[Online Database]**, indexed at the USGenWeb site for Clinton Co IA. See
http://files.usgwarchives.net/ia/clinton/history/dir/1939farm.txt.

1940. *The Iowa Press Association's Who's Who in Iowa: a Biographical Record of Iowa's Leaders in Business, Professional and Public Life* **[Microfilm & Digital Capture]**, from the original book published by the Iowa Press Association, Des Moines, IA, 1940, 1,361 pages, filmed by the W.C. Cox Co., Tucson, AZ, 1974, FHL film #934929. To access the digital images, see the online FHL catalog page:
www.familysearch.org/search/catalog/316526.

1940 Iowa Federal Census: Population Schedules **[Digital Capture]**, digitized images and every-name index taken from the microfilm of original records held by the Bureau of the Census in the 1940s. After microfilming, Congress allowed the Census Bureau to destroy the originals to free up space for WWII-related files. Digitizing of the 1940 census schedules microfilm images was done for the National Archives and made public on April 2, 2012. No microfilm copies were distributed. To access the digital images, see the online FHL catalog page:
www.familysearch.org/search/catalog/2057755.

1940 Federal Census Finding Aids **[Online Database]**. The National Archives prepared a special website online with a detailed description of the 1940 federal census. Included at the site are descriptions of location finding aids, such as Enumeration District maps, Geographic Descriptions of Census Enumeration Districts, and a list of 1940 City Directories available at the National Archives. The finding aids are all linked to other National Archives sites. The National Archives website also has a link to 1940 Search Engines using Stephen P. Morse's "One-Step" system for finding a 1940 E.D. or street address conversion. See
www.archives.gov/research/census/1940/general-info.html#questions.

1940 Telephone Directory, Pocahontas County, Iowa **[Online Database]**, indexed at the USGenWeb site for Pocahontas Co IA. See
http://iagenweb.org/pocahontas/1940pkyphone.htm

1941 WPA Survey. See *Guide to Public Vital Statistics Records in Iowa* **[Printed Book]**, prepared by the Iowa Historical Records Survey, Division of Community Service Programs, Work Projects Administration, published 1941, Des Moines, IA, 113

pages, FHL book 977.7 V2h. For access to a digital version of this book, see the online FHL catalog page for this title:
www.familysearch.org/search/catalog/2727869.

1941-1945. See *Webster County Citizens in World War II* **[Online Database]**, text at the USGenWeb site for Webster Co IA. See
http://web.archive.org/web/20081010132319/http://iagenweb.org/webster/wwii.htm.

1942. *(Iowa) U.S. World War II Draft Registrations Cards, 1942* **[Online Database],** digitized and indexed at the Ancestry.com website. Source: WWII Fourth Registration, Selective Service System records at the National Archives. The entire U.S. is indexed by surname, location, keyword, etc., but you can browse the images just for Iowa, within a surname range, e.g., Dittmer, Henry – Donini, Luigi. Each index record includes: Name, Gender, Race, Age, Birth date, Birth place, Residence date, and Residence place. This database has 15,283,470 records. See
https://search.ancestry.com/search/db.aspx?dbid=1002.

1946. *World War II Honor Roll, Hancock County, Iowa* **[Online Database]**, indexed at the USGenWeb site for Hancock Co IA. See
http://iagenweb.org/hancock/military/WWII.html.

1947-1954. *Iowa, World War II Bonus Case Files* **[Online Database],** digitized and indexed at the Ancestry.com website. Source: State Historical Society of Iowa, Des Moines. In May 1947, the Iowa Legislature approved bonus payments of up to $500 for men and women who served on active duty in the U.S. armed forces between 16 September 1940 and 2 September 1945. To qualify, applicants had to be legal residents of Iowa for at least the six months prior to their service. This database contains applications for those payments. Information on the forms includes name, birth date and place, place of residence for six months prior to enlistment or induction, and address where a check could be sent. This database has 240,951 records. See
https://search.ancestry.com/search/db.aspx?dbid=8825.
- See also *Iowa, World War II Bonus Case Files for Beneficiaries, 1947-1959* **[Online Database],** indexed at the Ancestry.com website. This database is a separate listing of applicants for the WWII bonus from beneficiaries of veterans. This database has 19,760 records. See
https://search.ancestry.com/search/db.aspx?dbid=61186.

1948 Farm Directory, Pocahontas County, Iowa **[Online Database]**, originally indexed at the USGenWeb site for Pocahontas Co IA. For an archived version, see
http://web.archive.org/web/20120402032940/http://iagenweb.org/pocahontas/1948resa.html.

1951 Jurors, Hardin County, Iowa **[Online Database]**, indexed at the USGenWeb site for Hardin Co IA. See
http://iagenweb.org/hardin/HCJURORS.HTM.

1951 Telephone Directory, Pocahontas County, Iowa **[Online Database]**, indexed at the USGenWeb site for Pocahontas Co IA. See
http://iagenweb.org/pocahontas/1951phone.htm.

1961 Farmers Directory, Calhoun County, Iowa **[Online Database]**, indexed at the USGenWeb site for Calhoun Co IA. Included are 1961 Plat Maps from this directory. See
http://iagenweb.org/calhoun/records/directories/farmers/1961.php.

1962 Farm Directory Township Maps, Keokuk County, Iowa **[Online Database]**, indexed at the USGenWeb site for Keokuk Co IA. See
http://iagenweb.org/keokuk/directories/1962farmdirectory.htm.

1962 Farm Directory, Mitchell County, Iowa **[Online Database]**, indexed at the USGenWeb site for Mitchell Co IA. See
http://iagenweb.org/mitchell/data/1962fdir.htm.

1963 Rural Residents of Worth County, Iowa **[Online Database],** indexed at the USGenWeb site for Worth Co IA. See
http://files.usgwarchives.net/ia/worth/history/rurwor63.txt.

1965 Rural Directory, Humboldt County, Iowa **[Online Database]**, indexed at the USGenWeb site for Humboldt Co IA. See
http://iagenweb.org/humboldt/ruraldirectory1963.html.

1965-1966 Farm Directory, Dubuque County, Iowa **[Online Database]**, indexed at the USGenWeb site for Dubuque Co IA. See
http://iagenweb.org/dubuque/directories/1965-1966farm.htm.

1966 Farm Directory, Pocahontas County, Iowa **[Online Database],** indexed at the USGenWeb site for Pocahontas Co IA. See
http://iagenweb.org/pocahontas/ruralres.htm.

1967 Farm & Ranch Directory, Delaware County, Iowa **[Online Database]**, indexed at the USGenWeb site for Delaware Co IA. See
http://iagenweb.org/delaware/directories/1967/index.htm.

1972 Farm Directory, Pocahontas County, Iowa **[Online Database],** indexed at the USGenWeb site for Pocahontas Co IA. See
http://iagenweb.org/pocahontas/1972res.htm.

1973 Farm Directory, Pocahontas County, Iowa **[Online Database]**, indexed at the USGenWeb site for Pocahontas Co IA. See
http://iagenweb.org/pocahontas/1973res.htm.

1975 County Directory, O'Brien County, Iowa **[Online Database]**, originally indexed at the USGenWeb site for O'Brien Co IA. For an archived version, see
http://web.archive.org/web/20080704155429/http://iagenweb.org/obrien/1973_Directory/Main.htm.

1975 Universal Directory, Lyon County, Iowa **[Online Database]**, indexed at the USGenWeb site for Lyon Co IA. See
http://iagenweb.org/lyon/miscellaneous/rdir1975.htm.

1988 Rural Residents of Worth County, Iowa **[Online Database],** indexed at the USGenWeb site for Worth Co IA. See
http://files.usgwarchives.net/ia/worth/history/1988list.txt.

1992-2008. *Iowa, Divorce Index* **[Online Database]**, indexed at the Ancestry.com website. Source: IA Bureau of Vital Statistics, Des Moines. This database is an index to over 64,000 divorce cases filed in Iowa from 1992-2008. Each index record includes: Husband's name, Wife's name, Divorce date, and county. This database has 128,978 records. See
https://search.ancestry.com/search/db.aspx?dbid=61022.

1992-Current. *Iowa Recent Newspaper Obituaries* **[Online Database]**, digitized and indexed newspaper obituaries at the GenealogyBank website, including newspapers from Adel, Algona, Ames, Anamosa, Atlantic, Bettendorf, Boone, Burlington, Cedar Rapids, Centerville, Charles City, Clarinda, Clinton, Council Bluffs, Creston, Davenport, Decorah, Denison, Dubuque, Fairfield, Forest City, Fort Madison, Glenwood, Hamburg, Kalona, Keokuk, Knoxville, Logan, Lone Tree, , Mason City, Mount Pleasant, Muscatine, Nevada, New Hampton, Newton, Osage, Osceola, Oskaloosa, Ottumwa, Pella, Perry, Red Oak, Riverside, Shenandoah, Sioux City, Story City, Washington, and Waterloo. See
www.genealogybank.com/gbnk/obituaries/explore/USA/Iowa/.

224 • *Census Substitutes & State Census Records*

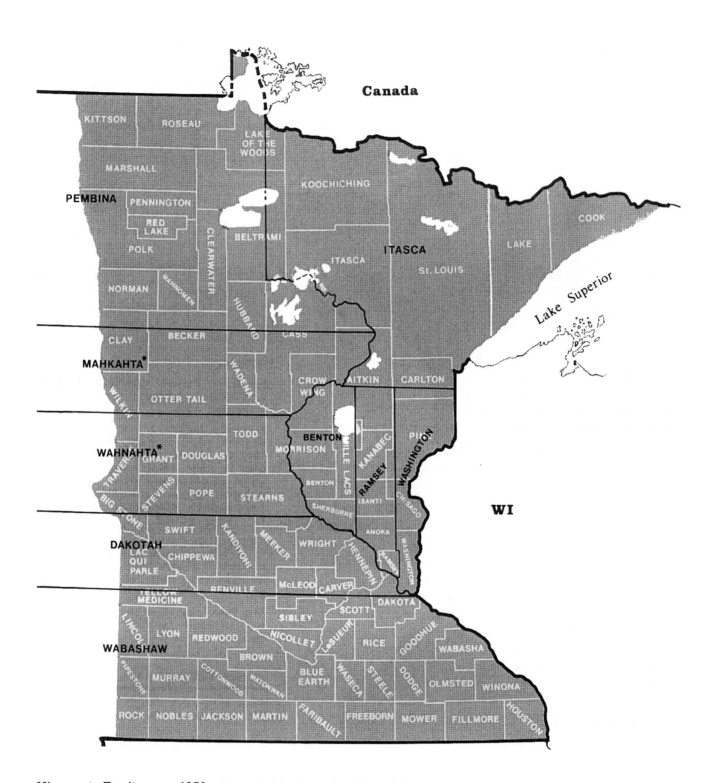

Minnesota Territory • 1850. Shown in black are the nine original counties of Minnesota Territory at the time of the 1850 Federal Census. The 87 current Minnesota counties are shown in white. In 1851, both Mankatah and Wahnahta counties were dissolved, their areas included in Pembina and a newly formed Cass County. Minnesota Territory's western boundary was the Missouri River (not shown). Minnesota became a state in 1858 with the same boundaries as today.

Minnesota
Censuses & Substitute Name Lists

Historical Timeline for Minnesota, 1612-1858

1612-1615. French explorers Etienne Brule and Samuel de Champlain were the first Europeans to see the Great Lakes. Brule explored Lake Huron in 1612. He was followed by Champlain in 1615.

1682. French Louisiana. René-Robert Cavelier (Sieur de LaSalle) erected a cross near the confluence of the Mississippi River and the Gulf of Mexico, after floating down river from the Illinois Country. He claimed the entire Mississippi Basin for Louis XIV of France, for whom Louisiana was named. All of the rivers and streams flowing into the Mississippi were part of the Mississippi Basin and included in the Louisiana claim.

1717. French Louisiana. The Illinois Country was officially added to the French Louisiana jurisdiction within New France. At that time *la Louisiane Française* extended from the Wabash River, down the Ohio and Mississippi Rivers to include several ports on the Gulf of Mexico. Any trading posts or forts north of the Highlands (Terra Haute) were administered as part of French Québec.

1763. Treaty of Paris. This was the end of the French and Indian war. (In Europe it was called the "Seven Years War.") At the 1763 Treaty, the French surrendered all their claims in North America. Spain acquired the former French areas west of the Mississippi, renamed *Spanish Louisiana*. Great Britain gained all of Québec, which they immediately renamed the *Province of Canada*. Britain also gained control of the rest of North America east of the Mississippi River, including an exchange with Spain, wherein Britain swapped Cuba for Florida. They immediately divided it into West Florida and East Florida, then named their entire area *British North America*.

1774. Québec Act. In response to increased American colonial rebellions, the British sought to solidify loyalty from their French communities in British Canada. The British Parliament passed the Québec Act, which restored the name Québec, allowed the French Canadians to retain French laws and customs, and permitted the Catholic Church to maintain all of its rights. The early French settlements in the Great Lakes region were by the act included in the Province of Québec, now under British rule.

1783. The Treaty of Paris recognized the United States of America as an independent nation and defined its borders from the Atlantic Ocean to the Mississippi River. Although the settlements in the Great Lakes region (formerly part of the Province of Québec) were to be included within the United States, British military forces continued to maintain control over parts of the Great Lakes area for several years after the Revolution. Notably, Fort Detroit remained in British control until 1796. And, Prairie du Chien, on the Mississippi River at the mouth of the Wisconsin River, was a strategic post that did not become American until after the War of 1812. The Isle Royale in Lake Superior was a mustering point for the British and their allied Indians, and also remained in British control until after the War of 1812.

1784. Ohio Country. New York, Connecticut, Virginia, and Massachusetts relinquished their claim to lands in the Ohio Country. Title transferred to the "public domain" of the United States Government. Connecticut retained ownership of the "Western Reserve" on Lake Erie, then later sold the tract to the

Connecticut Land Company. Virginia retained ownership of the "Virginia Military District."

1787. Jul 13. Northwest Territory. The Ordinance of 1787 established the "Territory Northwest of the River Ohio," and defined the procedure for any territory to obtain statehood. Present states carved out of the original area of the Northwest Territory include Ohio, Indiana, Illinois, Michigan, Wisconsin, and that part of Minnesota east of the Mississippi River.

1800-1803. Louisiana. In 1800, Napoleon gained title to Louisiana again after trading Spain a duchy in Italy. However, Napoleon's troops in the Caribbean were under siege and unable to provide any help in establishing a French government in Louisiana. Several months later, when American emissaries showed up trying to buy New Orleans, Napoleon offered the entire tract to them. In 1803, President Thomas Jefferson urged Congress to vote in favor, and the U.S. purchased the huge tract from France, doubling the size of the United States.

1804. Louisiana District. The United States had purchased Louisiana from France in 1803, land described as "the drainage of the Mississippi and Missouri Rivers." The Louisiana District, created in 1804, included that portion of present-day Minnesota west of the Mississippi River.

1814. Treaty of Ghent. The War of 1812 ended, freeing up American settlement of the Old Northwest.

1818. Anglo American Convention. At this treaty with Britain, the northern U.S. boundary was set at the 49th parallel, from the Lake of the Woods (Northwest Angle) in present Minnesota to the Continental Divide. - Also in 1818, the northern portions of both Illinois Territory and Indiana Territory were added to Michigan Territory, which now stretched across the Great Lakes region from Lake Erie to the Mississippi River, including the part of present Minnesota east of the Mississippi.

1819-1824. Fort Saint Anthony was founded by the U.S. Army, located at the confluence of the Minnesota and Mississippi Rivers (between present St. Paul and Minneapolis). The first steamboat to navigate the Mississippi into present Minnesota arrived at Fort St. Anthony in May 1823. The fort was renamed **Fort Snelling** in 1824, to honor its first commander and architect.

1832. Henry Schoolcraft discovered the source of the Mississippi River, a lake he named Itasca.

1836. Wisconsin Territory was created in 1836, taken from Michigan Territory. Its area included the lands of present Wisconsin, and extended west to the Missouri River, including all of present Minnesota.

1838. Iowa Territory was created, reducing the western area of Wisconsin Territory to end at the Mississippi River. Fort Snelling, on the west side of the Mississippi River, was now in Clayton County, Iowa Territory.

1840. Federal Census. Population within the areas of present Minnesota was limited to a few residents of St. Croix County, Wisconsin Territory, and Clayton County, Iowa Territory. A few fur traders located in Lake Pepin Precinct (near present Wabasha) were named in the census. But, the 96 inhabitants of Fort Snelling, also in Clayton County, Iowa Territory, were counted but not named.

1844. Iron ore was discovered in the Mesabi Range, the first of several more iron ranges that would become known as the Iron Range of Minnesota, the largest iron ore mining district in the U.S.

1848. Wisconsin became a state with the same boundaries as today. After WI statehood, the residents of the area between the Mississippi and St. Croix rivers (present-day eastern Minnesota) were left without a territorial government or legal system. About 4,500 people were living in the area of the present Minnesota counties of Benton, Ramsey, and Washington. They immediately began petitioning Congress to become a territory.

1849. Mar 3. Minnesota Territory was created by Congress, with St. Paul as the territorial capital. The original area included all of present Minnesota, extending west to the Missouri River, and included that portion of present North and South Dakota east of the Missouri River.

1858. May 11. Minnesota became the 32nd state admitted to the Union, with boundaries the same as today. St. Paul was the state capital. The orphaned area of old Minnesota Territory west of the Red River was enumerated in the 1860 federal census as *Unorganized Dakota*.

Resources at the Minnesota Historical Society

Online searching for resources at the MHS is enhanced by a special *People Finder* index with searches in all materials of the State Archives of the Minnesota Historical Society. For any item associated with a person, use a direct or key word search. For an instruction page and link to the People Finder, see http://sites.mnhs.org/library/search-help-people-finder-and-searchmnhsorg.

MHS People Finder - Types of Records
- Birth records, 1900-1934; 1935-2002
- Death records, 1908-2002
- Territorial/State census records, 1849-1905
- Veteran's grave registrations
- World War I Bonus Records
- Objects, books and photos
- Collection inventories (Finding aids)
- And much more!

MHS Search Tips & Guides Available
- Video Tutorial on the new searches
- Search Help
- Family History Research Guide
- Birth Certificate Index FAQ
- Death Certificate Index FAQ
- State Census Index FAQ
- Veterans' Grave Index FAQ
- Library Video Tutorials

MHS Library Catalog: A search of the MHS library catalog is also useful to find titles of resources not obviously part of the collections. A separate search screen is at
http://mnhs.mnpals.net/F?RN=590157597&func=file&file_name=basic.

Bibliography
Minnesota Censuses & Substitutes

Early Census Jurisdictions: The area of present Minnesota east of the Mississippi River was included in the formation of the United States per the Treaty of Paris of 1783. The western area of Minnesota was part of la Louisiane Française, 1717-1762; part of Spanish Louisiana, 1762-1802; part of (Napoleon's) Louisiana, 1802-1803; and part of the Louisiana Purchase of 1803, when the rest of Minnesota became American territory.

- At the time of the 1820 and 1830 federal censuses, present Minnesota east of the Mississippi River was part of Michigan Territory. No census enumerators made the 700-mile trip from Detroit to see if there were any people living there. Missed was the fur trading post at Fond du Lac (now Duluth) established in 1817 by John Jacob Astor's fur company, and a busy community in the 1820s and 1830s.
- The area west of the Mississippi was part of the Unorganized Territory, 1820-1830, and was assumed to be uninhabited. Although ignored by the census takers, there were a good number of French-Canadian fur traders known to be concentrated in the Pembina/Red River region in the 1820s and 1830s.
- The first census that recorded people living in present Minnesota was the 1836 Wisconsin Territory Census, as part of St. Croix Co, WI Terr.
- In the 1840 federal census, present Minnesota was part of two territories, with a few people counted along the Mississippi River at Ft. Snelling and Wabasha as part of Clayton County, Iowa Territory. Still part of unceded Indian lands, the fur trading posts on Lake Superior were enumerated as part of St. Croix County, Wisconsin Territory.

Minnesota Territory Censuses. Wisconsin became a state in May 1848, leaving the area between the St. Croix River and the Mississippi River without any government. The approximately 4,500 residents of the area immediately began petitioning Congress to become a territory, and in March 1849, Minnesota Territory was born. The area of the new territory spanned between the present Wisconsin border and the Missouri River.
- The first Minnesota Territory census was taken in June 1849, with two counties (St. Croix and La Pointe) inherited from Wisconsin Territory. By the end of 1849, the two were replaced with nine original Minnesota Territory counties: East of the Mississippi River: 1) Benton, 2) Ramsay, 3) Washington, and 4) Itasca counties; West of the Mississippi: 5) Pembina, 6) Mahkahta, 7) Wahnahta, 8) Dakotah, and 9) Wabashaw counties.
- The 1850 federal census taken for MN Territory survives complete for the nine original counties with a total population of 6,077 people. (See the 1850 county map of Minnesota on page 224).
- The next territorial censuses were taken in 1853, and again in 1855; but both are very incomplete.
- Just prior to statehood, the U.S. federal government funded a special Minnesota Territory census in 1857.

- From 1850 to 1860, Minnesota's population increased from 6,077 people in nine counties to 172,023 people in sixty counties.
- The surviving manuscripts for Minnesota's territorial censuses were microfilmed by the Minnesota Historical Society (MHS) in St. Paul. The 1857 special federal census was microfilmed by the National Archives.
- **Territorial Censuses Online:** The microfilms of the 1849, 1853, 1855, and 1857 censuses taken during the territorial period of Minnesota have all been digitized and indexed at the MHS website as well as the Ancestry.com and FamilySearch.org websites.

Minnesota State Censuses. After statehood in 1858, Minnesota took state censuses for 1865, 1875, 1885, 1895, and 1905. All of these microfilmed censuses (with digital images) are at the Family History Library (FHL) in Salt Lake City. The Minnesota state censuses on microfilm can be borrowed on interlibrary loan through the MHS.
- **State Censuses Online:** The MN State Censuses from 1865, 1875, 1885, 1895 and 1905 have all been digitized and indexed at the MHS website, as well as the Ancestry.com website and the FamilySearch.org website.

Minnesota Federal Censuses (Federal Copies). The 1850 federal census for Minnesota Territory is complete for all nine original counties, and the special 1857 federal census for Minnesota Territory is also complete (but with some strange anomalies, see the *1857 Note* in the bibliography for details). The state of Minnesota is complete for 1860-1880; lost for 1890 (like all states); and complete for 1900-1940.

Minnesota Federal Census (State Copies). The MHS also holds the original 1850 and 1860 federal censuses for all Minnesota counties – the state copies. For these census years, researchers have two versions to compare: the federal copy and the state copy. Unfortunately, there is no microfilm of the state copies. None of the state copies have been digitized, and the only copies are the MHS's originals. But, the 1850 state copy was extracted and indexed in a book published by the MHS; and, the MHS has a microfilmed card index to the 1860 state copy. The 1860 state copy has non-population schedules mixed in with the population schedules, and page numbers for the schedules do not agree with those on the federal set.

Census Substitutes: Because of the great number of Minnesota census name lists, the need for census substitutes between federal census years may seem less demanding – but this bibliography has many extra name lists. Together, they include Territorial, State, and Federal Censuses, Court Records, Directories, County Indexes, State Military Lists, Tax Lists, Vital Records, and Voter Lists. The censuses and substitute name lists begin below in chronological order:

♦ ♦ ♦ ♦ ♦

1830s-1925. *Minnesota, Wills and Probate Records* **[Online Database],** indexed at the Ancestry.com website. Source: MN county, district, and probate courts. In most cases, probates reveal the names and residences of beneficiaries and their relationship to the decedent. An inventory of the estate assets can reveal personal details about the deceased's occupation and lifestyle. There may also be references to debts, deeds, and other documents related to the settling of the estate. This database has 689,918 records. See http://search.ancestry.com/search/db.aspx?dbid=9070 .

1830-1850s. *Minnesota Cemetery Inscription Index, Select Counties* **[Online Database],** indexed at the Ancestry.com website. Source: book, same title, by John Dalby, publ. 2003. This is an index of cemeteries in Blue Earth, Carver, Dakota, Dodge, Goodhue, Hennepin, Le Sueur, McLeod, Olmsted, Rice, Scott, Sibley, Steele, and Waseca counties and also in the cities of St. Paul and Winnebago Minnesota; and Beloit, Illinois. This database has 338,304 records (and nearly 600,000 names). See http://search.ancestry.com/search/db.aspx?dbid=3775.

1830s-1900s. See *Minnesota USGenWeb Archives* **[Online Database].** The MNGenWeb Archives site offers free genealogical databases with searchable statewide name lists and for all Minnesota counties. Databases may include Bibles, Biographies, Cemeteries, Censuses, Court Records, Deaths, Deeds, Directories, Histories, Marriages, Military, Newspapers, Obituaries, Photos, Schools, Tax Lists, Wills, and more. See http://usgwarchives.net/mn/mnfiles.htm.

1830s-1900s. *Linkpendium – Minnesota: Family History & Genealogy, Census, Birth, Marriage, Death Vita Records & More* **[Online Databases].** Linkpendium is a genealogical portal site with links to state, county, town, and local databases. Currently listed are selected sites for Minnesota statewide resources (434), Independent Cities, Renamed Counties, Discontinued Counties (29), Aitkin County (140), Anoka County (211), Becker County (207), Beltrami County (158), Benton County (171), Blue Earth County (352) and 81 more Minnesota counties. See **www.linkpendium.com/mn-genealogy.**

1830s-1900s Minnesota Original Land Owners. See the *Family Maps* series for Minnesota counties, maps of all original land patents, compiled by Greg Boyd and published by Arphax Publishing Co., Norman, OK. These privately-produced computer-generated maps show the first property owners for an entire county, produced as a book of maps, each map laid out on the federal township grid, and includes indexes to help you locate a person, place-name, or cemetery. Additional maps are added for each county to show roads, waterways, railroads, selected city centers, and cemeteries within a county. At this writing, *Family Maps* books have been published for the following Minnesota counties: Carlton, Douglas, Hennepin, Houston, Hubbard, Kandiyohi, Lac qui Parle, Marshall, Martin, McLeod, Mille Lacs, Murray, Norman, Otter Tail, Pennington, Pope, Red Lake, Roseau, Swift, Todd, Wadena, Washington, and Winona County, Minnesota. Visit the publisher's information and ordering website for more details and updated county coverage. See **www.arphax.com/**.

1830s-1907. *Minnesota, Homestead and Cash Entry Patents, Pre-1908* **[Online Database],** indexed at the Ancestry.com website. Source: BLM's GLO Automated Records Project. A patent is the first-title deed and the true beginning of private ownership of the land. The patent describes in legal terms the land to which the title is given. Information recorded in these records includes: Name, Land Office, Sequence Document number, Total acres, Signature, Canceled document, Issue date, Mineral rights reserved, Metes and bounds, Statutory reference, Multiple warrantee and patentee names, Act or treaty, Entry classification, and Land description (Section/Range/Township). This database has 160,634 records. See
http://search.ancestry.com/search/db.aspx?dbid=2076.

1830s-1907. *Card Files (Index to Land Entry Files of General Land Offices, Eastern States)* **[Microfilm & Digital Capture],** from the original index cards at the Bureau of Land Management (BLM), Eastern States Office, Washington, DC. The card files serve as an index to the Tract Books, Plat Books, and Case Files relating to ten million public land sales in America. **Content:** Each card contains the Certificate Number, District Land Office, Kind of entry (cash, credit, warrant, etc.), Name of Patentee (Buyer, Entryman, etc.), and county of origin, Land description, Number of acres, Date of patent, Volume, and Page where document can be located. Filmed by the Bureau of Land Management, Washington, DC, c1970, 160 rolls , including 1 roll for Minnesota, FHL film #1501676 (Townships 3N, 20N, 25N-42N, 49N, 90N, 101N, 9, 16, 27, 36, 41, 45 Ranges 20W-32W, 34W, 21-23, 26, 31). To access the digital images, see the online FHL catalog page:
https://familysearch.org/search/catalog/511740.
- **NOTE:** The index cards in this database are arranged by township and range within each state, not by name of purchaser. An online index at the BLM website can be used to find the name of a purchaser with the land description for that person.
- See also **Bureau of Land Management – General Land Office Records [Online Database],** search for the name of any land purchaser of public land in the U.S. To access the search screen, see
https://glorecords.blm.gov/search/default.aspx.

1835-1890. *Minnesota, Compiled Census and Census Substitute Index* **[Online Database],** indexed at the Ancestry.com website. Originally edited by Ronald Jackson, Accelerated Indexing Systems, Salt Lake City, UT. This collection contains the following indexes: 1835-39 Tax Lists Index; 1849 Territorial Census Index; 1850 Federal Census Index; 1860 Federal Census Index; 1870 Federal Census Index; 1880 Federal Census Index; and 1890 Veterans Schedule. This database has 337,169 records. See
http://search.ancestry.com/search/db.aspx?dbid=3555.

1835-1990. *Minnesota Deaths and Burials* **[Online Database],** indexed at the FamilySearch.org website. Source: FamilySearch extractions of death and burial records from microfilm at the Family History Library, Salt Lake City, UT. This database has 1,434,142 records. See
https://familysearch.org/search/collection/1680831.

1836 Wisconsin Territorial Census [Microfilm & Digital Capture], from an article in *Collections of the Wisconsin State Historical Society*, v. 13, p. 247-270. People living between the St. Croix and Mississippi Rivers (now Minnesota) were enumerated as part of St. Croix County, Wisconsin Territory. Filmed by the Genealogical Society of Utah, 1980, 1 roll, FHL film #1293922. To access the digital images, see the online FHL catalog page:
www.familysearch.org/search/catalog/235270.

1836. *The First Census of the Original Counties of Dubuque and Demoine (Iowa) Taken in July 1836* **[Microfilm & Digital Capture],** from the book edited by Benjamin F. Shambaugh, originally published by the Historical Department of Iowa, Des Moines, IA, 1897-1898, 93 pages. Contents: pt. 1. Dubuque County,

pt. 2. Demoine County. From the original manuscript returns preserved in the office of the Secretary of State of Wisconsin. Census taken in accordance with the act of Congress erecting the territory of Wisconsin (of which these two counties at the time formed a part) comprising the present states of Iowa, Minnesota and part of North and South Dakota. Filmed by the Genealogical Society of Utah, 1978, 1 roll, FHL film #989450. To access the digital images, see the online FHL catalog page:
www.familysearch.org/search/catalog/2223215.

1840 Federal Census of Clayton County, Iowa Territory and St. Croix County, Wisconsin Territory (now Minnesota), indexed in *Minnesota 1840 Census Index* **[Printed Index],** another impossible title by Ronald Vern Jackson, publ. Accelerated Indexing Systems, Bountiful, UT, 1981, 57 pages. FHL book 977.6 X22m.

1840-1980. *Minnesota Births and Christenings* **[Online Database],** indexed at the FamilySearch.org website. Source: FamilySearch extractions of birth, baptism and christening records from microfilm at the Family History Library, Salt Lake City, UT. This database has 1,203,969 records. See
https://familysearch.org/search/collection/1680827.
- For Ancestry's version of this database, see
http://search.ancestry.com/search/db.aspx?dbid=2550.

1841-1855. *Early Settlers of Washington County, Minnesota* **[Online Database],** indexed at the RootsWeb site for Washington Co MN. See
www.rootsweb.ancestry.com/~mnwashin/settlers.htm.

1849 Minnesota Territorial Census **[Online Database],** indexed at the Park Genealogical Books website. The originals are located at the State Archives at the MN Hist. Soc. The names are listed by precincts within St. Croix County and La Pointe County (the two counties inherited from Wisconsin Territory, but reorganized a few months later into the nine original counties of Minnesota Territory). See
www.parkbooks.com/Html/res_18~1.html.

"1849 Territorial Census of Minnesota" [Printed Article], in *Minnesota Genealogist*, Vol. 11, No. 3 (Sep 1980); and *Minnesota Genealogical Journal*, Vol. 17 (Mar 1997).

1849 Census of Minnesota Territory **[Printed Abstract],** a typescript located at the Minnesota Historical Society, St. Paul, MN. FHL book 977.6 A1 No. 3 and FHL film #908224. Indexed in *Minnesota 1849 Census Index* **[Printed Book],** edited by Ronald Vern Jackson, et al, published by Accelerated Indexing Systems, Bountiful, UT, 1981, 34 pages. FHL book 977.6 X22m 1849.

1849-1858. *Territorial Papers of the U.S. Territory of Minnesota, 1849-1858* **[Microfilm],** from the originals at the National Archives, Washington, DC. Includes bills and resolutions originating in the Senate; bills and resolutions originating in the House; committee papers; petitions and memorials, resolutions of State Legislatures, and related documents; president's messages: Executive nominations; president's messages: Indian relations; and other miscellaneous information. For complete explanation of information contained herein see beginning of each film. Filmed by the National Archives, 1977, 11 Rolls, beginning with FHL film #1695152 (Senate records, 30th Congress – 33rd Congress).

1849-1905. *Minnesota, Territorial and State Censuses* **[Online Database],** indexed at the Ancestry.com website. Source: MN Hist. Soc., St. Paul, MN. This combined database of territorial and state censuses is also accessible at the MHS website. Each record may include: Name, Enumeration place, Age, Gender, Race, and Birthplace.
- **Contents, Territorial Censuses: 1849:** includes the counties of St. Croix and La Pointe inherited from Wisconsin Territory (from which nine original Minnesota counties were created by the end of 1849: Benton, Dakota, Itasca, Mankatah, Pembina, Ramsey, Wabashaw, Wahnahta, and Washington counties). **1853:** Dakota and Washington counties only. **1855:** surviving counties include Chisago, Doty, Superior, and Wright counties only. **1857:** Includes Anoka, Benton, Blue Earth, Brown, Buchanan, Carlton, Carver, Cass, Chisago, Cottonwood, Crow Wing, Dakota, Dodge, Faribault, Fillmore, Freeborn, Goodhue, Hennepin, Houston, Isanti, Itasca, Jackson, Lake, Le Sueur, Mahnomen, Martin, McLeod, Meeker, Morrison, Mower, Murray, Nicollet, Nobles, Olmsted, Pembina, Pierce, Pine, Pipestone, Ramsey, Renville, Rice, Rock, Scott, Sherburne, Sibley, St. Louis, Stearns, Steele, Todd, Wabasha, Waseca, Washington, Winona, and Wright.
- **Contents, State Censuses: 1865, 1875, 1885, 1895, & 1905:** Complete for all MN counties. Includes all members of a household, with names, ages, birthplaces, etc. In 1865, "Soldier in service on June 1, 1865" was included. The 1875 census gives the birthplaces of father and mother. The 1895 and 1905 censuses included the length of time an individual had lived in the state. This database has 5,710,993 records:
http://search.ancestry.com/search/db.aspx?dbid=1058.

Minnesota • 231

1849-1923. *Minnesota Newspaper Archives* **[Online Databases]**, digitized and indexed newspapers at the GenealogyBank website, for over 360 Minnesota cities, e.g., Duluth, Minneapolis, Red Wing,. Saint Anthony, and St. Paul. Minnesota. See www.genealogybank.com/explore/newspapers/all/usa/minnesota.

1849-1950. *Minnesota Marriages* **[Online Database]**, indexed at the FamilySearch.org website. Source: FamilySearch extractions of marriage records from various collections at the Family History Library, Salt Lake City, UT. This database has 438,331 records. See https://familysearch.org/search/collection/1680832.

1849-1950. *Minnesota, Marriages Index* **[Online Database]**, indexed at the Ancestry.com website. Source: FamilySearch extractions from original and compiled records on microfilm at the Family History Library. This database has 778,376 records. See http://search.ancestry.com/search/db.aspx?dbid=2561.

1849-1985. *Minnesota Will Records* **[Online Database]**, indexed at the FamilySearch.org website. Source: court records at the MHS, St. Paul. This project was indexed in partnership with the Minnesota Historical Society. Name indexes of the Probate Court will books for the counties of the state and territory of Minnesota. This database has 189,458 records. See https://familysearch.org/search/collection/1607922.

1850. *Minnesota, 1850 Federal Census: Population Schedules* **[Microfilm & Digital Capture]**, filmed by the National Archives, 1964, 1 roll, FHL film #14834. To access the digital images, see the online FHL catalog page: www.familysearch.org/search/catalog/744486.

1850. *Minnesota Territorial Census, 1850* **[Printed Book]**, edited by Patricia C Harpole and Mary D Nagle. This is a complete extract and index to the Minnesota Secretary of State's copy of the 1850 federal census. Publ. MHS, St. Paul, MN, 1972, 115 pages, FHL book 977.6 X2ph 1850.

1850-2001. *Minnesota, County Deaths* **[Online Database]**, digitized at the FamilySearch.org website. Source: FamilySearch imaging from county records on microfilm at the Family History Library. This image only database includes digital images of birth records from various county courthouses. Browse the collection, organized by county, then by the county's death index books. This database has 367,790 records. See https://familysearch.org/search/collection/2185953.

1851-1977. *Index to Gravestones of Benton County, Minnesota, as of 1975-1977* **[Microfilm & CD-ROM]**, from the original typescript at Hill Monastic Manuscript Library, Saint John's University, Collegeville, MN. Filmed by the library, 1982, 1 roll, FHL film #1527304. Also available on FHL CD-ROM No. 1559.

1853 Minnesota State Census (Fragments). See *Mendota Township, Dakota County Assessment Record and Census of Families, 1853* **[Printed Book]**, compiled by Mary Bakeman, publ. MHS, St. Paul, 1995. MHS call no CS42 M553 no. 13; and *List of Inhabitants in the Town of Stillwater, 1853* **[Printed Book]**, by Mary Bakeman, publ. MHS, St. Paul, 1993. MHS call no. CS42 M553 no.9;

1854-1957. *Minnesota, Naturalization Records Index* **[Online Database]**, indexed at the Ancestry.com website. Source: *Minnesota, Naturalization Records Index, 1854-1957,* edited by Conrad Peterzen. This is an index to the name of each person requesting citizenship and includes Spouses name, county of residence, microfilm reel reference, print volume, and page number. The index also includes records of people who were denied citizenship and those who never completed the process. The index contains 61 counties and roughly 865,000 records. See http://search.ancestry.com/search/db.aspx?dbid=3826.

1855 Minnesota Territory Census [Original Manuscript] at the Minnesota Historical Society, St. Paul, MN. Surviving counties include Chisago, Doty, Superior, and Wright counties only. Not on microfilm, but a digital version is included with Ancestry's *Minnesota, Territorial and State Censuses, 1849-1905* **[Online Database]**.
- See also, *Minnesota Population Census Schedule for Chisago, Doty, and Superior Counties, Manuscript 1855* **[Printed Book]**, State Archives Notebooks (Barcode 192489-10).
- See also a few printed abstracts from what appears to be names from the 1855 census: *Census of Winona Prairie and Town Proper, 1855* **[Printed Book]**, compiled by Mary Bakeman, publ. MHS, St. Paul, 2001. MHS call no CS42 M553 no. 26; which may be the same as "*Census, 1855, Winona Prairie*" **[Printed Article]**, in *Minnesota Genealogical Journal,* Vol. 26 (Sep 2001); and *The Lost "1855" Census* **[Printed**

Book], by Mary Bakeman, publ. MHS, St. Paul, 1992. MHS call no. CS42 M553 no.8; which may be the same as **"Census, 1855" [Printed Article]**, in *Minnesota Genealogical Journal*, Vol. 8 (Sep 1992).

1857. *Schedules of the Minnesota (Federal) Census of 1857* **[Microfilm & Digital Capture]**, from the original records located at the National Archives, Central Plains Region., Kansas City, MO. This special federal census taken in Minnesota Territory in 1857 contains a listing of families by Dwelling No. and Family No. in order of enumeration); names of each member of a family (starting with the assumed head of household, but with no relationships given) whose usual abode was in this household on 21 September 1857; each individual's age; sex; color, place of birth; whether a native voter or a naturalized voter; and occupation (of every male over 15 years of age). Filmed by the National Archives, 1973, series T1175, 8 rolls, available from the FHL as follows:
- Counties of Anoka – Dodge, FHL film #944283.
- Counties of Fairbault – Freeborn, FHL film #944284.
- Counties of Goodhue – Hennepin, FHL film #944285.
- Counties of Houston – Murray, FHL film #944286.
- Counties of Nicollet – Pipestone, FHL film #944287.
- Counties of Ramsey – Sibley, FHL film #944288.
- Counties of Stearns – Waseca, FHL film #944289.
- Counties of Washington – Wright, FHL film #944290.

To access the digital images, see the online FHL catalog page:
www.familysearch.org/search/catalog/90983.
- See also, *1857 Minnesota Territorial Census* **[Online Database]**, indexed at the FamilySearch.org website. Source: National Archives microfilm series T1175. This database has 156,888 records, see
https://familysearch.org/search/collection/1503055.

✓ **1857 NOTE:** In May 1857, the MN territorial legislature created seven new "paper" counties in the southwestern part of present Minnesota. The entire region was unceded Indian land and had no white population. In September 1857, the federal government mandated and funded a census to be taken in Minnesota Territory. That census included the seven paper counties (Cottonwood, Jackson, Martin, Murray, Nobles, Pipestone, and Rock) that had no population; yet the names of several thousand people were recorded. How could this be? Well, the ruling political party of Minnesota fabricated census schedules complete with names, ages, occupations, etc. Having previously stuffed ballot boxes with made-up names of voters, the census schedules were falsely created to cover their ballot fraud. For the history of this census fraud, see Robert J. Forrest, "Mythical Cities of Southwestern Minnesota," in *Minnesota History*, Vol. 14 (1933), pp243-52.

1857-1930. *Dakota County, Minnesota Census Combined Index, 1857, 1865, 1860, 1865, 1900, 1920, and 1930 Censuses* **[Online Database]**, a combined index available at the Dakota County Historical Society website. See
www.dakotahistory.org/genelogy-research.

1860. *Minnesota, 1860 Federal Census (Federal Copy)* **[Microfilm & Digital Capture]**, from the original records at the National Archives, Washington, DC. Filmed twice by the National Archives, 1950, 1967, 13 rolls, beginning with FHL film #803567 (2nd filming, Anoka, Becker, Benton, Blue Earth, Brown, Buchanan, Carver, Crow Wing, Morrison, Cass, and Itasca Counties). To access the digital images, see the online FHL catalog page:
https://familysearch.org/search/catalog/705415.

1860. *Index to the 1860 Federal Census Schedules for Minnesota (State Copy)* **[Microfilm]**, from the original card index at the State Archives at the Minnesota Historical Society, St. Paul, MN. The 1860 census card index was filmed by the MHS, 31 rolls. Available from the FHL in Salt Lake City, beginning with FHL film #1373881 (Aakers, Anna - Bacon, William). Interlibrary loan of the microfilm is available from the Minnesota Historical Society only.
To see if this microfilm has been digitized yet, see the FHL catalog page:
www.familysearch.org/search/catalog/276458.
- For more information, including roll contents, see Dennis E. Meissner, *Guide to the use of the 1860 Minnesota Population Census Schedules and Index*, publ. MHS, 1978; FHL book 977.6 A1 no. 28).

1860-1949. *Minnesota, County Marriages* **[Online Database]**, indexed at the FamilySearch.org website. Source: FamilySearch extractions from county courthouse records from Anoka, Blue Earth, Brown, Carver, Cottonwood, Dodge, Faribault, Fillmore, Freeborn, Goodhue, Hennepin, and Kanabec counties, Minnesota. See the FamilySearch Wiki for this title for the years of coverage for each county. This database has 870,856 records. See
https://familysearch.org/search/collection/1803974.

1860, 1870 & 1880 Mortality Census Schedules, Minnesota **[Microfilm & Digital Capture]**, filmed by the MN Hist Soc., 1977, 2 rolls, FHL film #485345

(1860, 1870, 1880 Atkin – Hennepin counties) & #485346 (1880 Houston – Yellow Medicine counties). To access the digital images, see the online FHL catalog page:
www.familysearch.org/search/catalog/98340.

1860-1895. *Rice County, Minnesota Marriages* **[Online Database],** indexed at the Ancestry.com website. Source: Book, same title, by John Dalby, publ. 2003. Each index record includes: Given name, Surname, Spouse, and Marriage date. This database has 1,540 records. See
http://search.ancestry.com/search/db.aspx?dbid=3754.

1861-1865. *Minnesota Civil War Records* **[Online Database],** indexed at the Ancestry.com website. Source: *MN Civil War Muster Rolls,* MHS, St. Paul. This database has 107,586 records. See
http://search.ancestry.com/search/db.aspx?dbid=1715.

1861-1865. *Minnesota Civil War Soldiers* **[Online Database],** indexed at the Ancestry.com website. Book, same title, by John Dalby, publ. 1999.
This database has 26,088 records. See
http://search.ancestry.com/search/db.aspx?dbid=3729.

1862-1866 Internal Revenue Assessment Lists for Minnesota **[Microfilm & Digital Capture],** from the originals at the National Archives, Washington, DC, series M0774. FHL Catalog title: *Bound Tax Revenue Assessment Lists for Minnesota, 1862-1866.* The first roll indicates location of county name lists, 3 rolls, beginning with FHL film #1602225 (District 1, division 1-6, Annual, monthly lists Jan-Dec 1866). To access the digital images, see the online FHL catalog page: www.familysearch.org/search/catalog/589214.

1863-1983. *Minnesota, County Birth Records* **[Online Database],** digitized at the FamilySearch.org website. Source: FamilySearch imaging from county records on microfilm at the Family History Library. This image only database includes digital images of birth records from various county courthouses. Some birth registers are for cities or townships. The year range varies by county. Browse the collection, organized by county, then by county's birth index books (for a range of years). This database has 150,669 records. See
https://familysearch.org/search/collection/1920099.

1865 Minnesota State Census **[Microfilm & Digital Capture],** from the original manuscripts. Filmed by the Minnesota State Library and Records Service, 1969, 3 rolls, available at the Family History Library:

- 1865 Counties of Blue Earth, Brown, Carlton, Lake, St. Louis, Carver, Cass, Chisago, Clay, Crow Wing, Dakota, Dodge, Faribault, Fillmore, Freeborn, and Goodhue, FHL film #565714.
- 1865 Counties of Hennepin, Houston, Insanti, Kanabec, Le Suer, McLeod, Mahnomen, Martin, Meeker, Morrison, Mower, Nicollet, Olmsted, Pine, Ramsey, Rice, FHL film #565715.
- 1865 Counties of Scott, Sherburne, Sibley, Stearns, Steele, Todd, Wabasha, Waseca, Washington, Watonwan, Winona, Wright - FHL film #565716.

To access the digital images, see the online FHL catalog page:
www.familysearch.org/search/catalog/166096.

1865 Minnesota State Census **[Online Database],** digitized and indexed at the FamilySearch.org website. Source: MHS-State Archives, St. Paul. The 1865 census contains a listing of families (by Family No. in order of enumeration); names of each member of a family (starting with the assumed head of household, but with no relationships given) whose usual abode was in this household on 1 June 1865; whether male or female; the color of each person; whether any member of household was deaf, dumb, blind, or insane; and whether any male of the household was serving in the military on June 1, 1865. This database has 246,591 records. See
https://familysearch.org/search/collection/1503054.

"**1865 Minnesota State Census, Carlton County**" **[Printed Article],** in *Genealogical Society of Carlton County Quarterly,* Vol. 12, No. 1 (Oct 1989).

"**1865 Minnesota State Census, Clay County**" **[Printed Article],** in *Northland Newsletter,* Vol. 1, No. 3 (Jul 1969).

"**1865 Minnesota State Census, Civil War Soldiers & Officers**" **[Printed Article],** in *La Crosse Area Genealogical Quarterly,* Vol. 21, No. 1 (Feb 1999).

1865-2006. *Minnesota, Clay and Steele County Obituaries* **[Online Database],** indexed at the FamilySearch.org website. Index and images of newspaper obituary files filmed by FamilySearch at the Clay County Historical Society and the Steele County Historical Society in Minnesota. This database has 29,797 records. See
https://familysearch.org/search/collection/2281907.

1866. *Minnesota Adjutant General's Report of 1866* **[Printed Book],** by the Adjutant General's Office, 1866, reprint by Park Genealogical Books, Roseville,

MN, 1997, 464 pages. Gives soldier's name, age, birthplace, rank, regiment, company, date and place mustered in, date and place mustered out, and other information. Arranged in alphabetical order by soldier's name. FHL book 977.6 M2ma.

1866-1916. *Minnesota Death Records* **[Online Database],** indexed at the FamilySearch.org website. Source: extractions from microfilmed records of the MN Dept of Health. This is a name index of municipal death records in St. Paul (Ramsey County) and Minneapolis (Hennepin County), Minnesota. The collection includes death registers, mortuary records, and death certificates. This database has 383,230 records. See
https://familysearch.org/search/collection/1858352.

1869-1940. *Minnesota, Grand Army of the Republic Membership Records* **[Online Database],** indexed at the FamilySearch.org website. Source: MHS, St. Paul. This database includes membership records of the Minnesota Department Grand Army of the Republic, an organization of Union army and navy veterans of the Civil War. The collection consists of registers, lists, adjutant and quartermaster reports and descriptive books of local posts (chapters). Records include town of residence, military unit, date of enlistment, date of discharge, age and birthplace. This database has 164,338 records. See
https://familysearch.org/search/collection/2239221.

1870. *Minnesota, 1870 Federal Census: Population Schedules* **[Microfilm & Digital Capture],** filmed by the National Archives, 1964, 31 rolls, beginning with FHL film #830421 (Aitken, Cass, Anoka, Becker, Beltrami, Benton, Big Stone, Blue Earth, Brown, Carlton, and Carver counties). To access the digital images, see the online FHL catalog page:
www.familysearch.org/search/catalog/698904.

1870-1874. Rice County, Minnesota, Births [Online Database], indexed at the Ancestry.com website. Source: Book, same title, by John Dalby, publ. 1999. Each index record includes: Given name, Surname, Birth date, Sex, Township, Father's name, Mother's name, and Parent's birthplace. This database has 2,114 records. See
http://search.ancestry.com/search/db.aspx?dbid=3735.

1872-1930. *Minnesota, Itasca County Land Records* **[Online Database],** digitized at the FamilySearch.org website. Source: Itasca County Recorder, Grand Rapids, MN. Land records, including grantee and grantor indexes. Browse the images, organized by record type, date range, and volume. This database has 7,328 records. See
https://familysearch.org/search/collection/2030516.

1872-1962. *Minnesota Naturalization Records and Indexes* **[Online Database],** digitized and indexed at FamilySearch.org. Source: National Archives records of U.S. district courts, Kansas City, MO. This database has 88,691 records, see
www.familysearch.org/search/collection/2632486.

1872-1947. *Minnesota, Clay County Land and Property Records* **[Online Database],** digitized at the FamilySearch.org website. Images of records from the courthouse in Moorhead, Minnesota. The land records include grantor indexes, grantee indexes, deeds, abstract books, and other books. Some indexes go beyond the year 1947. Browse the records, organized by Record Type, Year Range, and Volume. This database has 31,590 records. See
https://familysearch.org/search/collection/1762576.

1873 Minnesota State Business Directory: Alphabetic List of Business Firms, Proprietors and Artisans, State and County Officers—With Town and County Locations **[Printed Book],** compiled by Antona Hawkins Richardson, reprint by Paduan Press, St. Paul, MN, 2001, FHL book 977.6 E4.

1873-1961. *Obituary Index Card File, ca. 1873-1961* **[Microfilm & Digital Capture],** from the original card file at the Prairieland Genealogical Society, Southwest State University, Marshall, MN. Abstracts of obituaries for people from southwest Minnesota. Filmed by the Genealogical Society of Utah, 2003, 7 rolls, beginning with FHL film #2367279 (A to Butler, Alice). To access the digital images, see the online FHL catalog page:
https://familysearch.org/search/catalog/1197864.

1875 Minnesota State Census **[Microfilm & Digital Capture],** from the original manuscripts (all MN counties). Filmed by the State Library and Records Service, 1969, 16 rolls, available at the FHL in Salt Lake City, beginning with FHL film #565717 (Counties of Aitkin, Anoka, Becker, Benton, Blue Earth, and Brown). To access the digital images, see the online FHL catalog page:
www.familysearch.org/search/catalog/166104.

1875 Minnesota State Census **[Online Database],** digitized and indexed at the FamilySearch.org website. Source: MHS-State Archives, St. Paul. The 1875 census contains a listing of families (by Family No. in

order of enumeration); names of each member of a family (starting with the assumed head of household, but with no relationships given) whose usual abode was in this household on 1 June 1875; the individual's age; sex, color, nativity (state or country); and nativity of a person's father and mother. This database has 612,847 records. See
https://familysearch.org/search/collection/1503053.

"1875 Minnesota State Census, Lincoln County" [Printed Article], in *Prairieland Pioneer*, Vol. 9, No. 2 (Summer 1992) through Vol. 10, No. 4 (Winter 1993).

"1875 Minnesota State Census, Lyon County" [Printed Article], abstracts by townships, in *Prairieland Pioneer,* Vol. 3, No. 3 (Spring 1987), and various issues through Vol. 9, No. 4 (Summer 1993).

1876-2006. *Minnesota, Stevens County Genealogical Society Records* **[Online Database],** digitized at the FamilySearch.org website.
Images of records housed at the Morris Public Library in Donnelly, MN. The records include a marriage card index, obituary index, and obituaries. This database has 63,363 records. See
https://familysearch.org/search/collection/1419635.

1877-1948. *Minnesota County History Name Index* **[Online Database],** indexed at the Ancestry.com website. Source: John Dalby's *Minnesota County History Name Index*, publ. 1999. This database is a name index of eleven county histories and plat books for the area immediately south of St. Paul. Researchers will find the name of county resident, the book in which the person's name appears, and the page number. Where information is available, town of residence is also given. Dakota, Dodge, Goodhue, Le Sueur, Olmsted, Rice, Steele, and Winona counties are covered in this collection. This database has 216,812 records. See
http://search.ancestry.com/search/db.aspx?dbid=3721.

1880. *Minnesota, 1880 Federal Census: Soundex and Population Schedules* **[Microfilm & Digital Capture],** filmed by the National Archives, c1970, 71 rolls, beginning with FHL film #1254605 (Aitken, Anoka, Polk, Beltrami, Benton, Big Stone, and Blue Earth).To access the digital images, see the online FHL catalog page:
www.familysearch.org/search/catalog/673574.

1880-1881. *Minneapolis City Directory for 1880-1881: Comprising a Complete List of the Citizens of Minneapolis, With Place of Business* **[Online Database],** digitized and indexed at the Ancestry.com website. Full textual digital page images with an OCR index. This database has 512 pages. See
http://search.ancestry.com/search/db.aspx?dbid=23857.

1880-1901. *Minnesota, Dakota County, Tax Records* **[Digital Capture],** from the originals at the MN State Archives, digital capture by the Genealogical Society of Utah, 2015. To access the digital images, see the online FHL catalog page:
https://familysearch.org/search/catalog/2524795.

1880-1920. *Minnesota, Federal Naturalization Records* **[Online Database],** indexed at the Ancestry.com website. Source: National Archives microfilm, MN district and circuit court records. Records include petitions, declarations, and certificates. This database has 71,368 records. See
http://search.ancestry.com/search/db.aspx?dbid=61202.

1882-1883. *Minneapolis City Directory* **[Online Database],** digitized and indexed at the Ancestry.com website. Full textual digital page images with an OCR index. This database has 643 pages. See
http://search.ancestry.com/search/db.aspx?dbid=23859.

1885 Minnesota State Census **[Microfilm & Digital Capture],** from the originals (all MN counties). Filmed by the State Library and Records Service, St. Paul, MN, 1969, 28 rolls. Available at the FHL beginning with FHL film #56733 (Counties of Aitkin, Carlton, Kanabec, Hubbard, Cass, Anoka, Becker, Beltrami, Cook, Lake, Pipestone, and Benton). To access the digital images, see the online FHL catalog page:
www.familysearch.org/search/catalog/166180.

1885 Minnesota State Census **[Online Database],** digitized and indexed at the FamilySearch.org website. Source: MHS-State Archives, St. Paul. The 1885 census contains a listing of families (by Family No. in order of enumeration); names of each member of a family (starting with the assumed head of household, but with no relationships given) whose usual abode was in this household on 1 June 1885; the individual's age; sex, color, nativity (state or country); whether father of foreign birth; whether mother of foreign birth, and whether a person "served as a soldier in the federal army during the Rebellion." This database has 1,133,198 records. See
https://familysearch.org/search/collection/1503044.

"**1885 Minnesota State Census, Lyon County**" **[Printed Article]**, in *Prairieland Pioneer*, Vol. 4, No. 2 (Winter 1988).

"**1885 Minnesota State Census, McLeod County**" **[Printed Article]**, in *Prairieland Pioneer*, Vol. 1, No. 2 (Nov 1984).

"**1885 Minnesota State Census, Lake Sarah Township, Murray County**" **[Printed Article]**, in *Prairieland Pioneer*, Vol. 4, No. 3 (Spring 1988).

"**1885 Minnesota State Census, Surnames in Girard Township, Otter Tail County**" **[Printed Article]**, in *Otter Tail County Genealogical Society Newsletter*, Vol. 19, No. 1 (Mar 2001).

1885-1886 Minneapolis City Directory **[Online Database]**, digitized and indexed at the Ancestry.com website. Full textual digital page images with an OCR index. This database has 925 pages. See http://search.ancestry.com/search/db.aspx?dbid=23856.

1886-1887. *Minneapolis City Directory: Comprising a Complete List of the Citizens of Minneapolis, With Place of Business* **[Online Database]**, digitized and indexed at the Ancestry.com website. Full textual digital page images with an OCR index. This database has 956 pages. See http://search.ancestry.com/search/db.aspx?dbid=23858.

1887-2001. *Minnesota Deaths* **[Online Database]**, from MN State Dept. of Health records now at the MN Hist. Soc., St. Paul, MN. Digitized and indexed at FamilySearch.org. This database has 126,202 records, see **www.familysearch.org/search/collection/339846**.

1888-1953. *Rice County, Minnesota Directories* **[Online Database]**, indexed at the Ancestry.com website. Source: R.L. Polk and Co, all years. Specifically it includes the following years: 1888, 1899, 1903, 1911, 1915, 1921, 1926, 1929, 1936, 1939, 1945, 1948, 1952, and 1953. Information contained in this database includes first and last name of resident, occupation, address, and year of directory. The Rice County cities whose directories are included in this database are Berg, Bridgewater, Dean, Cannon City, Dundas, Eklund, Faribault, Hazelwood, Lester, Little Chicago, Lonsdale, Mazaska Lake, Millersburg, Moland, Morristown, Nerstrand, Northfield, Richland, Roberds Lake, Ruskin, Shieldsville, Tenod, Trondjem, Veseli, Walcott, Warsaw, Webster, and Wheatland. This database has 125,406 records. See http://search.ancestry.com/search/db.aspx?dbid=7585.

1889-1891. *Minneapolis, Minnesota Directories* **[Online Database]**, indexed at the Ancestry.com website. Source: Minneapolis Directory Co, 1889-1889, and 1890-1891. This database has 77,037 records. See http://search.ancestry.com/search/db.aspx?dbid=4561.

1889-1891. *St. Paul, Minnesota City Directories* **[Online Database]**, indexed at the Ancestry.com website. Source: R.L. Polk Directories, 1889-1890 and 1890-1891. This database has 71,443 records. See http://search.ancestry.com/search/db.aspx?dbid=4491.

1890 Census Substitute **[Online Database]**, indexed at the Ancestry.com website. This is nationwide collection of city directories for the time of the 1890 federal census (lost in a fire in Washington DC in 1921). A global search includes directories from several Minnesota cities. See http://search.ancestry.com/search/group/1890census.

1890-1963. *U.S., Northern Pacific Railway Company Personnel Files* **[Online Database]**, indexed at the Ancestry.com website. Source: MHS, St. Paul. This collection of personnel files from the Northern Pacific Railway Company in Minnesota includes company correspondence, job history, salary and promotion documents, and leaves of absence, and more. This database has 167,628 records. See http://search.ancestry.com/search/db.aspx?dbid=2157.

1892-1930. *Minnesota, Roseau County Land Records* **[Online Database]**, digitized at the FamilySearch.org website. Images of deeds, mortgages, bonds, probate records, homesteads, quit claims, U.S. Patent records, and Misc. Records from the courthouse in Roseau, MN. Browse the records, organized by Record Type, Date Range, and Volume. This database has 109,958 records. See https://familysearch.org/search/collection/2019834.

1893-1901. *Minnesota, Ramsey County, Tax Records* **[Digital Capture]**, from the microfilm of the originals at the MN State Archives. Digital capture by the Genealogical Society of Utah, 2015, 1 roll, DGS #100744017 (Tax lists, personal property, 1893-1901). To access the digital images, see the online FHL catalog page: https://familysearch.org/search/catalog/2524815.

1895 Minnesota State Census **[Microfilm & Digital Capture]**, from the originals (all MN counties). Filmed by the State Library and Records Service, St. Paul, MN, 59 rolls. Available at the FHL beginning with FHL film #565761 (Counties of Aitkin, Anoka, Becker (thru the

township of Green Valley). Includes all members of a household, with names, ages, birthplaces, etc., and includes the length of time an individual lived in the state. To access the digital images, see the online FHL catalog page:
www.familysearch.org/search/catalog/166265.

1895 *Minnesota State Census* **[Online Database]**, indexed at the FamilySearch.org website. Source: MHS-State Archives, St. Paul. The 1895 census contains a listing of families (by Family No. in order of enumeration); names of each member of a family (starting with the assumed head of household, but with no relationships given) whose usual abode was in this household on 1 June 1895; the individual's age; sex, color, nativity (state or country); for males over 21: length of residence in MN in years and months, and residence in the enumeration district in year and months; regular occupation; number of months employed at regular occupation; whether a soldier or sailor in the War of the Rebellion; father of foreign birth (yes or no); and mother of foreign birth (yes or no). This database has 1,570,739 records. See
https://familysearch.org/search/collection/1503031.

"1895 Minnesota State Census, Menahga, Becker County" [Printed Article], in *Heart O'Lakes Genealogical Newsletter,* Vol. 16, No. 1 (Mar 1993) and Vol. 16, No. 2 (Jun 1993).

1898. *R.L. Polk & Co.'s St. Paul City Directory, 1898: Comprising an Alphabetically Arranged List of Business Firms and Private Citizens* **[Online Database]**, digitized and indexed at the Ancestry.com website. Full digital page images with an OCR index. This database has 1,614 records:
http://search.ancestry.com/search/db.aspx?dbid=23870.

1898-1899. *Minnesota Volunteers in the Spanish American War and the Philippine Insurrection* **[Online Database]**, indexed at the Ancestry.com website. Source: Book, same title, by Franklin F. Holbrook, publ. 1923. There are a total of 9,846 records which each include the Name, Unit, Company, Rank, Age (if given), Birthplace (if given), Residence, and Page Number (from original book). The additional information in the book is a description of his military service. Index also includes Army, Navy and Marine personnel as well as Minnesotans who served in other state units. This database has 9,847 records. See
http://search.ancestry.com/search/db.aspx?dbid=4816.

1898-1899. *Minnesota, Spanish American War Muster Rolls and Casualty Lists* **[Online Database]**, indexed at the Ancestry.com website. Source: Adjutant General's report at the MHS. This database includes muster-in and muster-out rolls for the four Minnesota regiments that served in the Spanish-American War: the 12th, 13th, 14th, and 15th regiments. Some field returns and casualty reports are also included. Details listed can include name, date, rank, place, residence, regiment, and death date where applicable, depending on the form. This database has 3,992 records. See
http://search.ancestry.com/search/db.aspx?dbid=6070.

1900. *Minnesota, 1900 Federal Census: Soundex and Population Schedules* **[Microfilm & Digital Capture],** filmed by the National Archives, c1970, 223 rolls, beginning with FHL film #1240756 (Aitken, Anoka, Becker and Beltrami counties).To access the digital images, see the online FHL catalog page: www.familysearch.org/search/catalog/636810.

1900-1934. *Minnesota Birth Index* **[Online Database]**, indexed at the Ancestry.com website. Source: MN Birth Certificates Index, MHS). This database is also accessible at the MHS website. Each record includes the child's full name, father's full name, mother's maiden name, birth date, birth county, and state file number. Most of the records are linked to the People Finder at the MHS website. This database has 1,820,984 records. See
http://search.ancestry.com/search/db.aspx?dbid=9196.

1900-1999. *Minnesota, Cemetery Index* **[Online Database]**, indexed at the Ancestry.com website. This database is also accessible at the Iron Range Research Center website. This database has 15,567 records. See
http://search.ancestry.com/search/db.aspx?dbid=9746.

1902-1923. *Minnesota, Hennepin County, Register of Electors* **[Digital Capture]**, from the originals at the MN State Archives. Digital capture by the Genealogical Society of Utah, 2015, 1 roll, DGS #100744015. To browse the images online, see https://familysearch.org/search/catalog/2524800.

1904. *R.L. Polk & Co.'s St. Paul City Directory: Comprising an Alphabetically Arranged List of Business Firms and Private Citizens* **[Online Database]**, indexed at the Ancestry.com website. Full digital page images with an OCR index. This database has 2,013 records. See
http://search.ancestry.com/search/db.aspx?dbid=23873.

1905 *Minnesota State Census* **[Microfilm & Digital Capture]**, from the originals (all MN counties). Filmed by the State Library and Records Service, St.

Paul, MN, 58 rolls. Available at the FHL in Salt Lake City, beginning with FHL film #928767 (Aitkin, Anoka, Becker Counties). To access the digital images, see the online FHL catalog page:
www.familysearch.org/search/catalog/41411.

1905. *Minnesota State Census, 1905* **[Online Database],** indexed at the FamilySearch.org website. Source: MHS-State Archives, St. Paul. The 1905 census contains a listing of families (by Family No. in order of enumeration); names of each member of a family (starting with the assumed head of household, but with no relationships given) whose usual abode was in this household on 1 June 1905; the individual's sex; age; color, nativity (state or country); nativity of father; nativity of mother; length of residence in MN in years and months, and residence in the enumeration district in year and months; regular occupation; Army Service (Sold. or Sail.); and Wars (Civil War, Spanish War). This database has 1,973,884 records. See
https://familysearch.org/search/collection/1503056.

"1905 Minnesota State Census, Chippewa County, by Townships" [Printed Article], in *Chippewa County Clippings*, Vol. 1, No. 1 (Sep 1994) through various issues to Vol. 6, No. 4 (Dec 1999).

"1905 Minnesota State Census, Tyler, Lincoln County" [Printed Article], in *Prairieland Pioneer*, Vol. 3, No. 1 (Fall 1986) and Vol. 3, No. 2 (Winter 1986).

"1905 Minnesota State Census, Lyon County" [Printed Article], in *Prairieland Pioneer*, Vol. 1, No. 2 (Nov 1984) through Vol. 4, No. 2 (Winter 1988).

1905-1960. *Pines, Mines and Lakes: The Story of Itasca County, Minnesota* **[Printed Book],** by James E. Rottsolk, published by the Itasca County Historical Society, 1960, 155 pages. Includes a transcription of the 1905 state census for the county and a list of 50-year residents living in 1958. FHL book 977.678 H2r.

1908 History. See *Minnesota in Three Centuries, 1655-1908* **[Printed Book],** by Lucius Frederick Hubbard, et al, published New York, 1908, 4 vols., FHL book 977.6 H2mi. Indexed in *An Every-Name Index to Minnesota in Three Centuries* **[Printed Index],** compiled by Rod & Marie Nordberg for the Southern California Genealogical Society, 1990, 17 pages, FHL book 977.6 H2mi index.

1907-1952. *Minnesota, Manifests of Alien Arrivals* **[Microfilm & Digital Capture],** filmed by the National Archives, digitized by the Genealogical Society of Utah, 2014. Contain digital images of the originals of Passenger Lists of Vessels arriving at Baudette, Warroad, and International Falls, Minnesota. The records usually include the person's name, gender, age, marital status, citizenship, race, place of last permanent residence, and destination, how long they intend to remain in the U.S., and whether they intend to become a U.S. Citizen. To access the digital images, see the online FHL catalog page:
www.familysearch.org/search/catalog/2443340.

1908-2017. *Minnesota Death Index* **[Online Database],** indexed at the FamilySearch.org website. Source: MN Dept of Health (indexed by Ancestry). The index may include: Name of the deceased, City and county of death, Date of death, Birth date, Birthplace, Mother's maiden name, and State file number. This database has 4,897,032 records. See
https://familysearch.org/search/collection/1937234.
- For the Ancestry version of this database, see
http://search.ancestry.com/search/db.aspx?dbid=7316.

1909. *R.L. Polk & Co.'s St. Paul City Directory: Comprising an Alphabetically Arranged List of Business Firms and Private Citizens* **[Online Database],** digitized and indexed at the Ancestry.com website. Full digital page images with an OCR index. This database has 2,065 records;
http://search.ancestry.com/search/db.aspx?dbid=23871.

1909-1962. *Minnesota, Clay County, School Census Records* **[Online Database],** digitized at the FamilySearch.org website. Images of school census records arranged by district number. The records include the pupil's name, age, and name of a parent or guardian. This database has 14,457 records. See
https://familysearch.org/search/collection/1760963.

1910. *Minnesota, 1910 Federal Census: Population Schedules* **[Microfilm & Digital Capture],** filmed by the National Archives, c1970, 42 rolls, beginning with FHL film #1374702 (Aitken, Anoka, Cook, Becker and Clearwater counties).To access the digital images, see the online FHL catalog page:
www.familysearch.org/search/catalog/638144.

1910-1923. *Minnesota, Baudette, Warroad, and International Falls Passenger Lists* **[Online Database],** indexed at the FamilySearch.org website. Source: National Archives microfilm series A3490. The records usually include the person's name, gender, age, marital status, citizenship, race, place of last permanent residence, and destination, how long they intend to remain in the U.S or become a U.S. citizen. This database has 793 records. See
https://familysearch.org/search/collection/2443340.

1914. *Davison's Minneapolis City Directory: Vol. XLII, 1914: Containing an Alphabetical List of Business Firms, Corporations* **[Online Database],** digitized and indexed at the Ancestry.com website. Source: Full textual digital page images with an OCR index. This database has 2,456 records. See http://search.ancestry.com/search/db.aspx?dbid=25424.

1914. *Winona and Wabasha Counties, Minnesota Farmers Directory* **[Online Database],** indexed at the Ancestry.com website. Source: Database compiled by Ann Kurth, 2000. Each index record includes: Given name, Surname, Spouse, Children, Section, Years in county, County, Township, and Post office. This database has 2,867 records. See http://search.ancestry.com/search/db.aspx?dbid=5019.

1914-1943. *Minnesota, World War I Military Records* **[Digital Capture],** digitized by FamilySearch International, 2014, from original records at the MN Hist. Society, St. Paul. The records appear to be in three groups: 1) Gold Star Roll (also available at the MHS website); 2) Army, Navy, and Red Cross Nurses; and 3) World War I Military Service Records. To access the digital images, see the online FHL catalog page: www.familysearch.org/search/catalog/2520543.

1915-1925. *Veterans of Foreign Wars of the United States, A.R. Patterson Post No. 7, Membership Applications, Minneapolis, Minnesota* **[Microfilm],** from the originals at the A.R. Patterson Post #7, Minneapolis, MN. The applications are from veterans wishing to join the Veterans of Foreign Wars organization, arranged in alphabetical order by first letter of surname. The applications are printed forms with handwritten information for veterans of World War I. Gives age, birth date, birthplace, applicant's address, occupation, spouse's name, enlistment date, unit and branch of service, rank, date and place of discharge, reason for discharge, who recommended them for membership, character witnesses, and other information. Filmed by the Genealogical Society of Utah, 1 roll, FHL film #1425299. To see if this microfilm has been digitized yet, see the FHL catalog page: www.familysearch.org/search/catalog/980076.

1917-1918. *Minnesota, World War I Selective Service Draft Registration Cards* **[Microfilm & Digital Capture],** the cards are arranged alphabetically by state, then by county or city, and then by the surname of the registrant. filmed by the National Archives, 1987-1988, 94 rolls, beginning with FHL film #1675275. To access the digital images, see the online FHL catalog page: www.familysearch.org/search/catalog/746982.

1917-1919. *Minnesota, YMCA World War I Service Cards* **[Online Database],** digitized at the FamilySearch.org website. Source: Univ. of Minnesota, Kautz Family YMCA Archive, Minneapolis, MN. Images of approximately 27,600 index cards with the names of individuals who served with the YMCA during WWI. Cards are arranged alphabetically by surname and include age, home address, and occupation. This database has 27,364 records. See https://familysearch.org/search/collection/2513098.

1917-1919. *Minnesota, World War I Expeditionary Forces, Deaths* **[Digital Capture],** digitized by FamilySearch International, 2018, from the originals at the National Archives, College Park, MD. Number of records not noted. To access the digital images, see the online FHL catalog page: www.familysearch.org/search/catalog/3023933.

1918. *Minnesota, Alien Registration Index* **[Online Database],** indexed at the Ancestry.com website. This database is also accessible at the Iron Range Research Center website. This database has 111,827 records: http://search.ancestry.com/search/db.aspx?dbid=70801.

1918. *Minnesota, Hennepin County, Naturalization Records* **[Digital Capture],** from microfilm of the originals at the MN State Archives. Digital capture by the Genealogical Society of Utah, 2014, from 101 rolls of microfilm, beginning with DGS #101318314 (Alien registration forms and declaration of holdings, roll 168, Bloomington-Deephaven, 1918). To browse the images online, see https://familysearch.org/search/catalog/2520521.

1918-1943. *Minnesota, Military Records: World War I Bonus Application Files [Digital Capture],* digitized by FamilySearch International from originals at the MN Hist. Soc., St. Paul. FHL catalog has no description of contents, etc., except to note that this database has 917 digital folders (1 folder for 1 applicant?). To access the digital images, see the online FHL catalog page: www.familysearch.org/search/catalog/2831720.

1919. *Minnesota, Women in Industry* **[Online Database],** indexed at the Ancestry.com website. This database is also accessible at the Iron Range Research Center website. This database has 41,684 records. See http://search.ancestry.com/search/db.aspx?dbid=70787.

1920. *Minnesota, 1920 Federal Census: Soundex and Population Schedules* [Microfilm & Digital Capture], filmed by the National Archives, c1970, 220 rolls, beginning with FHL film #1820822 (Aitken, Big Stone, Anoka, Beltrami counties). To access the digital images, see the online FHL catalog page:
www.familysearch.org/search/catalog/574009.

1922-1958 Minnesota, Duluth and Wisconsin, Superior Crew Lists [Microfilm & Digital Capture], from the originals at the National Archives, digitized by the Genealogical Society of Utah, 2013. To access the digital images, see the online FHL catalog page:
www.familysearch.org/search/catalog/2140606.

1929-1956. *Minnesota, Crew Lists* [Online Database], indexed at the Ancestry.com website. Source: National Archives microfilm: *Crew Lists of Vessels Arriving at Two Harbors, Minnesota, August 1929-October 1956*. And *Crew Lists of Vessels Arriving at Baudette, Grand Marais, International Falls, Ranier, and Warroad, Minnesota, 1946-1956*. Passengers are not included. This database has 12,671 records. See
http://search.ancestry.com/search/db.aspx?dbid=8987.

1930. *Minnesota, 1930 Federal Census: Population Schedules* [Microfilm & Digital Capture], filmed by the National Archives, c1970, 59 rolls, beginning with FHL film #2340813 (Aitken, Anoka, and Benton counties). To access the digital images, see the online FHL catalog page:
www.familysearch.org/search/catalog/1037428.

1930-1988. *Minnesota Naturalization Card Index* [Online Database], indexed at the FamilySearch.org website. Source: National Archives microfilm of two card indexes from the District Court 3rd Division and 4th Division (Minnesota). The index cards Certificate number, Name, Residence, Birth date, Admission date, Certificate date, Name of court, Place of court, Petition number, and Alien registration number. This database has 71,367 records. See
https://familysearch.org/search/collection/2120721.

1930-1988. *Minnesota, Naturalization Card Index, 1930-1988* [Online Database], indexed at the Ancestry.com website. Source: FamilySearch, from National Archives microfilm. The collection consists of two naturalization card indexes from the District Court of Minnesota 3rd division and 4th division. The index cards include: Certificate number, Name, Residence, Birth date, Admission date, Certificate date, Name of court, Place of court, Petition number, Alien registration number, and Signature of immigrant. This database has 71,367 records. See
http://search.ancestry.com/search/db.aspx?dbid=60723.

1935-2000. *Minnesota Birth Index* [Online Database], indexed at the FamilySearch.org website. Source: MN Dept of Health. Each record includes the child's full name, father's full name, mother's maiden name, birth date, birth county, and state file number. Most of the records are linked to an order form to obtain copy of the original document. This database has 12,420,767 records. See
https://familysearch.org/search/collection/1949334.

1935-2002. *Minnesota Birth Index* [Online Database], indexed at the Ancestry.com website. Source: MN Dept of Health. Each record includes the child's full name, father's full name, mother's maiden name, birth date, birth county, and state file number. Most of the records are linked to an order form to obtain a copy of the original document. This database has 4,267,629 records. See
http://search.ancestry.com/search/db.aspx?dbid=8742.

1940. *Minnesota, 1940 Federal Census: Population Schedules* [Digital Capture], digitized images from the microfilm of original records held by the Bureau of the Census in the 1940s. After microfilming, Congress allowed the Census Bureau to destroy the originals to free up space for WWII-related files. Digitizing of the 1940 census schedules microfilm images was done for the National Archives and made public on April 2, 2012. To access the digital images, see the online FHL catalog page:
www.familysearch.org/search/catalog/2057765.

1940 Federal Census Finding Aids [Online Database]. The National Archives prepared a special website online with a detailed description of the 1940 federal census. Included at the site are descriptions of location finding aids, such as Enumeration District maps, Geographic Descriptions of Census Enumeration Districts, and a list of 1940 City Directories available at the National Archives. The finding aids are all linked to other National Archives sites. The National Archives website also has a link to 1940 Search Engines using Stephen P. Morse's "One-Step" system for finding a 1940 E.D. or street address conversion. See
www.archives.gov/research/census/1940/general-info.html#questions.

1940-1947. *Minnesota, World War II Draft Registration Cards* [Microfilm & Digital Capture], digitized by FamilySearch International, 2017, includes all registrations during WWII except the fourth registration. Images by Ancestry.com, index by FamilySearch. To access the digital images, see the online FHL catalog page:
www.familysearch.org/search/catalog/2759155.

1946. *Minnesota, World War II Honor List of Dead and Missing* [Printed Book & Digital Version], digitized at FamilySearch.org. To access the digital version, see the online FHL catalog page:
www.familysearch.org/search/catalog/2330654.

1958-2001 Minnesota Marriage Index [Online Database], indexed at the FamilySearch.org website. Source: MN Dept of Health (indexed by Ancestry). The index may contain any of the following information: Name of bride and groom, Birthplace and estimated year of birth for bride and groom, Ages, Parents' names, Previous spouses, Marriage place and date, and Race. This database has 2,414,040 records. See https://familysearch.org/search/collection/1949335.
- For the Ancestry version of this database, see http://search.ancestry.com/search/db.aspx?dbid=8721.

1970-1995 Minnesota Divorce Index [Online Database], indexed at the FamilySearch.org website. Source: MN Dept of Health (indexed by Ancestry). The index lists the following information: Name of husband, Name of wife, Docket number, Divorce date, Divorce place, and Reference number (page, volume, entry number). This database has 366,350 records. See https://familysearch.org/search/collection/1967743.

1970-1995 Minnesota Divorce Index [Online Database], indexed at the Ancestry.com website. Source: MN Dept of Health. Each record includes: Husband's name, Husband's age, Wife's name, and Wife's age. This database has 734,109 records. See http://search.ancestry.com/search/db.aspx?dbid=1081.

1986-Current. *Minnesota Recent Newspaper Obituaries* [Online Database], digitized and indexed newspaper obituaries at the GenealogyBank website, including newspapers for Albany, Albert Lea, Apple Valley, Austin, Apple Valley, Austin, Blooming Prairie/Ellendale, Brooklyn Center, Brooklyn Park, and more Minnesota cities. See
www.genealogybank.com/explore/obituaries/all/usa/minnesota .

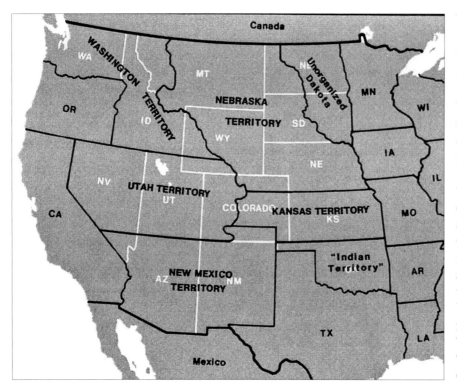

Western United States in 1860: Nebraska Territory and Kansas Territory were created in 1854, essentially west of the Missouri River to the Continental Divide. The 1860 Census of both Kansas and Nebraska Territories included a good number of people looking for gold in present Colorado. The Denver area was in the KS census, the Boulder area was in the NE census. "Unorganized Dakota" was a label invented by the Census Office. For convenience, several forts and posts along the Missouri and Yellowstone rivers in NETerr. were enumerated as part of Unorganized Dakota. An area remaining from the Unorganized Territory, was unofficially called "Indian Territory" (now Oklahoma).

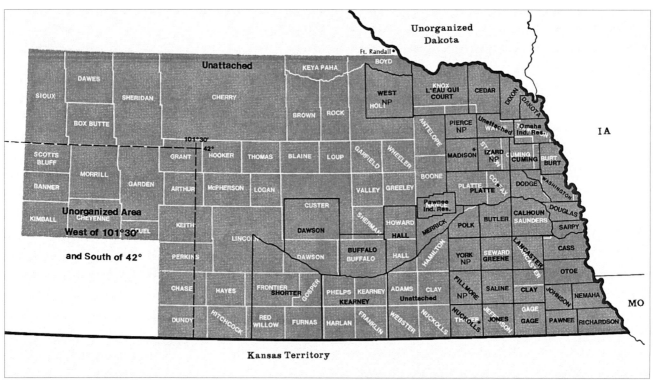

Nebraska Territory • 1860. The current 93 counties of Nebraska are shown in white. Those in black are for the time of the June 1860 Federal Census. The upper map shows the extent of Nebraska Territory to the northern U.S. border, and west to the Continental Divide. Although technically in Nebraska Territory, the various forts and trading posts along the Missouri River were enumerated in Unorganized Dakota. All other people enumerated in the 1860 census outside of the modern Nebraska area were at Fort Randall; or at Boulder, Altoona, and other northeastern Colorado towns enumerated as the *Unorganized area west of 101^0 30' and south of 42°*. *Map Note: County name changes are not explained here, except note that by 1870 the name Nuckolls had moved west one full county.

Nebraska
Censuses & Substitute Name Lists

Historical Timeline for Nebraska, 1682-1867

1682. Louisiana. French explorer René-Robert Cavelier (Sieur de LaSalle) erected a cross near the confluence of the Mississippi River and the Gulf of Mexico, after floating down river from the Illinois Country. He claimed the entire Mississippi Basin for Louis XIV of France, for whom Louisiana was named.

1682-1720. Louisiana. During this period, the jurisdiction of Louisiana ran from the Gulf of Mexico to the junction of the Arkansas River with the Mississippi River. The French administered Arkansas Post, Natchez, Baton Rouge, New Orleans, Mobile, and Biloxi as part of Louisiana. Fort Louis de la Louisiane (now Mobile), was the capital of Louisiana, 1702-1720.

1720-1762. Upper and Lower Louisiana. By 1720, The Illinois Country was separated from Québec and added to Louisiana. The original Louisiana area became known as *Lower Louisiana*. The capital of Lower Louisiana was at New Orleans, 1720-1762. *Upper Louisiana* extended from the Highlands (Terra Haute) on the Wabash River down the Ohio and Mississippi Valleys to the Arkansas River. The fur trading settlements of Upper Louisiana included Vincennes (now Indiana), Prairie du Chien (now Wisconsin); Cahokia, Kaskaskia, Chartres, Saint Philippe, and Prairie du Rocher (now Illinois); Ste. Genevieve (now Missouri), and Fort de Chavagnial on the Missouri River (now Kansas).

1763. Treaty of Paris. This was the end of the French and Indian war. (In Europe it was called the "Seven Years War.") At the 1763 treaty, the French surrendered all their claims in North America. Spain acquired the former French areas west of the Mississippi, renamed *Spanish Louisiana*. Great Britain gained all of Québec, which they immediately renamed the *Province of Canada*. Britain also gained control of the rest of North America east of the Mississippi River. They named their entire area *British North America*.

1783. Treaty of Paris. As the official end of the Revolutionary War, the 1783 treaty recognized the United States as an independent republic, with borders from the Atlantic Ocean to the Mississippi River. The treaty also reaffirmed the claims of Britain to present-day Canada; and Spain's claim to lands west of the Mississippi River.

1800. Louisiana. Napoleon acquired title of Louisiana from Spain. At the Third Treaty of San Ildefonso, the Spanish acknowledged that it was too costly to explore the country and could not see the rewards being worth the investment. Spain retroceded Louisiana to France in exchange for the Grand Duchy of Tuscany (now part of Italy).

1803. Louisiana Purchase. The United States purchased Louisiana from France. Sent by President Jefferson to attempt the purchase of New Orleans, the American negotiators (James Madison and Robert Livingston) were surprised when Napoleon offered the entire tract to them. The Louisiana Purchase was officially described as the "drainage of the Mississippi and Missouri River basins." Adding the area doubled the size of the United States.

1804. On an expedition ordered by President Thomas Jefferson, Captains Meriwether Lewis and William Clark's Corps of Discovery left St. Louis in search of an overland passage to the Pacific Ocean. Based on bad information from his spies, the Spanish governor of New Mexico dispatched soldiers from Santa Fe to the Arkansas River to intercept the party and arrest them. But, the Lewis and Clark party had taken a more northern route, following the Missouri River.

1804-1805. In 1804, Congress divided the Louisiana Purchase into two jurisdictions: **Louisiana District** and **Orleans Territory**. The latter had north and south bounds the same as the present state of Louisiana but did not include land east of the Mississippi River, and its northwestern corner extended on an indefinite line west into Spanish Tejas. For a year, Louisiana District was attached to Indiana Territory for judicial administration but became Louisiana Territory with its own Governor on July 4, 1805.

1812. Missouri Territory. On June 4th Louisiana Territory was renamed Missouri Territory by Congress This was to avoid any confusion after Orleans Territory became the State of Louisiana on April 30, 1812. The General Assembly of the Territory of Missouri met in St. Louis in October and converted the first five original districts into counties: Cape Girardeau, New Madrid, St. Charles, St. Louis, and Ste. Genevieve. A year later, the territorial legislature created Arkansas County from lands ceded by the Osage Indians.

1812. Spaniard Manuel Lisa built Fort Lisa on the Missouri River near present Omaha. He was credited with establishing the earliest fur trading posts along the Missouri River, from Montana to Nebraska.

1819. Nebraska Country. The U.S. Army established Fort Atkinson on the west side of the Missouri River (now the town of Fort Calhoun in Washington Co NE).

1820. Major Stephen Long explored the Platte and South Platte river routes of present Nebraska and Colorado. His official report referred to the central plains as the "Great American Desert" and had the effect of diverting interest in the area for several years. Long's report ignored the fact that over one million bison depended on the Nebraska Country for survival, and that the prairie had an abundance of fertile soil. Eighty years later, the Ogallala Aquifer, the largest aquifer in the world, began irrigating the "Great American Desert," including the entire state of Nebraska.

1820. The *Missouri Compromise* in Congress allowed Missouri to enter the Union as a slave state and Maine as a free state, thus keeping the balance of slave and free states equal in Congress. The Act dictated that the remaining area of old Missouri Territory north of Latitude 36° 30' was to be free of slavery (that area included present Kansas, Nebraska, Iowa, Minnesota, North Dakota, South Dakota, Wyoming, and Montana).

1821. Aug 10th. **Missouri** was admitted as a state with St. Louis as the capital. After Missouri became a state, the remaining part of old Missouri Territory was officially described as *Unorganized Territory*. The entire region was inhabited exclusively by American Indian tribes, except for a few left-over French-Canadian voyageurs roaming the rivers.

1823. Bellevue became the fist permanent settlement in Nebraska. The town is now a suburb of Omaha.

1827. Independence, Missouri. The frontier town of Independence was founded in 1827, the farthest point westward on the Missouri River where steamboats could travel at that time. Independence immediately became a supply point, staging area, and primary starting point for the growing number of trappers and traders using the Santa Fe Trail.

1829 Sublette's Trace/Oregon Trail. Before 1829, access to the Platte River Trail from Independence, Missouri, was via the Missouri River to the mouth of the Platte River in present Nebraska. But steamboat traffic ended at Independence and travel up river at that time required human-powered keel boats. The overland route of the Santa Fe Trail now started at Independence as well, heading west several miles into present Kansas, then southwest towards Santa Fe. A few miles into the Santa Fe Trail in present Kansas, at a point later called the Oregon Trail Junction, fur trader William Sublette blazed a cut-off from the Santa Fe Trail, turning northwest and connecting with the Platte River in present Nebraska. The new route across present northeast Kansas was more direct than the river route, and later became the first leg of the Oregon Trail.

1832. After dredging projects near the mouth of the Kansas River, steamboat traffic could continue up the Missouri River. In 1832, the steamboat *Yellowstone* began the first of its annual fur-trading voyages up the Missouri River, reaching Fort Union (present North

Dakota/Montana line). More steamboats going up river generated the need for docking, loading, and refueling facilities, and the development of new river ports along the entire length of the Missouri River.

1842. Nebraska Country. The word "Nebraska" first began to appear in publications in 1842 after John C. Fremont explored the Platte Valley and Nebraska areas.

1843. May. Oregon Trail. A wagon train with over 120 wagons, a large herd of livestock, and 1,000 pioneers left Elm Grove, MO and headed out on the Oregon Trail. The largest wagon train to date, it became the model for the thousands of wagon trains that followed. For an online list of the members of the 1843 Wagon Train, see the OR RootsWeb site:
http://freepages.history.rootsweb.ancestry.com/~mransom/pioneers.html

1846. The Utah-bound Mormons sent work parties ahead of their wagon trains to plant crops in Nebraska a year before the main body of immigrants passed through. This was when Nebraska was first discovered to be a great place to grow things.

1849. The onset of the California Gold Rush was when Nebraska was discovered as the best way to get there. A natural wagon route across the entire length of present Nebraska was the Platte River Trail (aka Mormon Trail, Oregon Trail, or Immigrant Trail).

1852. In this one year, over 250,000 people passed through Nebraska en route to California. Few stopped for any length of time, because the area was not legally open for settlement yet.

1854. Nebraska Territory was created in 1854 as part of the *Kansas-Nebraska Act*, landmark legislation relating to free versus slave states prior to the Civil War. The Act authorized the first land surveys west of the Missouri River, opening both territories for settlement. Both Kansas and Nebraska were expected to vote on the slavery issue, and both territories immediately began taking annual censuses to determine their numbers of qualified voters.
- Beginning in 1854, A large portion of eastern Nebraska Territory was surveyed for public land sales. The first GLOs were established at Brownsville, Dakota City, Nebraska City, and Omaha City. After the first year of land sales, about 4,500 people had settled in Nebraska Territory.

1863. During the Civil War, and towards the end of President Lincoln's first term in office, the Lincoln administration offered a quick approval to any proposed state constitution submitted from Nebraska. Lincoln saw the strong Union support of Nebraska Territory as a way to ensure enough votes for reelection – the matter was still not a certainty in Congress. Lincoln made the same offer to Nevada and Colorado. Only Nevada took up his offer. Both Nebraska and Colorado took the matter to their territorial legislatures, and both rejected statehood as "premature."

1867. Mar. Two years after the end of the Civil War, **Nebraska** joined the Union as the 37th state, with Omaha as the capital until a year later, when Lincoln was chosen.

Online Resources at the Nebraska State Historical Society

The NSHS presence on the Internet includes both online archives collections and online indexes. See http://nebraskahistory.org/databases/more_databases.htm.

In addition to the Nebraska Virtual Exhibits, searchable databases include the following:
- Atlases / Plat Books Name Index.
- BLOG - Search the Nebraska State Historical Society blog for recent posts.
- Cemetery Registry.
- City / County Directories.
- Civil War Veterans.
- Gazetteer Index, 1890 and 1911.
- Hastings Regional Center Cemetery, 1889-1959.
- Wyuka Cemetery Burials, (Lincoln, NE), 1877-1881.
- Norfolk Regional Center Cemetery Records, 1888-1954.
- U.S. General Land Office Tract Books – Search. homestead applications, proofs, & final certificates.
- Land Entry Files - Nebraska: Name Index to Cancelled, Rejected, and Relinquished Files (National Archives website).
- Nebraska - Our Towns (University of Nebraska database).
- Newspaper Project - over 200,000 names indexed from Nebraska newspapers. (NEGenWeb website).
- Newspapers on Microfilm. Indexed by town and newspaper name – PDF.
- Orphan Train riders.
- Prison Records, 1870-1990.
- Sherard's Nebraska Place Names.
- Telephone Directories.
- WWI Draft Registration Cards: 1917-1918, Nebraska Over 276,000 records, arranged by county.

Bibliography
Nebraska Censuses & Substitutes

Territorial Censuses, 1854-1865. The first Nebraska Territory censuses were taken in 1854, 1855, and 1856. They were heads of household name lists covering the eastern half of present-day Nebraska. The first three census years are mostly complete for all counties in place at the time. The fourth (and last) territorial census was taken in 1865, but only two full county name lists survive today. The originals of all surviving territorial census schedules are located at the Nebraska State Historical Society (NSHS) in Lincoln.

State Censuses, 1869-1884. After statehood in 1867, the Nebraska legislature passed a law that called for annual censuses, including lists of births and deaths to be gathered by the county tax assessors. It is not known how diligent the counties were in complying with the law, and only a few of the county census name lists have survived. The NSHS has some original annual name lists for 1869-1870, 1874-1879, and 1882-1884, but for just a few counties.

State Census, 1885. The Nebraska state census law was repealed in 1885. In that year, the Federal Government offered any state or territory an option for an assisted state census, providing federal money to defray up to half of the cost. Nebraska was one of only five states or territories that took up the offer. An 1885 state census of Nebraska was completed using a similar format as the 1880 federal census. The 1885 proved to be the last state census in Nebraska and stands complete for all counties in place in 1885, except for one missing county (Chase). Nebraska's original state copy of their 1885 census was lost – but as part of the deal with the Federal Government, a transcription copy had been made and sent to Washington, DC. That copy was microfilmed by the National Archives.

Censuses Online: The NE Territorial censuses for 1854, 1855, and 1856 are indexed in Ancestry's Compiled Census Index database. Full extractions of the NE 1854, 1855, and 1856 Terr. censuses are at the USGenWeb site for Nebraska. One county (Lancaster) of the 1865 NE Territory Census was digitized and indexed at Ancestry's NE State Census collection. Two more 1865 counties (Otoe & Cuming) have full extractions at the USGenWeb site for Nebraska. The NE State Censuses, 1870-1884 are online at Ancestry (1 or 2 counties only for each census year). Both Ancestry.com and FamilySearch.org have the 1885 NE State Census, the only NE State Census that is mostly complete.

Federal Censuses. The 1860 federal census taken in Nebraska Territory included mining camps in present-day Colorado (Boulder, Altoona, and a few other northeastern Colorado towns). They were added at the end of the enumeration lists for Nebraska towns, identified on the census schedules as *Unorganized West of 101° 30'*. The 1870-1940 federal censuses for Nebraska are complete for all counties (with the exception of the 1890, lost for all states). The 1950 federal census will open to the public in 2022.

Census Substitutes: Because of the number of Nebraska census name lists, the need for census substitutes between federal census years may seem less demanding – but this bibliography has many extra name lists. Together, they include Territorial, State, and Federal Censuses, Court Records, Directories, County Indexes, State Military Lists, Tax Lists, Vital Records, and Voter Lists. The censuses and substitute name lists begin below in chronological order:

♦ ♦ ♦ ♦ ♦

"1854 Nebraska Territory Census" [Printed Article], in *Roots and Leaves* (Eastern Nebraska Genealogical Society, Fremont, NE), Jan 1978 issue.

"1854 Nebraska Territory Census, Nemaha County" [Printed Article], in *Genealogist's Post* (R. T. Williams, Miami, FL), Vol. 4, No. 11 (Nov 1967) through Vol. 5, No. 2 (Feb 1968).

1854, 1855, 1856 Nebraska Territory Censuses **[Printed Index, Microfilm & Digital Version],** extracted by E. Evelyn Cox, published by the author, Ellensburg, WA, 1977. FHL book 978.2 X2p 1854-1856, and FHL film #1036024. To access the digital images, see the online FHL catalog page: **www.familysearch.org/search/catalog/183518.**

1854, 1855, 1856 Nebraska Territorial Census Index **[Printed Index],** edited by Ronald Vern Jackson, publ. Accelerated Indexing Systems, Salt Lake City, UT, 1980, 57 pages, FHL book 978.2 X2jrv 1854-56.

1854-1857. *Pioneers, Douglas County, Nebraska* **[Online Database],** indexed at the Genealogy Trails website. See **http://genealogytrails.com/neb/douglas/pioneers_1854-57.htm.**

1854-1860. *Nebraska, Compiled Census Index* **[Online Database],** indexed at the Ancestry.com website. Source: Accelerated Indexing Systems databases, acquired by Ancestry in 1999. The 1854, 1855, and 1856 NE Territorial Census name lists were indexed in separate databases by A.I.S. This collection also includes the A.I.S. index to the 1860 NE Territory Federal Census. The cited 1870 NE Federal Censuses could not be confirmed. Any search for an 1869, 1870, or 1871 date could not be found, and brought up an 1860 date instead. Each index record includes: Name, State, County (1854 was by District), Township, Year, Page, and Database title. This database has 8,303 records. See
http://search.ancestry.com/search/db.aspx?dbid=3559.

1854-1869. *Census Records of Nebraska* **[Online Database].** Extant lists for 1854, 1855, 1856, 1865 (Territorial), and 1869 were extracted and published in *Nebraska & Midwest Genealogical Records* (N&MGR), a publication of the Nebraska Genealogical Society, 1922-1944. The USGenWeb site for Nebraska has put all of the census articles from the N&MGR online. See
www.usgennet.org/usa/ne/topic/resources/OLLibrary/Journals/NMGR/censindx.html.

- Contents: The 1854, 1855, and 1856 territorial censuses are fairly complete for all counties. The 1865 territorial has name lists for Cuming and Otoe counties only; and the 1869 state census has lists for Butler and Stanton counties only. Direct links to the name lists by Year, N&MGR Vol. No. & Issue No. are organized as follows:
  - 1854 NE Territorial: District 1 (includes Pawnee & Richardson Co, and parts of current Gage, Johnson, Nemaha Co)
  - 1854 NE Territorial: District 2 (primarily Nemaha & Otoe counties)
  - 1854 NE Territorial: District 3 (Cass Co)
  - 1854 NE Territorial: District 4 (Douglas & Sarpy Co)
  - 1854 NE Territorial: District 5 (Dodge Co plus)
  - 1854 NE Territorial: District 6 (Burt & Washington Co)
  - 1855 NE Territorial: Cass Co
  - 1855 NE Territorial: Dodge Co
  - 1855 NE Territorial: Douglas Co
  - 1855 NE Territorial: Nemaha Co
  - 1855 NE Territorial: Otoe Co
  - 1855 NE Territorial: Pawnee Co
  - 1855 NE Territorial: Richardson Co.
  - 1855 NE Territorial: Washington Co
  - 1856 NE Territorial: Burt Co
  - 1856 NE Territorial: Cass Co
  - 1856 NE Territorial: Clay Co (area that is now Lancaster & Gage Co)
  - 1856 NE Territorial: Colfax Co (see Platte Co)
  - 1856 NE Territorial: Cuming Co
  - 1856 NE Territorial: Dakota Co (includes Dixon Co)
  - 1856 NE Territorial: Dixon Co (see Dakota Co)
  - 1856 NE Territorial: Dodge Co
  - 1856 NE Territorial: Douglas Co (Southern district – now Sarpy Co)
  - 1856 NE Territorial: Douglas Co (Northern District)
  - 1856 NE Territorial: Gage Co (see Clay Co)
  - 1856 NE Territorial: Johnson Co (see Nemaha Co)
  - 1856 NE Territorial: Lancaster Co
  - 1856 NE Territorial: Lancaster Co (also see Clay Co)
  - 1856 NE Territorial: Nemaha Co
  - 1856 NE Territorial: Otoe Co
  - 1856 NE Territorial: Pawnee Co
  - 1856 NE Territorial: Platte Co
  - 1856 NE Territorial: Richardson Co
  - 1856 NE Territorial: Sarpy Co (see Douglas Co, Southern District)
  - 1856 NE Territorial: Washington Co
  - 1865 NE Territorial: Cuming Co
  - 1865 NE Territorial: Otoe Co
  - 1869 NE State: Butler Co
  - 1869 NE State: Stanton Co

1854-1881. *Douglas County, Nebraska Marriages* **[Online Database],** indexed at the Ancestry.com website. Source: Book, same title, by Greater Omaha Genealogical Society and Friends, publ. 2002, GPC, Baltimore. This database has the scanned images from the text of the book, with OCR index. This database has about 50,000 records. See
http://search.ancestry.com/search/db.aspx?dbid=49043.

1854-1983. *Nebraska Newspaper Archives* **[Online Database],** digitized and indexed newspapers at the GenealogyBank website for Bloomington, Lincoln, Nebraska City, and Omaha, Nebraska. See
www.genealogybank.com/explore/newspapers/all/usa/nebraska.

1854-1900s Nebraska Original Land Owners. See the *Family Maps* series for Nebraska counties, maps of all original land patents, compiled by Greg Boyd, publ. Arphax Publishing Co., Norman, OK. These privately-produced computer-generated maps show the first property owners for an entire county, produced as a book of maps, each map laid out on the federal township grid, and includes indexes to help you locate a person, place-name, or cemetery. Additional maps are added for each county to show roads, waterways, railroads, selected city centers, and cemeteries within a county. *Family Maps* books have been published for Arthur, Blaine, Garden, Garfield, Grant, Hooker, Logan, Loup, McPherson, Scotts Bluff, Sioux, and Thomas County, Nebraska. See **www.arphax.com**.

1854-1900s. *Nebraska GenWeb Archives* **[Online Database].** The NEGenWeb site offers free genealogical databases with searchable statewide name lists and for all Nebraska counties. Databases may include Bibles, Biographies, Cemeteries, Censuses, Court Records, Deaths, Deeds, Directories, Histories, Marriages, Military, Newspapers, Obituaries, Photos, Schools, Tax Lists, Wills, and more. See
http://usgwarchives.net/ne/nefiles.htm.

1854-1900s. **Biographies - Douglas County, Nebraska [Online Database],** indexed at the Genealogy Trails website. See
http://genealogytrails.com/neb/douglas/bios_index.htm.

1854-1900s. *Database Search: Lincoln Lancaster County Genealogical Society* **[Online Database],** search all databases, including Cemetery, Marriage, Mortuary, Probate, Newspaper, Naturalization records, and more. Indexed at the LLCGS.net website. See www.llcgs.net/searchhome.php.

1854-1986. *Nemaha County, Nebraska* **[Printed Book],** written by the people of Nemaha County, compiled by the Nemaha County Book Committee and sponsored by the Nemaha Valley Museum, publ. 1987, 338 pages, FHL book 978.2278 D3n.

1854-1996. *Nebraska Newspaper Abstracts* **[Printed Book],** compiled and publ. Nebraska State Genealogical Society, Alliance, NE, 1984-1996. Contains abstracts arranged in alphabetical order by surname, giving name of person, type of event (birth, marriage, death, obituary, divorce, etc.), date of publication, newspaper name, contents of event, page, town and county.10 Vols., See FHL book 978.2 B32n.

1854-2000. *Linkpendium – Nebraska: Family History & Genealogy, Census, Birth, Marriage, Death, Vital Records & More* **[Online Databases].** Linkpendium is a genealogical portal site with links to state, county, town, and local databases. Currently listed are selected sites for Nebraska statewide resources (398), Renamed/Discontinued Counties (9), Adams County (602) Antelope County (329), Arthur County (82), Banner County (92), Blaine County (96), Boone County (270), Box Butte County (147) and 86 more Nebraska counties. See
www.linkpendium.com/ne-genealogy.

"1855 Nebraska Territory Census, Dodge County" [Printed Article], in *Roots and Leaves*, (Eastern Nebraska Genealogical Society, Fremont, NE), Vol. 17, No. 3 (Fall 1994).

"1855 Nebraska State Census, Washington County" [Printed Article], in *Roots and Leaves*, (Eastern Nebraska Genealogical Society, Fremont, NE), Vol. 3, No. 3 (Fall 1980).

1855-1867. *Index to Marriage Book A (from Nov 29, 1855 to Feb 18, 1867), Richardson County, Nebraska Territory* **[Microfilm & Digital Version],** from a typescript manuscript by Mr. and Mrs. Harvey Mobley. Filmed by the Genealogical Society of Utah, 1976, 1 rolls, FHL film #928359. To access the digital version, see the online FHL catalog page:
https://familysearch.org/search/catalog/55451.

1855-1870. *Douglas County, Nebraska, Naturalization Records* **[Microfilm],** from the originals at NSHS, Lincoln, NE. Filmed by the Genealogical Society of Utah, 1999, 1 roll, FHL film #2168455. To see if this microfilm has been digitized yet, see the FHL catalog page:
www.familysearch.org/search/catalog/1040670.

1855-1940. *Irish and Scotch-Irish Who Made a Declaration of Intention to Naturalize From Cass, Douglas, Lancaster, Nemaha, Otoe, Richardson, Sarpy and York Counties in Nebraska* **[Printed Book],** compiled by Ellen M. and Raymond D. DeVries, publ. 1997, Lincoln, NE, 152 pages, FHL book 978.22 P4d.

1855-1908. Nebraska, Marriage Records [Online Database], digitized and indexed at Ancestry.com. Source: NSHS, Lincoln, NE. Information that may be found in this database includes: Groom's name, Groom's parents' names, bride's name, Bride's parents' names, Birth date, Birth place, Marriage place, and Marriage date. This database has 1,452,885 records, see
www.ancestry.com/search/collections/61335.
- See also, *Nebraska Marriages, 1855-1995* **[Online Database],** indexed at the FamilySearch.org website. Source: NSHS, Lincoln, NE. Each index record includes: Name, Birth place, Residence, Marriage date, Marriage place, and Spouse. Each record includes a link to the images of these marriage records available at the NSHS website. This database has 193,370 records. See
https://familysearch.org/search/collection/1708654.

"1856 Nebraska Territory Census, Burt County" [Printed Article], name list in *Roots and Leaves*, (Eastern Nebraska Genealogical Society, Fremont, NE), Vol. 3, No. 3 (Fall 1980).

"**1856 Nebraska Territory Census, Dodge County**" **[Printed Article],** name list in *Roots and Leaves*, (Eastern Nebraska Genealogical Society, Fremont, NE), Vol. 17, No. 4 (Winter 1994).

"**1856 Nebraska Territory Census, Pawnee County**" **[Printed Article],** name list in *Genealogist's Post*, (R. T. Williams, Miami, FL), Vol. 4, No. 6 (Jun 1967).

"**1856 Nebraska Territory Census, Sarpy County**" **[Printed Article],** name list in *Remains to be Found*, (Greater Omaha Genealogical Society), March 1986 issue.

"**1856 Nebraska Territory Census, Washington County**" **[Printed Article],** name list in *Roots and Leaves,* (Eastern Nebraska Genealogical Society, Fremont, NE), Vol. 4, No. 1 (Spring 1981).

1856-1864. *Douglas County, Nebraska, Marriage Applications* **[Microfilm],** from the originals at the NE Historical Society. Filmed by the Genealogical Society of Utah, 1999, 1 roll, FHL film #2156455. To see if this microfilm has been digitized yet, see the FHL catalog page: **www.familysearch.org/search/catalog/1040666.**

1856-1874. *Washington County, Nebraska Marriage Records* **[Printed Book],** publ. Eastern Nebraska Genealogical Society, Fremont, NE. Includes index at the front of the book. Contents: v.1. April 20, 1856-September 6, 1865 -- v.2. October 21, 1867-July 2, 1874. FHL has v. 1-2 and bound them together. Se FHL book 978.2245 V2w.

1856-1898. *Nebraska, Marriage Index* **[Online Database],** indexed at the Ancestry.com website. Source: Liahona Research extractions from microfilmed records at the Family History Library, Salt Lake City, UT. This database has marriage records from Adams, Buffalo, Cuming, Dodge, Sarpy, and Washington County, Nebraska only. Each record includes: Name, Spouse's name, Marriage date and place, and source information. This database has 9,214 records. See **www.ancestry.com//search/collections/7871.**

1856-1951. *Marriage Records, Dodge County, Nebraska* **[Microfilm],** from the originals at the Dodge County Courthouse, Fremont, NE. Filmed by the Genealogical Society of Utah, 1997, 15 rolls, beginning with FHL film #2079549 (Index to Books A thru C 1856-1877; Marriage Book 1, 1856-1868; Marriage Books A, B, B1, 1856-1871; Marriage Book 2, 1871-1877; Marriage Book 3, 1877-1882). To see if this microfilm has been digitized yet, see the FHL catalog page: **www.familysearch.org/search/catalog/740384.**

1856-1989. *Nebraska, Wills and Probate Records* **[Online Database],** digitized and indexed at the Ancestry.com website. Source: Ancestry extractions from Nebraska county, district, and probate courts. Bound and loose papers may include Letters of Administration, Inventories, Distribution and Accounting, Bonds, and Guardianships. (Note: the 1806 date in the title was a mis-interpretation of one date appearing in the digitized images). See the Browse Collection box for the list of counties included in this database. The index to each record includes: Name, Probate date, Probate place, Inferred death year, Inferred death place, and Item description/type of record. The digitized image may have much more detail about the deceased and heirs, etc. This database has 2,703 records. See **http://search.ancestry.com/search/db.aspx?dbid=9073.**

1856-1993. See *Marriage Records, 1856-1993; Indexes, 1856-1986 (Dakota County, Nebraska)* **[Microfilm],** from the originals at the Dakota County Courthouse, Dakota City, Nebraska. Filmed by the Genealogical Society of Utah, 1995, 15 rolls, beginning with FHL film #2021908 (Index to marriage records, Vol 1-5). To see if this microfilm has been digitized yet, see the FHL catalog page: **www.familysearch.org/search/catalog/776781.**

1857-1930. *Naturalization Records, District Court, Sarpy County, Nebraska* **[Microfilm],** from the originals at the NE Historical Society, Lincoln, NE. Includes Declarations of Intentions, Petitions, Certificates, and Final Papers. Filmed by the Genealogical Society of Utah, 1995, 2 rolls, FHL #2027533 & #2027534. To see if this microfilm has been digitized yet, see the FHL catalog page: **www.familysearch.org/search/catalog/761302.**

1857-1950. *Marriage Records, Licenses, and Certificates, Sarpy County, NE* **[Microfilm],** from the originals at the Sarpy County Courthouse, Bellevue, NE. Filmed by the Genealogical Society of Utah, 1997, 28 rolls, beginning with FHL film #2107860 (Marriage records, 1857-1925). To see if this microfilm has been digitized yet, see the FHL catalog page: **www.familysearch.org/search/catalog/740728.**

1857-1896. *Sarpy County, Nebraska Marriages* **[Printed Book],** edited by Sylvia Nimmo, Joyce Cook, and Alice Clopton, publ. Omaha, NE, 1982, 140 pages, FHL book 978.2256 V2h.

1858-1898. See *Burt County, Nebraska, Probate Records, 1858-1898; Index, 1858-1895* **[Microfilm]**, from the originals at the NE State Historical Society, Lincoln, NE. Includes Probates, Estate Books, Administrator, Executor, Guardian Petitions, Inventories, and Settlements. Filmed by the Genealogical Society of Utah, 1999, 4 rolls, beginning with FHL film #2166410 (General Index, 1858-1895). To see if this microfilm has been digitized yet, see the FHL catalog page: www.familysearch.org/search/catalog/1040475.

1858-1900. *Early Nebraska Marriages and Cemetery Inscriptions: For the Following Counties: Cass, Dodge, Douglas, Fillmore, Lancaster, Otoe, Richardson, Saline, Wayne* **[Printed Book 7 Microfilm]**, compiled by E. Evelyn Cox, copied from volumes of the Nebraska and Midwest Genealogical Record, 19915, FHL book 978.2 V28ce. Also on microfilm, FHL film #1440415. To see if this microfilm has been digitized yet, see the FHL catalog page: www.familysearch.org/search/catalog/727320.

1858-1907. *Original Land Entries of Lancaster County, Nebraska 1858-1907, as taken from U.S. Land Office Tract Books* **[Printed Book]**, compiled and publ. DAR, Deborah Avery Chapter, Lincoln, NE, 97 pages, FHL book 978.2293 R2o.

1858-1986. *Index to Marriage Records, Otoe County, Nebraska,* **[Microfilm]**, from the originals at the Otoe County Courthouse, Nebraska City, NE. Filmed by the Genealogical Society of Utah, 1994, 16 rolls, beginning with FHL film #1977319 (Index to Marriage Records, 1858-1980, Aardappel, Deltone – Bek). To see if this microfilm has been digitized yet, see the FHL catalog page: www.familysearch.org/search/catalog/720786.

"1859 Nebraska Territory Census, Saunders County, Salt Creek" **[Printed Article]**, name list in *Nebraska Ancestree,* (Nebraska State Genealogical Society, Lincoln, NE), Vol. 2, No. 1 (Summer 1979).

1860. *Nebraska, 1860 Federal Census: Population Schedules* **[Microfilm & Digital Capture]**, filmed by the National Archives, 1950, 1967, 2 rolls, 2nd filming: FHL film #803665 (Entire Territory). To access the digital images, see the online FHL catalog page: www.familysearch.org/search/catalog/705444.

1860 Federal Census of the Nebraska Territory; Surname Index (Soundex Sort) **[Online Database]**, compiled by Ted & Carole Miller for the USGenWeb site for Nebraska. For the index, A-F, see: http://files.usgwarchives.net/ne/state/census/1860/sdx-idx1.txt. For the G-N index, see http://files.usgwarchives.net/ne/state/census/1860/sdx-idx2.txt. For the O-Z index, see http://files.usgwarchives.net/ne/state/census/1860/sdx-idx3.txt.

1860-1885. *Nebraska, State Census Collection* **[Online Database]**, digitized and indexed at the Ancestry.com website. Source: 1860-1884, NSHS, Lincoln; 1885, National Archives microfilm series M352. This database includes an index and images of an 1860 Federal Census (1 county); an 1865 NE Territorial Census (1 county); countywide NE State Censuses for 1870, 1874-1879; 1880, and 1881-1884; and the statewide 1885 NE State Census – for the following years and counties:
- **1860** Federal: Lancaster Co only
- **1865** NE Territorial: Lancaster Co only
- **1870** NE State: Cass and Lancaster Co only
- **1874** NE State: Lancaster Co only
- **1875** NE State: Lancaster Co only
- **1876** NE State: Cass Co and Lancaster Co only
- **1877** NE State: Cass Co and Lancaster Co only
- **1878** NE State: Cass Co, Lancaster Co, and Saunders Co only
- **1879** NE State: Cass Co and Lancaster Co only
- **1880** NE State: Cass Co and Lancaster Co only
- **1881** NE State: Cass Co only
- **1882** NE State: Cass Co only
- **1883** NE State: Cass Co only
- **1884** NE State: Cass Co only
- **1885** NE State: All counties that existed at the time, except for Chase Co. Blaine Co was created in 1885, but not organized in time to make it into this census).

The census schedules usually include: Name, Race, Gender, Age, Birthplace, Location (town, county, state), Enumeration district number, Date the census was taken, and the Census page number. Additional information may be found on the actual census image. This database has 851,345 records. See http://search.ancestry.com/search/db.aspx?dbid=1668.
- NOTE: The one 1860 federal census digitized as part of this series was from Lancaster Co NE. This original set was used to make the copy that was sent to Washington, DC - the one later microfilmed by the National Archives. Therefore, it would be possible to compare the two digitized versions and look for copying errors. Also, note that both Cass and Lancaster Cos NE have state census name lists for 1870 and 1880.These can be compared with the 1870 and 1880 federal censuses for such things as name spellings, places of birth, and other persons living within a family, etc.

1861-1865. *Index to Compiled Service Records of Volunteer Union Soldiers Who Served in Organizations from the Territory of Nebraska*

[Microfilm], from the originals at the National Archives, Washington, DC. Filmed by the National Archives, 1964, 2 rolls, FHL film #821905 (Surnames A-La); and FHL film #821906 (Surnames Le-Z).
- This database was included in *United States Civil War Soldiers Index* [Online Database], see www.familysearch.org/search/collection/1910717.

1861-1865. *Nebraska Civil War Service Records of Union Soldiers* **[Online Database]**, indexed at the FamilySearch.org website. Source: National Archives microfilm series M1787. Union service records of soldiers who served in organizations from the Territory of Nebraska. The records include a jacket-envelope for each soldier, labeled with his name, his rank, and the unit in which he served. The jacket-envelope typically contains card abstracts of entries relating to the soldier as found in original muster rolls, returns, rosters, payrolls, appointment books, hospital registers, prison registers and rolls, parole rolls, inspection reports; and the originals of any papers relating solely to the particular soldier. Each index record includes: Name, Event type, Event year, Age, and Military unit. This database has 74,800 records. See
https://familysearch.org/search/collection/1932417.

1861-1869. *Nebraska Volunteers* **[Online Database]**, indexed at the Ancestry.com website. This is an index to the book, *Roster of Nebraska Volunteers from 1861 to 1869*, publ. 1888. The index includes: Given name, Surname, Company, Regiment or Battalion, Rank, and Residence. This database has 5,169 records. See
http://search.ancestry.com/search/db.aspx?dbid=3734.
- See also *Roster of Nebraska Volunteers from 1861 to 1869* **[Online Database]**, digitized and indexed at the Ancestry.com website. Source: Book, same title, by Edgar S. Dudley, from documents at the Nebraska Adjutant General's office, publ. 1888. This database has the scanned images from the text of the book, with an OCR name index for searching. This database has 237 pages. See
http://search.ancestry.com/search/db.aspx?dbid=29983.

1861-1948. *Nebraska, Grand Army of the Republic, Burial Records* **[Online Database]**, digitized and indexed at FamilySearch.org. The collection consists of burial records of Union veterans of the Civil War living in Nebraska. Many of the veterans served in Union regiments from other states, see
www.familysearch.org/search/collection/2721451.

"1865 Nebraska Territory Census, Cuming County" [Printed Article], name list and annotations in Roots and Leaves, (Eastern Nebraska Genealogical Society, Fremont, NE), Vol. 3, No. 1 (Spring 1980).

1866-1909. *An Index to the Early Marriage Records of Lancaster County, Nebraska* **[Printed Book]**, compiled and publ. Lincoln-Lancaster County Genealogical Society, 1987, 3 vols. Vol. 1: Books 1-13; Vol. 2: Books 14-26; Vol. 3: Books 27-31. See FHL book 978.2293 V22i 1866-1906 v.1-3.

1866-1921 Omaha and Douglas County Directories **[Microfilm]**, from the originals at various libraries and societies, filmed by Research Publications, Woodbridge, CT, 1980-1984, 25 rolls, beginning with FHL film #1377220 (1866 Collins' Omaha Directory). For a complete list of roll numbers and contents of each roll, see the online FHL catalog page for this title. See
https://familysearch.org/search/catalog/545787.

1867-1909. *Naturalizations (Nebraska), Some Petitions for Naturalization & Some Declarations of Intention, 1867-1909* **[Microfilm & Digital Capture]**, from the originals at the National Archives, Kansas City, MO. Many of the documents pertain to Douglas County and the city of Omaha. Filmed by the Genealogical Society of Utah, 1994, 1 roll, FHL film #1954068. To access the digital images, see the online FHL catalog page:
www.familysearch.org/search/catalog/711661.

1867-1944. *Lancaster County, Nebraska District Court Records: Intention to Naturalize* **[Printed Book]**, compiled by Ellen M. DeVries, publ. Lincoln-Lancaster Co Genealogical Society, 1995, 176 pages, FHL book 978.293 P4d.

1868-1896. *Butler County – Genealogy Trails* **[Online Database]**, this is the home page to the following databases related to Butler County, Nebraska: County Data, County Organization, Early History, County Firsts, 1860 Federal Census, 1880 Schedules of Defective, Dependent and Delinquent Classes, and Butler, The Banner County. See
http://genealogytrails.com/neb/butler/countydataindexpage.htm.

1868-1943. *Naturalization Records, Burt County, Nebraska* **[Microfilm]**, from the originals at the NE State Archives. Includes Declarations of Intent, Petitions, and Naturalization records and Certificates. Filmed by the Genealogical Society of Utah, 1994, 4 rolls, beginning with FHL film #1977260 (Index to

Naturalizations, 1871-1932). To see if this microfilm has been digitized yet, see the FHL catalog page: www.familysearch.org/search/catalog/720790.

1869-1994. *Hall County, Nebraska, Marriage Records* [Microfilm], from the originals at the Hall County Courthouse, Grand Island, NE. Some volumes have indexes at the beginning. Filmed by the Genealogical Society of Utah, 1995, 27 rolls, beginning with FHL film #2027084 (Index cards, brides: Alborg – Melch, 1987-1994). To see if this microfilm has been digitized yet, see the FHL catalog page: www.familysearch.org/search/catalog/783615.

1870. *Nebraska, 1870 Federal Census: Population Schedules* [Microfilm & Digital Capture], filmed by the National Archives, 8 rolls, beginning with FHL film #552327 (Gage, Black Bird, Buffalo, Burt, Butler, Cass, Cedar, Cheyenne, Clay, Colfax, Cuming, Dakota, Dawson, Dixon, and Dodge counties). To access the digital images, see the online FHL catalog page: www.familysearch.org/search/catalog/698908.

1870. *Nebraska, 1870 Federal Census: Mortality Schedules* [Microfilm & Digital Capture], from the originals at the NE St. Hist. Soc., Lincoln, NE. NSHS title: *Census Schedules in the Custody of the Nebraska State Historical Society, 9th Census 1870 Nebraska.* Filmed by the National Archives, series T1128, 1 roll, FHL film #1405500. To access the digital images, see the online FHL catalog page: www.familysearch.org/search/catalog/343849.

1871-1907. *Marriage Records, Hall County, Nebraska* [Printed Book & Digital Version], compiled by Vonna J. Jackson, publ. in 8 volumes, 1998-2003. Volumes are individually indexed. FHL combined 8 vols into 5 bound books. Contents: v. [1-2]. Marriage Books 1 & 2, 22 Dec. 1871 - 25 Feb. 1886 -- v. [3-4]. Books 3 & 4, 2 Mar. 1886 - 11 Aug. 1892 -- v. [5]. Book 5; 12 Aug. 1893 - 5 Nov. 1896 -- v. [6-7]. Books 6 & 7, 6 Nov. 1896 - 24 Mar. 1904 -- v. [8]. Book 8, 29 Mar. 1904-1 Jan. 1907. Contains abstracts of original marriage records, giving names of grooms and brides, ages, birth places, current residence, names of parents, date and place of marriage, marriage record book and page numbers. FHL has v. [1-2] and [3-4] bound together in one volume. See FHL book 978.241 V28j v.1-8. Also available on microfilm, 2 rolls, FHL film #1440521 & #1573511. To access the digital version, see the online FHL catalog page: https://familysearch.org/search/catalog/818784.

1871-1937. *Burt County, Nebraska: Marriages, Brides-Grooms Index A-Z* [Printed Book & Digital Version], compiled by Joy L. Snow, publ. 2000, 161 pages, FHL book 978.2243 V22s. To access the digital images, see the online FHL catalog page: https://familysearch.org/search/catalog/2120924.

"1872 Tax List, Antelope County, Nebraska" [Printed Article], in *Nebraska Ancestree*, (Nebraska State Genealogical Society, Lincoln, NE),Vol. 9, No. 3 (Winter 1987), and Vol. 11, No. 1 (Summer 1988).

1872 Personal and Property Taxes, Burt County, Nebraska, [Online Database], indexed at the RootsWeb site for Burt Co NE. See www.rootsweb.ancestry.com/~neburt/olres/burttax1872.html.

1873-1900. *Sittler Index of Surnames: For Which Information has been Abstracted from the (Lincoln) Nebraska State Journal* [Printed Book], by Melvin Sittler, publ. Lincoln-Lancaster County Genealogical Society, 1983-1993, 5 vols: Vol. 1: 1873-1899, A-D; Vol. 2: 1873-1899, E-K; Vol. 3: 1873-1899, L-R; Vol. 4: 1873-1899, S-Z; and Vol. 4: 1900. See FHL book 978.2293 D22sl v. 1-5.

"1875-1877 Tax Receipts, Dawson County, Nebraska" [Printed Article], in *Dawson County Genealogical Newsletter,* (Dawson Co Genealogical Society, Cozad, NE), Vol. 12, No. 2 (Summer 1998) and Vol. 12, No. 3 (Fall 1998).

1875-1899. *Nebraska, Church Records* [Online Database], includes church records from the Reorganized Church of Jesus Christ of Latter-Day Saints chapels in Elkhorn and Antelope, Nebraska, see www.familysearch.org/search/collection/2790263.

1876 Tax List, Dodge County, Nebraska [Printed Book], compiled and published by the Eastern Nebraska Genealogical Society, Fremont, NE, 2000, 26 pages. Includes surname index. Contains name of property owner, taxation number, description of property, amount of tax liability. Includes Dodge County tax books, nos. 6, 8 and 10. FHL book 978.2235 R4d.

1876-1885. *1876 Nebraska State Census, Sarpy County, with Mortality Schedule; and 1885 State Census* **[Printed Book],** compiled and published by the Eastern Nebraska Genealogical Society, Fremont, NE, 1989, 63 pages. Contains an abstract of the 1885 and 1876 Sarpy County census, arranged in alphabetical order by surname, showing name of head of household, names of other persons in the household, ages, places of birth, other information, township where living, and frame number on microfilm of original census. See FHL book 978.2256 X22s.

1878-1927 School Census Records, Lancaster County, Nebraska **[Online Database],** indexed at the sites.google.com webpage for Lancaster Co NE. See https://sites.google.com/site/lancastercountyne/school-census-records.

"**1879 Tax Assessors Book, Center Township, Buffalo County, Nebraska**" **[Printed Article],** in *Buffalo Chips,* (Fort Kearney Genealogical Society, Kearney, NE), Vol. 14, No. 1 (Spring 1991).

1880. *Nebraska, 1880 Federal Census: Soundex and Population Schedules* **[Microfilm & Digital Capture],** filmed by the National Archives, c1970, 37 rolls, beginning with FHL film #1254743 (Adams, Antelope, Blackbird, Boone, Buffalo, and Burt counties). To access the digital images (Population Schedules), see the online FHL catalog page: www.familysearch.org/search/catalog/676486.

"**1881 Tax Assessors Book of Personal and Real Estate, Buffalo County, Nebraska**" **[Printed Article],** in *Buffalo Chips,* (Fort Kearney Genealogical Society, Kearney, NE), Vol. 17, No. 2-3 (Summer 1994).

"**1881 Personal Tax List, Greeley County, Nebraska**" [Printed Article], in *Nebraska Ancestree,* (Nebraska State Genealogical Society, Lincoln, NE),Vol. 11, No. 1 (Summer 1988).

"**1882 Personal Property Tax List, Shelton Precinct, Buffalo County, Nebraska**" **[Printed Article],** in *Buffalo Chips,* (Fort Kearney Genealogical Society, Kearney, NE), Vol.. 8, No. 1 (Winter 1985) and Vol. 8, No. 2-4 (Spring 1985).

1882 History. See *History of the State of Nebraska: Containing a Full Account of its Early Settlements; Also an Extended Description of its Counties, Cities, Towns and Villages. and Biographical Sketches* **[Printed Book, Microfilm & Digital Capture],** by A. T. Andreas, published by Western Historical Co., Chicago, 1882, 2 vols., 1,506 pages. This is the standard history of Nebraska. In the "Military History" section are complete rosters of those persons serving in Nebraska units during the Civil War and Indian campaigns on the Plains, 1861-1869. These rosters list names, dates of service, Nebraska residence, and remarks about their service. Contents: Part 1: Early History of Nebraska to Dundy County; Part 2: Fillmore County to York County. FHL book 978.2 H2h and FHL film #1000178. To access the digital images, see the online FHL catalog page:
www.familysearch.org/search/catalog/2840982.

- See also, *Index to History of the State of Nebraska: Published in Chicago by the Western Historical Company, A.T. Andreas, Proprietor, 1882, and Commonly Known as Andreas' History of Nebraska* **[Microfilm & Digital Capture],** compiled by Raymond E. Dale, originally published by the Nebraska State Historical Society, 1963, 500 pages. Filmed by the Genealogical Society of Utah, FHL film #1689292. To access the digital images, see the online FHL catalog page:
www.familysearch.org/search/catalog/744724.

"**1882-1885 Poll Tax, Dawson County, Nebraska**" **[Printed Article],** in *Nebraska Ancestree,* (Nebraska State Genealogical Society, Lincoln, NE),Vol. 20, No. 1 (Summer 1987) and Vol. 20, No. 2 (Fall 1997).

1883. See *Federal Pensioners, 1 January 1883* **[Online Database],** indexed at the USGenWeb site for Nebraska. The statewide lists are broken into four alpha groups, and there is one list for each Nebraska county:
www.usgwarchives.net/ne/state/military/penstabl.htm.

1883-1935 Lincoln (Nebraska) City Directories **[Microfilm],** from the original records located in various libraries and societies, filmed by Research Publications, Inc., Woodbridge, CT, 199?, 15 rolls, beginning with FHL film #2156801 (1883-1884 Wolfe's Lincoln city directory). For a complete list of roll numbers and contents of each roll, see the online FHL catalog page for this title. See
https://familysearch.org/search/catalog/993193.

1884-1897. See **Lancaster County Probate Records, 1884-1897 [Printed Index & Microfilm],** compiled by Ellen DeVries, publ. Lincoln-Lancaster Co Genealogical Society, 2000, 99 pages, FHL book 978.2293 P22d. Also on microfilm, FHL film #1440468.

1885 Nebraska State Census **[Online Database],** digitized and indexed at the FamilySearch.org website. Source: National Archives microfilm series M352. This Nebraska 1885 state census set was copied from the state's original set (now lost) and sent to Washington, DC. The 1885 enumeration was prompted by the Federal Government, who offered to pay up to half the cost . This Federal copy includes all Nebraska counties that existed at the time, except Chase Co NE is missing. Each index record includes: Name, Birth year, Spouse, Children, Other persons living in a family, and Residence. At each index record, the full image of an 1885 census page is accessible, adding considerable information, e.g., occupation, birth place of each person and birth place of the parents of each person. This database has 747,367 records. See **https://familysearch.org/search/collection/1810728**.

- See also, *Nebraska State Census, 1885 (Index)* **[Online Database],** indexed at the Ancestry.com website. Source: National Archives microfilm series M352. This is an every-name index to the NE 1885 State Census (no images), separate from Ancestry's 1860-1885 collection. For each person listed, the index includes: Name, Age, Birth year, Birth place, Race, Census date, Census location, Enumerator, Film roll, and Page. This database has 737,606 records. See **http://search.ancestry.com/search/db.aspx?dbid=6585**.

- See also *Schedules of the Nebraska State Census of 1885* **[Microfilm & Digital Capture],** from the originals located at the Central Plains National Archives Branch, Kansas City, MO. This 1885 state census was taken on the same forms used for the 1880 federal census. However, first names were not always shown, sometimes given as initials only, followed by the surname. The Federal Government proposed this census to all states and territories with an offer to help financially. Nebraska was one of five states and territories that took up the offer. But this was a state census, not a federal census. The feds also provided the printed forms and asked that a copy of the enumeration be kept in Nebraska, another sent to Washington, DC. The state copy was lost. This is the federal copy, which is missing Chase county only. Filmed by the National Archives, 1961, 56 rolls, beginning with FHL film #499529 (Adams County, vol. 1). To access the digital images, see the online FHL catalog page: **https://familysearch.org/search/catalog/181869**.

1885 Lincoln County, Nebraska State Census **[Printed Book]**, transcribed and published by Gloria Pressnall, aided by members of the North Platte Genealogical Society, 1987, 150 pages. Includes index and reprints of 1885 maps of North Platte and Lincoln County. FHL book 978.282 X2p. Also on 3 microfiche, FHL film #6050983.

1885 Washington County, Nebraska State Census **[Printed Book]**, compiled and published by the Eastern Nebraska Genealogical Society, Fremont, NE, 1989, 97 pages. Contains an abstract of the Washington County, Nebraska 1885 census arranged in alphabetical order by surname. FHL book 978.2245 X28w.

1886 Douglas County, Nebraska Voter Registration List **[Printed Book]**, published by the Greater Omaha Genealogical Society, 1981, 84 pages. Includes index. FHL book 978.2254 N4d.

- NOTE: 1886-1891 Directories. The Nebraska State Historical Society (NSHS) has an *1886* and an *1890-91 Nebraska Gazetteer and Business Directory* that lists farmers and businessmen by towns and counties. Both provide name, occupation, post office address, and county of residence. The 1886 Gazetteer is indexed, the 1890-1891 Gazetteer is online at the USGenWeb site for Nebraska. The NSHS has Nebraska gazetteers for other years that list businessmen, but not farmers, by towns and counties only. These were published irregularly between 1879-1917. Microfilm copies of the gazetteers are available through interlibrary loan. None of these directories are available at the FHL in Salt Lake City. For information about borrowing materials on microfilm from the NSHS, visit their Web site relating to interlibrary loans at:
www.nebraskahistory.org/lib-arch/services/refrence/loans.htm.

1866-1909. *An Index to the Early Marriage Records of Lancaster County, Nebraska* **[Printed Book]**, compiled and publ. Lincoln-Lancaster County Genealogical Society, Lincoln, NE. 2-Vols., FHL book 978.2293 V22i 1866-1906 v. 1-2.

1887 Abstract of Tax List, Box Butte County, Nebraska **[Printed Book]**, compiled by Janella Guthrie, published by the Northwest Genealogical Society, Alliance, NE, 1980, 49 pages.

1887-2015. *Nebraska, Box Butte County Marriages* **[Online Database]**, digitized and indexed at FamilySearch.org. This database has 9,346 images, see **www.familysearch.org/search/collection/2549789.**

"*1888 Tax List, Fillmore County, Nebraska*" **[Printed Article]**, in *Nebraska Ancestree*, (Nebraska State Genealogical Society, Lincoln, NE),Vol. 7, No. 2 (Fall 1984).

"*1889 Tax List, Personal Property, Brown County, Nebraska, (by Precinct)*" **[Printed Article]**, in *Nebraska Ancestree*, (Nebraska State Genealogical Society, Lincoln, NE),Vol. 5, No. 2 (Fall 1982) through Vol. 8, No. 2 (Fall 1984), and Vol. 23, No. 3 (Spring 2001).

1889-1906 Scotts Bluff County, Nebraska, Index of Head of Family Names, Personal Property Assessment; Incomplete: Castle Rock Precinct, Ford Precinct, Gering Precinct, Highland Precinct, Kiowa Precinct, Mitchell Precinct, Rose Precinct, Robidoux Precinct, Tabor Precinct, and Winter Creek Precinct **[Printed Book]**, compiled and published by the Rebecca Winters Genealogical Society, Scottsbluff, NE, 1 vol., 1998, FHL book 978.298 R4.

1890 Census Substitutes (Nebraska Locations) **[Online Database]**, indexed at the Ancestry.com website. This is Ancestry's collection of city directories (and other name lists) from all over the U.S. for the time of the lost 1890 federal census. Included are city directories for Adams Co NE; Beatrice, NE; Buffalo Co NE; Fremont, NE; Kearney, NE; McCook, NE; Omaha, NE; and the full 1885 NE State Census. Go to *View All Collections Included in this Search* for an alpha list of databases, by place (county, city, state), and year(s). See
http://search.ancestry.com/search/group/1890census.

1890 Banner County Farmer List **[Online Database]**, indexed at the RootsWeb site for Banner Co NE. See **www.rootsweb.ancestry.com/~nebanner/farmer.html.**

1890-1891 Nebraska State Gazetteer, Business Directory and Farmer List, Lancaster County, Nebraska **[Online Database]**, indexed at the USGenWeb site for Lancaster Co NE. See
www.usgennet.org/usa/ne/topic/resources/NSHS/1890Gaz/lancfarm.htm.

1890-1957. *Nebraska, Federal Naturalization Records* **[Online Database]**, digitized and indexed at the Ancestry.com website. Source: National Archives microfilm (NE Declarations & NE Petitions). Includes index and images of Declarations of Intentions, Petitions for Naturalization, and Naturalization Certificates. The index includes: Name, Gender, Age, Record type, Birth date, Birth place, Date of Petition,

Petition place, Spouse, and Petition No. This database has 32,628 records. See
http://search.ancestry.com/search/db.aspx?dbid=61205.

1890-1908. *Nebraska, Broken Bow Homestead Records* **[Online Database]**, indexed at the FamilySearch.org website. Source: National Archive microfilm series M1915. This database consists of 1,824 Homestead Land Entry Case Files of the Broken Bow (Nebraska) Land Office. The records are unbound documents that include final certificates, applications with land descriptions, affidavits showing proof of citizenship, Register and Receiver receipts, notices and final proofs, and testimonies of witnesses. The files were arranged chronologically and assigned a final certificate number. The index record includes: Name Event date, Certificate number, State, Township, Range, and Section. At each record there is a link to the images, located at the Fold3 website. Generally, the case files can be very mundane; but once in a while, the records explode. For example, if a person applying for a homestead were not born in the U.S. a proof of citizenship was required, either a petition/declaration of intention to become a citizen, or an actual naturalization certificate. In some cases, original documents can be found in the case files, because the applicant brought the original document to the land office for proof, but never got it back. The index does not indicate the quantity or quality of documents in the case files, so the accessible images are a godsend to review what may be stored there. This "treasure chest" database has 39,373 records. See
https://familysearch.org/search/collection/1840496.

1891. See *Nebraska Resident Military Roster on June 1, 1891* **[Online Database]**, indexed at the Ancestry.com website. Source: *Roster of Soldiers, Sailors, and Marines of the War of 1812, the Mexican War, and the War of the Rebellion, Residing in Nebraska on June 1, 1891*, Nebraska Secretary of State, publ. 1892 The index includes: Given name, Surname, Rank, Company, City (Nebraska residence), State (of military service). This database has 14,972 records. See
http://search.ancestry.com/search/db.aspx?dbid=4755.

1892-1961. *Probate Records, Hall County, Nebraska* **[Microfilm]**, from the originals at the North Platte Genealogical Society. Filmed by the Genealogical Society of Utah, 1995, 1 roll, FHL film #1598326. To see if this microfilm has been digitized yet, see the FHL catalog page:
www.familysearch.org/search/catalog/728371.

1893 Roster of Nebraska Veterans – Nebraska Enlistees **[Online Database]**, indexed at the USGenWeb site for Nebraska. The list includes the Name, Rank, Unit, 1893 Residence, and State of enlistment. See
www.usgennet.org/usa/ne/county/holt/1893/nebraska.html.

1892-1896 Poll & Personal Taxes, Buffalo County, Nebraska **[Printed Book]**, typed by Wilma Holderness Burgland; printed by Lynnda Wohleb Shaffer, published by the Fort Kearny Genealogical Society, Fort Kearny, NE, 1985, 141 pages. From introduction: "In this book, you will find the names of the heads of the household that were levied a personal or poll tax during 1892-96 in Buffalo County, Nebraska. We have not indicated whether the tax was for personal or poll in this index. We felt it more important to just get the list of the names of people living in the area." See FHL book 978.245 R4p.

1895. *Roster of Soldiers, Sailors, and Marines of the War of 1812, the Mexican War, and the War of the Rebellion, Residing in Nebraska* **[Online Database]**, indexed at the Ancestry.com website. Source: Newspaper reproduction of the 1892 report, publ. York, NE: Nebraska Newspaper Union, 1895. This database has the scanned images from the text of the newspaper reproduction, with an OCR name index for searching. This database has 551 pages. See
http://search.ancestry.com/search/db.aspx?dbid=23886.

1900. *Nebraska, 1900 Federal Census: Soundex and Population Schedules* **[Microfilm & Digital Capture]**, filmed by the National Archives, c1970, 134 rolls, beginning with FHL film #1240916 (Adams, Antelope, Blackbird, Banner, Blaine, and Boone counties). To access the digital images (Population Schedules), see the online FHL catalog page:
www.familysearch.org/search/catalog/637409.

1902-1906. See *School Attendance Register; District 81; Antelope County, Nebraska* **[Online Database]**, indexed at the USGenWeb site for Antelope Co NE:
http://files.usgwarchives.net/ne/antelope/sch001.txt.

1903. *Plat Book of Lancaster County, Nebraska: Containing Carefully Prepared Township Plats, Village Plats, Analysis of U.S. Land System, Leading Farmers Directory, Reminisces of Old Settler..* **[Printed Book]**, publ. Brown-Scoville Co., Des Moines, IA, 1903. See FHL book 978.2293 E7b.

1903-1904. See *Index to Selected Information From Lincoln Evening News* **[Printed Book]**, by Teresa Sullivan, et al. This database contains an alphabetical

listing by surname of persons taken from notices of birth, death, marriage, divorce and other notices published in the *Evening News*. Each index record gives full name, place of event or residence, type of event, date of publication, newspaper page and column number. Publ. Lincoln-Lancaster Co Genealogical Society, 2002, 220 pages,
FHL book 978.2293/L1B32L 1903-1904.

1906-1916 York City/County Directories [Microfilm], from the original records located in various libraries and societies, filmed by Primary Source Microfilm, Woodbridge, CT, 199?, 1 roll, containing R.L. Polk & Co.'s York City directory, including a list of taxpayers in York County, 1906-1907; FHL film #2310390 Item 1; R.L. Polk & Co.'s York City directory, 1908, and list of taxpayers in York County, FHL film #2310390 Item 2; R.L. Polk & Co.'s York City directory, 1911 FHL film #2310390 Item 3 ; R.L. Polk & Co.'s York City directory, 1913-1914, FHL film #310390 Item 4; and R.. Polk & Co.'s York City directory, 1915-1916 and taxpayers in York County, FHL film #10390, Item 5.

1906-1956. *Probate Records, Buffalo County, Nebraska* **[Microfilm]**, from the originals at the North Platte Genealogical Society. Filmed by the Genealogical Society of Utah, 1995, 1 roll, FHL film #1598327. To see if this microfilm has been digitized yet, see the FHL catalog page:
www.familysearch.org/search/catalog/728305.

1908-1909. *R. L. Polk & Co.'s Kearney City Directory* **[Online Database]**, indexed at the RootsWeb site for Buffalo Co NE. See
www.rootsweb.ancestry.com/~nebuffal/krny1908/index.htm.

1910. *Nebraska, 1910 Federal Census: Soundex and Population Schedules* **[Microfilm & Digital Capture]**, filmed by the National Archives, c1970, 20 rolls, beginning with FHL film #1374851 (Adams, Antelope, Banner, Blaine, Boone, and Box Butte counties). To access the digital images (Population Schedules), see the online FHL catalog page:
www.familysearch.org/search/catalog/638153.

1910-1946. See *Probate Records, Cass County, Nebraska* **[Microfilm]**, from the originals at the North Platte Genealogical Society. Filmed by the Genealogical Society of Utah, 1995, 1 roll, FHL film #1598327. To see if this microfilm has been digitized yet, see the FHL catalog page:
www.familysearch.org/search/catalog/728311.

1913-1929. See *Court Records, Washington County, Nebraska* **[Microfilm]**, from the originals at the North Platte Genealogical Society. Filmed by the Genealogical Society of Utah, 1995, 1 roll, FHL film #1598325. To see if this microfilm has been digitized yet, see the FHL catalog page:
www.familysearch.org/search/catalog/728416.

1915. *Rosters of Veterans of the Mexican, Civil, and Spanish-American Wars: Residing in Nebraska, 1915* **[Printed Book & Digital Version]**, official report of NE Secretary of State, publ. 1915. Digitized by FamilySearch International, 2016, To access the digital images, see the online FHL catalog page:
www.familysearch.org/search/catalog/2615723.

1917-1918. *Nebraska, World War I Selective Service System Draft Registration Cards* **[Microfilm & Digital Capture]**, filmed by the National Archives, 1988, 51 rolls, beginning with FHL film #1684016 (Adams Co). To access the digital images, see the online FHL catalog page:
www.familysearch.org/search/catalog/746984.

1917-1919. *Nebraska, World War I American Expeditionary Forces, Deaths* **[Digital Capture]**, from the originals of the U.S. Adjutant General's Office, now at the National Archives, College Park, MD. Digitized by FamilySearch International, 2018. To access the digital images, see the online FHL catalog page:
www.familysearch.org/search/catalog/3023937.

1919-1976. *Nebraska, Box Butte County, Funeral Home Records* **[Online Database]**, digitized and indexed at FamilySearch.org. Includes records from the Miller and Landa Funeral Home (1919-1976) and from the Wildy Funeral Home (1920-1950). This database has 3,591 records, see
www.familysearch.org/search/collection/2549775.

1920. *Nebraska, 1920 Federal Census: Soundex and Population Schedules* **[Microfilm & Digital Capture]**, filmed by the National Archives, c1970, 120 rolls, beginning with FHL film #1820979 (Adams, Deuel, Antelope, Arthur, and Box Butte counties). To access the digital images (Population Schedules), see the online FHL catalog page:
www.familysearch.org/search/catalog/576337.

1921. See *Alphabetical Index of the Rural Residents and Family Members as listed in the Atlas of Lancaster County, Nebraska, 1921* **[Printed Book]**, by Lincoln-Lancaster Co Genealogical Society, 84 pages, FHL book 978.2293 E72a. For a digital version of this book, see the online FHL catalog page: https://familysearch.org/search/catalog/91833.

1930. *Nebraska, 1930 Federal Census: Population Schedules* **[Microfilm & Digital Capture],** filmed by the National Archives, c1970, 31 rolls, beginning with FHL film #2341000 (Adams, Antelope, Arthur, Banner, and Boyd counties). To access the digital images (Population Schedules), see the online FHL catalog page: www.familysearch.org/search/catalog/1037448.

1940. *Nebraska, 1940 Federal Census: Population Schedules* **[Digital Capture],** digitized images from the microfilm of original records held by the Bureau of the Census in the 1940s. After microfilming, Congress allowed the Census Bureau to destroy the originals to free up space for WWII-related files. Digitizing of the 1940 census schedules microfilm images was done for the National Archives and made public on April 2, 2012. To access the digital images, see the online FHL catalog page: www.familysearch.org/search/catalog/2057769.

1940 Federal Census Finding Aids **[Online Database].** The National Archives prepared a special website online with a detailed description of the 1940 federal census. Included at the site are descriptions of location finding aids, such as Enumeration District maps, Geographic Descriptions of Census Enumeration Districts, and a list of 1940 City Directories available at the National Archives. The finding aids are all linked to other National Archives sites. The National Archives website also has a link to 1940 Search Engines using Stephen P. Morse's "One-Step" system for finding a 1940 E.D. or street address conversion. See www.archives.gov/research/census/1940/general-info.html#questions.

1940. *Who's Who in Nebraska* **[Online Database],** index to biographies published by the Nebraska Press Association, Lincoln, NE. The biographies are organized by county. Search the county list, which includes some historical background on each county, and then a list of Who's Who for that county. Indexed at the USGenWeb site for Nebraska. See www.usgennet.org/usa/ne/topic/resources/OLLibrary/who1940/whowho40.html.

1940-1947. *Nebraska, World War II Draft Registration Cards* **[Digital Capture],** from the originals at the National Personnel Records Center, St. Louis, MO; digitized by FamilySearch International, 2017. To access the digital images, see the online FHL catalog page: www.familysearch.org/search/catalog/2769514.

- See also, *Nebraska, World War II Draft Registration Cards, 1940-1945* **[Digital Capture],** from the originals at the National Personnel Records Center, St. Louis, MO; digitized by FamilySearch International, 2017. To access the digital images, see the online FHL catalog page: www.familysearch.org/search/catalog/2759156.

- See also, *Nebraska, Military Records: World War II 4th Draft Registration Cards, 1942* **[Digital Capture],** from the original records at the National Personnel Records Center, St. Louis, MO, digitized by FamilySearch International, 2015. These cards represent older men, ages 45 to 65 in April 1942, that were registered for the draft. They had birth dates between 28 Apr 1877 and 16 Feb 1892. Each card includes a name of the individual, date and place of birth, address, age, telephone number, employer's name and address, name and address of a person who would know where the individual can be located, a signature, and physical description. To access the digital images, see the online FHL catalog page: www.familysearch.org/search/catalog/2624869.

1950 Tomahawk Yearbook, University of Omaha **[Online Database],** the complete book was digitized at the RootsWeb site for Douglas Co NE. See www.rootsweb.ancestry.com/~nedougla/html/uom1950/UOM50-1.htm.

1951 Tomahawk Yearbook, University of Omaha **[Online Database],** the complete book was digitized at the RootsWeb site for Douglas Co NE. See www.rootsweb.ancestry.com/~nedougla/html/uom1951/.

1957 Tomahawk Yearbook, University of Omaha **[Online Database],** the complete book was digitized at the Univ. of Omaha website. See **www.e-yearbook.com/sp/eybb?school=72560&year=1957**.

1958-1965. *Omaha, Nebraska, Passenger and Crew Manifests of Airplanes* **[Online Database],** digitized and indexed at the FamilySearch.org website. Source: National Archives microfilm series A3541. This is a set of handwritten index cards, almost totally unreadable. The index for each record needs to be trusted, because the image can not be read for verification or added information. Each index record includes: Name, Nationality, Age, Birth date, Birth place, Arrival date, Arrival place, and Airline. This database has about 400 images. See http://search.ancestry.com/search/db.aspx?dbid=60979.

1964-1965. *Nebraska City (Otoe County, Nebraska) Directory: Including Otoe County Taxpayers* **[Printed Book],** publ. R. L. Polk & Co, Kansas City, MO. 1964. Includes index. See FHL book 978.2273/N1 E4p.

1976 Bicentennial Album of Pawnee County: Containing Plats of the Precincts, Directory, Pictures, Histories, Cattle Brands, etc. **[Printed Book],** compiled by Brand Irons Pictorial County Albums, McPherson, KS, 1976, 406 pages. Includes biographical sketches of many Pawnee County families. FHL book 978.2284 H2b

1996-Current. *Nebraska Recent Newspaper Obituaries* **[Online Database],** digitized and indexed newspaper obituaries at the GenealogyBank website, including newspapers for Ashland, Beatrice, Bellevue, Broken Bow, Chadron, Columbus, David City, Fremont, Gering, Grand Island, Gretna, Hemingford, Kearney, Lexington, Lincoln, Nebraska City, North Platte, Omaha, Papillion, Plattsmouth, Ralston, Schuyler, Scottsbluff, Syracuse, Tekamah, Wahoo, Waverly, and York, Nebraska. See **www.genealogybank.com/explore/obituaries/all/usa/nebraska.**

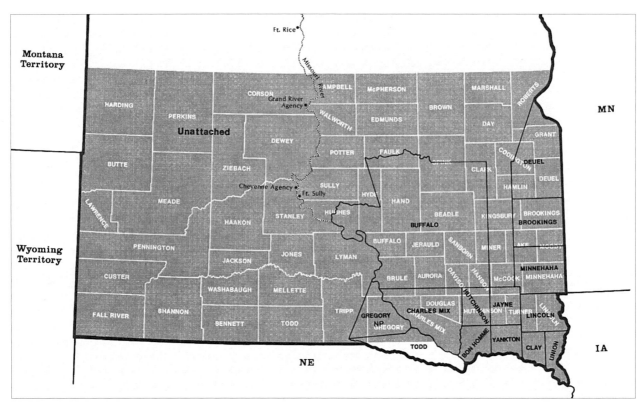

South Dakota • 1870 (as part of Dakota Territory) The paper county of Gregory is shown as NP (no population). The agencies and forts follow Yankton County on the microfilmed census.

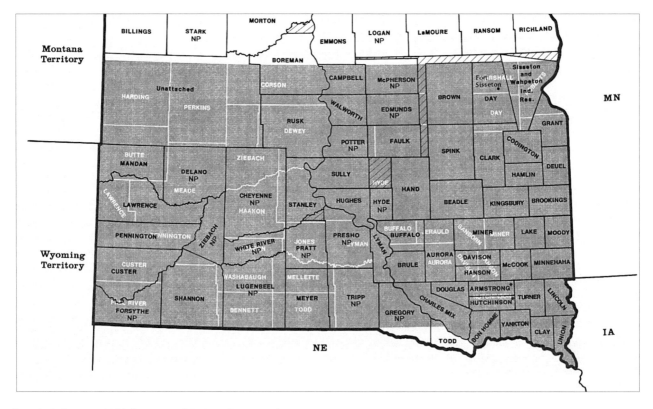

South Dakota • 1880 (as part of Dakota Territory). The counties of the South Dakota area at the time of the 1880 federal census are shown in black. South Dakota's 66 current counties are shown in white. Cross-hatched areas were unattached by statute. Paper Counties are shown as NP (no population).

South Dakota
Censuses & Substitute Name Lists

Historical Timeline of South Dakota, 1738-1889

1738. Dakota Country. French explorer Pierre Gaultier de la Vérendrye visited Mandan villages near the Missouri River. This was the first known white expedition into the Dakota Country.

1763. Treaty of Paris. This was the end of the French and Indian war. (In Europe it was called the "Seven Years War.") At the 1763 treaty, the French surrendered all their claims in North America. Spain acquired the former French areas west of the Mississippi, renamed *Spanish Louisiana*. Great Britain gained all of Québec, which they immediately renamed the *Province of Canada*. Britain also gained control of the rest of North America east of the Mississippi River. They named their entire area *British North America*.

1783. Treaty of Paris. As the official end of the Revolutionary War, the 1783 treaty recognized the United States as an independent republic, with borders from the Atlantic Ocean to the Mississippi River. The treaty also reaffirmed the claims of Britain to present-day Canada; and Spain's claim to lands west of the Mississippi River.

1792. Dakota Country. French-Canadian trader Jacques D'Englise opened trade on the Missouri River between Mandan villages and his Spanish employers located at St. Louis.

1797. Dakota Country. North West Company fur trader Jean Baptiste Chaboillez of the Red River Settlement (present Manitoba), established a trading post at Pembina (present North Dakota).

1800. Louisiana. Napoleon acquired title of Louisiana from Spain. At the Third Treaty of San Ildefonso, the Spanish acknowledged that it was too costly to explore the country and could not see the rewards being worth the investment. Spain retroceded Louisiana to France in exchange for the Grand Duchy of Tuscany (now part of Italy).

1803. Louisiana Purchase. The United States purchased Louisiana from France. Sent by President Jefferson to attempt the purchase of New Orleans, the American negotiators (James Madison and Robert Livingston) were surprised when Napoleon offered the entire tract to them. The Louisiana Purchase was officially described as the "drainage of the Mississippi and Missouri River basins." Adding the area doubled the size of the United States.

1804. On an expedition ordered by President Thomas Jefferson, Captains Meriwether Lewis and William Clark's Corps of Discovery left St. Louis in search of a passage to the Pacific Ocean. Based on bad information from his spies, the Spanish governor of New Mexico dispatched soldiers from Santa Fe to the Arkansas River to intercept the party and arrest them. But the Lewis and Clark party had taken a more northern route, following the Missouri River.

1804-1805. In 1804, Congress divided the Louisiana Purchase into two jurisdictions: **Louisiana District** and **Orleans Territory**. The latter had north and south boundaries the same as the present state of Louisiana but did not include land east of the Mississippi River, and its northwestern corner extended on an indefinite line west into Spanish Tejas. For a year, Louisiana District was attached to Indiana Territory for judicial administration but became Louisiana Territory with its own Governor on July 4, 1805.

1805. 1st Pike Expedition. U.S. Army Lieutenant Zebulon Pike led a small party of soldiers to investigate the Mississippi River above St. Louis. He was given specific orders to find the source of the Mississippi, and while doing so, to note "…any rivers, prairies, islands, mines, quarries, timber, and any Indian villages and settlements encountered."

1805. Louisiana Territory in 1805 had five original subdivisions: St. Louis District, St. Charles District, Ste. Genevieve District, Cape Girardeau District and New Madrid District. The unpopulated area north of these original districts was referred to as Upper Louisiana and included all lands north to the U.S./British border and west to the Continental Divide.

1812. June 4th. Louisiana Territory was renamed **Missouri Territory**. This was to avoid any confusion after Orleans Territory became the State of Louisiana on April 30, 1812. The General Assembly of the Territory of Missouri met in St. Louis in October, and converted the first five original districts into counties: Cape Girardeau, New Madrid, St. Charles, St. Louis, and Ste. Genevieve. A year later, the territorial legislature created Arkansas County from lands ceded by the Osage Indians.

1818. Anglo-American Convention. The 49th parallel was agreed to as the boundary between the U.S. and the British territory of Rupert's Land. In the treaty, the United States acquired part of the Red River drainage in present Minnesota and North Dakota, and ceded part of the Missouri River drainage in present North Dakota and Montana.

1832. After dredging projects near the mouth of the Kansas River, steamboat traffic continued up the Missouri River. In 1832, the steamboat *Yellowstone* began the first of its annual fur-trading voyages up the Missouri River, reaching Fort Union (present North Dakota/Montana line).

1833. June 1st. Black Hawk Cession. After the Black Hawk War of 1832, the Sauk and Fox tribe of present-day Iowa was forced to cede land on the west side of the Mississippi River to the United States. The cession opened a large area of the Ioway Country for legal white settlement for the first time.

1836. Wisconsin Territory was created, taken from Michigan Territory. Its area extended from its present Lake Michigan border to the Missouri River.

1838. Iowa Territory was created, encompassing all lands north of the state of Missouri between the Mississippi and Missouri Rivers.

1854. May 30th. Kansas-Nebraska Act passed the U.S. Congress. The territories of Kansas and of Nebraska were established. The act also allowed residents of the two territories to decide for themselves whether to allow slavery within their borders. Separated on their present common boundary, Nebraska Territory and Kansas Territory both extended from the Missouri River to the Continental Divide. Nebraska Territory included parts of present North Dakota, South Dakota, Montana, and Wyoming. Kansas Territory included present Kansas and parts of present Colorado.

1858-1861. Minnesota and Unorganized Dakota. When Minnesota was admitted as a state in 1858 with its present boundaries, part of Dakota was orphaned. The area from the western Minnesota line to the Missouri River was enumerated in the 1860 federal census as *Unorganized Dakota*. This was not an official jurisdiction, but one invented by the Census Office to gather census data for the Red River/Pembina settlements, plus a series of outposts along the Missouri River.

1861. Mar. Dakota Territory was created by Congress. The original area included all of present North Dakota, South Dakota, and the parts of present Montana and Wyoming east of the Continental Divide. Yankton was the first territorial capital, replaced by Bismarck in 1863.

1889. Nov. South Dakota and **North Dakota** both admitted as states with the same boundaries as today. Although Dakota Territory had petitioned Congress to be a single state, that would have caused two Democratic senators to be added, which would have upset the balance in Congress. By splitting Dakota Territory into two states, two Republican senators and two Democratic senators were added to Congress, maintaining the balance of power.

1889. Nov. As part of the statehood legislation, South Dakota lost most of Todd County and part of Gregory County to Nebraska. As an adjoining state, Nebraska had veto power over statehood if there were a dispute regarding boundaries with the proposed state. Essentially, South Dakota acquiesced to Nebraska's claim as a price of statehood. See the 1880 map on page 260 showing the disputed area.

Online Resources at the South Dakota State Historical Society

South Dakota Digital Archives. This online collection includes Photos, Manuscripts, Government Documents, Land Survey Field Notes, and more. Searchable databases of interest to genealogists include the following.

South Dakota State Surname Search Form. The South Dakota State Archives Surname Research Form allows a search through a database of birth, marriage, death, and other notices printed in South Dakota newspapers. This database is not complete and currently only recent newspapers are being added. Most newspaper surname entries are from 2000 to present, but some earlier entries were included as well. http://history.sd.gov/forms/surname/SurnameArchive.aspx.

1905 State Census Index. The images and index to the 1905 census cards are at the FamilySearch.org website. The 1905 SD State Census was also indexed at the Ancestry.com website. This is another database, indexed by the SDSHS and can be used to compare the results. See http://history.sd.gov/archives/Data/1905census/1905Search.aspx.

Cemetery Record Search. This searchable database includes records that were cataloged as part of the WPA Cemetery Project (pre-1940s) plus any cemetery updates that SDSHS has received. It is not a complete listing of all the burials in South Dakota.
See **https://apps.sd.gov/dt58cemetery**.

South Dakota State Newspapers Search Form. Use this form to search for SD state newspapers. You can search using as many or as few criteria as you want. Be sure that a field is blank if you do not want to enter it as a search criterion. To see a listing of all newspapers, just leave all the fields blank. By only specifying a year you will see all the reports pertaining to that particular year. See
http://history.sd.gov/forms/NewspaperArchive.aspx.

Biographical File Index is an alphabetical listing of offline files on individuals kept by the SD Archives. Search for a surname by a letter of the alphabet. See **http://history.sd.gov/Archives/Data/Biofile/default.aspx**.

Gold Star Volume: American Legion Auxiliary South Dakota World War I. This is an index of 549 South Dakotans who lost their lives in World War I. http://history.sd.gov//archives/Data/goldstar/default.aspx.

Naturalization Records Index: First Papers. See the **information page** for details. To start a search, see http://history.sd.gov/Archives/Data/naturalization/FirstPapersSearch.aspx.

South Dakota Farmer's Alliance. This searchable index includes over 17,500 names of South Dakotans who were dues paying members of the South Dakota Farmer's Alliance from 1890 to 1894. The Farmers Alliance was an organized agrarian economic movement amongst U.S. farmers. Information found in the index includes: Last Name, First Name, Post Office Address, County, Organization Name and Number, and the year dues were paid. See http://history.sd.gov/Archives/farmers/Search.aspx.

General Federation of Women's Clubs Pioneer Daughters Collection. This collection came from a statewide GFWC effort to collect and preserve the stories of female pioneers in South Dakota. Arranged by county, married name, and maiden name, this collection of nearly 6,000 stories is the largest body of women's histories in the State Archives. At the main information page, select County List, Married Name, Maiden name, or Request a File. See http://history.sd.gov/Archives/Data/gfwc/default.aspx.

Other Online Indexes. Visit the Genealogists page to access more searchable databases, such as the Fourth SD Infantry 1917, the 1870 Agricultural Census, the Library of Congress Digitized Newspapers Database, the 1885 Civil War Veterans Census, SD G.A.R. Annual Journal Deaths, American Indian Research, SD Sons of American Revolution, Spanish American War Roster, SD Brand Book Index, 1898-99, and SD Legislator Historical Listing. See http://history.sd.gov/Archives/genealogists.aspx.

Bibliography
South Dakota
Censuses & Substitutes

Censuses for the South Dakota area began with the Dakota Territory census of 1885, which was later divided by northern and southern counties. The originals for the southern portion are located today at the South Dakota State Historical Society (SDSHS).

State Censuses: After statehood in 1889, South Dakota began taking state censuses as a means of apportionment of their state legislature. The first one was for 1895, taken with a page format with names of persons listed without relationships, ages in categories, and nationalities. Unfortunately, only six counties for the SD 1895 State Census have survived. Subsequent state censuses taken every ten years, 1905 through 1945, are virtually complete for all counties, the originals located today at the SDSHS. The 1905, 1915, 1925, 1935, and 1945 censuses were all tabulations compiled on 3 x 5 index cards, one card per person, giving a full name and detailed personal information for each. The ingenious South Dakotans made use of college and high school students to take their censuses, using sortable index cards for each person enumerated. The cards were then arranged in alphabetical order by surname for the entire state, which is how the censuses are still organized and stored today at the SDSHS archives.

The digitized card index database allows for a global search within the state, and is very convenient for finding an individual, regardless of name, age, or place of residence. But, using the digitized index cards to recreate a family grouping is rather daunting. Since the card sequence numbers are not part of the search criteria, one cannot recreate the original order the cards were prepared house to house. A search for one name needs to be followed by a search for people at the same street address, or perhaps common keywords, but, there is no proof of relationship possible, because the individual cards do not indicate a name of a parent, or the names of any children.

In spite of the family grouping limitation, the South Dakota state censuses all have details about a person rarely found in other state censuses, e.g., for 1915, 1925, and 1935, the SD index cards ask for the maiden name of a wife, a census question found only in South Dakota.

Censuses Online:
- **Ancestry.com:** Digitized and Indexed 1885 Dakota Territory Census (southern counties); and digitized and indexed 1895 SD State Census (partial); and indexed only 1905, 1915, 1925, 1935 & 1945 SD State Census.
- **FamilySearch.org:** Digitized and Indexed SD State Censuses: 1905, 1915, 1925, 1935 & 1945.
- **SDSHS Website:** Indexed SD State Census: 1905 only.

Census Substitutes: Because of the number of South Dakota census name lists, the need for census substitutes between federal census years may seem less demanding – but this bibliography has many extra name lists. Together, they include Territorial, State, and Federal Censuses, Court Records, Directories, County Indexes, State Military Lists, Tax Lists, Vital Records, and Voter Lists. The censuses and substitute name lists begin below in chronological order:

♦ ♦ ♦ ♦ ♦

1856-1917. *South Dakota Birth Index* **[Online Database],** indexed at Ancestry.com. This collection was obtained from the South Dakota Health Department. The recording of vital records began in South Dakota in 1905. Live births were recorded, as well as delayed births recorded for persons needing an official birth record. From the delayed birth records, the earliest births recorded (those taking place in the South Dakota area) were from 1856. Information that may be found among these records includes the birth date, sex, mother's maiden name, father's name, and city or county of birth. This database has 929,883 records, see www.ancestry.com/search/collections/6996.

1859-1995. *South Dakota Land Patents Database* **[Online Database],** indexed by county, then surnames in alpha groups. This database was extracted from data provided by the Bureau of Land Management. It includes every homestead, mining and timber claim, as well as cash sales and Indian allotments. Not included are parcels still owned by the U. S. Government, including the Bureau of Indian Affairs, the Forest Service, and the National Park System. Indexed at the USGenWeb site for South Dakota. See www.usgwarchives.net/sd/land/sdland.htm.

1860. *Unorganized Dakota, 1860 Federal Census: Population Schedules* **[Microfilm & Digital Capture],** from the originals at the National Archives, Washington, DC. The name *Unorganized Dakota* was used only by the U.S. Census Office to describe the area. The main population centers of Unorganized Dakota were the communities of Sioux Falls, Yankton Agency, and the Pembina settlements on the Red River, with about 4,800 people total. For convenience, this 1860 federal census included a few inhabitants of the western frontier, even though the outposts were part of Nebraska Territory, e.g., Ft. Union, on the Missouri River; and Ft. Alexander on the Yellowstone River, were both included with Unorganized Dakota. Ft. Alexander was in present-day Rosebud County, Montana; while Ft. Union was located almost exactly on the present-day North Dakota/Montana line. Other outposts enumerated in the Unorganized Dakota census were the Missouri River outposts at Ft. Clark, Ft. William, and Ft. Stevenson; as well as the "Orphan's Village" on the Red River; and the "Old Trading House" on the Niobrara River. Filmed by the National

Archives, 1950, 1967, 2 rolls, FHL film #803094 (2nd filming: Dakota, entire territory). To access the digital images, see the online FHL catalog page: www.familysearch.org/search/catalog/704550.
- See also, *United States Census, 1860* [Online Database], digitized and indexed at the FamilySearch.org website, for all states and territories, including "Unorganized Dakota."
- *See also, 1860 Federal Census Images (Unorganized Dakota)* [Online Database], digitized 1860 census pages, organized by Post Office, town, or area descriptions, such as "between Red River and Big Sioux." The images are the actual census forms, where the *County of* and *State* headings are replaced with "Unorganized Dakota," see www.usgwarchives.net/sd/census/1860images.html.
- See also, *Dakota Territory 1860 Census – Interactive Search* [Online Database]. Type a couple letters of a surname to search the entire database. See www.rootsweb.ancestry.com/cgi-bin/sdcensus/sd1860cen.pl.
- See also, *Dakota Territory 1860* [Printed Book], edited by Ronald Vern Jackson, publ. Accelerated Indexing Systems, North Salt Lake, UT, 55 pages, FHL book 978 X22.

"1861 Dakota Inhabitants, A-D," in *Wy-Mon-Dak Messenger* (Tri-State Genealogical Society, Belle Fourche, SD), (Summer 1989).

"1861 Dakota Inhabitants, D-M," in *Wy-Mon-Dak Messenger,* (Tri-State Genealogical Society, Belle Fourche, SD), (Fall 1989).

"1861 Dakota Inhabitants, M-Z," in *Wy-Mon-Dak Messenger* (Tri-State Genealogical Society, Belle Fourche, SD), (Winter 1990).

1861-1865. *Index to Compiled Service Records of Volunteer Union Soldiers Who Served in Organizations from the Territory of Dakota* [Microfilm & Digital Capture], from the original records at the National Archives, Washington, DC, series M0536, 1 roll, NARA film #M536-1, FHL film #881616. To access the digital images, see the Online FHL catalog page: www.familysearch.org/search/catalog/313567.
- See also: *Civil War Soldiers Index, 1861-1865* [Online Database], Index of soldiers who served in the Civil War, 1861-1865 culled from 6.3 million soldier records in the General Index Cards to the Compiled Military Service Records in the National Archives. This index was a joint project of the U.S. National Park Service, the Federation of Genealogical Societies (FGS), and the Genealogical Society of Utah (GSU). Each record provides the full name, regiment, whether Union or Confederate, the company, the soldier's rank, sometimes alternate names, the NARA publication and roll numbers. See https://familysearch.org/search/collection/1910717.

1861-1865. See *Dakota Territory Civil War Service Records of Union Soldiers, 1861-1865* [Online Database], indexed at the FamilySearch.org website. Source: National Archives microfilm series M1960. Includes Union service records of soldiers who served in the 1st Battalion Dakota Cavalry from the Territory of Dakota. The records include a jacket-envelope for each soldier, labeled with his name, his rank, and the unit in which he served. The jacket-envelope typically contains card abstracts of entries relating to the soldier as found in original muster rolls, returns, rosters, payrolls, appointment books, hospital registers, prison registers and rolls, parole rolls, inspection reports; and the originals of any papers relating solely to one soldier. This database has 4,693 records. See https://familysearch.org/search/collection/1932393.

1861-1865. *Dakota Territory Civil War Service Records of Union Soldiers* [Online Database], indexed at the FamilySearch.org website. Source: National Archives microfilm series M1960. This database consists of Union service records of soldiers who served in the 1st Battalion Dakota Cavalry from the Territory of Dakota. The records include a jacket-envelope for each soldier, labeled with his name, his rank, and the unit in which he served. The jacket-envelope typically contains card abstracts of entries relating to the soldier as found in original muster rolls, returns, rosters, payrolls, appointment books, hospital registers, prison registers and rolls, parole rolls, inspection reports; and the originals of any papers relating solely to the particular soldier. This database has 4,693 records. See https://familysearch.org/search/collection/1932393.

1861-1889. See *History of Dakota Territory* [Online Database], digitized and indexed at the Ancestry.com website. Source: Book, same title, by George W. Kingsbury, 2 Vols., publ. 1915. This book includes a good read about the battle between the Republicans and the Democrats in Congress, and the split of Dakota Territory into North and South Dakota. This database has 5,248 records. See http://search.ancestry.com/search/db.aspx?dbid=25507.

1861-1900s South Dakota Original Landowners [Printed Books]. See the *Family Maps* series for South Dakota counties, maps of all original land patents, compiled by Greg Boyd, publ. Arphax Publishing Co.,

Norman, OK. These privately produced computer-generated maps show the first property owners for an entire county, produced as a book of maps, each map laid out on the federal township grid, and includes indexes to help you locate a person, place-name, or cemetery. Additional maps are added for each county to show roads, waterways, railroads, selected city centers, and cemeteries within a county. At this writing, *Family Maps* books have been published for Clark County, and Davison County, SD. See www.arphax.com.

1861-1941. *South Dakota Grand Army of the Republic Membership Records* **[Online Database],** indexed at the FamilySearch.org website. Source: SDSHS, Pierre, SD. Images of G.A.R post records from the Dakota and South Dakota Departments. The collection includes membership rosters, attendance registration books of various encampments (some include Women's Relief Corps.), post descriptive books, member deaths, adjutant reports, muster rolls, lists of officers, applications to form a post, reunion rosters, etc. The descriptive books are arranged by post name and number. Most records include item number, name, post name and number. The descriptive books may list name, age, state of birth, residence in South Dakota, occupation, date-rank-company-regiment of service and final discharge, cause of discharge, when mustered into G.A.R., status, and date of death. This database has 75,635 records. See
https://familysearch.org/search/collection/2239227.

1861-1900s. *South Dakota GenWeb Archives* **[Online Database].** The SDGenWeb site offers free genealogical databases with searchable statewide resources and a link to all county files. The following categories are accessible at the Welcome Page, see
http://usgwarchives.net/sd/sdfiles.htm.
- **County Files:** A listing of files arranged and organized primarily by county
- **State Files:** A listing of files from state, regional, ethnic, and other non-county sources

1861-2002. *South Dakota Newspaper Archives* **[Online Database],** digitized and indexed newspapers at the GenealogyBank website for Aberdeen, Artesia Deadwood, Eureka, Fort Randall, Miner, Pierre, Sioux Falls, Vermillion, and Yankton, South Dakota. See www.genealogybank.com/explore/newspapers/all/usa/south-dakota.

1862-2008. *South Dakota, Cemetery Index* **[Online Database],** indexed at the Ancestry.com website. This database is also accessible at the SDSHS Digital Archives website. This was an indexing project of the WPA for pre-1940s burials and added to by the SDSHS. The date of 1831 was for a Bon Homme County burial (Bon Homme County was created in 1862, it is unlikely that a cemetery was there much before then). Each record includes: Name, Death date, Burial place (city, county, state), and Cemetery. This database has 251,619 records. See
http://search.ancestry.com/search/db.aspx?dbid=9253.

1862-2014. *South Dakota, Department of Health, Index to Births 1843-1914 and Marriages 1950-2014* **[Online Database],** indexed at the FamilySearch.org website. Source: SD Dept of Health, Pierre, SD. The recording of statewide vital records began in South Dakota in 1905. **Births:** This database contains all the records that were filed for births from 1905 to 1914 and births that occurred before 1905, filed as delayed birth records. (The starting 1843 date was probably for a delayed birth record filed in South Dakota, but for a birth that occurred somewhere else). Each birth index record includes: Birth date, Sex, Mother's maiden name, Father's name, and Place of birth. **Marriages:** From the actual marriage certificates, information includes Certificate number, Registration number, Marriage county, Marriage date, and Names of husband and wife, and their Gender, Residence, and age. From the marriage registers, this database includes Certificate number, Date of marriage entry into the index, Marriage place, Marriage date, and Names of husband and wife, their Age, and Residences. This database has 693,053 records. See
https://familysearch.org/search/collection/2549807.

1865-1972. *South Dakota, County Naturalization Records* **[Online Database],** indexed at the FamilySearch.org website. Source: County Circuit and District court naturalization records from county courthouses in South Dakota. Coverage dates vary by county. The records were acquired from the South Dakota State Historical Society. Includes Declarations, Petitions, and Naturalization Records. This an image only database. Browse through the records, organized by county, then Record Type, Year Range, and Volume Number. This database has 124,277 records. See
https://familysearch.org/search/collection/2078640.

1865-2000. *Linkpendium – South Dakota: Family History & Genealogy, Census, Birth, Marriage, Death, Vital Records & More* **[Online Databases].** Linkpendium is a genealogical portal site with links to state, county, town, and local databases. Currently listed are selected sites for South Dakota statewide resources (312), Renamed / Discontinued Counties

(26), Aurora County (138), Beadle County (255), Bon Homme County (272), Brookings County (301), Brown County (334), Brule County (161), and 60 more South Dakota counties. See www.linkpendium.com/sd-genealogy.

1870. *Dakota Territory, 1870 Federal Census: Population Schedules* [Microfilm & Digital Capture], filmed by the National Archives, 1968, 1 roll, FHL film #545617 (Bon Homme, Brookings, Buffalo, Charles Mix, Clay, Deuel, Hutchinson, Jayne, Lincoln, Minnehaha of South Dakota, Pembina of North Dakota, Todd, Union, and Yankton of South Dakota Counties). To access the digital images, see the online FHL catalog: www.familysearch.org/search/catalog/698889.

1873-1935. *South Dakota, Minnehaha County, Probate Case Records* [Online Database], indexed at the FamilySearch.org website. Source: SDSHS, Pierre, SD. Minnehaha County (Sioux Falls) is South Dakota's largest county, created by Dakota Territory in 1862. This is an image only database. Browse through the records, organized by Record Type (Probate Case Files), then Box and File Number, and Year Range. Many of the images begin with a typed index to the names of people in a probate case. This database has 71,073 records. See https://familysearch.org/search/collection/1392773.

1875-1993. *South Dakota Church Records* [Online Database], digitized and indexed at FamilySearch.org, from a database compiled by the Sioux Valley Genealogical Society. This database has 3,759 records, see www.familysearch.org/search/collection/2790269.

1878-1928. See *North Dakota and South Dakota, Wills and Probate Records, 1878-1928* [Online Database], digitized and indexed at the Ancestry.com website. Source: North Dakota and South Dakota County, District, and Probate Courts. The contents of a probate file can vary from case to case, but usually includes names and residences of beneficiaries and their relationship to the decedent. An inventory of the estate assets can reveal personal details about the deceased's occupation and lifestyle. There may also be references to debts, deeds, and other documents related to the settling of the estate. This database has 5,121 records. See http://search.ancestry.com/search/db.aspx?dbid=9081.

1879-1955. *South Dakota, Death Index* [Online Database], digitized and indexed at the Ancestry.com website. Source: SD Dept of Health, from state registrations, 1905-1955; and from county registrations from 1879 (Dakota Territory). This is an index and images of death certificates (state registrations) and death registers (county registrations). The index contains the following information: Death certificate number, Name of deceased, County or county code, and Date of death. Ancestry's webpage for this title has the list of counties and their code numbers. This database has 322,632 records. See http://search.ancestry.com/search/db.aspx?dbid=8659.

1879-1970. *South Dakota, School Records* [Online Database], digitized and indexed at the FamilySearch.org website. Source: SDSHS, Pierre, SD. This database includes an index and images of School records, including teacher's term reports, school census and attendance records. The records are generally arranged by county, year and school district number. Each index record includes: Name, Event type, Event place, Gender, Age, and Birth year (estimated). This database has 4,753,816 records. See https://familysearch.org/search/collection/1389778.

1879-1971. *Rapid City, South Dakota, Mortuary Indexes* [Online Database], indexed at the Ancestry.com website. This database is also accessible at the Rapid City Society for Genealogical Research website. Each record includes: Name, Birth year, Death date, Age at death, Burial Place, Cemetery, and Mortuary. This database has 16,222 records. See http://search.ancestry.com/search/db.aspx?dbid=9752.

1880. *Dakota Territory, 1880 Federal Census: Soundex and Population Schedules* [Microfilm & Digital Capture], filmed by the National Archives, c1970, 11 rolls, beginning with FHL film #1254111 (Clay, Codington, Custer, Davison, Day, Deuel, Emmons, Forsyth, Shannon, Foster, Faulk, Grand Forks, Grant, Hamlin, Hand, Hanson, Hughes Stanley, Hutchinson, Armstrong, and Kidder counties). To access the digital images (Population Schedules), see the online FHL catalog: www.familysearch.org/search/catalog/670376.

1880-1937. *South Dakota, Pennington County Probate Case Files* [Online Database], indexed at the FamilySearch.org website. Source: SDSHS, Pierre, SD. Pennington County (Rapid City) is South Dakota's second largest (after Minnehaha), created by Dakota Territory in 1875. This is an image only database. Browse through the records, organized by Case File Number and Year Range. This database has 69,017 records. See https://familysearch.org/search/collection/1389957.

1885 Dakota Territory Census [Microfilm & Digital Capture], from the original records (for southern Dakota Territory counties) at the SDSHS, Pierre, SD. Most of the 1895 Census has been lost or destroyed. The only known county schedules are for Beadle, Brule, Charles Mix, Edmunds, Fall River, Faulk, Hand, Hanson, Hutchinson, Hyde, Lake, Lincoln, Marshall, McPherson, Moody, Roberts, Sanborn, Spink, Stanley, and Turner counties. Filmed by the SDSHS in 1971, 2 rolls at the FHL, as follows:
- Beadle, Butte, Charles Mix, Edmunds, Fall River, Faulk, Hand, Hanson, Hutchinson and Hyde Counties, FHL film #1405268.
- Lake, Lincoln, Marshall, McPherson, Moody, Roberts, Sanborn, Spink, Stanley and Turner Counties, FHL film #1405269.

To access the digital images, see the Online FHL catalog page:
www.familysearch.org/search/catalog/361027.

- See also *1885 Dakota Territory Census (Southern Counties)* [Online Database], digitized and indexed at the Ancestry.com website. Source: SDSHS, state archives microfilm collection. This database is an index and images of the 20 surviving southern counties of the 1885 Dakota Territory census. Index entries include name, race, age, and birthplace for everyone enumerated on the census. More information is shown on the census page image. The following counties are represented in this database: Beadle, Edmunds, Hand, Hyde, Marshall, Roberts, Stanley, Butte, Fall River, Hanson, Lake, McPherson, Sanborn, Turner, Charles Mix, Faulk, Hutchinson, Lincoln, Moody, and Spink counties. This database has 76,472 records. See
http://search.ancestry.com/search/db.aspx?dbid=6247.

- See also, *South Dakota 1885 Census Index* [Printed Index], compiled by Ronald Vern Jackson, Scott D. Rosenkilde, and W. David Samuelsen, published by Accelerated Indexing Systems, 1984, 296 pages. FHL book 978.3 X22j.

1889-1989. *South Dakota Historical Collections Cumulative Index: Lasting Legacy Project* [Printed Book], compiled by Suzanne Julin, publ. 1989, SDSHS Press, 469 pages, FHL book 978.3 H2sh index.

1889-1990. *Pioneer Certificates, Sioux Valley Genealogical Society (Sioux Falls, South Dakota)* [Microfilm & Digital Capture], from the original records of the society. Some records include pioneer certificate applications, application letters, genealogy charts, memo letters, certificates of pioneer, marriage, baptism and death, biographical, naturalization and deed records, marriage licenses, personal notes and checks. Filmed by the Genealogical Society of Utah, 1990, 20 rolls, beginning with FHL film #1710503 (Index, A-Berreth). To access the digital images, see the online FHL catalog:
https://familysearch.org/search/catalog/441686.

1890 Federal Census Fragments, Population Schedules, Jefferson Township, Union County, South Dakota [Microfilm & Online Database], from the original records at the National Archives, Washington, DC. Most of the 1890 population schedules were so badly damaged by fire in the Washington DC Commerce Department Building in January 1921 that they were disposed of. Only a few schedules are extant. Included on the microfilm are all surviving census pages from Jefferson Township, Union County, South Dakota on FHL film # 926499. To access the online index, see the FHL catalog:
www.familysearch.org/search/catalog/231212.

1895 South Dakota State Census [Microfilm & Digital Capture], from the originals located at the SDSHS, Pierre, SD, filmed by the society, 1971, 1 roll. FHL title: *Partial South Dakota 1895 Census Population Schedules*. Most of the 1895 schedules were destroyed. Surviving counties: Beadle, Brule, Pratt, Presho, Campbell and Charles Mix counties. See FHL film #1405183. To access the digital images, see the online FHL catalog:
www.familysearch.org/search/catalog/319716.

- See also, *South Dakota, State Census, 1895* [Online Database], digitized and indexed at the Ancestry.com website. Source: SDSHS, state archives microfilm collection. This database is an index with images of the first official state census in 1895. Of the 66 current counties of South Dakota, only six counties survived for this census year: Beadle, Brule, Campbell, Charles Mix, Pratt (now Jones), and Presho (now Lyman). On some of the printed census schedules, some enumerators took leave of the rules and listed people and facts differently, but the information is generally readable and understandable. This database has 21,007 records. See
http://search.ancestry.com/search/db.aspx?dbid=6120.

1897. *Memorial and Biographical Record (South Dakota): an Illustrated Compendium of Biography Containing a Compendium of Local Biography.* [Printed Book & Digital Version), publ. Chicago: G.A. Ogle & Co., 1897, 680 pages, FHL book 978.3 D3mb. To access the digital version, see the online FHL catalog:
https://familysearch.org/search/catalog/27906.

1897-1929. *Order of The Eastern Star, South Dakota Deceased Members* [Online Database], indexed at the RootsWeb site for South Dakota. See
www.rootsweb.ancestry.com/~sddaviso/OESMemoriam1897_1929.htm.

1899. *History of Minnehaha County* [Online Database], includes the full text of *History of Minnehaha County, South Dakota*, by Dan R. Bailey, publ. 1899. An added index to biographies is also available. Digitized and indexed at the USGenWeb Archives site for Minnehaha Co SD. See http://usgwarchives.net/sd/minnehaha/bailey.htm.

1900. *South Dakota, 1900 Federal Census: Soundex and Population Schedules* [Microfilm & Digital Capture], filmed by the National Archives, c1970, 55 rolls, beginning with FHL film #1241546 (Armstrong, Aurora, Beadle, Bon Homme, Brookings, and Brown counties). To access the digital images (Population Schedules), see the online FHL catalog: www.familysearch.org/search/catalog/650604.

1904-1928. *South Dakota, Federal Naturalization Records* [Online Database], digitized and indexed at the Ancestry.com website. Source: National Archives records of District Courts. Includes images and index to Declarations of Intention, Petitions, and Oath of Allegiance-Naturalization Records. The index to petitions includes: Name, Age, Record type, Birth date, Birthplace, Arrival date, Arrival place, Petition date, and Petition place. Index to naturalizations are similar. This database has 2,453 records. See http://search.ancestry.com/search/db.aspx?dbid=61209.

1905 *South Dakota State Census* [Microfilm & Digital Capture], from the original records at the SDSHS, Pierre, SD. Consists of cards containing statistical data for all individuals enumerated in the state. The cards are arranged alphabetically by surname. Information given includes the individual's name, address, age, sex, color, nationality, occupation, ability to read and write, whether blind, deaf and dumb, idiotic or insane, place of birth, years in South Dakota, years in United States, birthplace of father and birthplace of mother. Filmed by the Genealogical Society of Utah, 2002, 125 rolls, beginning with FHL film #2139869 (Aaberg, Albert – Aldous, William). To access the digital images, see the online FHL catalog: https://familysearch.org/search/catalog/1116537.
- See also, *South Dakota State Census, 1905* [Online Database], digitized and indexed at the FamilySearch.org website. Source: SDSHS, state archives microfilm collection. This database is an index and images to the 1905 census cards, filed in alphabetical order for the entire state. This database has 472,575 records. See https://familysearch.org/search/collection/1477737.
- See also, *South Dakota, State Census, 1905* [Online Database], indexed at the Ancestry.com website. Source: FamilySearch index (no images), extracted from the FHL microfilm of the originals at the SDSHS, Pierre, SD. This database has 472,575 records. See http://search.ancestry.com/search/db.aspx?dbid=60159.

1905-2017. *South Dakota, Marriages* [Online Database], indexed at the Ancestry.com website. This index was compiled from two sources. The first is from actual marriage certificates (covering 1905-49), and the second is from marriage certificates indexes created by the South Dakota Department of Health

1910. *South Dakota, 1910 Federal Census: Population Schedules* [Microfilm & Digital Capture], filmed by the National Archives, c1970, 15 rolls, beginning with FHL film #1375488 (Armstrong, Dewey, Sterling, Washabaugh, and Bennett counties, Wounded Knee District, Porcupine District, and Washington, Shannon, Mellette, Todd, Schnasse, and Bon Homme counties). To access the digital images, see the online FHL catalog: www.familysearch.org/search/catalog/646856.

1917-1918. *South Dakota, World War I Selective Service System Draft Registration Cards* [Microfilm & Digital Capture], from the originals at the National Archives, Washington, DC. The draft cards are arranged alphabetically by state, then alphabetically by county or city, and then alphabetically by surname of registrants. Filmed by the National Archives, 1987-1988, 22 rolls, beginning with FHL film #1877785 (South Dakota: Aurora Co, Bon Homme Co, and Brown Co). To access the digital images, see the online FHL catalog: https://familysearch.org/search/catalog/747000.
-See also, *South Dakota, World War I American Expeditionary Forces, Deaths, 1917-1919* [Digital Capture], from the original records at the National Archives, College Park, MD, digitized by FamilySearch International, 2018. To access the digital images, see the online FHL catalog: www.familysearch.org/search/catalog/3023951.

1920. *South Dakota, 1920 Federal Census: Soundex and Population Schedules* [Microfilm & Digital Capture], filmed by the National Archives, c1970, 62 rolls, beginning with FHL film #1821714 (Armstrong, Aurora, Bennett, Beadle, and Custer counties). To access the digital images (Population Schedules), see the online FHL catalog: www.familysearch.org/search/catalog/555234.

1924-1928. See *Fox's Who's Who Among South Dakotans: A Biographical Directory of Citizens Who are Prominent in Professional, Political, Business*

and Civic Affairs of the State [Book, Microfilm & Digital Version], from the book edited by Lawrence K. Fox, publ. 1924-1928, 2 vols. Contents: Vol. 1: 1924-1925; Vol. 2: 1928, FHL book 978.3 D3f. Also on microfilm, FHL film 1000589. For a digital version of this 2-vol. book, see the online FHL catalog page for this title. See
https://familysearch.org/search/catalog/184399.

1925 South Dakota State Census [Microfilm & Digital Capture], from the original records at the SDSHS, Pierre, SD. Consists of cards containing statistical data for all individuals enumerated in the state. The cards are arranged alphabetically by surname. The last name on each roll is repeated as the first name on the next roll. Each card contains: name of person, county, post office where person received mail; town or township name (if in a town, ward number); person's age, occupation, whether owner or renter, place of birth, years living in SD, years living in US; if foreign born, whether naturalized; birthplace of father and birthplace of mother; extent of education; military service, including wars fought, state, company, regiment, and division; marital status, maiden name of wife, year married, church affiliation; sex, ethnicity (color); misc. (read, write, blind, deaf, idiotic, insane); and the name of the enumerator. Filmed by the Genealogical Society of Utah, 2003, 213 rolls, beginning with FHL film #2368063 (Aabelson, Magnus - Afrank, Mollie). To access the digital images, see the online FHL catalog:
https://familysearch.org/search/catalog/1130131.
- See also, ***South Dakota State Census, 1925*** [Online Database], indexed at the FamilySearch.org website. Source: SDSHS, state archives microfilm collection. This database is an index and images to the 1925 census cards, filed in alphabetical order for the entire state. This database has 705,319 records. See
https://familysearch.org/search/collection/1476077.
- See also, ***South Dakota, State Census, 1925*** [Online Database], indexed at the Ancestry.com website. Source: FamilySearch index (no images), extracted from the FHL microfilm of the originals at the SDSHS, Pierre, SD. This database has 705,319 records. See
http://search.ancestry.com/search/db.aspx?dbid=60161.

1930. ***South Dakota, 1930 Federal Census: Population Schedules*** [Microfilm & Digital Capture], filmed by the National Archives, c1970, 16 rolls, beginning with FHL film #2341951 (Armstrong, Aurora, Bon Homme, and Beadle counties). To access the digital images, see the online FHL catalog:
www.familysearch.org/search/catalog/1037514.

1935 South Dakota State Census [Microfilm & Digital Capture], from the original records at the SDSHS, Pierre, SD. Consists of cards containing statistical data for all individuals enumerated in the state. The cards are arranged alphabetically by surname. The last name on each roll is repeated as the first name on the next roll. Each card contains: name of person, county, post office where person received mail; town or township name (if in a town, ward number); person's age, occupation, whether owner or renter, place of birth, years living in SD, years living in US; if foreign born, whether naturalized; birthplace of father and birthplace of mother; extent of education; military service, including wars fought, state, company, regiment, and division; marital status, maiden name of wife, year married, church affiliation; sex, ethnicity (color); misc. (read, write, blind, deaf, idiotic, insane); and the name of the enumerator. Filmed by the Genealogical Society of Utah, 2003, 733 rolls, beginning with FHL film #2369161 (Aaberg, Adoph – Adolph, Ina). To access the digital images, see the online FHL catalog:
https://familysearch.org/search/catalog/1143646.
- See also, ***South Dakota State Census, 1935*** [Online Database], indexed at the FamilySearch.org website. Source: SDSHS, state archives microfilm collection. This database is an index and images to the 1935 census cards, filed in alphabetical order for the entire state. This database has 673,322 records. See
https://familysearch.org/search/collection/1614831.
- See also, ***South Dakota, State Census, 1935*** [Online Database], indexed at the Ancestry.com website. Source: FamilySearch index (no images), extracted from the FHL microfilm of the originals at the SDSHS, Pierre, SD. This database has 673,322 records. See
http://search.ancestry.com/search/db.aspx?dbid=60162.

1940. ***South Dakota, 1940 Federal Census: Population Schedules*** [Digital Capture], digitized images from the microfilm of original records held by the Bureau of the Census in the 1940s. After microfilming, Congress allowed the Census Bureau to destroy the originals to free up space for WWII-related files. Digitizing of the 1940 census schedules microfilm images was done for the National Archives and made public on April 2, 2012. To access the digital images, see the online FHL catalog page:
www.familysearch.org/search/catalog/2057789.

1940 Federal Census Finding Aids [Online Database]. The National Archives prepared a special website online with a detailed description of the 1940 federal census. Included at the site are descriptions of location finding aids, such as Enumeration District maps, Geographic Descriptions of Census Enumeration Districts, and a list of 1940 City Directories available at the National Archives. The finding aids are all linked to other National Archives sites. The National Archives website also has a link to 1940 Search Engines using Stephen P. Morse's "One-Step" system for finding a 1940 E.D. or street address conversion. See www.archives.gov/research/census/1940/general-info.html#questions.

1942. *South Dakota, World War II 4th Draft Registrations Cards, 1942* **[Microfilm & Digital Capture],** from the originals at the National Personnel Records Center, St. Louis, MO. These cards represent older men, ages 45 to 65 in April 1942, that were registered for the draft. They had birth dates between 28 Apr 1877 and 16 Feb 1892. Includes name of individual, date and place of birth, address, age, telephone number, employer's name and address, name and address of person who would know where the individual can be located, signature, and physical description. Film located at the FHL was digitized in 2015. To access the digital images, see the online FHL catalog:
https://familysearch.org/search/catalog/2624776.

1945 South Dakota State Census **[Microfilm & Digital Capture],** from the original records located at the SDSHS, Pierre, SD. Consists of cards containing statistical data for all individuals enumerated in the state. The cards are arranged alphabetically by surname. The last name on each roll is repeated as the first name on the next roll. Each card contains: name of person, county, post office where person received mail; town or township name (if in a town, ward number); person's age, occupation, whether owner or renter, place of birth, years living in SD, years living in US; if foreign born, whether naturalized; birthplace of father and birthplace of mother; extent of education; military service, including wars fought, state, company, regiment, and division; marital status, maiden name of wife, year married, church affiliation; sex, ethnicity (color); misc. (read, write, blind, deaf, idiotic, insane); and the name of the enumerator. The 1945 census cards were microfilmed by the Genealogical Society of Utah, completed in late 2004, 193 rolls, beginning with FHL film #2370848. To access the digital images, see the online FHL catalog:
https://familysearch.org/search/catalog/1174457.
- See also, *South Dakota State Census, 1945* **[Online Database],** indexed at the FamilySearch.org website. Source: SDSHS, state archives microfilm collection. This database is an index and images to the 1935 census cards, filed in alphabetical order for the entire state. This database has 570,085 records. See
https://familysearch.org/search/collection/1747589.
- See also, *South Dakota, State Census, 1945* **[Online Database],** indexed at the Ancestry.com website. Source: FamilySearch index (no images), extracted from the FHL microfilm of the originals at the SDSHS, Pierre, SD. The original 1945 census cards are complete for all counties in place at that time. This database has 570,085 records. See
http://search.ancestry.com/search/db.aspx?dbid=60163.

1958-1961. *Sioux Falls, South Dakota, Passenger Manifests of Airplanes* **[Online Database],** digitized and indexed at the Ancestry.com website. Source: National Archives microfilm series A4072. This database includes an index and images of passenger manifests. Each index record includes: Name, Birth date, Birthplace, Departure date, Departure place, Nationality, and Airline. The image record may add information, including a place of residence, and a date a visa was issued. This database has 149 records. See
http://search.ancestry.com/search/db.aspx?dbid=60613.

1968-2012. *Rapid City, South Dakota, Obituary Index* **[Online Database],** indexed at the FamilySearch.org website. This database is also accessible at the Rapid City Society for Genealogical Research website. Each record includes: Name, Birth year, Age, Death date, Death place, Cemetery, and Obituary date. There are several obituaries for surrounding areas, including Wyoming. This database has 124,313 records. See
http://search.ancestry.com/search/db.aspx?dbid=9754.

1999-Current. *South Dakota Recent Newspaper Obituaries* **[Online Database],** digitized and indexed newspaper obituaries at the GenealogyBank website, including newspapers for Aberdeen, Belle Fourche, Brookings, Hot Springs, Madison, Pierre, Rapid City, Spearfish, and Sturgis, South Dakota. See
www.genealogybank.com/explore/obituaries/all/usa/south-dakota.

272 • *Census Substitutes & State Censuses*

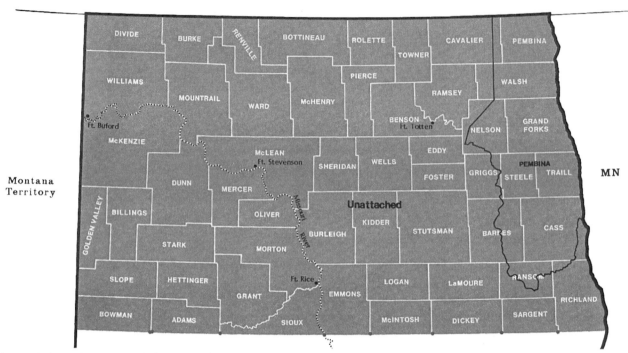

North Dakota Area • 1870 (as part of Dakota Territory) Pembina County, created in 1867, had the same area as the first Indian Cession in the region of the Red River of the North. (Cession No. 445, 1863, Red Lake & Pembina Bands of the Chippewa). For a detailed map see **http://usgwarchives.net/maps/cessions/ilcmap11.htm**. The various agencies and forts shown on the map above follow Yankton County (now South Dakota) on the microfilmed Dakota Territory 1870 census.

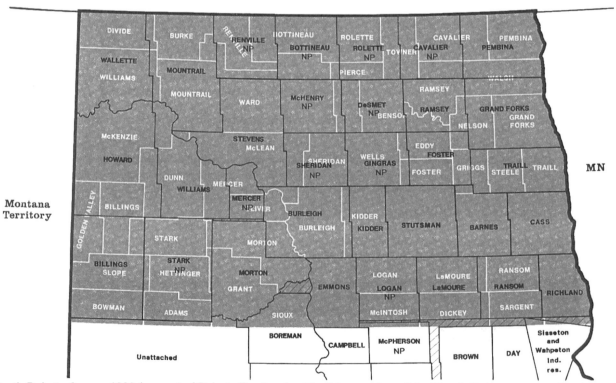

North Dakota Area • 1880 (as part of Dakota Territory). The 32 counties of the North Dakota area at the time of the 1880 federal census are shown in black. North Dakota's 53 current counties are shown in white. Crosshatched areas were unattached (by statute error). Paper Counties are shown with "NP" (No Population).

North Dakota
Censuses & Substitute Name Lists

Historical Timeline of North Dakota, 1738-1961

1738. Dakota Country. French explorer Pierre Gaultier de la Vérendrye visited Mandan villages near the Missouri River. This was the first known white expedition into what is now North Dakota.

1763. Treaty of Paris. This was the end of the French and Indian war. (In Europe it was called the "Seven Years War.") At the 1763 treaty, the French surrendered all their claims in North America. Spain acquired the former French areas west of the Mississippi, renamed *Spanish Louisiana*. Great Britain gained all of Québec, which they immediately renamed the *Province of Canada*. Britain also gained control of the rest of North America east of the Mississippi River. They named their entire area *British North America*.

1783. Treaty of Paris. As the official end of the Revolutionary War, the 1783 treaty recognized the United States as an independent republic, with borders from the Atlantic Ocean to the Mississippi River. The treaty also reaffirmed the claims of Britain to present-day Canada; and Spain's claim to lands west of the Mississippi River.

1792. Dakota Country. French-Canadian trader Jacques D'Englise opened trade on the Missouri River between Mandan villages and his Spanish employers located at St. Louis.

1797. Dakota Country. North West Company fur trader Jean Baptiste Chaboillez of the Red River Settlement (present Manitoba), established a trading post at Pembina (present North Dakota).

1800. Louisiana. Napoleon acquired title of Louisiana from Spain. At the Third Treaty of San Ildefonso, the Spanish acknowledged that it was too costly to explore the country and could not see the rewards being worth the investment. Spain retroceded Louisiana to France in exchange for the Grand Duchy of Tuscany (now part of Italy).

1803. Louisiana Purchase. The United States purchased Louisiana from France. Sent by President Jefferson to attempt the purchase of New Orleans, the American negotiators (James Madison and Robert Livingston) were surprised when Napoleon offered the entire tract to them. The Louisiana Purchase was officially described as the "drainage of the Mississippi and Missouri River basins."

1804. On an expedition ordered by President Thomas Jefferson, Captains Meriwether Lewis and William Clark's Corps of Discovery left St. Louis in search of a passage to the Pacific Ocean. Based on bad information from his spies, the Spanish governor of New Mexico dispatched soldiers from Santa Fe to the Arkansas River to intercept the party and arrest them. But the Corps of Discovery had already reached the Mandan villages of present North Dakota in the fall of 1804; where they built an encampment named Fort Mandan and stayed the winter there.

1804-1805. In 1804, Congress divided the Louisiana Purchase into two jurisdictions: **Louisiana District** and **Orleans Territory**. The latter had north and south boundaries the same as the present state of Louisiana but did not include land east of the Mississippi River, and its northwestern corner extended indefinitely into Spanish Tejas. For a year, Louisiana District was attached to Indiana Territory for judicial administration but became Louisiana Territory with its own Governor on July 4, 1805.

1805. 1st Pike Expedition. U.S. Army Lieutenant Zebulon Pike led a small party of soldiers to investigate the Mississippi River above St. Louis. He was given specific orders to find the source of the Mississippi, and while doing so, to note "…any rivers, prairies, islands, mines, quarries, timber, and any Indian villages and settlements encountered."

1805. Louisiana Territory in 1805 had five original subdivisions: St. Louis District, St. Charles District, Ste. Genevieve District, Cape Girardeau District and New Madrid District. The unpopulated area north of these original districts was referred to as Upper Louisiana and included all lands north to the U.S./British border and west to the Continental Divide.

1812. June 4th. Louisiana Territory was renamed **Missouri Territory**. This was to avoid any confusion after Orleans Territory became the State of Louisiana on April 30, 1812. The General Assembly of the Territory of Missouri met in St. Louis in October and converted the first five original districts into counties: Cape Girardeau, New Madrid, St. Charles, St. Louis, and Ste. Genevieve. A year later, the territorial legislature created Arkansas County from lands ceded by the Osage Indians.

1818. Anglo-American Convention. The 49th parallel was agreed to as the boundary between the U.S. and the British territory of Rupert's Land. In this treaty, the United States acquired part of the Red River drainage in present Minnesota and North Dakota, and ceded part of the Missouri River drainage above present North Dakota and Montana.

1827. Independence, Missouri. The frontier town of Independence was founded in 1827, the farthest point westward on the Missouri River where steamboats could travel at that time. Independence immediately became a supply point, staging area, and primary starting point for the growing number of trappers and traders using the Santa Fe Trail.

1832. After dredging projects near the mouth of the Kansas River, steamboat traffic continued up the Missouri River. In 1832, the steamboat *Yellowstone* began the first of its annual fur-trading voyages up the Missouri River, reaching Fort Union (present North Dakota/Montana line).

1833. June 1st. Black Hawk Cession. After the Black Hawk War of 1832, the Sauk and Fox tribe of present-day Iowa was forced to cede land on the west side of the Mississippi River to the United States. The cession opened a large area of the Ioway Country for legal white settlement for the first time.

1836. Wisconsin Territory was created, taken from Michigan Territory. Its area extended from its present Lake Michigan border to the Missouri River.

1838. Iowa Territory was created, encompassing all lands north of the state of Missouri between the Mississippi and Missouri Rivers.

1842. Nebraska Country. The word "Nebraska" first began to appear in publications in 1842 after John C. Fremont explored and mapped the Platte Valley and Nebraska areas.

1854. May 30th. Kansas-Nebraska Act passed the U.S. Congress. The territories of Kansas and of Nebraska were established. The act also allowed residents of the two territories to decide for themselves whether to allow slavery within their borders. Separated on their present common boundary, Nebraska Territory and Kansas Territory both extended from the Missouri River to the Continental Divide. Nebraska Territory included parts of present North Dakota, South Dakota, Montana, and Wyoming. Kansas Territory included present Kansas and parts of present Colorado.

1858-1861. Minnesota and Unorganized Dakota. When Minnesota was admitted as a state in 1858 with its present boundaries, a large part of the Dakota Country was orphaned. The area from the western Minnesota line to the Missouri River was enumerated in the 1860 federal census as *Unorganized Dakota*. This was not an official jurisdiction, but one invented by the Census Office to gather census data for the Red River/Pembina settlements, plus a series of outposts along the Missouri River.

1861. Mar. Dakota Territory was created by Congress. The original area included present North Dakota, South Dakota, and the parts of present Montana and Wyoming east of the Continental Divide. Yankton was the first territorial capital, replaced by Bismarck in 1863.

1889. Nov. South Dakota and **North Dakota** were both admitted as states with the same boundaries as today. Although Dakota Territory had petitioned Congress to be a single state, that would have caused two Democratic senators to be added, which would have upset the balance in Congress. By splitting Dakota Territory into two states, two Republican senators and two Democratic senators were added to Congress, maintaining the balance of power.

Bibliography
North Dakota
Censuses & Substitutes

The French-Canadian trading posts known as the Red River Settlements were mainly in what is now Manitoba. The area was home to numerous Métis voyageurs who followed the Red River south into the Dakota Country to establish trade with the Indians. In 1797, Jean Baptiste Chaboillez, working for the North West Fur Company, established a trading post at Pembina (present North Dakota). Soon after, a Hudson's Bay Company trading post was established near Pembina as well. The Pembina settlements were not American territory until the Anglo-American Convention of 1818, when the U.S. and Britain agreed on the 49th Parallel as the international boundary.

Manitoba Censuses, 1832-1870. There are several extant censuses available at the Provincial Archives of Manitoba relating to the Red River Settlements. The people identified therein include those who traveled back and forth into the Dakota Country.

American Censuses, 1836-1857. The first American census taken in the Dakota Country was the 1836 Wisconsin Territory census, which included the Pembina settlements on the Red River (2 miles south of the Canadian border). In the 1850 federal census, the Dakota Country areas east of the Missouri River were part of Pembina County, Minnesota Territory. The same area was included in the 1857 MN Territory Census.

Dakota Country, 1858-1861: When Minnesota became a state in 1858, a part of the Dakota Country was orphaned, and remained without jurisdiction for three years. The area from the Minnesota line to the Missouri River was enumerated as *Unorganized Dakota* in the 1860 federal census, while Dakota areas west of the Missouri River were part of Nebraska Territory.

Dakota Territory, 1861-1885: Dakota Territory was created in 1861. The original area included present North Dakota, South Dakota, and the parts of present Montana and Wyoming east of the Continental Divide. Yankton was the first territorial capital, replaced by Bismarck in 1863. The territory took only one territorial census, a special enumeration taken in 1885 with federal assistance. The original manuscripts for the 1885 Dakota Territory census schedules were later divided, the northern counties now kept at the State Historical Society of North Dakota in Bismarck; the southern counties at the South Dakota State Historical Society in Pierre.

North Dakota Censuses, 1885-1925:
- The North Dakota censuses begin with the Dakota Territory census of 1885, which was later divided into northern and southern counties. 50 of the 56 counties in place in the North Dakota area in 1885 have survived.
- After admission to the Union in 1889, the state of North Dakota conducted three state censuses, in 1905, 1915 and 1925. Only a statistical summary of the 1905 state census survives, but the full census schedules for the 1915 and 1925 censuses are extant. The original state censuses are located at the State Historical Society of North Dakota in Bismarck. There are no complete printed indexes, but both censuses were microfilmed by the SHSND and are available on interlibrary loan. Copies of the microfilm are also at the Family History Library in Salt Lake City.

Censuses Online: The North Dakota portion of the 1885 Dakota Territory census was indexed online at the ND State Univ. website; and indexed as well at the Ancestry.com website. The 1915 and 1925 North Dakota Sate Censuses are digitized and indexed online at both Ancestry.com and FamilySearch.org.

Census Substitutes: In addition to North Dakota censuses, this bibliography identifies many extra name lists. Together, they include Territorial, State, and Federal Censuses, Court Records, Directories, County Indexes, State Military Lists, Tax Lists, Vital Records, and Voter Lists. The censuses and substitute name lists begin below in chronological order:

◆ ◆ ◆ ◆ ◆

1832-1870. *Red River Settlement and Province of Manitoba: A Typed Card Index to the Nominal Census Returns* [Microfilm & Digital Capture], from records at the Provincial Archives of Manitoba, Winnipeg, Canada. The early censuses were taken by the Hudson's Bay Company, which had taken over the North West Company in 1821. The Red River Settlements were in the Red and Assiniboine Rivers area of Manitoba. Early French trappers, traders, and settlers were known to move up and down the Red River between present Manitoba and North Dakota. They were the founders of the Pembina settlements of present North Dakota. This is a combined index to the nominal (head of household) census returns for 1832, 1833, 1838, 1840, 1843, 1846-47, 1849, 1856 (incomplete) and every-name 1870, for the Lower Settlement, Grant Town and Indian villages. Filmed by the Genealogical Society of Utah, 1985, 3 rolls, beginning with FHL film #1420272. To access the digital images, see the online FHL catalog: www.familysearch.org/search/catalog/629379.

- **NOTE:** The 1870 Manitoba/Red River census names all members of a family, relationship to head, age, sex, occupation, religion, whether Métis (French & Indian blood), or other race; and identifies the full name of a father and full maiden name of a mother for each person. It is one of the most detailed censuses ever done in North America.

1836 Wisconsin Territory Census. See *the First Census of the Original Counties of Dubuque and Demoine (Iowa) Taken in July 1836* [Microfilm & Digital Version], from a book edited by Benjamin F. Shambaugh, published by the Historical Department of Iowa, 1897-1898, 93 pages. Includes Pembina settlements in present-day North Dakota. Names were extracted from the original manuscript returns preserved in the office of the Secretary of State of Wisconsin. The census taken in accordance with the act of Congress erecting the territory of Wisconsin (of which these two counties at the time formed a part) comprising the present states of Iowa, Minnesota and part of North Dakota and South Dakota. Filmed by the Genealogical Society of Utah, 1978, 1 roll, FHL film ##989450. To access the digital images, see the online FHL catalog: www.familysearch.org/search/catalog/2223215.

1838. *Iowa 1838 Territorial Census Index* [Printed Index], edited by Ronald Vern Jackson, et al, publ. Accelerated Indexing Systems, Bountiful, UT, 1984, FHL book 977.7 X22ji 1838. Includes the Pembina settlements in present-day North Dakota.

- See also, Marie Haefner, **"The Census of 1838,"** in *The Palimpsest* (IA State Hist. Soc., Des Moines), Vol. 19 (May 1938) pp 185-192.

1840 Federal Census, Iowa Territory. In 1840, Iowa Territory included lands between the Mississippi and Missouri Rivers, from its present boundary with Missouri to the western part of present Minnesota, and North and South Dakota.

- An extract was done as *The 1840 Iowa Census* [Printed Book & Digital Version], compiled by Rowene Obert, Helen Blumhagen, Wilma Adkins, published Salt Lake City, UT 1968. Includes index. Includes the 18 original counties and several precincts which comprised the entire area of Iowa Territory. FHL book 977.7 X2p 1840 and FHL film #844885. To access the digital version, see the online FHL catalog: www.familysearch.org/search/catalog/193563.

1850 Federal Census, Minnesota Territory. See *Dakota Census Index; 1850 Pembina District,* [Printed Index] edited by Ronald Vern Jackson, published by Accelerated Indexing Systems, Bountiful, UT, 1982, 61 pages. The names from Pembina County were extracted from the state copy of the Minnesota Territory 1850 census, located at the Minnesota State Historical Society in St. Paul. FHL book 978 X22d 1850.

- See also, *Minnesota Territorial Census, 1850* [Printed Book], edited by Patricia C. Harpole and Mary D. Nagle, published by the Minnesota Historical Society, 1972, 115 pages. FHL book 977.6 X2ph 1850. The federal copy of the *1850 MN Territory Census* schedules can be found on FHL film #14834.

1857 Federal Census, Minnesota Territory [Microfilm & Digital Capture], from the original records located at the National Archives, Central Plains Region, Kansas City, MO. Filmed by the National Archives, 1973, series T1175, 8 rolls, available from the FHL, including Pembina County (present North Dakota) on FHL film #944287. To access the digital images, see the online FHL catalog: www.familysearch.org/search/catalog/90983.

1857 Federal Census Abstracts, Minnesota Territory [Printed Book], county-wide abstracts by Mary Bakeman, published by the Minnesota Historical Society, 1994-2003 for all counties, including 1857 Pembina County, MHS call no. CS42 .M553 no. 21-23.

1860. *Unorganized Dakota, 1860 Federal Census: Population Schedules* [Microfilm & Digital Capture], from the originals at the National Archives,

Washington, DC. The name *Unorganized Dakota* was used only by the U.S. Census Office to describe the area. The main population centers of Unorganized Dakota were the communities of Sioux Falls, Yankton Agency, and the Pembina settlements on the Red River, with about 4,800 people total. For convenience, this 1860 federal census enumerated a few inhabitants of the western frontier, even though the outposts were part of Nebraska Territory. Ft. Union, on the Missouri River; and Ft. Alexander on the Yellowstone River, were both included with Unorganized Dakota. Ft. Alexander was in present-day Rosebud County, Montana; while Ft. Union was located almost exactly on the present-day North Dakota/Montana line. Other outposts enumerated in the Unorganized Dakota census were the Missouri River outposts at Ft. Clark, Ft. William, and Ft. Stevenson; as well as the Orphan's Village on the Red River; and the Old Trading House on the Niobrara River. Filmed by the National Archives, 1967, 1 roll, FHL film #803094 (2nd filming: Dakota, entire territory). To access the digital images, see the online FHL catalog:
www.familysearch.org/search/catalog/704550.
- See also *Dakota Territory 1860* **[Printed Book]**, edited by Ronald Vern Jackson, publ. Accelerated Indexing Systems, North Salt Lake, UT, 55 pages, FHL book 978 X22.

1860 Federal Census Images (Unorganized Dakota) **[Online Database]**, digitized 1860 census pages, organized by Post Office, town, or area descriptions, such as "between Red River and Big Sioux." The images are the actual census forms, where the County of and State are replaced with "Unorganized Dakota," See www.usgwarchives.net/sd/census/1860images.html.

1860. *Dakota Territory 1860 Census – Interactive Search* **[Online Database]**. Type a couple letters of a surname to search the entire database. See www.rootsweb.ancestry.com/cgi-bin/sdcensus/sd1860cen.pl.

"1861 Dakota Inhabitants, A-D," in *Wy-Mon-Dak Messenger* (Tri-State Genealogical Society, Belle Fourche, SD), (Summer 1989).

"1861 Dakota Inhabitants, D-M," in *Wy-Mon-Dak Messenger,* (Tri-State Genealogical Society, Belle Fourche, SD), (Fall 1989).

"1861 Dakota Inhabitants, M-Z," in *Wy-Mon-Dak Messenger* (Tri-State Genealogical Society, Belle Fourche, SD), (Winter 1990).

1861-1862. *Gazetteer of Pioneers and Others in North Dakota Previous to 1862* **[Online Database]**, extracted from "Collection of the State Historical Society," Vol. 1, 1906. Alpha list and annotations at the Genealogy Trails website. See
http://genealogytrails.com/ndak/earlysettlers.html.

1861-1865. *Index to Compiled Service Records of Volunteer Union Soldiers Who Served in Organizations From the Territory of Dakota* **[Microfilm & Digital Capture]**, from the original records at the National Archives, Washington, DC, series M0536, 1 roll, NARA film #M536-1, FHL film #881616. To access the digital images, see the online FHL catalog:
www.familysearch.org/search/catalog/313567.

1861-1865. *Dakota Territory Civil War Service Records of Union Soldiers* **[Online Database]**, indexed at the FamilySearch.org website. Source: National Archives microfilm series M1960. This database consists of Union service records of soldiers who served in the 1st Battalion Dakota Cavalry from the Territory of Dakota. The records include a jacket-envelope for each soldier, labeled with his name, his rank, and the unit in which he served. The jacket-envelope typically contains card abstracts of entries relating to the soldier as found in original muster rolls, returns, rosters, payrolls, appointment books, hospital registers, prison registers and rolls, parole rolls, inspection reports; and the originals of any papers relating solely to the particular soldier. This database has 4,693 records. See
https://familysearch.org/search/collection/1932393.

1861-1889. *History of Dakota Territory* **[Online Database]**, digitized and indexed at the Ancestry.com website. Source: Book, same title, by George W. Kingsbury, 2 Vols., publ. 1915. This book includes a good read about the battle between the Republicans and the Democrats in Congress, and the split of Dakota Territory into North and South Dakota. This database has 5,248 records. See
http://search.ancestry.com/search/db.aspx?dbid=25507.

1861-1900s. *North Dakota Biography Index* **[Online Database]**, indexed at the ND State Univ. website. This database is an ongoing project of the NDSU Institute for Regional Studies to provide access to biographical sketches found in a wide variety of North Dakota publications. It currently contains some 250,000 names to published biographical sketches of North Dakotans

found in over 800 publications. Additional names continue to be added on a regular basis. Consult the Institute's **information page** for the scope and content of the records and for ordering copies. See
https://library.ndsu.edu/db/biography.

1861-1900s. *Original Landowners, Burleigh County, North Dakota* **[Online Database],** index of the BLM Landowner records by surname, at the USGenWeb Archives site for Burleigh Co ND. See
www.usgwarchives.net/nd/burleigh/burlland.html.

1861-1900s. *North Dakota GenWeb Archives* **[Online Database].** The NDGenWeb site offers free genealogical databases with searchable statewide name lists and for all North Dakota counties. Databases may include Bibles, Biographies, Cemeteries, Censuses, Court Records, Deaths, Deeds, Directories, Histories, Marriages, Military, Newspapers, Obituaries, Photos, Schools, Tax Lists, Wills, and more. See
http://usgwarchives.net/nd/ndfiles.htm.

1861-1900s North Dakota Original Landowners. See the *Family Maps* series for North Dakota counties, maps of all original land patents, compiled by Greg Boyd, publ. Arphax Publishing Co., Norman, OK. These privately produced computer-generated maps show the first property owners for an entire county, produced as a book of maps, each map laid out on the federal township grid, and includes indexes to help you locate a person, place-name, or cemetery. Additional maps are added for each county to show roads, waterways, railroads, selected city centers, and cemeteries within a county. At this writing, *Family Maps* books have been published for Barnes County, North Dakota, Kidder County, North Dakota. See www.arphax.com.

1865-1931. *North Dakota Newspaper Archives* **[Online Database],** digitized and indexed newspapers at the GenealogyBank website for Bismarck, Fargo, Fort Rice, Grand Forks, Mandan, Michigan, and Tower City. See
www.genealogybank.com/explore/newspapers/all/usa/north-dakota.

1865-2000. *Linkpendium – North Dakota: Family History & Genealogy, Census, Birth, Marriage, Death, Vital Records & More* **[Online Databases].** Linkpendium is a genealogical portal site with links to state, county, town, and local databases. Currently listed are selected sites for North Dakota statewide resources (304), Renamed/Discontinued Counties (19), Adams County (97), Barnes County (182), Benson County (124), Billings County (97), Bottineau County (132), Bowman County (101), and 47 more North Dakota counties. See
www.linkpendium.com/nd-genealogy.

1868-1924. *North Dakota, Naturalization Records* **[Online Database],** from the originals at the National Archives, Kansas City, MO. Digitized and indexed at FamilySearch.org. This database has 1,864 records, see www.familysearch.org/search/collection/3241359.

1870 Dakota Territory, 1870 Federal Census: Population Schedules **[Microfilm & Digital Capture],** filmed by the National Archives, 1968, 1 roll, FHL film #295398 (2nd filming: Dakota Territory: Bon Homme, Brookings, Buffalo, Charles Mix, Clay, Deuel, Hutchinson, Jayne, Lincoln, Minnehaha, Pembina, Todd, Union, and Yankton counties). To access the digital images, see the online FHL catalog:
www.familysearch.org/search/catalog/698889.

1870-1890. *North Dakota, Compiled Census Index* **[Online Database],** indexed at Ancestry.com. Includes the 1870 Federal Census Index; 1885 State Census Index; and the 1890 Veterans Schedules Index for North Dakota. This database has 5,833 records, see www.ancestry.com/search/collections/3565.

1872-1958. *North Dakota, County Marriages* **[Online Database],** digitized and indexed at FamilySearch.org. Name index and images of county marriage records acquired from local courthouses. Coverage dates and image availability vary by county. This collection is being published as images and records become available. This database has 91,457 images, see www.familysearch.org/search/collection/2550852.

1873-1900. *Early History-Pioneers of Burleigh County, North Dakota* **[Online Database],** indexed at the Genealogy Trails website. See
http://genealogytrails.com/ndak/burleigh/history.html#pioneers.

1873-1925. *Index, Pre-1 July 1925, Marriage Records, Burleigh County, North Dakota* **[Printed Book],** by Beth H. Bauman, and Don Smith, publ. Bismarck-Mandan Historical and Genealogical Society, 2004, 91 pages, FHL book 978.477 D22b.

1873-1976. *Grand Forks County Heritage Book: A History of Rural Grand Forks County, North Dakota* **[Printed Book],** compiled by the Grand Forks Heritage Book Committee, 1976, 534 pages, FHL book 978.416 H2.

1873-1943. *Cass County, North Dakota, Divorce Index* [Online Database], digitized and indexed at Ancestry.com. This database was acquired from the Institute of Regional Studies, North Dakota State University, Fargo, ND. See
www.ancestry.com/search/collections/70840.
- See also, http://library.ndsu.edu/db/cassdivorce.

1874-1952. *North Dakota Naturalization Records Index* [Online Database], indexed at the ND State University website. The North Dakota Naturalization Records index was compiled at the State Historical Society of North Dakota, where all original county naturalization records are preserved and have been microfilmed. In cooperation with the NDSU Institute for Regional Studies, the index is made available as a searchable database. The database contains over 212,000 names, giving the county where the declaration of intention (1st papers) was filed and the naturalization occurred, the date of both events, and from what country the person emigrated. Consult the State Historical Society of North Dakota's Naturalization Records' information sheet regarding the history of the naturalization laws, types of records and how to use them. See
www.history.nd.gov/archives/datanaturalization.html.
- See also: Institute for Regional Studies' information page for the scope and content of the records, and access to the database. See
https://library.ndsu.edu/ndsuarchives/north-dakota-naturalization-records-database.

1876-1950. *Cass County, North Dakota, Probate Index* [Online Database], indexed at Ancestry.com. This database was acquired from the Institute of Regional Studies, North Dakota State University, Fargo, ND. This database has 6,183 records, see
www.ancestry.com/search/collections/70842.
- See also, http://library.ndsu.edu/db/probate.

1877-1944. *North Dakota, Cass County, Marriage Records* [Microfilm & Digital Capture], from microfilm by the Genealogical Society of Utah, 2015, 28 rolls, beginning with DGS #101837580 (Index, 1877-1944). To access the digital images, see the online FHL catalog:
https://familysearch.org/search/catalog/2627418.

1877-1999. *North Dakota, Cemetery Records* [Online Database]. Index and images of cemetery transcriptions compiled by the Red River Valley Genealogical Society. This database has 234,725 records, see
www.familysearch.org/search/collection/1451475.

- See also, *North Dakota, Select Funeral Home Indexes, 1903-1997* [Online Database], indexed at Ancestry.com. This database has 29,420 records, see www.ancestry.com/search/collections/70788.
- See the Red River Valley GS website:
www.redrivergenealogy.com/htmls/indexes.htm.

1880. *Dakota Territory, 1880 Federal Census: Soundex and Population Schedules* [Microfilm & Digital Capture], filmed by the National Archives, c1970, 11 rolls, beginning with FHL film #1254111 (Aurora, Barnes, Boreman, Rusk, Walworth, Campbell, Beadle, Billings, Bon Homme, Brookings, Brown, Brule, Burleigh, Cass, and Clark counties. To access the digital images, see the online FHL catalog:
www.familysearch.org/search/catalog/670376.

1880-1953. *North Dakota, Red River Valley Genealogical Society, Pioneer Files* [Online Database], includes index and images of a Pioneer biography file name index compiled by the Red River Valley Genealogical Society in Fargo, ND. This database has 5,520 records, see
www.familysearch.org/search/collection/3155904.

1881-2015. *Public Death Index* [Online Database], indexed at the ND Dept of Health website. The search criteria include Last name, First name, Date of death, County of death, which can ordered by name, birth date, death date, or county. The records of the previous 12 months from the date of search are not available. Searching is a bit restrictive, because a name, date of death, and county of death is required. No global searching. Still, North Dakota has an enlightened policy about death records open to the public. See
https://apps.nd.gov/doh/certificates/deathCertSearch.htm.

"1882 Tax List, Burleigh County, Dakota Territory" [Printed Article], in *Bismarck-Mandan Historical and Genealogical Society Quarterly*, (Bismarck, ND), (Vol. 10, No. 1 (Mar 1981) through Vol. 12, No. 4 (Dec 1983); and Vol. 14, No. 4 (Dec 1985) through Vol. 15, No. 3 (Sep 1986).

1883 Directory. *The Leading Businessmen of Dakota Cities: Accompanying the Map of Dakota Territory, Name and Address* [Microfilm & Digital Capture], from the original published by Warner & Foote, Minneapolis, MN, 1883, 105 pages. Filmed for the FHL by the Library of Congress, 1984, 1 roll, FHL film #1464014. To access the digital images, see the online FHL catalog:
www.familysearch.org/search/catalog/502915.

1883. Pensioners on the Roll as of January 1, 1883 (Living in Dakota Territory) [Printed Book], an extraction from the U.S. Pension Bureau's publication for all states, compiled and publ. Park Genealogical Books, Roseville, MN, 26 pages, FHL book 976 M2pr.

1883-1934. Fargo (North Dakota) City Directories [Microfilm], from the originals filmed by Research Publications, Woodbridge, CT, 1980-1984, 5 rolls, beginning with FHL film #2156874 (1883 Fargo City Directory). There is a complete run of directories from 1883 to 1934, one per year, or one per two-year span. For a complete list of roll numbers and contents of each roll, see the online FHL catalog page for this title. See https://familysearch.org/search/catalog/620271.

1885 Territorial Census, Dakota Territory (North Dakota Counties) **[Microfilm],** from the original records located at the State Historical Society of North Dakota, Bismarck. Filmed by the SHSNC, 12 rolls, available on interlibrary loan. (Film not available at the FHL). 50 of the 56 northern counties that existed in 1885 are extant. For information about the Interlibrary Loan service at the SHSND, see http://history.nd.gov/archives/genealogy.html.
- See also, **"Dakota Territorial Census of 1885: From the Original Records on File at Bismarck, N.D." [Printed Article],** in *North Dakota Historical Quarterly,* Vol. 4 (1913), pages 338-448. Information includes name, sex, age, relationship to head of family, occupation, birthplace, father's birthplace, and mother's birthplace. Census returns for the North Dakota counties of Allred, Bowman, Buford, Dunn, McIntosh, McKenzie, Mercer, Mountraille, Oliver, Renville, Stanton, Towner, Villard, Wallace, Ward, Wells and Wynn. FHL book 978.4 B5h.
- See also, *1885 Census Index* **[Printed Index],** edited by Ronald Vern Jackson, publ. Accelerated Indexing Systems, Bountiful, UT, 1982, 61 pages, extracted from the ND Historical Quarterly article (17 counties only). FHL book 978.4 X22j 1885.
- See also, *1885 Dakota Territory Census (North Dakota Counties)* **[Printed Books],** published indexes by county. This project was a division of work between the North Dakota Institute for Regional Studies, North Dakota State University, Fargo, ND, and the Bismarck-Mandan Historical and Genealogical Society, Bismarck, ND. These countywide indexes were used to input the electronic database now online. The individual books produced are all available at the FHL in Salt Lake City:
- Barnes County, by NDIRS, FHL book 978.432 X22s and FHL film #2055549.
- Benson County, by B-MHGS, FHL book 978.439 X22b, and FHL film #1425174.
- Billings County, by B-MHGS, FHL book 978.494 X22b.
- Burleigh County, by B-MHGS, FHL book 978.494 X22b and FHL film #2055286.
- Cass County, by NDIRS, FHL book 978.432 X22s.
- Dickey County, by B-MHGS, FHL book 978.454 X22b.
- Emmons County, by B-MHGS, FHL book 978.447 X22b.
- Fargo (city), by NDIRS, FHL book 978.413/F1 X22s.
- Griggs County (with Steele Co.), by NDIRS, FHL book 978.433 X22s.
- Kidder County, by B-MHGS, FHL book 978.457 X22b.
- La Moure County, by B-MHGS, FHL book 978.453 X22b.
- Logan County, by B-MHGS, FHL book 978.456 X22b.
- McLean County, by B-MHGS, FHL book 978.475 X22b.
- Morton County, by B-MHGS, FHL book 978.485 X22b.
- Nelson County (with Ramsey Co.), by NDIRS, FHL book 978.435 X22b.
- Ramsey County (with Nelson Co.), by NDIRS, FHL book 978.435 X22b.
- Richland County, by NDIRS, FHL book 978.412 X22s.
- Rolette County, by B-MHGS, FHL book 978.4592 X22b.
- Stark County, by B-MHGS, FHL book 978.4844 X22b.
- Steele County (with Griggs Co.), by NDIRS, FHL book 978.433.X22s.
- Traill County, by NDIRS, FHL book 978.414 X22b.

- See also, *1885 Dakota Territory Census* **[Online Database],** indexed at the ND State Univ. website. The NDSU Institute for Regional Studies headed a statewide cooperative project to index the entire original Dakota Territory 1885 Census schedules for the counties that today form North Dakota. The database contains over 151,500 names. Each entry includes name, age, nativity, occupation, county of residence, and exact location of the entry in the census schedule. Consult the Institute's information page for the scope and content of the records, ordering copies, and access to the database. See https://library.ndsu.edu/ndsuarchives/dakota-territory-1885-census-database.

1885, 1915, 1925 North Dakota, Territorial and State Censuses [Online Database], digitized and indexed in a combined database at Ancestry.com. Location of the originals: The 1915 and 1925 ND State Censuses are at the State Archives and Historical Research Library, State Historical Society of North Dakota, Bismarck, ND. The 1885 Territorial Census (Index) is at the North Dakota State Univ. Archives,

Fargo, ND. Each index record includes a Place of enumeration (locality, county, state), date of enumeration, Name, Gender, Race, and Age of each person. Additional information is available on the census image (linked to each index record). This database has 1,423,483 records, see www.ancestry.com/search/collections/1078.

1890-1900. *Records of Wills and Marriages from County Judge's Office, Burleigh Co., North Dakota* **[Microfilm & Digital Capture],** from a transcript written in 1955 at the Burleigh County Courthouse, Bismarck, ND. Filmed by the Genealogical Society of Utah, 1971, 1 roll, FHL film #859737. To access the digital images, see the online FHL catalog: www.familysearch.org/search/catalog/353846.

✓ **1890-1924 NOTE:** The *Declaration of Intention to become a U.S. Citizen* ("First Papers") gave an immigrant legal status in the U.S. as an alien. In most cases, the immigrant went on with the naturalization process, filing a **Petition**, a formal request to become a naturalization citizen, and finally, receiving a **Naturalization Certificate**, proving one's citizenship. But, with only the 1st Papers on file, an alien could legally stay in the U.S. indefinitely (unless they got in trouble with the law). The naturalization process could be initiated at any court of record in the U.S. (municipal, county, state, or federal). The specific Declarations databases listed below, 1890-1924, are from the U.S. Circuit Courts held at Fargo, Devil's Lake, Grand Forks, Bismarck, and Minot, ND.

1890-1924 *Declarations of Intention, North Dakota, Southeastern Division* **[Microfilm & Digital Capture],** from the originals at the U.S. Circuit Court, Fargo, ND. Filmed by the Genealogical Society of Utah, 1991, 2 rolls, FHL film #1737977 & #1737978. To access the digital images, see the online FHL catalog: www.familysearch.org/search/catalog/437978.

1890-1940. **Index to Oral History Collection [Online Database],** a PDF list of oral history interviews, located at the State Historical Society of North Dakota website. The collection has over 1,000 tapes created from 1974-1977, covering personal history from 1890-1940. This 50-page PDF list of the people involved in the interviews also explains how to access them. See http://history.nd.gov/archives/ORALHIST.pdf.

1891-1906 *Declarations of Intention, North Dakota, Northwestern Division* **[Microfilm & Digital Capture],** from the originals at the U.S. Circuit Court, Devil's Lake, ND. Filmed by the Genealogical Society of Utah, 1991, 1 roll, FHL film #1737978. To access the digital images, see the online FHL catalog: www.familysearch.org/search/catalog/438446.

1891-1910. *North Dakota Pioneers from the Banat* **[Printed Book],** by John M. Michels, publ. Univ. of Mary Press, Bismarck, ND, 1992, 44 pages. The Banat was a district in southeastern Austria-Hungary and was settled by Germans; later the area came under administration of the Hungarians. The Banat Germans immigrated from 1891 to 1910 when the Balkan wars restricted travel. These Germans settled in Stark and Hettinger counties, North Dakota. Includes a list of immigrants with their village of origin in the Banat. Also includes a list of Banat village names with German, Hungarian, and current names. The North Dakota township maps give names of homesteaders. Includes a discussion of farmhouses in the Banat and North Dakota. See FHL book 978.48 W 2m.

1892-1909 *Declarations of Intention, North Dakota, Northeastern Division* **[Microfilm & Digital Capture],** from the originals at the U.S. Circuit Court, Grand Forks, ND. Filmed by the Genealogical Society of Utah, 1991, 1 roll, FHL film #1737977. To access the digital images, see the online FHL catalog: www.familysearch.org/search/catalog/437961.

1892-1917 *Declarations of Intention, North Dakota, Southwestern Division* **[Microfilm & Digital Capture],** from the originals at the U.S. Circuit Court, Bismarck, ND. Filmed by the Genealogical Society of Utah, 1991, 2 rolls, FHL film #1737978. To access the digital images, see the online FHL catalog: www.familysearch.org/search/catalog/438466.

1900. *North Dakota, 1900 Federal Census: Soundex and Population Schedules* **[Microfilm & Digital Capture],** filmed by the National Archives, c1970, 45 rolls, beginning with FHL film #1241226 (Barnes, Benson, Billings, Botineau, Burleigh, and Cavalier counties). To access the digital images, see the online FHL catalog:
www.familysearch.org/search/catalog/640054.

1900-1996. *North Dakota, Funeral Home Records* **[Digital Capture],** digital images of originals at the Red River Genealogical Society, Fargo, North Dakota. Digitized by FamilySearch International, 2007. Includes the following Funeral home records
- J. O. Robertson & Evans & Knott, 1903-1969
- Eddy Funeral Home, 1905-1960
- Almklov, Quam, Plaisted, 1905-1960
- Lindsay-Carlson, 1914-1986
- Hanson-Runsvold, 1921-1956
- Vertin-Munson, 1911-1997
- Boulger, 1920-1992

- Richland County, 1900's
- Ransom County, Armstrong, 1949-1970; Challey, 1905-1948; Lozier, 1937-1970; Peterson, 1964-1990
- Cass County, Priewe, 1915-1950; West, 1917-1976; Gaard and Moore, 1913-1947; Hanson-Runsvold, 1957-1996; and Merril S. Moore, 1956-1963
- Early funeral records of Moorhead City, 1882-1993

To access the digital images, see the online FHL catalog: www.familysearch.org/search/catalog/1451476.

1906-1916 *Declarations of Intention, North Dakota, Western Division* [Microfilm & Digital Capture], from the originals at the U.S. Circuit Court, Minot, ND. Filmed by the Genealogical Society of Utah, 1991, 2 rolls, FHL film #1737976. To access the digital images, see the online FHL catalog:
www.familysearch.org/search/catalog/437953.

1906-1924 *Naturalization Records, North Dakota, Southeastern Division* [Microfilm & Digital Capture], from the originals at the U.S. Circuit Court, Fargo, ND. Includes Declarations, Petitions, and Certificates. Filmed by the Genealogical Society of Utah, 1991, 1 roll, FHL film #1737977. To access the digital images, see the online FHL catalog:
www.familysearch.org/search/catalog/438316.

1907-1948. *Index to over 2,000 Obituaries from Various Minot Area Newspapers* [Printed Book], compiled and publ. Mouse River Loop Genealogical Society, Minot, ND, 1994, 43 pages. The newspapers indexed were the *Minot Daily News, Berthold Tribune, Carpio Free Press, Democrat-Minot, Donnybrook Courier, Douglas Herald, Griggs County Sentinel, Kenmare News, Kenmare Journal, Oakes Times, Ryder Journal, Sawyer Telegraph, Stanley Run, Washburn Leader, White Earth Record, Mohall Tribune,* and *Ward County Independent.* See FHL book 978.463 V42m.

1910. *North Dakota, 1910 Federal Census: Population Schedules* [Microfilm & Digital Capture], filmed by the National Archives, c1970, 12 rolls, beginning with FHL film #1375151 (Adams, Barnes, Benson, and Billings counties). To access the digital images, see the online FHL catalog:
www.familysearch.org/search/catalog/639617.

1910-1921. *Manifests of Alien Arrivals at Northgate and Saint John, North Dakota* [Digital Capture], from the originals at the National Archives, College Park, MD. To access the digital images, see the online FHL catalog: www.familysearch.org/search/catalog/2526184.
- See also, *North Dakota, Manifests of Immigrant Arrivals, 1910-1952* [Online Database], indexed at the FamilySearch.org website. Source: National Archives microfilm series A3479 & A3560. This collection contains Arrival Manifests of Immigrants Arriving in Ambrose, Antler, Carbury, Fortuna, Noonan, Northgate, Portal, Saint John, Sherwood, and Westhope, North Dakota, 1910-1952. The records may include full name, age, gender, marital status, citizenship, last permanent residence, birthplace, and final destination. This database has 5,740 records. See https://familysearch.org/search/collection/2443935.
- See also, *Manifests of Alien Arrivals at Ambrose, Antler, Carbury, Fortuna, Noonan, Northgate, Portal, Sherwood, and Westhope, North Dakota, 1921-1952* [Microfilm & Digital Capture], from the originals at the National Archives, College Park, MD. Digitized by FamilySearch International, 2015. To access the digital images, see the online FHL catalog: www.familysearch.org/search/catalog/2526180.

1914. *Northwestern Gazetteer, Minnesota, North and South Dakota and Montana Gazetteer and Business Directory* [Microfilm], from the original publ. R. L. Polk Co, 1914. Filmed by the Genealogical Society of Utah, 1986, 2 rolls, FHL film #1321220 & #131221. To see if this microfilm was digitized yet, see the online FHL catalog:
www.familysearch.org/search/catalog/142321.

1914-1933. *Bismarck, North Dakota, City Directories* [Microfilm], from the originals pub. Kelter Directory Co (1914-1929) and R. L. Polk Co (1932-1933). Filmed by Research Publications, Woodbridge, CT, 1990, 1 roll, FHL film #2309664.

1915 *North Dakota State Census Schedules* [Microfilm & Digital Capture], from the original records at the State Historical Society of North Dakota, Bismarck. Filmed by the society, 1975. FHL has 25 rolls, no circulation to family history centers. Contents: To access the digital images, see the online FHL catalog: www.familysearch.org/search/catalog/413937.
Note: For information about the Interlibrary Loan service at the SHSND, see
http://history.nd.gov/archives/genealogy.html.
- See also, *North Dakota Census, 1915* [Online Database], digitized and indexed at the FamilySearch.org website. Source: State Historical Society of North Dakota, Bismarck. The index record includes: Name Birth, Parents, Spouse, Children, Other (names living in the household), and Residence. More details can be viewed on the digitized census page. This database has 619,486 records. See
https://familysearch.org/search/collection/2346284.
- See the sample page opposite →

CENSUS OF NORTH DAKOTA, 1915

Line	Dwelling #	Family #	Name	Native White Male	Native White Female	Native Colored Male	Native Colored Female	Foreign Male—All Other Nationalities	Foreign Female—All Other Nationalities	Children 5 Years Old and Under—Male	Children 5 Years Old and Under—Female	All Males 5 to 20 Years of Age	All Females 5 to 20 Years of Age	All Males 20 to 60 Years of Age	All Females 20 to 60 Years of Age	All Males Over 60 Years of Age	All Females Over 60 Years of Age
			TOTALS BROUGHT FORWARD	19	15			3	3	2	3	7	7	13	8		
41			Berkvam Clara		1								1				
42	9	9	Peterson Albert H.	1										1			
43			Peterson Clementine		1										1		
44			Peterson Vernon Jr.	1							1						
45	10	10	Sandvig Peter					1						1			
46	11	11	Snee Ole E.					1						1			
47			Snee Olena						1						1		
48			Snee Judith E.		1							1					
49	12	12	Colburn Charley N.	1										1			
50			Colburn Mary L.E.		1									1			
51			Colburn Donald W.	1								1					
52			Colburn Lola B.		1							1					
53			Colburn Audrie H.		1							1					
54	13	13	Swanson Clarence W.	1										1			
55	14	14	Darnell Samuel	1													1
56			Anderson John					1						1			
57	15	15	Vanhess Peter	1										1			
58			Vanhess Olive		1									1			
59	16	16	Ellefloot Elias					1						1			
60			Ellefloot Bernt					1						1			
61	17	17	Mathisen John					1						1			
62	18	18	Morton Charlie	1										1			
63			Morton Margret M.		1									1			
64			Morton Mary E.		1							1					
65			Morton Violet A.		1							1					
66			Morton Benjiman E.	1							1						

Sample page - 1915 North Dakota State Census. The census day was April 1, 1915. Although no relationships are given, the list of family members starts with the Dwelling No. / Family No. / Name of Head of Household first, followed by the Name of Spouse, then Names of Children, listed by order of their ages.

"**1915 North Dakota State Census, Bottineau County, Blaine Twp.**" [Printed Article], in *North Central North Dakota Genealogical Record*, (Mouse River Loop Genealogical Society, Minot, ND), No. 84 (Sep 2000).

"**1915 North Dakota State Census, Burke County**" [Printed Article], in *North Central North Dakota Genealogical Record*, (Mouse River Loop Genealogical Society, Minot, ND), Vol. 1, (Nov 1983).

"**1915 North Dakota State Census, Mountrail County**" [Printed Article], in *North Central North Dakota Genealogical Record*, (Mouse River Loop Genealogical Society, Minot, ND), No. 82, (Mar 2000); and Mar 2001.

1917-1918. *North Dakota, World War I Selective Service System Draft Registration Cards* [Microfilm & Digital Capture], from the original records at the National Archives branch at East Point, Georgia. The draft cards are arranged alphabetically by state, then alphabetically by county or city, and then alphabetically by surname of registrants. Filmed by the National Archives, 1987-1988, 30 rolls, beginning with FHL film #1819402 (Adams Co., A-Z; Barnes Co., A-S). To access the digital images, see the online FHL catalog: https://familysearch.org/search/catalog/746993.

1917-1918. See *Roster of the Men and Women Who Served in the Army or Naval Service Including the Marine Corps, of the United States or its Allies From the State of North Dakota in the World War, 1917-1918* [Printed Book, Microfilm & Digital Version], prepared and published under the direction of Brigadier General G. Angus Fraser, Legislative Assembly of North Dakota, printed by Bismarck Tribune Co., Bismarck, ND, 1931, 4 vols. Contents: vol. 1: Asberg to Flagg; vol. 2: Flagg to Lark; vol. 3: Larkee to Rice; and vol. 4: Rich to Zygmond. FHL book 978.4 M23a v. 1-4, and FHL film #982257 (vols. 1-2) and #982258 (vols. 3-4). To access the digital images, see the online FHL catalog:
www.familysearch.org/search/catalog/184980.
- See also, *North Dakota Military Men, 1917-1918* [Online Database], digitized and indexed at Ancestry.com, from "Roster of the Men and Women Who Served… from the State of North Dakota…" This database has 26,753 records, see
www.ancestry.com/search/collections/4569.

1920. *North Dakota, 1920 Federal Census: Soundex and Population Schedules* [Microfilm & Digital Capture], filmed by the National Archives, c1970, 62 rolls, beginning with FHL film #1821330 (Adams, Barnes, Benson, Billings, and Bowman counties). To access the digital images, see the online FHL catalog:
www.familysearch.org/search/catalog/553840.

1925 North Dakota State Census Schedules [Microfilm & Digital Capture], from the original records filmed by the State Historical Society of North Dakota, Bismarck, ND. FHL has 16 rolls, no circulation to family history centers. Contents:
- Adams, Barnes, Benson, Billings counties, FHL film #1731393.
- Bottineau, Bowman, Burke, Burleigh counties, FHL film #1731394 (another copy, FHL film #1433999).
- Bismarck (city), Cass County & Fargo (city), FHL film #1731395.
- Fargo (city), Cass, Cavalier, Dickey & Divide counties, FHL film #1731396.
- Divide, Dunn, Eddy, Emmons, Foster & Golden Valley counties, FHL film #1731397.
- Grand Forks, Grant & Griggs counties, FHL film #1731398.
- Hettinger, Kidder, La Moure, Logan & McHenry counties, FHL film #1731399.
- McHenry, McIntosh, McKenzie & McLean counties, FHL film #1731400.
- Mercer, Morton, Mountrail & Nelson counties, FHL film #1731401.
- Oliver, Pembina, Pierce & Ramsey counties, FHL film #1731402.
- Ransom, Renville, Richland & Rolette counties, FHL film #1731403.
- Sargent, Sheridan, Sioux, Slope, Stark & Steele counties, FHL film #1731404.
- Stutsman, Towner & Traill counties, FHL film #1731405.
- Walsh & Ward counties, FHL film #1731406.
- Wells & Williams counties, Fort Berthold (McLean County) & Devil's Lake Sioux Reservation. Includes list of townships with population in each county, FHL film #1731407.

To access the digital images, see the online FHL catalog:
www.familysearch.org/search/catalog/441185.
NOTE: For information about the Interlibrary Loan service at the SHSND, see
http://history.nd.gov/archives/genealogy.html.
- See also, *North Dakota Census, 1925* [Online Database], indexed at the FamilySearch.org website. Source: State Historical Society of North Dakota, Bismarck. The index record includes: Name, Date of

Birth, Names of Parents, Spouse, Children, and Other persons living in the household, and Residence. More details can be viewed on the digitized census page. This database has 678,504 records. See https://familysearch.org/search/collection/2351024.1930

North Dakota, 1930 Federal Census: Population Schedules **[Microfilm & Digital Capture]**, filmed by the National Archives, c1970, 15 rolls, beginning with FHL film #2341465 (Adams, Benson, Barnes, and Billings counties). To access the digital images, see the online FHL catalog:
www.familysearch.org/search/catalog/1037496.

1930-1990. *Polk's Grand Forks (Grand Forks County, N.D.) City Directory: Including East Grand Forks (Polk County, Minn.)* **[Printed Book]**, publ. R. L. Polk & Co., et al. FHL has 1930, 1956, 1967, 1980, 1986, 1987, 1988, 1989, and 1990 directories. See FHL book 978.416/G1 E4p.

1938-1996. *Fargo (Cass County, N.D.) and Moorhead (Clay County, Minn.) City Directory: Including Dilworth, West Fargo and West Fargo Industrial Park* **[Printed Book]**, publ. R.L. Polk & Co., St. Paul, MN. The FHL has 22 years of directories, publ. 1938, then jumps to the 1960s, 1970s, 1980s, and 1990s. For a complete list of titles and years, see the online FHL catalog page for this title. See https://familysearch.org/search/catalog/13548.

1940. *North Dakota, 1940 Federal Census: Population Schedules* **[Digital Capture]**, digitized images from the microfilm of original records held by the Bureau of the Census in the 1940s. After microfilming, Congress allowed the Census Bureau to destroy the originals to free up space for WWII-related files. Digitizing of the 1940 census schedules microfilm images was done for the National Archives and made public on April 2, 2012. To access the digital images, see the online FHL catalog page:
www.familysearch.org/search/catalog/2057776.

1940 Federal Census Finding Aids **[Online Database]**. The National Archives prepared a special website online with a detailed description of the 1940 federal census. Included at the site are descriptions of location finding aids, such as Enumeration District maps, Geographic Descriptions of Census Enumeration Districts, and a list of 1940 City Directories available at the National Archives. The finding aids are all linked to other National Archives sites. The National Archives website also has a link to 1940 Search Engines using Stephen P. Morse's "One-Step" system for finding a 1940 E.D. or street address conversion. See www.archives.gov/research/census/1940/general-info.html#questions.

1942. See *North Dakota, World War II 4th Draft Registrations Cards, 1942* **[Microfilm & Digital Images]**, from the originals at the National Personnel Records Center, St. Louis, MO. These cards represent older men, ages 45 to 65 in April 1942, that were registered for the draft. They had birth dates between 28 Apr 1877 and 16 Feb 1892. Includes name of individual, date and place of birth, address, age, telephone number, employer's name and address, name and address of person who would know where the individual can be located, signature, and physical description. Film located at the FHL was digitized in 2015. To access the digital images, see the online FHL catalog:
https://familysearch.org/search/catalog/2624775.

1958. *Fargo, North Dakota, Passenger Lists* **[Online Database]**, digitized and index at Ancestry.com. Source: National Archives microfilm series A3744. These passenger and crew lists from aircrafts were recorded on a variety of forms that were then turned over to the Immigration and Naturalization Service. They typically include the name of the vessel and arrival date, ports of departure and arrival, dates of departure and arrival, full name, age, gender, physical description, military rank (if any), occupation, birthplace, citizen of what country, and residence. This database has 280 records, see
www.ancestry.com/search/collections/9270.

1987-Current. *North Dakota Recent Newspaper Obituaries* **[Online Database]**, digitized and indexed newspaper obituaries at the GenealogyBank website, including newspapers for Beulah, Bismarck, Center, Devils Lake, Garrison, Grand Forks, Hankinson, Hazen, McClusky, New Town, Parshall, Turtle Lake, Underwood, Valley City, Velva, Wahpeton, Washburn, and Williston. See
www.genealogybank.com/explore/obituaries/all/usa/north-dakota.